Ethics:
Questions & Morality of Human Actions

Ethics:
Questions & Morality of Human Actions

Third Edition

Volume 3
Ethics & Professional Practices
Bioethics: Health, Medicine & Mortality
Economics & Business
Science, Technology & the Environment

Editors
George Lucas, PhD
John K. Roth, PhD

SALEM PRESS
A Division of EBSCO Information Services, Inc.
Ipswich, Massachusetts

GREY HOUSE PUBLISHING

Publisher's Cataloging-In-Publication Data
(Prepared by The Donohue Group, Inc.)

Names: Lucas, George R., editor. | Roth, John K., editor.
Title: Ethics : questions & morality of human actions / editors, George Lucas, PhD, John K. Roth, PhD.
Description: Third edition. | Ipswich, Massachusetts : Salem Press, a division of EBSCO Information Services, Inc.; Amenia, NY : Grey House Publishing, [2019] | Includes bibliographical references and index. | Contents: Volume 1. The Concepts of Ethics; Theories & Traditions; Theorists & Practitioners — Volume 2. Politics & Government; Law & Human Rights; War — Volume 3. Bioethics: Health, Medicine & Mortality; Economics & Business; Science, Technology & the Environment — Volume 4. Ethics & Human Identities; Religion & Ethics; Gender, Sexuality & Reproduction; Race, Ethnicity & Tribalism; Hope, Happiness & the Future.
Identifiers: ISBN 9781682179284 (set) | ISBN 9781682179291 (v. 1) | ISBN 9781682179307 (v. 2) | ISBN 9781682179314 (v. 3) | ISBN 9781642653335 (v. 4)
Subjects: LCSH: Ethics—Encyclopedias. | LCGFT: Encyclopedias.
Classification: LCC BJ63 .E54 2019 | DDC 170/.3—dc23

First Printing
PRINTED IN THE UNITED STATES OF AMERICA

Table of Contents

Volume 1
Wondering about Ethics

Volume 2
Politics, Government, Law, Human Rights, and War

Volume 3
Ethics & Professional Practices

Volume 4
Ethics & Human Identities

Gender, Sexuality & Reproduction

Race, Ethnicity & Tribalism

Volume 3

Ethics & Professional Practices

For the most part, the entries in this volume discuss *ethical issues* arising in the course of engaging in distinctive *practices*: we could say that these are shared activities which differentiate the human community into groups and organizations, and in which individual human moral agents cooperate to achieve specific *ends, objectives, or goals*. Because that is likely to prove a difficult abstraction to grasp, let us consider some very concrete examples of specific communities and the common practices in which they engage.

Take, for example, persons who are primarily engaged in the delivery of heath care—doctors or physicians, physician-assistants, nurses and nurse-practitioners, hospital orderlies and support staff, health insurers, pharmacists, medical researchers and medical school faculty. Notice right away that the more widely and inclusively we define the boundaries of membership in this specific group, the more diverse it becomes, and the more difficult it may be to link all the individuals together in pursuit of a single common goal or objective.

Nevertheless, we might start by offering a generic label to this community—healthcare professionals—with their various activities falling within the boundaries of the *healthcare profession.* We have already listed a variety of roles that individuals in this profession might occupy, each requiring different levels of expertise, training and education, practical experience, and so forth. Those different roles, and the requirements for occupying them, may also generate a kind of hierarchy or order within this community, with the most educated, expert, and experienced of these practitioners occupying the most senior ranks of the profession (exercising the most authority, and enjoying the most respect, and perhaps compensation), down to the lowest ranks requiring the least specialized training or experience (and accordingly, exercising less authority and independence, and enjoying a lesser degree of respect and/or compensation).

Notice that the same sort of organization and classifications of individuals can be developed for other kinds of practices such as education, the law, the clergy, journalism, engineering, and military service, among many others. The list may be lengthy, but not infinite, and it is not entirely clear whether some pursuits or vocations (such as auto repair, or plumbing, or carpentry—or for that matter, scientific research, or marketing and sales in business) would rightly be included among them.

Why, or why not? What difference does this classification make (other than appealing to someone's arbitrary and officious desire for order)? And *where, especially, does ethics come into this picture*?

One possible response, especially to the question of ethics in this context, is as follows. If we accept the rough descriptive classification, for example, of the healthcare profession offered above, including the description of its members, the various roles they occupy, and the implicit hierarchy or ranking among them, we would first want to examine *what it is that joins them together* into a community.

Despite vast differences among the individual members of this profession in terms of their roles and specific responsibilities (as well as in the degree of preparation required for holding them), all of these personnel seem to be properly characterized as being engaged in some kind of service to the wider public: especially to those they identify as their clients or patients. The most basic or fundamental feature of their various activities—their common practice—seems to be providing health care to those clients or patients. And despite a variety of different reasons or intentions harbored by each individual for making their way into the various roles of this profession, they might all agree that their underlying defining goal, purpose or end (as Aristotle would frame the matter) is promoting the good health and well-being—the flourishing—of those clients or patients (and accordingly, of the general public).

From this account of a profession as a community of individuals engaged in a common practice, aimed at achieving some final end or purpose in society at large, certain kinds of *aspirations and ideals* (best practices) may be identified. Likewise from this same account, certain *boundaries or constraints* may come to be recognized that define specific activities in which the profession's members may *not* engage (even when trying to attain the desired ends or goals—let alone when an individual member seems to be ignoring, forgetting, or forsaking those ideals).

It is the recognition of these best practices, as well as certain prohibited practices, that finally answers our questions about ethics: the list of aspirations, alongside the list of specific prohibitions on acceptable practice, define the ethics (or the ethical code) of (in this case) the healthcare profession.

For historically venerable and recognized professions like medicine, we find attempts at setting out the profession's ethical code stretching all the way back into antiquity. The Hippocratic oath, for example, is likely one of the most famous and widely recognized codes of ethics in the world. It is not meant to apply to every single human being in the world, but only to those who identify themselves as members of the group we are here calling the healthcare profession. Attributed to the ancient Greek physician, Hippocrates (often heralded as the father of the medical profession) the Hippocratic oath famously enjoins medical practitioners first to "do no harm" to their patients and subjects (*primum non nocere*). Deliberate harm or carelessness in medical practice are thus anathema to the healthcare profession, numbering among its most rigid prohibitions. The oath instead requires that physicians and healers practice their medical arts solely for the benefit of their patients, and, in their professional practice and even private personal lives, "abstain from mischief and corruption" and live "with purity and with holiness" (e.g., a life characterized by virtues like compassion and integrity).

This ancient code does not begin to encompass the full measure of contemporary responsibilities, not to mention moral challenges, that confront modern medical and healthcare professionals. These are taken up in greater detail in the topics and articles contained within first section of this volume, devoted to ethical standards and moral conundrums specific to health care and biomedical research. But it should now be reasonably clear that a similar approach can be taken with any other community of shared practices: journalism, for example (in which the responsibilities for truth-telling to the public, and respect for the dignity and privacy of subjects and sources would quickly come to the fore); the practice of law (in which the fiduciary duties to represent clients assiduously and competently in the overall pursuit of justice for all would play a central role); or military service (in which protecting, and never harming the nation and its citizens, and using deadly force only when necessary, and only to the degree required to attain security and protect the rule of law, are ethical norms of the highest priority).

The approach outlined above would likewise aid us in defining and discerning what we might call professional probity or moral rectitude (integrity and uprightness)for teachers, educators, or members of the clergy (priests, ministers, rabbis, imams and religious workers of all kinds), all of whom are required to place the welfare of their students or congregants as their highest priority, and to refrain from ever deceiving or taking inappropriate advantage of their vulnerable charges solely for the professional's own self-regarding purposes.

The approach to moral enquiry in the professional contexts above is, in fact, largely based upon how the Greek philosopher, Aristotle, approached his inquiry into ethics generally. He began, not by setting out rigid standards or absolute principles, so much as inquiring instead about how different communities of human beings organize themselves, live their lives, and carry out their affairs. Only through examining the shared practices (and the values they embody), together with the ends or goals sought in the pursuit of these practices, can we do for human beings generally what we did for professional practitioners (in health care particularly) above: namely, discern the best practices to achieve those ends, and dismiss or prohibit those practices that are inimical to the achievement of those ends or goals.

Aristotle emphasized *virtues* or forms of excellence to be sought and cultivated constantly and consistently throughout one's professional or personal life. In contrast, the prohibited practices, which fit with Aristotle's understanding of *vices*, are those forms of practice which ought to be avoided in one's self, and discouraged in others, as inimical to prospects for living a good life and making one's community flourish. This approach to examining moral beliefs and practices has been resurrected to widespread understanding and use in our own time by the Scottish philosopher, Alasdair MacIntyre.

This account may, however, seem to veer too sharply in favor of only one of the several fundamental approaches to moral reasoning outlined in the first volume of this series. But that turns out not to be the case. Rather, in the foregoing method of investigation we will quickly discover strict duties or obligations that must be upheld—such as the duty to refrain from harm—as well as other duties which we should strive to enact or achieve to the best of our individual abilities—such as the duty to work toward the benefit and welfare of those whom we serve professionally, or with whom we interact in our public lives generally. These are duties of justice and of virtue, respectively, as described by the Enlightenment philosopher, Immanuel Kant, constituting the substance of the so-called deontological approach to ethics generally.

And standing clearly in the background as the ultimate goal of such responsible and upright behavior, is the goal of achieving the greatest possible good for the greatest number of persons, the end of morality we have elsewhere described as utilitarianism, as outlined principally by philosophers like Jeremy Bentham and John Stuart Mill.

This confluence is no accident, as all these philosophers were thoroughly grounded in the moral philosophy of Aristotle and so-called virtue ethics. Their seemingly different accounts of ethics represent not so much rival approaches to moral reasoning and ethical behavior, as they do differing emphases on the three underlying elements of what we might term the moral situation, or the overall context of moral practice itself: *persons as "moral agents,"* cultivating the finest (and avoiding the worst) habits and traits of character that pave the path toward human flourishing; *the actions or practices in which those persons engage* (which should conform to the requirements and constraints of Duty and our clear obligations to others); and *the end result of living and acting in such a morally upright fashion*—namely, the flourishing and overall well-being of the entire community of moral agents (the greatest good for the greatest possible number).

That resonance or synergy between the components of our individual and social lives, and towards the kinds of moral reflection required to sustain ourselves and others, may seem to paint a rosy, optimistic picture of our human prospects. Yet our collective record of failures and shortcomings, as also recorded in these volumes, serves as caution even as it exhorts us to strive to improve our individual and collective lot. The topics of hope (and despair) in the pursuit of moral rectitude and the quest for human flourishing constitute issues that we shall take up in the final volume of this series.

For now, in the groupings of topics and articles that follow in this volume, scholars and experts will guide us toward more in-depth reflection on these virtues, duties, and goals of human flourishing as they arise—or are threatened or challenged—in medicine, health care, and biomedical research; in the conduct of scientific research and the pursuit of technological advancement (including the manner in which new technological innovations are utilized for military purposes, as well as in the efforts we undertake to protect our environment); and finally, in economics and business, in which key elements of our economic and social relations with one another—such as the practical welfare of employers, employees, customers, and the public generally—all figure centrally.

Bioethics: Health, Medicine & Mortality

In the general introduction to this volume, health care was cited as an example of a profession. It was portrayed as a community of individuals whose shared practices were aimed primarily at sustaining the health and well-being of individual patients, ultimately benefiting society at large. The moral rectitude of individual practitioners of this profession, in turn, seemed to be guaranteed through the explicit pledge or commitment of each, upon joining the profession, to uphold the morally justified ends or goals (what we termed their shared conception of the Good, attained through their shared practices). This commitment was symbolized by their individual or collective pledges always to adhere to the highest standards of professional probity—including the ethical standards or "Code of Ethics" of the profession.

With respect to health care specifically, however, our faith in this commitment can be compromised when we recognize that professional so encompasses important scientific inquiry and research. The broader ethical considerations and challenges (or moral dilemmas) unique to scientific inquiry and research, together with technological development and innovation, are reserved for the final section of this volume. But many of those primarily encountered in medicine and health care—especially, though not exclusively, those pertaining to the human quest to ward off human mortality—are examined in many of the articles in this section, under the heading of *bioethics*.

Ethical issues arise periodically because the ends or goals of greater medical knowledge and understanding to be gained through research may sometimes conflict with the goals of serving the best interests of individual patients. Such conflicts have sometimes come to the fore in dramatic and even tragic fashion, posing grave moral dilemmas for researchers and the wider public.

The pursuit of cures for serious diseases like malaria or syphilis may require biomedical researchers to perform a range of experiments, collect data, or engage in extensive clinical trials of potentially revolutionary medical treatments or medications in order to prove their safety and effectiveness for widespread use. If they perform these tests without the knowledge or consent of their test subjects, however, these researchers violate an important human right known as *autonomy*: namely, the freedom of each patient to knowingly choose both the risks they are willing to incur and the treatment they are to receive.

Simultaneously, the researchers also risk betraying their own code of ethics; namely, their fundamental professional commitment to "do no harm" to their patients (*primum non nocere*). Even if well-intentioned, the researchers might finally be placing their own scientific ambitions or aspirations above the individual rights and welfare of their human subjects by exposing the latter to harm or risk of harm entirely without their awareness, let alone their permission. The biomedical personnel would then have committed a serious violation of professional ethics, and would be rightly accused of engaging in grave *professional malfeasance*.

The underlying conflict in question is usefully portrayed as that between the researcher's desire bring some great benefit to the general public through their biomedical research (a *utilitarian* goal), but at the cost of ignoring or overriding the basic human rights of the particular patients or human subjects involved (a violation of duty, *deontology*). The specific moral error or act of malfeasance at issue in this important example has come to be known as a violation of the Principle of Informed Consent.

Perhaps the most famous—or rather, infamous—examples of such malfeasance occurred in German concentration camps during World War II. Medical researchers utilized prisoners in the camps, including children (many of whom were East Europeans of Jewish descent, incarcerated during the Holocaust) as research subjects in a range of medical experiments and investigations, some of which were themselves of questionable scientific or medical value. The experiments inflicted horrendous pain and suffering, often amounting to the worst imaginable kinds of torture (such a live vivisection), on the unwilling human subjects whose consent was never sought, and whose own welfare was never a consideration in the experimental procedures.

The details of such experiments emerged during the post-war Nuremburg trials of Nazi war criminals generally during 1945-46, particularly in what were termed the "Doctors' trials" (officially the "Subsequent Nuremburg Trials"), at which the "medical experiments" of Nazi physicians and military officials (like Josef Mengele at Auschwitz) were graphically and gruesomely presented. In addition to meting out punishment (including death by hanging) to those responsible, the allied war tribunal emphasized that the ancient Hippocratic oath needed to be supplemented with clear moral guidance for all biomedical practitioners in the future. The tribunal issued ten recommendations, now generally known as the Nuremburg Code.

The very first provision of that code is the absolute necessity that human subjects of biomedical research be granted the absolute right of informed consent. Subsequent biomedical and human subject research conventions (including the findings of the World Medical Association in Helsinki in 1975, and the Belmont Report of the U.S. National Commission for the Protection of Human Subjects of Biomedical and Behavioral Research in 1978) have continuously re-affirmed and reinforced the primacy of *Informed Consent* as the fundamental ethical principle to be observed in all future biomedical research on human subjects.

The field of bioethics thus incorporates the ethical code of the medical and healthcare *profession*, as well as these other important *ethical guidelines for biomedical research*. It also encompasses some wider public issues that fall under the headings of medicine and health care more generally, including what an early pioneer in bioethics, Paul Ramsey of Princeton University, termed *ethics at the edges of life*.

On one edge, we recognize that death eventually will claim us all. But its timing is highly contingent. Perhaps even its inevitability is at least open to question. Healthcare professionals and biomedical researchers frequently join forces to help "keep death at bay" through the discovery of ever-new forms of medical diagnosis and treatment, medication and vaccinations against deadly diseases, and even genetic experiments with the building blocks of human life. They do all this presumably in hopes of countering or even avoiding the onset of debilitating, life-shortening, genetically-transmitted diseases and disabilities (like sickle-cell anemia, cystic fibrosis, or Tay-Sachs disease)or to develop genetic weapons that will effectively combat otherwise-common life-threatening disorders (various forms of cancer and heart disease).

Medical science has made enormous strides over the years in treating such diseases, and thus prolonging human life expectancy. But in place of the tragedy of children and young adults cut down prematurely by plague and pestilence, a new horror has arisen in its stead: the prospect of an indefinitely-extended individual life span, increasingly absent the most precious features and experiences that make human life itself worth living. Friends and family die over decades, leaving the survivors alone and bereft of intimate companionship. One's cognitive faculties usually diminish with age, and precious memories, including the very identity of loved ones, fade and disappear. Physical capacities are lost even more quickly, and discomfort becomes an ever-present companion.

Is this the intended goal of medical advance? Rather than being gently "carried off" in older age by influenza or pneumonia—against which there are now effective vaccines for the elderly—is it our inevitable fate to spend decline years walking (with mechanical assistance) the halls of assisted-living and memory-care units like "the Walking Dead?" The eminent physician, philosopher, and medical ethicist, Leon Kass, used to confound his undergraduates at the University of Chicago with an opening question on their first day of his class: whether they thought, on the whole, that "Mortality might be a *good* thing?" He later reported their reactions, and his own reflections, in a famous essay entitled "Whether to Wither, and Why?" A number of the articles in this section likewise challenge readers to think about how our increasing medical prowess and the powerful reach of ever new biomedical technologies raise age-old questions about mortality itself in new and ever more disturbing ways.

In addition to death and dying, ethical questions arise when the healthcare profession tackles biomedical dilemmas at the "other edge" of human life: conception (and contraception), abortion, birth and premature birth, and the therapeutic prospects in present-day neonatal care. We can now fertilize human ova in a test tube and plant the fertilized egg in the mother's uterus. We may soon be able to bring that human zygote fully to term as a newborn infant entirely in an artificial environment. But should we attempt such things? To what end, or for what purposes?

Our ability over the past few decades, likewise, to care for prematurely-born infants of increasingly low birth weight has improved dramatically, exponentially. Doctors and nurses in those remarkable facilities sometimes wonder if they, and we as society, know precisely what we are doing. Prematurely born infants, sometimes after only a few weeks of uterine gestation, require extraordinary (and extraordinarily expensive) care—several weeks at minimum, at a cost of $10-20,000 per day) to "bring them to term," at which point they *might* be able finally to leave the hospital and survive with routine parental care alone. But often such babies are also born with serious birth defects, while others may suffer from drug addition passed on from the mother, who then abandons the child in the neo-natal intensive care ward after giving birth. What, exactly, have we managed to accomplish?

Readers hardly need be reminded how controversial, divisive, and morally troubling is the seemingly intractable problem of abortion in our society. All these early-life conundrums at the "other edge" of our existence are also essential topics of articles in this section.

If all this wasn't enough, finally, we might note in conclusion that health care itself is also increasingly understood as a business—the so-called heath care industry. This includes consideration of the costs of medical practice and treatment, in ways touched on in passing above—but also commercial and government investments in both scientific research and the industrial production of new medicines, vaccinations, and drug therapies. These are, at present, largely the province of large private pharmaceutical companies, whose stewardship of government-sponsored research funding, and commitment to public health alongside reasonable profits, are frequently a matter of critical scrutiny.

Should a patient's access to a vital, life-saving medicine be solely or even largely based upon his or her ability to afford it? Providing health insurance for individuals to protect against the unexpectedly high costs of such therapies and medical emergencies, but also against the ongoing costs of care in old age, is one approach to answering the foregoing ethical questions. But the healthcare insurance industry is itself largely a business enterprise, with limited access especially for those with serious medical conditions, or of modest financial means. Ought healthcare insurance of some sort be available to everyone who needs it? And if insurance firms, seeking to limit outlays for treatment in the interest of profit, partner increasingly with hospitals, medical personnel, and pharmaceutical firms to manage health care for their mutual benefit, who will protect the interests of vulnerable patients? These ethical challenges quickly balloon into massive political policy questions, as discussed in the remaining articles in this section. Such questions impact us all, and challenge us all, to formulate informed and intelli-

gent personal views, guide personal behavior, and support sensible and affordable public policies that aim at justice and full access to adequate health care, and through it, a more fully human quality of life for all.

Acquired immunodeficiency syndrome (AIDS)

Definition: Commonly known as AIDS, a physical condition believed to be caused by a virus of indeterminate origin that invades and seriously damages the body's immune system, leaving it vulnerable to a number of opportunistic infections and rare cancers

Date: Discovered in 1981

Type of ethics: Bioethics

Significance: The worldwide AIDS pandemic has highlighted a host of crucial policy issues including civil and human rights, confidentiality and privacy, accessibility to medical and social services, the drug trial and approval process, prisoners' rights, substance-abuse treatment, school-based sex education, equitable distribution of scarce resources, and international cooperation.

Acquired immunodeficiency syndrome, or AIDS, is a term given to a collection of life-threatening medical conditions that result from acquisition of the human immunodeficiency virus (HIV). Before 1981 the virus was unknown, and it is unknown how many cases of this disease occurred. In early 1981 eight cases of a rare, relatively benign tumor that affected older men, Kaposi's sarcoma, suddenly appeared in New York City. At the same time in New York and California, cases of a rare pneumonia caused by *pneumocystis carinii* were reported. Soon the Centers for Disease Control and Prevention (CDC) created a task force to study the situation. Many of the earlier cases occurred in gay men, and therefore the disease was initially dubbed the "gay compromise syndrome" or "gay-related immune deficiency (GRID)." Later the virus was also found among heterosexuals, and the syndrome's name was changed to acquired immunodeficiency syndrome, or AIDS. In 1984 the causative virus was isolated. By the first years of the twenty-first century, HIV disease was a worldwide pandemic.

The World Pandemic

By the beginning of 2003, 42 million cases of AIDS had been reported around the world, with 816,149 cases in the

United States. From the beginning of the epidemic in 1981 until December, 2002, 467,910 deaths attributed to AIDS had occurred in the United States alone, while at least 3.1 million deaths had occurred elsewhere in the world. During the mid- to late 1990's, the rate of progression from HIV to AIDS slowed in the United States, due to advances in treatment. The result was that increasing numbers of people were living with HIV. By 2003, it was estimated that there were 800,000 to 900,000 people with HIV living in the United States, with 40,000 new cases reported each year. Worldwide in 2002, 5 million new cases of HIV were identified, and the epidemic showed no signs of decline.

Issues of Liability

HIV is most commonly transmitted from one person to another through physical sexual contact. The second-most common method of transmission is blood-to-blood contact, followed by contacts between infected mothers and their children. Before 1985, HIV was transmitted through infected blood supplies and accidental needle pricks in health-care workplaces. Such accidents raise several issues of liability.

First, a person suffering from the disease may indulge in behaviors that purposely transmit the virus to others, leading to criminal liability. Any of three types of criminal laws may be applied in such cases: traditional (such as attempted murder, aggravated assault, assault with a deadly weapon, or attempted manslaughter); criminal violations of public health statutes; and AIDS-specific criminal statutes.

Criminal prosecutions often pose ethical challenges by being essentially punitive acts directed toward victims of HIV/AIDs that do little or nothing for public health. Several issues pertain to civil liability. Tort law is the area of law that governs harms allegedly caused by a private individual or group of individuals against other private individuals. Tort laws vary from state to state and are usually based on previous cases or precedents. Civil liability for transmitting HIV/AIDS may occur for any of four reasons: negligence or lack of use of reasonable care to avoid harm to others, battery involving unwanted touching or infliction of injury on other persons, intentional infliction of emotional distress, and fraud.

Issues of Discrimination

HIV/AIDS raises a number of issues relating to discrimination. At the societal level, it is a disease that has a great

CDC poster from 1989 highlighting the threat of AIDS associated with drug use.

stigma attached to it. That stigma is enhanced by the popular association of AIDS with homosexuals—a fact that also enhances negative images of gay people.

People carrying the HIV virus have also been discriminated against when they have sought health care. However, the federal Americans with Disabilities Acts (ADA) of 1990 bans discrimination against HIV-infected persons at any stage of their disease. In addition various professional codes such as the American Nurses Association Code also encourage respect for human dignity and prohibit discrimination against carriers of HIV. Nevertheless, there is evidence that many health care workers so fear HIV/ AIDS that they prefer not to care for persons with the disease.

Discrimination against people with HIV/AIDS has also been an issue in public accommodations, including hotels, restaurants, theaters, and nursing homes. Title III of the ADA protects HIV carries from such discrimination; however, violations of the law have been common. An even more serious issue is employment discrimination, which is also covered by the ADA. HIV infection is considered a disability, and employers are obligated to provide reasonable accommodations for persons carrying the virus. Another controversial issue is the placing of limits or caps by employers on the amount of health insurance coverage provided to HIV sufferers.

Housing discrimination is also an issue. Despite the fact that HIV cannot be transmitted through casual physical contact, people with HIV have been discriminated against in housing allotments. This, too, violates federal laws. For example, the Fair Housing Act of 1968 is designed to prevent landlords and real estate agents from discriminating against potential tenants on the basis of race, color, religion, sex, family status, national origin, or handicap. AIDS is considered a handicap under section 504 of the Rehabilitation Act of 1973. In addition there are state and local laws that prohibit housing discrimination due to HIV/AIDS.

Individual Liberties

The U.S. Constitution has many provisions protecting the rights of citizens to pursue their goals without restraints from others. Confidentiality and privacy are important ethical considerations within the broader framework of liberty. Health care professionals are ethically obligated to protect confidential information about their patients. Professionals who provide counseling before and after HIV testing procedures are also expected to maintain complete confidentiality of the results. However, diagnoses that turn up positive results can pose serious ethical dilemmas. The fact that health care professionals are expected to protect the privacy and confidentiality of their patients leaves open the question of who is ethically responsible for alerting the sexual partners of persons who test positive for HIV.

In HIV/AIDS, as for any medical condition, health care providers cannot perform examinations, conduct treatments, or even touch patients without their consent. This doctrine of informed consent is grounded under the overall principle of autonomy and respect for people. *Autonomy* is a Greek word that means self-governance or self-rule. Health care professionals are obligated to provide to their patients details of treatment and medical procedures to be performed, accurate descriptions of the potential risks and benefits of the procedures, explanations of alternative treatments or procedures, and assessments of the likelihood of success. After receiving this

information, patients who decide they do not want the procedures or treatments to be performed may choose to reject them. All adults with decision-making capacity who suffer from HIV/AIDS have the right to self-determination in their medical treatments and care.

The increasing numbers of women diagnosed with HIV/AIDS, many of whom become pregnant, raise additional ethical questions. For example, should legal restrictions on abortion be loosened for pregnant women?

Education and Research

Efforts to educate the public on the dangers of AIDS often collide with other public-education goals. For example, encouraging young people to practice safer sex and to use condoms is seen by some as condoning adolescent sexual activity. Providing drug users with free hypodermic needles to reduce the transmission of diseases may be seen as condoning illegal drug use.

Medical ethics require that researchers obtain the informed consent of their subjects. However, since no complete cures of HIV infection are know, persons carrying the virus may be inclined to accept unsafe risks in the hope of finding a cure. Researchers must be sensitive to that fact in evaluating their subjects' understanding of the risks they may take.

In any society there are some that have easy access to resources while others do not. Despite the illegality of discrimination in access to care, poor persons find it very hard to have access to enough resources. This disparity is even more glaring at the global level. Some of the poorer nations in Africa have a higher burden of this disease and very scarce resources to cope with the problem.

—*Manoj Sharma*

Further Reading

Adams, William E., et al. *AIDS Cases and Materials.* 3d ed. Durham, N.C.: Carolina Academic Press, 2002. Collection of case studies on legal and ethical issues relating to HIV/AIDS.

Ahmed, Paul I. *Living and Dying with AIDS.* New York: Plenum Press, 1992. Study of issues of coping with AIDS, including ethical and legal issues and the effects of AIDS on families and adolescents.

Almond, Brenda. *AIDS—A Moral Issue: The Ethical, Legal and Social Aspects.* London: Macmillan, 1990. Study of medical issues relating to AIDS and its effect on communities.

Dickson, Donald T. *HIV, AIDS, and the Law: Legal Issues for Social Work Practice and Policy.* New York: Aldine de Gruyter, 2001. Integrated approach to legal and social aspects of HIV/AIDS, with special attention to ethical issues.

Huber, Joan, and Beth E. Schneider. *The Social Context of AIDS.* Newbury Park, Calif.: Sage Publications, 1992. Overview of the directions that sociological research on AIDS has taken. Chapters are organized in three sections, which examine medical aspects of the disease, risky behaviors, and treatment.

Rubenstein, William B., Ruth Eisenberg, and Lawrence O. Gostin. *The Rights of People Who Are HIV Positive*. Carbondale: Southern Illinois University Press, 1996. Authoritative guide to the rights of people living with HIV or AIDS.

Stein, Theodore J. *The Social Welfare of Women and Children with HIV and AIDS: Legal Protections, Policy, and Programs*. New York: Oxford University Press, 1998. Ethical issues specific to women and children with HIV/AIDS are discussed.

See also: Americans with Disabilities Act; Health care allocation; Homosexuality; Medical ethics; Medical research; National Gay and Lesbian Task Force; Promiscuity; Sexually transmitted diseases.

American Medical Association

Identification: National professional organization of licensed physicians

Date: Founded in 1847

Type of ethics: Bioethics

Significance: The stated purpose of the American Medical Association (AMA) is to improve the quality of medical services provided to Americans and to maintain high standards of ethical behavior within the medical profession.

The AMA held its first official meeting in Philadelphia in 1847. The delegates to the meeting established a Code of Medical Ethics and set minimum requirements for medical education and training. To reflect changing times and conditions, major revisions were made to the Code of Medical Ethics in 1903, 1912, 1947, and 1994. The preamble, and primary component, of the code is known as the Principles of Medical Ethics. It contains nine fundamental ethical principles that have been applied to nearly two hundred different ethical issues in medicine, ranging from genetic testing to family abuse. Two other components of the Code of Medical Ethics are the Current Opinions with Annotations of the Council on Ethical and Judicial Affairs, which interprets the Principles of Medical Ethics, and the Reports of the Council on Ethical and Judicial Affairs. Together, the three components of the Code of Medical Ethics determine the AMA's overall position on ethical issues.

The Principles of Medical Ethics establish general rules of ethical conduct among doctors, between doctors and their patients, and between doctors and society at large. They require doctors to maintain secrecy within the requirements of the law, temperance, delicacy, punctuality, and respect for the rights of others. Physicians are requested to keep abreast of important medical developments that may benefit their patients, share relevant medical information with their patients, and consult and work with other medical professionals as necessary. The ethical behavior of physicians is determined by the overall content of the Principles of Medical Ethics. Although ethical values and legal principles are typically interrelated, the AMA advocates that ethical obligations of a physician usually supersede legal obligations.

—Alvin K. Benson

See also: Bioethics; Diagnosis; Ethical codes of organizations; Hippocrates; Medical bills of rights; Medical ethics; Medical research; *Principles of Medical Ethics*.

Behavior therapy

Definition: Collection of procedures for changing behavior based upon principles of learning

Date: Developed during the early 1950's

Type of ethics: Bioethics

Significance: Because behavior therapy techniques often involve extensive control of patients' environments and can include aversive procedures, they raise ethical concerns about manipulation, denial of rights, and the dehumanization of people.

Behavior therapy describes a set of specific procedures, such as systematic desensitization and contingency management, which began to appear during the early 1950's based on the work of Joseph Wolpe, a South African psychiatrist; Hans Eysenck, a British psychologist; and the American experimental psychologist and radical behaviorist B. F. Skinner. The procedures of behavior therapy are based upon principles of learning and emphasize the careful measurement of undesired behavior and the setting of objective goals. By the 1960's, behavior therapy and behavior-modification procedures were widely taught in colleges and universities and practiced in schools, prisons, hospitals, homes for the developmentally disabled, businesses, and in private practice offices. By the early 1970's, the ethical and legal status of behavior therapy was being challenged from several sources.

Ethical Challenges to Behavior Therapy

Behavior therapy techniques have associated with them the same concerns raised by any form of psychotherapy; namely, that informed consent be obtained from the patient, that the patient play the central role in the selecting of therapy goals, that the patient be primary even when a third party may be paying for or requiring the services, and that the least restrictive means (those that least restrict the freedom of the patient) be employed.

Behavior therapy procedures have been challenged on a variety of ethical grounds. Humanistic psychologists, most notably the late Carl Rogers, argued that behavior modification as practiced by the followers of Skinner led to treating people as objects to be manipulated by contrived rewards and denied patients the opportunity to find solutions to their problems through their own resources. Behavior modifiers reply that contrived reinforcers are already a part of our culture, that the learning of self-control techniques increases the client's or patient's freedom, that the patient or client is already controlled by the current environmental consequences, and that the client can select the desired goals of the behavior modification program.

Behavior therapy procedures that involve deprivation (withholding of desired objects and events) or aversive conditioning have come under special criticism. Aversive procedures (such as contingent electric shock) have been employed most often to lessen physically self-abusive behavior in the developmentally disabled and, during the 1970's, in attempts to change the behavior of persons with lengthy histories of sexual deviance. Time-out (a procedure in which a person is removed from all sources of reinforcement for a brief period of time) has also received criticism. Its use by school districts has been restricted in some states.

Legal authorities at two levels have singled out behavior therapy for regulation (again, nearly always techniques that involve aversive procedures or depriving a patient in some manner). Federal courts in several decisions have restricted the kinds of reinforcers (rewards) that may be withheld from patients and have required that in all circumstances the "least restrictive alternative" be employed in treating a patient. In addition, state legislatures and state divisions of mental health have established regulations limiting the use of aversive procedures and requiring review committees for certain behavior-modification techniques.

The Association for the Advancement of Behavior Therapy has developed a set of ethical guidelines for behavior therapists and has, along with the Association for Behavior Analysis, assisted states in developing appropriate regulations that ensure that patients have the right to effective treatment and the right to decline treatment. The associations have also been concerned that persons instituting behavior modification and therapy programs in fact have the requisite training to do so. Standards for claiming expertise in the field have been developed.

One of the unique aspects of behavior analysis and therapy is the attempt to develop ethical principles based upon theories of behaviorism and behavior analyses of the situations in which ethical constraints are necessary. For the most part, these efforts have been undertaken by followers of B. F. Skinner, who have tried to develop his ethical ideas.

—Terry Knapp

Further Reading

Barker, Philip J., and Steve Baldwin, eds. *Ethical Issues in Mental Health*. London: Chapman & Hall, 1991.

Bellack, Alan S., Michel Herson, and Alan E. Kazdin, eds. *International Handbook of Behavior Modification and Therapy*. 2d ed. New York: Plenum Press, 1990.

Keith-Spiegel, Patricia, and Gerald P. Koocher. *Ethics in Psychology: Professional Standards and Cases*. New York: McGraw-Hill, 1985.

Scotti, Joseph R., and Luanna H. Meyer, eds. *Behavioral Intervention: Principles, Models, and Practices*. Baltimore: Paul H. Brookes, 1999.

Stolz, Stephanie B. *Ethical Issues in Behavior Modification*. San Francisco: Jossey-Bass, 1978.

Van Hoose, William H., and Jeffery A. Kottler. *Ethical and Legal Issues in Counseling and Psychotherapy*. 2d ed. San Francisco: Jossey-Bass, 1985.

See also: Behaviorism; Family therapy; Group therapy; Psychology; Therapist-patient relationship.

Bioethics

Definition: Multidisciplinary study of ethical problems of humanity arising from scientific advances in medicine and technology

Type of ethics: Bioethics

Significance: As a discipline, bioethics seeks to develop a set of guidelines for moral decision making utilizing the resources of medicine, biology, law, philosophy, theology, and social sciences.

While the rudiments of bioethics are ancient in origin, modern bioethics—medical, scientific, and environmental—is a relatively young field, which emerged around 1970. Its growth has been necessitated by increasingly complex dilemmas brought about by sophisticated technological knowledge and capabilities. Bioethics deals with questions of moral dimension and professional responsibility involving all forms of life: issues of medical decision making, living and dying, withdrawing and withholding medical care, conducting research on human subjects, allocating scarce resources, transferring cells from one or several organisms to produce another with particular characteristics ("cloning"), and preserving natural resources by efficient use of energy to protect the atmosphere and counteract the deleterious effect of pollutants.

These are issues for which no single clear-cut or mechanical answers are possible. Proposed solutions involve reviewing the parameters of various options and selecting the most beneficial. Superimposed on that seemingly facile solution are overriding considerations such as the identity of the decision maker, his or her values, legal capacity, and priorities. Bioscience is based on principles of natural science and risk assessment, while bioethics is based on moral principles developed and applied in the context of professional ethics.

Historical Background

Ethical medical guidelines are rooted in the writings of the Greek physician Hippocrates, who was born about 460 bce. The Hippocratic oath taken by physicians reflects the traditional notions of paternalism of the medical profession, which regard the physician as the primary decision maker for the patient and the person best able to decide what course of action is in the patient's best interest. The oath requires physicians to act to benefit the sick and keep them from harm ("*primum non nocere*"). It also admonishes physicians to refrain from assisting patients in suicide or abortion. Most of the codes of ethics adopted by the American Medical Association (AMA) in 1847 and revised in 1903, 1912, 1947, 1955, and 1980 use a similar approach. In 1957, the AMA adopted *Principles of Medical Ethics*, a set of ten principles outlining the ethical mandate of the physician and requiring the medical profession to use its expertise to serve humanity. In 1973, the American Hospital Association adopted a "Patient's Bill of Rights," which ensures patient privacy and confidentiality. *Lectures on the Duties and Qualifications of a Physician*, written by John Gregory, professor of medicine at the University of Edinburgh, was published in 1772. The

book emphasized the virtues and dignity of the physician and further defined his responsibilities and duties. In 1803, Thomas Percival, an English physician, wrote *Medical Ethics*. Pragmatic in approach, it stressed the professional conduct of the physician, and his relationships with hospitals, medical charities, apothecaries, and attorneys. Percival encouraged physicians to act to maximize patients' welfare. His influence is reflected in the AMA codes of 1847 and 1957.

A changed focus from a theological approach to a growing secularization of bioethics began with Episcopalian theologian Joseph Fletcher's *Medicine and Morals* (1954), which introduced "situation ethics," emphasizing the uniqueness of moral choice. Protestant theologian Paul Ramsey's *The Patient as Person* (1970) examined the emerging moral issues. Environmentalism is derived from conservation and ecology. The former concept originated with forester Gifford Pinchot during the administration of President Theodore Roosevelt in the early twentieth century. At that time, the populace first became aware of conservation, but only in the context of how to manage natural resources; the consequences of the wasteful use of property were not considered. The term "ecology" was invented by Ernst Haeckel, a biologist and philosopher, and introduced in his 1866 book *General Morphology of Organisms*. Use of the term spread throughout the life sciences. Charles Elton, a founder of scientific ecology, explained that primitive men and women are actually ecologists who interpreted their surroundings. Therefore, environmentalism may be said to equate to primitivism. Ecology became a household word during the 1960's, when a public outcry arose concerning abuses of the environment.

Biotechnology evolved from biblical times. Noah's drunkenness, described in the Book of Genesis, indicates a requisite familiarity with the process of fermentation, which must have been used to produce the alcohol that Noah imbibed. Used in leavened bread, cheese, and pickling, the fermentation process was later utilized to isolate organisms capable of producing acetone and butanol and, in 1928, penicillin and streptomycin.

During the late 1940's, the study of deoxyribonucleic acid (DNA) began, for scientists recognized that every inherited characteristic has its origin somewhere in the code of each person's DNA. The structure of DNA was discovered during the early 1950's. Viewed as one of the major scientific accomplishments of the twentieth century, the study of DNA has significantly widened the horizons of biotechnology.

Principles of Biomedical Ethics Illustrated

The U.S. Constitution guarantees persons the right to exercise their liberty and independence and the power to determine their own destinies and courses of action. Autonomy is legally grounded in the right to privacy, guaranteed as a "penumbra," or emanation, of several amendments of the U.S. Bill of Rights. The philosophical origins of autonomy stem from John Locke's *Two Treatises of Government* (1690), Immanuel Kant's *Grundlegen Zur Metaphysik deu Sitten* (1785; *Groundwork for the Metaphysics of Morals)*, and John Stuart Mill's *On Liberty* (1989).

There is an inherent tension at the core of biomedical ethics, which springs from the need to balance the rights of patients to act in their own best interests without constraint from others (autonomy) and the obligation of health care professionals to act to promote the ultimate good of the patients, prevent harm, or supplant harm (beneficence). A conflict between patient autonomy and beneficence may arise in the context of medical treatment, acute care, or chronic care.

Acting in the patient's best interest may dictate a certain course of conduct that is medically indicated but whose result is unacceptable to the patient in terms of limitations in lifestyle. The President's Commission for the Study of Ethical Problems in Medicine and Biomedical and Behavioral Research (1983) declared that where conflicts between patients' self-interest and well-being remain unresolved, respect for autonomy becomes paramount. A weighing or balancing of the benefits against the burdens must be considered in order to arrive at an acceptable solution. Often, notions of paternalism are raised.

The principle of non-maleficence, or the non-infliction of harm or evil on the patient, may conflict with obligations to promote the good of the patient, because many medical courses of action may involve certain undesirable consequences yet result in an ultimate benefit. (An example is inflicting a negligible surgical wound to avoid death). In other circumstances, such as the continued futile treatment of seriously ill newborns, pointless treatment for the irreversibly comatose patient, or a decision to withdraw artificial nutrition or hydration from a patient in a persistent vegetative state, there must be a weighing of potential benefit versus potential harm. Quality of life considerations may influence the outcome of the analysis.

The principle of justice seeks a scheme whereby scarce resources may be allocated fairly and uniform criteria may be developed to determine, for example, an order for the allocation of organs for transplantation, space in intensive care units, participation as clinical research subjects, and access to health care for those who lack health insurance. Governed by a cost-benefit analysis, distributive justice issues arose as pressures for health care cost containment that emerged during the 1980's escalated during the 1990's.

Informed Consent

The most concrete example of autonomous decision making is contained in the doctrine of informed consent: an explanation of the patient's condition; an explanation of the procedures to be used, along with their risks and benefits; a description of available alternatives or options, if any; and reasonable opportunity for the patient to change his or her mind, withdraw consent, or refuse consent. Informed consent free from coercion or deception must be obtained before procedures that invade the body can be performed. In the normal setting absent an emergency, if proper consent is not obtained, a legal action for battery may ensue.

In the partnership model that characterizes the physician-patient relationship in pluralist Western society, variables may act as obstacles to the true exercise of autonomy. Individual circumstances and cultural, familial, and religious differences may color a person's moral judgment and influence that person's decision-making capacity. Because of patients' limited understanding of their medical conditions, they may make decisions that are ambivalent, contradictory, or detrimental to their own health. At the same time, they may be harmed by the fears and anxieties induced by a more accurate understanding of the risks and options they face. The health care professional may be required to make a determination about the extent of disclosure and the degree of assimilation of the information conveyed.

The most controversial exception to informed consent is the therapeutic privilege, which permits medical personnel to withhold information intentionally if in the exercise of sound medical judgment it is determined that divulging certain information would be harmful to the patient. The use of placebos for the welfare of the patient is an extension of the therapeutic privilege. Another instance of intentional nondisclosure or limited disclosure occurs in the context of clinical research, where "adequate" disclosure for purposes of consent does not necessitate "complete" disclosure. Resolution of these and other dilemmas of this nature are the subject of debate in this area.

Environmental Ethics

The steadily developing global environmental crisis is serving as a catalyst for the reexamination of human values and ethical concerns about moral responsibility for the common good. Questions of environmental concern include the propriety of exposing workers to substances whose toxicity is unknown or discharging pollutants into the air, the role of the government in preventing adverse activity, a determination of the steps to be taken to halt or slow the erosion of biological diversity, and the fair and equitable allocation of material resources.

Examples of serious environmental problems that threaten the earth and its inhabitants are overpopulation, an inadequate food supply, the threat of global warming or climate change caused by the release of greenhouse gases and the destruction of the ozone layer, deforestation, loss of biodiversity, threats of water and air pollution, and the depletion of mineral and energy resources. Wastes and poisons are threatening land, water, and air quality as well as mineral and energy resources. Soil erosion is the greatest threat to farmland. Chemical fertilization, once thought to provide a solution to the problem of the billions of tons of topsoil that are lost in runoff, is costly and does not accomplish its goal effectively. Worldwide dumping of litter has caused the loss of millions of sea birds and animals and contamination from crude oil residue. Freshwater lakes have become polluted from bacteria, sewage, groundwater contamination, and hazardous waste; drinking water has remained unprotected.

Acid rain is a damaging form of air pollution. Wind may cause acid rain to rise high in the air and travel many miles. A product of combustion, acid rain kills fish in lakes, destroys crops, corrodes pipes carrying lake water, and releases toxic metals from soil compounds into groundwater. The main sources of contaminants in acid rain are combustion fumes from industry and automobile and truck exhausts. Environmentalists have warned of a "greenhouse effect"—that is, a trend toward global warming—resulting from the buildup of carbon monoxide and other gases in the atmosphere. These climatic changes are expected to melt glaciers and ice caps, causing sea levels to rise, flooding cities and coastal areas. The decline in rainfall could potentially cause mass starvation and the extinction of plant and animal life unable to adapt to changed conditions. Depletion of the earth's ozone layer would permit potentially carcinogenic ultraviolet rays to escape into the atmosphere. Because of the worldwide deforesting of acres of trees, the earth's ability to reabsorb carbon dioxide has been reduced.

A general increase in energy efficiency is the fastest and cheapest solution to the problem. Energy efficiency reduces fuel consumption, thereby reducing the output of gases into the atmosphere. The development of automobiles that run on clean-burning natural gas or methanol will reduce emissions into the atmosphere. Using solar power, tidal power, and geothermal energy (natural steam produced by heat within the earth itself) as alternative energy sources have also been proposed as solutions. The use of atomic energy has also been debated.

In 1993, U.S. president Bill Clinton signed an international biodiversity treaty designed to protect plants and animals, committing the nation to reduce emissions of greenhouse gases to their 1990 levels by the year 2000. Earth Day, celebrated on April 22 of each year since 1970, calls attention to environmental problems. Community groups have instituted recycling programs. Activist groups such as the Sierra Club and Greenpeace and organizations such as Earthwatch and the Worldwatch Institute have flourished, alerting policy makers and the general public to emerging trends and the availability and management of resources.

The Environmental Protection Agency (EPA) is the federal governmental agency with the responsibility to enforce compliance with environmental standards through monitoring programs and inspections. Those who knowingly violate environmental laws may be subject to criminal sanctions. Under the Clean Water Act of 1972, negligent acts can also be construed as criminal violations (felonies or misdemeanors punishable by fine, imprisonment, or both).

Biomedical Technology

The use of new technological powers brings challenges to traditional notions of preserving human dignity, individual freedom, and bodily integrity. Scientific ability to prolong life through the use of respirators, pacemakers, and artificial organs; to conquer infertility and gestation through in vitro fertilization and fetal monitoring; and to practice birth control through abortion and techniques for reducing fertility make it possible to manipulate life. Genetic engineering and human genetic manipulation have unlimited potential. Overriding ethical considerations concerning problems of abuse and misuse of technological powers, must, however, be addressed.

Genetic Engineering

Ethical and social questions about experimenting on the unborn and the possible misuse and abuse of power have been raised since genetic engineering (also known as gene splicing, genetic manipulation, gene cloning, and recombinant DNA research) sparked the revolution in biotechnology. The debate was especially intense during the mid-1970's, when fear about the wisdom of interfering with nature in a fundamental way was thought to outweigh the possible benefits in biological and medical research. It was feared that genetic accidents could occur when someone with expertise deliberately constructed an organism with the potential to threaten human health. There was also the fear that gene therapy might be used to alter human attributes such as intelligence or physical appearance. As scientists demonstrated evidence of precautions and federal government guidelines regulating genetic engineering research and banning certain types of experiments were drafted, a majority of biologists concluded that the risks were negligible.

The industry most affected by biotechnology is the pharmaceutical industry. In September, 1982, insulin from bacteria became the first of many genetically engineered materials licensed for human consumption. The potential is enormous as better and cheaper antibiotics are developed, improved methods for matching organs for transplantation are found, and techniques for correcting body chemistry emerge. Transferring genes from one organism to another would reduce the cost and increase the supply of materials used in medicine, agriculture, and industry. Far-reaching benefits from the bioindustrial revolution include better health, more food, renewable sources of energy, more efficient industrial processes, and reduced pollution.

Genetic Screening and the Human Genome Project

The genome, or combination of genes acquired from one's biological parents, is central to a person's development. The three-billion-dollar, fifteen-year Human Genome Project, initiated during the 1990's to map human DNA, aims to study the total genetic endowment in the chromosomes, identify new markers for traits and diseases believed to have a genetic basis, and develop diagnostic tests to screen for hereditary diseases. Advances in human gene therapy could lead to the prevention of hereditary diseases and the alteration of inherited characteristics. Prenatal screening through amniocentesis or chorionic villus sampling makes possible informed choices about childbearing and alleviates the anxiety of noncarriers of diseases such as sickle-cell anemia and Tay-Sachs disease. Ethical issues and public policy dilemmas in this area involve the right to experiment, accessibility to organ and fetal transplants, and the imposition of controls in genetic testing.

—Marcia J. Weiss

Further Reading

Beauchamp, Tom L., and James F. Childress. *Principles of Biomedical Ethics.* 5th ed. New York: Oxford University Press, 2001. An important textbook and central resource in the study of bioethical theory.

Engelhardt, H. Tristram, Jr. *The Foundations of Bioethics.* New York: Oxford University Press, 1986. A critique of theoretical bioethics and a cogent issue-oriented explanation of the role of theories and values in the concepts of health and disease.

Gore, Albert. *Earth in the Balance: Ecology and the Human Spirit.* Boston: Houghton Mifflin, 1992. The former vice president of the United States discusses the environmental crisis on a global scale and alleges that every aspect of society, including political leaders, is involved in its consequences.

Holland, Stephen. *Bioethics: A Philosophical Introduction.* Malden, Mass.: Blackwell, 2003. This indispensable introduction to contemporary bio-ethical issues includes discussions of the moral status of biological tissue, the effects of biotechnology upon personal identity, and the natural or unnatural status of genetic modification, as well as the more traditional issues of life, death, and euthanasia.

Kass, Leon R. *Toward a More Natural Science: Biology and Human Affairs.* New York: Free Press, 1985. An issue-oriented discussion of the relationship between science and ethics in the light of new technologies and traditional democratic values.

Kogan, Barry S., ed. *A Time to Be Born and a Time to Die: The Ethics of Choice.* Hawthorne, N.Y.: Aldine De Gruyter, 1991. Proceedings of a thought-provoking conference dealing with the impact of current medical and technological advances on the ethics of controversies concerned with the beginning and the end of life from philosophical, religious, medical, and legal perspectives.

Olson, Steve. *Biotechnology: An Industry Comes of Age.* Washington, D.C.: National Academy Press, 1986. A basic book on the advances in biotechnology and their implications.

Pierce, Jessica, and Andrew Jameton. *The Ethics of Environmentally Responsible Health Care.* New York: Oxford University Press, 2004. This original and important text draws connections between bioethics and environmental ethics. Not only does it advocate environmentally responsible medicine, but it also argues that environmental degradation is making people sick and increasing the burden on the health care system.

Prentis, Steve. *Biotechnology: A New Industrial Revolution*. New York: George Braziller, 1984. A detailed book with diagrams and illustrations explaining basic concepts in biotechnology and their uses in medicine, agriculture, and industry.

Scheffer, Victor B. *The Shaping of Environmentalism in America*. Seattle: University of Washington Press, 1991. Explores the roots of environmentalism and examines progress in education, law, and politics in dealing with areas of concern.

See also: Biometrics; Biotechnology; Birth defects; Cloning; Eugenics; Euthanasia; Genetic engineering; Genetic testing; Global warming; Hippocrates; Human Genome Project; Stem cell research.

Biofeedback

Definition: Discipline that trains people to regulate physical functions of their bodies that are under involuntary control or are no longer under voluntary control

Date: Established during the early 1960's

Type of ethics: Bioethics

Significance: Biofeedback provides an alternative to painful and more extreme treatments for health problems, but it poses ethical questions in areas of human and other animal research.

Biofeedback has been used to treat a variety of health problems and to help people perform well. Among the health problems treated with biofeedback are gastrointestinal cramping, fecal incontinence, frequency and severity of epileptic seizures, high blood pressure, migraine headaches, tics, insomnia, bronchial asthma, bruxism (clenching and grinding of the teeth), sexual dysfunction, masticatory pain and dysfunction (MPD), temporomandibular joint (TMJ) syndrome, and Raynaud's disease (a functional disorder of the cardiovascular system characterized by poor blood circulation to the hands, feet, and face).

Biofeedback has also been used to treat patients whose muscles are no longer under voluntary control because of a stroke or an injury. Among the uses of biofeedback to improve performance are controlling test anxiety, improving athletic performance, controlling motion sickness in Air Force pilots, and reducing space adaptation syndrome (SAS) for astronauts. Biofeedback has also been used to help people quit smoking and to help people lose weight. Biofeedback trains people to regulate physical functions of their bodies. It provides continuous information about physiological responses so that individuals can learn to regulate these responses. Three types of biofeedback are inte-

grated electromyographic feedback (EMG), electrodermal response (EDR), and electroencephalographic response (EEG). EMG, in which muscular activity is recorded, is used for treatment of muscles and migraine headache. EDR, which records perspiration responses on the palms, is more often used for weight control, managing stress, or improved athletic performance. EEG biofeedback helps individuals gain voluntary control of their alpha rhythms.

Biofeedback is based on operant, rather than classical, conditioning. (In operant conditioning, desired behavior is rewarded with a stimulus; in classical conditioning, a conditioned stimulus precedes an unconditioned stimulus—for example, Pavlov's class heard the sound of the bell and then were shown food—until the conditional stimulus alone can elicit the desired behavior.) During the process of biofeedback, machines record physiological functions such as muscle movement, alpha waves, heart rate, blood pressure, or body temperature. The machines feed this information back to the patient in the form of numbers, gauges on a meter, lights, or sounds. Through this process, the patient learns to focus attention on controlling physical responses. The result, in part, is training of alpha waves that results in the calming effects of meditation.

Research and Experimentation

In the United States, experiments with operant conditioning of heart rate began in 1962. The first biofeedback studies of controlling blood pressure in humans were reported at Harvard in 1969. Such studies mark the early stages of biofeedback. Even though biofeedback, by historical standards, was first explored in the United States quite recently, Asian spiritual practitioners have, for centuries, been practicing conscious control of involuntary functions though meditation. Today, in clinics throughout the United States, biofeedback techniques are being taught to patients in as few as five to ten sessions.

According to Dr. Lilian Rosenbaum, in her 1989 book *Biofeedback Frontiers*, biofeedback research has moved into applications for diabetes, cancer, acquired immunodeficiency syndrome (AIDS), physical rehabilitation, education, vision disorders, improving performance in space, and developing superior athletes. Biofeedback is also being used to treat social disorders in criminals who voluntarily participate in the experiments. As researchers move into new areas, the machines that record the individuals' responses become more sophisticated. Among the most sophisticated of these machines is the computerized automated psycho-physiological scan (Capscan), developed by Charles Stroebel and his colleagues. The Capscan "combines advances in computers, computerized electroencephalography (brain-wave measurements) and biofeedback, according to Rosenbaum.

Concerning the ethics of biofeedback, it is relevant that much of the data on biofeedback comes from those who practice biofeedback and believe in its effectiveness. Several researchers, however, are exploring the ethical concerns in biofeedback research. Much of their concern focuses on the need for human subjects, since human consciousness is involved in the control of muscle responses that are usually regarded as involuntary. Testing the validity of biofeedback involves, in part, establishing control groups so that researchers can determine whether biofeedback or a placebo effect of psychotherapy is responsible for the results. Researcher Martin T. Orne observes that not only drugs but also treatment procedures themselves have "placebo components" that have "powerful effects on their own."

In summarizing the effects of biofeedback, Orne concludes that the effects of biofeedback are similar to the effects of relaxation therapy, self-hypnosis, or meditation. Nevertheless, he concludes, each of these techniques shows "considerable therapeutic effect" for various individuals, and such approaches "have been overlooked for many years, at least in this country."

Another ethical issue in biofeedback research involves the use of animal subjects. Research in biofeedback has often involved animal experimentation, especially with curarized animals—that is, animals in a state of drug-induced immobility. Some of the first studies with curarized animals involved rats that responded to stimulation of the pleasure center in the brain to slow down or speed up involuntary body functions. When the pleasure centers in the brain were stimulated, some of the rats responded by slowing down involuntary responses so much that death resulted. Other animal studies involved learning visceral and glandular (autonomic) responses. Additional animal studies have involved mice, golden hamsters, and baboons in Kenya.

Modern researchers have posed a number of complex ethical questions related to research in biofeedback, particularly questions involving the "justification for withholding therapy for research purposes."

John P. Hatch, in his discussion of ethics, lists a number of concrete ethical questions related to placebo therapy, fees for service, random selection of subjects, acceptable control treatment, and effects of biofeedback research on patients. He concludes that the "central ethical question is whether current knowledge allows a preferred treatment to be chosen, and whether the relative risk to a patient would be greater as a result of assigning treatments randomly versus basing treatment assignments on clinical judgment."

—Carol Franks

Further Reading

Hatch, John P., Johnnie G. Fisher, and John D. Rugh, eds. *Biofeedback: Studies in Clinical Efficacy.* New York: Plenum Press, 1987.

Lattal, Kennon A., and Michael Perone, eds. *Handbook of Research Methods in Human Operant Behavior.* New York: Plenum, 1998.

Rosenbaum, Lilian. *Biofeedback Frontiers.* Vol. 15 in *Stress in Modern Society.* New York: AMS Press, 1989.

Schwartz, Mark Stephen, and Frank Andrasik. *Biofeedback: A Practitioner's Guide.* 3d ed. New York: Guilford Press, 2003.

Van Hoose, William H., and Jeffrey A. Kottler. *Ethical and Legal Issues in Counseling and Psychotherapy.* 2d ed. San Francisco: Jossey-Bass, 1985.

White, Leonard, and Bernard Tursky, eds. *Clinical Biofeedback: Efficacy and Mechanisms.* New York: Guilford Press, 1982.

See also: American Medical Association; Bioethics; Biotechnology; Ethical Principles of Psychologists; Holistic medicine; Hypnosis; *Principles of Medical Ethics.*

Biometrics

Definition: Scientific techniques of measuring human biological data for purposes of identification

Type of ethics: Bioethics

Significance: Identifying people through biometrics reduces the incidence of false identification but at the same time poses ethical questions about how to protect such data from error and irresponsible dissemination.

As modern society grows more ever more complex, new questions of identification loom, especially for organizations that, for security reasons, must control access to their facilities and databanks. However, using biological data for human identification is not a new idea. In the late seventeenth century, a British physician noted that each human being has fingerprints that are wholly unique. Fingerprinting was perhaps the earliest form of biometrics but was not widely used by law enforcement and other agencies until the mid-nineteenth century. By the early twentieth century, fingerprinting was well entrenched as a means of identifying people, particularly those who left incriminating marks behind at the scenes of their crimes. Eventually, police departments began routinely finger-printing suspects and building files of their prints. By the 1920's, such agencies as the Federal Bureau of Investigation (FBI) had extensive fingerprint files. Local police departments could match prints they took from recently arrested prisoners against those collected in the huge FBI fingerprint archive.

Biometric Fundamentals

The word "biometrics" is derived from two Greek roots, *bio-*, for life, and *metrein*, for "to measure."

The science of biometrics rests on the supposition that no two living entities are wholly identical. Every living entity has physical and behavioral characteristics that distinguish it from every other living entity, including members of its own species. Underlying the implementation of biometrics to human beings is the presumption that every person, or at least the vast majority of people, share common characteristics, like fingers or eyes. Obviously, some people lack body parts for various reasons; however, because the vast majority of people have all the basic parts, reasonably accurate biological measurements involving these features have been devised.

Biometrics is ineffective unless elements of entities' features are unique to those entities, such as the whorls of individual fingerprints or specific characteristics of hands, eyes, or faces. These characteristics must be relatively constant. Characteristics that change over time often yield false readings if biometric measures are applied to them. Moreover, the physical features or behaviors being measured, such as handwriting or speech patterns, must be measurable by reliable devices.

Common Uses of Biometrics

Devices that can verify the identity of people have obvious practical uses. A device that can scan eyes, faces, or hands of people and identify them accurately in mere seconds, provides a more foolproof safeguard against identity theft and related problems than such measures as passwords, keys, and entry cards. As security has been increasingly necessary because of widespread international terrorism, those entrusted with protecting the national welfare have accelerated the use of biometrics to screen people in many contexts, most notably in airports and at border crossings.

Business corporations employ biometric devices to permit quick and easy entry of authorized personnel into

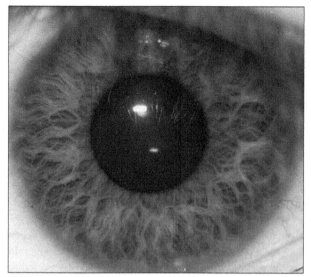

Iris recognition biometric systems apply mathematical pattern-recognition techniques to images of the irises of an individual's eyes. By Smhossei.

restricted facilities. One simple practical application is employee time clocks that identify people by having them insert their hands into slots to have their identities confirmed. Employees who arrive late or leave their jobs early thus cannot have friends punch in or out for them, as was sometimes done in the past.

Ethical Concerns

Because some biometric processes are conducted without the knowledge and consent of those being scrutinized, significant ethical questions arise. For example, a supermarket chain might gather information about its customers' shopping habits by identifying otherwise anonymous customers through eye scans—something it could do without its customers' knowledge. One might therefore justifiably ask how such information would be used and to whom and under what circumstances the information might be disseminated. Similar concerns are voiced about medical records that may in time come to haunt a person whose eye scans reveal, as they surely might, some health conditions, such as diabetes or hypertension, that could keeping them from getting jobs or insurance coverage. Questions regarding the individual privacy of people raise both ethical and constitutional concerns when biometric procedures make it possible for databases to be developed that might, if broadly available to employers or organizations, jeopardize individual rights to privacy.

As societies grow in complexity, trade-offs between individual rights and the protection of society often seem justifiable. When such trade-offs stay within bounds, many people accept them. The question arises, however, of whether some zealous officials might allow anticipated ends to justify the means of achieving them, perhaps for purely political reasons. In situations in which employers require employees to sign out by putting their hands into a scanner that will identify them, presumably unerringly, one can reasonably argue that employers have the right to verify that their employees are giving them the full measure of time for which they are being paid. Even if the use of scanners for this purpose appears to infringe on individual privacy, most people will realize the validity of such measures and will not strongly object to them.

However, if biometric devices gather and store data about individuals, the situation becomes more questionable. Even when safeguards are in place to protect the privacy of individuals, many people fear that such safeguards at some future point might be relaxed in ways that would compromise individual privacy rights. Those who use biometric devices for purposes of identification may vow that they will make no unethical uses of the information they gather, but a danger lurks in the minds of many people that public and private attitudes toward the inviolability of such information will eventually weaken, and that harmful information may become accessible to those who can justify their need for it in the name of assuring the national security or some vague greater good.

—*R. Baird Shuman*

Further Reading

Smith, Richard E. *Authentication: From Passwords to Public Keys.* Boston: Addison-Wesley, 2002.

Tocci, Salvatore. *High-Tech IDs: From Finger Scans to Voice Patterns.* New York: Franklin Watts, 2000.

Vacca, John R. *Identity Theft.* Upper Saddle River, N.J.: Prentice-Hall PTR, 2003.

Woodward, John D., Jr., Nicholas M. Orlans, and Peter T. Higgins. *Biometrics.* Boston: New York: McGraw-Hill/Osborne, 2003.

Zhang, David. *Automated Biometrics: Technologies and Systems.* Boston: Kluwer Academic Publishers, 2000.

See also: Bioethics; Biotechnology; Business ethics; Drug testing; Employee safety and treatment; Hiring practices; Identity theft; Invasion of privacy; Privacy.

Biotechnology

Definition: Application of science to the biological realm; the term is often used synonymously with genetic engineering, the artificial modification of the genetic codes of living organisms

Date: Concept first emerged during the 1960's

Type of ethics: Bioethics

Significance: Because of the great potential for changes that may have social, economic, political and environmental consequences, ethical principles must guide biotechnological choices.

A host of issues are subsumed under the rubric "biotechnology," including human and animal reproductive technologies such as cloning, the creation of genetically modified organisms and products, including food, xenotransplantation (the cross transplantation of human and animal genes and organs), human genetic testing and therapies, and stem cell research. As with most novel and highly complex technologies, no consensus obtains regarding the relevant ethical principles.

The Bases for Ethical Judgments

The utilitarian principle posits that when the potential exists for good and harm, the ratio of good to harm must be considered when developing, employing, and regulating technologies. Debates then may arise as to how benefits and risks should be prioritized. The "precautionary principle" would lead decision-makers to act with caution in advance of scientific proof of harm, to place the onus of proof on those who propose new technologies, and to promote intrinsic natural rights. Calculating potential benefits and harm is a formidable task given the novelty of these technologies, high levels of scientific uncertainty, the interconnected character of all natural phenomena, and the multiple economic, political, and social issues involved. Some fear that development of some biotechnologies increases moral hazard (or represents a "slippery slope") in that it increases the likelihood that humankind will cross fundamental thresholds with potential significant negative consequences for humankind.

The Human Genome Project well illustrates the potential benefits, risks, and moral hazards of biotechnology. This large research effort, funded by the United States and other governments, has now decoded the human deoxyribonucleic acid (DNA) sequence. This knowledge will ultimately allow scientists to understand diseases such as cystic fibrosis and conditions such as intelligence and aggression and to create drug therapies for specific genetic abnormalities. However, the success of the project raises the prospect of genetic profiling, which creates the possibility that employers may discriminate against applicants on the basis of their genetic profiles, or that corporations may adjust medical insurance rates to reflect policyholders' genetic predispositions. A potential moral hazard associated with this technology is that once an individual is classified by genotype, it is but a step to justify death for undesirable genetic traits.

Justice and Freedom

Universal principles of justice and autonomy may also serve as the bases for evaluating biotechnologies. When combined with utilitarian considerations, principles of distributive justice would dictate that the issue of potential benefit and harm be considered. It is important that the benefits of biotechnologies are distributed equitably: Potential risks should not fall disproportionately on those already burdened with various forms of discrimination, and powerful individuals, corporations, and states should not benefit disproportionately from development and use of these technologies. Moreover, the technologies' consequences for those without strong voices must be taken into account. Justice would also mandate careful consideration of who can legitimately make decisions about the development and regulation of biotechnologies. For example, what should be the role of the scientific community and profit-driven corporations relative to other stakeholders in deciding which technologies are developed?

The principle of autonomy recognizes that the right to self-determination and freedom from coercion as an inalienable right. This logic would allow individuals to consent or decline, to participate in the biotechnology research, or to consume bioengineered products. Openness and honesty are required if people are to understand the implications of their choices and exercise their freedom, so it is incumbent on all actors involved in creating, marketing, and regulating biotechnologies to educate the public as to the potential consequences of various biotechnologies and to ensure that political decision making be transparent and democratic. Concerns about freedom and autonomy are complicated when the rights of embryos, the gravely ill, or future generations are taken into account.

"Human" Thresholds

Biotechnologies may raise philosophical concerns about what it means to be human in that they may change or breach thresholds associated with bisexual reproduction, social entities and roles such as the family and child rearing, and taboos against homicide. While many boundaries serve vested interests and are not essential to human well-being, some thresholds may preserve the essence of "humanness," including the actualization of individual identity and beneficent communal interaction.

Physical attributes, such as genetic makeup and intelligence, and the assignment of dignity to life also distinguish human beings from other species. Xenotransplantation clearly blurs barriers between humans and other organisms. The medical advances achieved by the year 2100 are expected to allow physicians to transplant human heads. By the early twenty-first century, reproductive technologies were already allowing humans to select the genetic makeup of their offspring, create new organisms, and create embryos for reproduction and other medical and scientific research. Many people worry that the commonplace creation, manipulation, and destruction of life portend changes in what it means to be "human" and reduce respect for the dignity of humankind and life. Ethical biotechnologies demand that individuals and groups most affected by their advances be invited to participate in the discourse and decision making about which biotechnologies are developed and how they will be regulated. Science and technology are not ethically neutral; human beings can reflect upon and assume responsibility for ethical choice among biotechnologies.

—*M. Leann Brown*

Further Reading

Charles, Daniel. *Lords of the Harvest: Biotech, Big Money, and the Future of Food*. Cambridge, Mass.: Perseus Publishing, 2001.

Fukuyama, Francis. *Our Posthuman Future*. New York: Picador, 2002.

Kristol, William, and Eric Cohen, eds. *The Future Is Now*. Lanham, Md.: Rowman&Littlefield, 2002.

Sherlock, Richard, and John D. Morrey. *Ethical Issues in Biotechnology*. Lanham, Md.: Rowman& Littlefield, 2002.

Stock, Gregory. *Redesigning Humans*. Boston: Houghton Mifflin, 2002.

See also: Bioethics; Biofeedback; Biometrics; Cloning; Genetic testing; Genetically modified foods; Human Genome Project; Medical research; Stem cell research; Technology.

Brain death

Definition: Cessation of the organic functions of the human brain

Type of ethics: Bioethics

Significance: New definitions of what constitutes human death are integrally tied to ethical decisions relating to decisions about efforts to sustain life and the possibility of organ transplantation.

Throughout most of history, human death was defined in terms of cessation of the heart and lungs. Human beings were considered to be dead only after their hearts and lungs permanently ceased functioning. Those criteria sufficed until modern advances in medical technology required reconsideration of how death should be defined. The invention of the iron lung and artificial stimulation of hearts has made continued respiration and circulation possible long after hearts and lungs lose their normal functional capacities. Death has consequently come to be understood in terms of functional activity associated with the organs, not the organs themselves. A greater challenge to the traditional definition of death came to the fore during the 1960's. New medical technology made it possible for the first time to maintain the cardiopulmonary functions of patients whose entire brains—or at least large portions of them—were effectively dead. Since that time, brain-dead patients have never been able to regain consciousness, but their bodies have been maintained for long periods of time, sometimes years or even decades, in an unconscious state. Another important advance during the 1960's was the beginning of successful transplants of complex organs, including the heart.

Development

Maintaining patients in a permanent vegetative state is expensive and a drain on human personnel and medical resources. In addition, because of continued respiration and blood flow, the organs of such patients do not necessarily degrade if blood pressure and essential plasma and blood gas components are properly regulated. Medically speaking, the organs of such patients frequently are prime candidates for successful transplantation. The high costs of keeping comatose patients alive and the growing need for organs for transplants place a new urgency on the need to reconsider traditional definitions of death. Over the course of about ten years, many ethical, legal, and medical authorities explicitly rejected a definition based on cessation of the lungs and heart and embraced a brain-oriented

definition of death. During the first years of the twenty-first century, the prevailing view was a brain-death definition: A human being is dead when and only when the brain has permanently ceased functioning.

Despite the popularity of the new brain-oriented definition, two opposing schools of thought have arisen. One group advocates a whole-brain definition. This view holds that a human being is dead when and only when the entire brain, including the cerebrum (the outer shell of which is the cortex), the cerebellum, and the brain stem (which includes the mid-brain, the pons, and the medulla oblongata), permanently stops functioning.

The other group advocates a higher-brain definition. According to their view, a human being is dead when and only when the cerebrum (or cortex) permanently stops functioning. The latter view is the more radical of the two. The difference between the two views is important: A patient considered dead on a higher-brain definition might still be considered alive on a whole-brain definition. In some cases, brain stem function, for example, can continue in the absence of cortical activity. A patient with such a condition might even exhibit spontaneous respiration and heartbeat.

Controversy

Although brain death definitions have largely superseded the heart-lung definition, controversy still surrounds them. Advocates of a heart-lung definition argue that brain-death definitions represent no new or deeper insights into the nature of human death. They further charge that those definitions are motivated by attempts to redefine costly and inconvenient patients out of existence, coupled with medical opportunism on the part of transplant surgeons and potential organ recipients.

Even within the brain death camp there are disagreements. Advocates of the whole-brain definition have argued that the higher-brain view confuses the idea of a human being ceasing to be a person—permanent loss of consciousness, associated with permanent loss of cerebral function—with the idea of a human being ceasing to be alive—permanent loss of governing organic function, associated with permanent loss of all brain functions. On the other hand, advocates of a higher-brain definition have argued that once the heart-lung definition has been abandoned, there is tacit recognition that what human death really concerns is the loss of what is essentially significant to human existence—consciousness—and not mere organic function. Thus, brain stem function, as not intrinsically associated with consciousness, is no more relevant to the determination of human death than kidney function.

—*Michael J. Wreen*

Further Reading

Lamb, David. *Death, Brain Death and Ethics*. London: Croon Helm, 1985.

Potts, Michael, Paul A. Byrne, and Richard G. Nilges. *Beyond Brain Death: The Case Against Brain-Based Criteria for Human Death*. Boston: Kluwer Academic Publishers, 2000.

President's Commission for the Study of Ethical Problems in Medicine and Biomedical Behavioral Research. *Defining Death*. Washington, D.C.: U.S. Superintendent of Documents, 1981.

Youngner, Stuart J., ed. *The Definition of Death: Contemporary Controversies*. Baltimore: Johns Hopkins University Press, 1999.

See also: Bioethics; Life and death; Medical bills of rights; Medical ethics; "Playing god" in medical decision making; Right to die; Sentience; Stem cell research.

Child psychology

Definition: Diagnosis and treatment of children with mental, emotional, or behavioral disorders

Type of ethics: Bioethics

Significance: The practice of child psychology raises ethical questions about consent; confidentiality; values conflicts among parents, child, and therapist; guidelines for research, and the role of the professional in court cases.

Because persons under the age of eighteen (minors) are considered by American law to be incompetent to make decisions for themselves, proxy consent from parents or guardians is required for medical treatment. Involving the child in the decision when possible respects the child as a person and has the practical advantage of giving the child information and enlisting his or her cooperation, which may be very important for the success of the treatment. Parents may commit children to hospitalization against their will, however, and still have the admission labeled as "voluntary."

While the law seems to assume that parents always decide in the best interest of the child, ethical dilemmas may arise when parents refuse consent for treatment of children deemed in need by school officials or others. This raises the question of whether children have a right to needed treatment. Exceptions to the parental consent requirement may be made in cases of older adolescents who are legally emancipated minors—that is, living independently of parents, married, or in the armed services—or who are considered by the therapist to be mature minors and thus able to decide for themselves.

Confidentiality

The maintenance of confidentiality between therapists and adult patients is recognized as an important ethical rule, and there are many reasons why confidentiality should be respected for children as well.

Much of the material that becomes known to the therapist is very personal and may involve issues that are sensi-

Photograph of Jean Piaget at the University of Michigan campus in Ann Arbor. Piaget was a Swiss psychologist known for his work on child development.

tive for the child or family. Pledges to honor confidentiality can enhance trust between children and their therapists. Also, harm may be done to children by "labeling."

Revealing past status as psychiatric patients can be a factor in denying later educational or job opportunities. Despite the importance of confidentiality, parents often think that they have a right to know everything, and sometimes a therapist may have to break confidentiality to protect the child or others. A therapist should be honest and state ground rules before beginning treatment and inform the child or family before revealing information.

Conflicts in Values

Who should set the goals for psychiatric or behavioral therapy for a child? Parents may have unrealistic expectations for their children or want help in making them conform to cultural ideals of behavior that are different from societal norms or that the therapist may find inappropriate for a particular child.

The therapist must decide whether to accept the family's values and help the child adapt to them or to help the child develop the strength to stand against parental pressures. Even using the best interest of the child as the standard, this can be a difficult decision. It is the right of parents to make decisions for their children and to bring them up as they see fit, and many child-rearing practices and behavioral expectations are accepted in a pluralistic society. Although society does set limits and require that certain basic needs be met, and has legal standards of abuse or neglect, therapists must be careful not to impose their own personal values on families.

Research

Research in child psychology and psychiatry can run from totally nonintrusive observation of normal children in public places to surveys by questionnaire and interviews all the way to trials of new behavior modification techniques or clinical trials of psychotropic drugs. The use of children as research subjects presents ethical problems because as minors they cannot legally volunteer and because in many studies it is very difficult to assess potential risk. Thus, some questions are virtually unexplored and data about causes and effective treatment are lacking. The picture is improving, however, since in 1991 Congress approved a national initiative for increased research on child and adolescent mental health.

Ethical guidelines for medical research with children were adopted as federal regulations in 1983, and they provide that research be well-designed in order to give valid, nontrivial results, that trials be made on animals and adults rather than on children when possible, that risks be outweighed by expected benefits, and that informed consent of parents or guardian be given. It is recommended that children older than age seven be asked for their assent, as well. Nontherapeutic research, whose main goal is to obtain scientific information, has stricter standards than does therapeutic research, whose primary goal is to benefit the child-subject. Despite parental consent, in nontherapeutic research any child over age seven may refuse assent and veto participation, any child may withdraw from the research at any time for any reason, and except under very special conditions, no child may be subjected to anything greater than "minimal" risk, defined as the sort of experience likely to be encountered in everyday activities.

Forensic Issues

Courts often depend on the professional evaluations of psychiatrists or psychologists to determine the "best interest of the child" in custody or adoption suits, the reliability of child witnesses, or the competency of juvenile offenders to stand trial as adults.

One must beware of potential bias or conflict of interest in such cases, since the professional may be hired by one party and be expected to give favorable testimony. There is no general agreement on the age or standards of competency that apply to adolescents or tests to determine the truthful reporting of young children; thus, professionals may offer conflicting judgments, and there may be no clear way to resolve the conflict.

—Rosalind Ekman Ladd

Further Reading

Forman, Edwin N., and Rosalind Ekman Ladd. *Ethical Dilemmas in Pediatrics.* New York: Springer-Verlag, 1991.

Graham, Philip. "Ethics and Child Psychiatry." In *Psychiatric Ethics*, edited by Sidney Bloch and Paul Chodoff. Oxford, England: Oxford University Press, 1981.

Hoagwood, Kimberly, Peter S. Jensen, and Celia B. Fisher, eds. *Ethical Issues in Mental Health Research with Children and Adolescents.* Mahwah, N.J.: Lawrence Erlbaum Associates, 1996.

Koocher, Gerald P., ed. *Children's Rights and the Mental Health Professions.* New York: Wiley, 1976.

Koocher, Gerald P., and Patricia C. Keith-Spiegel. *Children, Ethics, and the Law.* Lincoln: University of Nebraska Press, 1990.

Melton, Gary B., G. P. Koocher, and M. J. Saks, eds. *Children's Competence to Consent.* New York: Plenum, 1983.

Stein, Ronald. *Ethical Issues in Counseling.* Buffalo, N.Y.: Prometheus, 1990.

See also: Child abuse; Child soldiers; Children; Children's rights; Confidentiality; Medical ethics; Psychology; Psychopharmacology; Therapist-patient relationship.

Cloning

Definition: Artificial production of identical copies of genes, at the molecular level, or production of genetically identical organisms at the macroscopic level

Date: First attempted in 1952

Type of ethics: Bioethics

Significance: In theory, any living organism can be cloned, resulting in genetically identical copies of the original organism. However, the concept of cloning human beings has raised both medical and philosophical questions as to the desirability of the procedure.

The basis for cloning dates to the early twentieth century, when German zoologist Hans Spemann found that individual embryonic cells from salamanders each contained the hereditary information necessary to create identical organisms. He later performed nuclear transfer experiments using amphibians and was eventually honored with the Nobel Prize in Physiology or Medicine for his work in 1935. Similar experiments were attempted by Robert Briggs and T. J. King in 1952 using tadpoles. Though initially unsuccessful, they were eventually able to clone tadpoles.

The first successful cloning of large life-forms occurred in 1984, when Danish scientist Steen Willadsen demonstrated the cloning of a lamb from embryonic sheep cells. Using similar techniques, others were subsequently able to clone a variety of other animals. Although categorized as "twinnings," none of these experimental procedures involved the transfer of hereditary material from one cell to another.

The first actual case of cloning a mammal using nuclear transfer techniques was reported in February, 1997. Ian Wilmut at the Roslin Institute in Scotland reported the cloning of an adult sheep by transplanting the nucleus obtained from cells of the sheep's udder into an enucleated egg cell. The cloned animal, nicknamed "Dolly," quickly became world famous. However, it soon became apparent that the procedure was not as straightforward as first

claimed. More than 250 separate attempts had been made prior to the successful experiment. By 2003, animals as diverse as cattle, mules, mice, and cats had reportedly been cloned, but no primates had been successfully cloned.

Cloning Humans

The question of whether it is desirable, or even possible, to clone humans has engendered two schools of thought. First is the question of reproductive cloning. In theory, this would involve the production of genetically identical individuals using either individual cells, or isolated nuclei in transfer experiments, their implantation into a female, and subsequent development. It is difficult to justify such a procedure, especially given the high rate of failure. Simply put, the creation of genetically identical offspring is arguably more in the realm of egotism than simple desire for children.

Given the early twenty-first century state of understanding how embryonic cells are regulated, as well as the limited technology that exists, it is questionable whether reproductive cloning of humans is even possible. Even when attempting the procedure with less evolved animals, the process is highly inefficient and subject to large numbers of chromosomal changes.

Successful nuclear transplantation requires both the inactivation of genes normally expressed in the donor cell, as well as activation, in the proper sequence, of genes necessary for proper embryonic development. The result has been that most animal clones do not survive implantation; those that do grow to term often have a variety of defects. Among such defects is the problem of premature aging that probably results from changes in the telomeres, the repeat sequences on the ends of chromosomes that shorten as cell division occurs. Even the famous Dolly was physically an old sheep in a young body.

A different school of thought addresses a second application of the procedure: therapeutic cloning. The difference between the two cloning procedures is that the first, reproductive cloning, is to generate an identical embryo. Therapeutic cloning is performed for the purpose of producing cells identical to those of the donor, not to produce embryos. Nuclear transfer experiments can therefore be applied to the understanding of regulation of both embryonic and adult genes.

In addition, the procedure would result in creation of embryonic stem cells genetically identical to that of the donor. Being identical, such cells could be transplanted back into the donor to serve as "seeds" or replacement

In Star Wars, *clone troopers were genetically engineered to fight the Clone Wars. By Pat Loika.*

cells for those which have died or undergone pathological changes. For example, such cells might replace brain or heart cells that had been damaged without the need of immune suppression, or dependency on not identical donors. Cell transplantation using cloned embryonic cells would thus not require immunosuppressive drugs to prevent rejection.

Since the fetus does not develop as a result of therapeutic cloning, those genes that are necessary for fetal differentiation are unnecessary. The embryonic cells that do develop are multipotential in that, in theory, they could be programmed to develop into any type of body cell. In effect, these can be considered as forms of embryonic stem cells. In the year 2003, science was still unable to program these cells into the desired differentiation pathway; however, it appeared to remain only a matter of time until this problem would be solved.

It is of interest that while most established churches object to the use of cloning procedures for the purpose of reproduction, most have expressed a willingness to accept therapeutic cloning as long as there are proper guidelines. For example, aborted embryos should not be a source of cells. Even Orrin Hatch, a conservative Republican senator from Utah and a man considered observant within the Mormon Church, introduced legislation to support research in the technique of therapeutic cloning in early 2003.

—*Richard Adler*

Further Reading

Gould, Stephen Jay, et al. *Flesh of My Flesh: The Ethics of Cloning Humans*. Lanham, Md.: Rowman & Littlefield, 1998.

Hochedlinger, K., and R. Jaenisch. "Nuclear Transplantation, Embryonic Stem Cells and the Potential for Cell Therapy." *New England Journal of Medicine* 349, no. 3 (2003): 275-286.

Kass, Leon R., ed. *Human Cloning and Human Dignity: The Report of the President's Council on Bioethics*. New York: Public Affairs, 2002.

Kass, Leon, and James Wilson. *Ethics of Human Cloning*. Washington, D.C.: American Enterprise Institute, 1998.

Silver, Lee. *Remaking Eden: How Genetic Engineering and Cloning Will Transform the American Family*. New York: Avon Books, 1998.

Snedden, Robert. *DNA and Genetic Engineering*. Chicago: Heinemann Library, 2003.

See also: Bioethics; Biotechnology; Genetic engineering; Human Genome Project; Medical research; Stem cell research; Technology.

Death and dying

Definition: Cessation of human physiological, psychological, and possibly spiritual existence

Type of ethics: Beliefs and practices

Significance: Defining death precisely has become crucial to such medical and moral issues as euthanasia, living wills, quality of life, abortion, organ transplantation, and cryonics.

The modern study of death and dying, thanatology (named for the Greek god of death, Thanatos), could be said to have begun in 1956, when the American Psychological Association held a symposium on death at its annual convention. This resulted in the publication in 1959 of an anthology of essays on death written by scholars from a wide range of disciplines. Popular attention focused on death and dying with the publication of Elisabeth Kübler-Ross's *On Death and Dying* (1969), a study of the stages of dying.

Biological Definitions

Historically, definitions of death have undergone a number of revisions. The earliest medical determination of death was the cessation of heart activity, respiration, and all functions consequent thereon (now commonly referred to as "clinical death"). With the advancement of respirators and other sophisticated medical equipment, however, it became possible for a patient with no brain activity to be artificially kept "alive." In 1970, Kansas became the first state to adopt a brain-based criterion for determining death in addition to the cessation-of-vital-functions definition.

A number of states followed that definition, while others eliminated the traditional definition altogether and focused solely on a "brain death" model. The term "brain death" in these legal documents referred to the total and irreversible cessation of the functions of the entire brain, including both the "higher brain," which is regarded as the seat of conscious mental processes, and the "brain stem," which controls cardiopulmonary activity. This usually takes place from three to five minutes after clinical death, although the process can take much longer in cases of death by freezing or barbiturate overdose.

In 1981, a presidential commission proposed a "Uniform Determination of Death Act," which defined death as either "irreversible cessation of circulatory and respiratory functions" or "irreversible cessation of all functions of the entire brain, including the brain stem." Such a determination, it added, must be made "in accordance with accepted medical standards." This legal definition was adopted by more than half the states within the first decade after its formulation. As is evident from this formulation, rather than viewing death as an "event," it is more accurate to define death as a process encompassing at least three different types of death: clinical death (the cessation of vital signs), biological death (including the cessation of brain activity), and cellular death (including the deterioration of all of the body's cells).

Proposed Changes

While state legislations have employed a "whole brain" definition of death, there have been attempts made by some states to define death in terms of the cessation of cerebral activity in the upper portion of the brain. Proponents of this position argue that an individual's "personhood" relies upon the cognitive faculties of the "higher brain." According to this definition, an individual in a "persistent vegetative state" in which only the brain stem, controlling heartbeat and respiration, is functioning would not be considered a living "person." Since no consensus can be reached regarding the proper definition of "person," however, and since reliance on cognitive awareness would exclude severely senile, mentally deficient, and anencephalic individuals from the category of "persons," a "higher-brain" definition of death has been almost universally rejected by the medical community and general public.

Autonomy over One's Death

The American Medical Association's position that one need not use "extraordinary means" to keep a person alive is almost universally accepted. This is commonly referred to as "passive euthanasia." ("Euthanasia" comes from the Greek phrase meaning "good death.") This position has led to the development of a "living will," which states that the individual does not want life-sustaining devices and extraordinary medical procedures used to prolong his or her life. Although the "living will" is not a binding legal document in all states, it is considered by most courts of law to be a valid expression of the signer's wishes.

A more extreme example of belief in the authority of the individual to determine his or her death can be seen in the practice of "active euthanasia." Defined as the act of directly bringing about a person's death by a means unrelated to the illness itself (for example, injection, anesthesia without oxygen, and so forth), active euthanasia is illegal in virtually all parts of the world. The practice became widespread during the 1980's in Holland, however, where one out of every five deaths of older patients was caused by active euthanasia. Although the usual argument for active euthanasia cites extreme physical suffering as an acceptable reason, other justifications, including psychological distress, old age, limited mental capacity, and an unacceptable "quality of life," also have been advanced.

In fact, in the latter half of the 1980's, Holland extended the practice to include Down syndrome infants and anorexic young adults. Those ethicists opposed to active euthanasia point to the danger that more and more categories of candidates would become acceptable, were it to be allowed.

Other Bioethical Issues

For many people, the debate over abortion hinges on how the fetus is to be categorized. If the fetus can be considered a human being at a particular point in its prenatal development, abortion after that point would be regarded as the unlawful taking of a human life. A precise definition of both life and death is, therefore, crucial to the issue. Some people argue that the determination of where human life begins should employ the same criteria that are used to define the absence of life, or death.

Even though the first organ transplant in the United States took place in 1954, early transplants did not meet with a great deal of success, because cadaveric organs were not widely available during the 1950's and 1960's as a result of the difficulty of defining death. With the establishment of brain-based criteria for determining death and with the discovery of the immuno-suppresive drug cyclosporine, organ transplantation increased dramatically during the 1980's.

In order for organs from cadavers to remain viable for transplantation, heart and respiratory functions must be sustained artificially until the procedure can be performed. This necessitates a definition of death that would allow for the artificial maintenance of vital functions.

Cryonics

During the late 1960's, the procedure called "cryonic suspension" was first attempted. The procedure involves freezing the human body immediately after clinical death in the hope that it can be thawed and resuscitated at a later date when a cure for the illness causing the death is available. Since the procedure depends upon freezing the body before deterioration of the brain and other organs takes place, it is crucial that death be pronounced immediately so that the procedure can begin. An additional ethical issue arose when, during the 1980's, a prominent mathematician who had been diagnosed with brain cancer was denied permission from a U.S. court to have his head removed prior to his clinical death. He had requested that his head be placed in cryonic suspension in order to halt the deterioration of his cerebral functions.

—Mara Kelly Zukowski

Further Reading

Brennan, Herbie. *Death: The Great Mystery of Life*. New York: Carroll & Graf, 2002.

Choron, Jacques. *Death and Western Thought*. New York: Collier, 1973.

Kübler-Ross, Elisabeth. *On Death and Dying*. New York: Macmillan, 1969.

Ladd, John, ed. *Ethical Issues Relating to Life and Death*. New York: Oxford University Press, 1979.

President's Commission for the Study of Ethical Problems in Medicine and Biomedical and Behavioral Research. *Defining Death: A Report on the Medical, Legal, and Ethical Issues in the Determination of Death*. Washington, D.C.: Government Printing Office, 1981.

Veatch, Robert M. *Death, Dying, and the Biological Revolution: Our Last Quest for Responsibility*. Rev. ed. New Haven, Conn.: Yale University Press, 1989.

See also: Abortion; Bioethics; Brain death; Euthanasia; Homicide; Immortality; Infanticide; Life and death; Quinlan, Karen Ann; Right to die; Suicide.

Diagnosis

Definition: Investigation of a problem, especially a medical problem, to determine its cause

Type of ethics: Bioethics

Significance: Successful diagnoses and care of patients may require physicians to make ethical judgments about their duty to disclose information to their patients and the confidentiality of information that must be shared with others in order to make their diagnoses.

For many physicians, the principle of confidentiality tends to produce a kind of knee-jerk reflex. The popular belief is that confidentiality is essential to the physician-patient relationship and must be safeguarded at all costs. Contrary to popular belief, however, it is not an absolute principle. In many cases, health care is now a product of teamwork, so that the physician is forced to pool information to some degree.

The advent of computers makes it far easier for the physician's duty of confidentiality to be abused. Thus, there is confusion among professionals and administrators about what should be and what should not be revealed. Attitudes among physicians have departed from absolute certainties to a confusion of views between those who would have no difficulty divulging information and those who feel that divulging information violates various ethical codes.

It is generally accepted that information gained by a professional in the course of a relationship with a client is the property of the client. Instances do occur, however, in which medical professionals must weigh their ethical duty against their secondary duty as citizens to prevent harm from befalling others. For example, physicians have a statutory obligation to disclose the existence of infectious diseases. In some way, however, disclosure should hinge around patient consent, whenever it is practicable.

There is a general consensus that physicians have an obligation to tell the truth. Some doctors assume that they also have a right, which they sometimes exercise, to withhold information from a patient about a condition. Many physicians find it difficult to tell their patients that they are terminally ill. Some believe that a failure to tell a patient the truth is a type of dishonesty. Various arguments for truthfulness apply in medical ethics in diagnosis. Medicine is practiced on the assumption that the patient consents to treatment, but consent becomes meaningless unless it is informed. Thus, truth telling is vital to medical practice and medical diagnosis. The right to be adequately informed is based upon patients' freedom of choice, which becomes compromised if they are not given adequate data about their conditions. Reaction to the truth (of a terminal diagnosis, for example) is varied and unpredictable, and physicians are aware of this, as are pastors. In fact, "privileged communication" between patient and physician is one of the priestly aspects of the doctor's role that have been left over from ancient times.

A sensitive person can sympathize with one physician who showed, in a plaintive remark, the duty to tell the truth, yet his dislike of it. "Devotion to the truth does not always require the physician to voice his fears or tell the patient all he knows. But, after he has decided that the process of dying has begun, only in exceptional circumstances would a physician be justified in keeping the opinion to himself." No one can better guard the ideal of absolute respect for the human person than the medical profession.

—*Jane A. Slezak*

See also: Confidentiality; Consent; Genetic testing; Illness; Medical ethics; Physician-patient relationship; Psychopharmacology; Therapist-patient relationship.

Electroshock therapy

Definition: Induction by electric current of convulsions in patients in order to alleviate severe depression and suicidal ideation

Date: 1938 to present

Type of ethics: Psychological ethics

Significance: Electroshock therapy intentionally causes pain and suffering in order to help patients with mental problems. This raises two fundamental ethical issues: First, is it ever acceptable to inflict pain, not as a by-product of treatment, but as a method of treatment, even if that pain brings about the desired benefits? Second, are patients with depression and other mental illnesses competent to consent to or refuse this type of treatment?

Depression is one of the most prevalent and most treatable life-threatening illnesses. As many as 5 percent of Americans are likely to experience at least one episode of clinical depression during their lifetimes. The most probable cause of death from depression is suicide: Indeed, approximately 15 percent of patients with major depression eventually take their own lives.

Electroshock therapy, or, more properly, electroconvulsive therapy (ECT), is used to treat severe depression that does not respond to drug therapy or that occurs in patients who cannot tolerate antidepressant drugs.

History

ECT was introduced in 1938 by two psychiatrists, U. Cerletti and L. Bini, who devised a means of inducing a convulsion in a patient by using an electric current delivered via electrodes fastened to one or both of the patient's temples. It had long been observed that some mental patients had temporary relief from their symptoms following a spontaneous seizure. Prior to Cerletti and Bini's work, seizures had been induced by the inhalation of various substances.

ECT enjoyed a peak of popular use during the 1950's and 1960's, when it was considered a virtual panacea for mental illness. It had the additional benefit of making otherwise "difficult" patients more manageable, causing it to be used in some cases for behavior control. Partly because of its misuse and its negative depiction in the popular media (such as in Ken Kesey's 1962 novel *One Flew Over the Cuckoo's Nest*), ECT has earned a reputation as a high-risk treatment with an enormous capacity for abuse and severe long-term side effects. This is not, in fact, the case.

Indications and Effects

ECT is extremely effective in the treatment of severe depression and the depressive phase of bipolar disorder. Patients with atypical depression, however, which includes features such as acute anxiety or vegetative symptoms, tend not to respond as well to ECT. The treatment is strongly indicated in cases in which suicide seems imminent. ECT is used primarily for patients who have not responded to, or who cannot tolerate, drug therapy. Studies have shown that between 50 percent and 80 percent of patients in this category respond positively to ECT.

There are no absolute contraindicators in the use of ECT. The treatment does raise blood and intracranial pressure, however, and therefore it must be used with caution in patients who already have high readings in these areas. ECT is often administered under anesthesia, and muscle relaxants are used to reduce the risk of bone fractures, so patients who have problems with these treatments need to be assessed carefully. Also, patients with cardiovascular problems are only rarely given ECT, because of reported complications. In studies to date, how-

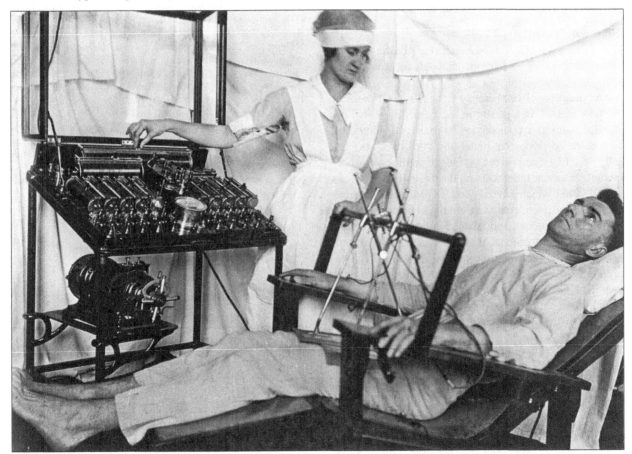

A Bergonic chair, *a device "for giving general electric treatment for psychological effect, in psycho-neurotic cases," according to original photo description. World War I era. By Otis Historical Archives National Museum of Health and Medicine.*

ever, the highest mortality rate associated with ECT has been 0.8 percent.

The major side effect of ECT is memory loss. The loss is primarily short-term. Studies indicate that there is little, if any, observable difference six months after treatment between the memory abilities of patients who have had ECT and those who have not. Since memory impairment is associated with depression in general, it is difficult to assess what loss is attributable to ECT.

Ethical Issues

The ethical issues involved with the administration of ECT revolve around the determination of what constitutes informed consent and competency to give consent or refuse treatment. In all psychiatric treatments, the question of the competency of a patient who suffers from some form of mental illness to give consent is raised. Other issues include the use of ECT for behavior control and decision making for patients considered not competent.

Informed Consent

The ethical issue of informed consent may be divided into two areas: consent by a competent adult and consent for an incompetent patient.

The question of competency is raised in all cases of mental illness. Can a person in the depths of severe depression, with its accompanying hindrances of judgment, be considered competent under any circumstances? Legally, yes. Legal competency is judged on the basis of observable behavior rather than on the basis of the patient's mental status, which can only be inferred. If a patient can make what is considered to be a rational decision, shows no signs of delusions, and is able to understand the risks and benefits of a treatment, that person is considered competent. The common negative societal view of ECT, however, often causes legally competent patients to refuse the treatment. Can their biased view of ECT, which is based on fictional portrayals, be considered delusional? Furthermore, consistency of consent becomes an issue because of the indecisiveness inherent in depression.

If a patient is judged to be incompetent, determining who will make treatment decisions becomes an issue. Most commonly these decisions are made by a close relative. It must be ascertained that the best interests and values of the patient have primacy in the decision, rather than such issues as ease of management by caretakers or punitive measures by other parties. In the case of the hospitalized patient, the aspect of voluntariness of consent must be considered. A patient does not automatically relinquish the right to refuse treatment upon hospitalization. If consent is sought, it must be clear that it is in no way coerced; for example, by telling a patient that release from the hospital will occur sooner if ECT is used.

Risks and Benefits

One of the important aspects of informed consent is the patient's ability to comprehend and evaluate the risks and benefits inherent in a given procedure. In the case of ECT, the risks of the procedure must be evaluated in the light of the continued risk of suicide in depressed individuals. A competent patient has the right to refuse ECT, however, if he or she considers that the risk of memory loss or other brain damage outweighs the possible benefits.

—Margaret Hawthorne

Further Reading

Abrams, Richard. *Electroconvulsive Therapy.* 4th ed. New York: Oxford University Press, 2002.

"American Psychiatric Association Practice Guidelines for Major Depressive Disorder in Adults." *American Journal of Psychiatry*, supp. 150 (April, 1993): 4.

Baldwin, Steve, and Melissa Oxlad. *Electroshock and Minors: Fifty-Year Review.* Westport, Conn.: Greenwood Press, 2000.

Bloch, Sidney, and Paul Chodoff, eds. *Psychiatric Ethics.* New York: Oxford University Press, 1981.

Childress, James F. *Who Should Decide? Paternalism in Health Care.* New York: Oxford University Press, 1982.

Edwards, Rem B., ed. *Psychiatry and Ethics.* Buffalo, N.Y.: Prometheus Books, 1982.

Keller, Martin B. "The Difficult Depressed Patient in Perspective." *Journal of Clinical Psychiatry*, supp. 54 (February, 1993): 4-8.

Kneeland, Timothy W., and Carol A. B. Warren. *Pushbutton Psychiatry: A History of Electroshock in America.* Westport, Conn.: Praeger, 2002.

Schoen, Robert E. "Is Electroconvulsive Therapy Safe?" *Postgraduate Medicine* 87 (May 1, 1990): 236-239.

See also: Consent; Mental illness; Psychology; Psychopharmacology; Suicide; Therapist-patient relationship; Torture.

Ethical Principles of Psychologists

Identification: Professional ethical code required of psychologists and enforceable through sanctions from various bodies

Date: First enacted in December, 1992; revised on June 1, 2003

Type of ethics: Psychological ethics

Significance: Health care professionals who deal with the mind and mental health face special ethical dilemmas over and above those common to all providers of care. The Ethical Principles set out by the American Psychological Association seek to aid practitioners in negotiating those issues, as well as reassuring the public that psychologists will not be permitted to abuse their position.

The Ethical Principles are primarily based on the potential for harming others through incompetence, improper emotional coercion, or misinformation that curtails free and informed thought and behavior.

Freedom of inquiry and expression is central to psychology, but discriminating against others or allowing the misuse of research is unethical. Psychologists have a particular responsibility to be self-aware, to be honest, and to use the methods of science, scientific explanation, and critique, rather than expressing mere personal opinion and authority. They must be aware of the basic and unique needs of other people and groups. Supervision, instruction, advisement, and treatment have considerable intellectual and emotional power.

Psychologists must avoid potential harm or exploitation by being candid about their services and fees, qualifications, confidentiality, allegiances, the requests they make of research volunteers (informed consent specifying risks and benefits, providing feedback, and minimizing deception), and avoiding potentially harmful multiple relationships. Psychologists do not engage in sexual relationships with students, supervisees, and patients because of the potential for biased judgment or exploitation through lack of interpersonal reciprocity. Tests, diagnoses, evaluations, and interventions must be based on scientific competence and avoidance of harm.

—John Santelli

See also: Animal research; Bioethics; Medical research; Metaethics; *Principles of Medical Ethics with Annotations Especially Applicable to Psychiatry*; Professional ethics; Psychology; Therapist-patient relationship.

Ethics of DNA analysis

Definition: Principles of conduct, moral duty, and obligation that guide professionals involved in the analysis of DNA.

Significance: In its use as a powerful tool for identifying the perpetrators of crimes, DNA analysis has revolutionized the field of forensic science. Many ethical is-

sues emerge from the use of DNA analysis, however, and forensic scientists must be aware of the potential for problems in the collection, use, and storage of DNA samples as well as the use of information gained from DNA analysis.

Because DNA (deoxyribonucleic acid) offers so much more information on individuals than either fingerprints or traditional serological evidence, serious concerns have been raised regarding the potential for abuses in the collection, storage, and analysis of DNA samples. At the forefront of these concerns is the conflict between law-enforcement agencies' legal power to collect evidence and individuals' rights to privacy and autonomy. In addition, it has been noted that because DNA analysis can reveal many intimate aspects of individuals and their families—including paternity, susceptibility to diseases, and predisposition to genetic anomalies—the information gained through DNA analysis could be used in discriminatory fashion by employers, health care institutions, insurers, and government and educational institutions.

Relative to the use of DNA analysis by forensic scientists, some ethical concerns have been raised regarding quality control in the handling of DNA samples, the reliability of interpretations of DNA analysis results, and access to DNA analysis. Some observers have expressed fears that human error in the analysis of DNA may contribute to the wrongful conviction of persons accused of crimes; it has also been noted that some individuals who have been wrongfully convicted of crimes may be denied access to DNA analysis that could exonerate them.

Individual Rights and Privacy

Many of the concerns that have been expressed about DNA analysis, particularly in the United States, are related to individuals' desire for privacy and autonomy. Because the information provided by a person's DNA to a large extent defines that person's physical being, many people are more concerned about keeping their DNA information private than they are about keeping their general medical information private. Any mandatory legal provision for collecting DNA from the public pool in order to solve crimes is thus met with resistance. Many observers have voiced doubts regarding the ability of law-enforcement authorities to safeguard DNA samples, and many fear the possible misuse of information gained through DNA analysis.

Many objections have also been raised to the forced or coerced collection of DNA samples from all persons considered possible suspects in criminal investigations. It is vital to distinguish coerced or forced submissions of DNA from truly voluntary submissions. Law-enforcement agencies have at times justified the use of "DNA dragnets" in which samples are collected from hundreds or even thousands of "volunteers" in communities where serial crimes have been committed. Such police activities are troubling because they involve the collection of DNA samples from people who are not suspects and who do not provide the samples in a truly voluntary way. In addition, the DNA information obtained in this way is often poorly controlled, as generally no provisions exist for destroying these DNA samples after analyses have excluded innocent persons from suspicion.

In practice, Law-enforcement investigators' collection of "voluntary" DNA samples can be questionable. No written provisions govern the consent process, and informed consent to provide DNA is possible only when the individual has a comprehensive understanding of the potential implications associated with the DNA analysis and the ultimate disposal or storage of the sample. In addition, the consequences of declining to "volunteer" a DNA sample when the police are collecting from a particular population can be too great for many people to bear; those who refuse may face social stigmatization or ostracization. In many cases, individuals who are unwilling to volunteer DNA samples may be forced to give them through search warrants.

Potential Misuses of DNA

The United States maintains the largest DNA database in the world, the Combined DNA Index System (CODIS). The rapid growth of CODIS has prompted many concerns over civil liberties. At first, the DNA profiles of convicted sex offenders constituted the bulk of the material in the local, state, and federal databases that make up CODIS, but many states then expanded to include all felons; some even take DNA samples from all persons arrested, even those who are not convicted. CODIS has expanded over the years to include the DNA profiles of suspects, victims, and many other people who were not originally intended to be included.

Although DNA databases play vital roles in criminal investigations and postconviction reviews, the necessity of solving crimes must be weighed against respect for civil liberties. Observers have noted that the sweeping expansion of DNA databases may lead to dangers of privacy invasion and even racial discrimination. Given that no effective policy or legal provisions are in place in the United States to ensure genetic privacy for those who have never been convicted of any crime, concerns about privacy issues in relation to DNA are legitimate. After a person's DNA makes its way into CODIS, it remains in that system whether the person is a model citizen or a violent criminal. For this reason, many have argued that the contents of DNA databases must be as limited as possible and that only those who have been convicted of crimes should be included.

Another ethical dilemma revolves around the potential for racial discrimination associated with the uses of these databases. The DNA analysis technique using short tandem repeats (STRs) was initially developed to enable the matching of a sample of unknown origin with a sample of known origin. The same kind of analysis, however, has been used to create suspect pools based on the linking of STR patterns with physical characteristics of certain races or ethnic groups. Given that numbers of arrests are already biased toward some racial and ethnic minorities, the increased inclusion of individuals from these groups in DNA databases raises the probability for future "identification" of members of these groups as seemingly established as perpetrators of crimes by what are actually probabilistic and scientifically evolving standards. It further compounds racial bias, given that many of the persons whose profiles are in the databases have never been convicted of any crime.

Quality Control and Equal Access

Some ethical concerns about DNA analysis center on quality control: in the collection of samples, in the isolation and analysis of DNA, and in the interpretation of results. For each of these stages to be accomplished properly, the persons involved—including detectives, lab technicians, forensic scientists, lawyers, and judges—must have a high level of professional competence.

The contamination of a DNA sample, for example, could jeopardize an otherwise strong prosecution case. The miscalculation of the probability of a profile match between evidentiary DNA and that of a suspect may lead to a wrongful conviction. An expert witness's neglect in presenting laboratory error rate may mislead jurors in one direction or another. To ensure that DNA analyses are carried out and interpreted to a high degree of quality, guidelines must be in place to ensure a standard acceptable error rate in DNA analysis for all laboratories, periodic review and certification of laboratories for forensic DNA analysis, and proper training of personnel, including scientists, police officers, lawyers, and judges.

The issue of equal access to the technology of DNA analysis has been raised by many observers. They have argued that fairness demands that persons who were convicted of crimes before this technology became available should have the opportunity to submit evidence for DNA analysis whenever circumstances warrant a review. The fair, just, and effective use of DNA analysis can aid in both convicting the guilty and exonerating the wrongfully accused.

—Ming Y. Zheng

Further Reading

Kobilinsky, Lawrence F., Thomas F. Liotti, and Jamel Oeser-Sweat. DNA: Forensic and Legal Applications. Hoboken, N.J.: Wiley-Interscience, 2005. Presents an informative overview of the uses of DNA analysis.

Lazer, David, ed. DNA and the Criminal Justice System: The Technology of Justice. Cambridge, Mass.: MIT Press, 2004. Collection of essays explores the ethical and procedural issues related to DNA evidence.

Rudin, Norah, and Keith Inman. An Introduction to Forensic DNA Analysis. 2d ed. Boca Raton, Fla.: CRC Press, 2002. Provides a good introduction to the use of biological evidence in forensics as well as the history and application of DNA fingerprinting in forensic investigations.

Scheck, Barry, Peter Neufeld, and Jim Dwyer. Actual Innocence: Five Days to Execution, and Other Dispatches from the Wrongly Convicted. New York: Random House, 2000. Describes some of the most prominent and successful cases taken on by Scheck and Neufeld's Innocence Project, providing comprehensive data on cases of wrongful conviction.

Williams, Robin, and Paul Johnson. "Inclusiveness, Effectiveness, and Intrusiveness: Issues in the Developing Uses of DNA Profiling in Support of Criminal Investigations." Journal of Law, Medicine, and Ethics 33, no. 3 (2005): 545-558. Discusses the use of DNA databases in England and Wales and the ethical issues raised by uses such as familial searching.

Eugenics

Definition: Attempt to alter human evolution through selection

Type of ethics: Bioethics

Significance: Even in its most benign form, eugenics raises serious ethical questions, since it almost unavoidably involves some people making reproductive choices for others, and making decisions about which genetic traits should be preserved, strengthened, and

eliminated from the human race. The darker forms of the science entail much clearer and more heinous transgressions, up to and including involuntary sterilization and genocide.

Although the idea of selective breeding dates back to antiquity, the first detailed exposition of eugenics founded in genetic and evolutionary science was produced by Sir Francis Galton in *Hereditary Genius* (1869). Two main strategies of eugenics are possible: increasing the gene contributions of those who have desirable traits (positive eugenics) and decreasing the gene contributions of those who have undesired traits (negative eugenics). Genetic testing must first determine what traits people have and to what extent each trait is heritable. Supporters of eugenics claim that intelligence is genetically determined, but most data concerning this claim are suspect, and the true heritability of intelligence is still hotly debated.

Positive eugenics encourages people with desirable traits to produce more numerous offspring. Encouragement may take the form of monetary rewards, paying the educational expenses for children, and so forth. Sperm of

Francis Galton, English polymath: geographer, statistician, pioneer in eugenics.

desirable men could be collected and stored for the future artificial insemination of selected women, but this suggestion has rarely been followed because of the expense of the procedure.

Negative eugenics applications may mean that individuals carrying undesired traits might be killed or sterilized. Advocates of eugenics say that this cruelty is for the greater good of humanity, but opponents strongly object. Beyond this issue, other ethical questions arise: Which traits are desired? Who will make the decisions? Since many traits vary by race, negative eugenics raises questions of racism and brings humanity close to the dangers of genocide. (The only nationwide eugenics laws in history were used in Nazi Germany to exterminate Jews and other non- "Aryans.") Geneticists have also determined that negative eugenics is very limited in its ability to change gene frequencies. Most genetic defects are rare, and selection against rare traits is very ineffective. Selection is especially ineffective if a trait is influenced by environment or education, as intelligence scores are. Also, if negative eugenics could succeed, it would reduce the genetic variability of the population, and variability may itself be desirable, especially if future environments change.

—*Eli C. Minkoff*

Further Reading

Black, Edwin. *War Against the Weak: Eugenics and America's Campaign to Create a Master Race.* New York: Four Walls Eight Windows, 2003.

Kevles, Daniel J. *In the Name of Eugenics: Genetics and the Uses of Human Heredity.* Cambridge, Mass.: Harvard University Press 1995.

Kline, Wendy. *Building a Better Race.* Los Angeles: University of California Press, 2001.

See also: Bioethics; Cloning; Evolutionary theory; Future-oriented ethics; Genetic counseling; Genetic engineering; Genetic testing; Genocide and democide; Intelligence testing; Nazi science; Social Darwinism; Sterilization of women.

Euthanasia

Definition: Active or passive encouragement of the death of a person to prevent further suffering

Type of ethics: Bioethics

Significance: Euthanasia continues to be an extremely controversial issue, since it engages one of the most fundamental moral questions: Under what circum-

stances, if any, is it ethical to cause the death of another person?

The term "euthanasia" is derived from the Greek phrase that means a pleasant or easy death. Relieving suffering was part of the Hippocratic oath, dating from the fourth century bce, when Greek physicians were sworn to preserve life and never willingly to take it. This sanctity-of-life principle was not, however, honored always and in all places. The Greeks and Romans, for example, ruled that slaves and "barbarians" had no right to life. In Sparta, the law required the death of deformed infants. The philosophers Plato and Aristotle regarded infanticide and abortion as acceptable, and Plato himself was a victim of compulsory suicide.

Before and during World War II, Nazi Germany practiced euthanasia on those viewed as socially unproductive: Jews, older people, the deformed, the chronically ill. Memories of these compulsory deaths have caused many people to resist the idea and practice of euthanasia, even by what would be considered humane methods. In 1969, however, Great Britain's House of Lords passed a voluntary euthanasia law; earlier bills had been defeated in 1938 and 1950. The main purpose of the British law was to authorize physicians to give euthanasia to a patient thought to be suffering from an incurable physical condition and who has made a declaration requesting euthanasia. A clause provides that a declaration may be revoked at any time. Passive euthanasia had been generally accepted, but Parliament by this act legalized active euthanasia.

Euthanasia is divided into two types: active and passive. Active euthanasia is direct intervention to bring about the death of one suffering from a terminal illness, while passive euthanasia is letting nature take its course. The intent to bring about death requires ethical analysis to find a moral consensus, since the rights of an individual and those of society come into play.

Christianity and Euthanasia

Throughout the twentieth century, Western churches—the Roman Catholic Church in particular—took strong stands against both types of euthanasia. During the medieval era, Saint Augustine of Hippo and Saint Thomas Aquinas affirmed that only God is the arbiter of life and death. They taught that pain and suffering have purpose in God's sight. In 1940, the Catholic Church officially condemned the administration of euthanasia for any reason as contrary to natural and divine law. In late 1957, however,

Pope Pius XII, speaking to an International Congress of Anaesthesiologists, stated that "morally one is held to use only ordinary means" to sustain life and that in cases of terminal illness, there is no obligation to continue lifesaving measures. Differences exist, however, regarding what constitutes ordinary versus extraordinary means and who should decide when death is preferable to treatment.

Ordinary means of treating a sick or dying person are means that are in common use, while extraordinary means involve nonstandard treatment, the new and the rare. Scientific and technological advances have transformed the extraordinary into the ordinary. This development complicates the issue, since such factors as scarce funds and facilities also come into play, introducing another ethical problem: the acceptability of utilitarianism.

The sanctity-of-life principle holds that it is absolutely prohibited either intentionally to kill a patient or intention-

Felix Adler, circa 1913, the first prominent American to argue for permitting suicide in cases of chronic illness. By Lewis Wickes Hine (1874–1940).

ally to let a patient die and to base decisions for the prolongation or shortening of human life on considerations of the quality of that life. Under no circumstances is there a "right to die." This is true irrespective of the competency or noncompetency of a person to decide for himself or herself whether to choose euthanasia.

Patients, doctors, and the patients' families are generally the decision makers in cases of possible euthanasia, whether active or passive. By 2004, virtually all states accepted living wills whereby competent adults give directions for the health care they want if they become terminally ill and cannot direct their own care. Those who believe in the sanctity of life fear that these living wills are a wedge that will allow nonvoluntary euthanasia to become acceptable. While staunchly opposed to euthanasia, some churches and courts accept the "double-effect" principle. This principle holds that an action whose primary effect is to relieve suffering may be ethically justified, although a secondary effect may be death. Physicians, they argue, have a duty to relieve pain as well as to preserve life—although doing so may shorten the person's life.

The Quality-of-Life Ethic

Much debate centers on the quality-of-life ethic. Some argue that if there is little hope that a given treatment prolonging a person's life will allow that person to live a beneficial, satisfactory life, then euthanasia is justified. In such cases, the sanctity-of-life principle is set against the quality-of-life approach. How can a proper quality of life be guaranteed to all citizens and an equitable distribution of medical care be ensured? Using utilitarianism as a guideline, providing high-quality life for a majority takes priority over prolonging the lives of a few. Cost-effectiveness becomes a major factor in the decision to choose or not to choose euthanasia. This is unacceptable to many persons, since it places an economic value on people.

The counterargument is made that while every person is equal to all others, not every life is of equal value. The case of Karen Ann Quinlan is cited as an example of the quality-of-life and sanctity-of-life dilemma. The victim of an accident, Quinlan went into a coma in 1975 and was kept on a respirator for several years. After repeated requests from her guardian, a court decision allowed discontinuance of the respirator. Quinlan's life was not benefiting her and was burdening her parents unduly. The quality-of-life judgment prevailed in that case.

In 1990, the U.S. Supreme Court ruled that patients have a constitutional right to discontinue unwanted life-sustaining medical treatment. In 1992, the Netherlands's parliament approved liberal rules on euthanasia and doctor-assisted suicide. The guidelines require, however, that the patient must be mentally competent, be suffering unbearable pain, and request euthanasia repeatedly; and the doctor must consult a second physician before proceeding. The right to die with dignity, free of terminal agony, is a concept that enjoys strong public support. Most of this support, however, is for passive euthanasia; support for active euthanasia is more moderate.

The notion of a right to die is still very controversial, making moral standards of judgment ever more imperative. Whether supporting the sanctity-of-life doctrine or the quality-of-life argument, there is general agreement among those most engaged with this issue that not every patient's life ought to be prolonged. The moral debate is over how this life should be ended. Individuals, families, courts, and ethics committees struggle over euthanasia, striving for justice for both patient and society.

—S. Carol Berg

Further Reading

Bernards, Neal, ed. *Euthanasia: Opposing Viewpoints.* San Diego, Calif.: Greenhaven Press, 1989.

Churchill, Larry R. *Rationing Health Care in America: Perspectives and Principles of Justice.* Notre Dame, Ind.: University of Notre Dame Press, 1987.

Kluge, Eike-Henner W. *The Ethics of Deliberative Death.* Port Washington, N.Y.: Kennikat Press, 1981.

Lammers, Stephen E., and Allen Verhey, eds. *On Moral Medicine: Theological Perspectives in Medical Ethics.* Grand Rapids, Mich.: William B. Eerdmans, 1987.

Van Zyl, Liezl. *Death and Compassion: A Virtue-Based Approach to Euthanasia.* Burlington, Vt.: Ashgate, 2000.

Weir, Robert F., ed. *Ethical Issues in Death and Dying.* 2d ed. New York: Columbia University Press, 1986.

See also: Health care allocation; Hippocrates; Homicide; Infanticide; Kevorkian, Jack; Medical bills of rights; Quinlan, Karen Ann; Right to die; Suicide; Suicide assistance.

Family therapy

Definition: Type of group psychotherapy that seeks to address the needs of families or individuals within families by analyzing and modifying relationships and dynamics within the family

Type of ethics: Psychological ethics

Significance: Family therapy raises all the ethical issues raised by individual psychotherapy, but it also raises special ethical concerns involving the need for evenhandedness in the relationship of the therapist to each member of the family group, the need for patients to balance honest work in therapy with the feelings of the other family members, and the confidentiality of information revealed between family members in therapy sessions.

Family therapy is guided by systems theory, which believes that psychological problems of the individual must be approached as a dysfunction of life within the family. Rather than attempting to promote behavioral and cognitive changes in the dysfunctional individual alone, the family therapist views the family unit as the agent or system for achieving change. It is through the family that understanding of individual behavior is achieved. Actions by any single family member have an effect on all other family members. Family therapists may work with individuals, couples, parents and children, siblings, the nuclear family, the family of origin, and social networks in order to understand their clients' problems and to formulate strategies for change.

Ethical Standards in Family Therapy

Gayla Margolin observed that the ethical questions facing the family therapist are even more different, numerous, and complicated than those faced by therapists who do individual therapy. In an attempt to provide guidance on how to deal with these ethical issues, the American Association of Marriage and Family Therapists published a code of ethics in 1991. The code addresses eight areas: (1) responsibility to clients; (2) confidentiality; (3) professional competence and integrity; (4) responsibility to students, employees, and supervisees; (5) responsibility to research participants; (6) responsibility to the profession; (7) fees; and (8) advertising.

Most of these areas (areas 3 through 8) are essentially the same for individual and family therapists because they focus on only the therapist: his or her qualifications and training, behavior, and income. It is in the first two areas of responsibility to clients and confidentiality that unique ethical issues confront the family therapist. These unique ethical concerns have been summarized by Gerald Corey, Marianne Schneider Corey, and Patrick Callanan (1993) in four general areas:

1. Treating the entire family. Most family therapists believe that it is crucial for all members of the family to participate. Ethical questions arise when a family member or members refuse to participate. Coercing militant members to participate is unethical.

Some therapists may withhold therapy until all members participate, but this strategy is controversial. Besides resembling coercion, it can be argued that this tactic denies therapy to the willing participants. Conversely, Rachel T. Hare-Mustin contends that involving the whole family may not always be in the best interests of a particular member. Giving priority to the good of the entire family may jeopardize the legitimate goals or desires of that member. Ethical considerations require the therapist to minimize risks for any family member.

2. Value system of the therapist. The therapist's value system crucially influences the course of family therapy in two ways: first, when the therapist has values that are different from those of a member or members of the family, problems can arise; second, value systems influence the formulation and definition of the problems that are presented, the goals and plans for therapy, and the course the therapy takes. For example, Irene Goldenberg and Herbert Goldenberg contend that family therapists generally believe in maintaining the family way of life. Such a belief could, however, be harmful or inappropriate under some circumstances.

Ethical considerations demand that the therapist make known his or her attitudes and commitments to each family member. Gerald Corey et al. further state that it is not the function of the therapist to make decisions for clients or dictate how they should change.

The therapist's role is to provide insight into family dynamics and to help and encourage the family to make necessary changes. The therapist must be aware of how his or her values can influence the course of therapy.

3. The ethics of consulting. This issue arises if one of the family members terminates joint sessions and begins therapy with another therapist. To complicate the situation further, Corey et al. pose a situation in which a person might persuade other family members to also consult with his or her therapist while still seeing their original therapist. Is this new therapist ethically obligated to consult with the original therapist? Are the two therapists ethically obligated to receive permission of their clients before talking with each other? Would it be ethical for the two therapists to ignore each other? These are difficult questions to answer.

4. The issue of confidentiality. In the course of family therapy, the therapist will see the family as a group and also individually. During individual sessions, of course, the client may divulge information that is not known to other family members. What is the ethically correct approach regarding the confidentiality of information revealed during these one-to-one sessions? Some therapists will not reveal such information. Other therapists believe that it is appropriate to reveal such information under appropriate circumstances that would benefit the rest of the family.

Again, this is a difficult issue to resolve. The implications of revealing confidences can be serious. Revealing confidences may, however, facilitate resolution of the family's problems. Corey et al. suggest a middle position. The therapist is ethically obligated to inform the family that information revealed during private sessions may be divulged, if in the therapist's opinion that shared information would benefit the family. This position allows the therapist maximum flexibility and options to act in the family's best interests.

In conclusion, the increasing popularity and usefulness of family therapy require sensitivity to and understanding of the unique ethical issues it can present to the family therapist.

—Laurence Miller

Further Reading

Corey, Gerald, Marianne Schneider Corey, and Patrick Callanan. *Issues and Ethics in the Helping Professions.* Pacific Grove, Calif.: Brooks-Cole, 1993.

Goldenberg, Irene, and Herbert Goldenberg. *Family Therapy: An Overview.* 6th ed. Pacific Grove, Calif.: Thomson, Brooks/Cole, 2004.

Margolin, Gayla. "Ethical and Legal Considerations in Marital and Family Therapy." *American Psychologist* 37 (July, 1982): 788-801.

Nichols, Michael P., and Richard C. Schwartz. *Family Therapy: Concepts and Methods.* 2d ed. Boston: Allyn & Bacon, 1991.

Patten, Christi, Therese Barnett, and Daniel Houlihan. "Ethics in Marital and Family Therapy: A Review of the Literature." *Professional Psychology: Research and Practice* 22 (April, 1991): 171-175.

Walsh, Froma, ed. *Normal Family Processes: Growing Diversity and Complexity.* 3d ed. New York: Guilford Press, 2003.

See also: Behavior therapy; Divorce; Ethical Principles of Psychologists; Family; Group therapy; Therapist-patient relationship.

Freud, Sigmund

Identification: Austrian pioneer in psychoanalytic theory
Born: May 6, 1856, Freiburg, Moravia, Austrian Empire (now Príbor, Czech Republic)

Died: September 23, 1939, London, England

Type of ethics: Psychological ethics

Significance: Freud founded the theoretical and clinical discipline of psychoanalysis, providing the twentieth century with one of its most powerful and influential models of psychological development, the formation of one's moral character, and the relationship between desire and culture. His many works include *The Interpretation of Dreams* (*Die Traumdeutung*, 1900) and *Civilization and Its Discontents* (*Das Unbehagen in der Kultur*, 1930).

Although Sigmund Freud has had a powerful impact on the field of ethics, he did not initially set out to study moral questions. Freud's original interest was medical research, and he was trained in Vienna as a physician. Financial constraints, however, forced him to abandon his chief interest in pure research, and he began to practice during the 1880's as a neurologist.

In 1884, Freud was introduced to Josef Breuer, a Viennese physician, who had developed a "cathartic" method for the treatment of hysterical symptoms. This method involved encouraging patients to talk in a completely free and unencumbered manner about the development of their symptoms. The talking alone seemed to produce a surprising improvement in patients' conditions. This discovery was the starting point of what later became the field of psychoanalysis. Freud and Breuer collaborated on *Studies in Hysteria* (1895), in which they described their groundbreaking work in this area.

Rise of Psychoanalysis

Freud continued this work alone, publishing such seminal volumes as *The Interpretation of Dreams* (1900), *Three Essays on the Theory of Sexuality* (1905), and *The Origin and Development of Psychoanalysis* (1910). In all these works, Freud developed a new way of examining the structure, nature, and diseases of the human mind. Freud's original focus was on the understanding and treatment of emotional disorders, but as the field of psychoanalysis rapidly progressed, Freud's ideas gradually took a broader perspective. Freud eventually left his followers with a theory of the human psyche, a therapy for the relief of its ills, and a method for the interpretation of culture and society. It was in his later works, such as *Totem and Taboo* (1913), *The Future of an Illusion* (1927), and *Civilization and Its Discontents* (1930), that Freud spoke most directly to ethical and social issues.

Ethical Implications

In many ways, Freud rejected the conventional ethics of his era. His focus on the egoistic, narcissistic, and aggressive roots of human behavior led some readers to conclude that Freudian psychoanalysis was an amoral discipline that left no room for either a philosophical or a practical theory of morality. It is true that Freud rejected many traditional religious values. He believed that a number of central religious beliefs were merely a misguided human effort to overcome infantile feelings of helplessness and dependence.

In *The Future of an Illusion*, Freud argued that the belief in God is a mythic attempt to overcome the human sense of powerlessness. Like an idealized parent, the concept of God is, for Freud, the projection of childish wishes for an omnipotent protector.

In *Civilization and Its Discontents*, Freud again argued that religious phenomena were merely the reflection of unresolved psychological needs from the early years of

Photographic portrait of Sigmund Freud, signed by the sitter ("Prof. Sigmund Freud"). By Max Halberstadt.

life. In the opening chapter of the book, Freud described the oceanic feeling, or sense of indissoluble oneness with the universe, which mystics have often celebrated as the most fundamental of all religious experiences. Freud believed that the origin of this feeling was the desire to re-create the undifferentiated infant's profound sense of fusion with its mother. By attempting to debunk such central aspects of religious belief, Freud called into question many religious notions of moral right and wrong.

In addition to his rejection of religious morality, Freud also disagreed with Immanuel Kant's position that reason and duty should be the central grounds for morality. While Freud believed that reason must play a part in the development of ethical guidelines, he also saw a place in ethics for the promotion of human happiness and welfare. Freud advocated a practical form of ethics that was designed to promote the general welfare of society while simultaneously allowing individuals a sufficient degree of instinctual gratification.

Freud's View of Human Nature

For Freud, this position grew logically from his rather mixed view of human nature. Freud believed that most individuals possessed powerful aggressive and egoistic tendencies, along with a capacity for self-observation and altruistic behavior. Freud consistently maintained that theorists who saw human nature as inherently good were seriously deluded. For this reason, Freud believed that the golden rule—to love one's neighbor as oneself—was a destructive and unrealistic goal. Freud also suggested that utopian schemes such as communism were destined to failure, because they called for humans to give more than they were capable of giving.

According to Freud, the best course for humanity was to establish civilizations in which the more destructive elements of instinctual drives were prohibited, in order to promote the common social good. People will be able to tolerate the rules of such social organizations if nondestructive outlets for aggressive and narcissistic wishes can be developed. This will not be an easy task, and Freud believed that individual and group needs will generally be in conflict.

Freud's hope was that society would adopt a realistic view of human nature and gradually learn more effective ways to manage the individual's need for instinctual gratification.

—*Steven C. Abell*

Further Reading

Deigh, John. *The Sources of Moral Agency: Essays in Moral Psychology and Freudian Theory*. New York: Cambridge University Press, 1996.

Freud, Sigmund. *Letters*. Edited by Ernst L. Freud. Translated by Tania Stern and James Stern. New York: Basic Books, 1960.

_____. *The Standard Edition of the Complete Psychological Works of Sigmund Freud*. Translated by James Strachey. London: Hogarth Press, 1953- 1974.

Hartmann, Heinz. *Psychoanalysis and Moral Values*. New York: International Universities Press, 1960.

Marcuse, Herbert. *Eros and Civilization: A Philosophical Inquiry into Freud*. Boston: Beacon, 1974.

Meissner, W. W. *The Ethical Dimension of Psychoanalysis: A Dialogue*. Albany: State University of New York Press, 2003.

Ricoeur, Paul. *Freud and Philosophy: An Essay on Interpretation*. Translated by Denis Savage. New Haven, Conn.: Yale University Press, 1970.

Rieff, Philip. *Freud: The Mind of the Moralist*. Garden City, N.Y.: Doubleday, 1961.

Roazen, Paul. *Freud: Political and Social Thought*. New York: Knopf, 1968.

Wallwork, Ernest. *Psychoanalysis and Ethics*. New Haven, Conn.: Yale University Press, 1991.

See also: Aggression; Alienation; Hypnosis; Jung, Carl; Motivation; Narcissism; Psychology; Psychopharmacology; Therapist-patient relationship; Violence.

Genetic counseling

Definition: Identification, explanation, and discussion of deleterious genes in potential parents

Date: Practiced began around 1960; formally defined in 1975

Type of ethics: Bioethics

Significance: Genetic counseling raises serious ethical questions in clinical practice, since reproductive decisions are central to conventional morality and the identification of inherited defects carries the possibility of discrimination.

Although it has roots in the eugenics movements of the early twentieth century, which have been justly criticized as being hampered by imperfect understanding of inheritance and tainted by racial and class prejudice, genetic counseling relies on landmark genetic discoveries of the 1950's—the elucidation of the structure of DNA and of the specific biochemical bases for a number of inherited disorders, including Tay-Sachs syndrome, sickle-cell anemia, and hemophilia.

Beginning in 1960, specialists in medical centers began advising couples who had already had a child with such a disorder or had close relatives who were affected. In 1975, the American Society of Human Genetics published a formal definition and guidelines on genetic counseling. The availability of these services and the number of conditions amenable to testing have risen steadily, although access is not universal even in the developed world. Most severe genetic diseases are recessive; carriers with one defective gene may or may not be identifiable. Gross chromosomal abnormalities and some metabolic disorders can be diagnosed *in utero* through amniocentesis.

U.S. government guidelines for genetic testing and counseling caution against using the process for perceived societal good and stress that the impetus for testing and reproductive decisions must come from the affected individuals, without outside compulsion. Nevertheless, many people perceive that a genetically abnormal individual places a burden on society and believe that it is immoral to bear a defective child; this attitude is seen by others as providing a justification for abandoning the handicapped. Voluntarily abstaining from conceiving children is morally acceptable to most people in Western society, but objections to abortion are widespread. Some heritable abnormalities are commonest among small, inbred ethnic minorities, in which case refraining from having children and marrying outside the group, the most prudent courses of action from a medical standpoint, have genocidal overtones. Not all genetic disorders are equally debilitating, and it is uncertain whether genetic counseling is appropriate for less severe conditions. Finally, there are many disorders (alcoholism, for example) that may be at least partially heritable, whose genetic basis is unknown, and for which the scientific basis for genetic counseling is tenuous.

Tests exist for some genetically transmitted conditions (for example, certain cancers) that manifest themselves late in life, and more are continually being developed. Although knowing of their existence is helpful to medical professionals, there is real concern that this information could be used to deny employment or insurance coverage to those who are affected. Maintaining confidentiality and respecting the rights of individuals are paramount in genetic counseling.

—Martha Sherwood-Pike

See also: Abortion; Bioethics; Birth defects; Eugenics; Genetic engineering; Genetic testing; Genocide and democide; Intelligence testing.

Genetic engineering

Definition: Branch of genetics that manipulates genetic material in living organisms, animal or vegetable

Type of ethics: Bioethics

Significance: As genetic engineering rushes toward eliminating genetic ills, it has produced such substances as industrial enzymes, the human growth hormone, and insulin and made possible the cloning of vertebrates and other sophisticated but ethically controversial procedures.

Long practiced by animal breeders and botanists, genetic engineering entered a new phase in the late 1950's when Francis Crick, James Watson, and Maurice Wilkins unraveled the mystery of the double helix structure of deoxyribonucleic acid, commonly called DNA, paving the way for research that seems almost a product of science fiction. The adult human genome contains approximately three billion chemical bases and some one hundred thousand genes, each with its function yet each containing the same DNA. The DNA from a single cell found in a person's saliva on the lip of a glass can identify with almost absolute certainty the person to whom it belongs. Every cell in a person's body possesses identical DNA. Every living organism has unique DNA except for identical organisms—in humans, identical twins. As the mysteries of DNA have continued to unfold, they have generated myriad ethical questions about the uses of genetic engineering.

Fundamental Concerns

Many religious organizations and their members actively resist supporting research in genetics and have expressed alarm that genetic engineering tampers with nature in indefensible ways. Contradictions underlie many such arguments. For example, if farmers turn rocky woodlands into cultivated fields in which crops can grow, are they not meddling with nature? Few would contest farmers' rights to cultivate land on a basis analogous to arguments objecting to genetic engineering. Nevertheless, considerable controversy surrounds such matters as the use of stem cells in genetic research.

Stem cells are harvested from human embryos, most of which have the potential of developing into humans but that exist unused in the freezers of fertility clinics. When a woman wishing to become pregnant receives fertility treatments, several of her egg cells are fertilized. The fertilized eggs that are not used to impregnate her are frozen and eventually discarded.

Stem cells are essential for research purposes because, as undifferentiated cells—that is, cells that have not yet assumed the specialized functions that distinguish more developed cells—they can adopt the characteristics of cellular material introduced into them and can reproduce rapidly. Animal experiments have revealed that neural or nerve stem cells not only replicate themselves but also, when placed in bone marrow, can produce several types of blood cells. These experiments provide hope that paraplegics may eventually have their spinal injuries repaired to the point of regaining the use of their paralyzed limbs and that genetic diseases may be contained or even cured.

Stem cell research offers hope that Parkinson's and Alzheimer's disease, diabetes, and heart trouble, as well as some cancers, will ultimately be controlled or wholly eliminated through the genetic engineering that such research makes possible. However, the question looms of whether it is ethically acceptable to use human embryos as sources of stem cells, inasmuch as the embryos that produce such cells have the potential to become human beings.

The stem cell controversy has become heated and fraught with political, religious, and moral implications. In 2001, President George W. Bush signed a bill permitting federal funds to be spent on stem cell research only on a limited basis. The bill restricts such research to the small number of stem cells currently available in a limited number of laboratories, but forbids any continuation of government-supported research once this supply has been exhausted.

Ironically, one of Bush's predecessors, President Ronald Reagan, opposed stem cell research during his administration, and such research might have provided a means of controlling the Alzheimer's disease that severely disabled him through the last years of his life after he left office. Very much aware of this fact, his wife, Nancy Reagan, publicly called for continuation of stem cell research in early 2004. Meanwhile, despite a lack of federal support, privately financed research organizations like the Howard Hughes Medical Institute continued crucial stem cell research.

The Human Genome Project

The systematic study of genetics, initiated in the mid-nineteenth century by Gregor Johann Mendel, an Augustinian monk, advanced greatly when, around 1869, a Swiss physician, Friedrich Miescher, discovered deoxyribonucleic acid, commonly called DNA, in pus from the wounds of German soldiers he was attending. Interest in the study of inherited traits increased steadily in the late nineteenth and early twentieth centuries.

A major breakthrough occurred in 1953 when Francis Crick and James Watson published a landmark article on the double-helix configuration of DNA in *Nature*, a well-respected scientific journal. Their work and that of Maurice Wilkins led to further DNA research for which this trio shared the Nobel Prize in Physiology or Medicine in 1962. In 1975, the first decoding of a gene from the DNA of a virus was accomplished. In 1977, the human gene that manufactures a blood protein was isolated.

In 1990, the Human Genome Project was launched with the expectation that it would, within fifteen years, map completely the human genome, the so-called blueprint of life. The project advanced with remarkable speed. By mid-2000, about 95 percent of the human genome had been sequenced using accelerated sequencing methods developed in the preceding decade and considered 99 percent accurate.

This research enabled scientists to uncover genetic problems in the cells of organisms and either correct them immediately or work toward discovering ways to culture antidotes or messenger cells that would, once introduced into the organism, eliminate defective cells. The implications of such work are enormous for the control and treatment of all sorts of genetic diseases as well as for such conditions as paraplegia resulting from accidents.

Prenatal Genetic Manipulation

Some of the ethical implications of advanced genetic research are daunting. Through assessment of the condition of cells in pregnant women, various genetic predispositions can be identified. Potential parents presently can learn of genetic abnormalities that are correctable in the unborn fetus. Prenatal microscopic surgery has already corrected serious genetic defects in fetuses.

Before the twenty-first century ends, it should be technologically possible for parents to select characteristics they consider desirable in their offspring. They may be able to choose sex, hair and eye color, height, and body structure as well as such characteristics as intelligence, disposition, athletic ability, and manual deftness. Although to do so would require expensive procedures not covered by health insurance, it would enable parents willing to bear the expenses to tailor to their own tastes the children they want.

One must inevitably address the ethical considerations this sort of genetic manipulation presents. For example, the creation of made-to-order children would be affordable only by the affluent. Class distinctions would surely arise from it. A genetically manufactured ruling class with which the rest of society would be unable to compete could result from such genetic meddling, spawning serious ethical dilemmas.

Cloning

Significant reservations accompany cloning, which genetic engineering has brought far beyond the simple cloning done by farmers taking slips of plants and rooting them to create genetically identical plants. Complex vertebrates, notably sheep and cows, have been cloned, and the technology exists to clone humans, although most industrialized countries prohibit human cloning.

Through genetic engineering, it should soon be possible to clone individual body parts—kidneys, livers, hearts, and other vital organs—that will be created from the donors' own DNA and, when sufficiently developed, be transplanted into donors without fear of rejection. Although few people have ethical reservations about this use of cloning, many view with alarm the possibility that some people might have identical whole selves cloned to provide spare parts when the organs of the original donors fail.

The U.S. Supreme Court ruled that a cloned human cannot be patented, although in 1980, in its *Diamond v. Chakrabarty* ruling, it affirmed the right of an inventor to patent a genetically altered life-form. The Court has forbidden patenting cloned humans because such patents would, in the Court's judgment, enable one person to own another person, constituting slavery.

Genetic Privacy

Genetic engineering can reveal potential physical and mental problems. Such revelations can result in finding ways to control and possibly overcome these problems, but a threat accompanies the use of information gained from this sort of genetic investigation.

If genetic information is not considered sacrosanct and strenuously protected, it could conceivably be made available to insurance companies, courts of law, potential employers, and others who might penalize people for their genetic predispositions even though there is no guarantee

that such predispositions would eventuate in illness or disability.

Although uncovering genetic information can be extremely valuable in meeting potential problems, the irresponsible dissemination of such information might destroy people's lives. What is sacrosanct today may not be considered sacrosanct tomorrow. A case in point concerns a disease such as Huntington's disease, a disabling and potentially fatal condition that is likely to afflict about half the offspring of parents suffering from it. At present, genetic testing can determine whether the children of people with Huntington's will develop the disease, whose onset typically occurs in middle age.

Many children of Huntington's disease victims decline to be tested. They resist knowing that they might eventually develop the disease. They are faced with an array of ethical dilemmas. Should they marry? Should they have children? Should they inform prospective mates or employers of their predisposition? How should they plan for their futures? How should they answer probing questions about their medical histories on insurance and employment applications?

Increased Life Expectancy

Life expectancy in the United States increased dramatically during the twentieth century. In 1900, the average man could anticipate living 44.3 years, the average woman 48.3 years. By 1950, those figures had grown to 65.6 years for men and 71.1 years for women. The figures for 1997 increased to 73.6 and 79.2 respectively.

Reliable sources indicate that genetic engineering and other technological advances may, by the year 2100, extend the life expectancy in the United States and Canada to as much as two hundred years. The thought that people may reach or surpass such an age poses thorny ethical questions, chief among them the question of how the elderly will survive economically. Will they be forced to work well into their second centuries? At present, the average American works from the age of about twenty to seventy. Given a theoretical life expectancy of eighty, they thus work for about two-thirds of their lives. If such a proportion is applied to a life span of two hundred years, people beginning to work at twenty would have to work until they are at least 160 years old. Even then, their least productive period, some of it probably involving costly disability and illness, would extend to forty years, whereas for most people currently it is between fifteen and twenty years.

It might be expected that social upheavals would be loosed by such increases in life expectancy as younger members of society question the ethics of saddling them with the socioeconomic responsibilities that are bound to ensue from such an extended life spans. The national economy in the early twenty-first century is already under severe pressure from a Social Security Administration faced with overwhelming economic problems and a health care system threatened by insolvency within two decades. Caring for the aged is costly.

In the brave new world that genetic engineering and other technological advances make possible, a major concern is a population explosion that exceeds the ability of society to support it. Questions of right and wrong arise as people ponder whether it is ethical to burden upcoming generations with decades of supporting, directly or indirectly, the elderly while, with increasing life expectancy, the economic security of their own futures remain in doubt.

—R. Baird Shuman

Further Reading

Boon, Kevin Alexander. *The Human Genome Project: What Does Decoding DNA Mean for Us?* Berkeley Heights, N.J.: Enslow Publishers, 2002.

Espejo, Roman, ed. *Biomedical Ethics: Opposing Views*. San Diego: Greenhaven Press, 2000.

Snedden, Robert. *DNA and Genetic Engineering*. Chicago: Heinemann Library, 2003.

Tagliaferro, Linda. *Genetic Engineering: Progress or Peril?* Minneapolis: Lerner Publications, 1997.

Toriello, James. *The Human Genome Project*. New York: Rosen Publishing, 2003.

Van DeVeer, Donald. *The Environmental Ethics and Policy Book: Philosophy, Ecology, Economics*. Belmont, Calif.: Thomson/Wadsworth, 2003.

Walker, Mark, and David McKay. *Understanding Genes: A Layperson's Guide to Genetic Engineering*. St. Leonards, New South Wales, Australia: Allen and Unwin, 2000.

See also: Bioethics; Cloning; Genetic counseling; Genetic testing; Genetically modified foods; Human Genome Project; In vitro fertilization; Stem cell research; Sustainability of resources; UNESCO Declaration on the Human Genome and Human Rights.

Genetic testing

Definition: Laboratory analyses of genetic materials designed to determine if subjects are carrying certain diseases, are likely to contract the diseases, or have other genetic disorders

Type of ethics: Bioethics

Significance: Genetic testing is a potentially powerful tool for the prevention, early detection, and improved treatment of diseases that have known genetic characteristics. However, such testing carries with it serious concerns about the ethical, social, legal, and psychological implications of how the information collected is used.

With the completion of the mapping work of the Human Genome Project, genetic information is rapidly moving into mainstream clinical medicine. Genetic testing is a powerful method of establishing diagnoses, and in some areas of medicine it is becoming a routine part of diagnostic testing.

Genetic Testing vs. Genetic Screening

Genetic testing that is used to predict risks of disease and influence individual clinical care should be distinguished from population-based genetic screening. An example of genetic screening is state-mandated newborn screening programs that are aimed at detecting genetic diseases for which early diagnosis and treatment are available. Population-based genetic screening is ethically justifiable when the benefits of screening outweigh the potential harms. Any such screening tests should provide clear diagnoses, and accurate information on risks and effective treatments for the conditions should be available. Screening is justifiable when the prevalence of the disease is high in the population screened, and when screening is acceptable to the population screened.

Population-based genetic screening is becoming increasingly common for adult-onset disorders for which known and accepted treatments are available. Population-based genetic screening to reduce the incidence of a disease, however, may sacrifice the values of individuals for the sake of social goals. Individuals may feel pressure to undergo genetic screening tests they would not otherwise have chosen.

The Privacy of Genetic Information

Maintaining the privacy of medical information is a concern that is not limited to genetic information. Privacy has instrumental value through the control that it affords individuals in providing protection from harm. For example, giving individuals absolute control over their own genetic information helps protect them from insurance or employment discrimination.

Laws that guarantee the privacy of genetic information are instrumental in allowing every individual to control who has access to potentially damaging genetic information.

As the number of genetic tests clinically available has increased there has been greater public concern about genetic privacy. One of the ironies of advances in human genetic research is that the very people who stand to gain most from this information may not seek genetic testing out of fear of discrimination. In a national telephone survey, 63 percent of participants said they probably would not or definitely would not take genetic tests for diseases if health insurers or employers were to have access to the test results. Such concerns about the potential for insurance and employment discrimination are at the heart of a national effort to accord genetic information special privacy protections.

By mid-2003, forty-two states had enacted legislation designed to protect against genetic discrimination in health insurance, and thirty-two states had legislated protection against genetic discrimination in employment. However, the specific provisions of these laws varied greatly from state to state.

On the federal level, President Bill Clinton signed an executive order prohibiting discrimination in federal employment based on genetic information. In addition, a new set of federal privacy regulations, issued pursuant to the Health Insurance Portability and Accountability Act of 1996 (HIPAA), created a minimum set of general privacy protections that preempt state law. Although multiple bills have been introduced into Congress, no federal legislation has been passed specifically relating to genetic discrimination in individual insurance coverage or to genetic discrimination in the workplace.

Efforts to enact legislation to ensure the privacy of genetic information stem from concerns that health insurers might use such information to deny, limit, or cancel insurance policies. There are also reasons for concern that employers might use genetic information to discriminate against their workers or to screen applicants for jobs. The use of genetic testing in the workplace presents employers with challenging decisions related to promoting health in the workplace while avoiding the potential misuse of genetic information. However, concerns about genetic discrimination may actually be out of proportion to the actual incidence of documented instances of information misuse.

Disclosure of Familial Genetic Information

Genetic test results of individuals have implications for other blood relatives. This feature of genetic information raises difficult ethical questions about the obligation of family members to share their genetic information with relatives, who may share the same genetic disorders, and the obligations of physicians to disclose information about disease risks with the relatives of patients who refuse to share the information themselves.

Studies of patients' attitudes toward disclosure of genetic information to at-risk family have documented varied attitudes toward disclosure of genetic information within families. Genetic information carries the potential for economic, psychological, and relational harm. For example, individuals who carry genetic alterations may see themselves as defective and feel guilty about the possibility of their transmitting genetic alterations to their offspring. There is an underlying fear that society will view those with genetic alterations as defective. Some perceive the identification of individuals with altered genes as the first step toward eugenics, or attempts to limit procreative freedom based on genotype.

Genetic testing should always be accompanied by the subjects' written informed consent to prevent misunderstanding and to minimize anxiety. The ethical, legal, social, and psychological implications of genetic testing are so complex that genetic counselors should be involved before, during, and after patients agree to undergo testing. Genetic counseling is a process of evaluating family histories to identify and interpret the risks of inherited disorders.

The mere fact that genetic tests are available does not mean that they should necessarily be ordered. Decisions to conduct tests should consider not only the possible benefits but also the potential social and psychological risks. Genetic counselors can be invaluable in helping individuals decide which tests are appropriate, deciphering complex test results, and helping individuals understand and reach decisions about what to do with the results of their tests.

Pre-implantation and Predisposition Genetic testing

Pre-implantation genetic diagnosis (PGD) has raised many ethical concerns. It is an alternative to prenatal diagnosis for individuals undergoing in vitro fertilization. PGD allows scientists to screen embryos for chromosome abnormalities and select unaffected embryos for implantation with the goal of reducing the transmission of genetic diseases. The process has been used for sex-linked disease and human leukocyte antigen matching. The ethical boundaries of employing this procedure are unresolved. It raises a variety of questions. For example, should parents be allowed to use the process to select the sexes of their offspring when no evidence of genetic diseases is present? Who should decide how this technology should be used?

Many of the earliest forms of genetic tests were designed to detect or confirm rare genetic diseases. Information obtained from single-gene disorders with high penetrance was relatively easy to interpret. However, later advances in genetics led to the discovery of gene alterations that contribute to common, complex diseases that develop later in life. These so-called predisposition tests determine the probabilities of healthy individuals developing the diseases. When unaffected family members are found to have genetic alterations that increase their risks of developing diseases, they may take measures to reduce their risk of developing the diseases. Such situations may also affect reproductive decisions and result in targeted medical diagnostics and therapeutics.

Appropriate uses of predisposition testing have been challenged. Predisposition genetic tests can identify alterations within genes, but they cannot always predict how severely the altered genes will affect the people who carry them. For example, finding an alteration on chromosome number 7 does not necessarily predict whether a child will have serious lung problems or milder respiratory symptoms.

Many ethical questions arise from predisposition testing. For example, should children undergo genetic testing for adult-onset disorders? Should predisposition testing be allowed prior to adoption decisions? Generally speaking the best interests of the children should guide decisions about genetic testing. When no immediate benefit to a child is evident, inessential testing should be avoided.

Genetic testing carries the promise of disease prevention, risk modification, and directed therapy. These benefits, however, are accompanied by the potential for discrimination and stigmatization. Informed consent and genetic counseling are essential to ensuring that genetic testing is appropriate and that the risks to individuals and social groups are minimized.

The greatest benefits of the Human Genome Project are yet to be realized, and as new genetic tests emerge new questions will certainly arise.

—Lisa Soleymani Lehmann

Further Reading

Andrews L. B., et al., eds. *Social, Legal and Ethical Implications of Genetic Testing: Assessing Genetic Risks*. Washington, D.C.: National Academy Press; 1994.

Kevles, Daniel J. *In the Name of Eugenics: Genetics and the Uses of Human Heredity*. Cambridge, Mass.: Harvard University Press, 1995.

Kristol, William, and Eric Cohen, eds. *The Future Is Now: America Confronts the New Genetics*. Lanham, Md.: Rowman and Littlefield, 2002.

Krumm, J. "Genetic Discrimination: Why Congress Must Ban Genetic Testing in the Workplace." *Journal of Legal Medicine* 23, no. 4 (2002): 491- 521.

Lehmann, L. S., et al. "Disclosure of Familial Genetic Information: Perceptions of the Duty to Inform." *American Journal of Medicine* 109, no. 9 (2000): 705-711.

Otlowski, Margaret F., Sandra D. Taylor, and Kristine K. Barlow-Stewart. "Genetic Discrimination: Too Few Data." *European Journal of Human Genetics* 11 (2002): 1-2.

See also: Bioethics; Biotechnology; Diagnosis; Eugenics; Genetic counseling; Genetic engineering; Human Genome Project; Intelligence testing; Surrogate motherhood.

Genetically modified foods

Definition: Foods artificially created by manipulating living organisms using methods involving the transfer of genetic information (DNA) from one source to another

Date: Began in the late twentieth century

Type of ethics: Bioethics

Significance: The emergence of genetically modified foods at the end of the twentieth century led to wide public debate regarding food safety and quality, consumer rights, environmental impact, the value of small-scale farming, and the potential need to regulate certain technological applications.

Human beings have been manipulating living organisms for food for thousands of years. Early examples were wine and bread production and the domestication of the ancestor to the modern corn plant. As scientists learned more about plant and animal biology, selective breeding practices became more efficient. Later, methods developed to alter DNA led to new traits important for commercial growing practices or that enhanced the quality of the food. With the development of genetic engineering, new ways

Plums genetically engineered for resistance to plum pox, a disease carried by aphids. By Scott Bauer, USDA ARS.

to modify plant and animal food sources became possible. In 1990, the U.S. federal Food and Drug Administration gave approval for the first food ingredient produced through recombinant DNA technology: chymosin or rennet, which is used in the production of cheese and other dairy products. Shortly afterward, Calgene, Inc. introduced the Flavr Savr tomato—the first genetically modified whole food approved for market.

By the early years of the twenty-first century, genetically modified (GM) foods had been altered for a variety of reasons including improving plant resistance to pests, disease, and such environmental stresses such as drought and frost. Other goals of genetically modifying foods have been to improve taste, quality, or nutritional value; to improve ability to transport or store the product; and to use

plants to produce novel products for industry, medicine, and consumer use.

Animals used as food sources have also been modified—most commonly by treating them with hormones produced through genetic engineering to increase their milk production or their muscle mass.

Hormone-treated dairy cows and the appearance of herbicide-resistant crops were particularly important in leading to public outcry against genetically modified foods. As a result, a new field of food and agriculture ethics emerged in which ethical principles related to general welfare, justice, and people's rights are applied. Environmental ethics and questions regarding what is considered "natural" enter into the assessment of this technology.

A Utilitarian Approach

One way to assess any new technology is to consider its potential benefits and harms. This approach, however, can lead to major dilemmas when considering genetically modified foods. Food is essential for survival of all animals, and thus has value. The Food and Agricultural Organization (FAO) of the United Nations has pointed out that access to safe, sufficient, and nutritious food is a universal right that impacts other values of enhanced well-being and human health. Proponents of genetically modified foods argue that they can contribute to sustainable agricultural systems and food of high nutritional quality—both of which are critical to support the expanding world population.

Opponents of genetically modified foods argue that genetic manipulation damages food quality by decreasing its nutritional value and increasing risk for the presence of dangerous chemicals in food that might cause allergic reactions or even cancer. Although regulatory agencies and scientists have deemed these foods safe, insufficient scientific data exist to conclusively address public concerns.

Genetically modified foods indirectly impact other aspects of human well-being including quality of life (the aesthetic value of rural settings and the natural environment) and satisfactory income and working conditions. Concerns about genetically modified food technology range from fears and uncertainties about the environmental and ecological impact of genetically engineered crops to the demise of small-scale farmers or possible disrespect for local customs and traditions. Given the ever-decreasing space available to grow food and the long history of environmental disturbances resulting from other agricultural practices, ethical analyses should compare the relative benefits and risks of both genetic modification technology and traditional practices.

Issues of Justice and Fairness

The world human population doubled between 1960 and 2000 and is expected to increase by an additional 50 percent by 2050. This increase, coupled with the growing gap between wealthy and less developed nations, forces consideration of new technologies and policies for food production and distribution. The value of enhanced well-being for all is intimately linked to the need for practical rural infrastructure and sustainable agriculture on a global basis.

Proponents of genetically modified foods argue that the technology may be the only way to address growing global food shortages and malnutrition. Opponents argue that other sound practices should be considered, that potentially unsafe food is being touted as a solution to world hunger, and that wealthy nations are forcing developing countries into abiding by patent rules and trade agreements to get the food supplies they need.

Certain business practices associated with genetically modified food production have been controversial. Widely differing public views on genetically modified foods in Europe versus the United States have led to international debates on fair trade laws and practices. Other concerns arise from patenting issues, the costs of genetically modified seed, and industry-imposed limitations on how farmers can use these products.

Interestingly, patent and intellectual property legal complications might actually lead to the underdevelopment and underutilization of genetically modified foods that could be applied for the greater public good. An example of this is "golden rice," a form of rice that was genetically modified to contain extra vitamin A in order to address nutritional deficiencies among Asian societies. The public views the intentions of businesses associated with genetically modified foods with skepticism, since many believe that corporate profit is valued more than either the condition of humankind or the long-term health and sustainability of the global environment.

Environmental ethicists question what is fair to the natural world. Will the technology that produces genetically modified organisms, including those used as food, negatively impact biodiversity—perhaps through the production of genetic pollution, "superweeds," or new pathogens—or will the technology actually enable scientists to help preserve biological diversity or perhaps even restore populations of endangered or extinct species? During the first years of the twenty-first century, genetically modified food technology was still too new to know whether there were unforeseen risks or to assess its impact on ecosystem balance and natural selection.

Other Issues

Another controversial issue surrounding genetically modified foods is whether the products should be labeled as such. Regulatory agencies in the United States have ruled that because such foods are essentially the same as natural and traditionally grown foods, they do not require special labeling. Companies producing genetically modified foods argue that given misperceptions and a lack of public understanding of the technology, such labeling would unfairly skew market competition. Consumer rights advocates argue the importance of the public's right to know and the need for freedom of informed choice in a democratic society.

As with the broader issue of genetically modified organisms, genetically modified food technology leads to concerns that science may have gone too far in intervening with nature. An underlying fear is that if humans continue to reduce living organisms to the status of manufactured goods, the standards set for genetically manipulating any organism, including humans, will also be relaxed. Traditional ethical principles and commonly used risk-benefit analyses do not readily apply to situations in which genetically modified crops begin to impact biodiversity, irreversibly change the concept of natural selection, or alter human activities involving basic needs and long-valued human interactions with the land.

—*Diane White Husic*

Further Reading

Doyle, Jack. *Altered Harvest: Agriculture, Genetics, and the Fate of the World's Food Supply.* New York: Penguin Books, 1986.

Lambrecht, Bill. *Dinner at the New Gene Cafe: How Genetic Engineering Is Changing What We Eat, How We Live, and the Global Politics of Food.* New York: St. Martin's Press, 2001.

Pinstrup-Anderson, Per, and Ebbe Schioler. *Seeds of Contention: World Hunger and the Global Controversy Over Genetically Modified Crops.* Baltimore: International Food Policy Research Institute, 2001.

Pringle, Peter. *Food, Inc.: Mendel to Monsanto—The Promises and Perils of the Biotech Harvest.* New York: Simon & Schuster, 2003.

Rissler, Jane, and Margaret Mellon. *The Ecological Risks of Engineered Crops.* Boston: MIT Press, 1996.

See also: Agribusiness; Bioethics; Biotechnology; Famine; Genetic engineering; Hunger.

Group therapy

Definition: Simultaneous psychotherapeutic treatment of several clients under the leadership of therapists who try to facilitate helpful interactions among group members.

Date: Term coined in 1932

Type of ethics: Psychological ethics

Significance: In addition to abiding by the same ethical strictures that bind all psychotherapists, group therapists must take special care not to aid one member of the group at the expense of another member. Moreover, all members of therapy groups are morally obligated to hold confidential everything that occurs within group sessions.

Typically, therapy groups consist of three to twelve members who meet once per week for twelve to an unlimited number of weeks. Formats of group therapy differ widely depending on the approach taken by the therapist, but all forms provide an opportunity for members to interact with other members and to learn from these interactions with the help of the therapist. Compared to individual therapy, group therapy provides a fuller social context in which an individual can work out social problems. Thus, group therapy affords a unique laboratory for working out interpersonal relationships. Members interact in a setting that is more representative of real life than is individual therapy.

Group therapy was developed over the first three decades of the twentieth century by several innovative mental health professionals. The term was coined by Jacob Moreno, also associated with the invention of psychodrama, at a psychiatric conference in 1932. The practice first became popular during World War II, when there were too few therapists available to treat all the psychological casualties of war. Many experienced therapists, however, have come to believe that group therapy has a number of advantages beyond the efficient use of a therapist's time (and lower cost to the individual).

One additional advantage of group therapy is that it encourages members to recognize quickly that they are not the only ones who feel the way they do; it gives them the opportunity to derive comfort, encouragement, and support from others who have similar, perhaps more severe, problems. This recognition tends to raise each member's expectations for improvement, an important factor in all forms of treatment. In addition, members have an opportunity to see themselves as others see them and to obtain more honest feedback about their behavior than they receive elsewhere in everyday life. They receive this feedback not only from the leader but also from other members, whose insights and observations can be very beneficial.

Members also have opportunities to try alternative responses when old ones prove ineffective. Thus, they can actually practice new behaviors in addition to talking about them. Further, members can learn vicariously by watching ho wothers behave and can explore attitudes and reactions by interacting with a variety of people, not only the therapist. Also, members often benefit from feeling that they are part of a group, from getting to know new people, from expressing their own points of view, and from becoming emotionally intimate with others. The group experience may make members less guarded, more willing to share feelings, and more sensitive to other people's needs, motives, and messages. Members may also experience increased self-esteem as a result of helping other members.

Group therapy poses several potential disadvantages. First, some people, because of insecurities or distrustfulness, may be unsuited to group therapy or may need individual therapy before they can function well in a group setting. Second, in some groups, the therapist's attention may be spread too thin to give each member the attention that he or she needs. Third, the pressure to conform to group rules may limit the therapy process. Fourth, some people may desire more confidentiality than a group can afford or may desire individual attention.

Some types of problems are more appropriate for group than individual therapy. Such problems include substance abuse, eating disorders, child abuse, problems with intimacy, compulsive behaviors (such as gambling), hypochondriasis, narcissism, and posttrauma adjustment (such as post-divorce adjustment or recovering from the effects of sexual victimization). Also, group therapy is a popular form of personal growth therapy; thus, groups are often composed of individuals who are essentially normal but who want to grow or develop more fully.

Types of Group Therapy

Some forms of group therapy currently in existence are sensitivity training or encounter groups, which promote personal growth by encouraging members to focus on their immediate relationships with other members; assertiveness training, in which leaders demonstrate specific ways of standing up for one's rights in an assertive but not aggressive manner; psychodrama, in which an individual acts out dramatic incidents resembling those that cause problems in real life; family therapy, in which two or more family members work as a group to resolve the problems of each individual family member (for example, school phobia in an eight-year-old) and to create harmony and balance within the family by helping each family member better understand the family's interactions and the problems they create; marriage encounter, in which couples explore themselves and try to expand and deepen their marriage relationships; and self-help groups such as Alco-

holics Anonymous, Parents Without Partners, and Weight Watchers, which often function within a specified structure but without a trained or formal leader.

People most likely to benefit from group therapy are those who can communicate thoughts and feelings and who are motivated to be active participants. Poor candidates are those who are withdrawn, uncommunicative, combative, antisocial, or so depressed or unreachable that they are likely to frustrate other group members.

—Lillian M. Range

Further Reading

Bowen, Murray. *Family Therapy in Clinical Practice.* New York: Jason Aronson, 1978.

Brabender, Virginia. *Introduction to Group Therapy.* New York: Wiley, 2002.

Haley, Jay, and Lynn Hoffman. *Techniques of Family Therapy.* New York: Basic Books, 1967.

Kline, William B. *Interactive Group Counseling and Therapy.* Upper Saddle River, N.J.: Merrill/Prentice Hall, 2003.

Lieberman, Morton A., Irvin D. Yalom, and Matthew B. Miles. *Encounter Groups: First Facts.* New York: Basic Books, 1973.

Minuchin, Salvador. *Families & Family Therapy.* Cambridge, Mass.: Harvard University Press, 1974.

Napier, Augustus, with Carl Whitaker. *The Family Crucible.* New York: Harper & Row, 1978.

Satir, Virginia. *Conjoint Family Therapy.* Rev. ed. Palo Alto, Calif.: Science and Behavior Books, 1967.

Yalom, Irvin D. *The Theory and Practice of Group Psychotherapy.* 4th ed. New York: Basic Books, 1995.

See also: Behavior therapy; Family therapy; Personal relationships; Psychology; Therapist-patient relationship.

Health care allocation

Definition: Distribution of health care resources to specific areas and to certain individuals in need of particular procedures

Type of ethics: Bioethics

Significance: Health care allocation raises questions of societal obligation and individual rights to health care, as well as values inherent in specific treatment choices

The allocation of scarce resources is an issue central to every political party, every government, and every organization and company. Whether to allocate 2 percent or 10 percent of the gross national product to health care, rather than defense, or education, or housing, or whatever other particular need is most pressing, is a decision that is central to the type of government and the values of those in power. Once a health care budget is established, the choices become progressively less global and more oriented to the individual recipient of health care. Although the values inherent in the original budget decisions can still be found, they are often less visible than the physician's personal opinions or the assessment of medical or social utility found in specific allocation decisions.

Certain salient issues include the need to balance ethical concerns with economic realities, the need to allocate scarce health resources, the call for heightened accountability, and the impact of various policies on vulnerable populations.

Macro- vs. Microallocation

Are patients individuals or members of populations? Should health care be regulated as part of the public good? Given a set amount of resources—funding, personnel, equipment, and so forth—to dedicate to health care, a particular system must then determine the allocation to different areas of health care. Preventive medicine, health care promotion, research, medical education, the physical establishment of new facilities, and technological advancement all compete for resources dealing with the treatment of injured and ill patients. This systemw-ide form of decision making, along with the initial allotment of resources, is usually considered macroallocation.

The macro level concerns the scope and design of basic health care institutions: the delivery and financing of personal medical services that comprise acute care, including the system of hightechnology hospital and clinic, support staff, research institutions, and public health programs involved in prevention.

Macro decisions generally determine the kinds of health care services that exist in society, who will receive them and on what bases, who will deliver them, and the distribution of financial burdens. In contrast, the individual determination of eligibility for a given procedure or selection of patients for treatment is called microallocation. Allocation in general is inextricably linked with societal and individual perceptions of justice. A society that considers inequities in health to be unjust, as opposed to unfortunate, will allocate a proportionately greater amount of its resources to mitigate health differences. If a society deems it a pity but not unjust that some people enjoy better health care than others, it will not feel such a societal obligation to correct these differences.

Theories of Justice

Distributive justice establishes principles for the distribution of scarce resources in circumstances in which demand outstrips supply and rationing must occur. Needs are to be considered in terms of overall needs and the dignity of members of society. Aside from the biological and physiological elements, the social context of health and disease may influence a given problem and its severity. Individual prejudices and presuppositions may enlarge the nature and scope of the disease, creating a demand for health care that makes it even more difficult to distribute scarce resources for all members of society. Principles of fair distribution in society often supersede and become paramount to the concerns of the individual. Questions about who shall receive what share of society's scarce resources generate controversies about a national health policy, unequal distributions of advantages to the disadvantaged, and rationing of health care.

Similar problems recur with regard to access to and distribution of health insurance, medical equipment, and artificial organs. The lack of insurance as well as the problem of underinsurance constitutes a huge economic barrier to health care access in the United States. Tom L. Beauchamp and James F. Childress have pointed out that the acquired immunodeficiency syndrome (AIDS) crisis has presented dramatic instances of the problems of insurability and underwriting practices, where insurers often appeal to actuarial fairness in defending their decisions, while neglecting social justice. Proposals to alleviate the unfairness to those below the poverty line have been based on charity, compassion, and benevolence toward the sick rather than on claims of justice. The ongoing debate over the entitlement to a minimum of health care involves not only government entitlement programs but also complex social, political, economic, and cultural beliefs.

Decisions concerning the allocation of funds will dictate the type of health care that can be provided for which problems. Numerous resources, supplies, and space in intensive care units have been allocated forspecific patients or classes of patients. A lifethreatening illness, of course, complicates this decision.

In the United States, health care has often been allocated by one's ability to pay rather than other criteria; rationing has at times been based on ranking a list of services or one's age. There are several theories of justice with regard to health care, some of which overlap, and others of which have different possible methods of distribution applicable to the overall concept. Three of the most general theories are the egalitarian, the libertarian, and the utilitarian.

Egalitarian Theories

Egalitarian theories of distributive justice advocate either the equal distribution of goods and resources to all people or the provision of equality of opportunity in obtaining care. Equal distribution has the major drawback of ignoring differences in health needs in a given population. For example, treatments appropriate to reasonably healthy individuals would certainly not be appropriate for people with diabetes or epilepsy, much less kidney disease or cancer.

Equality of opportunity emphasizes distribution of resources in accordance with what each individual person needs in order to function at a "normal" level. "Normal" in this sense is usually taken to mean that level that is species-typical. The assumption made is that no one should be denied medical treatment on the basis of undeserved disadvantaging properties such as social class, ability to pay, or ill health. The questions of what constitutes need and what constitutes an undeserved disadvantage, however, make the application of this theory very complicated. For example, does a person with a disfiguring feature, such as a birthmark or scar, need to have plastic surgery in order to enjoy the same social benefits as others?

Problems also arise when a particular system does not have enough resources to provide for all. At what level is it necessary to provide these resources? The range goes from the treatment of common diseases and injuries to the provision (at least theoretically) of heart and liver transplants to anyone who shows a need.

Libertarian and Utilitarian Theories

Libertarian theories of justice, when applied to health care, challenge the concept of health care as a right. If something is a right, society has an obligation to provide it to all people. Libertarians contend that justice results from allowing a society to participate in voluntary exchanges to obtain what they need; in other words, a free-market economy. A person is entitled to health care in proportion to his or her ability to exchange that which has been rightfully acquired.

Any redistribution of resources, such as taxing the wealthy to fund health care for the poor, is inherently unjust, because it denies the wealthy the right to use that which they fairly gained. These theories tend to ignore the fact that extreme wealth can give the rich the power to deny the poor the ability to exercise their rights freely.

Utilitarian theories focus on the principle of the greatest good for the greatest number. If x dollars could provide food for fifty starving people or openheart surgery for one, that money should be devoted to food. Utilitarians think that the government is responsible for enacting laws that promote the general public's happiness and that the legislature is responsible for inducing people to act in socially desirable ways through a system of incentives and disincentives. They feel that the law should focus on equality of opportunity for all people and that property rights should be protected because the security of property is crucial to attaining happiness. The problem with utilitarian systems in general is that they tend to lose sight of the individual in favor of the entire population as a whole.

Two-Tiered Systems

Many modern health systems are the results of a two-tiered philosophy. On the first level, a minimum of health care is provided to every person in a society, without regard to wealth or class. On the second level, goods are obtained on the basis of individual decisions and ability to pay. This is usually considered a fair compromise in the United States' health care system. Debate will always exist regarding where the tiers separate, and what decent minimum should be provided for all. There is a lack of consensus on principles for allocating resources.

—Margaret Hawthorne; Updated by Marcia J. Weiss

Further Reading

Beauchamp, Tom L., and James F. Childress. *Principles of Biomedical Ethics.* 5th ed. New York: Oxford University Press, 2001.

Beauchamp, Tom L., and LeRoy Walters, eds. *Contemporary Issues in Bioethics.* 4th ed. Belmont, Calif.: Wadsworth, 1994.

Danis, Marion, Carolyn Clancy, and Larry R. Churchill, eds. *Ethical Dimensions of Health Policy.* New York: Oxford University Press, 2002.

Garrett, Thomas M., Harold W. Baillie, and Rosellen M. Garrett. *Health Care Ethics: Principles and Problems.* Englewood Cliffs, N.J.: Prentice-Hall, 1989.

Greenberg, Warren. *Competition, Regulation, and Rationing in Health Care.* Ann Arbor, Mich.: Health Administration Press, 1991.

Roemer, Milton I. *National Health Systems of the World.* New York: Oxford University Press, 1991.

Van DeVeer, Donald, and Tom Regan, eds. *Health Care Ethics: An Introduction.* Philadelphia: Temple University Press, 1987.

Veatch, Robert M., ed. *Medical Ethics.* Boston: Jones & Bartlett, 1989.

See also: Acquired immunodeficiency syndrome (AIDS); Ageism; Cost-benefit analysis; Distributive justice; Holistic medicine; Illness; Medical bills of rights; Medical ethics; Medical insurance.

Hippocrates

Identification: Greek physician
Born: c. 460 bce, Greek island of Cos
Died: c. 377 bce, Larissa, Thessaly (now in Greece)
Type of ethics: Bioethics
Significance: Hippocrates is traditionally credited with the authorship of a collection of about sixty treatises on medicine and medical ethics, including the Hippocratic oath. This body of writings both created a standard of professional etiquette for the physician and formed the basis of the Western tradition of medical ethics

Although Hippocrates has traditionally enjoyed the reputation of being the father of Greek medicine, little is known about him. Only a few references to him by contemporary or near-contemporary authors exist. According to these references, he came from the island of Cos, off the southwestern coast of Asia Minor, and was a teacher of medicine. He was a member of the Asclepiads, a family or guild of physicians that traced its origins to the god of healing, Asclepius. For reasons that are not clear, Hippocrates came to be idealized after his death, and he became the subject of an extensive biographical tradition. Four short biographies exist, together with a collection of spurious epistles that are attributed to Hippocrates. They assert that Hippocrates learned medicine from his father, who was also a physician. He is supposed to have taught medicine in Cos (which later boasted a famous school of medicine) and to have traveled throughout Greece, dying at an advanced age at Larissa in Thessaly, in northern Greece. Many of the biographical details recorded in these later works must be regarded as legendary.

A large collection of about sixty medical treatises, the Hippocratic Corpus, came to be attributed to Hippocrates after his death. Most were written during the late fifth or fourth centuries bce, but some were composed much later. The works are anonymous and are marked by differences in style. Even in antiquity it was recognized that not all of them were genuine, and attempts were made to determine which were written by Hippocrates. There is no reliable tradition that attests the authenticity of any of the treatises, and the internal evidence is inconclusive. Most modern

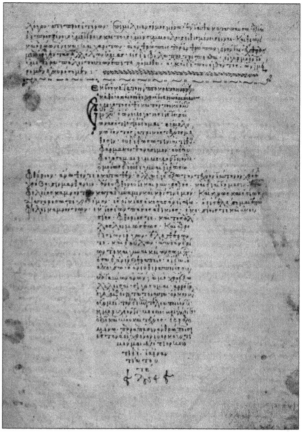

A 12th-century Byzantine manuscript of the Hippocratic Oath.

scholars believe that none of them can be attributed with certainty to Hippocrates.

Hippocratic Medical Ethics

The ethical or deontological treatises of the Hippocratic Corpus (*The Physician, Precepts,* and *Decorum,* dates unknown) constitute the earliest writings on medical etiquette. They define the professional duties that should be expected of Greek physicians.

Most of these principles of etiquette are the product of common sense. They recognize that certain types of conduct are inherently detrimental to the practice of medicine. Physicians should behave in a manner that will add dignity to their profession. Thus, they should look healthy and not be overweight. They should be gentlemen, cheerful and serene in their dealings with patients, self-controlled, reserved, decisive, and neither silly nor harsh. They should not engage in sexual relations with patients or members of their households. They are to be sensitive to the fees they charge, should consider the patient's means, and should on occasion render free treatment. Many of these precepts are meant to preserve the reputation of the physician, which (in the absence of medical licensure) was his most important asset in building and maintaining a medical practice.

The Hippocratic Oath

The best-known, though most puzzling, of the Hippocratic writings is the so-called Hippocratic oath. The oath is characterized by a religious tenor. It begins with an invocation of the healing gods Apollo and Asclepius and includes a pledge to guard one's life and art "in purity and holiness." It is divided into two parts: the covenant, which is a contract between the teacher and his pupil; and the precepts, which defines the duty of the physician to his patients. The oath prohibits, among other things, dispensing a deadly drug, performing an abortion, and practicing surgery (or at least lithotomy).

Several stipulations of the oath are not consonant with ethical standards prevalent elsewhere in the Hippocratic treatises, while some practices prohibited by the oath (induced abortion, euthanasia, and surgery) were routinely undertaken by Greek physicians.

It is difficult, moreover, to find a context in which to place the oath. Although it was traditionally attributed (like the other Hippocratic treatises) to Hippocrates, it is anonymous. It has been dated as early as the sixth century bce and as late as the first century of the Christian era (when it is first mentioned).

Most scholars assign it to the fifth or fourth century bce, making it roughly contemporaneous with Hippocrates. It has been suggested that it was administered to students who were undertaking a medical apprenticeship, but there is no evidence that it ever had universal application in the Greek world.

Greek and Roman physicians were not required to swear an oath or to accept and abide by a formal code of ethics. To be sure, ethical standards appear in the Hippocratic Corpus, but no one knows how widespread these standards were among medical practitioners in antiquity. The oath appealed to Christian physicians, however, who in late antiquity took over its precepts and infused them with new meaning. It was later adopted by Christian, Jewish, and Muslim physicians as a covenant by which physicians could govern their practices.

There have been a number of attempts to explain away the problem passages of the oath or to attribute it to an author whose views represented those of a group that lay outside the mainstream of medical ethics as described in the Hippocratic Corpus. The most notable is the attempt by Ludwig Edelstein to demonstrate that the oath originated in the Pythagorean community. Parallels can be found outside Pythagoreanism for even the most esoteric injunctions of the oath, however, and its Pythagorean origin cannot be said to have been conclusively proved.

The Influence of Hippocratic Ethics

The medical-ethical treatises of the Hippocratic Corpus have exercised great influence on the formulation and development of Western medical ethics. In establishing not only guidelines for the physician's deportment but also standards of professional obligation, they created both the basis of Greek medical ethics and an ideal of what the physician ought to be. Even in the rapidly changing field of bioethics, their influence continues to be felt to the present day.

—Anne-Marie E. Ferngren and Gary B. Ferngren

Further Reading

Cantor, David, ed. *Reinventing Hippocrates*. Burlington, Vt.: Ashgate, 2002.

Carrick, Paul. *Medical Ethics in Antiquity: Philosophical Perspectives on Abortion and Euthanasia*. Boston: Reidel, 1985.

Edelstein, Ludwig. *Ancient Medicine: Selected Papers of Ludwig Edelstein*. Edited by Owsei Temkin and C. Lilian Temkin. Translated by C. Lilian Temkin. Baltimore: Johns Hopkins University Press, 1967.

Hippocrates. *Hippocrates*. Translated by W. H. S. Jones and Paul Potter. 8 vols. New York: Putnam, 1923-95.

Sigerist, Henry E. *Early Greek, Hindu, and Persian Medicine*. Vol. 2 in *A History of Medicine*. Edited by Ludwig Edelstein. New York: Oxford University Press, 1961.

Temkin, Owsei. *Hippocrates in a World of Pagans and Christians*. Baltimore: Johns Hopkins University Press, 1991.

See also: American Medical Association; Bioethics; Confidentiality; Medical bills of rights; Medical ethics; Medical research; Mental illness; Physician-patient relationship; Professional ethics.

Holistic medicine

Definition: Approach to medicine that treats the whole person as a unity rather than isolating, attending to, or diagnosing only parts of the whole

Type of ethics: Bioethics

Significance: Holistic approaches to medicine usually emphasize noninvasive procedures, patient education, and nontraditional or non-Western practices such as acupuncture, homeopathy, and yoga. Advocates of such an approach see it as ethically admirable, because it humanizes the patient, whereas they believe mainstream medicine often treats patients as mechanical systems or objects

Holistic health practitioners regard patients as whole persons, teaching health maintenance, offering a wide choice of cures, and freely sharing expert knowledge. Holistic practitioners accept as valid knowledge from prescientific ages, as well as psychological and spiritual knowledge that is accessible to everyone. Therefore, for the holistic practitioner, the best possible health care makes use of ancient as well as modern healing arts from a variety of cultures. It treats people as psychological and spiritual beings as well as bodies and educates them in the care of their own psychological and physical health. Therefore, holistic health maintenance and disease curing typically involve teaching the patient actively to change habits of nutrition, exercise, and self-reflection.

In contrast, mainstream medicine is based on the premise that physical science is the most authoritative field of knowledge, though it can only be understood by trained experts such as medical doctors. Therefore, the mainstream physician offers the best possible care by acting as an expert authority, dispensing diagnoses and treatments of bodily diseases with the help of newtechnologies that are the fruits of science.

—*Laura Duhan Kaplan*

See also: Fairness and Accuracy in Reporting; Faith healers; Health care allocation; Illness; Medical ethics; Medical research.

Human Genome Project

Identification: International project launched by the U.S. National Institutes of Health and Department of Energy whose goal was to build a complete sequence map of the entire human genome, locating all the genes on their respective chromosomes

Date: Begun in 1990

Type of ethics: Bioethics

Significance: While the potential for good held out by the project is vast, it is recognized that firm legal, ethical guidelines for the use of human genetic information must be established and enforced

The Human Genome Project began in 1990 with the goal of better understanding the human genetic makeup and providing a free database to be used for the common good of everyone. The project released its first draft of the human genome sequence in February, 2001. The chemical structure of each gene sequence provides scientists with the necessary information to identify which genes are associated with specific human traits and with diseases such as cancer, diabetes, cardiovascular, arthritis, Alzheimer's, deafness, and blindness. Through ethical use of the human genome information, the hope is that serious diseases will be treated more effectively and eventually eliminated through the development of new drugs and gene therapy.

Although the results of the Human Genome Project are based on the principles of science and technology, the project itself is permeated with complex ramifications related to politics, public opinion, public relations, economics, and ethics. Issues of genetic privacy, genetic discrimination, and genetic determinism arise. One fundamental question that has arisen is who should be genetically tested to determine his or her risk for contracting a debilitating disease and what should be done to prevent the misuse of such information. People undergoing genetic testing might face significant risks by jeopardizing their employment or insurance status. Since the process involves genetic information, such risks could also be easily extended to other family members. Confidentiality and privacy of an individual's genetic formation must be protected.

Other ethical concerns raised by the project include human cloning and the possible manipulation of genes to produce superior traits. Animal cloning has proven to be inefficient and often produces animals with debilitating conditions. Many scientists and physicians strongly believe that it would be unethical to attempt human cloning.

Genetic information derived from the Human Genome Project is expected to help future researchers gain a better understanding of the human system, including particular organs, tissues, and the complete chemistry of life. As this progress continues, scientists and ethicists have pointed out that legal and ethical guidelines must be established, updated, and enforced to prevent the misuse of human genetics from leading to the abuse of human beings.

The U.S. Department of Energy and the National Institutes of Health have devoted about 5 percent of their annual Human Genome Project funding toward studying and dealing with the ethical, legal, and social issues associated with the availability of human genetic information.

Positive benefits of Human Genome research must be maximized, while social, economic, and psychological harm must be minimized.

—Alvin K. Benson

Further Reading

Munson, Ronald. *Outcome Uncertain: Cases and Contexts in Bioethics.* Belmont, Calif.: Thomson/Wadsworth, 2003.

Sulston, John, and Georgina Ferry. *The Common Thread: A Story of Science, Politics, Ethics and the Human Genome.* New York: Bantam, 2002.

Zilinskas, Raymond A., and Peter J. Balint, eds. *The Human Genome Project and Minority Communities: Ethical, Social, and Political Dilemmas.* Westport, Conn.: Praeger, 2000.

See also: Bioethics; Biotechnology; Cloning; Exploitation; Genetic engineering; Genetic testing; Medical research; Science; Technology; UNESCO Declaration on the Human Genome and Human Rights.

Hypnosis

Definition: State of consciousness, achieved through techniques of induction, in which a person is unusually open to suggestion

Type of ethics: Psychological ethics

Significance: Because hypnosis gives the appearance of yielding control of one's behavior and mind and conforming to the wishes of the hypnotist, a potential for abuse is perceived

Although the eighteenth century Viennese physician Franz Anton Mesmer no doubt hypnotized some of his patients ("mesmerism"), the concept of hypnosis was unknown before the work of the English physician James Braid. Braid invented the term "hypnosis" and conducted the first scientific studies of hypnotism. Braid devised numerous techniques for inducing the hypnotic state and extensively studied the psychological factors involved. Braid and the British physicians John Elliotson and James Esdaile made extensive use of hypnosis in their medical practices as an adjunct to surgery. Esdaile, for example, reported more than three hundred cases in which he performed major operations on unanesthetized but hypnotized patients who apparently experienced no pain.

The psychoanalyst Sigmund Freud found that hypnosis could be used to relieve symptoms of neurotic and abnormal behavior. Freud repudiated hypnosis as a therapeutic tool, however, because it could only relieve symptoms; it revealed nothing about the causes of the behavior.

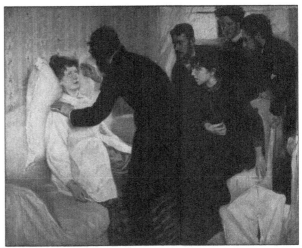

Hypnotic Séance *(1887) by Richard Bergh.*

Modern interest in hypnosis has passed from the physician and psychoanalyst to the experimental psychologist. Psychology's concern with hypnotism involves understanding its nature and mechanisms. Clark L. Hull's 1933 book *Hypnosis and Suggestibility* was the first systematic attempt to apply modern psychological methods to hypnosis, and Ernest R. Hilgard (b. 1904) and others added significantly to the understanding of this phenomenon.

Ethical Issues of Hypnosis

The aforementioned characteristics of the hypnotic state raise the question of whether the hypnotized person becomes unduly dependent upon, controlled by, or influenced by the hypnotist. While in the hypnotic state, could the person be persuaded by an unethical hypnotist to engage in behaviors that he or she otherwise would not perform? Is it possible to induce, for example, irrational, antisocial, criminal, unethical, immoral, or self-destructive behaviors such as impulsively buying a new car, robbing a bank, committing murder, injuring oneself, committing suicide, or having sex with one's hypnotherapist?

The consensus firmly states that hypnosis cannot induce or persuade a person to do anything that he or she would not otherwise do. The belief otherwise undoubtedly arises from the misconception that hypnosis is a condition induced in the person by the hypnotist. In fact, the hypnotist acts simply as a facilitator, guiding and teaching the person how to think and what to do to produce a particular behavior within the person's capabilities.

The person is responsible for and decides whether to perform that behavior. Before a behavior can occur, the person must be willing and able to produce it. Therefore, the question of ethics is really a pseudoethical issue. The hypnotist is not doing anything to which the person does not consent and cannot compel a person to commit an act that is repugnant to that person or beyond his or her capabilities. As Roy Udolf cogently observed, antisocial and self-destructive behavior can and has been obtained in hypnotized persons, but the hypnotist cannot induce the hypnotized person to commit those acts. The person had decided to do so already. An unethical hypnotist could, however, facilitate the performance of that act. For example, a hypnotist could make a criminal less nervous and more self-assured during the commission of a crime.

—Laurence Miller

Further Reading

Atkinson, Rita L., et al. *Introduction to Psychology.* 11th ed. New York: Harcourt Brace Jovanovich, 1993.

Gregory, Richard L., ed. *The Oxford Companion to the Mind.* New York: Oxford University Press, 1987.

Hilgard, Ernest R. *The Experience of Hypnosis.* New York: Harcourt, Brace & World, 1968.

Hilgard, Josephine R. *Personality and Hypnosis: A Study of Imaginative Involvement.* 2d ed. Chicago: University of Chicago Press, 1979.

Moss, C. Scott. *Hypnosis in Perspective.* New York: Macmillan, 1965.

Udolf, Roy. *Handbook of Hypnosis for Professionals.* New York: Van Nostrand Reinhold, 1981.

Weitzenhoffer, Andre M. *The Practice of Hypnotism.* 2d ed. New York: John Wiley & Sons, 2000.

See also: Behavior therapy; Biofeedback; Epistemological ethics; Freud, Sigmund; Pain; Psychology.

Illness

Definition: Lack of health; presence of disease

Type of ethics: Bioethics

Significance: An accepted definition of illness defines the parameters of the responsibilities of medical professionals, patients, and society in the treatment of both healthy and ill people

During the twentieth century, particularly after World War II, advances in medicine took place so rapidly that the health care profession ballooned. With this expansion has come consistently increasing, often unattainable, expectations about what can and should be treated by the medical profession. It is impossible to focus on a particular definition or viewpoint of illness without looking at its counter-part, health. Some people hold that illness is simply lack of health, but any definition of health is controversial.

The World Health Organization (WHO) in 1946 offered this definition: "Health is a state of complete physical, mental and social well-being." It is easy to see why this is controversial. This definition places in opposition to health such states as grief as well as such social problems as racial oppression and poverty. Simultaneously, by classifying these things as health problems, it obligates the health care profession to broaden its scope to include them. Many people have taken issue with the WHO definition of health, but no one has yet been able to formulate one that is any more widely accepted.

Views of Health and Illness

There are three predominant views of the concepts of health and illness. The first, the empirical view, proposes that the health of any organism is determined by whether that organism functions the way it was designed by nature to function. Illness, then, is any situation or entity that hinders the ability of the organism to function in the way in which nature intended.

Proponents of this view point out that this definition is equally applicable to plants, animals, and humans. An organism is determined to be ill or healthy without reference to symptoms subject to interpretation by either the patient or the evaluator.

Another view of health and illness holds that health is that which is statistically normal, and illness is that which is statistically deviant. The problem with this view is that it ends up classifying many things society sees as positive traits, such as extreme intelligence or strength, as illness. Proponents, however, point out that what nature intended for a specific organism is often determined by statistical evidence.

The third view is that of normativism. Normativists believe that the concepts of health and illness incorporate cultural and societal values, because what is viewed as illness depends on what the particular culture considers desirable or undesirable. For example, in seventeenth century America, there was a "disease" called drapetomania, which caused otherwise content slaves in the South to have the uncontrollable urge to escape. The designation of illness also depends on the ability or willingness of a society to recognize a situation as undesirable. A society without writing would not be likely to consider dyslexia an impairment.

The normative view is especially prevalent (and compelling) in the field of mental health. The designation of what is a disease is a product of the culture of the time. For example, in the nineteenth century, women who enjoyed sexual intercourse were considered mentally dysfunctional, while in the twentieth century, the opposite is true. Certain factions, such as advocates for alcoholics, have fought long and hard to have their particular problems labeled as disease. Others, such as homosexuals, have fought equally hard to keep themselves from being so labeled.

Implications of Definitions

Why is the label of illness so desirable or undesirable? When a particular set of symptoms or problems is labeled as an illness, its presence carries with it certain properties of the "sick role." Behaviors that would otherwise be seen as unacceptable or immoral are excused. Responsibility is diminished, both for actions and for inaction. The label of illness also carries with it, however, a certain stigma, that of the necessity to strive for a cure. This is why groups such as homosexuals have fought it so strenuously.

On a more general level, definitions of health and illness define the boundaries and obligations of the medical profession. It is reasonably clear that ideas about health care needs follow the line of ideas about health. The current conception of health care in Western society, the medical model, tends to support the paternalism of health care professionals as interventionists who relieve patients of their responsibility to care for themselves. A nonmedical model, however, tends to emphasize individual responsibility for health.

Disease vs. Illness

Most people consider the terms "disease" and "illness" to be synonymous. Some, however, separate illness into a subcategory of disease. This separation bridges the gap between the empirical and the normative definitions of health. Disease is seen as simply the impairment of natural function, as in the empirical view. Illnesses are diseases that incorporate normative aspects in their evaluations. An illness is a disease whose diagnosis confers upon its owner the special treatment of the sick role. Not all diseases are illnesses. Diseases such as sickle-cell anemia may not impair the health of the individual, and thus do not incur the sick role.

Generally accepted definitions of health, illness, and disease are becoming more necessary as the health care

profession grows. Until society clarifies these concepts, health care will be called upon to mitigate every problem society has, not only the enormous number it is traditionally expected to solve.

—Margaret Hawthorne

Further Reading

Beauchamp, Tom L., and LeRoy Walters, eds. *Contemporary Issues in Bioethics.* 6th ed. Belmont, Calif.: Thomson/Wadsworth, 2003.

Boorse, Christopher. "On the Distinction Between Disease and Illness." *Philosophy and Public Affairs* 5 (Fall, 1975): 49-68.

Callahan, Daniel. "The WHO Definition of 'Health.'" *The Hastings Center Studies* 1, no. 3 (1973): 77-88.

Caplan, Arthur L. "The Concepts of Health and Disease." In *Medical Ethics,* edited by Robert M. Veatch. Boston: Jones & Bartlett, 1989.

Engelhardt, H. Tristam, Jr. "Health and Disease: Philosophical Perspectives." In *Encyclopedia of Bioethics,* edited by Warren T. Reich. Rev. ed. Vol. 2. New York: Macmillan, 1995.

Foucault, Michel. *The Birth of the Clinic: An Archaeology of Medical Perception.* Translated by A. M. Sheridan Smith. 1973. Reprint. New York: Vintage Books, 1994.

McGee, Glenn, ed. *Pragmatic Bioethics.* 2d ed. Cambridge, Mass.: MIT Press, 2003.

Macklin, Ruth. "Mental Health and Mental Illness: Some Problems of Definition and Concept Formation." *Philosophy of Science* 39 (September, 1972): 341-364.

See also: Diagnosis; Health care allocation; Holistic medicine; Medical ethics; Medical insurance; Mental illness; Physician-patient relationship.

Institutionalization of patients

Definition: Involuntary confinement in mental health facilities of mentally ill individuals

Type of ethics: Psychological ethics

Significance: The involuntary institutionalization of people who are deemed to be mentally ill creates a conflict between the ethical values of personal autonomy on one hand and beneficence or care on the other. The question is when it is appropriate to violate the wishes of individuals for their own good. This question is made much more complicated by the fact that what has counted as mental illness and as legitimate grounds for institutionalization has changed significantly over time, which can cause any given standard to seem more arbitrary than it otherwise might

Religions teach that the least among us deserve aid and comfort. To apply this rule to the mentally ill often requires some degree of forced institutionalization. To fulfill the ethical rule not to restrict liberty without good cause means to allow people to live on the streets and to conduct costly court hearings. Many solutions to the problem of the seriously mentally ill have been tried, but all are flawed.

A History of Institutionalization

Various societies at various times have attempted to find humane solutions to the problem of mentally ill persons. Many homeless mentally ill persons wandered the towns and roads of the American colonies. In 1752, Benjamin Franklin influenced the Pennsylvania colony legislature to open the first mental hospital in the thirteen colonies. During the midnineteenth century, many people hailed Dorothea Dix as a great reformer because her efforts on the behalf of the homeless mentally ill resulted in the creation of thirty mental hospitals that soon were filled with patients. Placing people in mental hospitals deprived them of liberty. Common law principles allowed the taking of a person's liberty only if that person was dangerous to himself or herself or the community, required due process, and maintained that a defendant was innocent until proved guilty. Application of the common law rules could have stopped physicians from attempting to treat the mentally ill.

In 1849, the Association of Medical Superintendents of American Institutions for the Insane (now the American Psychiatric Association) appointed a well-known expert, Isaac Ray, to draft a model law for involuntary confinements. He proposed that the involuntary confinement of the deranged for treatment be treated as a medical decision without legal formalities. After several years, most states accepted Ray's idea. During the nineteenth century and the first half of the twentieth century, the states constructed many large mental asylums. In the United States in 1963, 679,000 persons were confined in mental hospitals, whereas only 250,000 were confined in state and federal prisons. From the medical viewpoint, confinement in mental institutions represented an opportunity to "help" those suffering from a disease.

The Deinstitutionalization Movement

By the 1950s, many critics, including the wellknown psychiatrist Thomas Szasz, attacked the involuntary confinement of the mentally ill unless the patients were dangerous to themselves or others. For Szasz, mental illness was a myth, a name for problems in living rather than a medical condition correctable by medical action. He proposed the deinstitutionalization of mental patients and the dismantling of community mental health centers. Szasz pointed to misuses of psychiatry in the former Soviet Union to institutionalize and "treat" political prisoners.

Patients' rights advocates who sued hospitals to release patients and improve conditions joined forces with fiscal conservatives who recommended the release of patients to more cost-effective community care. Judges forced mental hospitals to use more stringent criteria for involuntary admissions, to grant extensive rights to patients, to stop exploiting patients economically, and to improve conditions. The "need for treatment" criterion was rejected, and only the mentally ill who were a danger to themselves or others or were gravely disabled could be confined involuntarily and then only by means of a judicial decision. By 1984, the mental hospital population had dropped to roughly 125,000.

The courts also granted mental patients basic rights. Mental patients were to be treated as normal human beings, they were not to be embarrassed by disclosure of their patient status, and they were to be paid for work done in the institutions. They had a right to refuse most extreme treatments, such as shock therapy. Their rights included absolute access to an attorney and qualified rights for free communication. The restrictions on commitment and the new rights for mental patients made it more expensive and difficult to commit patients and more expensive to keep them. Mental hospitals had partially supported themselves by the unpaid labor of the patients, but this was now forbidden.

The theory behind deinstitutionalization was that community mental health facilities such as halfway houses would replace the large asylums, but legislatures did not fund adequate numbers of the new centers and communities resisted having the facilities in their midst. Outpatient care using chemotherapy was initiated, but most patients did not use such services.

Deinstitutionalization freed patients but did not improve their overall welfare. Many freed patients moved to the streets and endured terrible conditions. Some had children on the streets. Citizens complained about the activities of mental patients in their neighborhoods. The argument that the mentally ill should have the same legal protection as criminals is flawed. The consequences of confinement and freedom for each group of persons and for society are different.

Today, state laws specify the procedures for involuntary confinement of the mentally ill. The normal grounds for such confinement are that the patient is a danger to self or others or is gravely disabled. As patients' loss of liberty increases through longer confinements, the courts play a larger role and patients have more due process rights. The state must provide an appointed attorney if one is requested and must allow jury trials.

Treatment and a Clash of Values

Asecond factor that acted together with court rulings to promote the deinstitutionalization of the mentally ill was the discovery of powerful antipsychotic drugs during the 1950s. Chemotherapy treated symptoms but did not cure the mentally ill, and it often produced very unpleasant side effects. Because most patients could function as long as they took their medication, it made it possible to release many of them. Many patients improved during confinement because of therapy and drugs, won release, stopped taking their medication, and then relapsed.

Ironically, once the patients' rights advocates won the deinstitutionalization battle, they then attacked forced chemotherapy. Psychotherapists argued that chemotherapy liberated the mind from delusions. A majority of state courts granted patients rights to refuse chemotherapy, while the federal courts applied a "need-for-treatment" analysis and left the decisions in the hands of psychiatrists. As chemotherapy declined, hospital stays became longer and the use of physical restraints increased.

The basic institutionalization issue involves deciding which profession and which set of ethical values will control the treatment and confinement of the mentally ill. The patients' rights attorneys see themselves as being in conflict with arrogant physicians who deprive patients of civil rights. In fact, most therapists do tend to overdiagnose mental illness. The idea that judging a sick person to be well is more to be avoided than judging a well person to be sick is built into the medical model. Therapists are wary of public criticism and of lawsuits triggered by the violent acts of a fewdangerous released mental patients, and they view involuntary confinement and treatment as being ethically required to protect patients and the public.

—Leland C. Swenson

Further Reading

Appelbaum, Paul S. "The Right to Refuse Treatment with Antipsychotic Medications: Retrospect and Prospect." *American Journal of Psychiatry* 145 (April, 1988): 413-419.

Bartol, Curt R., and Anne M. Bartol. *Psychology and American Law*. Belmont, Calif.: Wadsworth, 1983.

Brooks, Alexander D. *Law, Psychiatry, and the Mental Health System*. Boston: Little, Brown, 1974.

Foucault, Michel. *Madness and Civilization: A History of Insanity in the Age of Reason*. Translated by Richard Howard. 1965. Reprint. New York: Vintage Books, 1988.

Lickey, Marvin E., and Barbara Gordon. *Medicine and Mental Illness: The Use of Drugs in Psychiatry*. New York: W. H. Freeman, 1991.

Roleff, Tamara L., and Laura K. Egendorf, eds. *Mental Illness: Opposing Viewpoints*. San Diego, Calif.: Greenhaven Press, 2000.

Schwitzgebel, Robert L., and R. Kirkland Schwitzgebel. *Law and Psychological Practice*. New York: Wiley, 1980.

Swenson, Leland C. *Psychology and Law for the Helping Professions*. Pacific Grove, Calif.: Brooks/Cole, 1993.

See also: Consent; Lobotomy; Mental illness; Psychology; Right to die; Sterilization of women; Therapist-patient relationship.

Intelligence testing

Definition: Measurement of human intelligence

Type of ethics: Bioethics

Significance: Intelligence testing raises ethical concerns involving potential cultural bias of tests as well as the differential treatment of people based on their test results

Alfred Binet and his colleagues first devised tests to assess the mental abilities of French children during the 1890s. A child's "mental age," divided by chronological age, gave an "intelligence quotient" (IQ). Binet thought that IQ scores could be improved through education, but many British psychologists insisted that intelligence was hereditary. Data on this issue were gathered by Cyril Burt, but some of his data were later shown to have been fabricated. American psychologists modernized Binet's tests but applied them, with considerable bias, against African Americans and immigrants.

Despite early claims that the tests measure "innate intelligence," careful studies show that educational influences are strong and that most early studies were flawed. In particular, a fifteen-point average difference between unselected whites and African Americans disappears when comparison is made between samples matched by social status, family income, and similar factors. African Americans who have attended good schools and have had similar advantages achieve higher scores than do students from disadvantaged backgrounds regardless of race.

Test bias occurs because the test is given in a particular language and because it assumes a middleclass cultural environment; the results are therefore biased against the poor and against those who speak a different language. More subtle bias includes questions about activities that are common to middleclass white males, thus discriminating against females and blacks. Bias-free exams are difficult to write.

Proponents of eugenics have advocated favorable treatment of high-IQ individuals and unfavorable treatment (including sterilization) of low-IQ subjects. Since test results can be modified by education and are subject to bias, such proposals have lost much favor since about 1940.

—*Eli C. Minkoff*

See also: Eugenics; Genetic counseling; Genetic testing; Psychology.

Kevorkian, Jack

Identification: American pathologist
Born: May 26, 1928, Pontiac, Michigan
Type of ethics: Bioethics
Significance: A medical doctor who has advocated the creation of a medical specialty ("obitiatry") for suicide assistance, organ harvesting, and experimentation on the moribund, Kevorkian personally assisted in the suicide of scores of terminally ill patients. Media coverage of his actions and ideas galvanized public debate on the issue of physician-assisted suicide

Jack Kevorkian's career-long focus on death—from trying to ascertain its onset in patients' eyes to trying to salvage some benefit from it—has alienated him from the medical establishment. Kevorkian advocated cadaver blood transfusions and lobbied along with death-row inmates for execution by lethal injection because it would be more merciful and would permit organ donation and experimentation under irreversible anesthesia. Kevorkian wrote various journal articles promoting his controversial ideas, but his objectives were repeatedly frustrated, and he turned his attention to patients who desired euthanasia.

In 1989, Kevorkian developed a saline drip by means of which a severely disabled person could activate a lethal drug, and he marketed this machine on talk shows. Kevorkian later developed another "suicide machine" that used carbon monoxide, which he used after his medical license was revoked and he no longer had access to pre-

scription drugs. On November 22, 1998, CBS's *60 Minutes* aired a video tape of Kevorkian injecting a patient named Thomas Youk with a lethal drug. The broadcast triggered renewed debate not only about the legality and morality of assisted suicide, but about journalistic ethics as well. Three days later, Kevorkian was arrested and charged with murder. He was convicted of second-degree murder in 1999 and sentenced to ten to twenty-five years in prison.

Kevorkian assisted in the deaths of at least 130 people. The media attention and controversy surrounding him throughout the 1990s made his name a household word. Besides questioning the propriety of assisted suicide, critics condemn Kevorkian's lack of medical experience with living patients; his brief relationships with the suicides; and the fact that many of the suicides were not terminally ill but merely in pain or afraid of advancing physical or mental disability, and possibly depressed. The number of people contacting him for assistance or openly endorsing his actions, however, demonstrates substantial dissatisfaction with available options for the terminally and chronically ill.

—*Ileana Dominguez-Urban; Updated by the editors*

See also: Abortion; Bioethics; Death and dying; Dilemmas, moral; Euthanasia; Homicide; Right to die; Suicide; Suicide assistance.

Life and death

Definition: Presence or withdrawal of the ineffable motive force that differentiates animate from inanimate matter
Type of ethics: Bioethics
Significance: Decisions regarding life and death are usually thought to be the most important and most difficult of all ethical issues. Specific definitions of life and death may determine the parameters of one's legal, ethical, economic, and personal obligations

Since humans do the defining, all life is defined from the standpoint of human life. Definitions of life reflect the complexity of human life and the various cultural contexts within which the definitions are sought. Definitions of life and death therefore symbolize the concerns of the individuals seeking a definition as well as the culture that supports their search. Definitions of life and death not only manifest the values and concerns of individuals and society but also determine who lives in that society. If a definition of death, for example, focuses on the irreversible loss of consciousness, then those who have irreversibly lost consciousness are no longer part of that human society because they are no longer considered human. If a definition of human life makes the possession of human DNA equal to being human, then every organism with human DNA is part of that human society.

Definitions also focus on one aspect of human existence rather than another. The word "death," for example, may refer to dying, the death event, or the time after the moment of death. People who say, "I am afraid of death" usually mean that they fear dying. Others, who say they look forward to death, usually mean an afterlife. Today, many people use "death" as it is used in this article to refer to the point at which a living entity changes from a living to a nonliving state. The focus of modern Western society is on the biological nature of life and death; therefore, its ethical concern is with the biological aspects of life and death. This concern will be the focus of this article.

Defining Life and Death
No society can exist without explicit or implicit definitions of life and death. People must know when someone is dead. Without such knowledge, wills could not be probated, burial could not take place, leadership positions in business and politics could not be clearly defined, and life-support systems could not be removed. Without clear definitions of human life and death, one would consider a thing (a cadaver) to be a human person. To treat things as human is not only an intellectual error but also an ethical one.

Western society has had, and still has in many situations, both implicit and explicit definitions of life and death. A person who steps off a curb and is run over by a truck is alive when he or she steps off the curb and dead afterward. One can point to a living person before the event and a corpse after the event. One "knows" both life and death in this situation. Since people need official recognition of what they know intuitively, common law developed a definition of death. In common law, death as the cessation of life is determined by "a total stoppage of the circulation of the blood." People's intuitive judgment and society's legal definition were adequate until modern technologies altered the ability to extend life.

In modern industrial societies, acute death, such as occurs in a truck accident, does not happen often. Most people die slowly, die old, and balance on the edge of death for a long time. The end of life today more properly may be described as "living-dying," because it is an extensive period of time during which individuals know that they will die and usually act differently in the light of this knowledge. This "living-dying" phase of life results in experiences and relationships that never have been dealt with in cultures that do not possess the technological ability to produce such a phase of life. This phase is not present when one is run over by a truck: one moment one is alive, the next one is dead.

Things are different today not only for those in the "living-dying" phase of their life but also for those who are "patients"—those who are ill but will probably get better. A significant number of patients will recover only if they receive a living human organ to replace one of their dead ones. The ability to transplant organs such as the heart, liver, and lungs leads modern society to deal with life and death in a different way. This ability produces a culture whose new definitions of death challenge the human view of life and ultimately determine who is human and who is not.

Redefining Life and Death
Since death is basically the cessation of life, a definition of death is also a definition of life. If one examines the corpse of an individual run over by a truck, one might notice that, although the person is dead, some parts of her or him are still alive. The heart may be beating and thus may be alive. The hair, fingernails, and many cells are also alive. If someone who was unaware of the person's death examined these human parts, that person would not know whether they came from a live human or a dead human. It could be said, therefore, that human death is a process in which it takes a long time for everything human to die. Yet society treats human death as an event. The laws and customs surrounding dying and death seek to mark a point before which the person is alive and after which the person is dead. Obviously, something more than cellular death is needed to indicate when a person is dead.

A medical doctor declares a person dead based on certain criteria. Modern criteria are the result of centuries of experience. A doctor who declares someone dead is saying that experience has shown that when certain criteria are fulfilled, this dead human will never again be a living human.

Commonsense observations that the person was dead in the truck accident are officially confirmed by someone who has the authority to do so, and after that confirmation has been made, people begin to then treat the corpse in a different way. For most of human history, commonsense observation was the only way to tell the difference between life and death. Part of that observation involved determining whether the person was breathing or not and whether his or her blood was flowing. The breath and the flow of blood were considered the criteria for life and death. Blood and breath, or spirit, are still central to many cultures' views of life. Commonsense observation told people that when their breath was gone, their life was gone. Common sense also demonstrated that if one lost a large quantity of blood, one's breathing stopped and one was dead. Certainly, human life was not only blood and breath, but without blood and breath one was not human.

The history of science has also been the history of challenging commonsense observations. The discovery of the human circulatory system and the invention of the stethoscope were challenges to commonsense observation. The discovery of the way in which the blood circulates demonstrated that when the heart stops pumping, there is effectively no blood; when the lungs stop functioning, there is no more breath. Commonsense observations were augmented by new scientific discoveries and inventions that showed that the previous criteria were ways of knowing that certain essential organs were dead. These criteria now were linked with certain places of death, such as the heart and/or lungs. People now believed that once these organs were dead, a corpse would never again be human.

Commonsense observation might lead one to believe that the lungs and the heart are not moving, whereas a stethoscope might indicate that they are. One no longer had to use a mirror held to a person's nose to knowwhether breathing had stopped; one did not have to see the loss of blood to knowthat the heart had stopped. The heart could stop for other reasons and still be dead. One could hear whether it was making noise and was alive. One could listen to the lungs to hear whether there was breath; if not, the person was considered dead. With the advent of the stethoscope, technology began to augment, and sometimes contradict, commonsense observations.

Death and Modern Technology
Modern technologies continue to augment and to defy commonsense observations, but the sequence of determining a death is the same: Certain criteria indicate that part of the human is dead; experience has shown that once these criteria are fulfilled, that person will never be alive again. Because humans developed the ability to keep the heart and lungs alive, former commonsense observations about death were challenged. Many investigators were led to conclude that if the brain were dead, the human would never again be alive. Since for most of human history the life of the organs was identical with the life of the human organism, the challenge of developing new criteria included determining new definitions of death, such as those that focused on the brain.

The meaning and definition of life were always concerns for philosophers and theologians. Scientists usually viewed these definitions as too abstract for scientific investigation because they could not be quantified and subjected to experimentation. To many biologists, it made no difference whether they were operating on a human heart or a pig's heart. A muscle was a muscle. A primary model for many scientists working with human anatomy is that of the machine. They speak of human parts in the same way that a mechanic would speak of automobile parts.

The realization that these parts form a conscious, willing, and loving machine is of little consequence to scientists using this model. This model's implicit definition of life seems to be that human life is equal to the efficient operation of the parts, which is indicated by the flow of blood and breath. Death occurs when there is an irreversible stopping of blood and breath; that is, when one of the parts no longer functions, the machine is dead. When one views the human being from a perspective other than that of the machine model, one arrives at different definitions. Robert Veatch, in *Death, Dying, and the Biological Revolution* (1989), provides an excellent summary of two modern definitions.

Other Definitions
One definition is that death is the irreversible loss of the capacity for bodily integration and social interaction. Death occurs when the entire brain is dead. The criteria for determining that the brain is dead are that there are no spontaneous movements, breathing, or reflexes and that such unreceptivity and lack of response are confirmed by a flat electroencephalogram. These same criteria might be met by someone who was suffering from hypothermia or who was taking a central nervous system depressant, so these possibilities must be ruled out before death is determined. It could be that a person whose heart and lungs were functioning with the aid of machines would be declared dead using this definition. For those accustomed to linking death with the circulation of vital body fluids, to remove the person from the machine would necessitate

the ethical decisions associated with euthanasia. For those who accept this definition of death, however, to continue to treat the person as if he or she were alive would be unethical.

Another definition of death is that death is the irreversible loss of consciousness or the capacity for social interaction. Notice that the capacity for bodily integration does not have to be irreversible according to this definition. If one's neocortex is dead, one has lost consciousness and cannot communicate with others. The easiest way to determine whether this is the case is with an electroencephalogram. Common sense is certainly challenged here, because a person in the living-dying phase of life could be breathing without a machine and still be considered dead.

In both of these definitions, human life is understood to be more than mere biological functions. The first definition assumes that both the biological function of spontaneous blood and breath circulation are necessary to be human, as is an ability to interact with others. If these are not present, then human life is absent.

The second definition goes further; it says that consciousness and social function are uniquely human. If both are absent, then human life is absent. The initial commonsense definition led to legal definitions of death. The new definitions also led to legal definitions. The common law definition was gradually redefined with the advent of the new technologies and discoveries. The most famous definition for legal purposes was that of the President's Commission for the Study of Ethical Problems in Medicine and Biomedical and Behavioral Research. The commission rejected the vague general definitions mentioned above for a more specific and biological definition, suggesting that the following definition be used in laws throughout the country: "An individual who has sustained either (1) irreversible cessation of circulatory and respiratory functions, or (2) irreversible cessation of all functions of the entire brain, including the brain's stem, is dead."

Refining Definitions of Life and Death

Definitions reflect the questions of persons and societies. These modern definitions reflect the concerns of the modern age: rational analysis and reductionism for the purpose of technological control. Other cultures have defined human life and death in terms of other concerns. Many times, the human life known and analyzed by the five senses was seen as limited in the face of something that transcended ordinary life. The sensual reality might be the spirit, or breath, but this sensual reality was a manifesta-

tion of a deeper reality that connected human beings with their past, present, and future. It has been called soul and *atman*. Many terms from many cultures attempt to define life and death. Modern arguments about definitions of life and death in Western culture are arguments about who human beings are and what they will become. Old views of life and death are no longer valid. Commonsense observation is insufficient. New views are still to be discovered. Modern definitions do not match human experience. Inevitably, there will be confusion as people search for definitions that reflect their experience and improve the quality of life in the face of its inevitable end.

Confusion as a Hopeful Sign

Modern popular literature uses four phrases that reflect definitional confusion: brain death, heart death, right to life, and right to death. The first two phrases reflect the difficulty experienced by many people who attempt to understand definitions of life and death. The last two phrases reflect attempts to argue for definitions within the political arena. Most people understand life and death not with the formal definitions stated here but within the parameters of "television-speak"; many decisions concerning social policy are made not by professionals but by the political process. These two phrases reflect the two major social constraints to definitions of life and death: the demand for simplicity in a very complex affair, and the unwillingness to change ideas about a very personal reality.

Modern Western society communicates through the media. The media need short and simple phrases to describe something. Such phrases show how one must think in using this technology. To use the phrases "brain death" and "heart death" as many reporters do is to suggest that there are two different kinds of death. This is inaccurate. A person is either dead or alive. To say that someone is "heart dead" is to refer to common, primitive definitions of death. To say that a person is "brain dead" indicates that the brain comes into the judgment about death—nothing more. The use of "heart death" and "brain death" to refer to the death of the person also gives the impression that a human being is identified with the heart and/or brain. Such an identification implicitly supports a materialistic view of the person that is not accepted by many philosophers.

The supporters of the "right to life" and those of the "right to die" use modern "rights" language to argue about life and death. They know what they do not want society to do. Right-to-life supporters do not want human life maximized in such a way that large groups of people who are defective, or perhaps lack full consciousness, will find themselves defined out of the human race. Right-to-die supporters do not want human life minimized in such a way that if any of a person's organs is alive, society would be obliged to sustain that person's life. Rights mean obligations.

Right-to-life supporters say that society is obliged to sustain human life under any circumstances. Right-to-die supporters say that society is obliged to allow an individual to choose a particular mode of death rather than experience a slowdeath of various organs. Most arguments about rights to life and death deal with the issue of euthanasia rather than the issue of definitions of death. The euthanasia issue concerns whether one may ethically hasten the death of someone in the living-dying phase of life. Definitions of death seek to determine whether a person is dead. These are two different issues.

Confusion and argument about definitions of life and death indicate that Western culture is undergoing significant change. They indicate that people are aware of the change that is taking place, thinking about it, and offering arguments for one side or the other. Being aware of these definitions means being aware of what arguments are offered and taking one's place in the conversation, not the confusion.

—*Nathan R. Kollar*

Further Reading

Chidester, David. *Patterns of Transcendence.* Belmont, Calif.: Wadsworth, 1990. A review of the concepts of death and life in various world cultures and religions.

Gervais, Karen Grandstrand. *Redefining Death.* New Haven, Conn.: Yale University Press, 1986. A review and critique of all the major definitions of death according to their methodologies.

Goldberg, Steven. "The Changing Face of Death: Computers, Consciousness, and Nancy Cruzan." *Stanford Law Review* 43 (February, 1991): 659-684. An extension of the life-death debate into the area of artificial intelligence. The changes in the legal definition of death are shown to occur as science progresses.

Heinegg, Peter, ed. *Mortalism: Readings on the Meaning of Life.* Amherst, N.Y.: Prometheus Books, 2003. An anthology of essays arguing for the finitude of human existence and examining the consequences of that finitude.

Searle, John. *The Rediscovery of the Mind.* Cambridge, Mass.: MIT Press, 1992. A review of the arguments that identify the human person with the brain.

Veatch, Robert M. *Death, Dying, and the Biological Revolution: Our Last Quest for Responsibility.* Rev. ed. New Haven, Conn.: Yale University Press, 1989. An exploration of the philosophical, ethical, legal, and public policy consequences of the radical changes in the definitions of death and life.

See also: Bioethics; Brain death; Death and dying; Homicide; Immortality; Life, meaning of; "Playing god" in medical decision making; Right to die; Right to life; Suicide.

Lobotomy

Definition: Destruction of tissue in the frontal lobes of the brain, or severing of the connection between those lobes and the rest of the brain

Date: First performed on human patients in 1935

Type of ethics: Bioethics

Significance: The use of lobotomy to treat mental disorders raises ethical questions as to the relative cost and benefits of the procedure, the possibility of destroying a personality, and the adequacy of the evidence supporting the technique. In the popular imagination and judgment, lobotomy has come to stand for all forms of psychosurgery

The lobotomy is based on the biomedical model of mental illness, which posits that mental disorders are caused by abnormalities in brain structure. If this is the case, surgically treating the brain should cure the disorder. The field that does so is called psychosurgery. The antecedent of the lobotomy was the prefrontal leukotomy, which was invented by the Portuguese neurosurgeon António Egas Moniz in 1935. In this procedure, a surgical device called a leukotome was inserted through a hole into the frontal lobe and rotated, destroying whatever nerve tissue it contacted.

The prefrontal leukotomy was replaced by the prefrontal lobotomy, which was developed by the American neurosurgeons Walter Freeman and James Watts in 1937. The limitation of the prefrontal leukotomy was that it did not permit precise determination of the area to be cut. In the prefrontal lobotomy, larger holes were drilled into both sides of the skull, after which a leukotome was inserted and precisely moved in a sweeping motion through the frontal lobe.

The prefrontal lobotomy was in turn replaced by the transorbital lobotomy, which was developed by Freeman in 1948. A knife was inserted through the top of the eye socket into the brain and then swung back and forth. This procedure was quick and efficient and could be performed as an office procedure.

The inspiration for these surgical procedures came from data presented by Carlyle Jacobsen that showed a marked change in the level of emotionality of a chimpanzee following destruction of a large part of the frontal lobe of the cerebral cortex. Formerly, the chimpanzee was highly emotional and obstinate. After the operation, the animal appeared calm and cooperative. Egas Moniz believed that this technique could be used on humans to relieve anxiety and other hyperemotional states. Egas Moniz claimed great success in alleviating extreme states of emotionality, and his work aroused worldwide interest, excitement, and practice. Psychosurgical techniques were seen as quick and effective methods for alleviating certain common mental disorders that could not be treated effectively and rapidly by other means, and as providing a partial solution to the problem of overcrowding in mental hospitals.

From 1936 to 1978, about 35,000 psychosurgical operations were performed in America, with perhaps double that number worldwide. Egas Moniz was awarded the Nobel Prize for Physiology or Medicine in 1949 in recognition of his work. The Nobel citation states: "Frontal leukotomy, despite certain limitations of the operative method, must be considered one of the most important discoveries ever made in psychiatric therapy, because through its use a great number of suffering people and total invalids have been socially rehabilitated."

Ethical Issues

Contrast Egas Moniz's Nobel citation, however, with David L. Rosenhan and Martin E. P. Seligman's assessment of the lobotomy in their 1989 textbook *Abnormal Psychology*: "Moreover, there is the danger that physicians and patients may become overzealous in their search for a quick neurological cure...the disastrous history of frontal lobotomies...should serve as a warning." In fact, Rosenhan and Seligman were correct and the Nobel Prize citation was wrong. The leukotomies and lobotomies were a disaster. Their sorry history is rife with ethical violations involving their rationale and the evidence that was used to justify their use on humans.

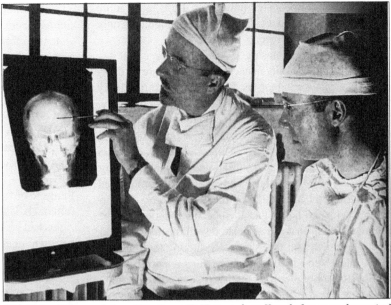

"Dr. Walter Freeman, left, and Dr. James W. Watts study an X ray before a psychosurgical operation. Psychosurgery is cutting into the brain to form new patterns and rid a patient of delusions, obsessions, nervous tensions and the like." Waldemar Kaempffert, "Turning the Mind Inside Out," Saturday Evening Post, *24 May 1941. By Harris A. Ewing.*

Within three months of hearing Jacobsen's account, Egas Moniz performed leukotomies. He did so despite the lack of clear evidence from animal experimentation to justify the procedure. Egas Moniz conducted no animal experimentation himself; in addition, his reading of the scientific literature to support his beliefs was spotty and selective, and he ignored contradictory evidence. Furthermore, there was a large animal and human literature that clearly demonstrated a range of serious side effects and deficits produced by lesions to the frontal lobe, such as apathy, retarded movement, loss of initiative, and mutism. With no supporting evidence, Egas Moniz insisted that these side effects were only temporary, when in fact they could be permanent. Egas Moniz's initial report on twenty patients claimed a cure for seven, lessening of symptoms in six, and no clear effect in the rest. An impartial review of these cases concluded, however, that only one of the twenty cases provided enough information to make a judgment.

There is also the question of whether it is ethical to destroy brain tissue as a means of treating cognition and action. Proponents of psychosurgery argue that newer techniques avoid the frontal lobes, the procedure is based upon a good understanding of how the nervous system functions, side effects are minimal, its use is much more strictly monitored and regulated, and it is undertaken only as a treatment of last resort.

Opponents of psychosurgery, however, argue that it is an ethically and morally unacceptable procedure of dubious value for several reasons. First, there are surprisingly few ethical or legal guidelines regulating psychosurgery. Second, psychosurgery has been used to treat a wide variety of disorders, such as schizophrenia, depression, obsessive-compulsive disorder, acute anxiety, anorexia nervosa, attention deficit disorder, uncontrollable rage or aggression, substance abuse and addictions, homosexual pedophilia, and intractable pain. Psychosurgery is performed with the belief that the specific locations in the nervous system that are associated with the above disorders are known and that surgically altering them will in turn alter the particular behavior. Opponents of psychosurgery argue, first, that such knowledge does not in fact exist and that the assumption that these behaviors are tied to specific locations in the brain has not been proved. Second, opponents argue, careful examination of the literature reveals psychosurgery to be an unpredictable, hit-or-miss procedure. Third, the destruction of brain tissue cannot be reversed, and undesirable side effects, which also cannot be reversed, are unavoidable.

—Laurence Miller

Further Reading

Kleinig, John. *Ethical Issues in Psychosurgery.* London: Allen & Unwin, 1985.

Marsh, F. H., and Janet Katz, eds. *Biology, Crime, and Ethics: A Study of Biological Explanations for Criminal Behavior.* Cincinnati: Anderson, 1985.

Pressman, Jack D. *Last Resort: Psychosurgery and the Limits of Medicine.* New York: Cambridge University Press, 1998.

Rodgers, Joann E. *Psychosurgery: Damaging the Brain to Save the Mind.* New York: HarperCollins, 1992.

Valenstein, E. S. *Great and Desperate Cures.* New York: Basic Books, 1986. _____, ed. *The Psychosurgery Debate.* San Francisco: W. H. Freeman, 1980.

See also: Bioethics; Institutionalization of patients; Mental illness; Psychology.

Medical bills of rights

Definition: Documents that explicitly list the rights of patients with regard to access to care, control over their care, privacy, or any other issues relevant to medical treatment

Type of ethics: Bioethics

Significance: Rights language shifts the focus of moral attention from the duty-bound caregiver to the patient to whom there is a duty—to the claims of the right holder

Although the express use of rights language in medicine is an artifact of the late twentieth century, deontological (duty-based) conceptions of medical ethics trace back to the Hippocratic oath, which explicitly obligates physicians to "abstain from all intentional wrong-doing and harm"—particularly "from [sexual] abus[e]"—and from "divulging [information about patients] holding such things to be holy secrets." Correlative to these obligations (although unstatable at the time, since the language of rights had yet to be invented), patients have the right not to be intentionally harmed, not to be sexually abused, and not to have confidential information divulged.

Duty-based conceptions of the physician-patient relationship were dominated by the Hippocratic oath until three eighteenth century British writers—the Reverend Thomas Gisborne, Doctor John Gregory, and Thomas Percival—developed theories of obligation deriving from physicians' social responsibilities and from their sympathy with patients. In 1803, Percival published a syncretic version of all three theories in the form of a code of ethics; that code, in turn, became the basis of codes of medical ethics issued by nineteenth century regional and national medical associations throughout the world. Although these writers were familiar with rights language, their primary focus was stating the duties of physicians. Consequently, even though their theories on physicians' duties generate correlative rights, they eschew the language of rights—as do the codes of medical ethics they inspired.

The first document to focus primarily on patients' moral claims is the 1947 Nuremberg Code, a set of ten principles issued by the Nuremberg Tribunal to justify its finding that the medical experiments conducted by twelve German physicians and their assistants were "crimes against humanity." The first Nuremberg principle opens by stating that for "moral, ethical, and legal [experimentation]...the voluntary consent of the human subject is essential." It closes by stating that "the duty...for ascertaining consent rests on each individual who initiates, directs, or engages in the experiment." The Nuremberg Code never uses the language of rights, yet most commentators treat it as the progenitor of patients' rights theory because its focus (exemplified in these quotations) is on the moral claims—the rights—of the subjects of research.

Rights language was first expressly used in major medical documents during the 1970s, when it surfaced in the American Hospital Association's 1972 *A Patient's Bill of Rights* and, concurrently, in the section "Rights and Responsibilities of Patients," in the *Accreditation Manual* of the JCAH(O), the Joint Commission on the Accreditation of Hospitals (later, Health Care Organizations)—the organization that accredits American medical hospitals, psychiatric hospitals, and nursing homes.

—Robert Baker

Further Reading

Annas, George. *The Rights of Patients: The Basic ACLU Guide to Patients Rights*. 2d ed. Carbondale: Southern Illinois University Press, 1989.

Annas, George, and Michael Grodin, eds. *The Nazi Doctors and the Nuremberg Code: Human Rights in Human Experimentation*. New York: Oxford University Press, 1992.

Baker, Robert, Dorothy Porter, and Roy Porter, eds. *The Codification of Medical Morality: Historical and Philosophical Studies of the Formalization of Western Medical Morality in the Eighteenth and Nineteenth Centuries*. Dordrecht, Netherlands: Kluwer, 1993.

Edelstein, Ludwig. *Ancient Medicine: Selected Papers of Ludwig Edelstein*. Edited by Owsei Temkin and C. Lilian Temkin. Translated by C. Lilian Temkin. Baltimore: Johns Hopkins University Press, 1967.

Wood, Marie Robey. "Patients' Bill of Rights." *The National Voter* 49, no. 4 (June/July, 2000): 16-19.

See also: American Medical Association; Health care allocation; Hippocrates; Medical ethics; Medical insurance; Medical research; Physician-patient relationship; *Principles of Medical Ethics*.

Medical ethics

Definition: Formal, informal, institutional, and personal codes of conduct for health care professionals

Type of ethics: Bioethics

Significance: Because medical workers deal with matters of life and death, as well as the most intimate details of their patients' lives, the ethics governing their actions are both especially important and especially complex

Health care professionals are faced with many situations that have moral significance. These situations are characterized by such questions as whether or when to proceed with treatment, which therapy to administer, which patient to see first, how to conduct research using human subjects, where to assign resources that are in short supply, and how to establish an equitable health care system. The discipline of medical ethics seeks to engage in a systematic and objective examination of these questions.

History

An ethical code of behavior is central to the writings collected in the *Corpus Hippocraticum*, attributed to an ancient physician known as Hippocrates and other writers of the fifth through third centuries bce. Medicine, according to these writings, should relieve suffering, reduce the severity of an illness, and abstain from treating that which is beyond the practice of medicine; the physician is defined as a good person, skilled at healing. The notion of a morally good dimension inherent in the medical practitioner has survived to this day. The Hippocratic texts were expanded upon by medieval physicians in the West so that, by the fifteenth century, rules of conduct had been established in the medical schools of the time. Eighteenth century physicians such as Benjamin Rush, Samuel Bard, John Gregory, and Thomas Percival stressed the need for primary moral rules of medical practice and began to wrestle with questions of truth-telling in the physician-patient relationship. Percival's writings would become the basis for the first American Medical Association Code of Ethics, issued in 1847.

Nineteenth century physicians such as Worthington Hooker, Austin Flint, Sr., and Sir William Osler continued to refine a primarily beneficence-based understanding of medical ethics (that is, a code based on taking action only for the patient's good). Osler argued that physicians should be broadly educated in the liberal arts so as to be able to practice medicine properly.

The enormous growth of medical research in the twentieth century led to remarkable advances in health care but also raised troubling ethical questions. In 1947, the Nuremberg Code established the first basic ethical requirements for the conduct of medical research. This document was a direct result of the Nuremberg Trials of Nazi war criminals who had engaged in human experimentation considered far outside the grounds of decency. The code was later expanded and revised to become the Declaration of Helsinki of the World Medical Association, originally issued in 1964.

During the 1950s, medical ethics began to move away from being primarily a set of internally generated rules of professional behavior. The writings of such nonphysicians as Joseph Fletcher and Paul Ramsey (both originally trained in theology) began to examine the impact of medicine and medical technology on the moral fabric of society.

The 1960s and 1970s brought an emphasis on patient autonomy to the consideration of biomedical ethics in the United States: Reverence for the wisdom of the medical doctor's decisions, which had been the rule during previous decades, was tempered by a growing respect for the patient's need to contribute to decisions affecting his or her future well-being. The ascendancy of autonomy parallels a rise in the technological capabilities of modern medicine, a time of unusually pronounced affluence in the West, and the appearance of what have since become paradigmatic legal challenges to the notion of the physician or medical institution as the sole participant in medical decision making.

Concurrent with these developments was the appearance of new institutions dedicated to the study of biomedical ethics, such as the Kennedy Institute of Ethics at Georgetown University and the Hastings Center in New York. At the same time, ethical theories developed by nineteenth century philosophers such as John Stuart Mill and Immanuel Kant began to be applied to situations arising out of medical practice by a number of individuals whose primary training was in philosophy and theology rather than clinical medicine.

With the 1980s and 1990s, the prospect of scarcity came to dominate ethical discussion in the United States, raising concern about such questions as health care rationing and public access to medical care. An emphasis on distributive justice began to temper the preceding two decades' concern with obligations of social justice to the individual.

Ethical Principles

Ethical analysis consists of the application of primary principles to concrete clinical situations. It also employs comparative reasoning, whereby a particular problem is compared to other situations about which a moral consensus exists. Principled reasoning rests on four fundamental principles of biomedical ethics. The principle of respect for autonomy requires that every person be free to take whatever autonomous action or make whatever autonomous decision he or she wishes, without constraint by other individuals. An example of respect for autonomy is the doctrine of informed consent, which requires that patients or research subjects be provided with adequate information that they clearly understand before voluntarily submitting to therapy or participating in a research trial.

The principle of nonmaleficence states that health care providers should not inflict evil or harm on a patient. Although straightforward in its enunciation, this principle may come into conflict with the principle of respect for autonomy in cases where a request for withdrawal of therapy is made. Similarly, the principle may come into conflict with obligations to promote the good of the patient, because many medical decisions involve the use of therapies or diagnostic procedures that have undesirable side effects.

The principle of double effect in the Roman Catholic moral tradition has attempted to resolve this latter conflict by stating that if the intent of an action is to effect an overriding good, the action is defensible even if unintended but foreseen harmful consequences ensue. Some commentators suggest, however, that intent is an artificial distinction, because all the consequences, both good and bad, are foreseen. As a result, the potential for harm should be weighed against the potential for benefit in deciding the best course of action. A formal evaluation of this kind is commonly referred to as a risk-benefit analysis. Individual interpretation of the principle of nonmaleficence lies at the heart of debates over abortion, euthanasia, and treatment withdrawal.

The principle of beneficence expresses an obligation to promote the patient's good. This can be construed as any action that prevents harm, supplants harm, or does active good to a person. As such, this principle provides the basis for all medical practice, be it preventive, epidemiologic, acute care, or chronic care. Not all actions can be considered uniformly beneficial. Certain kinds of therapy which may prove to be life-saving can leave a patient with what he or she finds to be an unacceptable quality of life. An examination of the positive and negative consequences of successful medical treatment is commonly called a benefit-burden analysis. In this context, the principle of beneficence most frequently comes into conflict with the principle of respect for autonomy. In such situations, the physician's appeal to beneficence is often considered paternalistic.

The principle of justice applies primarily to the distribution of health care resources in what can be considered a just and fair fashion. Because there are many competing theories of justice, there is no single, clear statement of this principle capable of being succinctly applied to all situations. However, the principle does require careful consideration of the means by which health care is allocated under conditions of scarcity. Scarce resources in the United States, for example, include transplantable organs, intensive care beds, expensive medical technologies in general, and in some circumstances basic medical care itself. Under conditions of scarcity, one's understanding of justice can easily come into conflict with the obligations to each of the three preceding principles. In general, the scarcer the resource, the more concerns about distributive justice influence the deployment of that resource.

Ethical Issues

Questions of medical ethics generally fall into two categories. A quandary is a moral question about which detailed ethical analysis yields a single undisputed answer. A dilemma, on the other hand, is a moral question to which there are at least two ethically defensible responses, with neither one taking clear precedence over the other.

Ethical issues in medicine can also be divided into macrocosmic (large-scale, societal) and microcosmic (small-scale, often individual) concerns. Macrocosmic issues are those that apply to a broad social constituency and therefore often involve both statutory and common law. Microcosmic concerns, on the other hand, are those that arise in the day-to-day practice of medicine, the discussion and resolution of which generally have less impact on society as a whole.

Primary among the macrocosmic ethical debates is the question of health care allocation, which centers largely on the development of health care delivery systems and health care financing. Proposals for reform of the U.S. health care system range from the creation of a single-payer national health insurance program, which would insure every citizen, to a series of proposals that would establish multiple requirements for private health insurance, often linking these requirements to employment. A problem common to all proposals for health care reform is the definition of what constitutes a basic minimum of health care to which each citizen is entitled. Even if consensus can be reached regarding a basic minimum, how and to whom scarce resources will be allocated remains to be determined. In both cases, solutions require an assessment of mechanisms for increasing supply and fairly distributing the resource in an ethically acceptable fashion.

Privacy

In medical ethics, respect for privacy stems both from the Hippocratic tradition and from the principle of respect for autonomy. Privacy also has been argued as a fundamental right of persons. All rightsbased theories imply a correlative obligation on the part of others to respect these rights. Debate, therefore, centers on when an individual's unbridled right to privacy begins to abrogate the public good. For example, does an individual's right to choose privately to have an abortion or to request euthanasia place an unacceptable burden on society to comply with these requests? If a physician considers a patient to be a public menace, what levels of justification are required before confidentially obtained personal information is divulged? To whom is it appropriate to release this information? Concerns of this nature lie at the center of public discussions surrounding the rights of persons infected with the human immunodeficiency virus (HIV).

Medical Research

Research ethics, as it applies to human subjects, deals primarily with two questions. First, does the proposed research appear to provide important information of substantial value to society at minimal risk to the research subject? Second, is the research subject completely aware of the personal risks and benefits of participation in the project so that consent is fully informed? In order to answer these questions, research involving human subjects must undergo ethical review at both the macrocosmic and the microcosmic levels. Nationally, it is regulated by agencies such as the U.S. Food and Drug Administration (FDA). At the microcosmic level, the FDA mandates and supervises the administration of institutional review boards (IRBs), which are charged with the responsibility of ensuring that human subjects are involved in creditable research, are treated in a humane manner, are not subjected to undue risks, and are fully cognizant both of the nature of the project in which they are participating and of any potential risks and benefits associated with it.

A third concern in biomedical research ethics, which does not directly apply to human subjects, is the question of what constitutes a conflict of interest on the part of the principal investigator or research institution. This becomes an increasing problem as more research is funded by private rather than public sources.

The Nature of Life and Ethical Decision Making

This is perhaps the thorniest of all issues in that it revolves around definitional questions about which no consensus exists. Is human life consistently of greater value than all other forms of life? Is the value of human life defined primarily by consciousness? Is human life defined by genetic information, and if so, is alteration of this information a moral enterprise? If genetic engineering is in principle morally acceptable, are there circumstances under which it becomes unacceptable? When precisely does life begin and end? Each of these questions has a profound effect on an individual's opinion of issues such as abortion, the appropriate circumstances for treatment withdrawal, brain death, organ transplantation, euthanasia, animal research, and allocation of health care.

Although some commentators tend to assign primacy to one of the four principles of medical ethics—autonomy, nonmaleficence, beneficence, or justice—relegating others to subordinate roles, the prevailing approach to principled reasoning interprets each principle as being *prima facie* binding; that is, each principle confers a binding obligation upon the medical professional to the extent that it does not conflict with another, equally binding principle. When two *prima facie* principles require actions that are diametrically opposed, there is an appeal to proportionality that allows the requirements of each principle to be evaluated in the light of circumstances at hand. On a case-by-case basis, one principle may be judged to be more binding than another, depending on the context of the problem.

An alternative form of ethical analysis employs the technique of casuistry, or case-based analysis. Using this method, the circumstances of a particular ethical quandary or dilemma (the "reference case") are compared to those of a case about which it is abundantly clear what the correct moral decision should be (the "paradigm case"). The degree to which the reference case resembles or differs from the paradigm case provides guidance as to what the ethically appropriate course of action might be. This method of analysis has the advantage of being similar to the way in which conclusions are reached both in common law and in clinical medicine. Clinical decisions are regularly made in medical practice by comparing the facts of a particular case about which the treatment may be in question with those of similar cases in which the correct treatment is known.

A problem for those who favor casuistic analysis is the wedge argument, sometimes known as the "slippery slope." Detractors suggest that the use of a particular logical argument, such as the defense for withholding or withdrawing certain kinds of therapy, will drive a wedge further and further into the fabric of society until an undesirable consequence (for example, active nonvoluntary euthanasia) ensues. Proponents of casuistry respond that the undesirable consequence is far enough removed from the paradigm case to no longer resemble it.

Most clinical ethicists combine principle-based analysis with case-based reasoning to answer the specific ethical questions that arise in the practice of medicine. In addition, clinical ethicists benefit from training in law, sociology, and psychology, as well as the primary studies of medical science and philosophy.

Public Policy

Macrocosmic, public issues are addressed publicly by a number of mechanisms. Blue-ribbon panels, such as the New York State Task Force on Life and the Law, can study a problem in depth, after which a consensus report with policy recommendations is issued. Such panels have the advantage of bringing together people who represent a wide range of opinion. Another avenue is the formation of grassroots organizations, such as Oregon Health Decisions, that attempt to generate a public consensus on ethically sensitive issues.

In one fashion or another, issues of public concern often are argued on the floors of both federal and state legislatures. Numerous state laws regulate the withholding and withdrawing of therapy; federal legislation, such as the Patient Self-Determination Act, also governs the disclosure of patients' rights to determine the course of their care when they cannot make decisions.

Even with legislative guidance, individual institutions often find themselves beset by microcosmic ethical questions such as when to terminate lifesustaining therapy or who should be admitted to intensive care units. Other common microcosmic dilemmas involve maternal-fetal conflict, wherein the autonomous requests or medical best interests of the mother do not coincide with the presumed best interests of her unborn child. In such situations, health care facilities often solicit the assistance of institutional ethics committees. Such committees are characteristically composed of individuals representing a broad spectrum of professional disciplines as well as community members not directly employed by the facility. In situations that require an institutional response, these committees will often assist in policy development. Ethics committees also serve as primary educational resources for both the institutional staff and members of the surrounding community. Many committees have established mechanisms for case consultation or case review for patients whose care raises ethical questions. Consultations of this type involve review of the patient's clinical condition as well as pertinent social, religious, psychological, and family circumstances. Consultants investigate the ethical arguments that support alternative courses of action before issuing a final recommendation. In most cases, the recommendations are not binding; however, certain models do require that consultative recommendations determine the outcome in specific settings.

Although intervention by an ethics committee often allows for the resolution of ethical disputes within the walls of an institution, sometimes irreconcilable differences require judicial review by a court of law. Under these circumstances, the court's decision becomes a matter of public record, providing precedent for similar cases in the future. Microcosmic cases can thereby generate a body of common law that has profound effects at the macrocosmic level.

—*John A. McClung*

Further Reading

Bandman, Bertram. *The Moral Development of Health Care Professionals: Rational Decisionmaking in Health Care Ethics.* Westport, Conn.: Praeger, 2003. Employs both classical and contemporary moral philosophy to construct a model of moral development based on rights and virtues and apply it to the medical professions.

Beauchamp, Tom L., and James F. Childress. *Principles of Biomedical Ethics.* 5th ed. New York: Oxford University Press, 2001. A lucidly written textbook. Although some commentators are critical of a primarily principle-based approach to bioethics, this remains the major introductory resource.

Beauchamp, Tom L., and Laurence B. McCullough. *Medical Ethics: The Moral Responsibilities of Physicians.* Englewood Cliffs, N.J.: Prentice-Hall, 1984. An excellent introduction to common problems encountered in clinical ethics. Each chapter opens with a case study that illustrates the focal topic. One of the best references for people completely new to the field.

Beauchamp, Tom L., and LeRoy Walters, eds. *Contemporary Issues in Bioethics.* 6th ed. Belmont, Calif.: Thomson/Wadsworth, 2003. A composite of readings culled from legal decisions, seminal legislation, ethical codes of conduct, and the writings of well-known ethicists. Readings are organized by topic and are preceded by a summary of ethical theory.

Jonsen, Albert R., Mark Siegler, and William J. Winslade. *Clinical Ethics: A Practical Approach to Ethical Decisions in Clinical Medicine.* 5th ed. New York: McGraw-Hill, 2002. A handbook of medical ethics aimed primarily at the physician in training. The authors present a method for evaluating the ethical dimensions of clinical cases, after which the book is organized lexically so that commonly encountered problems can be easily located. A concise reference that concentrates on practical rather than theoretical priorities.

Jonsen, Albert R., and Stephen Toulmin. *The Abuse of Casuistry: A History of Moral Reasoning.* Berkeley: University of California Press, 1988. A wellconstructed history of the technique of case-based analysis that concludes with a practical description of how this approach can be used as an alternative to principle-based analysis in clinical situations.

Miles, Steven H. *The Hippocratic Oath and the Ethics of Medicine.* New York: Oxford University Press, 2004. A work of history and ethics; provides cultural analysis of the original meaning and context of the Hippocratic Oath and demonstrates its relevance and application to contemporary medical practice.

Post, Steven G., ed. *Encyclopedia of Bioethics.* 3d ed. 5 vols. New York: Macmillan Reference USA, 2004. A broad look at the entire field of bioethics and one of the most comprehensive collections of readings available under one title.

Veatch, Robert M. *Case Studies in Medical Ethics.* Cambridge, Mass.: Harvard University Press, 1977. A good survey of ethical issues, illustrated by 112 separate case presentations. Excellent for group discussions.

See also: Bioethics; Diagnosis; Health care allocation; Hippocrates; Holistic medicine; Medical insurance; Medical research; Physician-patient relationship; *Principles of Medical Ethics*; Therapist-patient relationship.

Medical insurance

Definition: Provision of or payment of costs incurred by health care services when needed, given to a particular group whose membership is limited by factors such as payment of premiums, employment, income, or citizenship

Type of ethics: Bioethics

Significance: Inequities in health insurance coverage are both indicative of, and contribute to, unjust and inequitable policies and practices for the poor

At the beginning of the twenty-first century, health insurance was possibly the greatest cause of the rapidly escalating cost of medical care in the United States. The lack of regulation, the control of the industry by those who profit from it rather than those who purchase services, and the openness to abuse by both the insured and the providers of care combine to charge the insurance industry with helping have caused one of the most unfair aspects of modern American society: lack of access to needed care by a large portion of the population.

Access to health care has two major components: the patient's ability to pay and the availability of accessible and culturally acceptable facilities capable of providing appropriate care in a timely manner. Lack of health insurance is the greatest barrier to health care accessibility. In the absence of insurance coverage, people often postpone or forgo treatment. In 1980, 25 million Americans were uninsured; by 1999, over 42 million, or nearly one in six, people were uninsured according to the 2000 U.S. census. In 2002 the figure jumped to 43.6 million. By 2017, the number of uninsured Americans following the adoption of the Affordable Care Act (despite attempts to dismantle it by the Trump administration) stood at 28.5 million people.

Generally employment-related and -financed, health insurance is a relatively recent development in the medical field. Only within the twentieth century did access to health care become of general concern, primarily because earlier systems of health care were for, the most part, ineffectual. Historically, the care of the sick was the responsibility of families and churches, and the costs of such care consisted mainly of lost wages, rather than payments to outside providers.

Skyrocketing costs and a shift in the workforce from the highly paid, largely unionized full-time manufacturing sector with employer-sponsored health insurance to a low-wage, increasingly part-time nonunionized service and clerical workforce whose employers are less likely to provide insurance account for the widespread lack of insurance. Many people who are not provided with employer-sponsored insurance plans choose not to seek health insurance. The recessionary cycles in the mid-1970s to mid-1990s resulting in massive layoffs also accounted for lack of insurance coverage or underinsurance (lack of insurance for catastrophic illness, preexisting illness, gaps in Medicare, lack of coverage for long-term care, deductibles, and co-payments).

In a survey conducted by the Commonwealth Fund, a private foundation supporting independent research in health and social issues, 26 percent of American adults aged nineteen to sixty-four (or an estimated 45.4 million people) experienced a period of time when they were uninsured in 2003. In addition to instability in insurance coverage, the survey found evidence of a decline in the quality of coverage among those who were insured. Premiums increased as cuts or new limits in benefits emerged. Instability in insurance coverage and declines in the quality of private health benefits appear to impede Americans' ability to obtain necessary health care. Health insurance premiums increased 13.9 percent in 2003, faster than the 8.5 percent growth in health care costs. Health care expenditures in 2002 were $1.6 trillion, or 14.9 percent of the nation's gross domestic product.

The United States has the highest health care spending of any country, yet it is the only major industrialized nation not to provide health insurance coverage for everyone. The uninsured generally have higher mortality rates. They are also three times more likely than the insured to experience adverse health outcomes and four times more likely to require avoidable hospitalizations and emergency hospital care.

History

In 1883, Germany enacted laws providing compulsory national health insurance to all workers. This was done to produce a more productive labor force and to enhance national defense rather than out of concern for the individual. Other countries in Western Europe quickly followed suit. In the United States, commercially provided insurance policies were available from the turn of the twentieth century, but it was not until the Great Depression that health insurance became a major industry. At that time, since few people had money to spend on anything but necessities, all but the most crucial medical treatments were neglected. Hospitals, finding themselves in increasingly difficult financial situations, banded together to form Blue Cross, an organization designed to elicit prepayment of hospital costs to insure against future need. Soon afterward, a similar organization was formed by local and state medical associations in order to collect funds to reimburse physicians for expenses incurred in service. This organization was known as Blue Shield.

The commercial insurance industry (as opposed to the "nonprofit" nature of Blue Cross and Blue Shield) expanded after World War II, with the increasing demands of labor unions to provide health insurance for all workers. The federal government got involved in 1965, when the plans for Medicare, which provides coverage for people over the age of sixty-five, and Medicaid, designed to give access to health care to the poor, were enacted as amendments to the Social Security Act. During the early 1990s Medicaid coverage expanded to include children and pregnant women.

Health Care in the Twenty-first Century

During the first years of the twenty-first century, the United States was the only industrialized nation to provide total health care protection for less than 25 percent of its population. Only two other industrialized nations, Libya and Cyprus, provide for less than 90 percent of their populations. The majority of completely uninsured people in the United States are young people working at low-income jobs. Most are employed but work at jobs that do not provide group health coverage.

In most states, Medicaid does not provide care for employed persons, and the cutoff income for coverage is lower than the national poverty level; therefore, many people who are living in poverty do not have any form of medical insurance. Low-income Hispanic adults are particularly affected: 37 percent of this group were never insured with private coverage. As many as 80 percent of low-income Hispanics were uninsured sometime during 1996 through 1999 compared with 66 percent of low-income African Americans and 63 percent of low-income whites.

Unstable work patterns and part-time employment increase the risk that families will experience gaps in coverage or periods of time without insurance. Gaps in coverage impede people's ability to obtain needed care and increase the risk of burdensome medical bills. The U.S. Department of Health and Human Services has said that closing the health gap for minorities is a key public policy priority. Lawmakers and polticians in some places have floated the idea of "Medicare for all," a sort of single-payer approach that would move toward the assumption that medical care is a right, rather than a privilege, but the debate continues.

Benefits of Insurance

The greatest benefit derived from health insurance is security from financial risk in case of illness, security that health care will be available if needed. The other, more global benefit is ethical. Health insurance provides some equity by spreading the costs of undeserved illness between the sick and the healthy. While this does not compensate the ill person for the loss of health, it does allay some of the financial burden. Insurance also allows people the immediate gratification of providing for the possibility of bad times by spending a little less during the good.

Health insurance is considered among life's most important commodities. In fact, significant numbers of employed individuals were reluctant to change jobs because they feared loss of health insurance. The Health Insurance Portability and Accountability Act (HIPAA) of 1996—which became effective on April 14, 2003—guaranteed "portability," or the ability of people with preexisting conditions to retain their insurance coverage when changing jobs.

Costs of Insurance

Aside from the actual premiums for insurance, there are several hidden costs. There are the administrative costs and risk of liability to the insurer. More ethically significant are the consequences of insurance. Insurance companies, as third-party payers, set limits as to the types of treatments or procedures that they will cover for a particular illness or condition. The medical community is obligated to respect the limits set forth by insurance companies, although the latter are not trained in medicine. Managed care is a system that strives to provide the cheapest option available for care, without regard to efficiency, quality, or cost-effectiveness. Financial incentives exist to undertreat, although the underlying framework of managed care is improving the health of the population, instead of focusing on an individual patient. Cost is the major concern.

In response to this decreased incentive, insurers have instituted cost-sharing plans including deductibles, coinsurance (in which the patient pays a certain percentage), and copayment (in which a flat fee is paid at the time of service). These cost-sharing means are much harder on the poor, because they take a larger portion of their income.

Medical insurance can be said to be an inherently unfair means of providing health care. If health care is considered to be a right, it cannot depend on individual ability to pay. Medical treatment for the uninsured is often more expensive than preventive, acute, and chronic care of the insured, because the uninsured are more likely to receive medical care in the emergency department than in a physician's office. Those higher costs are passed on to the insured by cost shifting and higher premiums or to taxpayers through higher taxes to finance public hospitals and public insurance programs.

Improved access to health care is a vital and politically divisive issue. Presidential candidates, federal and state legislators, and health care industry leaders have all proposed ways to increase health insurance coverage, ranging from incremental expansions to various approaches that promise near-universal coverage.

—Margaret Hawthorne; Updated by Marcia J. Weiss

Further Reading

Bodenheimer, Thomas S., and Kevin Grumbach. *Understanding Health Policy: A Clinical Approach.* 3d ed. New York: McGraw-Hill, 2002.

Daniels, Norman. "Accountability for Reasonableness in Private and Public Health Insurance." In *The Global Challenge of Health Care Rationing*, edited by Angela Coulter and Chris Ham. Philadelphia: Open Press University, 2000.

Daniels, Norman, and James E. Sabin. *Setting Limits Fairly: Can We Learn to Share Medical Resources?* New York: Oxford University Press, 2002.

Danis, Marion, Carolyn Clancy, and Larry R. Churchill, eds. *Ethical Dimensions of Health Policy.* New York: Oxford University Press, 2002.

Garrett, Thomas M., Harold W. Baillie, and Rosellen M. Garrett. *Health Care Ethics: Principles and Problems.* Englewood Cliffs, N.J.: Prentice-Hall, 1989.

Kovner, Anthony R., and Steven Jonas, eds. *Jonas and Kovner's Health Care Delivery in the United States.* 7th ed. New York: Springer, 2002.

Lee, Philip R., and Carroll L. Estes. *The Nation's Health.* 5th ed. Sudbury, Mass.: Jones and Bartlett, 1997.

Menzel, Paul T. *Medical Costs, Moral Choices.* New Haven, Conn.: Yale University Press, 1983.

Phelps, Charles E. *Health Economics.* New York: HarperCollins, 1992.

Roemer, Milton I. *National Health Systems of the World.* New York: Oxford University Press, 1991.

See also: American Association of Retired Persons; Cost-benefit analysis; Employee safety and treatment; Health care allocation; Holistic medicine; Illness; Medical bills of rights; Medical ethics; "Playing god" in medical decision making; Product safety and liability; Tobacco industry.

Medical research

Definition: The application of bioethical principles to investigations whose goal is generalizable knowledge rather than individualized treatment

Date: Fifth century bce to present

Type of ethics: Bioethics

Significance: Ethical medical research attempts to ensure that human subjects understand risks, while minimizing harm to them and distributing the benefits of research equitably within the context of social morality; it also promotes the humane treatment of animals

Medical research, like other types of scientific inquiry, seeks either to discover patterns or to test proposed solutions (hypotheses) to problems. Broadly, the research entails observation and experimentation in accordance with the scientific method. Observation may be entirely passive—for example, an epidemiological study that tracks the spread of a disease through a population. Experiments depend upon intervention, that is, introducing some variable, such as a new drug or surgical procedure, in order to define that variable's effect on a disease.

Whether involving animal or human subjects, research poses complex ethical problems. In the case of human subjects, both the individual subject and the physician-researcher may face dilemmas if the social benefit of increased knowledge comes at the expense of the subject's health or societal moral principles. The trend in contemporary medicine has been to limit or eliminate ethical conflicts through defined principles, governmental regulation, and oversight panels.

The Need for Research

Every time physicians treat patients, some experimentation is involved, since however well tested a medicine or procedure may be, its use on the unique physiology of an individual patient amounts to a new test and carries some risk. In daily practice, however, physicians intend treatments to improve only the individual patient's health. By contrast, researchers hope to acquire generalized knowledge either to increase the basic understanding of the human psyche and soma or to treat all people who have a given disease. Accordingly, research has even broader social and scientific implications than does treatment.

The social implications of medical research become particularly important when such research contravenes a basic moral conviction held by the public in general or by a particular group. Beginning in the 1990s, advances in genetic engineering, stem cell research, and mammalian cloning provoked objections from diverse religious and humanitarian groups in the United States and prompted legislation by state and federal governments. To receive government funding and to protect their research from political pressures, scientists increasingly must accommodate research to extra-scientific moral issues.

History

In Western medicine, the Epidemics, traditionally attributed to the fourth century bce Greek philosopher Hippocrates, presented the first preserved general guidelines for physicians; its dictum to help patients or at least not harm them acquired pervasive moral authority. (Similar strictures appear in early Hindu and Chinese medical treatises.) The Hippocratic method stressed that physicians should observe patients and their surroundings and assist nature in restoring their health. The method was not innately experimental in the scientific sense.

Although Hippocrates' prestige was great, many early physicians approved of experimental procedures, and so the conflict between research and preserving patients from harm began early. The third century bce Alexandrian physicians Herophilus and Erasistratus believed that understanding the body's structures must precede effective treatment of diseases. Accordingly, they practiced vivisection on condemned prisoners to study anatomy, reasoning that the pain inflicted on them could lead to knowledge that would benefit humanity in general, which to them justified the vivisection. Later classical writers often disagreed. Celsus and the Christian philosopher Tertullian, for example, considered vivisection to be murder.

During the European Middle Ages, the teachings of the second century Greek physician Galen dominated medicine. Galen taught that nature does nothing without a purpose and that the physician simply must discover that purpose. Medicine was primarily the application of the four-humors theory to specific cases, a method that was congenial to medieval Christian philosophy. Empirical experimentation was considered unnecessary and immoral.

After the Renaissance, when physicians began to abandon the humors theory and investigated the pathology of disease, biochemistry, and anatomy, the impetus to experiment grew. Little research was rigorous, and most of it involved experiments on patients, sometimes resulting in a public outcry. Such was the case in Boston during the smallpox epidemic of 1721-1722. Learning from England that small amounts of infected material stimulated immunity to the disease, Cotton Mather and Zebdeil Boylston inoculated 250 healthy Bostonians; 2 percent died, while 15 percent of plague victims died among the general population. However, the immunization experiment was decried. Not only did the procedure meddle with the workings of God, opponents claimed, but the 2 percent who died might not have contracted smallpox otherwise.

Modern Developments

The debate over the welfare of patients and the need for validated medical knowledge began to assume its modern shape during the second half of the nineteenth century. In 1865 Claude Bernard, a French physician, published his *Introduction to Experimental Medicine*, a fundamentally influential treatise. In it he argued that researchers must force nature to reveal itself; since experimental trials and procedures, including vivisection, are the surest means to produce verifiable knowledge, the physician has a duty to employ them. He added, however, that all research must benefit the test subjects. Those experiments that do only harm must be forbidden.

Bernard's book appeared as an antivivisection movement was spreading, intent upon exposing the cruelty of medical experiments on both animals and humans. Antivivisectionists criticized researchers for looking upon research subjects as objects rather than living, individual beings and for using subjects for the researchers' own ambitions with careless disregard of the pain and injury they may inflict. Such attitudes, according to the argument, are immoral because they conflict with the Christian principle of benevolence and the physicians' Hippocratic oath.

Efforts to codify ethical principles increased following World War II, mainly in reaction to grisly experiments performed in concentration camps by Nazi doctors. The post-World War II Nuremberg Code sought to prohibit experiments upon humans against their will or when death is the likely outcome; most subsequent codes were modeled upon it. The World Medical Association's Declaration of Helsinki (1964; revised 1975) suggested methods of protecting human subjects and urged researchers to respect animals' welfare and be cautious about the effect of experiments on the environment. In the United States, various federal agencies published regulations for experiments financed by public funds, especially the Food and Drug Administration (FDA) (1981) and the Department of Health and Human Services (1983), which required that institutional review boards (IRBs) approve research proposals before projects begin and monitor their execution.

In 1978, the National Commission for the Protection of Human Subjects of Biomedical and Behavioral Research released *The Belmont Report*, which proposed broad ethical principles to guide researchers in designing ethical studies. While widely influential, this brief document provided only a framework. Upon researchers and IRBs falls the task of interpreting and applying the principles to resolve ethical problems, sometimes in unprecedented contexts. For example, subsequent epidemics, such as acquired immunodeficiency syndrome (AIDS), challenged the ethics of clinical trials and research funding and raised concerns about public safety.

By 2000, IRBs in their traditional form were increasingly considered inadequate to handle ethical problems. With an estimated two million to twenty million people enrolled in clinical research projects, sometimes tens of thousands in a single drug trial, the case load for monitoring experiments threatened to be overwhelming. Additionally, the complexity of modern experiments and the potential effects on test subjects require understanding a broad range of research protocols and extensive scientific and technical expertise, difficult requirements for many local review boards to meet. At the same time, there was a trend for researchers or their academic institutions to seek profits in the research outcome, especially in patenting and licensing the applications of therapeutic innovations produced by genetic engineering.

For these reasons, the Institute of Medicine recommended that IRBs be reconstituted to enhance protection of subjects, rigorously to exclude potential conflicts of interest, and to increase training in the ethics of human studies for board members and researchers. Furthermore, although some government agencies regulate animal experiments, animal rights advocates condemn tests that harm animals for the benefit of humans, and groups such as the People for the Ethical Treatment of Animals (PETA) have sought legislative and judicial intervention to restrict the practice.

Ethical Principles

The Belmont Report draws from assumptions about equity and autonomy that are common in modern cultures: Each human is to be treated as an individual, rather than as a component of a group; no individual is inherently superior; and no individual can be used primarily as the means to an end. The report's three *prima facie* principles—respect for persons, beneficence, and justice—assert these values' primacy when they conflict with the central value of scientific research, the acquisition of knowledge.

Respect for persons, also called autonomy, rests upon ensuring the self-determination of research subjects. Prospective subjects must not be enrolled in a study through coercion or deceit. Investigators must explain the nature of their study and its potential to harm subjects; then the subjects' formal, written consent must be obtained. For those subjects incapable of informed consent, such as children, the mentally impaired, and the brain dead, responsible guardians must consent to the enrollment. During the course of a study, researchers must protect the well-being and rights of subjects and permit them to end their participation at any time. In effect, researchers are to treat subjects as partners and collaborators, not as objects.

Beneficence obligates researchers to design a study protocol (the plans and rules for a study) so that the risk of harm to subjects is minimized and the potentiality for benefits is maximized. (Some ethicists divide this principle into beneficence, which assures the well-being of subjects, and nonmaleficence, which requires avoidance of harm. The division, they argue, reduces confusion and emphasizes the tenet in the Hippocratic oath against harming patients.) The Department of Health and Human Services has defined minimal risk as the risk one runs in daily life or during routine physical or psychological tests. Beneficence entails a dual perspective: Not only should each subject expect benefits to health to be greater than harms, but there should also be a reasonable expectation that the study's findings will benefit society.

Because research risks the health of a few subjects, even if volunteers, in order to improve medicine for everyone, an innate inequity exists. The principle of justice seeks to moderate this inequity. No class of people, as defined by poverty, race, nationality, mentality, or condition of health, is to be exploited as research subjects so that they assume a disproportionate burden. The subjects are to be treated fairly; that is, their general human rights must be guarded. The benefits of research must be distributed equally among all groups in the society.

Ethical Norms

Six norms, or standards, are widely used to verify that a study adheres to the principles of respect for persons, beneficence, and justice.

First, the design of the study should be rigorously defined and based upon the null hypothesis (also called equipoise). The null hypothesis assumes that none of the treatments involved in a study is known to be superior when the study begins; likewise, if a placebo (inert drug or innocuous procedure) is used, there must be no persuasive evidence beforehand that the treatment is superior to the placebo. This norm protects subjects, especially those with disease, from receiving treatments known to be inferior, and it helps physician-researchers overcome their central dilemma in medical research: withholding the best available treatment in order to test new treatments. Thereby, good research design supports respect for persons and beneficence.

Second, researchers must be competent, possessing adequate scientific knowledge and skill to conduct the study and to give subjects proper medical care. This norm also supports respect for persons and beneficence.

Third, the study should either balance possible benefits with harms or expect more benefits. Furthermore, if in the course of the study one treatment proves to be superior to another or to the placebo, researchers must terminate or modify the study so that all its subjects receive the better treatment. This norm incorporates all three ethical principles.

Fourth, researchers must obtain documented informed consent from each subject before a study begins, which assures respect for persons.

Fifth, to affirm the justice of a study, the selection of subjects must be equitable, drawing at random from the eligible population.

Sixth, again for the sake of justice, researchers should compensate subjects for any injuries incurred because of a study.

Ethical Issues

The most common form of medical research is the three-phase clinical trial, which usually tests new drugs. To eliminate possible biases toward the data and to provide equal treatment of subjects, researchers may incorporate one or more of the following four techniques.

First, randomization assigns subjects by a lottery system, rather than on the basis of health, group affiliation, or economic condition.

Second, one group of subjects receives the treatment under study, while a second, the control group, receives a placebo. When the first group reacts favorably to the treatment and there is no change to the control group, the researchers can conclude that the treatment causes the reaction, and it is not just an accident.

Third, studies are blinded, which means that either the researchers, the subjects, or both (doubleblinded) do not have access to documents recording which subjects are receiving treatment and which placebos.

Fourth, the groups can exchange roles (crossover); that is, the first group changes from treatment to placebo and the second group from placebo to treatment.

A study employing all these techniques is usually called a randomized, double-blinded, placebo-controlled clinical trial with crossover.

Phase I and Phase II

Ethical issues trouble every step of such studies. For example, government regulation requires that a new drug be tested on animals before humans try it, and animal rights advocates have long denounced this procedure as cruel and exploitative. A phase I study determines the toxicity, side effects, and safe dosage of a drug on a small group of people in good health. Since an experimental drug can confer no health benefit on these "normals," the study lacks beneficence; however, the trend has been to conduct phase I tests on subjects who have a disease for which a drug or procedure is a potential treatment, which obviates the ethical objection.

Phase II studies are controlled clinical trials on a small number of patients to determine whether a drug has a beneficial effect and is safe. Phase III trials, either with or without a control group, compare the effect of the new treatment with that of the standard treatment on a large group of subjects, while defining the medicinal properties and adverse effects as precisely as possible. When patients in a clinical trial are desperately ill, they may grasp at any new treatment with hope, so the use of randomization, blinded dispensation of treatment, and placebos can seem a deprivation of well-being.

Such was the case in the 1980s when azidothymidine (AZT)was tested on subjects carrying the human immunodeficiency virus (HIV) associated with AIDS; the phase I trial showed clinical improvements in some patients. Federal regulations called for a placebo-controlled phase II follow-up, yet scientists were sharply divided over the morality of withholding AZT from HIV-infected persons, because AIDS, once fully developed, was then thought to be universally fatal. A controlled study would be selective and would involve rationing of the drug, which they argued was unjust. Other scientists contended that only a thorough, controlled study could determine whether AZT had side effects more debilitating than the disease itself, and therefore the beneficence of the experimental treatment would remain in doubt.

When federal regulations made AZT the control drug for all further studies, concerns about confidentiality were raised. By selecting subjects for AIDSrelated trials, researchers exposed the fact that these subjects were infected, and many subjects worried that they would face discrimination. Furthermore, the large amount of public funds devoted to AIDS research in the late 1980s brought complaints from scientists that other projects were left underfunded as a consequence. Some of these issues apply to studies of other widespread, deadly diseases, such as cancer and heart disease.

Ethical issues literally arise before subjects' births and continue after their deaths. For example, using the bodies of the brain-dead persons, even if legal wills explicitly grant permission, is potentially unethical if the family members object. Some right-to-life advocates, whose convictions demand that all human life is sacred, object to the use of fetuses or fetal tissue in research. Their beliefs come into direct conflict with stem cell research, one of the most promising lines of investigation at the beginning of the twenty-first century. Stem cells possess the capacity to self-renew and to differentiate into more than one type of cell. There are differing types of stems cells with disparate capacities, but the best for research and therapy are those human stem cells with the ability to become all types of cells, called pluripotent stem cells. They are harvested only from the embryo in an early stage of development. Such cells can be cultured indefinitely and hold great promise in testing pharmaceutical products, regenerating damaged organs, treating cancer, and investigating birth defects and fertility problems.

Genetic Research

Because many religions accord full human status to embryos, harvesting embryonic cells following abortion is judged abhorrent, and the abortion itself is regarded as murder. Even the use of excess embryos from in vitro fertilization raises troubling questions about the moral and legal status of the human embryo to many observers. In 2001 President George W. Bush ordered that federal funding be restricted to embryonic stem cell research involving the cells lines already developed from sixty-four embryos.

Research into transgenic organ transplantation, genetic engineering, and the possibility of cloning humans raise even more basic ethical and moral questions than does embryonic stem cell research. By altering a basic natural process in some way, each challenges the nature of human identity and uniqueness. For example, scientists succeeded in introducing specially designed fragments ofDNAinto patients to treat genetic disorders. Transplanting a baboon's heart into a human baby can keep the child alive until a human organ can be found. Thus, clon-

ing—making copies of embryos—promises to help elucidate basic cellular processes, simplify the testing of pharmaceuticals, create rejuvenation therapy, and provide treatments for infertility, genetic syndromes, and cancer.

Few dispute the potential benefits of such modern technologies. However, theologians, ethicists, and some scientists object to them for three basic reasons. The first is often characterized as the "playing god" accusation. Some religions find that the genetic engineering of novel DNA and cloning (should it occur) are impious human attempts to replace the natural processes created by God and accordingly efface the complicated natural chain of events that makes each human unique. Scientists similarly worry that manufactured novelties, untested by the slow process of evolution through natural selection, may introduce counterproductive, even deadly, features into the human genome and accidentally eliminate some that are needed. The second objection comes from a general unease concerning the misuses of technology.

The therapeutic effects, the argument runs, are admirable, but the power to intervene could escalate little by little into the power to dominate and change, a form of "technotyranny." So, genetic engineering and cloning, critics contend, might eventual produce designer children, eliminate politically unpopular traits, end diversity, and even create a newsubspecies of *Homo sapiens*. This argument is sometimes called the "slippery slope" thesis. The third objection concerns matters of choice and justice. If it is possible to eliminate or replace human traits, who should decide which traits and on what basis? Moreover, since the technology involved is very expensive, there is the risk it will remain available only to a limited number of privileged persons. Although transgenic transplantation and genetic engineering weathered such critics for the most part, cloning research did not. By 2003, the United States, Great Britain, and many other countries considered partial or outright bans on human cloning.

Purely observational research may also be unethical when it withholds treatment and allows a disease to progress. For example, the Tuskegee Syphilis Study (1932-1972), designed to define the natural history of syphilis, illustrates harm by omission. The study followed four hundred black men with syphilis and about two hundred without it to determine the occurrence of untreated symptoms and mortality. The study continued even after penicillin, an effective treatment, became available during the late 1940s.

Regulation

Scientists applying for public funding and pharmaceutical companies seeking FDA approval of a newdrug must comply with federal regulations, many of which are designed to satisfy the ethical principles enunciated in *The Belmont Report*. The initial responsibility for compliance belongs to IRBs, which act on behalf of their parent institutions (mainly hospitals and universities), not as agents of the government. Composition of IRBs varies, but all must have doctors and scientists capable of reviewing the scientific merit of a proposed study; clergy, nurses, administrators, ethicists, and members of the public may also participate to safeguard the rights, well-being, and privacy of subjects. Even institutions that do not rely on public funds routinely convene IRBs to review research proposals. Since federal agencies lack the resources to scrutinize every research project, medical research is largely self-regulated from a project's beginning, through IRBs, to its final product: publication. Medical journal standards call for editors to reject articles written by researchers who have not adhered to *The Belmont Report*'s principles, although some editors do publish such articles but follow them with editorials calling attention to ethical problems.

In the United States, the courts have also begun to provide ad hoc review of medical research as a result of litigation. Both individual and class-action civil suits seek redress, usually monetary awards, for injury sustained in research, but there have also been allegations of fraud or deception, which can involve punitive judgments as well. Researchers, institutions, and IRBs have been named as plaintiffs. As a result, research designers and IRBs must anticipate possible legal liabilities as part of their analysis of ethical issues.

—Roger Smith

Further Reading

Beauchamp, Tom L., and James F. Childress. *Principles of Biomedical Ethics.* 5th ed. New York: Oxford University Press, 2001. General philosophical treatment of medical ethics, of which research ethics forms an appreciable part, and one of the most frequently cited investigations of the subject. Attempts to educe the ethical theory that best serves American health care.

Cohen, Carl. "The Case for the Use of Animals in Biomedical Research." *New England Journal of Medicine* 315 (October 2, 1986): 865-870. Argues that animal experimentation reduces risks to human subjects while accumulating much knowledge that is beneficial to human and veterinary medicine; urges also that animals be used humanely. While sympathetic to research, Cohen provides a good introduction to the animal rights controversy.

Espejo, Roman, ed. *Biomedical Ethics: Opposing Viewpoints.* Farmington Hills, Miss.: Greenhaven Press, 2003. The book offers reprinted articles that debate the ethics of human cloning, organ donations, reproductive technologies, and genetic research. It is well suited for readers unfamiliar with medical or bioethical terminology.

Holland, Suzanne, Karen Lebacqz, and Laurie Zoloth, eds. *The Human Embryonic Stem Cell Debate: Science, Ethics, and Public Policy.* Cambridge, Mass.: MIT Press, 2001. The reprinted and original articles in this collection provide sophisticated considerations of stem cell research in four parts. The first explains the science and its potential benefits to medicine. The second summarizes basic ethic issues. The third offers secular and religious perspectives on the controversy. The fourth discusses the role of public policy in the research. With a helpful glossary.

Kass, Leon R., ed. *Human Cloning and Human Dignity: The Report of the President's Council on Bioethics.* New York: Public Affairs, 2002. The President's Council on Bioethics provides this committee-generated report as an introduction to the moral significance of cloning and the ethical and policy questions raised by it in order to clarify its recommendations to President George W. Bush. It also supplies an explanation and history of cloning and a glossary.

Levine, Robert J. *Ethics and Regulation of Clinical Research.* 2d ed. Baltimore: Urban & Schwarzenberg, 1986. Levine, a consultant to the National Commission for the Protection of Human Subjects in Biomedical and Behavioral Research, interprets and expands upon the principals enunciated in *The Belmont Report*, drawing also upon such documents as the Nuremberg Code and the Declaration of Helsinki. A valuable, thorough discussion of specific issues as well as theory.

National Commission for the Protection of Human Subjects of Biomedical and Behavioral Research. *The Belmont Report.* Washington, D.C.: Government Printing Office, 1978. Brief document that has widely influenced research ethics in the United States. Far from exhaustive, it nevertheless describes the basic principles that underlie most subsequent discussions.

See also: Animal research; Bioethics; Biotechnology; Cloning; Experimentation; Genetic engineering; Human Genome Project; Medical ethics; National Commission for the Protection of Human Subjects of Biomedical and Behavioral Research; Nazi science; Science; Stem cell research.

Mental illness

Definition: Nondevelopmental psychological or behavioral disorders

Type of ethics: Psychological ethics

Significance: Responses to mental illness by medical professionals, criminal justice systems, public policy experts, and society at large engage issues of paternalism, confidentiality, the right to privacy, individual autonomy, informed consent, the right to treatment, the right to refuse treatment, and the limits of criminal responsibility

By conceptualizing mental disorders as illness, physicians are awarded primacy in regard to treatment decisions. Persons who suffer from mental illness may be viewed as requiring treatment, even when they do not desire such care. Under certain circumstances, persons who are mentally ill may be declared not responsible for their actions.

History

Historically, persons with mental disorders have been beaten, driven from their homes, subjected to inhumane treatments, and put to death. Early views of mental disorders were founded on a mixture of demonology and theories of organic causality. Demonology is founded on the idea that evil spirits or an angry god can dwell within or directly influence a person. Organic theories attribute the development of mental disorders to physical causes—injuries, imbalances in body fluids, or abnormal body structures.

Skulls dating back as far as 500,000 years show evidence of trephining, a technique using stone instruments to scrape away portions of skulls. It is assumed that these operations were performed to allow evil spirits to escape from the bodies of the people whose skulls were found. A modified form of trephining was revived in Europe in the Middle Ages. As late as the sixteenth century, some patients were subjected to surgical procedures in which a physician would bore holes in a patient's skull and an attending priest would remove stones that were assumed to be a cause of insanity.

An Egyptian papyrus of 3000 bce describes recommended treatments for war wounds and shows that the Egyptians recognized the relationship between organic in-

Dr. Philippe Pinel at the Salpêtrière, 1795 by Tony Robert-Fleury. Pinel ordering the removal of chains from patients at the Paris Asylum for insane women.

jury and subsequent mental dysfunction. Another papyrus, of the sixteenth century bce, shows that in regard to diseases not caused by obvious physical injuries, the Egyptians were likely to rely on magic for their explanations and incantations for their cures. Still, superstition was tempered with humane care—dream interpretation, quiet walks, and barge rides down the Nile.

The Hebrews viewed insanity as resulting from God's wrath or the withdrawal of his protection. Without God's protection, a person was subject to invasion by evil spirits, which could cause madness. For the Hebrews, mental disease was a consequence of not living according to God's word.

Prior to the fifth century bce Greek beliefs concerning mental illness were founded on a mixture of religion and superstition. While the most typical responses to persons with mental abnormalities were banishment and stoning, some individuals received humane and supportive care. As did the Egyptians, the Greeks built temples devoted to healing and medicine. Baths, changes in diet, moderate exercise, and dream interpretation were aspects of the early Greek treatment regimen.

Subsequent to the fifth century bce, Greek thought concerning diseases came under the influence of the physician Hippocrates. Hippocrates rejected the prevailing belief that attributed disease to possession. The writings of Hippocrates, nearly all of which were authored by his followers, are very clear in attributing diseases to natural processes. While many healthful remedies followed the Hippocratic idea that mental disorders could be traced to imbalances in body fluids, this same theory also led to many improper and inhumane interventions, such as bloodletting and the forced consumption of foul potions.

In addition to the deductions of Greek physicians, Greek philosophers also speculated concerning mental disturbances. The Greek philosopher Plato addressed the need to treat persons afflicted with mental disorders with compassion and argued that persons who commit a crime as a result of madness or disease should pay a fine but otherwise should be exempt from punishment.

The early Romans expanded upon and refined Greek ideas in regard to mental diseases. After the death in c. 199 ce of the Greek physician Galen, who practiced in Rome for most his lifetime, Roman medicine stagnated. While Europeans abandoned scientific explanations for mental disorders, Islamic countries continued the inquiries initiated by the Greeks. In 792, the first hospital devoted exclusively to the care of mentally ill persons was opened in Baghdad. Humane treatment and a concern for the dignity of disturbed persons were key aspects of treatments recommended by Islamic physicians.

European Traditions

In contrast to the Islamic tradition, Europeans routinely expelled, tortured, abused, and murdered the mentally disturbed. With the rise of Christianity, insanity was variously ascribed to demonic possession, hormonal imbalances, and folk superstitions. While some monasteries offered healing rituals based on incantations and prayer, it was far more common to view the mentally disturbed as abandoned by God or in league with Satan and in need of redemption rather than assistance.

During the mid-thirteenth century, the Church focused on the need to search out and identify witches and warlocks. Mentally ill persons were perfect targets for the papal inquisitors, although it is believed that many more sane than insane persons died as a result of the Inquisition. Commonly, the accused were tortured until they confessed, after which they were burned to death.

The fifteenth century also saw a major movement that was directed toward the confinement of the mentally ill. The institutions for the mentally disturbed were administered by physicians, and as a result, doctors assumed primacy in the care of the mentally disturbed. While the care of persons with mental disorders was transferred from the clergy to physicians, the quality of the patients' lives showed little improvement. Bloodletting, emetic potions, straitjackets, chains, dunking chairs, spinning devices, and terror were the most frequently prescribed treatments.

It was not until the late eighteenth century that positive changes occurred in regard to the treatment of the mentally ill. In 1793 a French physician, Philippe Pinel, was put in charge of a Paris asylum. Dismayed by the treatment that was provided the inmates, Pinel initiated a series of reforms that became the foundation for what was later called the Moral Treatment Revolution. The Moral Treatment Revolution was founded on the principles that mental patients should be treated with compassion, provided with supportive counseling, housed in comfortable surroundings, and given purposeful work. While a number of existent asylums adopted the Moral Treatment approach and new hospitals were dedicated to its principles, it did not take long for economics and neglect to make a mockery of the stated principles. Over time, mental hospitals became little more than warehouses where the mentally ill were admitted, diagnosed, and forgotten.

The Modern Era

While the late nineteenth century saw the development of new theories and techniques for the treatment of mental disorders that were based on free association and catharsis, only a few affluent persons with mental disorders received these treatments. Still, by the early twentieth century, bloodletting, purging, terror, and treatments designed to cause disorientation were being abandoned. These treatments were replaced by somatic therapies and pharmacological interventions. Major problems existed, however, in that the somatic therapies caused brain damage, and the drugs that were available prior to the 1950s were sedatives that caused extreme lethargy and sometimes death.

By the early 1930s, psychiatrists began experimenting with various types of somatic therapy. Insulin coma therapy involved administrations of toxic doses of insulin to nondiabetic patients. Electroconvulsive therapy (ECT) involved passing an electric current through a patient's brain, causing a seizure. Between the late 1930s and the 1960s, several hundred thousand mental patients were involuntarily treated with ECT.

During the mid-1930s, the Portuguese physician António Egas Moniz introduced a surgical procedure that evolved into the prefrontal lobotomy. Between 1935 and 1955, more than fifty thousand mental patients were subjected to lobotomies, in which healthy brain tissue was destroyed in a misdirected effort to treat mental illness.

By the mid-1950s, new pharmacological agents became available. The first of the drugs to be used was reserpine. Although the effects of reserpine on the behavior of psychotic patients were profound, the drug had dangerous side effects. Reserpine was soon replaced by the drug Thorazine. Over the next several years, hundreds of thousands of patients, some voluntarily and many involuntarily, were given Thorazine and other major tranquilizers. One side effect of Thorazine and other drugs of its class is tardive dyskinesia, a disfiguring disturbance that manifests as facial grimacing, palsy, and a staggering gait. For most patients, the tardive dyskinesia disappears when the drug is discontinued, but for some the symptoms are irreversible.

Partially as a result of the availability of psychotropic medications and as a result of changes in social policy, the 1960s saw the beginnings of the community mental health movement. The community mental health movement promoted the concepts of deinstitutionalization, treatment in the least restrictive environment, and treatment as close to the person's home community as possible. Deinstitutionalization involved discharging as many patients as possible from state hospitals and discouraging new admissions. As a result of deinstitutionalization, state hospital populations went from a peak of more than 500,000 during the mid-1950s to fewer than 130,000 during the late 1980s.

Clarification of Terms

Throughout the preceding narrative the terms "mental illness," "mental disease," "insanity," "madness," "mental abnormality," "mental disturbance," "mental dysfunction," and "mental disorder" have been used interchangeably. While this is a common practice, it can lead to misunderstandings. While medical practitioners, legal documents, and the general public frequently refer to aberrant behavior and mental disorders as mental illness, this is a misuse of the term "illness." Illness implies that some underlying disease process exists. The American psychiatrist Thomas Szasz has argued that the complaints that are called symptoms of mental illness are simply communications concerning beliefs, discomfort, or desires that an individual experiences in regard to self or others. Labeling such communications as symptoms of mental illness is a sociopolitical process that vests authority in physicians to control and abuse persons whose communications make others uncomfortable or who are presumed to be dangerous.

While "insanity" is used interchangeably with "mental illness," it would be best if the term "insanity" were reserved to describe a mental state pertinent to legal proceedings. Most countries mitigate punishment if it is determined that a person was insane at the time of committing an illegal act. In fact, most states in the United States allow a finding of not guilty by reason of insanity. This means that a person who commits an illegal act while insane should be found not guilty of any criminal offense.

The terms "madness," "mental abnormality," "mental disturbance," and "mental dysfunction" are simply descriptive in nature. They have no particular standing in regard to the legal system or the medical establishment.

The term "mental disorder" is the official term adopted by the American Psychiatric Association and the American Psychological Association to describe abnormal behavioral or psychological states that cause personal distress, impaired functioning, or conflict with society. The Diagnostic and Statistical Manual of Mental Disorders catalogs the symptoms and behaviors of the various types of mental disorders. Only a minority of the several hundred disorders listed fit the criteria for identification as diseases. That is, it is not possible to identify infectious processes, biochemical imbalances, organ malfunctions, or physical trauma as causes of most disorders. Therefore, it is questionable to refer to them as illnesses.

Ethical Issues

The treatment of persons with mental disorders brings into consideration a number of ethical issues. Among the ethical issues that are of importance in regard to the treatment of persons identified as mentally ill are the following: paternalism, confidentiality, right to privacy, autonomy, informed consent, right to treatment, right to refuse treatment, and criminal responsibility.

In the United States, persons may be involuntarily confined in mental hospitals if they are "mentally ill" and a danger to self or others. Additionally, many states allow the commitment of "mentally ill" persons who are likely to deteriorate mentally or physically if they do not receive care. While at one time simply having a mental disorder could serve as grounds for loss of freedom, states now require an additional finding of dangerousness or probability of deterioration. The right of the state to confine selected citizens involuntarily is based on the concepts of paternalism and police power. Paternalism, or *parens patriae*, allows the state to protect citizens from themselves.

Confidentiality

Confidentiality is central to the practice of psychotherapy. Professional codes and legal procedures require that certain communications be held in confidence. Still, all states provide exceptions to confidentiality, which include the following: when criminal charges have been filed, in child custody cases, when a criminal offense is planned, when the client is a danger to self or others, and when the client has been informed that certain communications are not privileged. While the right to privacy is a fundamental right that most citizens enjoy, it is frequently denied persons who have been diagnosed as mentally ill. If the mentally ill person does not cooperate with treatment, divulge personal secrets, and participate in routine hospital activities, he or she will be identified as an uncooperative patient and will find it very difficult to obtain his or her freedom.

Autonomy is the right to act in a manner that is consistent with one's personally held beliefs and to make decisions that affect one's fate and destiny. This is a right that is refused many mentally ill persons. Through involuntary commitment and forced treatment, persons deemed to be suffering from mental diseases are denied the right to make key decisions that affect their quality of life and their personal survival. Concerning personal survival, only two states have laws making suicide illegal. Furthermore, all states allow a competent adult to make decisions regarding the continuation of life-support devices. Most states either allow or are mute on the right of a competent person to terminate his or her life. Still, all states allow the forced incarceration of a mentally ill person who attempts suicide.

Patient Rights

Informed consent requires that persons understand the nature of the procedures they are to experience, that their participation be voluntary, and that possible consequences be explained. Involuntary commitment, forced treatment, and failure to discuss side effects of psychotropic medications are examples of violations of informed consent in regard to mentally ill persons.

Right to treatment refers to the concept that persons involuntarily confined in mental institutions have a right to humane care and therapeutic treatment. During the 1971 Alabama case *Wyatt v. Stickney*, Judge Frank Johnson stated, "to deprive any citizen of his or her liberty upon an altruistic theory that the confinement is for humane and therapeutic reasons and then fail to provide adequate treatment violates the very fundamentals of due process."

During the 1975 case *O'Connor v. Donaldson*, the Supreme Court ruled that Donald Donaldson, who had been confined to a mental hospital in Florida for fourteen years, deserved a periodic review of his mental status and could not be indefinitely confined if he was capable of caring for himself and was not a danger to himself or others. While not directly ruling on the issue of right to treatment, the court let stand an earlier decision that if Donaldson was not provided treatment, he should have been discharged from the hospital.

The right to refuse treatment is an issue that causes a great deal of controversy. Prior to the 1960s, it was common practice to force patients to undergo dangerous and disabling treatments. Involuntary sterilizations, electroconvulsive therapy, and psychosurgery were frequently prescribed for recalcitrant or difficult patients. While patients now have specific rights in regard to certain invasive treatments, their right to refuse unwanted medications was undefined as late as the early 1990s. During the 1979 case *Rogers v. Okin*, a patient who had been committed to the Boston State Hospital complained that he should not be required to take psychotropic medications against his will. While the initial court finding was that Rogers should have had a right to refuse medication, the case was appealed, and no clear precedent emerged from the case.

The issue of criminal responsibility is bound up with the concept of insanity. If a person, because of mental defect or state of mind, is unable to distinguish right from wrong, then most states would find the person exempt from criminal punishment. Beginning in 1975, however, Michigan adopted an alternate verdict of "guilty but mentally ill." As of 2000, twenty states had followed the Michigan example. The option of finding a person guilty but mentally ill increases the probability that incarceration will follow a crime committed by a person who previously would have been declared insane. Additionally, it allows for mitigation of the length of sentencing and provides for specialized treatment in a prison hospital.

—*Bruce E. Bailey*

Further Reading

Bednar, Richard L., et al. *Psychotherapy with High-Risk Clients: Legal and Professional Standards*. Pacific Grove, Calif.: Brooks/Cole, 1991. Discusses legal and ethical issues related to the practice of psychotherapy. Topics related to client rights and therapist responsibilities are reviewed.

Foucault, Michel. *Madness and Civilization: A History of Insanity in the Age of Reason*. Translated by Richard Howard. 1965. Reprint. New York: Vintage Books, 1988. A seminal work on the cultural history of mental illness, detailing the origins of the category of madness and the uses to which that category has been put.

Goffman, Erving. *Asylums: Essays on the Social Situation of Mental Patients and Other Inmates*. Garden City, N.Y.: Anchor Books, 1961. Explores sociological and environmental influences within institutions that inappropriately shape and change behavior.

Medvedev, Zhores. *A Question of Madness*. Translated by Ellen de Kadt. New York: Knopf, 1971. Provides an account of the involuntary confinement and forced psychiatric treatment of the Russian biochemist Zhores Medvedev. Documents how Soviet psychiatrists collaborated with other agents of the state to silence his criticism of the government.

Roleff, Tamara L., and Laura K. Egendorf, eds. *Mental Illness: Opposing Viewpoints*. San Diego, Calif.: Greenhaven Press, 2000. An anthology of essays written on both sides of the central ethical issues facing contemporary mental health workers.

Szasz, Thomas S. *The Myth of Mental Illness: Foundations of a Theory of Personal Conduct*. Rev. ed. New York: Harper & Row, 1974. Explores issues and ethics related to the diagnosis and treatment of mental disorders. Promotes the concept that individuals and members of the medical establishment must assume responsibility for their behavior.

Valenstein, Elliot S. *Great and Desperate Cures*. New York: Basic Books, 1986. Examines the historical, social, scientific, and ethical issues that led to the development and use of psychosurgery as a cure for mental illness.

See also: Child psychology; Confidentiality; Electroshock therapy; Hippocrates; Institutionalization of patients; Lobotomy; Psychology; Psychopharmacology; Soviet psychiatry; Suicide.

National Commission for the Protection of Human Subjects of Biomedical and Behavioral Research

Identification: Interdisciplinary body that formulated ethical guidelines governing the treatment of human subjects in federally funded research

Date: Established in July, 1974

Type of ethics: Bioethics

Significance: The commission was the earliest and most successful government effort to establish a basic code of ethical conduct regulating scientific inquiry

From 1966 through 1972, several revelations that reputable scientists had routinely risked the health and well-being of subjects without their knowledge eroded public confidence in science. Many incidents involved poor, institutionalized, old, military, or prison populations. Most notorious were the 1972 Tuskegee Syphilis Study revelations. For forty years, Public Health Service researchers had studied the natural course of syphilis in poor African American men from Tuskegee, Alabama; the researchers kept the men unaware of the study's purpose, failed to treat them, even when penicillin became available, and actively prevented outside treatment. In 1974, Congress established the commission and provided that its recommendations were to be accepted by the U.S. Department of Health, Education, and Welfare unless the reasons for rejecting them were made public.

The commission issued several reports, including the *Belmont Report: Ethical Principles and Guidelines for the Protection of Human Subjects of Research* (1978), which led to the establishment of comprehensive regulations. The basic regulations require that most federally funded researchers obtain informed consent, protect confidentiality, and minimize risks to subjects. Additional safeguards were implemented from other reports to govern research on children, pregnant women, prisoners, and other special populations. The commission's impact extends beyond directly funded research. Since institutions receiving federal funds must ensure that all research is conducted ethically, most institutions review all research under the same guidelines, which have become the accepted standard for ethical research.

—*Ileana Dominguez-Urban*

See also: Bioethics; Experimentation; Medical research.

Opioid epidemic

Category: Social issues

Definition: Opioids are a class of drugs that includes pain relievers such as oxycodone, hydrocodone and fentanyl, as well as heroin. Opioids may be naturally occurring in the opium plant or synthetic. An epidemic is defined as an increase in the number of cases of a disease or condition that exceeds the normal levels expected for the particular population.

Description: The opioid epidemic refers to the high rate of misuse of opioid drugs, which includes prescription painkillers, synthetic opioids and heroin.

Prevalence

The misuse of opioids has exploded in prevalence in the U.S. in the past decade. In 2015, 2 million people in the U.S. misused prescription opioid painkillers and approximately 600,000 were addicted to heroin. Every day, 115 people die from opioid overdose in the U.S, with more than 350,000 deaths from opioid overdose occurring from 1999 to 2016. In 2015 alone, the number of deaths from overdose of opioid drugs was more than 33,000.

History

The increase in overdose deaths occurred in three waves. The first wave started in 1999 and was mainly due to over-prescription and misuse of opioid drugs. The second wave of overdose deaths in 2010 was due to heroin overdoses, while the third wave in 2013 was caused by the advent of synthetic opioids such as illicitly manufactured fentanyl. Fentanyl is often mixed with other drugs such as heroin and cocaine.

In the first wave of the opioid epidemic, clinicians overprescribed opioid painkillers. An estimated 255 million total prescriptions for opioid drugs have been written in U.S., with the peak of 81 prescriptions per 100 persons

occurring in 2012. This high prescription rate was partly due to the large number of people who report symptoms of pain in the U.S. According to the Functioning and Disability Supplement of the 2012 National Health Interview Survey, more than 126 million adults reported some pain in the previous 3 months, 25 million of which reported experiencing pain every day (chronic pain). According to the National Institute on Drug Abuse, 21 to 29 percent of patients who are prescribed opioids for chronic pain misuse these drugs.

Risk factors

The Substance Abuse and Mental Health Services Administration (SAMHSA) classifies risk factors for prescription drug (especially opioids) misuse into factors acting at the individual, relationship, social and community levels. Individual-level factors include mental illness, acute and chronic pain, physical health problems (e.g., fatigue and headaches), heightened physiological reactions to some types of drugs, a history of drug or alcohol misuse, and greater access to opioid drugs (e.g., receiving prescriptions of high dosages or multiple prescriptions). Surprisingly, higher education is not always linked to lower risk of opioid addiction, with one study showing that college-educated residents of New York City had an increased risk of unintentional overdose from opioids at home.

At the relationship level, the adolescent children of parents who express disapproval of drug use are less likely to misuse opioids and other prescription drugs. Conversely, adolescent children of parents who express favorable views on drug use are more likely to misuse prescription drugs, including opioids. People with many friends who misuse drugs and college students in fraternities and sororities are also more likely to misuse prescription drugs.

Community-level risk factors are features of the neighborhood and community that influence drug use. For example, in children 12 to 17 years of age, moving 3 or more times in a year or living in an urban setting increase the risk of opioid drug misuse.

Society-level risk factors for prescription drug misuse include stressors such as being a victim of discrimination and unfair treatment because of lower social status or being a member of a marginalized group.

Assessment and Diagnosis

National government organizations such as the Federal Drugs Administration (FDA) and the Centers for Disease

Control and Prevention (CDC) assess the prevalence of opioid prescriptions, use and misuse annually.

Thorough evaluation by a psychiatrist, psychologist or licensed alcohol and drug counselor. According to the American Psychiatric Association, opioid misuse may be diagnosed when there is a problematic pattern of opioid use causing clinically significant impairment over a 12-month period. Clinically significant impairment is defined as at least two of the following features:

- Opioids are frequently taken in larger amounts or for longer than was intended.
- Persistent desire or unsuccessful efforts to reduce or control opioid use.
- A lot of time spent obtaining and using the opioids or recovering from their effects.
- Craving to use opioids.
- Repeated use of opioids, causing problems in fulfilling obligations at work, school or home.
- Social, occupational or recreational activities have been reduced or stopped because of opioid use.
- Continued use of opioids in spite of social or interpersonal problems caused by or exacerbated the opioid use.
- Repeated use of opioids in situations where it is physically hazardous.
- Continued use of opioids despite knowing that it is causing or exacerbating physical or psychological problems.
- Tolerance to opioids, as evidenced by a much lower response to the continued use of the same amount of opioid or a need to use higher doses of opioids to achieve the desired effect.
- Withdrawal, as evidenced by either opioid withdrawal syndrome or the taking of opioids or other drugs to relieve withdrawal symptoms.

Treatment

The FDA has taken steps to address the opioid epidemic, which can be categorized under four aims: 1) decreasing exposure and preventing new addiction; 2) supporting treatment of people with opioid use disorder; 3) fostering the development of novel pain therapies; and 4) improving enforcement and assessment of benefits and risks.

At the same time, the FDA set up an Opioid Policy Steering Committee in 2017 and held public meetings in September 2017 to consult the public on their opinions and ideas about possible solutions that the FDA could implement.

Aim 1 focuses on evaluating and facilitating appropriate doses of opioid drugs for various indications, as well as education of prescribers (including doctors, nurses and pharmacists) about the risks of opioid misuse. The FDA has now tightened the regulations associated with opioid drugs and their prescription.

Aim 2 centers round treatment of opioid misuse, including medication-assisted therapy, which has been shown to be the most effective means of treating opioid misuse disorder. The FDA is implementing efforts to encourage the use of over-the-counter naloxone (Narcan®, Evzio®) to save more lives. Naloxone is the medication of choice in emergency overdose situations, and traditionally has been only administered by healthcare professionals, including emergency room doctors and paramedics.

In Aim 3, the FDA is partnering with other organizations such as the National Institutes of Health to help promote the development of new pain therapies as alternatives to opioid medications, and the development of misuse-deterrent formulations. One of these drugs that is being evaluated is hydrocodone (Hydexor®). The FDA is also examining options for using Fast Track and Breakthrough Therapy designations to speed up the process of approval for promising new pain therapies.

Finally under Aim 4, the FDA is exploring how to collaborate with agencies such as Customs and Border Protection to seize illegal opioids brought into the U.S. and to recommend withdrawal of opioids from the market that have a high risk of misuse.

Future Trends

Although some reports mention that the rate of opioid prescriptions has been decreasing in the past few years, the rate of opioid misuse and overdose has been on the rise. According to the National Institute on Drug Abuse, overdoses from opioid drugs rose by 30% in 45 states from July 2016 to September 2017. Thus, in the near future, the opioid epidemic will likely continue. However, if the plans to address the epidemic are successful, including the FDA strategies outlined above, the prevalence of opioid misuse should start declining.

—*Ing-Wei Khor, PhD*

Further Reading
Center for Behavioral Health Statistics and Quality (CBHSQ), Substance Abuse and Mental Health Services Administration

(SAMHSA), U.S. Department of Health and Human Services (HHS). National Survey on Drug Use and Health. https://www.samhsa.gov/data/sites/default/files/NSDUH-Det Tabs-2016/NSDUH-DetTabs-2016.htm. This report provides the annual statistics for prevalence of opioid misuse and deaths due to opioid overdose.

National Institute on Drug Abuse, National Institute of Health. "Opioid Overdose Crisis." Available at: https://www.drugabuse. gov/drugs-abuse/opioids/opioid-overdose-crisis. Updated March 2018. Accessed July 6, 2018. The page gives an overview of the opioid epidemic and some statistics about its prevalence and causes.

Centers for Disease Control and Prevention. "Opioid Overdose: Understanding the Epidemic." Available at: https://www.cdc.gov/drugoverdose/epidemic/index.html. Updated August 30, 2017. Accessed July 1, 2018. This summary page on the CDC website lists statistics about the opioid epidemic.

Substance Abuse and Mental Health Services Administration. "Preventing Prescription Drug Misuse: Overview of Factors and Strategies." Available at: https://www.samhsa.gov/capt/sites/default/files/resources/preventing-prescription-drug-misuse-overview.pdf. This report from Substance Abuse and Mental Health Services Administration (SAMHSA) discusses the issues, challenges and concerns related to prescription opioid misuse.

American Psychiatric Association. Diagnostic and Statistical Manual of Mental Disorders, Fifth Edition. 2013. Available at: https://pcssnow.org/wp-content/uploads/2014/02/5B-DSM-5-Opioid-Use-Disorder-Diagnostic-Criteria.pdf. This PDF presents the diagnostic criteria for opioid misuse disorder from the most recent edition of the DSM (DSM-V).

Throckmorton DC, Deputy Director for Regulatory Programs, Center for Drug Evaluation and Research, FDA. "FDA's Actions to Address the Opioid Epidemic." Presented at the CBI Abuse-Deterrent Formulation Summit, March 14, 2018. https://www.fda.gov/downloads/AboutFDA/CentersOffices/OfficeofMedical ProductsandTobacco/CDER/UCM601178.pdf. This presentation by the Deputy Director for Regulatory Programs at the FDA discusses the evolution of the opioid epidemic in the U.S. and the steps that the FDA has taken to help contain and manage the epidemic.

Organ transplants

Definition: Replacement of worn-out, diseased, or injured organs and tissues with healthy substitutes

Date: Begun in early twentieth century

Type of ethics: Bioethics

Significance: Organ transplantation and substitution raises ethical issues regarding the definition of death, the equitable distribution of scarce resources (including the ethics of selling body parts), and the quality of life of the transplant patient

For centuries, humans have longed to be able to replace the diseased or injured parts of the body with healthy organs. Stories abound from ancient civilizations of attempts at organ and tissue transplantation, but until recently these seem to have been mostly dreams. Finally, during the early nineteenth century, there were successful skin grafts. These were autografts in which a patient's own tissue was used, and thus there was little danger of rejection. When material was taken from one member of a species and placed in another (an allograft), however, it was rejected by the recipient.

This was not the only problem faced by these early medical pioneers. Before organ transplantation could be done on a routine basis, it was necessary to develop better methods of tying up weakened arteries, aseptic surgery, anesthesia, and tissue typing.

By 1913, the French physician Alexis Carrel transplanted a kidney from one cat to another and later developed a profusion machine that drenched a removed organ in blood, thus sustaining its life. However, a major obstacle remained; namely, the rejection of the transplanted organ. The mechanics of this little-understood process were discovered by Peter Medawar at Oxford University during the 1940s. He found that this process was caused by the immune system's rejection of the body's lymphoid organs. Thus, the recipient's system recognized the donor tissue as foreign and responded by destroying the transplant.

The amount of genetic disparity of the two individuals determines the degree and speed of this rejection. Attempts to limit the activity of the immune system eventually led to the use of a combination of a corticosteroid (prednisone) with the antileukemia drug (azathioprine). A third medicine, cyclosporine, discovered in 1972, was particularly important because it took less of a scattergun approach than the others. Rather than suppressing the entire immune response, cyclosporine targets the T cells, the particular parts of the system that attack alien tissues. The most effective treatment of transplant patients includes daily doses of these three drugs.

Types of Organ Transplants

The human body contains twenty-one different transplantable organs and tissues, including the heart, liver, kidneys, lungs, pancreas, cornea, bone marrow, and blood vessels. In 1954, a team of Boston physicians led by Joseph E. Murray successfully transplanted a kidney from one twin brother to another. Cardiac transplantation began in 1967, when Christiaan Barnard performed a human-to-human operation, but the first fully successful heart transplant was done by Norman Shumway in the United States. Although lung transplants were attempted as early as 1964, because of problems with infection that are peculiar to this organ it was not until the 1980s that John D. Cooper of Toronto made the process feasible. The work of Thomas E. Starzl led in 1967 to successful transplanting of the liver. Also during the decade of the 1960s, the pancreas, bone marrow, cornea, and blood vessels were transplanted with increasing frequency.

By the turn of the twenty-first century, more than 16,000 kidney, liver, pancreas, heart, heart-lung, and lung transplants were being performed each year in the United States alone. These operations seem to be the only treatment that can transform individuals from a near-death condition to a relatively normal life in a matter of days.

Ethical Concerns

Such procedures raise a number of ethical and moral problems. Those that concern organ donation often result from worry that individuals will not receive adequate treatment if they sign donor agreements. An understanding of the modern definition of death can deal with much of this confusion. Until the 1960s, cessation of brain function inevitably followed cessation of cardiopulmonary function. Individuals did not live for extended periods with the heart and other organs functioning after the brain activity ceased. New medical techniques such as the use of respirators made this condition possible. Machines could maintain blood and oxygen circulation even when the body could never again operate on its own.

The notion of "brain death" was therefore proposed. In 1966, Pope Pius XII defined death as the departure of the spirit from the body through the cessation of brain function rather than the loss of pumping action of the heart. The United States and other countries have passed laws that have given legal sanction to this definition. Patients who are brain dead may be kept alive for a few days, but not permanently. A physician can confirm this situation beyond a doubt through neurological examination. Public support for this position has gained wide acceptance, and currently very few people oppose organ donation.

More difficult problems remain that involve the recipient. Some of these concern the selection of those who are to receive transplants. Despite the thousands of operations performed in 1991, there were still more than 30,000 individuals listed by the United Network for Organ Sharing (UNOS) who needed one or more of the major organs. In an attempt to alleviate this shortage, UNOS, an organiza-

Alexis Carrel: 1912's Nobel Prize for his work on organ transplantation.

tion of transplant centers, was founded. It has established a national waiting list to ensure equitable organ allocation according to policies that forbid favoritism based on race, sex, financial status, or political influence. The only considerations are the medically determined conditions of the patients. This organization has been quite successful in raising awareness of the need for donor organs.

Even if a person receives a transplant, there is a continuing need for a more healthy lifestyle and the constant cost and bother of daily medication. Finally, the entire situation of the expense and availability of transplants is a microcosm of the macrocosm of health care for everyone. How can scarce resources be allocated? Who is wise or caring enough to decide who will die and who will have a chance at a new life? Such questions must be addressed by the general field of medical ethics.

—Robert G. Clouse

Further Reading

Fox, Renee, and Judith P. Swazey. *The Courage to Fail: A Social View of Organ Transplants and Dialysis.* 2d rev. ed. Chicago: University of Chicago Press, 1978.

Price, David. *Legal and Ethical Aspects of Organ Transplantation.* New York: Cambridge University Press, 2000.

Sheil, A. G., and Felix T. Rapapport. *World Transplantation.* 3 vols. East Norwalk, Conn.: Appleton & Lange, 1989.

Shelton, Wayne, ed. *The Ethics of Organ Transplantation.* New York: Elsevier Science, 2001.

Starzl, Thomas E. *The Puzzle People: Memoirs of a Transplant Surgeon.* Pittsburgh: University of Pittsburgh Press, 1992.

Veatch, Robert M. *Transplantation Ethics.* Washington, D.C.: Georgetown University Press, 2000.

Warshofsky, Fred. *The Rebuilt Man.* New York: Thomas Y. Crowell, 1965.

See also: Bioethics; Health care allocation; Life and death; Medical ethics; *Principles of Medical Ethics.*

Pain

Definition: Fundamentally unpleasant physical or emotional sensation; suffering

Type of ethics: Bioethics

Significance: Pain names the broad class of experience which all sentient beings are conditioned to avoid. It is the most primal negative influence on behavior, as pleasure is the most primal positive influence. In many ethical systems, to intentionally cause pain in another is among the most serious moral transgressions, and to alleviate the pain of another is among the most morally admirable acts

The treatment and relief of pain is often considered to be a central goal of the medical profession, at least by those who seek care. People usually think of pain as a warning sign that something has gone wrong in the body's systems; however, not all pain serves this function, and not all pain is indicative of physical malfunction.

Physiology

Pain is usually separated (somewhat arbitrarily) into two diagnoses: acute and chronic. While chronic pain is often defined clinically as acute pain persisting longer than six months, there are differences in perception and meaning that go beyond merely temporal distinctions.

Acute pain is also of two types, classified by the speed with which the actual nerve impulses reach the brain. When an event, such as a burn, triggers signals to be sent to the brain, one set of signals travels much faster. These are the initial impulses, "fast" pain, that travel on myelinated (sheathed in a protein-lipid layer) A delta fibers. These impulses reach the brain in a fraction of a second, while the "slow" pain, which travels on unmyelinated C fibers, takes up to a couple of seconds to register in a person's consciousness.

The further the site of stimulus is from the brain, the greater the difference in the times these signals register. Fast pain is sharp and bright. Slow pain is dull and aching, and ultimately more unpleasant. In addition to the nerve impulses sent to the brain, for which the chemical neurotransmitter seems to be substance P (for pain), chemicals are released at the site of stimulus. Prostaglandins draw blood to the area to gain the healing and infection-fighting power of white blood cells. Prostaglandins also increase the sensitivity of the nerves in the immediate vicinity of the injury, as do bradykinins and leukotrienes, which are also released.

Psychological Components of Pain

Pain cannot, however, be relegated to mere physical perception. The knowledge of the consequences of pain is inextricably entwined with the feeling and assessment of pain. In a now-famous study published in 1946, Henry K. Beecher found that men who were severely wounded in battle reported far less pain (and some no pain at all) than did civilian patients with comparable wounds caused by surgery. The reason for this seems clear: For men in battle, severe wounds are the ticket home. Pain cannot be separated from the personal and social consequences of its presence.

Many people take pain and suffering to be synonymous, yet they are different and distinct. Pain can occur without causing suffering, as does the pain that athletes endure during competition. There can certainly be suffering without pain, either physical, such as severe itching, or mental, as in grief. (Some authorities do not distinguish between physical and mental suffering, believing them to be so linked as to be inseparable.) Pain is usually taken to be a physical perception, while suffering is psychological distress. Intrinsic to suffering is a threat to the integrity of a person as a whole. The anticipation of pain and loss can cause as much suffering as the actuality thereof.

Meanings of Pain

Pain has had different interpretations in different cultures and periods of history. While today Western culture ostensibly reaches toward the eradication of pain, this has by no means always been the case. Aside from medical inability to eliminate pain in the past, pain and suffering have themselves been considered valuable in many cultures. The Christian religion, in particular, has traditionally deemed experiencing pain, in some circumstances, a virtue.

Suffering, especially suffering for others, is considered one of the highest forms of sanctity, as can be seen from the litany of saints by martyrdom throughout the ages. In other religious traditions, pain and suffering are, or can be, due punishment for sins or wrong actions committed either in this life, as in Judaism and Islam, or in past lives, as in Hinduism and Buddhism. The word "pain" in English is derived from the Latin word *poena*, meaning "punishment."

The English word for one who seeks medical care, "patient," also comes from the Latin. Its root, *pati*, means "the one who suffers." Underlying these derivations, and extending beyond the words themselves, is the cultural acceptance that pain and suffering are an inevitable part of life and as such are not intrinsically evil. This attitude is the basis for medical hesitancy to consider pain a problem to be treated in and of itself, rather than simply as a symptom of other disease or injury.

Treatment of Pain

Because of these deep-rooted cultural attitudes toward pain and those who suffer, only recently has aggressive treatment of pain become an issue in medical ethics. Studies have shown surprising underutilization of pain-relieving medication for sufferers of severe pain, especially among terminal cancer patients. This seems to be because of fears of addiction to narcotics and a lack of knowledge of proper use. The use of heroin for terminal patients has long been accepted in Great Britain but continues to be prohibited in the United States.

Alternative forms of treatment are becoming more acceptable, although the efficacy of some remains to be substantiated. Biofeedback techniques, chiropractic, hypnosis, and TENS (transcutaneous electrical nerve stimulation) are generally accepted to be of value for many patients. Acupuncture is gaining ground in the United States. For millions of people, however, effective pain relief still lies in the future.

—*Margaret Hawthorne*

Further Reading
Bendelow, Gillian. *Pain and Gender*. New York: Prentice Hall, 2000.
Bowker, John W. "Pain and Suffering: Religious Perspectives." In *Encyclopedia of Bioethics*, edited by Warren T. Reich. Rev. ed. Vol. 4. New York: Macmillan, 1995.
Care, Norman S. *Living with One's Past: Personal Fates and Moral Pain*. Lanham, Md.: Rowman & Littlefield, 1996.
Ganong, William F. *Review of Medical Physiology*. 21st ed. New York: Lange Medical Books/McGraw-Hill, 2003.
Hardcastle, Valerie Gray. *The Myth of Pain*. Cambridge, Mass.: MIT Press, 1999.
Morris, David B. *The Culture of Pain*. Berkeley: University of California Press, 1991.

See also: Biofeedback; Cruelty; Harm; Hypnosis; Illness; Sentience.

Principles of Medical Ethics

Identification: American Medical Association's official guidelines on professional conduct
Date: Adopted in 1957; revised in 1980 and 2001
Type of ethics: Bioethics
Significance: Principles of Medical Ethics formally codifies professional standards of conduct that are applicable to all physicians practicing in the United States.

In 1957, the AMA replaced its *Code of Ethics*—which had, since the organization's founding in 1847, stated the duties that American physicians owed to their patients, to their society, and to one another—with a statement of moral principles, supplemented by commentary. The reform was consonant with the appeal to basic moral principles by the 1948 Nuremberg Tribunal and the World Medical Association. It also lessened physicians' malpractice liability under the explicit obligations stipulated by the code and, at the same time, provided a more flexible format for advising physicians on conduct.

The *Principles* require physicians to provide competent, compassionate medical service, respectful of human dignity; to deal honestly with patients and colleagues; to expose fraud and deception; to respect the law; to respect the rights of patients and to safeguard their confidences; to respect the rights of colleagues and other health care professionals; to advance scientific knowledge; to share information with patients, colleagues, and the public; and to recognize a responsibility to contribute to the community.

Revised in 1980 and again in 2001, the *Principles* are largely unchanged but have shifted in subtle ways. They have tended toward a slightly more explicit enumeration of physicians' rights as well as their responsibilities, and they have expunged certain financial rules (for example, a prohibition against referral fees).

—Robert Baker

See also: American Medical Association; Medical bills of rights; Medical ethics; Physician-patient relationship; *Principles of Medical Ethics with Annotations Especially Applicable to Psychiatry.*

Principles of Medical Ethics with Annotations Especially Applicable to Psychiatry

Identification: Addendum to *Principles of Medical Ethics* published by the American Psychiatric Association to address unique ethical issues confronting psychiatrists

Date: First published in September, 1973; revised in 1981, 1986, 2001, 2003, and 2004

Type of ethics: Psychological ethics

Significance: The *Principles* sets out the issues particular to practitioners in the mental health field and codifies standards of ethical conduct in matters not covered by the American Medical Association's code.

The 1973 statement of *Principles* recognized that, although psychiatrists have the same goals as all physicians in adhering to the American Medical Association's code of ethics, psychiatrists also face particular ethical questions that differ in kind and degree from those of other medical specialties. The annotations given in the *Principles* were viewed as being open to revision from time to time to reflect current issues and problems. An extensive revision was published in 1986. The most relevant sections of the 1973 document dealt with contractual relationships with other mental health professionals and physicians, the waiving of confidentiality, and speaking out on social issues not related to psychiatry.

The thrust of the document was that psychiatrists must maintain the trust of their patients and other medical and nonmedical professionals. The 1986 revision maintains this basic thrust, but its seven sections contain much more lengthy, detailed, and specific annotations and focus in particular on the various aspects of the psychiatrist-patient relationship, such as confidentiality, consultation with other psychiatrists, and honesty. In 2001, the AMA adopted a revised version of its *Principles*. The APA fol-

lowed suit and added a series of amendments in November, 2003.

—Laurence Miller

See also: Ethical Principles of Psychologists; Medical ethics; *Principles of Medical Ethics*; Psychology; Therapist-patient relationship.

Psychopharmacology

Definition: Study of the effects that drugs have on emotion, thought, and behavior

Type of ethics: Psychological ethics

Significance: Psychopharmacology is the basis for the medical treatment of mental illness. As such, it raises ethical questions involving the rights of the mentally ill to determine their own course of treatment or to refuse medication, as well as the long-term risks of medications that produce short-term benefits.

While many physicians and biologically oriented psychiatrists have had a long-standing commitment to the use of psychotropic medications for the treatment of some emotional disorders, others have questioned their use in particular cases. From an ethical perspective, some people have questioned whether such interventions are demonstrably superior to other treatment forms—such as psychotherapy, for example—in view of the known side effects of medications. In addition, it is not always clear that patients are able to give fully informed consent, and it is not always clear that patients are fully informed of all the risks inherent in psychopharmacological interventions.

History

While the use of psychoactive drugs designed to treat mental disorders is relatively recent, the use of drugs as pain relievers and sleep producers goes back for many hundreds of years. Alcohol and opiates are good examples of drugs that have been used for such purposes. The use by the medical community of drugs to treat mental symptoms goes back to the 1840's, when bromides were first used to treat anxiety. Later in the nineteenth century, Sigmund Freud, the father of psychoanalysis, suggested that cocaine was a psychoactive drug that could be helpful, and in the first part of the twentieth century, barbiturates were introduced to treat anxiety.

Alan Gelenberg, Ellen Bassuk, and Stephen Schoonover point out in their book *The Practitioner's Guide to Psychoactive Drugs* (3d ed., 1991) that in 1949, with the synthesis of chlorpromazine, the medical community began to focus on the use of drugs to treat mental illness. At about the same time that chlorpromazine was developed, reserpine (another tranquilizer synthesized from the root of the plant *Rauwolfia serpentina*) came into use. Lithium chloride was used as early as 1940, but its ability to counter manic behavior was not established until 1949 and lithium itself was not approved for use in the United States until 1970.

Prescription Privileges

While physicians and some other health professionals (for example, nurse practitioners and optometrists) do have the authority to prescribe medications, nonphysicians, including psychologists, do not have prescription privileges, although on the federal level psychologists have legally prescribed within the Indian Health Service. Since the 1990's, there has been a spirited debate among psychologists regarding whether prescription privileges should be sought by psychologists on a state-by-state basis. The focus of the argument has been on psychotropic medications and their judicious use. Some people have argued that nursing home residents are often treated with drugs that are designed to treat mental disorders when, in fact, most of these patients are not mentally ill. Conversely, while there is agreement that some children with symptoms of hyperactivity and/or attention deficit disorder should be treated with psychotropic medications, it is important to diagnose such problems carefully, since such problems may involve parents' ineffectiveness in coping with the child.

Objections to Psychotropic Drugs

In his book *Toxic Psychiatry* (1991), Peter Breggin argues that many patients may not have been fully apprised of the negative (addictive and dangerous) side effects of many psychotropic medications. In addition, he argues that the use of drugs even for the severely mentally ill is not unequivocally supported by research and that the results of positive drug studies are countermanded by evidence that some psychotropic drugs cause brain impairment. Mary Lee Smith, Gene Glass, and Thomas Miller, in their book *The Benefits of Psychotherapy* (1980), analyzed 112 experiments that studied the separate and combined effects of drug therapy and psychotherapy. They found that even for serious psychological disorders, psychotherapy was nearly even with drug therapy in terms of overall effectiveness. While drug therapy and psychotherapy taken to-

The common muscimol-bearing mushroom Amanita muscaria (fly agaric). By Onderwijsgek at nl.wikipedia.

gether produced greater effects than did either drug therapy or psychotherapy alone, the effects of these therapies in combination were only slightly greater than their separate effects.

The Combined Use of Pharmacotherapy and Psychotherapy

In his book *The Psychotherapist's Guide to Psychopharmacology* (1990), Michael J. Gitlin raises the question of whether there are negative interactions between drug therapy and psychotherapy. To the extent that successful drug therapy reduces symptoms, some patients may not wish to continue in psychotherapy for their emotional problems. There is also concern that dependence on drugs may make patients unusually passive and relatively unwilling to explore their problems in psychotherapy. Finally, some patients may become distressed at the notion that they could benefit from medications in addition to psychotherapy, since they may perceive medications as a kind of crutch. Some patients, however, are convinced that they have some kind of chemical imbalance that needs to be "fixed" by means of psychotropic drugs. These patients do not believe that it is important to explore their problems in psychotherapy.

Gitlin also describes who should have a medication consultation. He points out that patients with such psychiatric symptoms as delusions, hallucinations, or psychosis should be considered, as well as patients with appetite or sleep disturbances and those with significant suicidal tendencies. Patients with significant medical disorders and patients with a family history of more than minor psychiatric disorders are candidates for drug therapy. Finally, patients presenting confusion, concentration problems, and other cognitive symptoms are also good candidates for medication consultations.

The Right to Refuse Treatment

In his book *Law, Psychiatry, and Morality* (1984), Alan Stone raises an important moral and ethical issue. Should hospitalized mentally ill patients be required to take antipsychotic medications? Critics of forcing hospitalized patients to take antipsychotic medications argue that this is an invasion of privacy or that these drugs are mind altering and thus violate First Amendment rights. It is known, for example, that some antipsychotic drugs can affect speech and thought. Stone cites a case in which the court was asked to decide whether the state can impose the use of antipsychotic drugs in the absence of an emergency.

In that case (*Rogers v. Commissioner of Mental Health*), a federal judge decided that the patient did have the right to refuse medication, since the patient was not likely to harm himself or others. Stone argues that the real issue that should be addressed is whether a patient's mental illness will respond to antipsychotic medications, rather than assuming that antipsychotic drugs are chemical restraints. Some organizations, such as the National Association for the Mentally Ill, strongly agree with Stone. Others, including many psychologists, agree with the judge's decision. Time will tell how this topic will be resolved.

—Norman Abeles

Further Reading

Breggin, Peter. *Toxic Psychiatry*. New York: St. Martin's Press, 1991.

Gelenberg, Alan J., and Ellen L. Bassuk, eds. *The Practitioner's Guide to Psychoactive Drugs*. 4th ed. New York: Plenum, 1997.

Ghaemi, S. Nassir, ed. *Polypharmacy in Psychiatry*. New York: Dekker, 2002.

Gitlin, Michael J. *The Psychotherapist's Guide to Psychopharmacology*. New York: Free Press, 1990.

Smith, Mary L., Gene V. Glass, and Thomas I. Miller. *The Benefits of Psychotherapy*. Baltimore: Johns Hopkins University Press, 1980.

Stone, Alan A. *Law, Psychiatry, and Morality*. Washington, D.C.: American Psychiatric Press, 1984.

See also: Diagnosis; Drug abuse; Electroshock therapy; Institutionalization of patients; Jung, Carl; Psychology; Therapist-patient relationship.

Quinlan, Karen Ann

Identification: Comatose patient who was the focus of a well-publicized ethical controversy

Born: March 29, 1954, Scranton, Pennsylvania

Died: June 11, 1985, Morris Plains, New Jersey

Type of ethics: Bioethics

Significance: Despite the fact that Karen Ann Quinlan remained alive for almost ten years after she was taken off life support, the removal of her respirator set an important precedent for legal battles over euthanasia.

On April 15, 1975, Karen Ann Quinlan, then twenty-one years old, was taken to a hospital in a critical comatose state. She had had a few drinks, passed out, and temporarily quit breathing. There was a small amount of alcohol in her body as well as a nontoxic level of aspirin and Valium. Part of her brain had died because of oxygen depletion. She was moved to St. Clare's Hospital in Denville, New Jersey, where it was determined that she had extensive brain damage. Karen began to deteriorate physically and coiled into a fetal position. She was attached to an MA-1 respirator.

In July, Quinlan's parents asked that the respirator be removed and signed papers absolving the hospital from legal liability. The doctors refused. Karen was twenty-one, so her parents were not her legal guardians. Joseph Quinlan went to court to be appointed guardian so that he could have the respirator removed. The lower court ruled against the Quinlans, but the New Jersey Supreme Court ruled in their favor.

Six weeks later, Karen was still on the respirator; however, the doctors agreed to wean her from it. She continued to breathe without the respirator. In June, 1976, she was moved to a nursing home where she was given high-nutrient feedings and antibiotics. She lived for ten years in a persistent vegetative state. Her case is important in discussions of the right to die, the ordinary/extraordinary care distinction, the active/passive euthanasia distinction, and the need for a living will.

—Rita C. Hinton

See also: Death and dying; Euthanasia; Life and death; "Playing god" in medical decision making; Right to die.

Right to die

Definition: Just or legitimate claim to be allowed to die rather than submit to necessary medical treatment

Type of ethics: Bioethics

Significance: Claims that terminally ill persons have a right to die are founded upon the notion of human dignity. Proponents claim that forcing someone to stay alive and to continue suffering against their will violates their dignity, whereas allowing them to die restores or preserves it. Opponents may assert that suicide, even passive suicide, is an absolute moral wrong, or they may point out that extremely ill people are often not in their right minds and may not be competent to make such a difficult and irrevocable decision.

"Right to Die" was the title of a debate in the journal *Forum* on legalizing euthanasia. Later, the term was used to refer solely to voluntary euthanasia. Viewed narrowly, the right to die is merely the application of autonomy-based legal principles of self-determination and informed consent developed in the nineteenth century: If treatment cannot be given without consent, even for the individual's own good, then the individual must have a right to refuse treatment. During the 1970's and 1980's, the right to die was used in this sense, as a synonym for voluntary passive euthanasia.

History

After World War II, several factors led to the recognition of the right to die. Medical advances and social prosperity reduced sudden deaths, resulting in a growing population of older people, greater incidence of senility, and greater incidence of death from degenerative diseases. Meanwhile, health care costs soared and smaller, more dispersed families led to increased institutionalization of older people. By means of respirators and other forms of technology, life could be continued indefinitely despite failing organs.

Although the number of patients in "a limbo between life and death" had increased, these issues remained private as physicians discontinued treatment or withheld resuscitation for some hopelessly ill patients. With the advent of transplants, however, particularly heart transplants, the established definition of death became inadequate. Public debate began with a Harvard committee's 1968 recommendation that brain death be included in the "definition" of death. Meanwhile, civil and human rights movements emphasizing self-determination, bodily integrity, and individual empowerment were reflected in a movement away from "mercy killing" to a focus on voluntary euthanasia.

Then, in 1975, the case of Karen Ann Quinlan galvanized the public consciousness in the battle for end-of-life decision-making control. The family sued to have Karen, who was in a persistent vegetative state (a coma with minimal brain function and no anticipated recovery of consciousness), removed from a respirator. The New Jersey Supreme Court held in 1976 that under the Constitution, acceptance or refusal of any treatment was to be made by the patient, or in the case of incompetency, by her guardians in accordance with her expressed desire. The Quinlan case also suggested that "ethics committees" could assist families and physicians in medical decision making. Such committees, staffed by physicians, ethicists, and lawyers, later became common. Afterward, courts consistently found a "right" to die in the common law or federal or state constitutions.

In 1990, the U.S. Supreme Court confirmed a federal constitutional "liberty" basis for the right to refuse life-sustaining treatment, including possibly artificial nutrition and hydration.

Ethical Issues

Society has long held legal and moral prohibitions against the taking of human life. Early discussions centered on whether allowing a human being to die when that death could be prevented or forestalled was tantamount to killing. In 1957, Pope Pius XII distinguished between permissible forgoing of treatment in "hopeless cases" and active euthanasia, which was killing or suicide, but who was to determine which was which? The pope intimated that the individual's duty to accept, and society's duty to provide, medical treatment extended to ordinary treatment but not to extraordinary (or "heroic") measures.

Although popular during the 1970's, these categories were later dismissed as unworkable. Other attempts to distinguish killing from permitting "natural death," distinguishing between withholding and withdrawing treatment and between acts and omissions, were also rejected as morally indefensible and tending to discourage the initiation of treatment.

Committing suicide cannot be distinguished from refusing treatment on the basis of an action versus nonaction distinction. Thus, the fundamental question is whether an individual should ever be allowed to forgo life-sustaining treatment.

The right to die is often justified along utilitarian grounds and opposed on the basis of deontological, beneficence-based principles. Some utilitarians oppose any euthanasia, however, believing that the harms from potential abuse and from accepting incursions into the sanctity of life outweigh the benefits.

Conversely, some deontologists support the right to die by defining "benefit" to encompass not only prolonged life but also freedom from suffering, or the protection of individuals' liberty interests. Some suggest that autonomy cannot be overridden, others that decisions in extremis are not autonomous.

Opponents of Euthanasia

Opponents of euthanasia often argue the "slippery slope"—that allowing some to die will lead to further "justified" endings of lives. Some cite various eugenics movements as evidence for this view. Proponents counter that all moral choices involve drawing lines with a potential for abuse. Another objection raised is that the slippery slope entails accepting a recognized evil, disregarding the autonomy, dignity, and suffering of the dying patient in favor of possible future evils.

Some argue that human life is inviolable and that acceptance of a decision to forgo any amount of life necessarily requires a societal recognition that some lives are not worth living. Others counter that this inviolability is negated by causes throughout history that have been deemed worthy of self-sacrifice.

Some fear that passive euthanasia will insidiously change the treatment of older people and dying; individuals may be subtly coerced into dying because they perceive themselves as burdens to their families, or because they see others who are younger, healthier, or even in comparable positions refusing treatment.

Passive euthanasia for the terminally ill enjoys overwhelming societal and judicial support, though popularity in the polls does not foreclose the need to address the ethical concerns surrounding the issue.

The public and the media characterize the issue as one of not unduly "prolonging life" or of allowing individuals to die "naturally" and "with dignity"; such characterizations beg the question of what is a dignified and natural death in the context of advancing medical technology.

Even if passive euthanasia is acceptable, a number of issues remain unresolved: Can the right be invoked on behalf of incompetent patients? For formerly competent individuals, treatment decisions can be made on the basis of previously expressed wishes. For the never competent (including children), recognizing an equal right to refuse treatment produces thornier questions of how to carry out that right without committing involuntary euthanasia.

Is a slow, painful, and lingering death or an indefinite existence under sedation dignified? Can artificially administered nutrition and hydration be withheld to hasten the end? Are feeding tubes or intravenous drips another form of medical treatment? Is it dignified to allow individuals to starve to death? Does the right to die include the right to assistance in suicide? Finally, should the right to die be extended to individuals suffering from painful chronic or degenerative illnesses?

—*Ileana Dominguez-Urban*

Further Reading

Beauchamp, Tom L., and Robert M. Veatch, eds. *Ethical Issues in Death and Dying.* 2d ed. Upper Saddle River, N.J.: Prentice Hall, 1996.

Humphry, Derek, and Ann Wickett. *The Right to Die: Understanding Euthanasia.* New York: Harper& Row, 1986.

Kleespies, Phillip M. *Life and Death Decisions: Psychological and Ethical Considerations in End-of-Life Care.* Washington, D.C.: American Psychological Association, 2004.

Meisel, Alan. *The Right to Die.* New York: John Wiley & Sons, 1993.

Rothman, David J. *Strangers at the Bedside: A History of How Law and Bioethics Transformed Medical Decision Making.* New York: Basic Books, 1991.

Russell, O. Ruth. *Freedom to Die: Moral and Legal Aspects of Euthanasia.* New York: Human Sciences Press, 1975.

United States President's Commission for the Study of Ethical Problems in Medicine and Biomedical and Behavioral Research. *Deciding to Forgo Life-Sustaining Treatment: A Report on the Ethical, Medical, and Legal Issues in Treatment Decisions.* Washington, D.C.: GPO, 1983.

See also: Euthanasia; Infanticide; Institutionalization of patients; Life and death; Medical ethics; Quinlan, Karen Ann; Right to life; Suicide; Suicide assistance.

Soviet psychiatry

Definition: Use of psychiatric techniques and facilities in the Soviet Union as tools of political oppression

Date: Approximately 1862 to the 1990's

Type of ethics: Psychological ethics

Significance: The confinement of religious and political dissidents by Soviet psychiatrists was been a vivid reminder of theways in which a profession can function unethically as an agent of social control.

The persecution of both political and religious dissidents by mental health authorities in the former Soviet Union was long a source of great concern to organizations that monitor human rights violations. Extensive evidence exists that hundreds if not thousands of mentally healthy dissidents were involuntarily committed to Soviet psychiatric hospitals. These individuals were committed in order to remove them from society and thus suppress their dissenting ideas and opinions.

History

Although psychiatric facilities in the Soviet Union practiced this type of abusive social control for many years, Soviet psychiatry was not always an ethically compromised profession. The field of psychiatry was founded in the Soviet Union by Ivan Belinski, a Russian physician, who formed the first Russian psychiatric society in 1862. Belinski promoted psychiatric training and worked to establish outpatient treatment for the mentally ill. Under his leadership, the profession of psychiatry grew rapidly. In 1887, the first Congress of Russian Psychiatrists met in Moscow and endorsed the humane, scientifically informed treatment of mental patients as well as the notion that, if possible, psychiatric patients should be cared for in their home environments. Such ideas put Russian psychiatrists on an equal plane with their fellow practitioners in the rest of the world.

Positive developments continued to take place in the field of Soviet psychiatry after the Communist Revolution of 1917. At the time of the revolution, a People's Commissariat of Health was formed, with a special division devoted to psychiatry. Under the commissariat's leadership, many types of services were offered free of charge to the mentally ill, such as crisis intervention, sheltered workshops, and home care programs. Many Soviet psychiatrists also began to develop an interest in the young field of psychoanalysis, and the major works of Sigmund Freud were widely distributed.

The Advent of Abuse

Problems began to develop during the late 1920's, as Joseph Stalin consolidated his hold on the government of the Soviet Union. Stalin had little concern for the rights of the mentally ill, and he viewed involuntary psychiatric commitments as an effective way to control his ideological opponents. Although psychiatric hospitals continued to treat individuals who suffered from genuine forms of mental illness, they also became a place of involuntary confinement for individuals who openly disagreed with the political or religious doctrine of the government. Labor organizers and artists who advocated creative freedom were favorite targets of the psychiatric establishment. Placing such dissidents in psychiatric facilities served both to remove them from society and to discredit their ideas by allowing the government to label them as insane.

A special diagnostic category, known as "sluggish schizophrenia," was developed. Anatoly Snezhnevsky, a notorious Russian psychiatrist who rose to a position of high authority under the Stalinist regime, defined sluggish schizophrenia as delusions of reforming the country's social system in the mind of an otherwise normal individual. This type of false diagnosis enabled psychiatrists such as Snezhnevsky to label mentally stable individuals as insane and have them involuntarily committed to psychiatric facilities.

Even if such an individual was eventually fortunate enough to be discharged, his or her name was maintained on a national list of mental patients. This registry was distributed to prospective employers and schools, ensuring that the individual would suffer from lifelong discrimination. Doctors who refused to follow the unethical practices of this system were routinely disciplined or even imprisoned. Over time, Soviet psychiatrists became virtual servants of the state, with no professional autonomy and little room for ethical judgment.

The Use of Torture

Psychiatric treatment in the Soviet Union eventually became so abusive that some dissidents were actually tortured during their hospitalization. A convincing account of such treatment has been provided by Anatoly Koryagin, a Soviet psychiatrist who was himself hospitalized involuntarily because he refused to carry out government policy. Throughout his fifteen-month hospitalization, Koryagin was kept on a virtual starvation diet, so that he was severely emaciated and in a constant state of hunger. He was forced to take various psychiatric medications and also reports having had a probe smeared with acid placed in his stomach in order to induce excruciating pain. This type of torture was apparently designed to force Koryagin and other dissidents to renounce their ideological beliefs. Because of such extreme violations of human rights, the World Psychiatric Association (WPA) condemned Soviet psychiatry in 1977. Six years later, the All-Union Society of Soviet Psychiatrists resigned from the WPA rather than face certain expulsion.

Such international condemnation, however, did little to change the field of psychiatry in the Soviet Union. Peter Reddaway, a political scientist who has written extensively about Soviet psychiatric abuse, has noted that only *glasnost* and the reorganization of Soviet society has brought about genuine reform. In what was once the Soviet Union, the reorganized profession of psychiatry appears to be returning to its humanitarian roots.

—*Steven C. Abell*

Further Reading

Amnesty International, USA. *Political Abuse of Psychiatry in the USSR: An Amnesty International Briefing.* New York: Author, 1983.
Bloch, Sidney, and Peter Reddaway. *Psychiatric Terror: How Soviet Psychiatry Is Used to Suppress Dissent.* New York: Basic Books, 1977.
_____. *Soviet Psychiatric Abuse: The Shadow over World Psychiatry.* Boulder, Colo.: Westview Press, 1985.
Fireside, Harvey. *Soviet Psychoprisons.* New York: W. W. Norton, 1979.
Kanas, Nick. "Contemporary Psychiatry: Psychiatry in Leningrad." *Psychiatric Annals* 22 (April, 1992): 212-220.
Koryagin, Anatoly. "The Involvement of Soviet Psychiatry in the Persecution of Dissenters." *British Journal of Psychiatry* 154 (March, 1989): 336-340.
Smith, Theresa C., and Thomas A. Oleszczuk. *No Asylum: State Psychiatric Repression in the Former USSR.* New York: New York University Press, 1996.

See also: Farrakhan, Louis; Human rights; Institutionalization of patients; Mental illness; Oppression; Psychology; Stalin, Joseph.

Stem cell research

Definition: Scientific studies of undifferentiated cells derived from fertilized human embryos less than one week old that have the ability to develop into virtually any other human cell
Date: First discoveries announced in November, 1998
Type of ethics: Bioethics
Significance: Stem cells are uniquely valuable to medical research because they can be directed to become specific types of cells or tissues useful to treat such diseases as juvenile diabetes and heart disease. They can also yield new methods for screening and testing new drugs and provide insights into the earliest stages of human development. However, they are at the center of a major ethical debate over definitions of the beginning of human life.

In 1998, biologist John Gearhart of John Hopkins University and researcher James Thomson of the University of Wisconsin announced that they had isolated embryonic stem cells and induced them to begin copying themselves without turning into anything else. They had apparently discovered how to manufacture cells that could become human tissue.

Both Gearhart and Thomson called on the U.S. Congress to enact clear legal guidelines for future stem cell research. Instead, Congress placed a moratorium on federal funding for experimentation on most fetal tissue. However, no law governed what scientists could do using private funding. A situation then arose in which most stem cell research was in the hands of corporate-backed researchers. This proved to be a mixed blessing. While the situation permitted stem cell research to continue, albeit more slowly, the research was being done by privately funded scientists and was therefore not subjected to the multiple levels of peer review and disclosure normally required of publicly funded researchers.

Producing even greater anxiety was the fact that stem cell research can make human cloning possible. Because stem cell research uses cells from human embryos, controversy developed over the ethical question of when human life begins. Roman Catholic, evangelical, and Islamic religious theorists say that life begins at the moment sperm meets egg. By this view, a single cell can have sacred rights. Scientists counter, however, that technically that process is not what happens. DNA (deoxyribonucleic acid) sets from egg and sperm do not in fact immediately merge, as the egg divides once before the onset of genetic recombination.

Obstetricians sometimes mark the time when life begins at about two weeks after conception—when the fertilized egg implants itself in the mother's womb. *Roe v. Wade*, the 1973 Supreme Court decision permitting women to choose to terminate their pregnancies through abortion, held that viability (the moment when the fetus is capable of existing outside the mother) was significant. Other authorities argue that life begins at the moment when fetal brain activity commences, around the twenty-fifth week of gestation, indicating that the fetus has become human.

The Clinton Administration

In September, 1999, the National Bioethics Advisory Commission appointed by President Bill Clinton released its final report recommending federal funding for research on the derivation and use of human embryonic stem cells. The commission recommended that voluntary consent to the research should be sought only from individuals or couples who have already decided to discard their embryos instead of storing them or donating them to other couples. It further recommended that the sale of embryos remain illegal, and that professional standards should be developed to discourage fertility clinics from increasing the numbers of embryos remaining after infertility treatments that might subsequently become eligible for research.

Ethical and moral problems are associated with manufacturing embryos in the laboratory to be used in research. Most members of American society do not want to see embryos treated as products or as mere objects, fearing that such a development will diminish the importance of parenting, risk commercialization of procreation, and trivialize procreation.

Society, it is argued, has granted embryos a special standing in American law and culture because of their potential to become human beings. Manufacturing embryos for stem cell research would violate that status.

During the early years of the twenty-first century, several clinical trials were utilizing mature stem calls taken from adult human beings. There were, however, severe limitations to this line of research because adult cells are already functionally specialized and their potential to regenerate damaged tissue is thus limited. Adults do not have stem cells in many vital organs, so when those tissues become damaged, scar tissue develops. Only embryonic stem cells, which have the capacity to transform into any kind of human tissue, have the potential to repair vital organs.

Moreover, embryonic stem cells have the ability to reproduce indefinitely in laboratories, while adult stem cells are difficult to grow, and their potential to reproduce diminishes with age. In 2003, a study indicated that deciduous (baby) teeth were a source of stem cells.

Bush Administration and Stem Cell Research in the Twenty-first Century

In a speech delivered on August 9, 2001, President George W. Bush announced that he would allow research on only existing human embryonic stem cell lines, provided that the stem cells came from embryos that no longer had the possibility of developing into human beings. He specifically referred to organs and tissues "harvested" from executed Chinese prisoners and stated that he was limiting federal subsidies to the more than sixty genetically diverse stem cell lines that already existed. (At the time of Bush's speech, the National Institutes of Health identified thirty diverse stem cell lines). Some commentators applauded Bush's decision because it could be used to justify policies such as organ harvesting. Others denounced it because they felt it justified the taking of human life. Today, however, stem cell research involves other avenues with less potential for controversy: adult stem cells, amniotic stem cells, and induced pluripotent stem cells do not involve creating, using, or destroying human embryos. In addition, other less controversial means of acquiring stem cells include cells from the umbilical cord, breast milk, and bone marrow.

—Marcia J. Weiss

Further Reading

Engendorf, Laura K., ed. *Medicine: Opposing Viewpoints.* Farmington Hills, Mich.: Greenhaven Press, 2003.

Holland, Suzanne, Karen Lebacqz, and Laurie Zoloth, eds. *The Human Embryonic Stem Cell Debate: Science, Ethics, and Public Policy.* Cambridge, Mass.: MIT Press, 2001.

Kristol, William, and Eric Cohen, eds. *The Future Is Now: American Confronts the New Genetics.* Lanham, Md.: Rowman and Littlefield, 2002.

Ruse, Michael, and Christopher A. Pynes, eds. *The Stem Cell Controversy: Debating the Issues.* Amherst, N.Y.: Prometheus Books, 2003.

Torr, James D., ed. *Medical Ethics: Current Controversies.* San Diego, Calif.: Greenhaven Press, 2000.

See also: Bioethics; Biotechnology; Brain death; Cloning; Genetic engineering; Human Genome Project; Life, meaning of; Life and death; Medical research; "Playing god" in medical decision making; Pro-life movement.

Suicide assistance

Definition: Active provision of help to a person committing suicide

Type of ethics: Bioethics

Significance: Decisions to assist other human beings end their own lives pose difficult moral dilemmas, and suicide assistance is illegal in most U.S. states.

Terminally ill patients often openly express the wish to hasten their deaths. Such requests may pose dilemmas for persons in the position to assist with the suicides. Historically, the self-induction of death among persons who are severely ill and suffering has been justified by a number of philosophers including Plato, Seneca, and David Hume.

The concept of having a physician assist with a patient's suicide was not widely discussed until after the twentieth century discovery of analgesics and anesthetics. When administered in sufficient quantities, these substances permit the inducement of painless deaths.

Assistance to commit suicide became an increasingly important issue as Americans began to grow significantly older and advances in health care extended life spans among terminally ill patients. Over the second half of the twentieth century, a shift from dying in the home to dying in clinical-care settings and hospitals developed. By the early twenty-first century, approximately 80 percent of American deaths were occurring in medical-care settings. Consequently an increasing number of persons have begun seekingways to die with dignity and in physical comfort.

There has been a growing demand for modern medicine to provide comfortable, pain-free deaths and merciful ends of lives. Studies have shown that approximately 70 percent of the American public favors legalization of physician-assisted suicides or aids in dying. Health-care proxies and advance directives routinely include provisions to ensure that individual patients retain autonomy and control over their dying.

Although committing suicide is not in itself a crime, assisting or failing to take steps to prevent a person's suicide can result in ethical and legal actions. The double effect of providing medications that relieve suffering while at the same time inadvertently shortening a patient's life is an ethically accepted part of medical practice. The withdrawal of life-sustaining but burdensome treatments that leads to death is also an accepted part of medical care, even when such actions hasten death. However, in 2004, *voluntary* active euthanasia was illegal in the United States, and assisted suicide was against the law in the majority of states.

In June, 1977, the U.S. Supreme Court ruled that persons have no right to assistance in committing suicide. However, the Court did not rule out the possibility that state law could legalize physician-assisted suicide. The ruling addressed a narrow federal constitutional question that affects the mentally competent, terminally ill patient who seeks the assistance from a physician to prescribe medication for the purpose of committing suicide. However, states were permitted the right to publicly debate the issue and pass laws that either prohibit or allow physician-assisted suicide. At the federal level, this Supreme Court decision clarified the role of the physician in handling requests from a patient to hasten death. The Supreme Court did not address the role of other health care professionals such as social workers and psychologists. Following the Court's decision, a law to legally sanction physician-assisted suicide in the state of Oregon was passed.

—Frank J. Prerost

Further Reading

Humphry, Derek. *Final Exit: The Practicalities of Self-Deliverance and Assisted Suicide for the Dying.* 2d ed. New York: Dell, 1996.
Quill, T. *Caring for Patients at the End of Life: Facing an Uncertain Future Together.* Boston: Oxford University Press, 2001.
Snyder, Lawrence, and T. Quill, eds. *Physician Guide to End-of-Life Care.* New York: ACP-ASIM Publishing, 2001.

See also: Death and dying; Dilemmas, moral; Euthanasia; Homicide; Infanticide; Kevorkian, Jack; Right to die; Self-preservation; Suicide.

Therapist-patient relationship

Definition: Association between a psychotherapist and client

Type of ethics: Psychological ethics

Significance: Ethical aspects of the therapist-patient relationship are governed both by codes of professional conduct and by statutory law. The relationship raises issues involving paternalism, autonomy, confidentiality, and informed consent.

There are often disagreements among therapists regarding what constitutes the best treatment for a given individual. At last count, almost three hundred different forms of treatment had been described for the alleviation of emotional disorders. Samuel Perry, Allen Frances, and John Clark in group treatments into three broad categories in their book *A DSM-III Casebook of Differential Therapeutics* (1985). These categories are exploratory, directive, and experiential.

Exploratory techniques include psychoanalysis and treatments that are not as lengthy or as frequent as psychoanalysis but utilize at least some psychoanalytic techniques. Proponents of these psychodynamic treatments argue that their treatments are useful for many patients and can be adapted to the requirements of individual patents better than can traditional psychoanalysis, which requires the patient to come to therapy four to five days a week.

Directive techniques include the use of principles derived from the study of how people learn and may utilize reward, punishment, advice giving, or other methods designed to change maladaptive behaviors. For example, some directive therapists argue that patients have learned misconceptions about themselves or others that must be unlearned. Other therapists attempt to reduce patient anxieties by gradually exposing them to frightening situations in order to reduce and eliminate the impact of the anxiety-provoking situation.

Experiential techniques utilize a different perspective. Advocates of these techniques emphasize the expression of feelings. They see little, if any, value in diagnosis or psychiatric classifications. They also object to the power differential found in most therapist-patient relationships. Instead, experiential therapy is viewed as an encounter between two equal individuals who care for each other as real people. Experiential therapists tend to focus on the present and believe that personal growth is an important aspect of therapy. Thus, it is not necessary to be emotionally disturbed to benefit from experiential treatment.

It should be pointed out that these descriptions are necessarily brief and are designed to give the reader an overview rather than a detailed understanding of techniques used in therapist-patient relationships. They are helpful, however, for providing a foundation for understanding some of the ethical issues involved in such relationships.

Informed Consent and Confidentiality

The American Psychological Association's "Ethical Principles and Code of Conduct" (1992) discusses a number of topics relevant to therapist-patient relationships. The code of conduct requires therapists to discuss with patients such topics as the nature and anticipated course of therapy, fees, and confidentiality. Thus, the beginning of a therapist-patient relationship involves the informed consent of the patient.

Daniel R. Somberg, Gerald L. Stone, and Charles D. Claiborn (1993) suggest that this includes discussion of the potential risks of therapy, the length of treatment, the procedures to be used, alternatives to therapy, and the limits of confidentiality. Therapists need to be sure that the patient has given consent freely, and if the patient is unable to give consent legally (for example, if he or she is a young child), permission must be obtained from those who are able to give legal consent. Even with individuals who are not capable of giving informed consent, however, psychologists have an obligation to explain the proposed

intervention and to seek cooperation and agreement. In addition, the therapist must take into account that person's best interest.

With regard to confidentiality, the limits of confidentiality must be discussed. In many jurisdictions, for example, there are limitations on confidentiality when treatment is done in a group or family setting.

There may also be limitations on confidentiality whenever more than one therapist and one patient are present, as in marital therapy, for example. Disclosures of confidential information are not permitted without the consent of the individual unless permitted by law. Usually, disclosures are limited in order to obtain professional consultations and to provide needed professional services. In addition, disclosures can be made in order to protect a patient or others from harm. Such disclosures are discussed further under the duty to warn.

Duty to Warn

This requirement arose out of a suit brought by the parents of Tatiana Tarasoff in the 1970's. Tatiana had been killed by an individual who had been in treatment at the student health facility at the University of California at Berkeley. The patient had revealed to the therapist that he was extremely attached to Tatiana and that he planned to purchase a gun.

The therapist, after consulting with colleagues, concluded that the patient was both mentally ill and dangerous and should be hospitalized. Police interviewed the patient and decided there was no need for hospitalization after the patient agreed not to contact Tatiana. The parents of Tatiana sued, and their attorney eventually came before the California Supreme Court, arguing that the treating therapist should have warned Tatiana Tarasoff or her family and that the patient should have been committed involuntarily to an inpatient facility. Initially, the court decided that not only did the therapist have a duty to warn because of the special relationship between therapist and patient but also that the police might be liable, since their questioning of the patient probably resulted in the patient's decision to terminate treatment. In a later opinion, the same court broadened the duty of the therapist to protect others from dangerous actions of patients but no longer held the police liable.

Since that time, a number of states have passed laws requiring therapists to breach confidentiality in the face of patient threats to harm others. Alan Stone, in his book *Law, Psychiatry, and Morality* (1984), argues that therapists are not effective in consistently evaluating the dangerousness of their patients. Nevertheless, he believes that when a therapist is convinced of the dangerousness of a patient, the special relationship between patient and therapist does justify the legal duty to protect both the patient and the public. Thus, therapists are called upon to balance the interests of society against the interests of patient-therapist relationship.

—Norman Abeles

Further Reading

American Psychological Association. "Ethical Principles of Psychologists and Code of Conduct." *American Psychologist* 47 (December, 1992): 1597-1611.

Crits-Christoph, Paul, and Jacques P. Barber, eds. *Handbook of Short-Term Dynamic Psychotherapy.* New York: Basic Books, 1991.

Perry, Samuel, Allen Frances, and John A. Clarkin. *A DSM-III Casebook of Differential Therapeutics.* New York: Brunner/Mazel, 1985.

Slovenko, Ralph. *Psychotherapy and Confidentiality: Testimonial Privileged Communication, Breach of Confidentiality, and Reporting Duties.* Springfield, Ill.: Charles C. Thomas, 1998.

Somberg, Daniel R., Gerald L. Stone, and Charles D. Claiborn. "Informed Consent: Therapists' Beliefs and Practices." *Professional Psychology: Research and Practice* 24 (May, 1993): 153-159.

Stone, Alan A. *Law, Psychiatry, and Morality.* Washington, D.C.: American Psychiatric Press, 1984.

Syme, Gabrielle. *Dual Relationships in Couseling and Psychotherapy: Exploring the Limits.* Thousand Oaks, Calif.: Sage Publications, 2003.

See also: Confidentiality; Diagnosis; Electroshock therapy; Group therapy; Institutionalization of patients; Medical ethics; Physician-patient relationship; *Principles of Medical Ethics with Annotations Especially Applicable to Psychiatry;* Professional ethics; Psychology; Psychopharmacology.

Triage

Definition: Process of sorting victims of war, accident, or disaster to determine priority of medical treatment
Type of ethics: Bioethics
Significance: Triage is perhaps the most extreme single instance of ethically difficult resource allocation.

It requires immediate, life-and-death decisions to be made about whose injuries will be treated first and who will be left to wait. The major ethical question raised by triage is whether severity of injury is the only appropriate criterion for determining priority, or whether other considerations such as age, occupation, social status, membership in the enemy military, and criminal record may be considered.

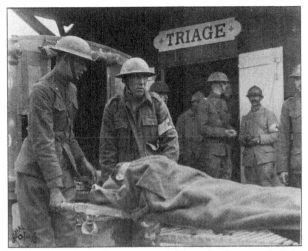

Triage station, Suippes, France, World War I. by Otis Historical Archives.

Triage employs a utilitarian calculation concerning how to do the most good with whatever resources are available, determining which patients will be helped at all, and in which order those to be helped will be treated. Triage may be employed in any situation in which all the injured, sick, or wounded cannot be treated: on the battlefield, at the site of a natural disaster, in the first moments of a traffic accident, in the emergency room of a large hospital, or in a country suffering from mass starvation. Triage is more easily defended than are some other types of utilitarian calculations, since there is no intent to sacrifice the innocent for the greater good of the majority. Since triage does require that one make a "quality of life" judgment before one decides which victims will be helped, however, it may be an ethically objectionable practice.

If it is wrong to judge who is worth helping and who is not, then it is arguable that triage should be replaced with a "first-come-first-helped" principle.

—Daniel G. Baker

See also: Lifeboat ethics; Medical ethics; Military ethics; "Playing god" in medical decision making; Utilitarianism.

UNESCO Declaration on the Human Genome and Human Rights

Identification: First universal instrument in the field of biology and ethics
Date: Adopted on November 11, 1997

Type of ethics: Bioethics

Significance: Written in several iterations by representatives from around the world, this statement aims at striking a balance between the rights and freedoms of human beings and the goal of ensuring freedom of research.

In early 1995 the Bioethics Unit of the United Nations Educational, Scientific, and Cultural Organization (UNESCO) prepared a draft declaration regarding human genome research. The purpose was to prepare a universal instrument designed to safeguard cultural diversity while presenting an ethical stand on genetic research. In September, 1995, that draft was revised by a committee that met in Paris. The revised draft was given to the meeting of government experts in July, 1997, for their comments. The fifth session of the UNESCO International Bioethics Committee reconvened in October, 1997, in Cape Town, South Africa.

The final version that emerged was the Universal Declaration on the Human Genome and Human Rights, which was adopted unanimously by the 188 members of the general conference of UNESCO on November 11, 1997. Five years later, the International Society for Bioethics (SIBI) awarded its SIBI Award to UNESCO for the declaration.

The preamble of the declaration presents UNESCO's mandate and previous declarations regarding human rights, discrimination, research, and related issues ratified by member states. The declaration's first section is about human dignity and the human genome. It underscores the unity of all human beings and calls for scientists to respect their subjects, not reduce individuals to genetic characteristics or base their work solely on financial gain. The second section, about the rights of concerned persons, calls for informed consent, rigorous preliminary research, nondiscrimination, confidentiality, and punitive damages for violation of an individual's genome.

The third section is about research on the human genome and has three articles that call for respect of human rights over research; forbidding practices contrary to human dignity, such as human cloning and making universally available the results of research.

The fourth section deals with the conditions under which scientific research is conducted. Its four articles pertain to meticulousness in inquiry, intellectual freedom, restriction of uses to peaceful purposes, and committee assessments. The fifth section pertains to solidarity and international cooperation, with two articles about global cooperation. The sixth section is about the promotion of principles in the declaration, and the final section is about implementation of the declaration by each of the member states.

—Manoj Sharma

Further Reading

Boon, Kevin Alexander. *The Human Genome Project: What Does Decoding DNA Mean for Us?* Berkeley Heights, N.J.: Enslow, 2002.

Roberts, Leslie. "Controversial from the Start." *Science* 291 (2001): 1182-1188.

Sulston, John, and Georgina Ferry. *The Common Thread: A Story of Science, Politics, Ethics and the Human Genome.* New York: Bantam, 2002.

Toriello, James. *The Human Genome Project.* New York: The Rosen Publishing Group, 2003.

See also: Biotechnology; Genetic engineering; Genetic testing; Human Genome Project; International Covenant on Civil and Political Rights.

World Health Organization

Identification: International agency that initiates and coordinates efforts to solve global health problems

Date: Founded in 1948

Type of ethics: Bioethics

Significance: Also known as WHO, the World Health Organization was founded in response to the perceived need for an entity capable of addressing medical and health problems that cross national boundaries to affect entire regions, continents, or the planet as a whole.

International health organizations have existed from the first decade of the twentieth century, but WHO's scale is far larger than that of anything that existed earlier. It admits and provides services to all states, regardless of whether they are U.N. members. Its tasks fall by their nature into three categories. The first, carried out mainly at headquarters in Geneva, might be called "minding the store": maintaining international drug standards and sanitary and quarantine regulations, and disseminating information regarding epidemics, drug addiction, chemical residues, radiation hazards, and so forth. The second involves providing education and technical assistance for member nations, experts to help plan and set up local health centers, teachers, temporary medical personnel, and so forth. The third is mobilization to deal with specific diseases, including services provided by the central organization, national health bodies, medical laboratories, and other entities.

Smallpox was declared eradicated from the world in 1980. The list of other diseases that WHO has targeted for eradication is striking. In 1988, the organization set the year 2000 as the target date for eradicating polio. That goal was not met, but by the year 2004, only 530 cases of polio were reported worldwide, and those cases were confined to six nations: India, Pakistan, and Afghanistan in South Asia, and Nigeria, Niger, and Egypt in Africa. WHO also set 2000 as the target date for eradicating leprosy. Progress in eradicating that bacterial disease has not been nearly as dramatic as has been the case for polio, but the incidence of leprosy through the world was dramatically reduced by 2004 and was continuing to decline. Other diseases that WHO has targeted for eradication include AIDS, tuberculosis, malaria, yellow fever, cholera, and diphtheria.

In the nondisease category, WHO's goals include the providing of new contraceptives, chemical and mechanical, male and female; the promotion of health practices for mothers and children in developing countries; and even antismoking campaigns. As its charter states, WHO aims for "the highest possible level of health" for all people.

—Robert M. Hawthorne, Jr.

See also: Bioethics; Geneva conventions; International Red Cross; League of Nations; United Nations.

Economics & Business

Economics involves the study of the production, distribution, and consumption of goods and services. A great many of its practitioners see it as a science, not much different than physics or chemistry in that they are engaged in the collection and analysis of data—in this case, specific facts and information concerning the various commercial activities on which this science focuses (such as income and income distribution, indebtedness, employment trends and job growth, and a nation's overall "gross domestic product" or GDP). Economists also engage (as do physicists and chemists) in the development of theories explaining some of the trends observed in those data.

Economic activities are essential and inescapable features of the lives of every individual, as well as of families and of other larger groups or communities of individuals (like towns and cities)—and ultimately of nations involved collectively in the production and exchange (trade) of their citizens' and communities' commercial goods and services. Economists generally group these complex economic relationships into two categories: microeconomics (treating the financial and commercial activities and relations among individuals, families, and local communities), and macroeconomics (focused on large scale financial and commercial relationships of states and nations, as well as the commercial interactions among these large-scale entities. The relationship and interactions (the "causal impacts") between the two branches of differently-scaled economic activity are themselves matters of extensive study and debate.(For example, what impact will tariffs or trade barriers imposed by one nation-state upon another's goods and services ultimately have on those individuals, families, and distinct communities dwelling within each of those nations?)

Students of human history and anthropology recognize, of course, that such production and exchange (trade) of goods and services is a principle characteristic of human social behavior, likely originating with "hunter-gatherer" civilizations stretching back into "prehistoric" ages. Presumably, the barter, exchange, and trade of goods and even services between individuals and social groups "caught on" and became commonplace because it generally redounds to the mutual benefit of all parties to the exchange.

But the organized and systematic examination of these activities (and the corresponding attempts to understand, predict, and control them through the formulation and advocacy of rival theories about economic relationships) originated only comparatively recently. Credit as the "first economist" or "Father of Economics" usually is accorded to a Scottish academic scholar at the University of Glasgow, Adam Smith (1723-1790). His great work, the *Wealth of Nations* (1776) is likewise credited as being the first truly thorough, scientific examination of both the micro and macro-economic relationships among individuals and communities dwelling within a single nation-state.

Smith is certainly credited (and quite frequently praised, or sometimes denounced) for having been the first to formulate important economic concepts like "the free market," "the invisible Hand," and "gross domestic product" (GDP) as a measure of a nation's total overall production of "wealth" (goods and services). It is often overlooked, however, that he himself was not, strictly speaking, an "economist" (there were no such individuals at the time), but an ethicist. Smith held the Chair of Moral Philosophy at the University of Glasgow during a period of intellectual flowering known as the "Scottish Enlightenment." The fundamental question underlying the detailed analysis of economics in *Wealth of Nations* is: "What structure of fundamental economic relationships ought to be instituted and practiced by individuals and organizations, and encouraged by governments and politicians, so as to promote the greatest possible benefit for all involved or affected?"

Readers who consult the introduction and selected articles in Volume One of this resource will quickly recognize that Smith is implicitly invoking a form of moral reasoning known as "utilitarianism," stressing that the correct, morally sound practice or policy is that which promotes the greatest possible good distributed amongst the greatest possible number, when compared to every possible alternative. Smith's surprising (if now famous) answer at first seems paradoxical from the standpoint of ethics: the greatest benefit accruing to all members of a nation, he claims, is achieved by allowing each individual or organization participating in the nation's economy complete freedom to pursue his or her own immediate self-interests.

Smith is suggesting that "selfishness" or self-interest (an orientation thought by most people to be amoral, if not downright immoral), when pursued on a microeconomic scale by individuals and small groups of people engaged in "business" (commercial activities and transactions of various kinds),will invariably lead at the macroeconomic level to the benefit—the wealth and prosperity—of all citizens residing within the nation that permits or encourages such "free market" or *laissez-fair* commercial practices. In Smith's case, the objective measure of this claim was precisely a nation's gross domestic product (GDP). Scientifically speaking, his hypothesis, as examined in detail in his book (and to be verified or refuted, at least in principle, by evidence), was how the GDP would be maximized in any nation that refrained from overly interfering in or controlling its citizens' economic interactions. ("Let them be," or "let it alone," is the approximate meaning of the French idiom, *laissez-faire*.)

Economics, and economic relationships among individuals, communities, and organizations (like private commercial firms or "businesses" engaged in the production and distribution of goods and services) are thus firmly grounded in ethics and moral philosophy. Economics (and business) involve fundamental moral questions, such as: How should we interact with and treat one other? For what should we strive in our own personal lives, or attempt to achieve on behalf of our families, fellow citizens (including employees and customers), and communities as a whole? And ultimately, how can we organize and arrange our economic practices so as to allow human life itself to flourish, and our material well-being to prosper?

Economic relationships and policies obviously figure centrally in such questions, since they have material and concrete effects on our health, security, and happiness—and so are properly regarded as involving ethics. The articles in this section examine specific ethical questions, challenges, obstacles, and critiques of economic practices and relationships, as well as of economic theories (like Smith's free market) and the political policies that influence them. These concepts and issues include questions about the extent to which "material well-being" and financial prosperity are essential ingredients in human happiness and flourishing.

One strident and searing moral critique of Smith's theory of *laissez-faire*, free market capitalism, for example, argues that this form of economic organization in any society does not ultimately produce the results promised in its moral self-justification. Instead, the "capitalist" feature of that theory and its practice—namely, the private, unregulated ownership and operation of businesses as "the means of production" of goods and services—tends to concentrate the wealth derived from these commercial activities in the hands of comparatively few persons who actually own these organizations and institutions, rather than allowing the wealth to flow more or less equitably to members of the wider public at large (as Smith presumed it would finally do). Workers, and in particular, employees, in particular, do not benefit nearly as much as they should for their own individual efforts and contributions to economic productivity. Instead, it is in the self-interest (at least, narrowly conceived) of the owner of capital, or the employer in the business, to exact as much labor as possible from employees and to maximize his or her own profits by paying them as little as possible in exchange (in the form of wages paid for their labor). This result, some critics object, is an inherent structural defect in the free market itself, leading inevitably to unfortunate and morally unjustifiable outcomes.

That ultimate social consequence is extreme (and morally unjustifiable) economic inequality in any society characterized by free market economic relationships. The free market promotes the concentration of vast wealth in the hands of the few (the "capitalists"), while leading to impoverishment and virtual enslavement (immiseration) of the vast majority of rank-and-file workers, who are wholly dependent for their individual and family livelihood upon wages paid for their labor. Most famous among the critics of free-market capitalism was the German economist and social reformer, Karl Marx (1818-1883), whose work in sociology, political philosophy, and economic theory (e.g., *The Communist Manifesto*, 1848; *Capital*, 1867) came to exert enormous influence on subsequent worldwide political debates surrounding the relationship between forms of economic organization and the achievement of social justice. Articles in this section explore the wide-ranging criticisms of prevailing economic theories, as well as moral arguments advocating more just and fair alternative policies in their place.

Businesses and industries, as the principal entities composing any sort of economy based upon broad scale production and exchange, come in for a large share of this critical examination. In Adam Smith's account, their unfettered activity holds the key to wealth and prosperity for all. They, and their workers and laborers, driven by personal self-interest, are engines of creativity and innovation. Their most successful owners and managers are visionary, risk-taking entrepreneurs whose competitive spirit drives the growth of overall domestic production, resulting in affordable goods and services that are finally available to everyone, including the workers and employees whose efforts produce them in abundance. The latter are enabled to participate and prosper in this economy through the availability of useful employment, resulting in the wages they garner for their productive activity.

Critics, however, see precisely the opposite: workers (as Marx complained) indeed engage in demeaning labor under harsh and unsafe condition to produce goods and services, but their own meager wages do not enable them to afford these comparative luxuries. Moreover, the businesses themselves are otherwise engaged in consuming vital resources and destroying the surrounding environment—polluting cities, fouling the atmosphere, and ravaging the surrounding countryside of precious land, timber and water, without penalty and without contributing their proportionate share of the costs (economic and otherwise) accruing to society at large from this ongoing environmental damage and resource depletion.

Not surprisingly, these sharply contrasting portraits of business and industry set the stage for highly fraught and emotional conflicts of moral and political opinion that are not always fair or accurate portrayals of the legitimate underlying concerns of either side. But useful and important questions are posed by these conflicts. Some, like the overall welfare of the natural environment, or the role of technological advances and innovations in this process, are taken up separately in a subsequent section of this volume. But a plethora of significant moral issues remain that are addressed in the remaining articles in this section devoted to a specific field of moral inquiry known as business ethics.

What, finally, is the proper role of business within larger society? Is it merely the production of goods and services, the provision of useful work, employment, and livelihood for wage earners, and the production of wealth for owners or shareholders? Those are tall orders in themselves, even if nothing more is demanded or expected of business organizations. Is the work provided indeed productive, useful, and adequately compensated to afford

employees and their families at least a minimally acceptable standard of living? Is the workplace safe, and free from hazards to the health of workers and the surrounding population? Do the individual workers, supervisors, managers and owners treat each other (not to mention their customers, clients, and the general public) with decency and mutual respect—in particular, do they circumspectly refrain from deceiving, coercing, abusing or otherwise attempting to take unfair advantage of one another for financial gain, let alone exploiting their supervisory or employment powers for the gratification of unsavory personal appetites? And are the opportunities for employment and promotion equally open to all who seek them, and are these finally awarded solely on the basis of relevant, job-related qualifications or achievements, free from arbitrary (and usually irrelevant) prejudices (such as race or gender)?

And for that matter, do societies truly need all the immense varieties of goods and services produced and offered for sale in a fully free market? Or does marketing and advertising by organizations competing with their business rivals tend to create illusory needs, or aim to deceive customers or disguise vital information needed to make informed choices about what to buy and what to use or consume (let alone assess the likely impact of those choices upon the health and safety of the consumer)? In particular, do marketing and advertising strategies aim to exploit the weakness or ignorance of vulnerable populations (like children, or the elderly)? Are the actual sales and exchange procedures engaged in to purvey these goods and services fully forthcoming and truthful, or do they rely on fraud, disinformation, or deception? These, and a host of related issues and questions, comprise the field of business ethics, and constitute the principal foci of the remaining articles in this section.

Accuracy in Media

Identification: Politically conservative nonprofit watchdog group that critiques news media coverage of political, social, legal, and economic issues
Date: Founded in 1969
Type of ethics: Media ethics
Significance: One of the best-known American news media pressure groups, Accuracy in Media has been criticized for being more biased than the liberal news media that it criticizes.

Accuracy in Media (AIM) raises the issue of defining ethical news coverage of public issues. It has been financed through donations and dues paid by members and major conservative donors, such as billionaire Richard Mellon Scaife. AIM's staff and supporters monitor daily media coverage and provide news outlets immediate criticism of what they regard as instances of biased or otherwise unethical reporting.

Staff members also solicit and regularly receive citizen complaints about perceived biased news coverage. The organization's nationwide activities include providing media guides, holding conferences, providing books and tapes to members, maintaining an intern program, and maintaining an information site on the World Wide Web (www.accuracyinmedia.org).

AIM publishes a twice-monthly newsletter, the *AIM Report*. It also broadcasts a daily news commentary program, *Media Monitor*, over more than 150 radio stations throughout the United States; publishes a syndicated weekly newspaper column; and supports a speaker's bureau. AIM members are encouraged to attend the annual shareholder meetings of large media organizations and initiate mass letter-writing campaigns to newsrooms to complain about specific acts of biased or incomplete news coverage.

The organization also presents annual awards for what members judge to be outstanding examples of fair and accurate news coverage. Criticisms of AIM, often from activists on the political Left, charge the organization with being more biased and less accurate than the media they monitor. In part in response to AIM, political liberals established a rival media monitoring organization, Fairness and Accuracy in Reporting (FAIR), in 1986.

—Robert E. Dewhirst

See also: American Society of Newspaper Editors; Fairness and Accuracy in Reporting; Journalistic ethics; Media ownership; News sources; Photojournalism.

Advertising

Definition: Public promotion of goods or services designed to increase their sales, directly or indirectly

Type of ethics: Media ethics

Significance: Advertisers have a financial stake in crafting their messages in ways that persuade consumers to buy their products. At the same time, they also have a responsibility to craft their messages in ways that do not take unfair advantage of prospective consumers or competitors, or negatively influence vulnerable populations, such as children.

The ethics of advertising are professional ethics, not theoretical ethics. They operate to serve various loyalties, to clients, advertising agencies, consumers, and society in general. Often, the identified constituents have different—and conflicting—needs that must be balanced. Moreover, advertising is ubiquitous, pervasive, and influential, so its potential effects should be considered when determining what level of corresponding responsibility should accompany it.

Advertising as Communication

Advertising is one of the oldest forms of mass communication. Since the days of the European town crier, advertising has carried messages of people who things to sell to people who might want to buy those things. The modern American advertising industry is a multibillion-dollar business, and advertising messages are inescapable. In addition to advertising's role in providing information to potential consumers, it may be argued that advertising can have a profound influence on societal values and norms.

Advertising influences the target audience's worldview. Consumers who routinely see stereotypical images and unrealistic depictions of physiques and relationships in radio and television commercials, magazine ads, and other forms of advertising may blur the lines between reality and fantasy. Advertising can promote materialism by keeping images of bigger, better, new, advanced, and the latest "must haves" in front of consumers. Advertising can also influence the self-images of people who receive its messages. Advertisements usually depict beautiful, young people enjoying life with the help of such products as the right toothpastes, the right shampoos, the right clothes, and the right cars, and against the glamour of the people using those products in advertisements, the average person rarely measures up.

Advertising as Business

Advertising supports the free market. Businesses attempt to increase their profits by increasing sales, and advertising can place sales messages in front of the audiences who are most likely to respond. Increased sales of products can lead to lower prices, and that in turn can aid consumers. It is thus clear that both marketers and consumers both can benefit from advertising.

According to social contract theory, businesses exist not only for their own profit but also for the benefit of their consumers, and they are thus accountable to their consumers. In addition, much advertising is the product of advertising agencies, and advertising agencies expect practitioners to be loyal to the agencies, which are also businesses that operate for profit in their own right.

Professional Codes of Ethics

The advertising industry has several professional organizations that publish codes of ethics as industry guidelines. These organizations include the American Association of Advertising Agencies, the American Advertising Federation, the Promotional Products Association International, and the Outdoor Advertising Association of America. Professional journalism organizations also publish guidelines on advertising as well. Guidelines may be stated as "action-guides," moral statements that are prescriptive, are normative, and direct people toward particular actions while keeping them from other actions.

The American Association of Advertising Agencies developed a creative code to support healthy competition. Specifically, the code stipulates that association members should not knowingly create false, misleading, or exaggerated claims; dishonest testimonials; misleading price claims; unsupported claims; or content offensive to decency or members of minority groups. The code also stipulates that comparative advertising be truthful, substantiated, and tasteful.

Ads that compare an advertiser's products and services with those of the competition may be helpful to consumers but must be handled fairly. Dishonest testimonials are from people who do not actually use the products that they tout or who have hidden conflicts of interest.

The American Advertising Federation created "The Advertising Principles of American Business," a document that cautions members in eight areas. It stipulates that advertisers should be truthful, be prepared to substantiate claims, avoid untruthful comparisons, refrain from bait-and-switch advertising, offer specific information about guarantees and warranties, avoid false or misleading price claims, limit testimonials to real and competent witnesses, and avoid content that is offensive or indecent. Substantiation is a legal consideration as well, and advertisers are expected to have prior proof before making claims in advertising.

The Promotional Products Association International, a specialty advertising trade group, focuses its guidelines

on customer service. It asks its members to offer quality products and services and to work toward complete customer satisfaction. The Outdoor Advertising Association of America is an organization of owners and operators of standardized outdoor advertising displays. Its code focuses on the responsibility of advertisers to ensure that outdoor displays do not detract from their surroundings. It specifically stipulates that members refrain from placing advertising displays in areas of natural scenic beauty, parks, or historical monuments and requires that members follow regulations and zoning laws. Members may erect advertising displays only on properties that they lease or own, and the displays must be truthful, attractive, and consistent with high moral standards.

Sweepstakes competitions are often attention-getting promotions used by advertisers, and the Magazine Publishers of America even has a code for ethical sweepstakes promotions. Critics have charged that the advertising industry has marketed sweepstakes in ways that are confusing to consumers. The guidelines outline specific components of contest solicitations and state that each component should be easy to read and understand, that the individual's chances of winning should not be overstated, and that recipients of the promotions should not be duped into ordering or extending their magazine subscriptions by being led to believe that doing so will enhance their changes of winning the competitions.

Twenty-first Century Issues

The codes of ethics outline valuable lists of do's and don'ts for advertising professionals. However, as society has evolved, additional ethical issues have emerged. For example, only during the late twentieth century did the advertising industry begin to make a large-scale effort to depict members of racial minorities in advertisements targeting the general population. Minorities had long been token representatives in popular media, but the failure to include them in general interest advertisements projected narrow views of American society.

Ads also long employed stereotypes to make points. For example, the Frito-Lay Corporation once used a character called the "Frito Bandito" to advertise its corn chips. The Frito Bandito provided an attention-getting and easily remembered product icon, but at the cost of reinforcing negative stereotypes of Mexican Americans as criminals. Advertisements that objectify women and men are common. For example, ads may depict human bodies without heads or show a satiny-smooth human shoulder and arm that are not connected to the rest of a body. Critics charge that such ads are destructive in that they promote the practice of viewing individuals as body parts rather than as whole people.

Political advertising has its own issues. Political advertising plays an important role in society and can directly influence political outcomes. Political ads that commonly receive criticism are those that rely only on emotional appeals rather than providing information that can be evaluated by the receiver and those that distort opponents' records. Subliminal messages have also been criticized, although it is unclear whether or not subliminal messages have any impact on the audience.

During the 2000 election, the George W. Bush presidential campaign pulled a Republican National Committee ad that criticized opponent Al Gore's plan on prescription drugs and used subliminal messages to tell television viewers that the opponents were the "bureaucRATS."

Another controversial issue is the manner in which advertisers target vulnerable populations, particularly children. Advertisers have been criticized for targeting children through ads promoting movies they are too young to view and through ads promoting cigarettes to children too young to buy tobacco products legally. RJ Reynolds's Joe Camel campaign ended because of the cartoon character's popularity with the younger set. Young children spend a lot of time watching television and, in some cases, listening to the radio. Many advertisers are cognizant of their younger audience members and refrain from exposing them to vulgar, age-inappropriate content.

Some debate has centered on advertising to older persons and members of minority groups. Direct mail, in particular, has been used to get the attention of older people who are in the habit of opening official-looking envelopes and who may confuse advertising materials with official business documents. On the other hand, because older persons are not children, many people would argue that they should not need to be protected from advertisers.

Another controversial type of advertising is "advertorials"—advertisements packaged to look like news. Advertorials blur the lines between advertising and news and can confuse people who are exposed to a diverse variety of nontraditional sources of news. For example, audiences who are accustomed to network news, cable news channels, entertainment news, and other sources may not readily distinguish advertorial programming from genu-

ine news programs because the presentations are similar. To avoid confusion, most advertorials, or "infomercials," include disclaimers. In addition, many news departments have guidelines designed to protect the editorial process from the influence of the advertising department.

Unusual situations may develop when advertisers try to get audience attention with shock tactics. People for the Ethical Treatment of Animals (PETA) once produced an advertising campaign called "The Holocaust on Your Plate," which showed pictures of naked concentration camp inmates alongside pictures of abused animals. Its caption read, "To animals, all people are Nazis." The ad succeeded in attracting attention but offended many people, especially Jews, who thought that it trivialized the Holocaust. PETA supporters maintained that people are animals, too, and that animals should get similar protection.

The terrorist attacks of September 11, 2001, negatively affected many businesses in America. After the attacks, many corporations ran ads to offer condolences for the victims of the attacks and to express hope for the future of the country. However, some of these advertisements also tied into commercial pitches that critics saw as attempts to capitalize on tragedy. For example, General Motors ran a "Keep America Rolling" campaign that offered consumers zero percent financing on new vehicles. The ad attempted to link buying a new American car with being patriotic, but the link was weak.

Pharmaceutical companies have long advertised their products to doctors and other medical professionals. During the mid-1990's, the industry began greatly increasing direct advertising appeals to consumers. This trend spurred a debate in the medical community, because some say that direct-to-consumer advertising puts incomplete information in the hands of people with medical problems who may not be trained to interpret it. Other observers, however, have said that it is valuable for patients to know their medical options and to be able to ask their doctors about advertised medications that may help them.

Finally, Internet advertising has opened up a new way for advertisers to reach audiences, and a new set of issues has arisen. Unsolicited e-mail, or spam, clogs the in-boxes of millions of Internet users daily, and companies are devising ways to help users filter out unwanted messages. Opt-in options give users the opportunity to ask to be added to e-mail mailing list. Opt-out options give the user the opportunity to ask to be deleted or unsubscribed from e-mail lists, but they assume tacit approval unless the messages are received. Opt-out options require users to take steps to avoid receiving unsolicited e-mail.

Legal Considerations

The Federal Trade Commission regulates the American advertising industry and has the power to constrain and punish advertisers who create ads that are deceptive, fraudulent, or misleading. In addition to ethical considerations, advertisers must consider legal ramifications of their advertising. Many consumers are suspicious of advertisers who have financial stakes in their buying decisions; however, ethical advertising can serve needed functions for businesses and consumers alike.

—Alisa White

Further Reading

Bivens, T., ed. *Mixed Media: Moral Distinctions in Journalism, Advertising, and Public Relations.* Mahwah, N.J.: Lawrence Erlbaum, 2004. Examines ethical issues in the mass media in view of social responsibility, truth, and harm.

Day, L. A. *Ethics in Media Communications.* Belmont, Calif.: Wadsworth, 2000. Provides an ethical decision-making model to help readers decide how to resolve moral dilemmas presented in hypothetical cases and in real life. Also covers ethical theories and includes the ethics codes of the American Advertising Federation and other professional organizations.

Donaldson, Thomas. *Corporations and Morality.* Englewood Cliffs, N.J.: Prentice-Hall, 1982. Sets forth a social contract theory for corporations based on loyalties to consumers and society as a whole.

Fink, Conrad C. *Media Ethics: In the Newsroom and Beyond.* New York: McGraw-Hill, 1988. Case studies and examples of moral dilemmas that arise in journalism and other media professions. Offers a framework whereby readers can make moral decisions.

Jamieson, K. H., and K. K. Campbell. *The Interplay of Influence: News, Advertising, Politics and the Mass Media.* 5th ed. Belmont, Calif.: Wadsworth, 2000. Examines the relationship among media outlets and the influence the messages they carry have on the public.

Leslie, L. *Mass Communication Ethics: Decision Making in Postmodern Culture.* Boston: Houghton Mifflin, 2000. Establishes an ethical framework in theory and philosophy, and discusses cases in cultural context.

Rotzell, K. B. "Persuasion in Advertising." In *Media Ethics: Cases and Moral Reasoning,* edited by C. Christians et al. 6th ed. New York: Longman, 2001. Considers moral dilemmas that confront media practitioners through the framework of the Potter Box, a four-step ethical decision-making model that asks subjects to define dilemmas and identify values, principles, and loyalties before making decisions.

See also: Applied ethics; Business ethics; Children's television; Choice; Consumerism; Electronic mail; Infomercials; Journalistic ethics; Marketing; Sales ethics; Tobacco industry.

Advice columnists

Definition: Journalists who offer advice on wide-ranging topics in columns that are typically syndicated in many newspapers and magazines

Date: The first advice column appeared in 1901

Type of ethics: Media ethics

Significance: Influential columnists can profoundly affect the attitudes and behavior of their readers, even though the columnists may lack expertise in their subjects or exhibit bias.

In 1901, the *New York Journal* began publishing the first nationally recognized advice column, "Dorothy Dix Talks." For fifty years, Dix dispensed advice to lovelorn, confused, and worried readers. For the most part, she avoided difficult and taboo subjects. However, by the 1950's, when Ann Landers and her twin sister, Abigail Van Buren, began their long careers as advice columnists, America had changed. Landers and Van Buren were able to take on more sensitive issues than Dix ever discussed,

Esther "Eppie" Pauline Friedman Lederer, a.k.a. 'Ann Landers', 1961. By Fred Palumbo, World Telegram staff photographer.

such as homosexuality, abortion, abusive parenting, and premarital sex. The two women enjoyed immense success, but not without criticism. While neither Landers nor Van Buren had any formal training in psychology or counseling, their status as widely syndicated and respected columnists gave them the appearance of authority. Their popularity alarmed many mental health professionals, who often disagreed with the advice the columnists provided. For example, Landers initially regarded homosexuality as an illness, even though the American Psychiatric Association had concluded otherwise. Landers later softened her stance on that subject, but only after homosexuality began to gain wider acceptance in America.

Twenty-first century advice columns are more popular than ever; they also tend to be more specialized. Readers want specific advice from experts in health, the law, technology, investing, and other subjects. Even personal advice columns—the successors of Dix, Landers, and Van Buren—have become more narrowly focused, targeting limited demographic groups. This has raised new issues. Columnists, unlike other journalists, deal in opinions as well as facts. However, while facts may be checked, opinions are easily subjected to manipulation. With the proliferation of specialized and technical columns, it has become more difficult for newspaper and magazine editors to "backstop" their columnists, challenging assertions and rooting out bias.

Columnists are particularly prone to conflicts of interest. Lawyers writing columns on law may suggest that home buyers should hire lawyers to review their sales documents, knowing full well that this may bring new business to their own law firms. However, this relatively benign form of conflict of interest pales in comparison to scandals in the securities industry, where investment columnists have touted specific stocks that they themselves, or their employers, own and from which they hope to profit from future eventual sales.

Technology is providing a sea change for advice columnists. With the Internet, anyone can claim to be an expert and give advice. In consequence, ethical constraints on advice columnists will be further eroded.

—*Robert L. Palmer*

Further Reading

Fink, Conrad C. *Media Ethics*. Boston: Allyn and Bacon, 1995.

Grossvogel, David I. *Dear Ann Landers: Our Intimate and Changing Dialogue with America's Best-Loved Confidante*. Chicago: Contemporary Books, 1987.

Paul, Pamela. "Dear Reader, Get a Life." *Psychology Today* 36, no. 4 (2003): 56-71.

Winans, Foster R. *Trading Secrets: An Insider's Account of the Scandal at the "Wall Street Journal."* New York: St. Martin's Press, 1986.

Zaslow, Jeffrey. *Tell Me About It: A Personal Look at the Advice Business*. New York: William Morrow, 1990.

See also: Cohen, Randy; Confidentiality; Ethical Principles of Psychologists; Homosexuality; Insider trading; Journalistic ethics; Tabloid journalism.

Affirmative action

Definition: Aspect of government programs designed to increase the participation of statistically underrepresented groups in education, employment, and public works

Date: Concept developed during the mid-1960's

Type of ethics: Civil rights

Significance: Affirmative action programs have promoted cultural diversity and reduced invidious discrimination against women and members of particular racial minorities; however, other persons frequently feel threatened by the programs.

The federal Civil Rights Act of 1964 and similar laws of the states prohibit employers and educational institutions from discriminating against individuals on the basis of race, national origin, or sex. Initially, the term "affirmative action" referred simply to employment policies designed to enforce these laws and ensure equal opportunities for members of groups that had historically encountered prejudicial attitudes and discriminatory practices. However, as these groups, especially African Americans, continued to experience subtle forms of discrimination, regulatory agencies and courts began to consult statistical data when assessing compliance with the laws.

By the early 1970's, the term "affirmative action" was being applied to aggressive programs of recruitment that could be evaluated on the basis of quantitative results. Most programs included racial and gender preferences, and some utilized "quotas" or "goals and timetables." Arguing that the programs contradicted the principle of equal opportunity, white men often claimed to be victims of "reverse discrimination."

Moral Arguments

Almost all modern ethicists endorse the ultimate goal of an equality of opportunity for every individual, without regard to characteristics such as sex, ethnicity, or religion, except in special situations in which such characteristics are relevant. Because of the pernicious consequences of past discrimination, however, defenders of affirmative action policies argue that some preferences will be necessary for a limited period of time in order to level the playing field. In contrast, opponents insist that discriminatory practices are inherently unjust, even when used as a means toward a just goal.

Proponents tend to believe that racism and sexism are profoundly entrenched in American beliefs, practices, and attitudes. Believing that white males are beneficiaries of unacknowledged privileges, moreover, they typically assume that women and minorities, except for invidious discrimination, would occupy prestigious positions in rough proportion to their numbers. Some radical proponents justify affirmative action as atonement for past discrimination and argue that justice demands "equality of results" rather than "equality of opportunity."

Opponents, in contrast, usually argue that the relative successes of various groups are more influenced by culture than by invidious discrimination. As an example, they point to the conspicuous achievements of Jewish Americans and Asian Americans in the liberal professions, in spite of continuing discrimination. Believing that some groups will always excel in particular endeavors, the opponents conclude that preferential treatment, once begun, will continue indefinitely. From their perspective, it is wrong to penalize an individual person because of membership in a group judged to be excessively successful.

Many libertarians view affirmative action as a pernicious example of "social engineering" that denigrates individual freedom, and they insist that the value of liberty is more basic than equality. Persons committed to the idea of meritocracy usually concede that government has a legitimate interest in promoting equal opportunity, but they strongly oppose the notion that government should decide on the statistical representation of groups in various professions. A basketball team, for instance, is more likely to win if it recruits its players strictly on the basis of their ability to play basketball.

Moral debates about affirmative action frequently deal with questions about which persons should be beneficiaries. One problem is that racial classifications are socially defined and constantly changing.

Another problem is that affirmative action tends to limit the opportunities of white males raised in poverty, while preferences sometimes go to women and minorities from relatively higher socioeconomic backgrounds. Proponents insist that race and socioeconomic class are closely correlated and that, in any case, discrimination has significantly limited the opportunities of women and minorities of all classes.

One suggested compromise is to base affirmative action programs primarily on socioeconomic status rather than race or sex.

Legal Controversies

The literal words of the "equal protection" requirement of the U.S. Constitution and almost all civil rights laws appear to require race neutrality and to extend equal rights to all citizens, including white men—who are generally regarded as the least disadvantaged people in the society. Proponents of affirmative action, however, argue that these legal documents must be interpreted in accordance with their primary objective, which is to achieve equality for African Americans and other victims of longstanding discrimination. Proponents emphasize that affirmative action programs, in contrast to earlier Jim Crow discrimination, do not totally exclude any persons or deny their full human dignity.

During the late 1970's, the U.S. Supreme Court approved several aggressive programs of affirmative action. In *Regents of the University of California v. Bakke* (1978), the Court examined a competitive medical school's policy of reserving a fixed percentage of admissions to members of disadvantaged minorities, even if those applicants' qualifications were less impressive than those of some white applicants who are denied admission. Although the Court disallowed the use of specific quotas, it endorsed admissions policies that gave some consideration to race in an attempt to promote a diverse enrollment. In *United Steelworkers v. Weber* (1979), the Court allowed a private employer to utilize a racial quota rather than seniority in order to achieve a minimum number of skilled African American workers.

By the 1990's, there was a strong public backlash against affirmative action programs. In 1996, California voters approved Proposition 209, which prohibits state institutions, including universities, from giving any preferences based on race, ethnicity, or sex. Likewise, the U.S.

Supreme Court held that a number of affirmative action programs were discriminatory. In *Adarand Constructors v. Peña* (1995), the Court ruled that all race preferences were inherently suspect and must be narrowly designed to further compelling governmental objectives. For several years it appeared that the Court might strike down all race-based preferences. In *Grutter v. Bollinger* (2003), however, it allowed educational institutions to take race into account as a "plus" factor in order to obtain a "critical mass" of minorities. However, it also prohibited rigid quotas, required individualized evaluation of each applicant, and called for the end of all preferences in twenty-five years. In 2013 the Supreme Court ruled on *Fisher v. University of Texas*, declaring that schools are permitted to use race-conscious admission practices so long as the school can prove that the practice is their only avenue for achieving a diverse student body and is specifically designed to achieve that goal. Most recently, in 2018 a case was raised by a conservative group, Students for Fair Admissions on behalf of Asian American students who claim Harvard University discriminates against students of Asian heritage. The decision in this case could likely reach the Supreme Court, and a new conservative majority among the panel could mean an end to the practice of affirmative action in college admissions.

—*Thomas Tandy Lewis*

Further Reading

Beckwith, Francis, and Todd Jones, ed. *Affirmative Action: Social Justice or Reverse Discrimination?* New York: Prometheus Books, 1997.

Cahn, Stephen, ed. *The Affirmative Action Debate.* New York: Routledge, 2002.

Eastland, Terry. *Ending Affirmative Action: The Case for Colorblind Justice.* New York: Basic Books, 1997.

Katznelson, Ira. *When Affirmative Action was White: An Untold History of Racial Inequality in Twentieth -Century America.* New York: W. W. Norton & Company, 2005.

Kennedy, Randall. *For Discrimination: Race, Affirmative Action, and the Law.* New York: Pantheon, 2013.

Kranz, Rachel. *Affirmative Action.* New York: Facts On File, 2002.

Leiter, Samuel, and William Leiter. *Affirmative Action in Anti-Discrimination Law and Policy: An Overview and Synthesis.* Albany: State University of New York Press, 2002.

Rosenfeld, Michel. *Affirmative Action and Justice: A Philosophical and Constitutional Inquiry.* New Haven, Conn.: Yale University Press, 1993.

Skrenty, John. *The Ironies of Affirmative Action: Politics, Culture and Justice in America.* Chicago: University of Chicago Press, 1996.

See also: Americans with Disabilities Act; Disability rights; Discrimination; Inequality; Integration; Political correctness; Reverse racism; Supreme Court, U.S.; Title IX.

Agribusiness

Definition: Term applied to the increasing integration of the world's food production—and consumption—into the processes of modern big business

Type of ethics: Business and labor ethics

Significance: The rationalization and coordination of agricultural production and distribution and their subordination to the requirements of global investment practices have combined with technological developments to transform the ethics of the world food supply.

According to its advocates, agribusiness methods have been vindicated by past successes and offer the only hope of being the world's continued ability to feed its people, as supplies of land and water dwindle while human population increases. The first Green Revolution may have confounded prophets of mass starvation, such as the early nineteenth century political economist Thomas Malthus, but new techniques are required if human lives, and particularly high-consumption lifestyles, are to survive.

Critics of agribusiness view its tactics as predatory and contrary to the long-term stability and wellbeing of human society. They view global agribusiness as disrupting local ecologies and economies, and restructuring and subordinating them according to the vicissitudes of high finance. Developing world famines are due, such critics claim, to inequities of distribution as international markets are manipulated to maximize profits. Apart from the impact on the hungry, critics have also focused attention on the effect of global corporate agricultural development on the prospects of the traditional family farm.

Ethical Debates

Broadly, the ethical debates about agribusiness can be seen as falling into four overlapping areas: business, international relations, environmental ethics, and biotechnology.

As a form of business, agribusiness involves the routine issues of business ethics, such as fairness in relation to employees, integrity in dealing with competitors, honesty toward customers, and decency in relation to society. This includes concerns about the working conditions of farm and factory laborers. In the light of its importance and worldwide impact, agribusiness is also part of the ethics of international relations, particularly the debate over globalization.

Critics question whether the opportunities that agribusiness opens up in countries outweigh new distortions introduced into local economies. As an enterprise based on the cultivation of domesticated fauna and flora, agribusiness represents one of humanity's most significant impacts on the natural environment. As such, agribusiness is deeply enmeshed in issues of environmental ethics, such as crop selection, soil depletion, and rain-forest reduction.

Critics question whether agribusiness decisions lead to sustainable development or merely quick profits. Factory farming is particularly subject to criticism.

Agribusiness is also becoming increasingly embroiled in the ethical quandaries of biotechnology, particularly vigorous debates about genetic engineering, such as cloning issues. Other issues include risk estimation, risk and benefit distribution, concerns about extending human control across "natural" boundaries, and the impact of human design and decision making on the diversity of the gene pool.

—*Edward Johnson*

Further Reading

Berry, Wendell. *The Unsettling of America: Culture and Agriculture.* San Francisco: Sierra Club Books, 1977.

Charles, Daniel. *Lords of the Harvest: Biotech, Big Money, and the Future of Food.* Cambridge, Mass.: Perseus Publishing, 2001.

Manning, Richard. *Food's Frontier: The Next Green Revolution.* New York: North Point Press, 2000.

See also: Animal rights; Biotechnology; Business ethics; Developing world; Ecology; Famine; Genetically modified foods; Globalization; Hunger; Lifeboat ethics; Multinational corporations.

American Federation of Labor

Identification: First permanent national-international federation of skilled trades

Date: Founded on December 8, 1886

Type of ethics: Business and labor ethics

Significance: The American Federation of Labor (AFL) asserted the rights of workers to organize on their own behalf and upheld the dignity of labor against the impositions of the business community.

A successor to the Federation of Organized Trades and Labor Unions, which was established in November of 1881 in Pittsburgh, Pennsylvania, the American Federation of Labor (AFL) became the first permanent American trade union federation. Earlier American national labor organizations, such as the National Labor Union (established in 1866) and the Knights of Labor (established in 1871), had been loosely structured industrial unions with polyglot memberships and broad economic and political programs. Despite some limited successes, they ultimately failed because of internal divisions, the dispersion of their energy, and the hostility of the public and the business community.

The AFL was founded largely through the efforts of Samuel Gompers and Adolf Strasser, both of whom were immigrant cigar makers and socialists. A pragmatic organization, it was tailored to American workers' lack of class consciousness and emphasized the improvement of wages, hours, and working conditions—that is, bread-and-butter unionism. Its constituent organizations—carpenters, coal miners, building tradespeople, and railroad workers—enjoyed almost complete autonomy and enlisted skilled workers almost exclusively.

The relatively high wages of skilled workers made it possible for the organization to accumulate substantial strike funds. AFL membership rapidly grew to two million by 1910 and more than tripled by 1950. Publicly, the AFL sought the mediation of labor disputes, the enactment of labor legislation, limits on immigration, protection from technological unemployment, and, whenever possible, collaboration with employers. The AFL's merger with its rival, the Congress of Industrial Organizations, in 1955 (founding the AFL-CIO) created the free world's largest labor union. The merger also resulted in diminished autonomy and the acceptance of industrial unionism and political action.

—*Clifton K. Yearley*

See also: International Labour Organisation; Knights of Labor; Labor-Management Relations Act; National Labor Union; Work.

American Society of Newspaper Editors

Identification: Organization that encourages newspaper editors to concern themselves with the ethics, quality, and history of editorial and news policy

Date: Founded in 1922

Type of ethics: Media ethics

Significance: Of the many groups monitoring the news media for fairness and accuracy, the American Society of Newspaper Editors is among the most influential because it is made up of editors themselves.

At the beginning of the twenty-first century, the American Society of Newspaper Editors (ASNE) had more than one thousand members. Its members are the directing editors who determine editorial and news policy on daily newspapers across the country. The organization has several goals: to improve the quality of journalism education and of newspaper writing and editing, to help newspaper managers work more effectively with employees, to encourage adequate minority representation on newspaper staffs, and to protect First Amendment rights and freedom of information. To achieve these goals, ASNE publishes several periodicals for editors, educators, and others, and presents awards for excellence in editing and writing.

ASNE monitors its own members to see how newspapers are responding to various needs. This often leads to controversy. During the late 1980's, ASNE began surveying daily newspapers to determine whether gay and lesbian journalists were being given fair treatment in hiring and promotion, and whether the AIDS epidemic was receiving fair and adequate coverage. During the same period, ASNE researched the hiring and promotion of members of racial and ethnic minorities, and debated whether to publicize the names of newspapers with poor minority-hiring records.

—Cynthia A. Bily

See also: Accuracy in Media; Journalistic entrapment; Journalistic ethics; Media ownership; News sources; Photojournalism; Tabloid journalism.

Antitrust legislation

Definition: Federal laws that define certain actions of large companies, or combinations of companies, as illegal because they give the actors too much power in the marketplace

Type of ethics: Business and labor ethics

Significance: Antitrust laws attempt to create marketplace conditions that are fair to all buyers and sellers.

Federal antitrust legislation regulates the behavior of American businesses, in particular large businesses and business combinations. The combinations that are regulated can take the form of agreements, formal contracts, and legally identified organizations such as trusts and holding companies. Through antitrust legislation, governments attempt to balance the goal of business, which is to control the market to earn profits, with the goal of providing all marketplace actors, including both buyers and sellers, with the opportunity to compete. By definition, noncapitalist societies do not have antitrust laws, since firms are owned and operated by the state rather than competing independently.

Federal law generally recognizes that size confers benefits on firms and can be beneficial to society, as in the case of "economies of scale." A firm with economies of scale can produce its product at a lower cost per unit the more it produces. The law also recognizes, however, that the existence of a large firm may make operation more difficult for smaller firms and that consumers generally benefit from having a choice among sellers. These considerations prompt the drafting of antitrust legislation.

History

One of the earliest pieces of antitrust legislation was the Statute of Monopolies, which was enacted in England in 1623. It stated that monopolies, or single firms producing a given product in a certain market, were not allowed. That law had many exceptions but did set the precedent for later antitrust legislation. The United States developed the most comprehensive antitrust legislation in the world. The Sherman Antitrust Act of 1890 represented the first clear statement that the U.S. government disapproved of abuse of market power by large firms. That law led to an era of "trust busting" over the next thirty years, particularly under the administration of Theodore Roosevelt. The Sherman Antitrust Act was somewhat vague in its prohibitions. The Clayton Antitrust Act of 1914 clarified the actions that would be subject to antitrust prosecution.

Two major cases in 1911 clarified judicial thinking on antitrust policy. The U.S. Supreme Court ordered the breakup of Standard Oil and of the American Tobacco Company. The Court established the "rule of reason" approach, whereby the law proscribed only actions that were "unreasonable" restraints of trade. The Court ruled that largeness of a company was not necessarily an offense but that both of those companies had used the power associated with their size in "unreasonable" ways.

Antitrust Issues

The history of antitrust legislation, both in the United States and elsewhere in the world, has been uneven. Actions prohibited at one time have later been allowed, and actions that were legal have been prohibited. In general, the law has come to specify particular actions that are not allowed and has clarified the conditions under which various actions are allowed.

In the United States, the Robinson-Patman Act of 1936 specified types of price discrimination that are illegal. Price discrimination consists of setting different prices for different customers when those differences are not justified by differences in the cost of serving customers. Price discrimination prevents each customer from being offered the best price on a product.

Other laws and regulations concern tie-in sales, in which a consumer has to buy one product before being allowed to buy another; resale price maintenance, whereby a manufacturer forces distributors to charge a minimum price; and base-point pricing, under which competitors agree to set prices as if their products were delivered from a given "base point," thereby not using a location that allows lower transportation costs to offer lower prices to customers.

The law covers both "horizontal" business combinations (those at the same stage of production or sale, such as a retailer forming a contract with or acquiring another retailer) and "vertical" combinations (those at different stages of production, such as a manufacturer buying a retail outlet for its product).

Ethical Principles

The most basic goal of antitrust legislation is to create a marketplace that produces the best results for society. Economists define an "efficient" marketplace as one that produces a given product at the least cost. In this sense of "good" results, a large firm can benefit society if it operates under economies of scale. A firm that has control over its customers because it is the only seller (or only one of a few sellers), however, may not pass those cost advantages on to customers. Antitrust legislation attempts to prevent that possibility. Some firms with economies of scale are allowed to operate under regulation by the government. Examples include telephone companies, cable television operators, and electric companies.

Most market economies respect freedom. Freedoms, however, can conflict. The freedom of businesses to get together and agree to charge the same price conflicts with the freedom of consumers to shop around to find the lowest price. Most governments that have consciously considered the issue have ruled in favor of the consumer, to at least some extent. The Sherman Antitrust Act, for example, outlaws every "contract, combination...or conspiracy" in restraint of trade. That means that firms are not allowed to hinder competition among themselves. Antitrust legislation seeks to clarify which actions constitute hindrances of competition.

—*A. J. Sobczak*

Further Reading

Armentano, Dominick T. *Antitrust and Monopoly: Anatomy of a Policy Failure*. New York: Wiley, 1982.
Hahn, Robert W., ed. *High-Stakes Antitrust: The Last Hurrah?* Washington, D.C.: AEI-Brookings Joint Center for Regulatory Studies, 2003.
Howard, Marshall C. *Antitrust and Trade Regulation: Selected Issues and Case Studies*. Englewood Cliffs, N.J.: Prentice-Hall, 1983.
Kintner, Earl W., and Mark R. Joelson. *An International Antitrust Primer*. New York: Macmillan, 1974.
Low, Richard E. *Modern Economic Organization*. Homewood, Ill.: Richard D. Irwin, 1970.
Posner, Richard A. *Antitrust Law: An Economic Perspective*. Chicago: University of Chicago Press, 1976.
Sherman, Roger. *Antitrust Policies and Issues*. Reading, Mass.: Addison-Wesley, 1978.
Wells, Wyatt. *Antitrust and the Formation of the Postwar World*. New York: Columbia University Press, 2002.
Whitney, Simon N. *Antitrust Policies: American Experience in Twenty Industries*. New York: Twentieth Century Fund, 1958.

See also: Business ethics; Capitalism; Communism; Economics; Monopoly; Price fixing; Profit economy.

Art

Definition: Human creative expression
Type of ethics: Arts and censorship
Significance: Issues of censorship and artistic freedom are raised by artistic production in virtually all human societies. In addition, some philosophers and artists believe that aesthetic creation is in itself a profoundly moral activity.

The earliest discussion of the relationship of art and ethics goes back to the Greek classical period, when philosophers such as Socrates, Plato, and Aristotle considered art and its goodness and importance in relationship to the search for truth and virtue in human life. Socrates believed that the beautiful is that which both serves a good purpose and is useful, therefore uniting the beautiful and the good. He viewed the arts as being only incidental to other concerns, however, not of primary importance. Plato considered the relationship of art to nature and truth, and its resulting ethical function, which led him to reject art. Art was imitation and therefore was not good because imitations were untrue. Plato loved beauty but hated painting.

Aristotle separated ethics and art by describing goodness as present in human conduct and beauty as existing in a motionless state. He saw moral good and aesthetic value as separate considerations. In the modern understanding, art—specifically, the fine arts of drawing and painting, sculpting, dance, music, theater, photography, and creative writing—is the act and process of creating. Works of art are the creations of the artistic process. It is the contact of the artist's work—the painting, dance, musical composition, and so forth—with the lives of other people that creates an ethical responsibility for the artist. Such contact invites participation by persons other than the artist in the artistic product, and it is this participation that implies an ethical responsibility.

Artistic Freedom

Artistic freedom is publicly determined by ethical values; art as a creative act is independent of morality, but the artist as a human being is not. By making artwork public, artists involve themselves in the lives of others, necessarily resulting in accountability for the contributions they are making to their lives. While artists are not responsible for every effect their work may have, tension can exist between their aesthetic interests and the moral interests of the community. The relationship of art and ethics is different from the relationship of art and aesthetics in that ethics deals with the concepts of what is good or bad, while aesthetics deals with the concepts of what is beautiful or ugly. These relationships are different yet closely related, because ethics raises questions of morality and propriety and aesthetics helps judge the aims and values of art: Is the end product beneficial for human life? Does it elevate the human spirit? Does the work of art respect the common good in intellect and conscience?

Answers to these questions involve the public in the role of censor when ethical standards are violated by the artist. Public censorship and self-censorship can determine the success or failure of a work of art but not the success or failure of the artistic process. It is generally not subject matter but the manner of its treatment that causes

art to be subject to moral ethical considerations. The very nature of art requires complete artistic freedom for the artist in order to "create," to bring about something new that is highly personal and unique. To impose limits on the creative process often stymies the goal of the process. Many people believe that art in itself is amoral, that the process cannot be subjected to ethical judgment because of its very nature. It is, however, the result of this process, the creative work of art, that is subject to ethical judgment. Moral value is judged by its contribution to the richness of human experience. Is it honest and fair-minded as well as aesthetically pleasing? Does it elevate the human spirit?

The issues of artistic freedom and artistic responsibility and the subordination of one to the other are at the heart of art and ethics. Using sensitivity, imagination, and inspiration, it is the responsibility of the artist to nourish the human spirit and express human emotion. Certain types of subject matter, such as nudity, cultural social taboos, religious concepts, and sexual perversion, can be difficult for the general public to accept. Art that utilizes such subjects is often subject to ethical examination and/or censorship. The issues of forgery, plagiarism, and honest business practices are also important to the relationship of art and ethics. Professional artistic standards in the modern world require that works of art be original if presented as such and that ethical business standards apply to the marketing of works of art.

The relationship of art and ethics touches the lives of all artists who share their work with others. The artist is often on the edge of cultural and societal changes, supporting as well as challenging traditional and modern ethical standards, broadening and enriching the human experience.

—Diane Van Noord

Further Reading

Barasch, Moshe. *Theories of Art: From Plato to Winckelman.* New York: New York University Press, 1985.

Benjamin, Walter. "The Work of Art in the Age of Mechanical Reproduction." In *Illuminations,* edited by Hannah Arendt. Translated by Harry Zorn. London: Pimlico, 1999.

Eldridge, Richard. *The Persistence of Romanticism: Essays in Philosophy and Literature.* New York: Cambridge University Press, 2001.

Haapala, Arto, and Oiva Kuisma, eds. *Aesthetic Experience and the Ethical Dimension: Essays on Moral Problems in Aesthetics.* Helsinki: Philosophical Society of Finland, 2003.

Hygen, Johan B. *Morality and the Muses.* Translated by Harris E. Kaasa. Minneapolis, Minn.: Augsburg, 1965.

McMahon, A. Philip. *Preface to an American Philosophy of Art.* Port Washington, N.Y.: Kennikat Press, 1968.

Marcuse, Herbert. *The Aesthetic Dimension: Toward a Critique of Marxist Aesthetics*. Boston: Beacon Press, 1978.

Maritain, Jacques. *The Responsibility of the Artist*. New York: Scribner, 1960.

Taylor, Harold. *Art and the Intellect*. Garden City, N.Y.: Doubleday, 1960.

Tolstoy, Leo. *What Is Art?* Translated by Aylmer Maude. Introduction by Vincent Tomas. Indianapolis: Hackett, 1996.

See also: Art and public policy; Book banning; Censorship; Christian ethics; Golden mean; *Index librorum prohibitorum*; Mapplethorpe, Robert; Plagiarism.

Art and public policy

Definition: Relationship between artistic freedom of expression and governmental and public policies and attitudes

Type of ethics: Arts and censorship

Significance: Public funding of the arts raises issues of freedom of speech, cultural bias, and appropriate uses of taxpayer money.

The legislation creating the National Endowment for the Arts (NEA) and the National Endowment for the Humanities (NEH), passed by the U.S. Congress in 1965, maintained that "it is necessary and appropriate for the federal government to help create and sustain not only a climate encouraging freedom of thought, imagination, and inquiry, but also the material conditions facilitating the release of this creative talent." In a speech at Amherst two years earlier, President John F. Kennedy had pledged support for artistic achievement, stating, "I look forward to an America which commands respect not only for its strength but for its civilization as well."

The Arts and American Culture

During the 1960's, there was widespread agreement across the United States that the time had come for federal, state, and local governments to subsidize the arts; however, the notion that public funds could properly be spent on art was never universally embraced. Traditionally, in the fabric of American life, the arts were considered marginal. Puritan contempt for artistry outlived colonial times. Among the grievances held against the British by Boston patriots during the 1770's was that the soldiers of King George III staged plays. The anti-obscenity campaigns of Anthony Comstock and others in the nineteenth century masked profound mistrust of artists, art, and free expression. Until Franklin D. Roosevelt's Works Progress Administration created programs to get artists off the relief roles, government support for the arts was restricted to funding for military bands, statuary in public spaces, and adornment of public buildings.

The National Endowment for the Arts, resulting from years of lobbying by arts organizations, was hailed as a wise first step toward cultural democracy. The endowment immediately contributed to a flowering of the arts at the local level, nudging state arts councils into being and fostering unprecedented attention to arts education. After President Richard M. Nixon came to power in 1969, however, his NEA Chairperson Nancy Hanks set about increasing the endowment's funding by favoring well-heeled elitist institutions such as symphony orchestras and large urban museums. The endowment began to back away from individual artists and small arts organizations. By 1981, when President Ronald Reagan took office, there was a serious movement to relegate funding for the arts to the private sector. This was thwarted by pressure from major arts institutions, and the endowment survived with some cuts.

Culture Wars

During Reagan's administration, powerful forces began to use the "immorality" of the arts as a rallying point for fund-raising and political gain. The failure of any meaningful public arts education ensured that much contemporary art would remain incomprehensible to the masses and that isolated examples of publicly supported art works that were difficult, heterodox, or sexually explicit could offend people whose previous exposure to art was minimal. The propaganda of the religious right exploited the belief that art was at best a frill and at worst a cause of moral turpitude and treason. A typical advertisement from Pat Robertson's Christian Coalition asked members of Congress: "Do you want to face the voters with the charge that you are wasting their hard-earned money to promote sodomy, child pornography, and attacks on Jesus Christ?"

Within the U.S. Congress, the most powerful adversary of the arts was North Carolina senator Jesse Helms, a former television personality who was given to taking the University of North Carolina to task for the teaching of such "filth" as Andrew Marvell's 1650 poem "To His Coy Mistress." In 1989, outraged by an NEA-supported exhibit of Robert Mapplethorpe's occasionally homoerotic photographs, Helms, a conservative Republican, attached to NEA funding legislation an amendment forbidding the funding of "obscene or indecent materials," work that "denigrates the objects or beliefs of a particular religion or nonreligion," or work that denigrates particular persons "on the basis of race, creed, sex, handicap, age, or national origin."

This Helms Amendment was stripped away from the appropriations bill by the House of Representatives, but its language was reflected in a pledge the NEA began to require of its grantees, who were asked to sign statements promising not to use NEA money to create anything obscene. Interpreted as a loyalty oath that exercised prior restraint on artistic expression, the anti-obscenity pledge sparked an uproar.

More than thirty grant recipients, including Joseph Papp of the New York Shakespeare Festival, refused to sign; some artists sued. The pledge was quietly retired at the end of the 1990 fiscal year. Congress, however, soon augmented the agency's enabling legislation with a clause stating that NEA-supported art must reflect "general standards of decency and respect for the diverse beliefs and values of the American public." Although blandly worded, the clause cast a wide net and had an insidious effect on grantmaking policy.

From 1989 through the 1990's, a succession of subsidized artists and arts organizations were effectively demonized by right-wing activists, both secular and religious. In response, President George Bush's appointee as NEA chairman, John Frohnmayer, and his successor, Anne-Imelda Radice, preemptively vetoed a number of grants that had been approved by peer panels. The artists most typically affected were gay men, lesbians, feminists, AIDS activists, and members of racial minorities: Robert Mapplethorpe, Andres Serrano, David Wojnarowicz, Todd Haynes, Mel Chin, Marlon Riggs, Kiki Smith, and many others. At the heart of this cultural strife was enmity between those who saw the NEA as custodian to a Eurocentrist tradition and those who believed that the NEA should nurture art at the grassroots level, acknowledging the diverse cultures that constitute the United States. The real issue was a clash of incompatible American dreams. In this context, concern for "your hard-earned tax dollars" was disingenuous.

Defunded performance artists Karen Finley, Tim Miller, Holly Hughes, and John Fleck—the "NEA Four," whose concerns included sexual issues—fought back by suing to reclaim their fellowships. After receiving out-of-court restitution of grant money in 1993, the NEA Four continued litigation in order to challenge the arts agency's "decency and respect" clause, which they viewed as an unconstitutionally vague measure that facilitated viewpoint discrimination. In 1993, when Democratic president Bill Clinton selected Jane Alexander to replace Radice as chair of the NEA, many believed the public-funding debate was over. A respected actress, Alexander was the first working artist to head the NEA; it was assumed that she would bring vision and integrity to the role of NEA chair. However, during Alexander's tenure, the Republican-dominated 104th Congress, led by House Speaker Newt Gingrich, sought aggressively to eliminate "socialistic" government services. In 1994, threatened with draconian cuts or extinction, the NEA's governing body, the National Council on the Arts, began preemptively vetoing grants awarded by peer panels in various disciplines, targeting anything conservatives could use as propaganda.

When Alexander resigned in 1997, the NEA's budget had been reduced to $99.5 million from its 1993 appropriation of $176 million. The agency's spending power had dipped below its late 1970's levels. Awards to individual artists had been eliminated in all but a few literary categories. The NEA had been restructured in a way that placed more emphasis on its administrative role in funding state, jurisdictional, and regional cultural agencies.

Meanwhile, the NEA Four's legal initiative, *Finley v. National Endowment for the Arts*, made its way through the judicial system. When lower courts ruled in favor of the artists, the Clinton administration appealed the case at every turn. In 1998, it reached the U.S. Supreme Court. To the dismay of many arts professionals and First Amendment advocates, the William Rehnquist court upheld the NEA's "decency and respect" clause. Writing for the majority, Justice Sandra Day O'Connor interpreted the clause as "merely hortatory" language that "stops well short of an absolute restriction."

In a rigorous dissent, Justice David Souter said the proviso "should be struck down on its face." He declared its language "substantially overbroad," with "significant power to chill artistic production." Souter noted that the high court was, in effect, giving the NEA permission to practice viewpoint discrimination, and he asserted that "the government has wholly failed to explain why the statute should be afforded an exemption from the fundamental rule of the First Amendment that viewpoint discrimination in the exercise of public authority over expressive activity is unconstitutional.... "

Once the decency clause had obtained the Supreme Court's imprimatur, oversight of artistic content by public officials became more overt. Following the *Finley v. National Endowment for the Arts* ruling, the best-known local censorship imbroglio took place in New York City in 1999. That year, Mayor Rudolph Giuliani targeted the Brooklyn Museum over an exhibit including Anglo-Nigerian artist Chris Ofili's iridescent, stylized painting of an African "Holy Virgin Mary." The work involved a lump of elephant dung, an African symbol of fertility and renewal that Giuliani interpreted as blasphemous. Failing to obtain court approval for shutting down the show or freezing the museum's city funding, the mayor eventually revived New York's dormant Cultural Advisory Commission and redirected its mission toward decency issues.

Most arts advocates consider such machinations superfluous. Institutions dependent in part upon government subsidy almost always play it safe. In the case of the NEA, its yearly per capita expenditure on "controversial" art was, in fact, infinitesimal. In 1992, when the agency was near its budgetary peak, the combined budgets of the National Endowments for the Arts and Humanities added up to about 0.024 percent of the total federal budget. In 2002, thanks to his skill at distancing the NEA from creation of art, the new chairman, William J. Ivey of the Country Music Foundation, who succeeded Jane Alexander, managed to obtain an NEA budget of $115.7 million—far below its appropriations during the first Bush administration. At the beginning of the twenty-first century, the United States government continued to spend less on the arts than any other Western industrialized nation.

At the start of the new century, the future of public arts funding hinged on whose vision of the United States will prevail, and on the availability of arts education. Former arts administrator Edward Arian had assessed the struggle in his 1989 book, *The Unfulfilled Promise*: "The stakes in the contest are high. The right to artistic experience cannot be separated from the quality of life for every citizen, the opportunity for full self-development for every citizen, and the creation of the open and tolerant personality that constitutes the underpinning of a democratic society."

—*James D'Entremont*

Further Reading

Alexander, Jane. *Command Performance: An Actress in the Theater of Politics*. New York: Da Capo Press, 2001.

Arian, Edward. *The Unfulfilled Promise: Public Subsidy of the Arts in America*. Philadelphia: Temple University Press, 1989.

Binkiewicz, Donna M. *Federalizing the Muse: United States Arts Policy and the National Endowment for the Arts, 1965-1980*. Chapel Hill: University of North Carolina Press, 2004.

Bolton, Richard, ed. *Culture Wars: Documents from Recent Controversies in the Arts*. New York: New Press, 1992.

Dowley, Jennifer, and Nancy Princenthal. *A Creative Legacy: A History of the National Endowment for the Arts Visual Artists' Fellowship Program*. Introduction by Bill Ivey. New York: Harry N. Abrams, 2001.

Frohnmayer, John. *Leaving Town Alive: Confessions of an Arts Warrior*. Boston: Houghton Mifflin, 1993.

Heins, Marjorie. *Sex, Sin, and Blasphemy: A Guide to America's Censorship War*. New York: New Press, 1993.

Zeigler, Joseph Wesley. *Arts in Crisis: The National Endowment for the Arts Versus America*. Chicago: Chicago Review Press, 1994.

See also: Art; Censorship; Mapplethorpe, Robert; Motion picture ratings systems; Song lyrics.

Betting on sports

Definition: Legalized gambling on the outcome of sporting events that is sanctioned by, and sometimes promoted by, governmental bodies

Type of ethics: Personal and social ethics

Significance: Although sometimes defended as a way of discouraging organized crime from dominating gambling, legalized betting on sports has created other ethical problems.

Wagering on sporting events has existed at least since the time of the ancient Greek Olympic Games, but it now pervades many parts of the world. In the early twentieth century, the influence of organized crime resulted in scandals in both professional and amateur sports and led to greater vigilance by governmental bodies. The sanctioning or tacit approval of betting on sports events by the media has reduced the involvement of organized crime but has undoubtedly made betting on sports more popular than ever.

The question of the advisability of allowing betting to flourish legally is part of the larger question of whether gambling should be permitted at all. In a society of religious diversity and widespread religious skepticism, prohibitions based on specific religious doctrines do not command widespread allegiance. In a country such as the United States, such prohibitions are likely to be condemned as violating the separation of church and state as well as being constitutional affronts to personal freedom. Important arguments remain, however, to the effect that betting on sports events is harmful both to the bettors and to the sports on which they bet.

Although liberal moralists are likely to argue that the follies of weak individuals may be addressed without impinging on the freedoms of others, gambling may be objected to as leading to personal dissolution and the neglect of family and other social responsibilities. Regardless of whether a given behavior is intrinsically wrong, however, it becomes a legitimate concern of citizens and lawmakers if it leads to criminal behavior that is costly or destructive to society. Compulsive betting, like addiction to drugs, may lead participants into levels of financial ruin that in turn offer strong temptations to commit actual crimes, such as larceny, to sustain the addiction.

With specific reference to sports betting, opponents of the routine modern publication of point spreads and betting odds on games in the sports pages of daily newspapers see these practices as encouragements to more widespread wagering than would otherwise be the case, thus increasing the numbers of bettors. Published point spreads offer inducements to bettors and sports participants alike. An individual athlete urged to shave the margin of victory may conclude that merely winning by a closer margin than expected is not as serious as "throwing" a game; however, such behavior poses a threat to the integrity of games such as basketball and football in which spreads are widely publicized and discussed.

A final objection to legalized betting is that emphasizing the importance of betting odds tends to persuade sports devotees of the dubious proposition that the most important measure of the worth of sport is the money that can be made, whether by playing or gaming.

—Robert P. Ellis

Further Reading

Pavalko, Ronald M. *Risky Business: America's Fascination with Gambling.* New York: Wadsworth, 1999.

Walker, Michael B. *The Psychology of Gambling.* New York: Pergamon Press, 1997.

See also: Family values; Lotteries; Medical ethics; Native American casinos; Relativism; Responsibility; Vice.

Book banning

Definition: Suppression of literary works deemed to be politically or socially unacceptable or otherwise threatening

Type of ethics: Arts and censorship

Significance: Books are generally banned when their contents are judged to be immoral; however, to many people, book banning itself is immoral.

As a result, it is an inherently controversial practice. Book banning is an ancient activity practiced throughout history and the world. The first recorded book banning occurred in Western civilization in 387 bce, when Plato recommended that Homer be expurgated for immature readers. Four hundred years later, the Roman emperor Caligula tried to ban Homer's *Odyssey* (c. 800 bce) because he feared that the book's strong theme of freedom and liberty would arouse the citizenry against his autocratic rule. In 1559, Pope Paul IV issued a list of prohibited books, the *Index librorum prohibitorum.*

Book Banning in the United States

In the United States, the First Amendment to the Constitution seems unequivocally and absolutely to guarantee freedom of speech, no matter how that speech is expressed, without interference by the government. The First Amendment states in part that "Congress shall make no law...abridging the freedom of speech." In fact, however, this freedom is by no means absolute or unfettered. Donna E. Demac correctly points out that the history of freedom of expression in the United States is a complex mixture of a commitment to personal rights and intolerance of ideas deemed subversive, dissident, or obscene. Certain books, by the very nature of their subject matter or writing style, will offend the values and attitudes of certain individuals or groups. As Kenneth Donelsen has observed: "Any book or idea or teaching method is potentially censorable by someone, somewhere, sometime, for some reason." A book's ideas may be disliked, the book may be perceived to ridicule certain individuals or to ignore others; or the book may be judged to be dangerous or offensive. If these parties believe the book has transgressed the bounds of acceptability, they may take action to have the book banned.

Book banning is in fact a common and everyday occurrence in the United States. More than a thousand incidents are recorded each year, and no doubt many other incidents go unrecorded or unrecognized. William Noble called book banning "a pervasive ethic" and noted that banning incidents arise throughout the country and in many forums—school board meetings, public libraries, legislative hearings, ad hoc parental complaints, governmental committees, private groups assessments, open court and even commercial publishing decisions. "Book banning is as much a part of our lives as the morning newspaper or...television; its cultural influence is strong enough to affect the way we think and the way we communicate."

Obscenity

The first anti-obscenity law passed in the United States was in 1712 by the colony of Massachusetts. The "composing, writing, printing, or publishing of any filthy, obscene, or profane song, pamphlet, libel or mock sermon" was prohibited. The first obscenity case in America occurred in 1821 in Massachusetts, when Peter Holmes was found guilty for publishing and circulating a "lewd and obscene" book, John Cleland's *Memoirs of a Woman of Pleasure*. The federal government effected its first anti-obscenity statute in 1842, and in 1865 Congress passed a law prohibiting the sending of obscene materials by mail.

The modern era of book censorship and book banning commenced after the U.S. Civil War, a period of urban upheaval, rootlessness, loosening of moral controls, and widespread circulation of graphic erotica. The most notable milestones of this era were the passage of the Comstock Act by Congress in 1873 and the passage of anti-obscenity legislation by most states by 1900. The Comstock Act prohibited using the U.S. mails to send any "obscene, lewd, or lascivious, indecent, filthy or vile book" through the mails and was responsible for the seizure and destruction of thousands of tons of books and court prosecutions.

The 1920's marked the end of an era for the book banners. The liberalizing influences of 1920's American culture resulted in a change in attitudes and values among the population and judiciary toward what had been formerly considered obscene. Three landmark court decisions occurred between 1933 and 1973. In 1933, James Joyce's *Ulysses* (1922) was declared to be a work of art that was not written for the purpose of exploiting obscenity. Also, in determining whether a book was obscene, the entire book now had to be considered, whereas previously obscenity charges could be based on a single page or paragraph. In 1957 in *Roth v. United States*, the Supreme Court specifically defined what constituted obscenity: "Obscenity is utterly without redeeming social importance." This definition was further refined in 1973 when the Supreme Court established three criteria to be used to determine if material is obscene:

(1) [The] average person, applying modern community standards would find that the work, taken as a whole, appeals to the prurient interest; (2) whether the work depicts or describes, in a patently offensive way, sexual conduct specifically defined by the applicable state law; and (3) whether the work, taken as a whole, lacks serious literary, artistic, political or scientific value.

These rulings had the effect of making it much more difficult to prove a work was obscene. Old bans were overturned (*Lady Chatterley's Lover* in 1959, *Memoirs of a Woman of Pleasure* in 1966), and although attempts at censorship and book banning continued to occur with frequent regularity, the early twenty-first century era is characterized by greater tolerance and openness in artistic and personal expression. To an extent, this greater tolerance and openness fostered by the judicial process can be circumvented by the political process. For example, a bill that prohibited the use of federal money for any work of art deemed obscene was passed by Congress and signed into law by President Ronald Reagan.

Secular Humanism and Anti-Religionism

Secular humanism has been characterized by an attorney as "a godless religion which rejects any notion of the supernatural or a divine purpose for the world" and which also "rejects any objective or absolute moral standards and embraces a subjective 'anything goes' approach to morals based on personal needs and desires." According to plaintiffs, secular humanism has been advocated in public school textbooks. Since secular humanism is a religion, it violates the constitutionally mandated separation of church and state, and therefore the books should be banned. Plaintiffs were upheld in a court case in 1987, but this decision was reversed by the Court of Appeals.

A much broader and more widespread attack on school textbooks has been instituted by various watchdog groups that believe that a number of textbooks are antireligious. For example, Beverly LaHaye of Concerned Women for America expressed the necessity "to preserve, protect, and promote traditional and Judeo-Christian values through education, legal defense.... The sad fact is that educational systems in most American schools has already removed any reference to God or teaching of Judeo-Christian values that is the most important information a child can learn." In a famous case, LaHaye's group supported seven families in Hawkins County, Tennessee, who were attempting to ban a series of textbooks. Purportedly, the books contained passages about witchcraft, astrology, pacifism, feminism, and evolution, while ignoring religion and creationism.

The trial judge agreed that the textbooks interfered with the parents' free exercise of religion, that the children were exposed to offensive religious beliefs that interfered with practice of their own religion and that put Tennessee in the position of favoring one religion over another. Ten months later, however, the court of appeals reversed this decision, stating that the Constitution was not violated and that exposure to offensive religious beliefs is not identical to requiring them to be accepted.

Self-Censorship by Publishers and Government

William Noble has observed that the absorption of many independent publishing houses into conglomerates has produced more reluctance to stir up controversy or to offend, resulting in self-censorship of what is published. Unlike the previously discussed situations, the publisher may be the only one who knows what has happened. Self-censorship takes several forms. Probably the mildest form occurs when an author is asked (not ordered) to change or eliminate some text. For example, Judy Blume removed text at her publisher's request in her young-adult book *Tiger Eyes*: "There was just one line in the book [about masturbation], but my publishers said it would make the book controversial and limit the book's audience. I took it out but I wish I hadn't."

Similar to Judy Blume's encounter with self-censorship is bowdlerism, named for Thomas Bowdler, a nineteenth century British physician who excised text from William Shakespeare's plays. These "bowdlerized" versions can still be found in schools, and in 1980 Harcourt Brace Jovanovich published an edition of William Shakespeare's *Romeo and Juliet* minus about 10 percent of the text. About two thirds of the omitted passages had sexual connotations.

A more severe form of self-censorship is to fail to publish a book or to withdraw it from publication under pressure once it has been published. Deborah Davis's unflattering 1980 biography of Katharine Graham, owner of the *Washington Post*, was pulled from circulation after Graham and the *Post*'s executive director, Ben Bradlee, protested in private to the publisher. When the Ayatollah Khomeini of Iran issued a death warrant on Salman Rushdie for his authorship of his "blasphemous" *The Satanic Verses* in 1989, worldwide book bannings and burnings occurred. In the United States, three of the largest book chains—Waldenbooks, B. Dalton, and Barnes and Noble—removed all copies of *The Satanic Verses* from open display (the book could still be bought by request). This action was justified in terms of protecting the safety and welfare of employees and patrons.

Frank W. Snepp, a former Central Intelligence Agency (CIA) agent, wrote a critical book (*Decent Interval*) about the CIA's involvement in the Vietnam War. The book was published in 1977 without prior CIA approval, to which Snepp had previously agreed in writing. In federal district court, Snepp's attorney argued that since no classified information was revealed in the book, the government was violating Snepp's rights under the First Amendment. The CIA argued that finding Snepp innocent would create a dangerous precedent and that the CIA would lose control and be unable to enforce the guarantee. Snepp was found guilty, but the decision was reversed in appeals court on the grounds that since no classified information was revealed, Snepp was protected by the First Amendment. The Supreme Court upheld the district court decision, however, stating that Snepp's book had "irreparably harmed the United States government," and Snepp was ordered to hand over more than $200,000 in royalties to the Department of Justice.

Racial and Sexual Subordination

Mark Twain's *Adventures of Huckleberry Finn* (1884) was considered to be racist by the National Association for the Advancement of Colored People, which sought to have it banned from New York City Schools in 1957. The book was said to demean African Americans but not whites, resulting in a loss of respect by the reader for African Americans. The book continued to be attacked. In 1984, an African American alderman in Illinois succeeded in having it removed from a high school reading list for its use of offensive language. Similarly, the British novelist William Golding's *Lord of the Flies* (1954) was branded as racist by the Toronto School Board for using the term "nigger" and for demeaning African Americans and was banned from schools.

Radical feminist writer Andrea Dworkin and lawyer Catharine MacKinnon attempted to regulate pornographic literature on the grounds that it discriminated against women and therefore was under the jurisdiction of civil rights laws. According to Dworkin, pornography produced "bigotry and hostility and aggression toward all women," and promoted the idea that "the hurting of women is...basic to the sexual pleasure of men." Legislation intended to allow a woman who perceived herself to be hurt by pornography to sue the bookstore owner for civil damage and have the materials banned was proposed in three cities but was never put into law. In Indianapolis, the case was appealed to the Supreme Court, which upheld a lower court's ruling that "to deny free speech in order to engineer social change in the name of accomplishing a greater good for one sector of our society erodes the freedoms of all and, as such, threatens tyranny and injustice for those subjected to the rule of such laws."

The Case Against Book Banning

Some Americans have interpreted the First Amendment literally to mean that book banning or censorship is not justifiable or permissible under any circumstances. The Supreme Court justices William O. Douglas and Hugo L. Black and the American Civil Liberties Union (ACLU) stated that the First Amendment protected all publications, without qualification, against either civil or criminal regulation at any level of government. Douglas tolerated "no exceptions...not even for obscenity." To Douglas, the First Amendment can have meaning and significance only if it allows protests even against the moral code that is the standard in the community. The ACLU declared that all published material is protected by the First Amendment unless it creates a "clear and present danger" of causing antisocial behavior.

George Elliot stated the case for removing all censorship for pornography: (1) No law can be stated clearly enough to guide unequivocally those who decide censorship cases. The ACLU has called such laws "vague and unworkable." The Supreme Court has for years grappled with defining obscenity and pornography with considerable disagreement among justices and changes in definition over the years. (2) There is no clear and unequivocal evidence that in fact pornography does severely injure many people, even adolescents. (3) The less power government has the better. As Justice Hugo L. Black wrote in 1966: "Criminal punishment by government, although universally recognized, is an exercise of one of government's most awesome and dangerous powers. Consequently, wise and good governments make all possible efforts to hedge this dangerous power by restricting it within easily identifiable boundaries."

The essence of the belief that reading materials should not be banned under any circumstance rests on the assumption that the citizenry has free will and is intelligent. Therefore, each citizen is free and able to reject material that he or she finds personally offensive, but no person has the right to define what is personally offensive for anyone else or to limit anyone else's access to that material. To do so is, to paraphrase the words of federal judge Sarah Backer, to erode freedom for the entire citizenry and threaten tyranny and injustice for those at whom the laws are directed.

The Case for Book Banning

An editorial in the April 2, 1966, issue of *The New Republic* commented on Justice William O. Douglas's position: "It would be nice if we could have a society in which nothing that others sold or displayed made anyone fear for the future of his children. But we are not that society, and it is hard to protect Mishkin's [a convicted pornographer] freedom to make a profit anyway he likes, when his particular way is a stench in the nostrils of his community, even though the community would perhaps be better advised to ignore him." The editorial advocated permitting Mishkin to cater to those who seek his product but not allowing him to display it in public.

That editorial represented the stance of most of the pro-censorship articles that have been published, as well as the position of the courts. It is a middle-of-the-road position. Censorship itself and the power vested in agencies to enforce it should be approached warily. Pornography does exist; however, many consider it to be a social evil that needs to be controlled. When material is perceived to destroy or subvert social and moral laws, undermine community standards, or offend decency without aesthetic justification, it may be banned.

The two situations of most concern are materials available to or directed at minors and material that is publicly displayed and available that is indecent and offensive to community standards. If such material is made unavailable to minors and kept from public view, it may be permissible to offer it to those who desire it. A more extreme and minority position is that the ban on pornography should be total, and the material should not be made available to anybody. Most of the debate about censorship and the banning of books has focused on pornography and obscenity. The other areas of book banning (self-censorship, religion, and sexual and racial subordination), however, would no doubt find adherents to each of the above positions. Probably the only area of censorship that comes close to finding a consensus is the revelation of classified material that would endanger lives or national security. Most people support the censorship and banning of such material.

Defining what kinds of books and other reading materials should be banned and the subject of banning itself are slippery issues. The reason is, as George Elliott noted, that these issues are not amenable to scientific analysis. They cannot be numerically defined or objectively measured. They are ambiguous matters of personal preference and consensus opinion. Censorship and book banning are psychological, aesthetic, and political phenomena.

—*Laurence Miller*

Further Reading

Demac, Donna A. *Liberty Denied*. New Brunswick, N.J.: Rutgers University Press, 1990. An excellent discussion of the different kinds of censorship and book banning and their effect on the authors and on society. Takes a strong anticensorship position.

Haight, Anne Lyon, and Chandler B. Grannis. *Banned Books, 387 B.C. to 1978 A.D.* 4th ed. New York: R. R. Bowker, 1978. A comprehensive list of book banning and related incidents through the years and in various countries.

Kravitz, Nancy. *Censorship and the School Library Media Center*. Westport, Conn.: Libraries Unlimited, 2002. An exhaustive study of censorship and book banning in schools, including historical background, a survey of contemporary pressures upon school libraries, and analysis of current laws and court decisions.

McClellan, Grant S., ed. *Censorship in the United States*. New York: H. W. Wilson, 1967. An excellent collection of magazine and newspaper articles that argue the pros and cons of censorship.

Noble, William. *Bookbanning in America*. Middlebury, Vt.: Paul S. Erickson, 1990. Highly recommended. A lively, very readable, thorough, and thoughtful discussion of the various forms of censorship. Takes a strong anticensorship position.

Rauch, Jonathan. *Kindly Inquisitors: The New Attacks on Free Thought*. Chicago: University of Chicago Press, 1993. A leisurely and very personal but insightful essay on the evils of censorship.

Woods, L. B. *A Decade of Censorship in America: The Threat to Classrooms and Libraries, 1966- 1975*. Metuchen, N.J.: Scarecrow Press, 1979. A detailed and thorough presentation of the censorship wars as fought in public schools and libraries. Presents both pro- and anticensorship points of view.

See also: Academic freedom; Art; Art and public policy; Censorship; First Amendment; Freedom of expression; *Index librorum prohibitorum*; Library Bill of Rights; Song lyrics.

Bribery

Definition: Illegally or improperly obtaining favors in exchange for money or other items of value
Type of ethics: Personal and social ethics

Significance: The concept of bribery focuses attention upon the relationship of special duties to general moral obligations.

Bribery involves paying somebody else in money or other things of value, whether objects or favors, to violate a special obligation or duty. Payments to violate general ethical duties, such as to refrain from murder or robbery, would not ordinarily be classified as bribery. Very often, however, general ethical duties and special obligations may be linked. For example, a prosecutor who through bribery is induced falsely to prosecute the briber's political opponent is violating both general and special obligations. It might be tempting to analyze bribery in terms of extrinsic morality, in which a morally neutral act is made wrong (or obligatory) by some just authority for the common good. Modern industrial societies have found bribery to be inconsistent with efficiency and have, therefore, outlawed bribery. Most ethicists, however, see true bribery as a violation of intrinsic morality—a wrong in itself—because it aims at luring persons to neglect or to trespass the obligations they have taken upon themselves by acceptance of public or private office with inherent duties.

The moral impermissibility of bribery arises out of two primary considerations: First, the bribers induce the bribees to violate their special duties, and second, evil consequences may flow from the actions undertaken for the bribes. Consider the employment manager of a corporation who accepts a bribe to hire a particular candidate for a job. Even if the candidate is fully qualified, if the bribe causes the choice of a less-than-best candidate, that manager makes his company slightly less competitive in the free market, potentially costing jobs, profits, and even the future existence of the enterprise. In the case of a scrupulous bribee, who will accept a bribe only from the candidate he considers best qualified for the position, the evil of the bribe rests on the violation of the duty alone, or that violation plus a kind of fraud against the briber (although the latter is problematical). Problems still arise, however, for the right to require payments for doing a good act remains uncertain. If the good deed is morally obligatory, it would seem that demanding payment for it would not be right unless the payment were actually necessary to carry on the good work. If, on the contrary, the good act were supererogatory, then perhaps a requirement of payment might be justifiable.

Bribery vs. Extortion

Another area of concern in regard to bribery involves payments made in response to demands by persons in authority (or otherwise influential) to prevent the conduct of business or to inflict other harms. Moral philosophers have established a useful distinction between bribery and extortion. Demands of payment to prevent harm are, properly speaking, extortion, and the theoretical considerations involved in such payments are extremely complex. Clearly, refusing to pay extortion must usually be regarded as praiseworthy, but under many circumstances such a principled approach must be judged to be supererogatory. The customs of many regions and nations support the making of moderate payments to public officials to perform their ordinary tasks. Persons seeking permits, licenses, visas, passage through customs, and so forth, may be required to pay small "bribes" to the appropriate officials, but where sanctioned by longstanding custom (even though technically illegal), such payments are more akin to tips than to bribes. In much of the world, furthermore, such practices may be accepted on account of the unrealistically low salaries of officials, which necessitate the supplementation of pay. In addition, gift giving to public officials has the beneficial effect of giving an incentive for the performance of duty when civic virtue does not suffice.

The offering of bribes, whether accepted or not, may be assumed to be morally reprehensible in circumstances in which the taking of bribes would be blameworthy. In a situation in which taking a bribe would be morally blameless, such as making nominal payments to public servants where custom sanctions it, the offering of such bribes must be held innocent. In Plato's *Crito*, Socrates refused to allow his friends to bribe his guards in order that he escape into exile, avoiding his execution. Socrates had numerous reasons for his principled stance, and among these was that bribery would cause the guards to fail in the duties they owed by virtue of their office. Simply stated, the moral maxim would be that nobody ought to induce (or attempt to induce) another to do wrong—that is, to violate his or her special obligations and duties.

The federal Foreign Corrupt Practices Act of 1977 was enacted by Congress to restrict both the payment of bribes and extortion by U.S. corporations operating overseas. Some ethicists praise the act as holding American corporations to the highest ethical standards, but others see it as an unrealistic imposition upon American businesses, damaging their competitiveness.

—Patrick O'Neil

Further Reading

Carson, Thomas L. "Bribery and Implicit Agreements." *Journal of Business Ethics* 6 (February, 1987): 123-125.

Noonan, John T. "Bribery, Extortion, and 'The Foreign Corrupt Practices Act.'" *Philosophy and Public Affairs* 14 (Winter, 1985): 66-90.

_____. *Bribes.* New York: Macmillan, 1984. Philips, Michael. "Bribery." *Ethics* 94 (July, 1984): 621-636.

_____. "Bribery, Consent, and *Prima Facie* Duty: A Rejoinder to Carson." *Journal of Business Ethics* 6 (July, 1987): 361-364.

Vincke, François, Fritz Heimann, and Ron Katz, eds. *Fighting Bribery: A Corporate Practices Manual.* Paris: ICC, 1999.

See also: Business ethics; Cheating; Duty; Hiring practices; Inside information; Lobbying; Politics; Professional ethics; Sales ethics.

Business ethics

Definition: Moral behavior of individuals and organizations in the performance of their business activities

Type of ethics: Business and labor ethics

Significance: Because the conduct of business has become such a pervasive part of human existence and because business organizations have grown so large and powerful, a study of ethical behavior in this dimension of the social fabric has become increasingly important.

The study of business ethics has a long history. Questions regarding the need for honest dealings between buyers and sellers, for example, have stirred ethical deliberation for every generation in all cultures. The Old Testament, from the fifteenth century bce, states that when buying from or selling to one another, "ye shall not oppress one another" (Leviticus 25:14) and that one must use "a perfect and just [weight] and measure," in one's business dealings (Deuteronomy 25:13-15).

As civilizations have evolved from pastoral and agrarian to highly industrialized societies and as humans have become increasingly interdependent, concerns about the proper way in which to conduct business have become more pressing. Especially since the Industrial Revolution, as business units have become huge corporate entities and as rapid changes in technology have led to extremely complex products and processes for producing them, imbalances in power between buyers and sellers, between employees and employers, and between businesses and the communities in which they operate have focused increased attention on business ethics.

During the late 1960's and early 1970's, American society began increasingly to question established institutions' business ethics. At the same time, the concept of corporate social responsibility started assuming ever-greater importance by business critics. Discussion of these subjects became more common in business school curricula and inside corporate boardrooms. As consumerism, feminism, environmentalism, and the Civil Rights movement gained strength, it was only natural that society would examine the extent to which members of the business community had been exacerbating the problems of consumer deception and harm, unequal treatment of women in the workplace, environmental degradation, and racial discrimination. More pressure began to be applied to encourage businesses to become a part of the solution to these social problems.

Frameworks of Analysis

Ethicists have generally used a number of different concepts—such as utility, rights, justice, virtue—to analyze and judge the morality of business behavior. Utilitarianism focuses on the results or consequences of any business decision. It requires managers first to identify all the costs and benefits to all of society of a given set of alternative business actions and then to choose the alternative that will result in the greatest net benefit to society. An important aspect of this framework is that it requires business managers to consider not only the consequences for their businesses, that is, the effects on company profits, but also the consequences to the greater society. An advantage of the utilitarian approach is that it corresponds closely with cost-benefit analyses so common to business decision making. There are, however, some decided disadvantages. It is difficult for managers to identify all costs and benefits to society. Moreover, it is difficult to measure certain social benefits such as improvements in the general level of health, aesthetic improvements, or greater enjoyment of life. Finally, utilitarianism ignores questions of rights, duties, fairness, and justice.

Using rights as the framework for analyzing business decisions requires that managers identify what stakeholders—that is, affected individuals or groups—will be involved in a particular decision, and then ask what rights those individuals or groups may have and what obligations the business may have to those stakeholders. As the late eighteenth century German philosopher Immanuel

Kant stressed, people must be considered as ends in themselves and not merely as means toward some other end. This is especially problematic for business managers who have traditionally thought of their employees as a "means of production" and of their customers as the ultimate source of their profits. Furthermore, this deontological framework of ethical analysis creates difficulties when managers must attempt to weigh and prioritize the rights of various competing stakeholder groups: for example, employees who feel they have a right to more generous health care plans versus their companies' owners and shareholders, who would like to see those funds distributed in the form of dividends.

A third framework for assessing the appropriateness or morality of business decisions involves focusing on justice or fairness. Justice requires an equitable distribution of life's benefits and burdens. The twentieth century American philosopher John Rawls was a leading proponent of this school. Using this approach, managers would be required to ask which of their alternative courses of action would be the most fair to all affected parties. The advantage here is that justice and fairness are widely accepted as desirable goals. The disadvantage is that there is little agreement on how to define them. A free, democratic, capitalistic system that prizes individualism, free choice, and the sanctity of private property allows its individual citizens—and its corporate citizens—to pursue their economic goals, that is, acquire wealth, according to their individual and differing abilities. This necessarily leads to unequal distribution of income and assets, and therefore, of benefits and burdens. There are no commonly accepted standards regarding what degree of inequality can still pass the justice and fairness test.

The issue of executive compensation vis-à-vis the average worker's pay is an interesting and contentious example of the concerns raised by this framework. Some business critics—and even a few socially conscious firms—have held that chief executive officers' compensation should be no more than seven times that of the average "shop floor" worker. Before the 1990's, the average chief executive officer of a U.S. firm was likely to earn forty times the salary of an average employee. However, by the beginning of the twenty-first century, that ratio had grown to a factor of four hundred times. There are partial explanations, such as the deferred compensation through stock options and the necessity of a major corporation to pay what the market demands for top-flight leaders. Nevertheless, this enormous differential in pay, especially when combined with poor corporate performance and lay-offs of thousands of workers, strikes many as patently unfair and, therefore, unethical.

Another approach to analyzing ethical dilemmas—the virtue ethics framework—entails identifying certain principles or virtues that are universally accepted as worthy behavior. Among those usually accepted are honesty, loyalty, integrity, making good on commitments, steadfastness, and the like. Viewed through this perspective, managers are called upon to act—to choose those alternatives—which reinforce and are in harmony with these virtues, regardless of the consequences. There is no agreement among business ethicists or business managers that any one of these frameworks is superior to the others. Each has its merits; each has its advantages and disadvantages. Managers need to be familiar with all these approaches and may need to analyze a given ethical dilemma through all these different lenses to arrive at the "best" decision.

Levels of Analysis

Scholars and managers can analyze business ethics problems on four different levels. First, at the individual level, unethical acts are seen as the results of individuals who make unethical decisions. If this is the case, corporation need only rid itself of its "bad apples" and do a better job of training and supervising its managers and employees. The second level is the corporation or organization, which allows for the possibility that a firm—such as Enron—may develop a culture that condones or perhaps even encourages unethical behavior. The third level is the industry. Some would argue that certain industries are, by the very nature of the products they produce, unethical. Examples might include the tobacco industry, the munitions industry, and perhaps even the fast-food industry—which has come under increasing criticism for fostering poor eating habits and contributing to obesity and associated health problems. Finally, there is the systemic level, which holds that there are fundamental flaws in the entire capitalistic, free enterprise system that inevitably lead to unethical behavior of one form or another.

Relevant Issues

The field of business ethics is often organized around specific issues, and these issues may be grouped according to the stakeholders that are most affected: employees, customers, shareholders, the environment, communities, and so forth. Managers faced with making decisions regarding one of these issues must ask themselves what the nature is of the relationship between the organization and a particular stakeholder group. What responsibilities does the organization have? What rights do these stakeholders enjoy? How best can competing claims or rights be resolved?

Due to changes in the social, technological, or political environments, new issues may appear and old issues may disappear. For example, because of the rapid growth of use of the Internet, the subject of intellectual property and the rights of musicians, film producers, and computer software creators became an important issue in the early years of the twenty-first century.

A company's employees constitute one of the company's most important stakeholder groups, and many ethical issues involve employees. For example, discrimination in all of its many forms is one of the most common. Since the passage of the federal Civil Rights Act of 1964, along with subsequent related legislation, American employers have been forbidden by law from discriminating on the basis of sex, race, national origin, age, religion, or disability in their employment policies: hiring, pay, promotion, benefits, or termination. Decisions in these matters must be made on each individual's ability to perform on the job, with only a minimum number of exceptions, such as seniority. From an ethical perspective, this is seen as necessary to satisfy society's view of fairness and to protect each individual's right to equal opportunity. The issue is complicated, however, by affirmative action programs that may lead to reverse discrimination against majority groups. The growing number of different minority groups as well as the growth of the overall minority population in the United States, the so-called glass ceiling that prevents women from achieving top management positions in numbers equivalent to their prevalence in the workforce, and discrimination against workers on the basis of sexual preference all continue to be important ethical issues for employers to address in the twenty-first century.

Employer-employee issues also include employees' right to privacy; relationships and responsibilities to union organizations; whistle-blowing; advance notice of large-scale layoffs or plant closings; the question of whether employers have the obligation to provide a minimum level of health insurance, child care, pension plans, and other benefits; and the question of whether workers have some right to participate in management decisions that affect their jobs. In all these issues, managers face questions about how far beyond minimum legal requirements they must go to satisfy prevailing social expectations.

Customer Relationships

Customers represent another vital stakeholder group for any organization, and the organization's relationship with them has its own set of complex ethical issues. One of the most enduring issues is the question of product liability: To what extent should manufacturers be held responsible for harm caused by their products or services? Caveat emptor (let the buyer beware) is no longer the guiding principle in transactions between buyers and sellers or between manufacturers and their customers. The courts and some state laws have moved steadily in the direction of placing on the manufacturer more and more of the liability for harm done by its products. Under the concept of strict liability, it is no longer necessary to prove that a manufacturer has been negligent in the production or the design of a product. Courts routinely expect manufacturers to anticipate any potential problems and have increasingly held producers responsible even though state-of-the-art scientific knowledge at the time of production could not have predicted the ensuing problems.

The asbestos industry has, in effect, ceased to exist in the United States. Virtually all the major asbestos producers have disappeared, often into bankruptcy, because of massive class-action lawsuits against them. During the 1990's, the tobacco industry came under severe legal and social pressure from a broad coalition of state governments, health associations, and advocacy groups. Cigarette manufacturers have been accused of conspiring to hide from their customers and from the public what they have known about the addictiveness and other harmful—often deadly—effects of smoking. While cigarettes have continued to be legal products, the tobacco companies have agreed to pay massive sums to the states in reimbursement for costs to the state health care systems. They have also agreed to serious restrictions in the way they market their products.

Alleged ethical violations cover a wide range of subjects including the falsifying of information regarding the effects of smoking on health and inappropriately targeting children with cigarette advertising, especially in the use of icons such as "Joe Camel" and the Marlboro Man. Once deemed invulnerable, the tobacco industry was being forced to accept responsibility for the harm caused by its products during the first years of the twenty-first century. Emboldened by developments in the tobacco industry, other advocacy groups have moved against the firearms industry in an attempt to hold gun manufacturers, especially handgun makers, responsible for deaths and accidents resulting from the use of their products. By the year 2004, moves against the firearms industry have had little success in the courts, but the ethical questions continued to be debated. Other advocacy groups have started claiming that the fast-food industry bears some of the responsibility for the growing problem of obesity in the United States. They have urged McDonald's and the rest of the industry to acknowledge and accept their ethical responsibilities by offering wider selections of healthy menu items and by providing more information to the public about the fat content of their hamburgers and french fries.

Advertising

Another major category of ethical problems associated with the buyer-seller relationship stems from the advertising and other promotional tactics that sellers employ. Advertisers are often tempted to make claims about their products and services that are either blatantly fraudulent or that can be easily misconstrued by the public. Such claims are unethical because they do not respect the rights of customers to be fully and properly informed, and they do not measure up to societal expectations that business dealings be conducted in an honest (virtuous) manner. Various governmental agencies, such as the Food and Drug Administration and the Federal Trade Commission, have the statutory responsibility for protecting against dishonest advertising, while nongovernmental groups such as Better Business Bureaus and the American Association of Advertising Agencies provide a modest level of self-policing.

As the persuasive power of advertising messages has become more subtle, some businesses have been accused of exploiting certain "vulnerable" groups. Targeting children, especially for products such as breakfast cereals and violent video games, has been criticized frequently. The argument is made that children lack the experience and the maturity to evaluate advertising messages, especially when manufacturers blur the lines between commercials and entertainment programs. Cigarette, alcoholic beverage, and handgun advertisers have also been sharply criticized, notably when they have targeted women and racial minorities.

Other Issues

Another major category of business ethics problems is related to environmental concerns. By the early twenty-first century, it was widely reported and understood that business, in its normal functions of manufacturing and transporting products, contributes to environmental problems around the world: air pollution, water pollution, solid and toxic wastes, and so on. A number of ethical questions are then posed: What responsibilities must business assume for the clean-up of polluted water and dump sites? What responsibilities does the business community have to redesign its products and processes to reduce waste and consume fewer natural resources? To what extent must business protect endangered species and respect the rights of animals, for example, in testing the safety of pharmaceuticals and personal care products?

In the early years of the twenty-first century, the United States was rocked with a series of highly publicized business ethics scandals involving such corporations as Enron, Arthur Anderson, WorldCom, and Tyco. These situations tended to fall into the subject of accounting issues or into the subject of governance, which involves the role of the board of directors and its relationship to management. In the former category, ethical issues were raised when information was either withheld or falsified by internal or external auditors to the point that shareholders and the investing public could not use the accounting information available to them to make sound judgments about the company. In the latter category, it was becoming apparent that the boards of directors in a large number of publicly held companies were not exercising independent judgment in monitoring and evaluating the work of management.

Transnational Problems

As the globalization of business has continued to grow in importance, so too have the business ethics issues related specifically to doing business in and with other countries. One set of ethical problems derives from the old maxim, "When in Rome, do as the Romans do." This may be fine advice under most circumstances for business managers venturing out into other countries and other cultures, but does it, or should it apply, to ethical matters?

Bribery—under all its different names and different forms—has been the most often debated issue. Since the passage of the Foreign Corrupt Practices Act in 1977, it has been illegal under United States law to offer bribes to foreign officials in return for business contracts or other favors. However, the law specifically condones "facilitating payments," and so managers are called on to distinguish such payments from outright bribes. At the heart of this debate, however, is this question: If an act is deemed to be wrong—that is, absolutely immoral—in this country, why should it be considered acceptable to perform the same act in a different country or culture?

A quite different set of questions is raised when companies from developed countries do business in developing nations. Do such firms have special obligations and responsibilities? Nestlé was widely criticized during the late 1970's for the tactics it used to market its infant formula in developing countries. A variation of this issue regards the responsibility of manufacturers and retailers for the working conditions and wages in the factories of its suppliers. Nike and Wal-Mart are examples of large international firms that have been criticized for using developing world suppliers who employ child labor, pay wages so low that they cannot provide even the bare essentials of food and shelter, and where the working conditions and treatment by supervisors is inhumane. Under these circumstances manufacturers and retailers are called upon to be responsible not only for their own employees but for the employees of their suppliers and contractors as well.

The early twenty-first century also witnessed a growing world debate over the responsibility of pharmaceutical companies to make their patented drugs for acquired immunodeficiency syndrome (AIDS) and other life-threatening diseases available to poor African and Asian nations at greatly reduced prices.

Attention to Ethical Issues

Interest in business ethics in the academic community began increasing during the mid-1980's. Since then, colleges and universities have incorporated growing numbers of ethics courses and modules into their graduate and undergraduate business curricula. A number of professional academic societies such as the Society for Business Ethics, the International Association for Business and Society, the Social Issues in Management division of the Academy of Management, and the Marketing in Society division of the American Marketing Association hold annual meetings and encourage the writing and publication of scholarly papers. The Center for Business Ethics at Bentley College has sponsored a series of national conferences on the subject.

Within the business community itself, there has also been a marked increase in the recognition of ethical problems. A number of companies have created the new position of "ethics officer." Most large companies have adopted "codes of conduct," programs that are designed to clarify their policies regarding ethical behavior, and systematically inculcate their managers and employees at all levels with these policies. Johnson & Johnson credits the company-wide understanding of and respect for its Credo with helping the organization through its Tylenol crisis in 1982, still regarded as one of the great exemplars of ethical corporate behavior.

Throughout the economic history of the United States there have been periods of corporate misconduct followed by periods of heightened concern for business ethics and government regulation. There is no reason to think that this wavelike pattern of scandal and ethical reform will not continue.

—D. Kirk Davidson

Further Reading

Acton, H. B. *The Morals of Markets: An Ethical Exploration.* Harlow, England: Longmans, 1971. This work covers the systemic level of business ethics in presenting a defense of capitalism, especially as it has developed in the United States.

De George, Richard T. *Business Ethics.* 5th ed. Englewood Cliffs, N.J.: Prentice Hall, 1999. An exposition on moral reasoning in business that includes good coverage of the important issues by a widely respected professor in the field.

Donaldson, Thomas. *The Ethics of International Business.* New York: Oxford University Press, 1989. Donaldson is one of the leading business ethicists in the United States. This work focuses only on international issues and defends the position that there are certain absolute standards or "hyper-norms" that transcend all countries and all cultures.

Donaldson, Thomas, Margaret Cording, and Patricia Werhane, eds. *Ethical Issues in Business: A Philosophical Approach.* 7th ed. Englewood Cliffs, N.J.: Prentice Hall, 2001. This book includes an excellent group of case studies and sets forth an analysis of the most important ethical issues facing businesses today.

Donaldson, Thomas, and Thomas W. Dunfee. *The Ties That Bind: A Social Contract Approach to Business Ethics.* Boston: Harvard University Business School Press, 1999. An important work from two noted scholars at the University of Pennsylvania grounding business ethics in a broader ethics concept.

Smith, N. Craig, and John A. Quelch. *Ethics in Marketing.* Homewood, Ill.: Richard D. Irwin, 1993. A very good collection of business case studies and articles from business periodicals on all aspects of marketing ethics: advertising, pricing, product policy, research, and so forth.

Velasquez, Manuel G. *Business Ethics: Concepts and Cases.* 5th ed. Englewood Cliffs, N.J.: Prentice Hall, 2002. An excellent all-purpose text on the subject. Explains in readable, straightforward language the various frameworks for analyzing business behavior and uses those frameworks to analyze the most impor-

tant ethical issues such as honesty in advertising and insider trading.

See also: Advertising; Antitrust legislation; Corporate compensation; Corporate responsibility; Corporate scandal; Downsizing; Ethical codes of organizations; Marketing; Multinational corporations; Sales ethics; Wage discrimination; Whistleblowing.

Cell-phone etiquette

Definition: Proper and improper use of cell phones in public places
Type of ethics: Personal and social ethics
Significance: The rapid growth of cell phones that began in the late 1980's has led to public debate on the ethics of using such in public.

Almost since the time that the first cell phones were introduced to the public in 1977, questions have been raised concerning the proper way to conduct cell phone conversations in public places. By the middle to late 1980's, the cell-phone industry and the number of cell-phone customers was growing rapidly, and the early years of the twenty-first century users in North America numbered more than sixty million. The widespread use of cell phones has led to what many people consider misuse of cell phones. Some of the main grievances concerning inappropriate use of this relatively new industry include people talking on their phones in restaurants, theaters, checkout lines in stores, and their cars. In addition, interruptions due to cell-phone calls often disrupt classrooms and business meetings.

A 2003 survey conducted by the web site LetsTalk.com found that only 57 percent of cell-phone users turn off their ringers while in movie theaters and even fewer—43 percent—turn off their phones while in restaurants. This behavior is considered by many people to be unacceptable and has raised the issue of the need to curb cell-phone use in public places. In 2004, many Americans cities and states were considering legislation to ban cell phones from public places such as restaurants, theaters, and public transportation.

A more important consideration in cell-phone use is public safety. Using cell phones while driving vehicles is believed by many people to be more than simply ethically wrong; it is also seen as a safety issue. In response to this concern, New York became, in June 2001, the first state to require motorists to use hands-free devices to talk on cell phones while driving. Meanwhile, as the cell-phone industry continues its rapid expansion, so too, does the debate over the need for legislation concerning the ethical uses of cell phones.

—*Kimberley M. Holloway*

See also: Computer technology; Confidentiality; Electronic mail; Electronic surveillance; Etiquette; Gossip; Invasion of privacy; Privacy.

Censorship

Definition: Official scrutiny and consequent suppression or alteration of publications, performances, or art forms that fail to meet institutional standards

Type of ethics: Arts and censorship

Significance: Justification of censorship in virtually all cultures is founded upon policies concerning public welfare and morals; arguments against censorship center on the moral values of free expression and the open exchange of ideas. The strength of ethical convictions on both sides of the issue continues to fuel controversy.

Since classical times, proponents of censorship have invoked religion or government to promote the repression of material that purportedly threatened public morals or controlling institutions. In this context, artistic expression has been targeted as potentially harmful by ancient philosophers, religious organizations, special-interest groups, and governmental bodies. Throughout the ages, the basic arguments for and against freedom of expression have remained remarkably consistent.

History

Plato was among the earliest proponents of censorship of the arts. His *Laws* (360 bce) argued for strict censorship of the literary and visual arts, particularly poetic metaphor, which he claimed interfered with achieving pure, conceptual truth. Early Christianity took a similar position concerning mythology and art. The Roman Catholic Church eventually utilized censorship to control philosophical, artistic, and religious belief generally. In 1521, Holy Roman emperor Charles V issued the Edict of Worms, which prohibited the printing, dissemination, or reading of Martin Luther's work. The *Index librorum prohibitorum* (1564), which was published by the Vatican, condemned specific books. The *Index* eventually included such works as Galileo Galilei's *Dialogue Concerning the Two Chief World Systems* (1632); Galileo was subsequently prosecuted for heresy during the Inquisition.

The scope of governmental censorship in Europe changed with the separation of powers between the church and state. When church courts were abolished and religious beliefs and mores were no longer subject to government control, censorship laws focused on political speech and writing. Works criticizing government practices ran the risk of prosecution for seditious libel in England; in France, Napoleon censored newspapers, publications, theatrical productions, and even private correspondence at will.

Politically motivated censorship became common in countries with totalitarian governments, from communism to fascism. *The Communist Manifesto* (1848) of Karl Marx and Friedrich Engels was banned throughout Europe, yet subsequently communist leaders from V. I. Lenin to Mao Zedong to Fidel Castro routinely practiced political censorship. In the Soviet Union, political censorship targeted the arts when it imposed the doctrine of Socialist Realism in 1932. The following year in Germany, Adolf Hitler organized nationwide book burnings in the name of the National Socialist government.

Soviet-bloc writers, artists, and scientists have been imprisoned, exiled, and have had their work confiscated, when it has been deemed ideologically impure. Aleksandr Solzhenitsyn was arrested in 1945 for a pejorative remark about Joseph Stalin, spent eleven years in prison, and was finally exiled in 1974. In Muslim fundamentalist countries, religious censorship is the norm. For example, the publication of Salman Rushdie's *The Satanic Verses* (1989) prompted Iran's Ayatollah Khomeini to pronounce a *fatwa*, calling for Rushdie's death and forcing the author into seclusion.

Public political debate was given constitutional protection in some jurisdictions. Article 5 of the Basic Law of West Germany (1949) and Article 10 of the European Convention on Human Rights and Fundamental Freedoms (1953) specifically provided for free speech rights. The First Amendment to the U.S. Constitution, ratified in 1791, expressly prohibited Congress from making any law that abridged freedom of speech, press, religion, assembly, or the right to petition the government for redress of grievances. This right to free speech was not, however, absolute. The First Amendment has generated an enormous amount of litigation over its interpretation, particularly when it has collided with other rights in American society.

The degree to which the principle of free speech has been extended to the arts has been a matter of case law in all jurisdictions in which censorship has been scrutinized. Most troublesome for the courts has been the issue of the protection of allegedly obscene or pornographic material.

When free expression has come into conflict with potentially overriding public policy concerns, the courts have engaged in complex legal reasoning, often guided by philosophical and political arguments, in order to determine which interests dominate. Despite the evolution of cultural values, vestiges of several arguments remain common to most court deliberations of the free speech principle.

The argument from truth (also referred to as the libertarian argument) has been associated with the works of John Stuart Mill, but it was also articulated by John Milton two hundred years earlier. It emphasizes the importance of open discussion to the discovery of truth as a fundamental good and invaluable to the development of society. To some extent, this philosophy has been utilized by the U.S. Supreme Court, first in Justice Oliver Wendell Holmes's now-famous dissent, in *United States v. Abrams* (1919), although its application is limited to speech with political, moral, aesthetic, or social content.

The argument from democracy views freedom of speech as a necessary component of any democratic society, in which public discussion is a political duty. Alexander Meiklejohn is one of its leading proponents, and similar theories are found in the works of Immanuel Kant, Baruch Spinoza, and David Hume. The constitutional scholar Alexander Meiklejohn considered the First Amendment a protection of the right of all citizens to discuss political issues and participate in government. Similarly, the German Constitutional Court and the European Court have recognized the importance of public debate on political questions. The argument from democracy has had little success in cases involving nonpolitical speech.

By contrast, the argument from individuality is rights-based rather than consequentialist, recognizing the interest of the speaker, rather than society, as being paramount. It asserts that there is an individual right to freedom of speech, even though its exercise may conflict with the welfare of society. A free expression rationale based solely on individual fulfillment has raised philosophical and legal quandaries when it has come into conflict with other equally important liberties.

The argument from the paradox justifies censorship in cases in which freedom of speech is exercised by those who would use it to eliminate the free speech principle itself. For example, in England, it was used to set regulations restricting the activities of the National Front. In the United States, those seeking to prohibit the marching of the Nazi Party in Skokie, Illinois, a predominantly Jewish suburb of Chicago, relied on this argument without success. The European Convention on Human Rights employed it as a fundamental consideration in Article 10, and it has been cited as authority for outlawing the German Communist Party.

The utilitarian argument suggests that the speech in question should be weighed for the balance of pleasure and pain. Its value is limited in assessing the extent of free speech protection contemplated by the U.S. Constitution, or other legislation with similar provisions.

The contractualist argument is a rights-based conception that excludes certain rights from state power, particularly the right to conscience. This argument asserts that the government violates this right when it superimposes its own value judgment on the speech at issue.

Censorship and the Arts in Europe

Artistic freedom is protected in Europe in all countries adhering to the European Convention of Human Rights and Fundamental Freedoms. Article 10 guarantees everyone the right to freedom of expression. Any prior restraints on publication must be justified as necessary in a democratic society in order to constitute permissible restraints on the free expression principle.

Germany's Basic Law, Article 5, provides for freedom of expression rights, specifically designating art, science, research, and teaching. This freedom of expression is, however, subject to a fundamental right to dignity and is limited by the provisions of the general laws. As a result, the German Constitutional Court has balanced the interests of free expression and other specific laws in a manner similar to that used by the U.S. Supreme Court.

Great Britain does not constitutionally protect speech; instead, it relies upon common law and administrative agencies to resolve issues involving free expression. Courts often articulate a common law principle of freedom of speech to limit the scope of other rules that impinge on this freedom. Prior restraint by licensing of the press was abolished in 1694, but films remain subject to scrutiny under the Video Recordings Act of 1985.

In 1979, a special committee, popularly known as "The Williams Committee," presented to the government its report containing studies and policies on obscenity and film censorship. Its findings, which recommended the restriction of material that is offensive to reasonable people, are frequently cited by the courts as well as by legal scholars.

Obscenity is prosecuted under the Obscene Publications Act of 1959, provided that the work is not justified as being for the public good or in the interest of science, literature, art, learning, or any other area of general concern. This exception to the obscenity law bears a strong resemblance to the balancing of interests tests utilized by American Supreme Court justices.

Censorship and the Arts in the United States

The constitutional guarantee of free speech was articulated in one simple phrase, yet its interpretation has been a matter of intricate, strenuous legal debate since its inception. When state laws are challenged as unconstitutional restraints on free speech, the ultimate determination of their legality rests with the U.S. Supreme Court. This court has established, on a case-by-case basis, both the scope and limitations of the free speech doctrine as well as its applicability to the states through the Fourteenth Amendment. It has been argued that the drafters of the First Amendment contemplated only the protection of political speech. The path that the Supreme Court took in extending the free speech principle to the arts was long, arduous, and occasionally winding. Most instances of repression of the literary and visual arts have occurred under the guise of preservation of moral standards, pertaining to blasphemy and obscenity. Anti-vice movements and groups have operated on the premise that society needed protection from exposure to material that those movements and groups considered threatening to public morals. Although not necessarily acting under the color of state law, organizations such as the Legion of Decency, the New England Watch and Ward Society, and various independent groups constituting what became known as the "moral majority" have pressured municipalities and businesses into tacitly censoring material deemed offensive.

The U.S. Supreme Court began to address the extension of First Amendment protection beyond political speech during the 1940's. Blasphemy prosecutions are all but obsolete in the United States, but it was not until 1952 that the Supreme Court ruled that a film (*The Miracle*) could not be censored for sacrilegious content. The Court also ruled that motion pictures were included within the free speech and press guarantee of the First and Fourteenth Amendments; the importance of films as organs of public opinion was not lessened by the fact that they were designed to entertain as well as inform.

Literary and visual arts in the form of erotica have been afforded the least First Amendment protection. Obscenity has always been criminally sanctioned and subjected to prior restraints in the United States, based on numerous policy considerations: that it corrupts the individual, that it leads to sex-related crime and illegal sexual activity, that it serves no socially redeeming purpose, and that it is lacking in any solid element of the search for truth.

Until 1934, American courts relied on the English common law Hicklin test when determining whether a given work was to be considered illegally obscene. *Regina v. Hicklin* (1868) defined the test of obscenity as whether the tendency of the matter is to deprave and corrupt those whose minds are open to such immoral influences and into whose hands a publication of this sort may fall. Thus, a publication was judged obscene if any isolated passage within it could corrupt the most susceptible person.

The Hicklin rule was replaced by the "Ulysses standard," first articulated in *United States v. One Book Entitled Ulysses* (1934), which required that the entire work, rather than an isolated passage, be evaluated for its libidinous effect. The Supreme Court continued to proclaim in *Chaplinsky v. New Hampshire* (1942) that there were certain well-defined and narrowly limited classes of speech that are of such slight social value as to be clearly outweighed by the social interest in order and morality. Such classes of speech included the lewd and obscene, the profane, the libelous, and insulting words that by their utterance inflict injury.

The first landmark case setting forth a standard for determining whether a work was to be considered obscene, and therefore undeserving of First Amendment protection, was *Roth v. United States* (1957). The Court, in upholding convictions for violations of California and federal obscenity statutes, found that the statutes did not violate constitutional standards. The Court stated that the test for obscenity was whether the average person, applying contemporary community standards, would find that the dominant theme of the material, taken as a whole, appealed to prurient interest.

Three years later, the Supreme Court found that a Chicago city ordinance requiring submission of film for examination as a prerequisite to obtaining a permit for public exhibition was not void as a prior restraint under the First Amendment. In *Times Film Corp. v. City of Chicago* (1961), the Court indicated that there is no complete and absolute freedom to exhibit, even once, any and every kind of motion picture. The Court limited the scope of the First Amendment, based on the overriding societal interest in preserving the decency of the community, assuming that the ordinance was directed at obscenity. In applying the "*Roth* standard" in *Jacobellis v. Ohio* (1964), the Court found the motion picture *Les Amants* not to be obscene and overturned the prosecution of a theater manager who had exhibited the film. The court stated that obscenity is excluded from constitutional protection only because it is utterly without redeeming social importance, and that the portrayal of sex in art, literature, and scientific works is not in itself sufficient reason to deny material the constitutional protection of freedom of speech and press.

In 1970, a presidential commission appointed to study the statistical correlation, if any, between crime and pornography published its conclusions, finding that there was no direct correlation. There was, however, considerable dissension among the members of the committee, who sought to lodge their conclusions separately.

In 1973, *Miller v. California* was decided, again refining an earlier standard set in *Memoirs v. Massachusetts* (1966). The test for obscenity established three standards that must be independently met in order for a work to be removed from the umbrella of First Amendment protection: whether the average person, applying contemporary community standards, would find that the work, taken as a whole, appeals to prurient interest; whether the work depicts or describes, in a patently offensive way, sexual conduct specifically defined by the applicable state law; and whether the work, taken as a whole, lacks serious literary, artistic, political, or scientific value.

Consequently, a work that had political value was protected, regardless of its prurient appeal and offensive depiction of sexual activities. Sexually explicit art was immune if it demonstrated serious artistic value. Subsequent cases have made it clear that works found by a reasonable person to have serious artistic value are protected from censorship, regardless of whether the government or a majority approve of the ideas these works represent.

A companion case to *Miller v. California*, *Paris Adult Theater I et al. v. Slaton*, held that a state could prohibit hard-core pornographic films. Although there were extensive dissenting opinions, the majority categorically disapproved the theory that obscene, pornographic films acquire constitutional immunity from state regulation simply because they are exhibited for consenting adults; they stated further that the states have a legitimate interest

in regulating the use of obscene material in local commerce and in all places of public accommodation. The Court concluded that a legislature could quite reasonably determine that a connection between antisocial behavior and obscene material does or might exist.

In October of 1989, the "*Miller* standard" of obscenity became controversial outside the courts. A censorious bill proposed by Senator Jesse Helms, which sought to restrict and punish the National Endowment for the Arts (NEA) for allegedly funding "obscene" art, was defeated. Congressional critics had assailed the NEA for funding two controversial projects: a photography exhibit by Robert Mapplethorpe that included homoerotic images and an exhibit by Andres Serrano entitled "Piss Christ," which was criticized as sacrilegious. Congress passed instead a compromise bill that removed most penalties against specific artists and institutions but required that the NEA observe legal bans on obscenity by employing standards reminiscent of the language in *Miller v. California*. Further, grant recipients were required to sign a nonobscenity oath.

Subsequently, many organizations and artists refused to sign the oath, and several initiated lawsuits against the NEA. *Bella Lewitzky Dance Foundation v. Frohnmayer et al.* (1991) held that the nonobscenity oath requirement was unconstitutional. Artists and legal scholars alike voiced strenuous objections to the *Miller*-style decency standards of the legislation, particularly because the determination of obscenity was made by NEA panelists and administrators rather than by peer review, and because the standards ignored the nature and purpose of postmodern art, which rejects the previous definition that art must be "serious."

In June, 1992, a United States District Court heard the suit of *Karen Finley et al. v. National Endowment for the Arts and John Frohnmayer*, in which four performance artists whose grant applications were denied by the NEA brought suit alleging improper denial of the grant applications. The governing statute as amended in 1990 provided that artistic merit was to be judged taking into consideration general standards of decency and respect for the diverse beliefs and values of the American public. The Court found that the decency provision violated the Fifth Amendment's due process requirement. It further held that the public funding of art is entitled to First Amendment protection and that the decency clause on its face violates the First Amendment on the basis of overbreadth.

The influence of ethical arguments throughout the constitutional case law concerning censorship and the arts is unmistakable. Throughout the twentieth century, the Supreme Court has labored to give contemporary meaning to the terms of the First Amendment, affording broad freedom of expression to the arts while balancing various community values and shifting interests in a pluralistic society.

—Kathleen O'Brien

Further Reading

Barendt, Eric. *Freedom of Speech.* Oxford, England: Clarendon Press, 1985. A comparative treatment of the protection afforded speech and other forms of expression in the United States, the United Kingdom, Germany, and countries adhering to the European Convention.

Egendorf, Laura K., ed. *Censorship.* San Diego, Calif.: Greenhaven Press, 2001. An anthology of opposing viewpoint essays arguing each side of controversial issues in censorship. Issues covered include the role of government in regulating popular culture, the existence of censorship in the educational system, and whether to censor speech or pornography.

Gerber, Albert B. *Sex, Pornography, and Justice.* New York: Lyle Stuart, 1965. A complete study of the topic from the Middle Ages to the twentieth century, including exhibits of the items that came before the courts. Updated supplements are available.

Hurwitz, Leon. *Historical Dictionary of Censorship in the United States.* Westport, Conn.: Greenwood Press, 1985. An overview of the types of expression subjected to repression in the United States, with cases, concepts, terms, and events listed alphabetically with brief summaries. An extensive bibliography and a table of cases make the book a useful reference tool.

Richards, David A. J. *Toleration and the Constitution.* New York: Oxford University Press, 1986. Provides a contractualist account of U.S. constitutional law regarding religious liberty, free speech, and constitutional protection of privacy.

Schauer, Frederick. *Free Speech: A Philosophical Enquiry.* Cambridge, England: Cambridge University Press, 1982. Draws extensively on legal rules and examples to present the author's political philosophy as well as his analysis of the right to free speech principle and the variety of communication that it includes.

See also: Academic freedom; Art; Art and public policy; Book banning; First Amendment; Freedom of expression; *Index librorum prohibitorum*; Library Bill of Rights; Mapplethorpe, Robert; Pentagon Papers; Political correctness.

Cheating

Definition: Willful violation of rules with the intent to benefit oneself

Type of ethics: Personal and social ethics

Significance: As an ethical violation for personal gain, cheating is one of the central issues addressed by any system of personal ethics.

Broadly speaking, cheating can be taken to mean any violation of known social norms, therefore encompassing all deliberate deception and lawbreaking. A narrower interpretation restricts cheating only to situations in which an individual has voluntarily agreed to behave according to a set of rules and willfully violates those rules for personal gain. Examples of such cases are games and marketplace behavior. In the former, rules are usually explicit; in the latter, rules may be implicit—taking the form of customs—or may be explicit or even established by law. Often, the punishment for cheating is limited to expulsion from the activity. Cheating is similar to breaking a personal promise in that a person willfully breaks an expected standard of behavior; it differs in that the standard was set socially rather than individually.

Forms of Cheating

All immoral action can be taken to constitute cheating, but most discussions limit cheating to several broad areas. Cheating is taken to mean willful breaking of rules. The breaking of formal established rules, such as laws, most often falls outside discussions of cheating. The innocent violation of rules is not considered to be cheating; even though "ignorance of the law is no excuse," a person is not said to have cheated by violating a rule of which he or she was unaware. Cheating is deliberate behavior. The clearest cases of cheating are those in which individuals deliberately violate rules that they have willingly agreed to follow. Games provide some examples. By participating in a game, a player agrees to follow the rules of the game. Cheating takes place when a player violates the rules with the intention of winning. This behavior takes advantage of other players who follow the rules. Clearly, if everyone cheated, games would cease to have any meaning and would cease to exist. This would deprive people of any enjoyment they derive from playing games. Societies have rules in the forms of laws and social conventions. Lawbreaking is usually, but not always, a clear violation of social norms. The exceptions occur in cases in which there is a perception that the law is widely violated or is irrelevant to the situation. Such cases include speeding, jaywalking, and cheating on taxes. Even though all of those behaviors are violations of laws, many people do not believe themselves to have behaved unethically by performing those behaviors, since "everyone does it." Unwritten social conventions include positive reinforcement for helping those in need and prohibitions against eavesdropping, spreading gossip, and skipping ahead in lines, to name only a few.

Ethical issues arise when people argue that they do not enter into social contracts voluntarily and thus are not bound by those contracts. Examples include taxpayers who argue that they did not vote for the tax laws and students who state that they are in school against their will and thus are not subject to its rules. As in games, when people violate social contracts, even those entered into implicitly (through citizenship in society) or against individuals' will, those contracts become meaningless and people become less certain of what they can expect of others. Behavior becomes less cooperative and more self-serving and protective.

Misrepresentation

Misrepresentation, or lying, is a particular

Cheater with the Ace of Diamonds, by Georges de La Tour.

case of violation of rules. One of the most basic social conventions is that people should tell the truth. In some cases, as in courts of law or on legal documents, that convention is enforced by threat of legal sanction. In many cases, people simply rely on each other to tell the truth.

In the United States, laws specifically cover many types of misrepresentation, including that in many sales contracts, employment contracts, and even the marriage contract. Cheating behavior involving any of these contracts gives the damaged party the right to dissolve the contract and possibly to claim damages. Other countries that rely less on the legal system to settle disputes have not codified prohibitions against misrepresentation to the same extent, instead relying on social conventions and social sanctions against those found to misrepresent themselves.

Ethical Implications

Cheating involves taking advantage of a situation to gain an unfair advantage. In competitions of all sorts, the objective is to win, but winning carries less meaning when the rules of the game are violated. A student who cheats on a test, for example, appears to have proved attainment of knowledge but instead has proved only the ability to defeat any monitoring system. To the extent that cheating is successful, it punishes those who behave ethically and honestly by giving rewards to those who cheat. This harm to society is one reason that many social conventions have

been codified into law. The same reasoning helps to explain why payment of taxes is not voluntary and is subject to rules, with punishment for violation. Individuals would believe themselves to be gaining by violating any voluntary system of taxation, but the society as a whole would lose because there would be insufficient money to allow the government to provide goods for the benefit of everyone. In cases where conventions are important to society, governments tend to mandate behavior through laws rather than relying on people to behave ethically.

—A. J. Sobczak

Further Reading

Brandt, Richard B. *A Theory of the Good and the Right*. Foreword by Peter Singer. Rev. ed. Amherst, N.Y.: Prometheus Books, 1998.

Callahan, David. *The Cheating Culture: Why More Americans Are Doing Wrong to Get Ahead*. Orlando, Fla.: Harcourt, 2004.

Gert, Bernard. *The Moral Rules: A New Rational Foundation for Morality*. New York: Harper & Row, 1970.

Harman, Gilbert. *The Nature of Morality: An Introduction to Ethics*. New York: Oxford University Press, 1977.

Lande, Nathaniel, and Afton Slade. *Stages: Understanding How You Make Your Moral Decisions*. San Francisco: Harper & Row, 1979.

Langone, John. *Thorny Issues: How Ethics and Morality Affect the Way We Live*. Boston: Little, Brown, 1981.

Shermer, Michael. *The Science of Good and Evil: Why People Cheat, Gossip, Care, Share, and Follow the Golden Rule*. New York: Times Books, 2004.

Weiss, Paul, and Jonathan Weiss. *Right and Wrong: A Philosophical Dialogue Between Father and Son.* New York: Basic Books, 1967.

See also: College applications; Conscience; Fairness; Fraud; Integrity; Lying; Moral education; Resumes; Taxes; Temptation; Universalizability.

Children's television

Definition: Television programming and advertisements designed specifically for children

Type of ethics: Media ethics

Significance: Numerous studies have indicated that children are particularly vulnerable to being influenced by messages contained in television programs and advertisements; for this reason, broadcasters of children's programming have a special ethical responsibility.

By the age of eighteen, most North American children have spent more than two solid years of their lives watching television—more time than many of them have spent in school. Studies dating back to the 1960's indicate that television programming and advertisements can have a strong influence on children, who are frequent viewers. Further, television and media violence, gender and race portrayals, and advertisements have been linked to a variety of adverse behaviors, including violence in later life, aggressive attitudes, and obesity.

Although children's television in the United States has been bound by few ethical codes beyond the broad mandate that broadcasters serve the "public interest, convenience, and necessity," two key pieces of U.S. congressional legislation have attempted to codify that directive. The Children's Television Act of 1990 required programming that met the educational and informational needs of children. The Telecommunications Act of 1996 mandated a program-rating system similar to that used by the film industry and also required manufacturers to install computer devices called V-chips on all new televisions. V-chips read ratings embedded in programs and allow owners of the sets—such as parents—to block shows with specific ratings. In addition, the 1996 law called for broadcasters to air a minimum of three hours of children's educational programming per week.

Although V-chip technology was widely publicized, the device was slow to catch on. By 2004, it was estimated that less than 20 percent of Americans who owned V-chip-equipped televisions were using the device. Further research suggested that broadcasters may not be providing enough information via the rating system, and the definition of educational television remained murky, at best.

Violence

More than one thousand studies have identified links between childhood exposure to television violence and real-life violent behaviors. Some studies have suggested that exposure to television violence, including the make-believe, or fantasy, violence associated with cartoons, may not only desensitize children to acts of real violence but also change their opinions about what constitutes right and wrong behavior. Several studies have found that childhood exposure to media violence predicts aggressive behavior in both male and female adults.

Saturday-morning television programming, typically consisting of cartoons and other shows targeting children, has been found to average twenty-five acts of violence per hour. In addition to programming content, more than a third of commercials airing on children's shows contain aggressive acts, and many advertisements linked to adult-related programming target children. For example, World Wrestling Entertainment, which produces such shows as *SmackDown* and *Raw*, also licenses a series of action figures modeled after wrestling stars.

Gender Roles

Although many children's shows reflect changing modern gender expectations, most programs continue to portray male and female characters with stereotypical traits. For example, male figures appear more frequently in cartoons than do female figures and are generally more action-oriented. Male characters are also more likely to use physical aggression, and female characters are more likely to demonstrate fear, romantic behavior, and supportive gestures. On the other hand, when female characters are portrayed in action roles, they often behave as violently as their male counterparts.

Advertisements targeting children showed similar characteristics. Boys typically appear more often and are placed in contexts in which they have traits of power, control, action, competition, and destruction. The content of commercials targeting girls generally emphasizes more limited physical activity, as well as feelings and nurturing.

Educational Television

Although U.S. federal law requires broadcast television stations to air at least three hours per week of educational programming, the Federal Communications Commission's definition of educational television is vague: "any television programming that furthers the educational and informational needs of children." Broadcasters have frequently pointed to their own studies, which indicate that their educational programming has increased 100 percent since 1990—more than complying with the federal law.

However, by the broadcasters' definitions, their educational programming has included such shows as *NBA: Inside Stuff*, *G.I. Joe*, *America's Funniest Home Videos*, *The Flintstones*, *The Jetsons*, and *Teenage Mutant Ninja Turtles*. At one point, ABC-TV even attempted to depict its program *Tales from the Crypt*, based on HBO's adult horror series, as a way to teach children a "wonder-filled morality lesson."

More traditional forms of educational television often appear on Public Broadcasting System (PBS) including *Sesame Street*, *Barney*, and *Wishbone*. Research studies have suggested that these shows do, indeed, provide young viewers with educational experiences. For example, children who watch *Sesame Street* generally know and understand more words, have a better grasp of mathematics, and are better prepared for school than children who watch only cartoons and general programming on commercial television.

Rogers and François Clemmons reprising their famous foot bath in 1993. The scene was a message of inclusion during an era of racial segregation. By Dr. François S. Clemmons.

Advertising

In 1750 bce, Hammurabi's code made it a crime punishable by death to engage in commerce with a child without first obtaining the permission of a parent. Historically most societies have implicitly understood the ethical questions raised by selling goods to children. Sweden has banned all advertising directed at children under twelve, and in Greece, commercials for toys are banned before 10 p.m.

In North America, however, children represent an exceptionally ripe demographic market. By the early twenty-first century advertisers were spending more than two billion dollars per year on commercials targeting children alone. Numerous studies have suggested that young children are typically unable to understand the intent of advertisements and frequently accept advertising claims as literally true. Many parents also voice concerns that advertising makes children too materialistic and encourages youths to define their self-worth by their possessions.

Health Implications

Around the turn of the twenty-first century, the number of overweight children in North America was double what it had been two decades earlier. Some authorities believed that television was at least partly to blame. Beyond promoting physical inactivity, food advertisements were a regular part of children's television. On Saturday-morning television, for example, 61 percent of commercials were for food, and more than 90 percent of those advertisements were for sugared cereals, fast foods, and other nutritionally questionable foods. Numerous studies have now documented that such advertising is very effective in increasing children's requests for junk food and fast food, and in changing their fundamental views of healthy nutrition.

—*Cheryl Pawlowski*

Further Reading

American Academy of Pediatrics: "Media Education." *Pediatrics* 104 (1999): 341-343.

Macklin, M. C., and L. Carlson, eds. *Advertising to Children: Concepts and Controversies*. Thousand Oaks, Calif.: Sage, 1999.

Robinson, T. N. "Does Television Cause Childhood Obesity?" *Journal of the American Medical Association* 279 (1998): 959-960.

Strasburger, V. C., and B. Wilson. *Children, Adolescents, and the Media: Medical and Psychological Impact*. Thousand Oaks, Calif.: Sage, 2002.

Villani, S. "Impact of Media on Children and Adolescents." *Journal of the American Academy of Child and Adolescent Psychiatry* 40, no. 4 (2001): 392- 401.

Walsh, D. *Selling Out America's Children.* Minneapolis: Fairview Press, 1995.

See also: Advertising; Censorship; Child psychology; Children; Head Start; Moral education; Reality television; Song lyrics; Violence.

Coercion

Definition: Manipulation of other persons, groups, or entities by force or by threat
Type of ethics: Personal and social ethics
Significance: In addition to being an ethical transgression on the part of the perpetrators, the fact of coercion may mitigate one's moral and legal responsibility for acts one was coerced into performing.

Reinhold Niebuhr, the most politically influential American theologian of the twentieth century, wrote in *Moral Man and Immoral Society* (1932) that "all social co-operation on a larger scale than the most intimate social group requires a measure of coercion."

Modern ethicists agree that coercion is present, if not necessary, in every area of social life. The task of ethicists is to lead in critical discussions that will help to identify the nature of coercion, assess responsibility for coerced acts, determine if and when coercion can be appropriately employed, and control coercion.

The Nature of Coercion

Although coercion is sometimes considered to be synonymous with force, they are in fact distinct. When force is used, the person is acted upon; the forced person does not act. In the case of a forced deed, the victim has no freedom to act otherwise. The victim of force is a medium of another person or power. Personal physical force (for example, being manacled or shot) and natural forces (for example, hurricanes, gravity, or illness) can override or remove an agent's ability to act.

If someone pushes another person out of the way of an oncoming car, the first person forces the other person to move but does not coerce that person. Coercive threats are, however, obstacles to self-determination. They limit one's freedom to act, but they are not overwhelming or insuperable. Some choice remains.

A coerced person still acts. Although autonomy is diminished, a measure of autonomy remains. A coercive threat is intended to motivate a person to act by stimulating in the person an irresistible desire to avoid a penalty although the act is also contrary to the person's will. Offers also intend to motivate a person to act by stimulating in the person an irresistible desire, though here the similarity stops. Scholars agree that threats and offers are different types of proposals. Threats can coerce; offers cannot. Even so, threats and offers (also incentives, rewards, bribes, and so forth) can be linguistically structured in terms of one another. A merchant could threaten a customer, saying, "Give me your money or I will deprive you of the merchandise." One could also construe a mugger's proposal, "your money or your life," not as a threat but as an offer to preserve one's life for a fee, but such machinations obscure the issues. The meaning of a proposal, not its linguistic structure, determines whether it is an offer or a coercive threat.

Coercive threats can be further understood and distinguished from offers by means of other characteristics. First, and most fundamental, is that victims of coercion perceive coercive threats as dangers, penalties, or some kind of loss. An offer is considered a beneficial opportunity. Second, a coercive threat cannot be refused without unwanted consequences. Moreover, the consequences of acting in accordance with a coercive threat are also undesired. Regardless of a coerced person's actions, an unwanted consequence is unavoidable. The recipient of an offer, however, can refuse without the recipient's life conditions being altered. Third, a coercive threat requires an imbalance of power, while an offer is usually proposed in a more egalitarian relationship. Fourth, with coercion, the will of the coercer predominates. The threat's recipient submits reluctantly

Responsibility

To be responsible for one's acts is to be accountable for their impact on oneself and on others. If a person were forced to perform certain actions, that person would be relieved of moral responsibility for those actions. Neither praise nor blame would apply. By contrast, when persons freely act, they are responsible for their behavior. Between these two poles is the moral territory of responsibility for coerced acts. Not forced, but not wholly free, coerced persons are only partially accountable for their actions. Coerced persons act with less freedom than normal, contrary to their will, and subject to the influence—not control—of a coercer. All apparent options are rendered morally undesirable. A coerced person's responsibility is therefore limited. The degree of this limitation depends upon the cultural context, the historic background, the immediate situation, and the moral framework.

Limiting Coercion

Because coercion can be personally beneficial and socially necessary, efforts must be made to control it, not eliminate it. To restrain coercion, regardless of the coercer's claim to benevolence, it must be subject to an impartial, third-party evaluation. Human beings are simply too self-interested to weigh their own acts of coercion impartially. Reducing the number of incidents of unjust coercion, however, is more fundamental than is controlling coercion. Unjust coercion can be limited by redressing the inequality from which it grows. History has shown that egalitarian social institutions such as democracy, income redistribution, and public education enhance equality and thereby reduce coercion.

—Paul Plenge Parker

Further Reading

Colvin, Mark. *Crime and Coercion: An Integrated Theory of Chronic Criminality.* New York: St. Martin's Press, 2000.

Frankfurt, Harry G. "Coercion and Moral Responsibility." In *Essays on Freedom of Action*, edited by Ted Honderich. Boston: Routledge & Kegan Paul, 1973.

King, Martin Luther, Jr. *Why We Can't Wait.* New York: Harper & Row, 1964.

McCloskey, H. J. "Coercion: Its Nature and Significance." *Southern Journal of Philosophy* 18 (Fall, 1980): 335-352.

Nozick, Robert. "Coercion." In *Philosophy, Science, and Method.* Edited by Sidney Morgenbesser, Patrick Suppes, and Morton White. New York: St. Martin's Press, 1969.

Wertheimer, Alan. *Coercion.* Princeton, N.J.: Princeton University Press, 1987.

Williams, Daniel Day. *The Spirit and the Forms of Love.* New York: Harper & Row, 1968.

See also: Autonomy; Consent; *Nicomachean Ethics*; Niebuhr, Reinhold; Power; Responsibility; Violence; Will.

College applications

Definition: Information that students seeking admission to institutions of higher learning provide so that their qualifications can be evaluated

Type of ethics: Personal and social ethics.

Significance: Obtaining a good college education is such a critically important matter to young people that many ethical issues arise from the process of applying—from the standpoint of both the applicants' honesty and the care and fairness with which colleges and universities treat their applications.

Formal applications are a standard feature of the admissions processes used by four-year American colleges that do not have "open admissions" policies that allow any high school graduate to enter simply by supplying a high school transcript. Most competitive four-year colleges require applicants to take national standardized tests, such as the Scholastic Aptitude Test (SAT) or the American College Test (ACT) and also require applicants to submit original essays on selected subjects to test their writing and thinking abilities. High school transcripts and national test results are considered to be so objective that they do not usually generate ethical issues, unless there is evidence of outright fraud.

Evaluations of application essays, by contrast, are more subjective and open the door to ethical issues, from the standpoint of both applicants and the institutions. Because most applicants to highly competitive colleges have strong transcripts and impressive national test scores, their essays may be the best opportunities they have to separate themselves from other candidates. To enhance their chances of admission, many applicants turn to Internet services that promise—for a price—to help them write "winning" essays. Is it ethical, however, for applicants to have others write their application essays or to give them so much help that the essays they submit will misrepresent their true writing abilities?

Students who gain admission to competitive colleges under false pretenses may find themselves in academic environments whose challenges go beyond their own capabilities, thus ensuring their chances of failure. It would seem to be clearly unethical for such students to take admission spots that would otherwise go to more capable students who have not paid others to write their application essays for them.

Members of college application evaluation committees should be, and often are, aware of the availability of essay-writing services and may discount essays they judge to have been written by people other than the actual applicants. The possibility of making incorrect judgments increases the chances of unfairly rejecting qualified candidates. In fact, the process itself becomes an imperfect guessing game in which the essay-writing services look for ever more clever deceptions to fool admissions boards, such as giving the essays they provide a less polished look.

The entire process of college admissions raises serious ethical questions that can affect applicants' entire futures. In their efforts to seek objective standards for admission or for finding new ways to evaluate applicants, colleges will continue to grapple with these serious issues.

—Richard L. Wilson

Further Reading

Allen, Andrew. *College Admissions Trade Secrets: A Top Private College Counselor Reveals the Secrets, Lies, and Tricks of the College Admissions Process.* New York: Writer's Press Club, 2001.

Fiske, Edward B., and Bruce G. Hammond. *The Fiske Guide to Getting into the Right College.* Napierville, Ill.: Sourcebooks, 2004.

Steinberg, Laurence. *Beyond the Classroom.* New York: Simon & Schuster, 1997.

See also: Academic freedom; Cheating; Hiring practices; Honesty; Honor systems and codes; Resumes; Title IX.

Computer misuse

Definition: Unauthorized use of computer hardware or software that may cause damage, regardless of intent, to persons, property, or services

Type of ethics: Business and labor ethics

Significance: The presence of computers in the workplace, libraries and other locations is almost universal. Therefore, businesses may face loss of productivity as a result of the misuse of the equipment and their digital resources.

Ethical issues arise when the misuse is not the direct or indirect cause of damage, such as unauthorized remote examination of records or files. Because of the rapid pace of technological innovation in computer technology and use in the late twentieth and early twenty-first centuries, many activities have become commonplace that several decades earlier would have seemed impossible. As the technology continues to develop, handling ethical questions relating to computer use have become increasingly important.

In *Computers, Ethics, and Society* (1990), M. David Ermann, Mary B. Williams, and Claudio Gutierrez offered a theoretical framework for discussions about which behaviors may be considered as blameworthy. For example, should it be considered as unethical simply to gain access to the computer files of other persons, without their permission and knowledge, even if there is no intention to destroy or alter those files? The authors suggest that utilitarian theorists might conclude that such acts are neither morally wrong nor morally right. No measurable harm actually results from the unauthorized access. An alternative approach would involve analysis of the act from the perspective of Immanuel Kant. The Kantian categorical imperative, that people must always treat other persons as ends in themselves and never merely as means to an end, might suggest the act of gaining unauthorized access to the files of another is morally wrong. By committing such an act, the actor fails to take into account the right of privacy of the person whose files have been accessed.

Workplaces, Libraries, and Academic Settings

Many activities in the workplace create opportunities for computer abuse. For example, an employee may have access to a computer with an Internet connection that enables the employee to perform tasks as assigned by the employer. The employer's expectation is that the computer will be used solely within the course or scope of employment. From time to time, however, this is not the case. Instances of computer misuse present ethical questions regarding the moral implications of those misuses.

Computer misuses in the workplace fall into at least three broad categories. First, there are misuses of a relatively benign, personal nature. Misuses in this category might involve online shopping, downloading files or trading stock in personal brokerage accounts, sending non-business-related electronic mail to relatives and friends, and so on. A second category might include such activities as downloading copyrighted material such as music or software, thereby potentially exposing the employer to copyright infringement liability. A third, and most severe, category of misuse would include forwarding or receiving pornography, producing and disseminating computer viruses, threatening or harassing others, committing fraud, hacking, or mishandling confidential information of the business itself or of its clients.

The misuses in the second two categories, while certainly posing serious ethical issues, may additionally expose the perpetrator to legal liability, either civil or criminal in nature. The activities in the first category, while not of a strictly illegal nature, nevertheless present questions of ethical import. While employees are involved in personal activities, they are not performing tasks assigned by their employers and may also be tying up limited office resources.

One ethical question arising from such behavior is how the blameworthiness of such activities be determined. Some might argue that these misuses should not be evaluated any differently than any other actions that decrease workplace productivity, such as arriving late to work, leaving early, and taking overly long lunch breaks. Others would suggest that because of the public nature of the latter forms of misbehavior, they are easier for employers to guard against. By contrast, computer misuse activities typically occur in the relative privacy of individual employee offices and cubicles, leaving much if not all of the policing of such activities to the individual employees. For this reason, questions of ethics and individual choice are of paramount importance.

In addition to the types of computer misuses that arise in the workplace, libraries and academic setting such as high schools, colleges and universities face additional potential for misuse. Computer users in such environments are frequently children or teenagers. The free access to the Internet afforded by library and school computers presents risks in the form of sites on the World Wide Web dedicated to pornography and pedophilia. As a result, librarians face ethical questions of whether access to such sites should be blocked completely, thereby protecting younger patrons. This action would also serve to deny access to older patrons, who might not feel that the library was receptive to their information needs.

In response to computer misuse, many companies, libraries, and academic institutions have developed written policies containing lists of authorized and unauthorized uses. These policies also set forth penalties for failure to comply with their requirements.

—Gloria A. Whittico

Further Reading

Baird, Robert M., Reagan Ramsower, and Stuart E. Rosenbaum, eds. *Cyberethics: Social and Moral Issues in the Computer Age.* Amherst, N.Y.: Prometheus Books, 2010.

Ermann, M. David, Mary B. Williams, and Claudio Gutierrez, eds. *Computers, Ethics, and Society.* New York: Oxford University Press, 1990.

Ermann, David, and Michele S. Shauf, eds. *Computers, Ethics, and Society.* 3d ed. New York: Oxford University Press, 2002.

Forester, Tom, and Perry Morrison. *Computer Ethics: Cautionary Tales and Ethical Dilemmas in Computing.* 2d ed. Cambridge, Mass.: MIT Press, 1994.

Hafner, Katie, and John Markoff. *Cyberpunk: Outlaws and Hackers on the Computer Frontier.* New York: Simon & Schuster, 1991.

Iannone, A. Pablo. *Contemporary Moral Controversies in Technology.* New York: Oxford University Press, 1987.

Weckert, John, and Douglas Adeney. *Computer and Information Ethics.* Westport, Conn.: Greenwood Press, 1997.

See also: Artificial intelligence; Computer crime; Computer technology; Electronic mail; Identity theft; Internet chat rooms; Napster; Plagiarism.

Consumerism

Definition: Movement aimed at improving the status and power of the consumer relative to the seller in the marketplace

Date: Began during the late 1960's

Type of ethics: Business and labor ethics

Significance: Consumerism is strongly associated with the introduction of morality into the otherwise amoral marketplace, since it emphasizes the responsibilities of manufacturers to consumers in such areas as product safety, fair pricing, and honest advertising.

The publication in 1965 of Ralph Nader's book *Unsafe at Any Speed*, which criticized the dangerous design features of the Chevrolet Corvair, is often viewed as the birth of modern-day consumerism. Since that time, Nader and others have founded such consumer organizations as the Center for Auto Safety, Public Citizen, the Health Research Group, and various buyers' cooperatives to promote safer products, lower prices, and full and honest disclosure in advertising.

Two important trends have encouraged the growth of consumerism: the fact that sellers (manufacturers and retailers) increasingly tend to be giant corporations with whom individual buyers have little influence; and the growing complexity of many consumer products, which prevents buyers from making informed judgments. Consumerism has led to the passage of such legislation at the federal level as the Child Protection and Safety Act, the Hazardous Substances Act, and the Fair Credit Reporting Act, as well as the creation of the Consumer Product Safety Commission. The movement has been unsuccessful, however, in lobbying for the establishment of a federal cabinet-level consumer protection agency.

—D. Kirk Davidson

See also: Advertising; Boycotts; Business ethics; Infomercials; Nader, Ralph; Price fixing; Product safety and liability; Sales ethics; Warranties and guarantees.

Corporate compensation

Definition: Salaries, stock options, bonuses, and other benefits received by top corporate officers

Type of ethics: Business and labor ethics

Significance: Many people think it unethical that chief executive officers (CEOs) and other high officers of many American corporations receive immense salaries, huge bonuses, the right to purchase company stock below market prices, and extravagant perquisites ("perks"); however, there are arguments on both sides of the issue.

Many people believe that huge gaps in income levels between corporate CEOs and their employees are unethical. An early twenty-first century analysis of corporate compensation found that the average CEO received slightly more than 280 times the amount earned by the average worker. In 2002, the highest-paid executives among Standard and Poor's five hundred top firms received compensation worth as much as $20 million apiece.

In addition to their salaries, many CEOs receive "golden parachute" packages at retirement or exit compensation packages that enable them to land safely in the event they get fired from their companies, or their companies are taken over or fail. CEOs also usually have unusually strong job security through multiyear contracts and the close relationships they enjoy with members of their boards of directors.

By contrast, most employees work under "employment-at-will" conditions and can be dismissed at any time and for any reason. The ethics of these distinctions can be considered from the perspectives to contrasting philosophical theories: libertarianism and distributive justice.

Libertarian philosopher Robert Nozick holds the view that since Americans live in a free market society, they should be willing to compensate people for goods and services they provide based on supply and demand, thereby maximizing individual rights. Inequalities in incomes are natural products of differing natural abilities and should not be subjected to moral or ethical judgments. It is natural that large and complex corporations are willing to offer CEOs high salaries and extravagant compensation packages in return for the rare and valuable skills that CEOs bring to their positions. Corporations must compensate their CEOs with extraordinary financial and other inducements if they expect to hire and retain them. In most cases corporate compensation is pegged to overall organizational performance and corporate organizational health, and serves as a baseline in calculating compensation for other employees.

Philosopher John Rawls, a proponent of the theory of distributive justice, represents a contrasting school of thought. He asks whether it is ethical for CEOs to receive high salaries and other corporate compensation schemes, while their employees face the possibility of losing their jobs through corporate downsizing. Huge disparities in income levels between management and ordinary employees make the lower-level employees cynical, foster morale problems, and cultivate feelings of inequality.

—*Joseph C. Santora*

Further Reading

Brancato, Carolyn Kay, and Christian A. Plath. *Corporate Governance Best Practices: A Blueprint for the Post-Enron Era.* New York: Conference Board, 2003.

Nozick, R. *Anarchy, State and Utopia.* New York: Basic Books, 1974.

Rawls, John. *A Theory of Justice.* Cambridge, Mass.: Harvard University Press, 1971.

See also: Business ethics; Corporate responsibility; Corporate scandal; Distributive justice; Downsizing; Greed; Income distribution; Minimum-wage laws; Professional athlete incomes.

Corporate responsibility

Definition: Moral accountability of corporations for their actions, including but not limited to their duty to conform to the laws of the state

Type of ethics: Business and labor ethics

Significance: Corporate responsibility raises important issues for ethics in regard to the nature of collective action and the division between personal and group morality. The disjunction between the ethical responsibilities and the legal accountability of large corporations may lead some to question the level of social justice available within late capitalist society.

Business corporations are collectivities of persons that are granted legal personhood and limited liability by the state for the purpose of carrying on commerce. The purposes for which a general corporation is created—primarily to make profit from commerce for its shareholders—raise questions about whether corporations ought to undertake supererogatory actions for the public good. This issue is further complicated by the issue of minority stockholders' rights, since there are few noncontroversial issues of public policy and the unanimous agreement of stockholders is scarcely to be anticipated in large, publicly traded corporations.

Nobel laureate Milton Friedman has argued eloquently for restricting the moral obligation of corporations to obeying the laws of their respective nations. In this view, minority stockholders' rights are a prime consideration, but the economic efficiency of the market is another desired aim of this policy. The purely economic arrangement of the market, this theory argues, would be damaged by the noneconomic behavior of altruistic corporations. The lessening of the profitability of some enterprises, the potential for boycott, counter-boycott, and so forth, threaten the normal functioning of the capitalistic market economy, in this view.

The contrary view would hold that it is absurd to separate financial profitability from questions of the general quality of life: Would it make sense for a businessman to indulge in some as-yet legal form of polluting if that pollution would significantly shorten his life and/or that of his family? Would it be "profitable" for one to make money by legally selling weaponry to a potential enemy who might be expected to use those weapons to conquer or to destroy one's nation?

—Patrick M. O'Neil

See also: Accountability; Boycotts; Business ethics; Consumerism; Corporate scandal; Duty; Employee safety and treatment; Leadership; Sales ethics; Self-regulation.

Corporate scandal

Definition: Highly publicized legal and ethical misconduct of corporate leaders

Type of ethics: Business and labor ethics

Significance: During the first years of the twenty-first century, a long string of financial frauds in public American corporations cast public doubt on the ethics of even untarnished corporations. Such trust, once lost, is slow to return. The immediate measure result was a slowdown in the financial markets.

President Theodore Roosevelt is credited with saying that to "educate a person in mind and not in morals is to educate a menace to society." Rarely has the truth of that observation been more apparent than in the early years of the twenty-first century, when numerous corporate scandals, perpetrated by highly educated and highly paid corporate officers, dominated the news media.

Corporate financial scandals are not new; they have been around since the dawn of the corporate form of business in the late nineteenth century. They have been called the "agency problem." As agents of their companies' stockholders, corporate officers utilize corporation assets on behalf of the stockholders. At the same time, the officers have a vested interest in maximizing their own well-being. The result is that stockholders need some form of governance over the officers of the corporations. Such governance is supposed to be provided by corporate boards of directors, audit committees, and internal auditors who oversee the activities of management. However, during the early years of the twenty-first century, several corporations, including Enron, WorldCom, Global Crossing, HealthSouth, Tyco, and others, were driven into bankruptcy or other financial embarrassments due to the overly greedy activities of their high-level executives.

In some cases, corporate stock options—the right to purchase shares of stock at a certain price—were the cause of the financial fraud. In other cases, opportunities to receive year-end salary bonuses were the incentive. After exercising their options to buy stock at low prices, corporate officers could then manipulate their companies' financial reports to make reported income appear to be higher than it actually was, thus raising the value of their own stock. The result was that many corporate officers benefitted at the expense of stockholders. In instances in which employees were offered bonuses for achieving specific income goals for their companies, officers used various methods to report greater revenues or lower expenses, or both. These actions were clearly unethical acts on the part of the officers, but the practice was widespread enough to dampen all stock market activity severely.

Enron and WorldCom

In most cases of corporate scandal, external auditors were blamed, either for agreeing to the questionable practices of the corporate officers, or for failing to uncover the illegal activities. One of the most highly publicized scandals, which affected the Enron Corporation, was uncovered in late 2001. After Andersen & Company (formerly Arthur Andersen & Company), the external auditor that had approved some questionable Enron transactions, was discovered to have shredded thousands of documents related to its audit of Enron, that venerable auditing firm was destroyed. By the spring of 2002, Andersen essentially ceased to exist—not merely because it had failed in conducting an audit, but because it attempted to hide its audit coverage by shredding key documents.

As the news coverage of the Enron scandal waned, a new fraud was uncovered at WorldCom, a major telecommunications firm in Clinton, Mississippi. Internal auditors at WorldCom discovered that the company's chief financial officer, controller, and other accounting employees had recorded expenses as assets, which resulted in ostensibly higher income and the consequent awarding of huge bonuses to top-level employees. The WorldCom scandal was essentially the straw that broke the camel's back. Investors prevailed upon Congress to do something about the unethical acts of corporate executives. The result was the passage on July 31, 2002, of the Sarbanes-Oxley Act, which limited the types of nonaudit work that external auditors are allowed to perform for their clients. The law also required corporate executives to certify to the accuracy of their company's financial statements.

Internal Auditors

One of the reasons that the Sarbanes-Oxley Act limited the types of work done by external auditors was that large audit firms were selling consulting services to their clients as well as conducting audits. Since auditors are supposed to be independent of their clients, their providing consulting services was regarded as a conflict of interest that inhibited their independence. This practice was particularly noted at Enron, where Andersen had either designed or approved the use of subsidiary organizations that would absorb losses that would otherwise have appeared on Enron's books.

Internal auditors are considered the first line of defense against questionable corporate ethics, but at Enron there were no internal auditors. Andersen had convinced Enron's board of directors that it could also handle the company's internal auditing duties. This concept of outsourcing the internal audit function to the external auditor had become a common American business practice during the late 1990's. However, the breakdown at Enron led to the prohibition against the practice in the Sarbanes-Oxley Act.

Enron Complex in Downtown Houston. By Alex.

Corporate Fraud in History

The perpetration of fraud by corporate insiders is not a new phenomenon. During the 1870's, half of the railroads in the United States were in receivership, many because of the immoral acts of insiders. In 1932, the bankruptcy of the Swedish financier Ivar Kreuger's scandal-ridden empire following his suicide led to a national outcry that resulted in Congress's passage of the 1933 Securities Act. During the 1980's, hundreds of financial institutions failed because of insider fraud, leading to a congressional investigation.

In many respects, Enron, WorldCom, and their ilk are merely extensions of the nineteenth century railroads and the Kreuger debacle. In every case, the governance system broke down or did not exist, and unethical individuals succumbed to greed. Laws cannot make individuals ethical, but by reducing opportunities for personal enrichment through the use of internal auditors, audit committees, and other forms of governance, unethical persons will have fewer opportunities for gain.

—Dale L. Flesher

Further Reading

Brancato, Carolyn Kay, and Christian A. Plath. *Corporate Governance Best Practices: A Blueprint for the Post-Enron Era*. New York: Conference Board, 2003.

Bryce, Robert. *Pipe Dreams: Greed, Ego, and the Death of Enron*. New York: Public Affairs, 2002.

Cruver, Brian. *Anatomy of Greed: The Unshredded Truth from an Enron Insider*. New York: Carroll& Graf, 2002.

Fox, Loren. *Enron: The Rise and Fall*. Hoboken, N.J.: Wiley & Sons, 2003.

Jeter, Lynne. *Disconnected: Deceit and Betrayal at WorldCom*. Hoboken, N.J.: Wiley & Sons, 2003.

Swartz, Mimi, and Sherron Watkins. *Power Failure: The Inside Story of the Collapse of Enron*. New York: Doubleday, 2003.

See also: Business ethics; Corporate compensation; Corporate responsibility; Corruption; Ethical codes of organizations; "Everyone does it"; Insider trading; Private vs. public morality; Stewart, Martha; Whistleblowing; White-collar crime.

Cost-benefit analysis

Definition: Method of deciding between alternative courses of action that weighs economic costs and benefits in order to ensure that net benefits outweigh net costs

Type of ethics: Environmental ethics

Significance: Cost-benefit analysis is a tool especially valued by environmental and regulatory agencies that must make choices in proposals for public land use. The ethical challenge is determining whether the assumption that preferences for such issues as wilderness and clean air protection can be measured in economic terms is valid.

Cost-benefit analysis was developed by economists in the early 1950's as a test for the desirability of government policies and projects. Just as a corporation maximizes profits, good government should maximize the benefits for society. Cost-benefit analysis is a procedure for decision making that emphasizes consequences. The procedure is simple: Given alternative courses of action, policy makers should choose the course that maximizes public benefits after subtracting associated costs, which are expressed in dollars.

Economists have touted cost-benefit analysis as an especially useful and rigorous way of thinking about issues such as health care and environmental and regulatory policies. Common sense seems to dictate a preference for choices that maximize benefits and minimize costs. However, cost-benefit analysis is not without its critics, notably environmentalists and philosophers who are concerned about the ethical implications of this thinking.

Estimating Value

Preferences for health care, clean water, environmental beauty, and safe consumer products, can be affected by regulation and policies. Cost-benefit analysis requires that such preferences be expressed in dollar amounts. For example, in a case in which the installation of pollution control equipment will result in the savings of human life, it should be easy to estimate the equipment costs. However, it is notoriously difficult to assign dollar values to the benefit of saving human lives. How can such costs be measured? For example, should the baseline be the annual salaries of the people whose lives are saved?

Critics also argue that cost-benefit analysis raises serious fairness issues by implying that people with higher incomes are more important than those with lower incomes. If society thinks of workers in terms of their incomes, because low-income workers cost less than higher income workers, they might consequently be afforded less protection because they are cheaper to replace.

Making Decisions

Cost-benefit analysis offers a procedure for resolving disputes between competing interests to everyone's benefit. An example might be one in which two parties disagree over the use of a piece of land—one party wishes to develop it, and the other to preserve it. To resolve the dispute one could ask what the parties are willing to pay to develop or to preserve the land.

Analysts claim that the party willing to pay more money is the party that desires the property more and consequently will benefit more from its acquisition. That line of reasoning seems to be intuitive—if one party is willing to pay more for something, then one must want it more. The "losers" in the bidding war could then be compensated for their losses, and no one would be worse off. However, this result is also controversial. If willingness to pay is equated to what a party can actually pay on demand, then the losing bidder must desire the outcome less. However, what if one party just has fewer financial resources than the other? It does not follow that that party wants the property less. Furthermore, financial compensation for "losers" may be irrelevant if their interest in the land is noneconomic and cannot be measured in dollar amounts.

—*Edward W. Maine*

Further Reading

Hausman, Daniel, Michael S. McPherson. *Economic Analysis and Moral Philosophy*. Cambridge, England: Cambridge University Press, 1998.

Kelman, Stephen. "Cost-Benefit Analysis: An Ethical Critique." *Regulation* (1981): 74-82.

Van DeVeer, Donald, and Christine Pierce. *The Environmental Ethics and Policy Book*. Belmont, Calif.: Wadsworth, 1998.

See also: Choice; Economic analysis; Free-riding; Future-oriented ethics; Health care allocation; Incommensurability; Medical insurance; Outsourcing; Pollution permits; Utilitarianism.

Downsizing

Definition: Reduction of a company's size through employee layoffs

Type of ethics: Business and labor ethics

Significance: Downsizing is a management decision that has ethical implications for managers, who must consider their responsibilities to maintain the financial health of their firms for shareholders and to honor the rights of their employees.

According to the federal Bureau of Labor Statistics, 11,947 mass layoff actions were implemented during the first half of 2003 alone, prompting 1,183,045 unemployment insurance benefits filings. Such downsizing decisions are management choices that have different ethical implications and perceptions depending on whether the affected people are managers formulating and implementing downsizing plans or employees losing their jobs.

It is generally believed that company managers have an ethical obligation to make sound business decisions that maintain the financial integrity of their firms and that are in the best interests of their firms' owners. Beyond the bottom-line impact of downsizing decisions, managers must consider, in varying degrees, the ethical implications that impact their employees in formulating and implementing downsizing decisions. At one extreme are managers who believe that any downsizing decisions are correct in light of their responsibilities to their firms' owners and that they have little or no ethical responsibility to employees in whatever subsequent actions result from their decisions.

At the other extreme are managers who factor in ethical considerations at every step of the downsizing process by exhausting every other alternative for maintaining the financial health of their organizations and choosing downsizing as their last alternative. Then, as they formulate and implement their decisions, they remain conscious of the ethical obligations they have to the employees who are affected by their decisions. For example, in addition to providing severance pay for employees who lose their jobs, the manages may also provide benefits packages that include outplacement assistance; personal, financial, and career counseling; and assistance with medical insurance coverage.

Studies have shown that employees believe that their employers violate their ethical responsibilities when management denies their rights on any of three aspects of downsizing. The first aspect is poor timing. Employers should not implement their downsizing decisions on dates near major holidays, and they should give their employees ample advance notice. Sixty days' notice is a standard used by many and is the law in some situations.

The second aspect is the method of communication through which the news is conveyed to employees. No person losing a job wants to learn the bad news while reading the morning newspaper. Finally, employees who lose their jobs want to know there are valid reasons for their firms' layoff decisions. When management provides adequate notice, communicates through appropriate channels, and provides cogent reasons for downsizing, employees are likely to believe they have received ethical treatment during the difficult downsizing process.

—*Stephen D. Livesay and Corinne R. Livesay*

Further Reading
De Meuse, Kenneth, and Mitchell Lee Marks. *Resizing the Organization*. San Francisco: Jossey-Bass, 2003.
Radin, Tara, et al. *Employment and Employee Rights*. Malden, Mass.: Blackwell Publishing, 2004.

See also: Business ethics; Corporate compensation; Corporate responsibility; Cost-benefit analysis; Employee safety and treatment; Hiring practices; Multinational corporations; Outsourcing.

Employee safety and treatment

Definition: Policies and procedures used by employers to protect the on-the-job safety and welfare of their workers

Type of ethics: Business and labor ethics

Significance: Employers have an ethical responsibility for the general workplace health and safety because they—and not their workers—control the facilities and equipment used. To place responsibility on workers would be to create a gap between responsibility and authority.

Worker treatment is generally seen as falling into two basic categories: the physical safety of employees in the workplace and the rights of workers to fairness and dignity with respect to hiring, compensation, promotions, job security, and discrimination.

Physical Safety

As approximately 10,000 workers are killed each year in American workplaces, and another 2.8 million workers are injured (these numbers do not include workers who suffer from occupational diseases, which can take decades to develop), safety is a critical issue in business. Ensuring physical safety requires the elimination of workplace hazards and implementation of safety standards. Although many hazards have been eliminated, many dangerous conditions still exist. Among these dangers are textile fibers that can cause brown lung disease, paint vapors that cause emphysema, excessive noise that may cause hearing loss, and debilitating carpal tunnel syndrome from computer keyboard operation.

To improve worker safety and to establish forums in which employees may seek remuneration, individual states began enacting legislation to guarantee payment for workplace injuries as early as 1920. This legislation, known as worker's compensation, or "worker's comp," compensated workers only for existing injuries and did not eliminate the conditions that caused injuries. To reduce workplace injuries, the federal government enacted the Occupational Safety and Health Act, which established the Occupational Safety and Health Administration (OSHA) in 1970.

With the creation of OSHA, employers had a new legal duty to maintain a safe working environment, provide proper supervision, and educate their employees about their products and their workplace. OSHA required all employers to conform to certain minimum safety standards and sought to reduce hazards in the workplace by establishing corporate responsibilities for improving worker safety and health. OSHA sometimes disciplines employers who think that compensating injured workers is cheaper than implementing costly safety standards to prevent accidents. OSHA may impose criminal penalties upon individuals within the corporate structure—rather than only upon the corporation itself—if it finds that corporate managers understood the risks to workers and ignored them.

One famous example of how disastrous it can be for a company to fail to provide for employee safety is Johns Manville, formerly the leading manufacturer of asbestos products. During the 1930's the company discovered that exposure to asbestos fibers could result in serious, even fatal, disabilities. However, the company kept this information private and did not inform its thousands of workers about the hazards of asbestos exposure. When the dangers of asbestos finally became known to the public in the early 1980's, thousands of lawsuits were filed by former employees of Manville and other companies that used asbestos products supplied by Manville. As a result, Manville declared bankruptcy, established a fund to help pay for injuries, and became widely vilified for its failure to warn workers. The result of Manville's negligence was catastrophe—for the injured workers and their families, and for the company, which was nearly destroyed. More even than OSHA, the common law character of American courts makes employers liable for negligent or malicious behavior on their part.

By the early twenty-first century, one of the important twentieth century assumptions about worker's compensation legislation had come under widespread attack. As American labor costs—including insurance premiums to pay for worker's compensation claims—rose, businesses increasingly found it cheaper to export jobs to low-wage environments in countries abroad. In an effort to save American jobs, business have pressured many state governments to reduce the benefits awarded under their worker's compensation laws or face the loss of jobs to other less protective American states or to overseas locations.

This growing trend raised new ethical issues, and not only for workers who may find themselves with reduced protection. If workers are injured in facilities controlled by irresponsible employers and the new worker's compensation laws do not provide adequately for medical costs or permanent disabilities, the injured workers will be forced into some form of state financed welfare. This is an ethical issue not only for the workers but also for responsible employers. Caring employers who attempt to maintain safe working environments for their employees will pay twice: once for the safety measures they provide and again when they pay increased taxes to cover the losses foisted on the taxpayers by less responsible employers.

Safety in the workplace is of paramount importance to all ethical employers, and ideas about what constitutes safety have evolved as new knowledge has become available. A classic example of how opinions can change regarding what constitutes a safe workplace is the issue of secondhand smoke. During the early 1980's, few employers saw a need to protect their employees from coworkers' secondhand smoke. By the early twenty-first century, however, secondhand smoke was recognized as a serious workplace concern. Although there is no doubt that the workplace has become safer and that employers' concern for the safety of workers has increased, the issue of safety merits continued close attention.

Workers' Rights and Fairness

All workers have the right to expect fairness from their employers and to be treated with respect and dignity. Fairness is especially important in the areas of hiring practices, compensation, promotions, privacy, discrimination, job security, and sexual harassment.

The federal government has enacted legislation to protect employees from discrimination in the workplace based on race, religion, sex, color, and national origin. Title VII of the Civil Rights Act of 1964 specifically protects women, African Americans, Hispanics, Native Americans, Asian Americans, and Pacific Islanders. In addition, some states and local communities have added to the list more protections, such as those relating to marital status, veteran status, and sexual orientation. The Pregnancy Discrimination Act of 1978 protects pregnant women from discrimination, and the Age Discrimination in Employment Act of 1975 extends protection to workers forty years of age or older. The 1990 Americans with Disabilities Act requires all companies with more than fifteen employees to provide reasonable accommodations for workers with disabilities. The goal of all this legislation is to incorporate fairness into the workplace so that ability will be the primary criterion in decisions that involve hiring, promotions, compensation, discipline, and firing.

Another twenty-first century issue in the workplace is sexual harassment, which is a form of gender discrimination. While a precise definition of sexual harassment is not always clear to employers, employees, or even lower courts, the U.S. Supreme Court has moved in the direction of greater clarity in successive cases. Sexual harassment is an ethical issue because it unfairly focuses job advancement or retention on a factor other than the ability to do a job. As a result of legislation and well-publicized lawsuits, many companies have adopted guidelines for dealing with sexual harassment as well as training programs to educate employees about the dangers of harassment and discrimination.

—*Jonathan Hugh Mann; Updated by Richard L. Wilson*

Further Reading

Broadhurst, Arlene Idol, and Grant Ledgerwood. *Environmental Ethics and the Corporation.* Houndmills, England: Macmillan, 2000.

Buchholz, Rogene A., and Sandra B. Rosenthal. *Rethinking Business Ethics.* New York: Oxford University Press, 2000.

Collins, Larry R., and Thomas D. Schneid. *Physical Hazards of the Workplace.* Boca Raton, Fla.: Lewis, 2001.

Des Jardins, Joseph R., and John J. McCall, eds. *Contemporary Issues in Business Ethics.* 4th ed. Belmont, Calif.: Wadsworth, 1999.

Hofmann, David A., and Lois E. Tetrick, eds. *Health and Safety in Organizations: A Multilevel Perspective.* San Francisco, Calif.: Jossey-Bass, 2003.

Nielsen, Richard P. *The Politics of Ethics: Methods for Acting, Learning, and Sometimes Fighting with Others in Addressing Ethics Problems in Organizational Life.* New York: Oxford University Press, 1996.

Pava, Moses L. *The Search for Meaning in Organizations.* New York: Quorum Books, 1999.

Solomon, Robert C. *A Better Way to Think About Business.* New York: Oxford University Press, 1999.

See also: Ageism; Biometrics; Business ethics; Downsizing; Dress codes; Fairness; Fear in the workplace; Medical ethics; Medical insurance; Product safety and liability; Sexual abuse and harassment.

Ethical codes of organizations

Definition: Guidelines adopted by professional organizations and businesses that seek to impose or encourage ethical conduct through either mandatory or permissive rules

Type of ethics: Business and labor ethics

Significance: Numerous organizations of all sorts have adopted or are adopting ethical codes. However, whether such codes have a meaningful impact or are designed merely to project positive images to the public continues to be debated.

Ethical codes for organizations have both a long history and a recent resurgence of interest in light of the corporate scandals of the early twenty-first century. Such codes can be broken down into codes adopted by trade or professional associations to guide the conduct of members and codes adopted by businesses, typically corporations.

The first category has a long and established history. There are, for example, long-standing codes governing the conduct of lawyers, psychologists, accountants, doctors, journalists, engineers, and many others. Some of these efforts, such as the famous Hippocratic oath taken by physicians, are of ancient vintage, while others began early in the twentieth century. The first attempt to institute an ethical code by the American Bar Association, for example, was in 1908.

The second category tends to be of more recent vintage and has become increasingly common. A prime reason for this movement is that companies that want to be perceived as good corporate citizens adopt codes of ethics, particularly in the wake of publicity surrounding corporate scandals involving WorldCom, Enron, and others. Moreover, the Sarbanes-Oxley Act, passed by the U.S. Congress as a response to corporate scandals, requires, among other things, that public companies adopt codes of ethics for their senior financial officers, and that their codes be made publicly available. In a similar vein, many stock exchanges mandate that the companies they list adopt codes of ethics for all their corporate employees. In light of these trends, the vast majority of Fortune 500 companies had codes of ethics by 2003.

The Content of Ethical Codes

Given the variety of organizations and issues ethical codes can address, on one code is typical. Many, perhaps most, address issues such as conflicts of interest, confidentiality of information, labor relations, and political contributions. Other codes cover such matters as business goals and aspirations and social responsibility.

A critical issue involving such codes has to do with how and when they are enforced. Some codes permit or mandate discharging employees or other disciplinary action if they are violated. Others, however, contain provisions allowing appropriate authorities within the organizations to waive the codes' prohibitions. With the passage of the Sarbanes-Oxley Act, such waivers may need to be publicly disclosed—an attempt by Congress to discourage corporate boards of directors from rubber-stamping unethical behavior, such as self-dealing among corporate senior executives.

Rationales and Critiques

Drafters of ethical codes justify them as a means of embodying best practices and ideals for a group. In a similar vein, codes raise group consciousness so that members of organizations are sensitized to ethical issues that may not be immediately obvious, such as subtle conflicts of interest. This is seen as especially important in light of what some perceive as a moral decline in culture generally. Moreover, in some instances, violations of a code can serve as the basis for discipline within or expulsion from a professional organization, thus maintaining the organization's integrity and reputation.

Ethical codes are not without their critics. Some people argue that ethics are, by definition, deliberative and collaborative—something that no code of ethics can be. Others question the ability of a code either to encourage ethical behavior or to discourage unethical behavior. Another critique is that such codes may foster a misleading sense of complacency; the very existence of such a code may be taken to mean that an organization and, by extension, its members take ethics seriously. An infamous example is that the Enron Corporation had its own code of ethics. That code, like many similar ones, had a conflict-of-interest provision that prohibited Enron employees from participating in both sides of any transaction taking place between Enron and other entities with which it did business. However, such forbidden practices were later found to have been done repeatedly within the organization.

Some people have argued that an organization's "culture"—the "way things are done" and the types of behavior that garner recognition and advancement within an organization—influences the behavior of its members far more than a written code of ethics ever could.

A major influence and perhaps disincentive in the adoption of codes of ethics is the looming threat of litigation. Many companies fear that their adoption of codes will enable litigants to sue them privately for violations of codes. As a matter of public policy, some argue that this is a good way to impose accountability on corporate behavior. Others, however, argue that such litigation will simply increase the cost of doing business, which is in the interest of neither the company nor the public.

—*Robert Rubinson*

Further Reading

Davies, Peter W. F. *Current Issues in Business Ethics*. London: Routledge, 1997.

Di Norcia, Vincent. *Hard Like Water: Ethics in Business*. Oxford, England: Oxford University Press, 1998.

Gorlin, Rena A. *Codes of Professional Responsibility: Ethics Standards in Business, Health, and Law*. 4th ed. Washington, D.C.: Bureau of National Affairs, 1999.

Manley, Walter W., II. *Executive's Handbook of Model Business Conduct Codes*. Englewood Cliffs, N.J.: Prentice-Hall, 1991.

See also: Applied ethics; Code of Professional Responsibility; Codes of civility; Corporate scandal; Dress codes; Ethical Principles of Psychologists; Honor systems and codes; Judicial conduct code; Medical bills of rights; *Principles of Medical Ethics*; Professional ethics.

Ethics in Accounting

Definition: Legal and moral obligations that govern the collecting, classifying, and summarizing of financial information about a given firm to record, report, and analyze that information honestly

Type of ethics: Politico-economic ethics

Significance: Ethics in accounting focuses on adhering to accurate and honest accounting practices, and scholars have identified a number of approaches and social norms that seek to explain how accountants make ethical decisions.

Accounting deals with the rules that govern the collecting, classifying, and summarizing of financial information about a given firm, and ethics is concerned with recording, reporting, and analyzing that information honestly, so that it reflects true market values. Ethics in accounting focuses on adhering to accurate and honest accounting practices, and scholars have identified a number of approaches and social norms that seek to explain how accountants make ethical decisions. Because employers and the public

expect new accountants to already be trained in ethical behavior, the federal government and professional accounting organizations have accepted responsibility for setting guidelines for ethics in accounting.

Overview

The accounting profession depends on the ability of its client base and relevant stakeholders to trust the information that accountants provide about their firms. A series of scandals in the early twenty-first century focused global attention on the ethics of accounting and led to an increased emphasis on teaching ethics to accounting students. In the United States, a number of states now require that accounting students be trained in the ethics of accounting before they are licensed as certified public accountants (CPAs).

Once in the workplace, however, new accountants are faced with ethical decisions that may determine the course of their entire careers. Just as business executives depend on accountants to provide them with information about the financial health of their firms, governments depend on that information to produce information about the health of the economy as a whole. Accountants who do not behave ethically may find themselves facing criminal charges that lead to heavy fines and prison terms.

While *ethical behaviors* are closely related to *morals*, the two terms are not always synonymous. Morals govern personal rather than professional behavior. The modern Occupy movement, which has been partially a response to corporate greed and unethical business behavior, has ignited a spark around the world with a grassroots movement dedicated to demanding more ethical behavior.

In the United States, there are 55 jurisdictions that license CPAs, and 35 of those jurisdictions require CPAs to either complete a stand-alone ethics course or prove ethical knowledge through an ethics examination. California, Illinois, Maryland, Texas, Indiana, and West Virginia require that CPAs present evidence of a stand-alone ethics course in order to be certified. California has gone further than any other state in promoting ethics in accounting, mandating ten units of ethics courses and requiring that at least three of those units be taken in accounting ethics. The American Institute of Certified Public Accountants has increased pressure on states to establish strict ethics accounting standards.

To explain ethical decision-making in accounting, scholars have identified such approaches as egoism, universalism, utilitarianism, and social norms that differ according to the goals involved in each, focusing variously on the interests of employers, society, and customs. The most common approach is utilitarianism, which considers consequences paramount to decision-making. In the late 1980s, scholars began focusing on cognitive-based models, paying close attention to psychological theories developed by Lawrence Kohlberg, who was the first to identify the stages of moral development.

Rest generated the Defining Issues Test (DIT), which depends on the concept of virtue for making ethical decisions. Rest's four models occur in sequence, beginning with the recognition that an ethical situation has occurred and considering possible actions and effects. Second, a desired course of action is decided on after examining all sides of the issue. Third, steps that must be taken to resolve the issue are identified. Last, the selected steps are put into practice. Martinov-Bennie and Mladenovic suggest that Rest's models do not pay sufficient attention to the moral intensity involved in decision-making in accounting.

Beginning in the 1990s and increasing significantly in the early years of the twenty-first century, the entire globe was plagued by a number of accounting scandals that shook the profession to its core. Names of companies and individuals such as Adelphia, AIG, Bernie Madoff, Dynergy, Enron, Fannie Mae, Freddie Mac, Global Crossing, Rite Aid, Tyco, and WorldCom became as well known for their unethical behaviors as for the products and services they provided. Accounting students were required to study such scandals to learn how accounting frauds were perpetrated and the consequences suffered in each instance.

Some accounting scandals have come to light as the result of auditors discovering firms engaging in such practices as misrepresenting revenues or losses, but others are discovered by outside agencies, such as the Securities and Exchange Commission. Whistleblowers have also played a role in uncovering accounting sandals. Sherron Watkins was responsible for blowing the whistle on Enron, a giant energy company whose unethical practices bankrupted the company and led to a 24-year prison sentence for CEO Jeff Skilling. Former CEO Ken Lay died before he could begin serving time.

Cynthia Cooper opened the gate for the WorldCom scandal in which investors lost $180 billion. CEO Bernie Ebbers was sentenced to 25 years in prison after company auditors discovered fraud amounting to $3.8 billion. One of the first whistleblowers to receive national attention

was James Alderson, a former CFO at North Valley Hospital. Alderson filed a lawsuit in 1993 under the False Claims Act (FCA) against HCA, the owner of North Valley Hospital, accusing them of defrauding the government of Medicare and Medicaid payments by keeping separate sets of books. The federal government joined Alderson's suit in 1998, and in 2001 HCA was forced to pay $745 million in civil damages, $95 million in criminal fines, and $881 to settle other charges.

In 2004, the collapse of the accounting firm Arthur Anderson after the public learned of frauds carried out by partners and managers resulted in a $457 million class action lawsuit and mounting public concern over ethics in accounting. David Costello, the president of the National Association of State Boards of Accountancy, and 160 charter members founded the NASBA Center for the Public Trust (CPT). In 2013, the group established the CPT Ethics Pilot Program, which provides online presentations, narrations, images, videos, and polls for use by teachers of accounting certification programs. The CPT online certification program is an eight-hour course composed of separate sections, and students are required to take a test after completing each section. In order to pass, at least 80 percent of all questions must be answered correctly.

Further Insights

The federal government has attempted to promote ethics in accounting through a series of laws. In 2002, Congress passed the Sarbanes-Oxley Act (SOX), which required American publicly traded companies to monitor accounting practices internally. Responsibility for honest reporting was assigned to CEOs and CFOs, who could face stiff punishment if convicted of unethical behaviors. SOX also established the Public Company Accounting Oversight Board to monitor ethics in auditing and accounting. The act banned auditors from being hired to provide non-auditing services to the companies they audit. SOX was not well received among American businesses, and it was dubbed "quack corporate governance" by its critics.

In 2010, Congress passed the Dodd-Frank Wall Street Reform and Consumer Protection Act, which significantly expanded the efforts made in SOX to ensure accountability of big business in the United States. Elements of Dodd-Frank included stricter standards for the accounting profession, more emphasis on peer reviews, and better methods for identifying accounting fraud. Increased attention meant that the pressure on accountants was increased even as firms demanded that auditing costs be reduced.

Recognizing the need, software developers responded by creating a plethora of applications for auditors that were designed to uncover unethical accounting behaviors and make the work of accountants easier. SOX has continued to be controversial, and Republicans and big business have attempted to mitigate what they see as interference in the market. In 2014, Congress passed the Jumpstart Our Business Startups Act, which allowed exemptions of new companies reporting revenues of less than $1 billion from the provisions of both Dodd-Frank and SOX.

In an effort to monitor itself, the accounting profession has created a number of state, national, and international organizations that attempt to establish guidelines for ethics in accounting. The United States has historically enforced accounting standards more stringent than those of other countries, but efforts to globalize accounting standards in the twenty-first century has led to some relaxing of those standards. The International Association for Accounting Education and Research (IAAER) was founded in 1984 to establish global standards for teaching professional ethics, and organizations such as the International Federation of Accountants (IFAC) continue to offer guidance for establishing ethical standards for accountants and auditors and for ensuring that accounting students are trained in making ethical decisions.

In 1986, the American Accounting Association's Committee on Future Structure, Content, and Scope of Accounting Education launched a campaign to improve ethics training in accounting programs in the United States. In 2008, NASBA announced that it was revising Rules 5-1 and 5-2 of the Uniform Accountancy Act to mandate that all accounting students take three semester hours of professional ethics classes.

In 2002, the American Institute of Certified Public Accountants began providing an Ethics Tree for accountants to use when determining the proper professional behavior, suggesting that accountants trust their instincts when discussing situations with management and treat all responses with "the necessary degree of professional skepticism." Accountants are encouraged to document all elements of the ethical situation, including questions asked and responses received in light of professional and legal standards. Based on the information as a whole, accountants are then advised to determine whether employment should continue and whether the situation needs to be reported to non-company accountants, regulatory agencies, banks, lending institutions, owners, investors, boards, and/or other stakeholders.

Issues

The alarming number of high-profile accounting scandals led Wall Street to attempt to shift some of the blame for unethical behaviors to colleges and universities, insisting that they had failed to train accountants adequately in the ethics of the profession. In the 1960s and 1970s, most training programs for accountants had spent only limited time on teaching ethics, offering students a few case studies of firms that had violated ethics laws and been charged with violations. In 1979, however, the Association to Advance Collegiate Schools of Business (AACSB) added an ethics requirement for business majors. A decade later, the organization began mandating ethics training in accounting and demanded that ethics education be integrated across the business curriculum.

As new scandals erupted, more schools added ethics to the curriculum. In 1990, the Academy of Management's Social Studies Issues in Management section conducted a study of ethics training for accountants, finding that one in three schools accredited under the AACSB offered no stand-alone courses dedicated to the ethics of business and society. Only half of the accredited schools had assigned full-time faculty members to teach ethics. In other schools, professors from others fields, particularly philosophy, taught ethics.

The debate over how ethics should be taught to accounting students has been intense, and researchers have devoted significant effort to analyzing efforts of colleges and universities to prepare new accountants to meet the demands of a profession that is in the global spotlight. Scholars suggest that ethics training should focus on the need for honesty, fairness, and justice as universal and inviolate concepts. In a 2012 study, (Ethics and Accounting), Thomas found that education was a major factor in sensitizing accounting students to ethical questions. The study indicated that fourth-year students were more attuned to deliberate reasoning than first-year students were and that first-year accounting students were more aware of different levels of decision-making than were first-year business students.

A 2015 study by Martinov-Bennie and Mladenovic suggested that ethical sensitivity of accounting students was greatest when the teaching of ethics was integrated throughout the curriculum. They were surprised to find that the students who exhibited the most sophisticated levels of ethical judgments were those who had not been exposed to frameworks that discussed the various viewpoints on ethics in accounting. Some studies have revealed that student accountants who are repeatedly exposed to ethics are better equipped to make ethical decisions on the job and in their personal lives. Overall, studies have demonstrated that the best ethics training for accountants is both cumulative and integrative. However, benefits from a single course dedicated solely to ethics are considered highly significant. The emphasis on accounting in ethics has led to an overall finding that accounting students express less tolerance for unethical behavior on the job than either business majors or non-business majors.

Since 2004, the AACSB has suggested that all ethics courses cover business responsibility, ethical decision-making, ethics in leadership, and corporate government leadership. In 2005, the education committee of NASBA began recommending that all accounting programs include three semester hours of accounting ethics and three semester hours of business ethics. The backlash forced NASBA to backtrack, reducing the recommendation to only three semester hours of ethics training that could be taught in a stand-alone course or integrated into the existing curriculum. Azusa Pacific University—a private evangelical Christian school located near Los Angeles, California—has gone further than most schools, establishing an endowed chair ($8.6 million) in ethical auditing within the Timothy Leung School of Accounting and providing a master's degree in ethical auditing. John Thornton was recruited from Washington State University to head up the program, which covers ethics from the ancient Greeks and the biblical period to modern philosophies of ethics. Methods for teaching ethics in college classrooms include written and video ethics cases, group learning, case studies, role-playing, film, and multimedia presentations. These methods may be used in stand-alone ethics classes and incorporated into other accounting and business classes.

The increased emphasis on ethics in accounting has not completely stopped firms from engaging in illegal practices, but it has made it more likely that such practices will be made public. In 2005, Refco, a commodities trading company, was engaged in a scandal when it was reported that its CEO and chairman of the board had prevented auditors and investors from learning about $340 million in bad debts. Three years later, it was learned that Lehman Brothers had engaged in off-balance sheet accounting.

The National Business Ethics Survey reported that between 2007 and 2013, incidences of unethical business behavior declined from 55 percent to 41 percent. However, more than one in four American firms is still believed to engage in some form of unethical behavior.

—*Elizabeth Rholetter Purdy*

Further Reading

American Institute of Certified Public Accountants. (2015). Ethics tree.

Carlino, B. (2011). The 21st century audit. *Accounting Today, 25*(4), 1-35.

Chawla, S. K., Khan, Z. U., Jackson, R. E., & Gray III, A. W. (2015). Evaluating ethics education for accounting students. *Management Accounting Quarterly, 16*(2), 16-25.

Lau, C. L. L. (2010). A step forward: Ethics education matters! *Journal of Business Ethics, 92*(4), 565-584.

Martinov-Bennie, N., & Mladenovic, R. (2015). Investigation of the impact of an ethical framework and an integrated ethics education on accounting students' ethical sensitivity and judgment. *Journal of Business Ethics, 127*(1), 189-203.

Mastracchio Jr., N. J., Jiménez-Angueira, C., & Toth, I. (2015). The state of ethics in business and the accounting profession. *CPA Journal, 85*(3), 48-52.

Meymandi, A. R., Rajabdoory, H., & Asoodeh, Z. (2015). The reasons of considering ethics in accounting job. *International Journal of Management, Accounting, and Economics, 2*(2), 136-143.

Rest, J. R. (1986). *Moral development: Advances in research and theory*. New York, NY: Praeger.

Romano, R. (2005). The Sarbanes-Oxley act and the making of quack corporate governance. *Yale Law Journal, 114*, 1521-1612.

Thomas, S. (2012). Ethics and accounting education. *Issues in Accounting Education, 27*(2), 399-418.

Chambers, D, Hermanson, D. K., & Payne, J. L. (2010). Did Sarbanes-Oxley lead to better financial reporting? *CPA Journal, 80*(9), 24-27.

Cooper, B. J., et al. (2008). Ethics education for accounting students: A toolkit approach. *Accounting Education: An International Journal, 17*(4), 405-430.

Gill, M. (2009). *Accountants' truth: Knowledge and ethics in the financial world*. New York, NY: Oxford University Press.

Goldberg, S., & Bettinghaus, B. Everyday ethics: Tougher than you think. *Strategic Finance, 97*(6), 46-53.

Stem, R. (2012). *Understanding moral obligation: Kant, Hegel, Kierkegaard*. Cambridge, UK: Cambridge University Press.

Ethics Reform Act of 1989, Public Law 101-194 (1989)

Congressional enactment, 30 November 1989, that revised the financial disclosure requirements for Congress first set forth in the Ethics in Government Act of 1978. The rules regarding honoraria and disclosure requirements were strengthened. As part of 18 USC § 207(e), the act broadened the list of officials subject to honoraria requirements. Prior to the 1989 revisions, only certain matters and certain people were subject to the restrictions. The act also for the first time restricted gifts and honoraria that could be received after an individual left office, whereas previously only current officeholders were covered. The act also named the Office of Government Ethics, located in Washington, D.C, as the "supervising ethics office" for the entire U.S. government.

When President George Bush signed the act into law on 30 November 1989, he stated:

"Today I have signed into law H.R. 3660, the Ethics Reform Act of 1989, which contains important reforms that strengthen Federal ethical standards. It is based on the legislation that I sent to the Congress last April, the recommendations of the President's Commission on Federal Ethics Law Reform, and the report of the House Bipartisan Ethics Task Force.

Key reforms in the Act include: the extension of post-employment "revolving door" restrictions to the legislative branch; a ban on receipt of honoraria by Federal employees (except the Senate); limitations on outside earned income for higher-salaried, noncareer employees in all branches; increased financial disclosure; creation of conflict-of-interest rules for legislative branch staff; and limitations on gifts and travel.

In 1995 the United States Supreme Court struck down part of the 1989 act as unconstitutional—that part that prohibited honoraria for executive branch employees. In *United States v. National Treasury Employees Union*, 115 S. Ct. 1003, 513 U.S. 454 (1995), the Court held that this provision violated the First Amendment of the U.S. Constitution since honoraria allows for free speech.

See also: Ethics in Government Act of 1978.

"Everyone does it"

Definition: Rationalization invoked to excuse, justify, or otherwise neutralize the moral bind of law, freeing one to commit acts deemed morally, legally, and socially undesirable

Type of ethics: Personal and social ethics

Significance: Originally thought to explain delinquency among delinquent youth, the idea that "everyone does it" has been shown to explain why white-collar offend-

ers commit crime and simultaneously maintain their sense of being upright citizens.

In his 1994 book *"Everybody Does It!,"* criminologist Thomas Gabor describes how people justify their involvement in dishonest, unethical, or immoral behavior, using phrases that "normalize" their actions to themselves and others. Phrases such as "everyone's doing it" were first identified by sociologists David Matza and Gresham Sykes during the late 1950's as techniques of "neutralization" for questionable behavior.

Neutralizations are words and phrases that negate the moral and ethical binds of law. Those who use them draw on the explicit exceptions to law such as "I was not myself at the time" or "I was acting in self-defense." Embezzlers commonly describe their stealing as "borrowing." Dishonest employees typically blame their excessive expense-account claims, time thefts, or thefts of company property on their companies or unscrupulous supervisors, claiming that their companies have treated them badly, their bosses have cheated them out of vacation days, or their managers have prevented them from receiving deserved raises or promotions.

Language of Neutralization

Similarly, corporations themselves use neutralizing words and phrases to explain that their fraudulent actions are necessary for them to remain competitive. Government agencies may explain their abuses of power as necessary to "protect the public." The use of such phrases is self-serving, in that they reduce the sense of moral culpability of wrongdoers, while also freeing them to commit further offenses, especially if they sense that their excuses will be accepted by judging audiences.

Neutralizations may be excuses that people use to acknowledge committing misdeeds, while denying responsibility for them; an example is "I was ordered to do it." Alternatively, neutralizations may be justifications offered to accept responsibility for misdeeds or to assert the rightfulness of the actions, such as "no one got hurt."

Most people use such "claims to normality" in varying degrees to excuse or justify their deviant behavior; some to negate serious deviant, and even criminal, behavior. As a claim of normality, saying that "everyone does it" promotes the commonality of the action over any principle of ethics or law.

A crucial issue of neutralizations is their timing. When they occur after the acts, neutralizations are seen merely as rationalizations seeking to minimize the culpability or consequences for questionable behavior. When they occur prior to the acts, they can motivate misbehavior by freeing potential wrongdoers from the moral and ethical bind of law.

Criminologists argue that to counteract the effect of neutralization that undermines morality and ethics, it is necessary continuously to point out the harm caused by the misdeeds—through the media, meetings, and interpersonal relations. It is also important to be clear that words and phrases used to neutralize are nothing less than self-deception, designed at best to minimize the consequences for the offenders, and at worst, to justify doing harm to others because of harm others have done in the past. An example of the latter would be to justify any action that undermines corporate power because of the damage corporations have done to the environment in the past.

—Stuart Henry

Further Reading

Gabor, Thomas. *"Everybody Does It!": Crime by the Public.* Toronto: University of Toronto Press, 1994.

Katz, Leo. *Bad Acts and Guilty Minds: Conundrums of the Criminal Law.* Chicago: University of Chicago Press, 1987.

See also: Bystanders; Choice; Conscience; Corruption; Hypocrisy; Role models; White-collar crime.

Executive Order 10988

Identification: Federal executive order that gave federal employees the right to collective bargaining

Date: Signed on January 17, 1962

Type of ethics: Business and labor ethics

Significance: Executive Order 10988 made the labor policies of federal offices and agencies consistent throughout the country and influenced the labor policies of state and local agencies.

Before the 1960's, federal agencies dealt with organized labor unions individually; some agencies recognized unions, and some refused to negotiate with them. The administration of President John F. Kennedy took a more favorable attitude toward unions.

On January 17, 1962, Kennedy signed Federal Executive Order (EO) 10988, giving federal employees the right to form unions and to bargain collectively through them. Under the terms of the order, employees had the right to form a union but could not be forced to join one. Federal

agencies were required to bargain with properly elected unions. These unions were forbidden to strike.

Once the order was signed, there was a tremendous increase in the number of federal employees represented by unions, especially among white-collar workers. Some groups, including postal workers, are represented by unions for all of their contract negotiations. The rights of federal employees were amended several times during the late 1960's and the 1970's. In 1978, the Civil Service Reform Act became the first unified code of federal sector labor relations, formalizing the bargaining rights first endorsed by the executive order.

—Cynthia A. Bily

See also: American Federation of Labor; Fair Labor Standards Act; Hasidism; Knights of Labor; Labor-Management Relations Act; National Labor Relations Act; Work.

Fair Labor Standards Act

Identification: Labor legislation regulating wages, hours of labor, and the use of child labor

Date: October 24, 1938

Type of ethics: Business and labor ethics

Significance: The Fair Labor Standards Act arose out of a progressive ideal that holds government responsible for protecting the economic and social welfare of laboring people by regulating business.

The Supreme Court ruled unconstitutional attempts such as the National Industrial Recovery Act of 1933 by the Roosevelt administration to regulate prices, wages, hours, and other labor conditions. In 1938, however, Congress passed wages and hours legislation as an omnibus bill, and the Supreme Court upheld it in 1941. The Fair Labor Standards Act regulated minimum wages, overtime pay, child labor, and the production of goods for interstate commerce.

Beginning with the third year after its effective date, the act raised the minimum wage to forty cents per hour, made it subject thereafter to review by a congressional committee, and required overtime pay of one and one-half times the employees' regular pay above forty hours work per week. The act eliminated child labor (by children under age sixteen) with certain exceptions. One of the most significant amendments to the act, which came in 1963, required equal pay for equal work without regard to sex. Although more than forty exemptions to the act exist, including the regulation of professional employees and out-

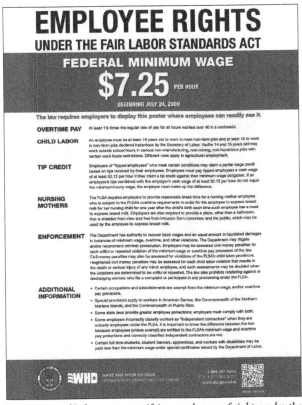

Department of Labor poster notifying employees of rights under the Fair Labor Standards Act. By U.S. Department of Labor, Wage and Hour Division, Washington, D.C.

side salespersons, the act is a milestone for labor, since in it Congress and the president recognized their responsibility to be the guardians of economic and social justice for labor.

—Stephen D. Livesay

See also: Child labor legislation; Congress; International Labour Organisation; Minimum-wage laws; National Labor Relations Act.

Fairness and Accuracy in Reporting

Identification: Left-leaning watchdog group that encourages the news media to report the diverse concerns and opinions of the American public rather than privileging mainstream conservative voices.
Date: Founded in 1986
Type of ethics: Media ethics

Significance: FAIR works to correct what it perceives as a conservative bias in news reporting.

FAIR believes that the national and local news media are increasingly influenced by political and economic powers—that instead of independently challenging and criticizing government and big business, the news media tend to accept and pass along official versions of events. For example, FAIR examined news coverage of the 1991 Gulf War and found that most news stories and editorials echoed official government press releases and statements, and reflected little or no attempt to confirm or refine government versions of events. When some official statements turned out to be exaggerated or false, corrections were given minimal attention. FAIR also found that on talk shows and other analysis programs, only a small range of views was presented, and the views of those opposed to the war were seldom heard.

In 1989, FAIR published an important report showing that the guest analysts on two of the most widely watched television news programs were overwhelmingly white males from large institutions. Representatives of labor, social movements, minority groups, and local civic groups were very rarely featured on these programs. FAIR maintains contact with the public through a magazine that is published eight times a year and through a weekly radio program.

—Cynthia A. Bily

See also: Accuracy in Media; Journalistic ethics; Media ownership; News sources; Photojournalism.

Fear in the workplace

Definition: Emotion experienced in the face of job-related threats
Type of ethics: Business and labor ethics
Significance: Fear can be both a cause and a result of unethical behavior.

Fear is fuel for unethical behavior, and unethical actions are fuel for fear. Fear is therefore both a cause of and a result of unethical behavior. When people manage ethically, they do not operate in an environment of fear. Fear is an emotion experienced in the face of threats or danger that one feels unable to control. It has two components: the presence or perception of a danger or threat and a lack of control over the danger or threat. Kathleen Ryan and Daniel Oestreich, in their book *Driving Fear Out of the Workplace* (1991), observe, "We see fear as a background phenomenon that undermines the commitment, motivation, and confidence of people at work. It is most easily observed as a reluctance to speak up about needed changes, improvements, or other important work issues."

Effects of Fear

Managers often do not see the impact of fear because it is hidden in the process of how the work gets done. The cost of having fear in the workplace can be figured out by examining the influence of negative emotions on people's work. Ryan and Oestreich's research indicates that the two greatest impacts fear has on an organization are negative feelings about the organization and decreased quality and productivity.

Fear translates into a loss of trust and pride, and employees often react to fear by increasing self-protective behavior. Negative feelings about the organization also result in sabotage (theft, fraud, and the destruction of company property). Fear translates into a lasting resentment, the making and hiding of mistakes, or failure to meet deadlines and budgets. W. Edwards Deming has said that quality is impossible to achieve when people are afraid to tell the truth. They fear being ethical. Scrap and breakage are hidden, numbers and schedules are misrepresented, and bad products are shipped to customers because someone is afraid to stop the production line.

Fear shows up in "falsifying" reports and overpromising customers. Employees may not ask for personal time off for fear that their supervisors will not understand and their requests will be denied, so they lie and call in sick. Falsifying reports, overpromising customers, and calling in sick when one is not soon become the norm. Employees become used to behaving unethically. There is an old saying, "It is easy to tell a lie, but difficult to tell only one." Negative feelings about the organization make unethical behavior easier to live with.

Fear is often at the center of "whistle-blowing." The employee fears the results of the improper activity (harm to employees, customers, or the community) and also management's reaction. He or she feels pushed to go outside to have the injustice resolved. The employee does not trust management to handle the problem.

What Creates Fear

The employee's relationship with his or her immediate supervisor has the most impact on creating fear. Ambiguous

Anita Hill testified her charge against Clarence Thomas for sexually harassing her at the Department of Education and the EEOC. By Tim Pierce.

or abusive behavior destroys trust. Other behaviors contributing to fear are blaming, insulting, and ignoring. A manager who is not fair, who plays favorites, or who takes credit for an employee's idea invites mistrust from subordinates and executives. Unethical actions such as asking employees to mislead and lie to customers send a signal that perhaps the employees are being misled and lied to as well. Ethical management is at the center of efforts to create an atmosphere in which fear cannot survive. A good relationship with one's manager is a start.

The systems, procedures, and culture of the organization also contribute to fear. Will the company support the employee or not? The employee asks, "My manager is okay, but if I complain to the human resources department about a sexual harassment incident, will I be labeled a troublemaker and laid off in the next round of cutbacks? Is top management really concerned about people, customers, and employees? Is the leadership honest and does it convey a sense of integrity? Is management honestly communicating to employees about the health of the company?" The prevalence of rumors signals a culture of fear.

In an atmosphere of fear, managers and employees do not trust one another. Managers believe that employees are manipulative and operate only on the basis of self-interest. Employees worry that their managers will put their own self-interest ahead of the needs of employees and customers. Each group fears the other and reacts out of fear. It becomes a self-propagating behavior. If I fear that you will act first in your self-interest, I will interpret all your actions in the light of that fear, and react accordingly with self-preserving behavior and retaliation. It is not difficult to imagine the unethical actions that permeate such an environment.

Fear and Unethical Behavior

Laura Nash says, in *Good Intentions Aside* (1990), "I cannot think of a single ethical problem in business that does not rest on a...betrayal of trust."

Which comes first, lack of trust and fear or unethical behavior? Fear is not the only cause of unethical behavior. Another cause is the lack of awareness of the ethical implications of decision making. Unethical behavior is not fear's only result. Good employees often leave a company in which there is an environment of fear. Fear is both a cause of and a result of unethical behavior. It is a red flag, a signal that the health of the organization needs attention. If company employees and managers look for the effects of fear and take action to develop an atmosphere of trust, the ethical pulse of the organization will improve accordingly.

Howard Putnam, in *The Winds of Turbulence* (1991), summarizes fear's effect: "Fear is the most imposing barrier to transformation. Fear flows from the feelings of instability caused by dealing with the unknown, and it can strangle creative thinking."

—Kathleen D. Purdy

Further Reading

Covey, Stephen R. *Principle-Centered Leadership*. New York: Simon & Schuster, 1992.

De George, Richard T. "Whistle-Blowing." In *Business Ethics*. 5th ed. Upper Saddle River, N.J.: Prentice Hall, 1999.

Dozier, Rush W., Jr. *Fear Itself: The Origin and Nature of the Powerful Emotion That Shapes Our Lives and Our World*. New York: St. Martin's Press, 1998.

Nash, Laura L. *Good Intentions Aside*. Boston: Harvard Business School Press, 1990.

Putnam, Howard D. *The Winds of Turbulence*. New York: Harper Business, 1991.

Ryan, Kathleen D., and Daniel K. Oestreich. *Driving Fear Out of the Workplace: Creating the High-Trust, High-Performance Organization*. 2d ed. San Francisco: Jossey-Bass, 1998.

See also: Business ethics; Corporate responsibility; Dress codes; Electronic mail; Employee safety and treatment; Equal pay for equal work; Hiring practices; Merit; Sexual abuse and harassment; Wage discrimination; White-collar crime.

Hiring practices

Definition: Methods used by employers to hire new personnel

Type of ethics: Business and labor ethics

Significance: The late twentieth century saw a significant increase in government oversight of hiring practices, pressure on employees by special interest groups, and greater efforts to develop fair hiring practices within private companies

During the last two decades of the twentieth century, hiring processes of private American entities came under increasing supervision by the federal government and various special interest or pressure groups in society. In addition, the presence of human resource departments within companies and their role in the hiring process became more evident and influential in the workforce. All signs pointed to greater efforts by employers to bring ethics into their hiring practices.

However, the task of incorporating ethical processes into hiring is not easy for several reasons. One of the biggest obstacles to ethical hiring practices is the simple fact that different people are sometimes not in agreement as to what constitutes an ethical decision. However, the difficulties that employers face in their attempts to bring ethical behavior to the hiring process should not stop them from trying to bring it about. Companies may not succeed to the extent that they wish when it comes to bringing ethical choices in the hiring process, but even a small amount of success is better than no success at all.

In contemplating how to incorporate ethical behavior into the hiring process, several issues need to be kept in mind. First, it has to be a major goal for employers. This means that its presence has to be foremost in the minds of employers as something they desire to achieve. However, companies must also be honest and demonstrate integrity in the hiring process. This implies that they clearly indicate to future employees what their reasons are for choosing one candidate over others. Employers must also be aware of their need to conform to the law when making employment decisions. The federal government has made it clear that it intends to provide equal employment opportunities to its citizens, and it is important that there be compliance with all legal provisions relating to hiring practices.

Employers must also be careful not to be influenced in the hiring process by subjective reasons and avoid any projection of personal gain. Perhaps one of the best ways to answer the question of whether employers have been successful at incorporating ethical behavior into the hiring process is to ask what an outside committee reviewing the employer's actions might indicate about how it made its choice regarding an employment position.

—*William E. Kelly*

Further Reading

Berenbeim, Ronald. "What Is Ethical? An American View." *Vital Speeches of the Day* 68, no. 18 (July 1, 2002): 549.

Brown, Fred. "Ethics vs. Law." *Quill* 88, no. 9 (October-November, 2000): 6.

Coates, Joseph F. "Updating the Ten Commandments." *Futurist* 37, no. 3 (May-June 2003): 68.

Militello, Frederick, and Michael Schwalberg. "Ethical Conduct: What Financial Executives Do to Lead." *Financial Leadership* 1911 (January-February, 2003): 49.

Sniderman, Joe. "When Good Hiring Is a Challenge." *Nation's Business* 87, no. 4 (April, 1999): 10. "White House Defends Faith-Based Hiring." *Christian Century* 120, no. 15 (July 26, 2003): 16.

See also: Biometrics; Business ethics; College applications; Downsizing; Equal pay for equal work; Fear in the workplace; Labor-Management Relations Act; Merit; Resumés; Wage discrimination; Work.

Index librorum prohibitorum

Identification: Now-defunct list of books forbidden by the Roman Catholic Church

Dates: 1559-1966

Type of ethics: Arts and censorship

Significance: Members of the Roman Catholic Church were forbidden, except in special circumstances, from reading or even possessing books included in the *Index librorum prohibitorum*, on the theory that such works were harmful to the faith and morals of practicing Catholics, and that it was the function of the church to protect its members from such moral harm

Title page of the first Papal Index, Index Auctorum et Librorum, *published in 1557 and then withdrawn.*

The *Index librorum prohibitorum was* never intended to be an exhaustive catalog of forbidden literature. Rather, it represented those works condemned by the Roman Catholic Church in response to specific requests from people around the world. The majority of works included in the *Index* were theological in nature. During the first century (1559 to 1649) of its four centuries of existence, 469 texts appeared in the *Index*; in its second century, 1,585 were added; in its third, 1,039 were added; and in its final century, 1,585 were added.

By the time the *Index* was suppressed in June, 1966, it contained 4,126 entries. Some entries denoted specific titles, whereas others designated authors with Latin notations such as *omnia opera dramatica* ("all dramatic works" [forbidden]) or, the most severe censure, *opera omnia* ("all works" [forbidden]). Among those whose writings were forbidden were such notables as Émile Zola (all works), Stendhal (all love stories), Samuel Richardson (*Pamela: Or, Virtue Rewarded*, 1740), Laurence Sterne (*A Sentimental Journey Through France and Italy*,1768), Edward Gibbon (*The History of the Decline and Fall of the Roman Empire*, 1776-1788), and the complete works of British philosophers Thomas Hobbes and David Hume. Only four American authors (whose writings were theological in nature) were ever listed on the *Index*.

—*Robin G. Hanson*

See also: Art; Art and public policy; Book banning; Censorship; Christian ethics; Library Bill of Rights.

Infomercials

Definition: Paid commercials that mimic the lengths and formats of conventional television programs and are typically designed to sell specific products

Date: First broadcast during the mid-1980s

Type of ethics: Media ethics

Significance: The dramatic rise in infomercial broadcasting at the end of the twentieth century posed ethical questions regarding truth in advertising and the blurring of lines between commercial and noncommercial television programming

The two- to four-minute television commercials for household gadgets that entrepreneur Ron Popeil began broadcasting during the mid-1950s are often considered precursors of modern infomercials, which typically devote thirty minutes or more to promoting a single product or line of products. In 1984, the administration of President Ronald Reagan relaxed federal guidelines limiting the time that television stations could devote to advertising, paving the way for lengthier and more detailed on-air sales pitches. Later that same year, the HerbaLife company aired a sixty-minute advertisement for its diet products that is commonly regarded as the first true infomercial. Infomercials then proliferated rapidly throughout the rest of the decade and into the 1990s, fueled by budget cuts that forced local television stations to increase their advertising revenues.

Infomercials are frequently designed to mimic news programs, talk shows, or public service announcements, creating the illusion that the information they present meets journalistic standards of credibility and objectivity.

Infomercial advertisers are often accused of utilizing these formats to reinforce outrageous claims and sell shoddy merchandise to consumers who are sometimes emotionally or intellectually vulnerable. Critics of this practice cite laws against deceptive advertising as well as the ethical tradition of the regulated market economies of Western nations, which holds that businesses and advertisers should not mislead consumers by lying or misrepresenting facts.

Defenders of infomercials argue that according to the dictates of the free market, infomercial producers and broadcasters have a fiduciary obligation to maximize profits that supersedes their obligation to consumers, that the disclaimers commonly included in these programs provide sufficient notification to viewers as to their content, and that consumers must assume at least partial responsibility for distinguishing between news and advertising.

—*Michael H. Burchett*

See also: Advertising; Children's television; Consumerism; Marketing.

Information access

Definition: Ability to obtain, utilize, and disseminate information, especially personal information, stored on computers

Type of ethics: Media ethics

Significance: The advent of one integrated set of technologies, the computer network, to both store and transmit information, renders information both less secure and more easily exploited or disseminated once it has been accessed, by an order of magnitude. As a result, new ethical principles are required to arbitrate and safeguard the traditional right to privacy in the Information Age

The ability to store and exchange computerized information about individuals raises ethical questions about access to that information. Who should have access to personal information? Does the right of the government to know take precedence over an individual's right to privacy? What kind of information should not be kept or shared? Complicating these issues is the tendency to accept information obtained from a computer as totally accurate. Given authorized access, how can the information be verified as accurate? Do people have a right to examine information pertaining to them?

Rise of Information Technology

Since World War II, computer and communications technologies have combined to produce a major influence on Western society. The first generation of electronic computers had thousands of vacuum tubes, required huge amounts of electricity for power and cooling, and cost so much that only governments and very large corporations could afford them. The development of the transistor, the integrated circuit, and the microprocessor led to generations of ever-more-affordable computers. By the 1980s, computer technology had reached virtually every level of the economic infrastructure. Computers became repositories for criminal and tax records, health and employment records, and credit and financial information.

The communications revolution parallels the computer revolution. Satellites and fiber-optic lines have made possible the almost instant transmission of data between geographically distant computers.

The first two decades of computer technology progressed without much public discussion of ethical issues. By 1965, the Federal Bureau of Investigation (FBI) had begun to develop the National Crime Information Center as a central repository of criminal arrest records. That same year, the proposed idea of centralizing government records of individual citizens in a National Data Center was met with strong opposition in Congress. Debate over the National Data Center focused national attention for the first time on the issue of invasion of privacy as people began to fear the prospect of an Orwellian all-seeing, all-knowing government becoming reality.

In *Menard v. Mitchell*, a landmark 1971 federal case, the U.S. Supreme Court ruled that a "compelling public necessity" had to be proved before an individual's arrest record could be widely disseminated. Legislation by Congress followed. The Privacy Act of 1975 regulated the use of criminal justice information, and the Freedom of Information Act of 1977 gave individuals the right to access nonclassified government records.

The Private Sector

The first attempt to regulate the retail credit industry's use of personal credit information had come with the Fair Credit Reporting Act of 1969. By the 1980s and 1990s, however, personal information had become a lucrative commodity driving a huge industry. The two largest credit bureaus maintained separate databases of more than 150 million files, which they made available to banks, credit card companies, and virtually any other business willing to pay for the service. Many people believed that the protection of the Fair Credit Reporting Act was no longer adequate. Reports by the news media and consumer advocates documented cases of individuals being victimized by false and ruinous credit information.

A 1991 Consumer Union study found inaccuracies in nearly half the records it sampled. Smaller companies specialized in providing demographic and consumer information to direct marketing firms. For a small monthly fee, customers had access to detailed information on millions of households, including address, telephone number, property ownership, and legal records. Manufacturers often routinely sold information taken from cards returned by consumers for product warranty registration to direct marketers, who used it to target potential customers more accurately.

Prospects for Regulation

Because access to personal information has reached virtually every level of modern society, regulation by a single law or agency is impossible. Federal and state governments struggle to sort out the questions of access versus privacy and enact appropriate legislation, while some critics question the government's ability to regulate itself. By 1982, U.S. government computers contained more than 3.5 billion personal files. The FBI continues to build a database of the arrest records of 25 million people, whether or not their arrests resulted in convictions.

During the 1970s, the National Security Agency (NSA) and International Business Machines (IBM) developed the Data Encryption Standard (DES) to ensure secure transmission of classified information over telephone and data lines. Data or conversations that are transmitted between two points are encrypted with a mathematical key. In 1993, the introduction of a DES integrated circuit chip, to be made available in commercial products, led the Clinton administration to support its widespread use. Privacy advocates hailed the advent of the DES chip but worried that a new standard with government control of the keys could trigger abuses of wiretapping and that computer hackers might be able to duplicate the new standard's classified algorithm. Meanwhile, groups such as the Consumer Union and the American Civil Liberties Union, as well as individual citizens, continued to press for protection against abuses by both the government and the private sector.

Summary

The ethics of information access began with the issue of privacy versus the government's right to acquire knowledge for the public good but expanded as businesses began to perceive their access to personal information as part of their right to do business in a free-market economy.

Some social analysts claim that the Information Age has brought a change in values to modern society, where the benefits and convenience of free access to information outweigh the individual's right to privacy. It has even been proposed that since an individual's personal information is a commodity with commercial value, that person should be compensated with a royalty whenever the information is sold.

The Industrial Revolution was welcomed as an unmixed blessing to humankind for many years before society began to consider such ethical issues as child labor and pollution. The Information Age has brought sweeping changes to society at a much faster pace. Sorting out the ethics of information access and creating systems for control is a slow process, with much opportunity for abuse in the meantime, because the very concepts of information and privacy are being redefined by this rapidly developing technology.

—*Charles E. Sutphen*

Further Reading

Allen, Dennis. "Ethics of Electronic Information." *Byte* 17 (August, 1992): 10.

Begley, Sharon, et al. "Technology: The Code of the Future." *Newsweek* 121 (June 7, 1993): 70.

Hoerr, John, et al. "Privacy." *Business Week*, March 28, 1988, 61-68.

Hunter, Richard. *World Without Secrets: Business, Crime, and Privacy in the Age of Ubiquitous Computing.* New York: J. Wiley, 2002.

Lacayo, Richard. "Nowhere to Hide." *Time* 138 (November 11, 1991): 34-40.

Marchand, Donald A. *The Politics of Privacy, Computers, and Criminal Justice Records: Controlling the Social Costs of Technological Change.* Arlington, Va.: Information Resources Press, 1980.

Mossberger, Karen, Caroline J. Tolbert, and Mary Stansbury, eds. *Virtual Inequality: Beyond the Digital Divide.* Washington, D.C.: Georgetown University Press, 2003.

Roszak, Theodore. *The Cult of Information.* New York: Pantheon Books, 1986.

Spinello, Richard A. *CyberEthics: Morality and Law in Cyberspace.* 2d ed. Boston: Jones and Bartlett, 2003.

Wayner, Peter. "Clipped Wings? Encryption Chip Draws Fire." *Byte* 18 (July, 1993): 36.

See also: American Civil Liberties Union; Arrest records; Computer databases; Computer technology; Confidentiality; Freedom of Information Act; Identity theft; Orwell, George; Privacy.

Inside information

Definition: Confidential knowledge possessed or obtained by people in positions of power or with privileged access to information within a company, organization, or government

Type of ethics: Media ethics

Significance: Inside information can be put to many uses with ethical implications. It can be used to profit the person who possesses or obtains it, it can be passed on to authorities or to a public whose interest in such knowledge is arguably legitimate, or it can be used to harm, or violate the privacy of, individuals, companies, or organizations. All of these uses are the subject of ethical codes and many are subject to legal regulation as well.

Confidential information that derives from the fulfillment of professional or civic duties is a valuable commodity. Misappropriation of such knowledge is a common occurrence in the banking and securities industry, where frequent opportunity exists to convert one's knowledge into a monetary profit through the buying and selling of stocks about which one has secret information. The Securities and Exchange Commission explicitly prohibits such practices and vigorously prosecutes violators.

Media professionals, too, have access to information that is proprietary in nature and that has the potential for misuse. The wide scope of the First Amendment and the privileges guaranteed to the press therein, however, preclude the existence of both a regulatory body and legal restrictions designed to control the use of information. Therefore, the press, as with other questions of conduct, is obliged to address the ethical issues on a situational basis, weighing circumstances along with values, loyalties, and journalistic principles.

Two central issues exist regarding the issue of inside information: how the information is obtained and how it is used. In regard to the securing of information, journalists are morally obligated to remain objective and uncompromised and to respect the boundaries of legal as well as ethical codes. Because a journalist's primary obligation is to distribute information, however, even these simple tenets must be weighed in the light of a situation's defining circumstances. *The New York Times*, for example, in the publication of the Pentagon Papers (the documents that exposed the illegal activities of the Nixon administration during the 1972-1973 Watergate Affair), knowingly accepted stolen materials in the light of what the editors reasoned was a greater moral good—the exposition of a governmental effort to misrepresent the realities of the Vietnam War.

The second question concerns how inside information can be ethically used by media professionals. The code of ethics of the Society of Professional Journalists states that journalists who use their professional status as representatives of the public for selfish or other unworthy motives violate a high trust. A vigorous and effective press relies on the public trust, so it is incumbent upon journalists to use information humanely, intelligently, and ethically. This process involves questioning the motives of both the reporter and the source of the information, any obligation that may be created on the part of the journalist in exchange for the information, and the nature of the relationship in which the information became known.

That the public interest is best served by making known everything that is knowable is a journalistic standard that justifies much of what is presented as news. When journalists become the recipients of confidential information, however, an ethical dilemma arises that challenges this utilitarian philosophy and the accompanying assertion that an action is just as long as it achieves the greatest good for the greatest number. The debate lies in an opposing belief that people are not to be treated as a means to a journalistic end. A corollary to this principle is that the journalist should not allow himself or herself to be so treated, which may well be the case when publishing information "leaked" from confidential sources. Journalists, therefore, are morally obligated to seek out competing perspectives and confirming information and to question whether they are being used by someone whose interest is counter to the public interest, such as a campaign worker who might provide information about an opponent's sexual history.

Journalists must also inquire about their own motives for pursuing confidential information. During the 1970s, Bob Woodward and Carl Bernstein of *The Washington Post* were guilty of unethical conduct when they sought to lure information from grand jurors hearing evidence on the Watergate case who were sworn to secrecy. Even though a corrupt administration was eventually driven from office partly as a result of their investigation of the Watergate break-in, they did not foresee this event at the time, and the means they employed to obtain information violated ethical codes.

Obligations of Reporters

A second ethical question raised by the use of inside information relates to the obligation it establishes on the part of the reporter. Does the journalist incur responsibility toward the informant when he or she has taken risks to provide the information? If he or she has broken the law to do so, does the reporter assume culpability as well? Such concerns refer again to the principle that people are to be treated with respect and not as a means to an end, and also begin to encroach into other ethical problems for journalists, those of source-reporter confidentiality and the use of anonymous sources.

Finally, the issue of respecting the nature of the relationship in which confidential information is learned presents yet another ethical challenge. Reporters, as representatives of the public trust, frequently find themselves privy to sensitive information that they are obligated to preserve in respect to their roles as journalists. Even seemingly insignificant violations of the public trust, such as providing friends with advance notice of an upcoming sale to be advertised in the local paper, are unethical by intention regardless of the consequences.

The press, by nature, is not governed by a concise, explicit code of professional conduct. The ethics codes that do exist offer guidelines for performance and not absolute standards of behavior. Journalists and other media professionals, therefore, are encouraged to weigh situational factors along with their principles of duty in a thoughtful, critical effort to determine the ethical use of inside information.

—*Regina Howard Yaroch*

Further Reading

Bain, George. "The Subtleties of Inside Information." *Mclean's* 102 (May, 1989): 48.

Black, Jay, Bob Steele, and Ralph Barney. *Doing Ethics in Journalism: A Handbook with Case Studies.* Greencastle, Ind.: Sigma Delta Chi Foundation and the Society of Professional Journalists, 1993.

Christians, Clifford G., et al. *Media Ethics: Cases and Moral Reasoning.* 5th ed. New York: Longman, 1998.

Day, Louis A. *Ethics in Media Communications: Cases and Controversies.* Belmont, Calif.: Wadsworth, 1991.

Donaldson, Thomas, and Patricia Werhane. "Introduction to Ethical Reasoning." In *Case Studies in Business Ethics*, edited by Thomas Donaldson and A. R. Gini. Englewood Cliffs, N.J.: Prentice-Hall, 1990.

See also: Confidentiality; Insider trading; Intellectual property; Journalistic ethics; News sources; Pentagon Papers; Privacy.

Insider trading

Definition: Use of information not available to the public to guide decisions to buy or sell publicly traded securities

Type of ethics: Business and labor ethics

Significance: Federal laws regulating insider trading in the United States are designed to create a level playing field for all investors, on the theory that for the stock market to be fair, it must in principle be both equally accessible and equally unpredictable to all participants

Insider trading has been prohibited in the United States since the passage of the Securities Exchange Act of 1934, whose Section 10(b) laid down restrictions. The federal regulations on securities were designed to prevent corporate executives, directors, attorneys, accountants, investment bankers, and other "insiders" from using their positions to gain unfair advantages in the market trading of their corporations' securities. To buy or sell securities on the basis of confidential information or to recommend trading to others on that basis constitutes a violation of federal securities regulations, potentially subjecting violaters to both criminal prosecution by the Security and Exchange Commission (SEC) and civil lawsuits by injured investors.

Over the years, the SEC and the courts developed a detailed description of insider trading in numerous individual cases, most notably in the U.S. Supreme Court's decisions in *United States v. Chiarella* (1980) and *Dirks v. Securities and Exchange Commission* (1983). Insider trading became widely publicized during the 1980s, when two prominent financiers, Ivan Boesky and Michael Milken, were convicted of numerous securities violations, sentenced to prison, and fined more than $700 million.

No formal definition of insider trading was written into federal law until 2002, when the U.S. Congress passed the Sarbanes-Oxley Act. That law spelled out the conditions constituting lawful and unlawful insider trading and established ground rules for legal insider trading. These rules required dealers to file insider transactions, electron-ically, within two business days to the SEC and to post the transactions on their companies' Web sites within one day of filing the information with the SEC. Under previous legislation, insider traders had at least forty-one days to report their transactions, making it nearly impossible to detect abuses until well after damage was done. For example, executives of the failing Enron corporation did not report they had sold off most of their own stock in the company in 2001 until after the company's collapse was made public. By the end of the calendar year, the value of the company's stock fell from more than eighty-one dollars per share to virtually nothing.

—W. Jackson Parham, Jr.; Updated by the editors

Further Reading

Lu Shen-Shin. *Insider Trading and the Twenty-Four Hour Securities Market: A Case Study of Legal Regulation in the Emerging Global Economy*. Hanover, Mass.: Christopher, 1999.

See also: Corporate scandal; Inside information; Profit taking; Retirement funds; Stewart, Martha; White-collar crime.

International Labour Organisation

Identification: Specialized agency of the League of Nations, and later of the United Nations, that attempts to improve global working conditions and standards of living

Date: Founded in 1919

Type of ethics: Business and labor ethics

Significance: Formation of the International Labour Organisation (ILO) served to recognize and legitimize the ethical ideals of international labor groups

As a result of lobbying by international labor unions and the governments of several countries, the Treaty of Versailles, which ended World War I, recognized the International Labour Organisation. Its declarations and resolutions were not, however, made enforceable. During the Great Depression, the ILO encouraged governments to plan for the reemployment of workers and to develop relief and unemployment insurance schemes. The United States joined the ILO in 1934. Other countries had delayed joining; some also dropped their membership.

The ILO was the first specialized agency to be affiliated with the United Nations, which was created in 1946. It took on a more proscribed role, with some of its concerns delegated to other agencies. Its membership also changed, including many more developing rather than industrialized countries. The ILO became more of a statistical and information center that also provided technical assistance to developing countries. It turned its attention more to problems of poverty and social conditions rather than narrow labor issues. The agency is concerned with international disparities in the treatment of workers, and it attempts to prevent exploitation. As part of that program, it promotes relatively free immigration and emigration of workers. The ILO is unique among intergovernmental agencies in that member states send representatives not only from their governments but also from worker and employer groups.

—A. J. Sobczak

See also: American Federation of Labor; Employee safety and treatment; Fair Labor Standards Act; Globalization; Knights of Labor; League of Nations; United Nations; Universal Declaration of Human Rights.

International Organization of Consumers Unions

Identification: Global non-governmental organization that seeks to protect and expand the rights of consumers

Date: Founded in 1960

Type of ethics: Business and labor ethics

Significance: The International Organization of Consumers Unions (IOCU) is the main vehicle through which national and regional consumers' groups share information and coordinate action

Headquartered in The Hague, Netherlands, the International Organization of Consumers Unions is affiliated with 175 national and local consumer organizations in sixty-eight countries. Its purpose is to bring together the efforts and results of these smaller organizations to increase the power of consumers worldwide. Specifically, the IOCU has worked on such issues as the safety and effectiveness of infant formulas, and the safe distribution and use of pesticides.

The IOCU gathers and shares published information from its affiliates; provides a forum for further sharing of information and problems; encourages nations to cooperate with one another in testing product safety and in sharing the results of these tests; and studies and interprets local, national, and international laws relating to consumers. Because it works closely with the United Nations and other international bodies but not with any individual national governments, the IOCU can be an important advocate for consumers in developing nations. These consumers have sometimes been deceived or coerced into buying products that have been judged too dangerous or ineffective for sale in the developed nations where they were manufactured. Working with the United Nations, the IOCU offers consumer education and protection programs in developing nations.

—Cynthia A. Bily

See also: Consumerism; Globalization; Product safety and liability; Public interest; United Nations; World Trade Organization.

Internet piracy

Definition: Unauthorized duplication and distribution of copyrighted materials taken from computer networks, usually to avoid paying for the use of commercially licensed materials such as music, motion pictures, photographs, computer software, and texts

Type of ethics: Business and labor ethics

Significance: Internet piracy is considered unethical because it prevents creators from being able to profit fairly from their works or regulate their use and distribution. The growing practice of Internet piracy raises issues concerning the ethical assumptions presupposed by intellectual property, fair use, and copyright laws

Perhaps no new technology has created a more daunting challenge to traditional notions of intellectual property rights and their relationship to personal privacy than the popularity and ready availability of file-sharing mechanisms on the Internet. Internet use worldwide skyrocketed in the 1990s, as did the use of free and easily accessible computer software that allows users to make and share digital copies of music, video, and other media.

A significant portion of the material that was being exchanged in the early years of the twenty-first century consisted of illegally pirated works, copies of commercially recorded music, software, and similar materials originally created and distributed for profit. Encryption technology that might prevent unauthorized duplication of digitized materials was not able to keep pace with the software allowing users to "rip," or digitally duplicate, copyrighted materials via the Internet. Industry estimates in the late 1990s put the number of computer users exchanging pirated music, not to mention other commercial electronic media, in the tens of millions.

The Piracy Phenomenon

In 1997, a small group of college students developed and made available free of charge on the Internet a software program that allowed its users to easily "rip" copies of music from compact discs and upload them to centralized storage servers. Other users could then access the servers to download the illegally copied music without charge. Initially used only by a handful of music enthusiasts, word of Napster's capabilities spread rapidly, and by 1999, Napster's developers estimated that their program had been downloaded about sixty million times. If even only a small fraction of Napster's users were robbing the entertainment industry of potential revenues, the courts viewed its existence as a potential disaster for the music industry. Consequently, Napster was shut down by a U.S. federal court injunction in 2002. However, by that time, similar renegade filesharing systems were proliferating the Internet.

Some of these systems allowed users to swap not only music with ease but also a range of other types of digitized files—computer software, games, and full texts of books. In contrast to Napster, the new systems were decentralized, not requiring the use of central servers for storage of pirated material. Consequently, illegal piracy became more difficult to trace back to its sources. Identifying and attempting to shut down even a small fraction of the users of pirated files proved impractical if not impossible. Despite government and entertainment industry campaigns to inform users of the unethical and illegal use of Internet file-sharing systems, Web-based piracy continued to grow even after Napster's highly publicized court battles.

Fair Use and Big Business

Many online file sharers have claimed that theirs is a victimless crime, asserting that they are merely sharing duplicated materials for their own personal use. Some have even argued that online file sharing actually leads to increased sales of music, games, and video materials because it increases exposure for commercial artists. However, representatives of the entertainment industry vehemently disagree. The Recording Industry Association of America (RIAA), a music industry trade group, attributed to the popularity of online piracy a significant plunge in music sales in the years following the proliferation of Internet file-sharing programs. In 2001, sales of compact discs (CDs) in the United States dropped 6.4 percent, and the following year, they plunged another 8.7 percent. During the same period, the number of Internet users who admitted downloading ever more music while buying less of it outnumbered those who claimed downloading led them to buy more music by a two-to-one margin.

Both the entertainment and software industries tend to regard virtually *all* unauthorized duplication of their products as acts of piracy. However, certain considerations complicate the issue. The copyright laws of most countries, including the United States, provide for the "fair use" of protected artistic and intellectual materials. In other words, it is legal for those who own copyrighted copies of music, movies, and in some cases computer software, to duplicate them for their own private use—provided they do not share their "personal" copies with others. It is legal for a person who has purchased a collection of compact discs to make CD collections of their favorite songs, provided they do not share the copies that they make. The ethical and legal problem lies in what constitutes "sharing" such copies. Surely, giving a friend a copy of one's "personal" CD would infringe on copyright. Nonetheless, if one makes a "personal" copy of a song and plays it in the presence of a visiting friend, does this infringe on the rights of the copyright holder to profit from the friend's hearing the music?

Privacy advocates strongly oppose what they see as the entertainment industry's draconian efforts to invade personal privacy by limiting "fair use." They also warn against allowing software companies to have almost absolute control over their software's source code, pointing out that in many cases this limits the individual's rights to fair personal use and impedes the natural course of technological progress.

A Happy Medium?

In 2003, the RIAA sued major Internet service providers Verizon and Earthlink, demanding that they turn over the names of their customers known to download or exchange copyrighted media files. However, in reality such lists only allowed the RIAA to verify the names of Internet subscribers from whose computers illegal file exchanges had occurred.

They could not verify which particular members of these households had been sharing pirated materials because no electronic mechanism exists that can pinpoint exact violators. In one highly publicized case, the RIAA sent a letter threatening a sizeable lawsuit against a grandfather whose name appeared on a list of Internet accounts from which illegal downloads had allegedly been made.

In truth the computer owner's grandson, who only visited his home occasionally, was actually downloading pirated music on the family computer. Privacy advocates view the RIAA's efforts at enforcing their rights as copyright holders as displaying an unethical disregard for personal privacy rights when taken to this extreme.

They place the responsibility for preventing piracy on the entertainment companies themselves, suggesting that they develop and market new ways of copy-proofing their products rather than playing Big Brother and haphazardly attempting to target individual copyright violators. They maintain that although copyright infringement takes place on a widespread basis on the Internet, targeting individuals has a serious cost—the potential sacrifice of personal privacy and the significant risk of punishing the undeserving.

—Gregory D. Horn

Further Reading

Graham, Jefferson. "Privacy vs. Internet Piracy." *USA Today*, June 6, 2003.

Hart-Davis, Guy. *Internet Piracy Exposed*. London: Sybex Press, 2001.

Manes, Stephen. "Copyright Law: Ignore at Your Own Peril." *PC World*, September, 2003, 182.

Monk, Bill. "Listen to Impartial Advice." *Computer Weekly*. July 29, 2003, 16.

Willcox, James K. "Where Have All the CDs Gone?" *Sound and Vision*, June, 2003, 87-89.

See also: Computer crime; Computer misuse; Computer technology; Copyright; Intellectual property; Napster; Plagiarism; Song lyrics.

Journalistic entrapment

Definition: Use of an undercover investigation to lure subjects into compromising or illegal acts they would not otherwise commit

Type of ethics: Media ethics

Significance: Reporters investigating wrongdoing may inadvertently or intentionally corrupt innocent people or cause the commission of crimes that would not otherwise have occurred

Investigative journalism was propelled into prominence during the 1970s as a result of the Watergate scandal uncovered by *The Washington Post*, the leaking of the Pentagon Papers to *The New York Times*, and the general adversarial tone that characterized the relationship between government and the media throughout the Vietnam War. In subsequent years, technological advancements and the proliferation of broadcast shows that relied on videotape footage to document undercover findings swelled both the number and the scope of such investigations. Issues subject to such treatments have included home and commercial lending practices, nursing home care, governmental corruption, abortion practices, and military information confirmation.

The Federal Bureau of Investigation (FBI) and other law enforcement agencies frequently use undercover operations to expose criminal wrongdoing. Their activities, unlike those in journalism, are subject to explicit guidelines and legal restrictions that help to establish the line between legitimate investigative work and coercing or abetting in the commission of a crime. For journalists, however, that line is largely one of interpretation because of the broad latitude and significant freedoms offered by the First Amendment. It is incumbent upon journalists, therefore, to wrestle with a number of ethical considerations, such as the morality of devising an enticement for illegal activity and the awareness that reporters themselves may become, if even indirectly, agents of wrongdoing.

Industry misgivings about the practice exist, as revealed in the Pulitzer Prize committee's reluctance to recognize stories that rely on undercover investigations because of their deceptive nature. The usage continues, however, because of the journalistic belief that news organizations have an overriding obligation to distribute information to a democratic society and a moral responsibility to consider society's needs, thereby providing the greatest good for the greatest number of people. This approach, with its emphasis on consequences, accepts the belief that the end justifies the means. Therefore, the media's "watchdog role" in preserving and protecting the public interest—a good and moral end—is justified in its aggressive pursuit of certain undercover investigations. Because the journalism profession also professes a strong commitment to accuracy and truthfulness, however, any use of deception must be carefully weighed.

Integrity of the Press

Recognizing that integrity is its greatest asset, the press is especially vigilant in upholding standards that do not erode or detract from its credibility, including the use of deception. Because codes of ethics among the media are more advisory than mandatory, however, much of the decision is left to interpretation by individual journalists who adjudge the specifics of individual situations. The long-standing reliance on consequential reasoning has typically emphasized the social benefit derived from an undercover investigation. For example, a series entitled "Abortion Profiteers" by the *Chicago Sun-Times* in November, 1978, relied on information obtained by reporters who, obscuring their identity as journalists, went to work for several outpatient abortion clinics where gross negligence as well as medical misconduct had been reported. The articles resulted in a number of new state laws regulating outpatient abortion clinics, the closing of two of the four clinics under investigation (one of them permanently), and the imprisonment of one doctor. Several other doctors left the state.

It was agreed by the editors and reporters involved that the overwhelming benefit to the community of such an investigation outweighed the price of the deception. Another case involving a different publication, however, reveals that a positive outcome is not the only measure in weighing the ethical considerations of going undercover. In 1988, *Newsday* conceived and planned—but did not execute—an undercover investigation designed to confirm the suspected practice of real estate "steering," a method of maintaining racially segregated neighborhoods by directing potential buyers only to those areas already populated by people of the same race. After a year of preliminary work, management decided that the operation was logistically untenable and that the same information could be obtained through other methods, such as interviews with buyers and real estate records. Anthony Marro, the editor at the time, also questioned the existence of probable cause, wondering if the appropriate level of presumed bad conduct merited the use of entrapment techniques.

The Society of Professional Journalists, whose code of ethics is widely invoked by individual journalists and news organizations, in 1993 introduced a new approach to ethical decision making that combined the long-used consequential reasoning with an effort to examine a number of other factors, such as the characteristics of the situation, as well as journalistic values, loyalties, and professional principles. In addition, the new code set forth a number of conditions, all of which must be met to justify deceptive information-gathering strategies:

1. The information sought must be of profound importance;
2. Other alternatives have been exhausted;
3. The reporter is willing to make public the deception;
4. Excellence has been pursued through full allocation of the news organization's resources;
5. The harm prevented by the deception outweighs the harm of the deception;
6. Conscious, thoughtful, moral, ethical, and professional deliberations have been made.

In addition, the revised code outlined specific rationalizations that do not meet ethical standards and may not be used to justify the use of deception. These include:

1. Winning a prize;
2. Beating the competition;
3. Saving costs or time;
4. Others have "already done it";
5. The subjects, themselves, are unethical.

Out of concern for their role as protectors of the public interest, journalists avoid concrete rules regarding the use of deception and undercover operations. They maintain the right to use such tactics ethically and morally on a situational basis when a greater good is served and when other methods have been exhausted.

—Regina Howard Yaroch

Further Reading

Black, Jay, Bob Steele, and Ralph Barney. *Doing Ethics in Journalism: A Handbook with Case Studies.* Greencastle, Ind.: Sigma Delta Chi Foundation and the Society of Professional Journalists, 1993.

Bovee, Warren G. "The End Can Justify the Means—But Rarely." *Journal of Mass Media Ethics* 6, no. 3 (1991): 135-145. "Cases and Commentaries: The Norfolk Abortion Case." *Journal of Mass Media Ethics* 5, no 2. (1990): 136-145.

Christians, Clifford G., et al. *Media Ethics: Cases and Moral Reasoning.* 5th ed. New York: Longman, 1998.

Dufresne, Marcel. "To Sting or Not to Sting?" *Columbia Journalism Review* 30 (May/June 1991): 49-51.

Englehardt, Elaine E., and Ralph D. Barney. *Media and Ethics: Principles for Moral Decisions.* Belmont, Calif.: Wadsworth Thomson Learning, 2002.

McQuail, Denis. *Media Accountability and Freedom of Publication.* Oxford, England: Oxford University Press, 2003.

See also: Internet chat rooms; Journalistic ethics; News sources; Photojournalism; Tabloid journalism.

Journalistic ethics

Definition: Formal and informal professional codes of conduct governing the practice of journalism

Type of ethics: Media ethics

Significance: Journalistic ethics seeks to balance the public's right to know with the moral responsibility of individual journalists to be truthful, objective, and fair both in their reporting and in their work to uncover and develop information. Moreover, because the First Amendment dictates that the press be virtually unregulated by the government and legal system, there is a greater than average need for journalists to regulate themselves

Unlike doctors and lawyers, journalists do not control who may practice in their field or police their own ranks; neither do they prescribe a body of knowledge with which those entering the field must be familiar. In this sense, journalists do not fit within the traditional definition of a "profession." Nevertheless, responsible journalists—like members of these other professions—do adhere to a set of occupational principles, many of which are addressed in the ethical code (the "Code") of Sigma Delta Chi, the Society of Professional Journalists.

Responsibility and Freedom of the Press

The first three sections of the professional code concern what many journalists regard as their occupational imperative: to observe a constitutional mandate to serve the public's right to know. Such a right is not, in fact, explicitly stated in the Constitution and has been discounted by such eminent legal authorities as former Chief Justice Warren Burger. Other media critics point to abuses—such as invasion of privacy and interference with the right to a fair trial—stemming from overzealous pursuit of the journalistic mission. Still, courts have consistently upheld the media's First Amendment rights, which are regarded as so central to the nation's democratic principles that they can overcome—as they did during the 1971 "Pentagon Papers" case, *United States v. New York Times Company*—a countervailing concern as compelling as national security.

The Pentagon Papers case illustrates the code's precept that "[journalists] will make constant effort to assure that the public's business is conducted in public and that public records are open to public inspection." Other, less august, journalistic exercises, such as traffic reports and celebrity gossip, illustrate not so much the public's right to know as its need or desire to know. In such contexts, there is perhaps less justification for the kind of aggressive, sometimes invasive techniques employed by journalists.

Accuracy, Fairness, and Objectivity

It would seem fundamental—and the professional code takes it for granted—that one of a journalist's primary duties is to report truth rather than falsehoods. Yet the news business has always been plagued with so-called "yellow journalism," which distorts or exaggerates facts in order to create sensationalism and attract consumers. In this sense, the blatant jingoism of William Randolph Hearst's papers during the 1890s is not unrelated to attempts on the part of modern television broadcasters to dramatize news through fictionalized "reenactments." Public skepticism about television news rose to new levels during the 2004 U.S. Presidential campaign, when CBS News was accused of using falsified documents to cast doubt on President Bush's service record in the National Guard during the 1970s.

Another method by which journalists can take liberties with the truth is through misattribution or misquotation. Although the plaintiff in *Westmoreland v. Columbia Broadcasting System* (1984), General William C. Westmoreland, commander of United States troops in Vietnam during the late 1960s, ultimately lost his libel action against CBS, the defendant clearly played fast and loose with the truth by deliberately misrepresenting a damaging cable regarding the deadly Tet offensive as Westmoreland's. In 1990, however, the Supreme Court permitted psychoanalyst Jeffrey Masson to proceed with his lawsuit against *New Yorker* magazine writer Janet Malcolm because her allegedly purposeful misquotation of him (for example, that he intended to turn the Freud Archives into "a place of sex, women, fun") could be libel.

Ironically, it was Malcolm herself, in her book about the relationship between convicted murderer Jeffrey MacDonald and his journalist/chronicler Joe McGinniss, who pinpointed one of the primary reasons that journalists sometimes violate the ethical imperative of fairness emphasized in the code: "The moral ambiguity of journalism lies not in its texts but in the relationships out of which they arise—relationships that are invariably and inescapably lopsided."

Malcolm's contention is that McGinniss insinuated himself into MacDonald's confidence in order to obtain exclusive information and then betrayed him by writing a damning portrait of him. Seen in this light, MacDonald is just as culpable as the reporter who fails to protect the confidentiality of his sources. If this evaluation is accurate—and if Jeffrey Masson's allegations about Malcolm are accurate—then clearly both McGinniss and Malcolm have violated the code's tenet that "Journalists at all times will show respect for the dignity, privacy, rights and wellbeing of people encountered in the course of gathering and presenting the news."

Just as MacDonald and Malcolm could be accused of not playing fair, they could also stand accused of bias, of failing to observe the journalistic objectivity that the code requires. They could, alternatively, be seen to be over-compensating for the intimate access they had to their respective subjects. The code states that "Journalists must be free of obligation to any interest other than the public's right to know."

The most obvious interpretation of this precept is that journalists should not compromise their integrity by accepting payoffs. It can also be seen, however, to apply to situations such as McGinniss's and Malcolm's and to journalist-celebrities, who can themselves influence and even become the stories they cover.

Most ethical principles espoused in the code are simply restatements of common sense and courtesy. Because of the media's ability to influence and shape society, however, it is of particular importance that purveyors of news take seriously not only their First Amendment rights but also their moral obligations.

—*Carl Rollyson*

Further Reading

Adams, Julian. *Freedom and Ethics in the Press.* New York: R. Rosen Press, 1983.

Elliott, Deni, ed. *Responsible Journalism.* Beverly Hills, Calif.: Sage, 1986.

Englehardt, Elaine E., and Ralph D. Barney. *Media and Ethics: Principles for Moral Decisions.* Belmont, Calif.: Wadsworth Thomson Learning, 2002.

Fink, Conrad C. *Media Ethics: In the Newsroom and Beyond.* New York: McGraw-Hill, 1988.

McQuail, Denis. *Media Accountability and Freedom of Publication.* Oxford, England: Oxford University Press, 2003.

Merrill, John C., and Ralph D. Barney, eds. *Ethics and the Press: Readings in Mass Media Morality.* New York: Hastings House, 1975.

Olen, Jeffrey. *Ethics in Journalism.* Englewood Cliffs, N.J.: Prentice-Hall, 1988.

See also: Accuracy in Media; Libel; News sources; Pentagon Papers; Privacy; Tabloid journalism.

Knights of Labor

Identification: Universal national labor union working to promote social reform

Date: Founded in December, 1869

Type of ethics: Business and labor ethics

Significance: The Knights of Labor was the first national union to seek economic justice for unskilled labor by promoting a classless society in which each worker would also be an entrepreneur

Established originally as a secret league, the Knights of Labor experienced tremendous growth when it became an open organization during the 1880s through the efforts of Terence Powderly, its grand master workman from 1879 to 1893. With the exception of professional workers, the Knights melded all labor, regardless of sex, race, creed, national origin, or skill level, into a single disciplined army that would check the power of concentrated wealth that, according to the Knights, was degrading labor.

The Knights of Labor believed that labor could regain its moral worth if it received a proper share of the wealth that it created and adequate leisure time to enjoy the blessings of a civilized society. The Knights sought to check the power of corporations through legislation to secure safe working conditions, equal pay for the sexes, an eight-hour day, a national banking system, public lands for settlers, weekly pay in full, the substitution of arbitration for strikes, and the abolition of contract labor and child labor. The Knights declined after 1886 when many

The Seal of the Knights of Labor.

skilled workers who desired less utopian reform joined the newly organized American Federation of Labor.

—Stephen D. Livesay

See also: American Federation of Labor; Executive Order 10988; International Labour Organisation; National Labor Union.

Labor-Management Relations Act

Identification: Federal law that attempted to check the power given to labor unions under the National Labor Relations Act of 1935 by specifying a set of unfair union practices

Date: Became law on August 22, 1947

Type of ethics: Business and labor ethics

Significance: The Labor-Management Relations Act sought to limit the power of labor partly to find a balance between labor interests and business interests and partly out of political fears that linked labor unions with communism

After the passage of the National Labor Relations Act (Wagner Act) in 1935, manufacturers began a decade-long media blitz to convince the public and Congress of the evils of the new state of industrial relations. Manufacturers extolled the virtues of the free enterprise system and blamed the Wagner Act for allowing an unregulated growth of organized labor and producing the social and industrial unrest of post-World War II America. Pro-business Republicans turned the Democrats out of office in 1946 and promptly amended the Wagner Act, detailing six unfair labor practices and monitoring officials of labor organizations.

Changes in the law included outlawing the closed shop, prohibiting unions from participating in secondary strikes, allowing for an eighty-day injunction for emergency disputes, and requiring union officials to renounce any Communist Party affiliation or belief. This legislation provided a necessary balance between the interests of business and labor and proved the viability of the American system of government to keep its traditional economic institutions intact while meeting the current needs of all of its people.

See also: American Federation of Labor; Executive Order 10988; National Labor Relations Act.

Libel

Definition: Defamation of a person or group by means of writing or visual images

Type of ethics: Media ethics

Significance: To be libelous, defamatory material must generally be both malicious and untrue, and it must be shown to cause actual harm. It must therefore be deemed to be morally indefensible in order to be legally prosecutable. In the United States, libel is one of the few classes of speech not protected by the First Amendment

Libel is often confused with slander, which is oral defamation rather than written or visual defamation. One's good reputation is usually among one's most valuable possessions. Since libel, by definition, damages the reputation of another, it does serious harm and thus is clearly unethical.

Criminal libel is the malicious publishing of durable defamation. In common law and under most modern criminal statutes, criminal libel is a misdemeanor (an infraction usually punishable by a year or less in prison) rather than a felony (a more serious infraction punishable by more than a year in prison). Libel is also a tort, a noncontractual and noncriminal wrongdoing. Libel is thus grounds for a civil lawsuit in which one may seek to recover money to compensate for the damage that the libel has caused to one's reputation.

Truth, however, is a defense against libel, and even if the damage is caused by a false claim, if the damaged person is a public figure, then one must show malice (intent to harm) or a reckless disregard for the truth in order to prove libel. Honest mistakes do not constitute libel against public figures. Civil lawsuits against libel and punishment for criminal libel are both limited by the First Amendment of the Constitution.

This was the upshot of the landmark Supreme Court case *New York Times Co. v. Sullivan* (1964) and its progeny. This landmark case was designed to preserve the vigor and variety of public debate in a democracy, balancing democracy against serious harms to reputations in order to avoid a chilling effect on the exercise of the constitutional right of free speech.

—Sterling Harwood

See also: Censorship; Freedom of expression; Journalistic ethics; Lying; *New York Times Co. v. Sullivan.*

Library Bill of Rights

Identification: Document of the American Library Association that sets forth policies on intellectual freedom meant to be followed by all U.S. libraries

Date: Adopted on June 18, 1948

Type of ethics: Arts and censorship

Significance: The Library Bill of Rights is designed to protect the rights of all citizens to free and equal access to information and creative expression. Some provisions of the document may be controversial, especially the insistence (reaffirmed in 1996) that people of all ages should have access to the same materials.

The original text of the Library Bill of Rights was drawn up by Forrest Spaulding. It was adopted for the American Library Association (ALA) at the ALA Council in San Francisco. Subsequently, the ALA Committee on Intellectual Freedom was established to recommend any steps necessary to protect the rights of library users in accordance with the Bill of Rights of the United States and the Library Bill of Rights. Through discussion and approved emendation by members of the ALA Committee on Intellectual Freedom and by the membership of the ALA, the document was adopted on June 18, 1948, and amended in 1961 and 1980.

The six basic policies that make up the Library Bill of Rights are summarized as follows: (1) library materials should be chosen for the interest and enlightenment of all people in the community; (2) libraries should provide materials that represent all points of view on issues and concerns; (3) censorship should be challenged; (4) libraries should cooperate with those concerned with resisting the abridgement of free expression and free access to ideas; (5) rights of individuals to use libraries should not be denied based on "origin, age, background, or views"; and (6) meeting rooms of libraries should be available to community groups regardless of the beliefs and affiliations of their members.

—Robin G. Hanson

See also: Book banning; Censorship; Computer misuse; Freedom of expression; *Index librorum prohibitorum*; Intellectual property; Pornography; Song lyrics.

Marketing

Definition: Promotion, sale, and distribution of commodities

Type of ethics: Business and labor ethics

Significance: Marketing in modern society entails identifying potential consumers, persuading them to purchase one's products, and designing, modifying, manufacturing, or providing those products with the target market in mind. All these practices require ethical decisions to be made, about everything from invasions of privacy to honesty in advertising to fairness in pricing

Various personal, societal, and environmental factors have led to an increased awareness of ethics in business practices. Frequently, this awareness is focused on marketing activities. Continual publicity about businesses involved with unethical marketing practices such as price fixing, unsafe products, and deceptive advertising has led many people to believe that marketing is the area of business in which most ethical misconduct takes place.

Marketing and Ethics

Broadly speaking, "ethics" implies the establishment of a system of conduct that is recognized as correct moral behavior; it concerns deciphering the parameters of right and wrong to assist in making a decision to do what is morally right. "Marketing ethics" is the application of ethical evaluation to marketing strategies and tactics. It involves making judgments about what is morally right and wrong for marketing organizations and their employees in their roles as marketers.

The American Marketing Association (AMA) is the major international association of marketers. It has developed a code of ethics that provides guidelines for ethical marketing practices. Marketers who violate the tenets of the AMA code risk losing their membership in this prestigious and influential association.

Marketing is involved with a variety of ethical areas. Although promotional matters are often in the limelight, other ethical areas deserving attention relate to marketing research, product development and management, distribution, and pricing.

The area of marketing that seems to receive most scrutiny with respect to ethical issues is promotion. Because advertising, personal selling, and other promotional activities are the primary methods for communicating product and service information, promotion has the greatest visibility and generally has the reputation of being one of the most damaging areas of marketing. Misleading and deceptive advertising, false and questionable sales tactics, the bribing of purchase agents with "gifts" in return for purchase orders, and the creation of advertising messages that exploit children or other vulnerable groups are some examples of ethical abuses in promotional strategy.

Marketing Research, Development, and Management

Marketing research can aid management in understanding customers, in competing, and in distribution and pricing activities. At times, however, it has been criticized on ethical grounds because of its questionable intelligence-gathering techniques; its alleged invasion of the personal privacy of consumers; and its use of deception, misrepresentation, and coercion in dealing with research participants and respondents.

Potential ethical problems in the product area that marketing professionals can face involve product quality, product design and safety, packaging, branding, environmental impact of product and packaging, and planned obsolescence. Some marketers have utilized misleading, deceptive, and unethical practices in their production or packaging practices by making unsubstantiated and misleading claims about their products or by packaging in a way that appeals to health-conscious or environmentally concerned shoppers. Ethical behavior involves using safe and ethical product development techniques, providing a product quality that meets customers' product specifications, using brand names that honestly communicate about the product, and using packaging that realistically portrays product sizes and contents.

Planned obsolescence represents an ongoing ethical question for marketers. Consumers are critical of it for contributing to material wear, style changes, and functional product changes. They believe that it increases resource shortages, waste, and environmental pollution. Marketers, on the other hand, say that planned obsolescence is responsive to consumer demand and is necessary to maintain sales and employment.

Distribution and Pricing

Many of the potential ethical problems in distribution are covered by laws such as those contained in the Robinson-Patman Act. Nevertheless, distribution involves some ethical issues that merit scrutiny. Deciding the appropriate degree of control and exclusivity between manufacturers and franchised dealers, weighing the impact of serving unsatisfied market segments where the profit potential is slight (for example, opening retail stores in low-income areas), and establishing lower standards in export markets than are allowed in domestic markets are examples of some distribution cases that have significant ethical implications.

Since pricing is probably the most regulated aspect of a firm's marketing strategy, virtually anything that is unethical in pricing is also illegal. Some of the primary ethical issues of pricing are price discrimination, horizontal/vertical price fixing, predatory pricing, price gouging, and various misleading price tactics such as "bait-and-switch" pricing, nonunit pricing, and inflating prices to allow for sale markdowns.

Social Responsibility

It seems tenable to suggest that the areas of marketing ethics and social responsibility should be seen as concomitant. If marketing is authentically concerned with meeting consumer needs and concerns, it should also entail carefully evaluating how decisions impact and affect consumer expectations and quality of life.

Marketing activities can have significant societal and environmental ramifications. The rise of ecological consciousness among consumers gives social responsibility increasing stature. Consumers now are very concerned about whether the products or services they buy cause air or water pollution, landfill expansion, or depletion of natural resources. Recognizing this increased ecological concern of consumers, many companies are reevaluating the ways in which they produce and package their products and are considering the alteration of other areas of their marketing mix.

—John E. Richardson

Further Reading

Boone, Louis E., and David L. Kurtz. *Contemporary Marketing, 1999.* Rev. 9th ed. Fort Worth, Tex.: Dryden Press, 1999.

Bovée, Courtland L., and John V. Thill. *Marketing.* New York: McGraw-Hill, 1992.

Davidson, D. Kirk. *The Moral Dimension of Marketing: Essays on Business Ethics.* Chicago: American Marketing Association, 2002.

Evans, Joel R., and Barry Berman. *Marketing.* 5th ed. New York: Macmillan, 1992.

Laczniak, Gene R., and Patrick E. Murphy. *Ethical Marketing Decisions: The Higher Road.* Boston: Allyn & Bacon, 1993.

Milne, George R., and Maria-Eugenia Boza. *A Business Perspective on Database Marketing and Consumer Privacy Practices.* Cambridge, Mass.: Marketing Science Institute, 1998.

Richardson, John E., ed. *Annual Editions: Business Ethics.* 5th ed. Guilford, Conn.: Dushkin, 1993.

_____. *Annual Editions: Marketing 93/94.* 15th ed. Guilford, Conn.: Dushkin, 1993.

Schlegelmilch, Bodo B. *Marketing Ethics: An International Perspective*. Boston: International Thomson Business Press, 1998.

Smith, N. Craig, and John A. Quelch. *Ethics in Marketing*. Homewood, Ill.: Richard D. Irwin, 1993.

See also: Advertising; Boycotts; Business ethics; Industrial research; Information access; Multinational corporations; Resumes; Sales ethics;Telemarketing.

Marketing Ethics

Definition: Promotion, sale, and distribution of commodities

Type of ethics: Business and labor ethics

Significance: Marketing in modern society entails identifying potential consumers, persuading them to purchase one's products, and designing, modifying, manufacturing, or providing those products with the target market in mind. All these practices require ethical decisions to be made, about everything from invasions of privacy to honesty in advertising to fairness in pricing

Companies that maintain marketing ethics sell their products or services in a way that does not harm, insult, or deceive consumers. Ethical marketing aims to persuade consumers in a truthful way and avoids trying to trick them into making a purchase. While many marketing managers would like to create ethical advertising campaigns, they often cannot do this because unethical advertising is effective and increases sales. To further complicate the dilemma, ethics are subjective; while some consumers might consider an ad unethical, others find it acceptable. Unethical marketing practices include targeting children in advertising, making subjective claims, and stereotyping women. Many companies that strive to maintain ethical marketing practices also integrate social and environmental concerns into their operations, a practice referred to as corporate social responsibility (CRS). These companies may invest in local communities and reduce their own carbon footprint.

Overview

Marketing ethics refers to the application of standards that define acceptable conduct for marketers and organizations engaging in marketing. According to the American Marketing Association Standard of Ethics, marketers must adhere to these norms: (1) doing no harm, which includes maintaining high ethical standards and obeying laws and regulations; (2) fostering trust in the marketing industry by striving for good faith with customers, promoting fairness, and avoiding deceptions in product designs, pricing, communication, and delivery and distribution; (3) embracing ethical values, which include honesty, responsibility, fairness, respect, transparency, and citizenship.

However, implementing these norms and values is difficult when doing the right thing does not make money for a company and might cause it to fail. Consider a company that manufactures and sells diet pills. While the company's marketing managers may understand that diet pills in general do not work, they may approve advertisements with testimonials from customers who exaggerate their effectiveness. To further promote their product, they may also approve the use of "fake news" websites designed to imitate real news websites such as Fox News and CNN. Without such advertising, the diet pills will not sell and the company, which might employ thousands of people, may go out of business. While the company's ads may trick consumers, they are not illegal.

The relationship between doing what is perceived as right and making money is complicated. Marketing managers are pressured to meet performance objectives—and sometimes, what is considered unethical results in high sales. To further complicate the situation, ethics are subjective. A behavior that one person considers wrong is considered acceptable by another. Those in the field of marketing must struggle to make decisions to balance what is perceived as morally acceptable with what is profitable.

The decision should be easier if the marketing practice under consideration is illegal, yet some major U.S. companies have been charged with illegal marketing practices, such as deceptive advertising. Deceptive advertising involves deliberately misleading consumers through false representation or the omission of information. In 2015, the Federal Trade Commission (FTC) filed a lawsuit against Volkswagen (VW) claiming that the car company deliberately deceived customers with its "Clean Diesel" ad campaign. According to the FTC, VW had been cheating emissions tests on its more than one-half million diesel cars in the United states for seven years. Customers who purchased or leased the cars believed they were low-emissions and environmentally friendly. In 2016, VW pleaded guilty and agreed to pay a $14.7 billion settlement to buy back or repair the vehicles and address the environmental harm caused by its cars.

In 2007, the New York Attorney General filed charges against the PC manufacturer Dell, Inc. for an illegal marketing practice known as bait and switch. According to the Attorney General, Dell advertised "no interest" and "no payment" financing. Yet even customers with excellent credit were denied these options and instead offered high-interest financing. The company also did not provide customers with the support services in their warranties. Dell agreed to pay $4 million in restitution and penalties and changed its advertising and promotions O'Leary, 2009).

Ethical Dilemmas

Ethical dilemmas arise for marketing practices that may be considered shady but are not illegal and will likely be profitable. Before the passage of the Public Health Cigarette Smoking Act in 1970, some cigarette companies launched advertising campaigns targeting young people to attract new customers to their brand. These advertisements made smoking look fashionable and sophisticated. While at this time the link between smoking and cancer was not yet proven, most advertisers were aware of the possibility of the negative health effects.

Selling products door to door is considered unethical because the practice invades customers' privacy, yet salespeople have successfully sold water filtration systems this way for years. Companies justify selling the water filtration systems door to door because they claim the privacy invasion is minimal and the customer always has the right to refuse the salesperson's pitch and close the door.

The following are considered unethical marketing practices:

- Targeting children in advertising—creating ads for sugary cereal or other products that appeal to children who are too young to make objective decisions;
- Making unverified claims—promising to deliver results without scientific evidence, as in "using this exercise machine for only ten minutes a day will get you in the best shape of your life";
- Making subjective claims (puffery)—making claims that cannot be proven, as in "America's favorite jam";
- Stereotyping women—portraying women as sex objects or housewives;

- Using surrogate advertising—finding a way to advertise a product that cannot be advertised legally, as in placing a bottle of water in an ad with a fictitious brand name that is the same as a brand of liquor.

Unethical marketing is more effective when a company's goal is to maintain a short-term relationship with a customer. If a company wants to inspire brand-loyalty and a long-term relationship with its customers, it should make only true claims about its products and try to persuade its customers in a truthful way. The Body Shop, which sells bath and body products, makeup, and fragrances, uses organic ingredients and does not test products on animals. The company promotes healthy body images in its advertisements and has a reputation for treating its workers fairly. The company advertises its ethical nature as a way to differentiate itself from competitors and to hopefully convince its customers to shop there again and again.

Corporate Philosophies

Marketing managers should establish a corporate policy regarding their company's marketing ethics. Before they can do this, though, they must first determine the principles that will guide the company; in other words, marketing managers and other executives need to decide how they feel about corporate responsibility. The following are three frames of reference described by Goodpaster and Matthews:

The Invisible Hand: According to this philosophy, "the true and only social responsibilities of business organizations are to make profits and obey the laws." Morality, responsibility, and conscience reside in the invisible hand of the free market system or the legal system rather than in the hands of individual organizations or their managers.

The Hand of Government: According to this philosophy, "the corporation would have no moral responsibility beyond political and legal obedience. Morality, responsibility, and conscience reside in the regulatory hand of the government rather than in the hands of individual organizations or their managers.

The Hand of Management: This philosophy "encourages corporations to exercise independent, non-economic judgment over matters that face them in their short- and long-term plans and operations. It calls for corporations to implement "moral reasoning and intent." This implies that the managers of corporations should determine the ethics the company will abide by when making decisions.

Corporate Social Responsibility (CSR)

Corporate social responsibility (CSR) refers to a company integrating social and environmental concerns into its operations. Consumers in the twenty-first century expect companies to work to support the world around them. CSR contends that a company can "do well by doing good." CSR is closely linked to marketing ethics because companies seeking to be held in high regard with consumers implement both.

Large corporations significantly harm the environment. They damage local ecosystems and even contribute to climate change via pollution. CSR encourages these corporations to use a portion of their profits to help the environment and the communities in which they operate.

Companies engaging in CSR aim to be transparent, meaning they disclose their actions not only to shareholders and investors but also to the public. These companies help the environment by reducing their carbon footprint by recycling and using renewable resources. They help their local communities by initiating employee volunteer programs, maintaining strict standards regarding product safety, and making charitable contributions, not only in the form of donations but in improvements to public structures such as schools and hospitals. CRS also dictates that companies treat their employees fairly and respectfully. This includes employees working for a company in other countries, where the labor laws may be more lax.

Further Insights

In the 2010s, marketing executives continued to struggle to create advertisements that are both successful and profitable. The following are some examples of advertising campaigns consumers considered unethical:

- In 2015, GoDaddy pulled its Super Bowl commercial because of consumer backlash. The advertisement showed a lost puppy who managed to find its way home to its owner, who decided to sell the puppy on her GoDaddy website.
- Also in 2015, McDonald's launched its "Carry On" advertising campaign. The advertisements featured McDonald's signs referencing public tragedies such as 9/11 and the Boston Marathon bombings along with birthday parties and other happy events while the music group Fun's song "Carry On" played in the background. The company's intent was likely to portray itself as being part of its community but consumers thought the ads were in poor taste.

- Dove soap's "Choose Beautiful" campaign angered women. The video showed women from different cities being asked to either walk through a door labeled "beautiful" or one labeled "average." Most women chose the "average" door at first but then realized that they can "choose beautiful" for themselves and walked through the first door.
- In 2016, the brain-training app Luminosity launched an ad claiming that using its app for more than 10 minutes, three times a week could prevent Alzheimer's disease and enable students to better perform in school. The FTC fined the company $2 million for making unfounded advertising claims.

—*Tracey Biscontini*

Further Reading

Acquier, A., et al (2011). Rediscovering Howard Bowen's legacy: the unachieved agenda and continuing relevance of social responsibilities of the business-man. *Business & Society*, 50, 580-606.

Gates, Guilvert et al. (2017). How Volkswagen's 'defeat devices' worked. The *New York Times*, May 16. 2015.

Lacziak, Gene R. and Patrick E. Murphy (2016). The relationship between marketing ethics and corporate social responsibility: serving stakeholders and the common good. *Marquette University E-publications*, Jan. 1, 2016.

Suggett, Paul (2016). What is unethical advertising? *The Balance*, Aug. 12. Retrieved from https://www.thebalance.com/what-is-unethical-advertising-38797.

Wallace, Gregory (2013). Johnson & Johnson to pay $2 billion for false marketing. *CNN Money*, Nov. 4. 2013

Media ownership

Identification: Owners and executive officers of print and broadcast media, such as newspapers, magazines, radio and television stations, and broadcast networks

Type of ethics: Media ethics

Significance: Ownership of multiple media outlets by single individuals or companies raises serious ethical concerns about the availability and fairness of news

Media ownership raises a number of interesting ethical questions. Of particular important are questions relating to whether owners of the media conduct their operations in a fashion that is objective, comprehensive, and ultimately in the best interest of the general public. When large numbers of media outlets are concentrated in the hands of a few owners, especially when the outlets are of various kinds of media, then these ethical questions become particularly acute. Such situations periodically occur in Western society.

During the late nineteenth century, sizable numbers of newspapers in both the United States and Great Britain became concentrated in the hands of a few individuals, known in the United States as "press magnates" and in Britain as "press barons." By the 1880s, the American publisher Joseph Pulitzer—after whom Pulitzer Prizes are named—had assembled a number of newspapers under his control; these included the *New York World*. Meanwhile, his great rival, William Randolph Hearst, took over the *San Francisco Examiner* from his father in 1887 and in 1895 bought the *New York Morning Journal*. The following year, Hearst established the *New York Evening Journal*.

Low priced, easy to read, and filled with eye-catching sensational stories, the Pulitzer and Hearst papers soon had large circulations and enormous influence on public affairs—influence that Pulitzer and Hearst, in particular, were not shy about using. Perhaps the most striking example of their influence occurred during the Spanish-American War of 1898, which was actively pushed by the two newspaper chains, especially by the Hearst papers. At one point, before war had been declared, the famous artist Frederic Remington asked if he could return from his assignment as a war illustrator in Havana, since war between Spain and the United States appeared to be unlikely. Hearst is reported to have responded, "You provide the pictures and I'll furnish the war."

Whether that story is literally true or not, Hearst's famous riposte accurately symbolized the considerable powers of media ownership and its ethical dilemmas. At the same time that Pulitzer and Hearst were battling for media dominance in the United States, two brothers named Harmsworth were gathering a media empire in Great Britain. Better known as Lords Northcliffe and Rothermere, the brothers came to own a sizable portion of the British press, including the famous *Times of London* as well as such high-circulation papers as the *Daily Mail*, *Daily Mirror*, *Weekly/Sunday Dispatch*, *London Evening News*, and *Glasgow Evening News*. They also owned the magazine group Amalgamated Press. Although such acquisitions, the Harmsworths became the dominant media power in the United Kingdom, and Lord Northcliffe in particular was recognized as highly influential.

In 1917, during the crisis of World War I, another press baron, Lord Beaverbook, was appointed minister of information by the British government, thus making him offi-cially responsible for wartime propaganda both at home and, increasingly important, in neutral countries such as the United States. After this, there could be little doubt about the power of media ownership and control.

Modern Media Consolidation

The question of media consolidation in the hands of a relatively few individuals or corporations arose again toward the end of the twentieth century, as a handful of key players came to dominate the international media market. In addition to owning traditional newspapers, these new press barons also owned varieties of other media, most notably book publishing companies; film, radio, and television outlets; and new media channels, such as sites on the World Wide Web. They also introduced new forms of media, such as twenty-four-hour all-news networks, which operated in cooperation with their other holdings. Never before in history had such a variety of media been collected and controlled by so relatively few persons or companies.

Chief among these players were giant media corporations such as AOL-Time Warner, which was created by a merger early in 2000 and which operated Cable News Network, or CNN; Rupert Murdoch's News Corporation, which started in Australia and spread throughout the world and which started Fox Television as a challenge to CNN and the existing big three networks; and Finivest, an Italian multimedia group owned by Silvio Berlusconi, who went on to become prime minister of that nation. Of these groups, News Corporation and Finivest were known for espousing and spreading the conservative, sometimes extreme right-wing thoughts of their owners. Not since the days of Hearst and Colonel Robert McCormick, reactionary owner of the *Chicago Tribune*, had media owners been so blatant in allowing their personal viewpoints to shape the reporting of their organizations. The ethical problems created by such a situation, while obvious to many media observers and members of the general public, did not seem to trouble Murdoch and others.

At the same time, non-news corporations were purchasing media outlets, chief among them the major television networks in the United States. During the 1980s, the American Broadcasting Corporation (ABC) was bought by Capital Cities Communications, the National Broadcasting Corporation (NBC) by General Electric, and the Columbia Broadcasting System (CBS) by Loews Corporation. In addition to cutbacks in their news budgets, with possible negative impacts on coverage, diversity, and objectivity, the networks also faced the delicate situation of reporting potentially negative stories about their corporate owners that could lead to possible loss of value in the stock of the parent company. Such situations were clearly filled with potential ethical dilemmas, most of which could be traced back to the problem of media ownership that influences not only what stories are covered, but how and to what purpose as well.

—Michael Witkoski

Further Reading

Christians, Clifford G., et al. *Media Ethics: Cases and Moral Reasoning.* 5th ed. New York: Longman, 1998.

Day, Louis A. *Ethics in Media Communications: Cases and Controversies.* Belmont, Calif.:Wadsworth, 1991.

Englehardt, Elaine E., and Ralph D. Barney. *Media and Ethics: Principles for Moral Decisions.* Belmont, Calif.: Wadsworth Thomson Learning, 2002.

Gorman, Lyn, and David McLean. *Media and Society in the Twentieth Century.* Oxford, England: Blackwell, 2003.

Kovach, Bill, and Tom Rosenstiel. *The Elements of Journalism.* New York: Crown, 2001.

Levy, Beth, and Denis M. Bonilla, eds. *The Power of the Press.* New York: H. W. Wilson, 1999.

Pavlik, John V. *Journalism and New Media.* New York: Columbia University Press, 2001.

Pritchard, David, ed. *Holding the Media Accountable: Citizens, Ethics, and the Law.* Bloomington: Indiana University Press, 2000.

See also: Accuracy in Media; American Society of Newspaper Editors; Fairness and Accuracy in Reporting; Journalistic ethics; News sources; Public's right to know; Tabloid journalism.

Minimum-wage laws

Definition: Laws requiring that workers' salaries fall no lower than specified hourly rates

Type of ethics: Business and labor ethics

Significance: The central ethical issue raised by minimum-wage laws is whether government has a duty to require employers to raise the wages of low-paid workers above what free market forces would dictate. In the background is the deeper problem of whether it is unjust for there to be unequal distribution of wealth

In medieval Europe, local governments often fixed wages at customary levels for various kinds of work. However, they typically imposed maximum wage levels, rather than minimum levels. During the nineteenth century, classical economists strongly opposed the fixing of wages by government, and comparatively little such wage-fixing occurred. During that period, however, workers, especially those in factories, often labored for low pay under bad conditions. As public concern for their well-being gradually increased, laws setting minimum wages were proposed as one way to help workers. Such laws were enacted first in Australia and New Zealand during the 1890s. Many other countries soon followed suit.

Massachusetts was the first U.S. state to set a minimum wage, in 1912. Afterward, other states enacted laws setting minimum wages for women and children; however, these laws had little effect. Finally, the federal Fair Labor Standards Act of 1938, one component of Franklin D. Roosevelt's New Deal, established a uniform minimum wage for all workers who were directly or indirectly engaged in interstate commerce. Later, Congress repeatedly raised minimum wage levels and extended them to cover ever more types of employment. Democrats usually have been eager to raise the minimum wage, while Republicans have been less eager to do so. In 2003 the U.S. federal minimum wage stood at $5.15 per hour.

Arguments for Minimum-Wage Laws

Advocates of minimum-wage laws hold that without this form of government intervention the lowestpaid workers would be paid less than they need to live on, and this would be unfair, when others are living well. Setting minimum wages is thus seen as a move toward greater justice in the distribution of wealth. Those who think this way tend to presuppose the view that society is more just when its wealth is more evenly distributed. Historically, one inspiration for this egalitarian view was the Judeo-Christian tradition that stressed the duty of the well-to-do to share with the poor. Another was criticism of the capitalistic system that came from socialists and communists; greedy employers, they said, exploited workers by taking, as profits, revenue that should rightly have belonged to the workers.

A modified version of egalitarianism, not based on religion or on communism, was formulated by the American philosopher John Rawls. He held that if a society is to be just, wealth and other advantages must be distributed equally, except when inequalities serve to raise the level of well-being of the least welloff group in the society. For example, paying physicians high salaries could be just, if that were the only way to ensure that health needs are met. Rawls's theory offers a rationale for minimum-wage laws, and for much else in the New Deal's program.

Advocates have often proposed as a guideline that minimum wage levels must be high enough to enable each worker to support a family of four.

Arguments Against Minimum-Wage Laws

Opponents of the minimum wage argue that it has bad economic consequences for others in society, especially in that it increases unemployment. Those who fail to notice this are wrongly overlooking the fact that in a free market economy, wage levels affect how many job openings there will be. If minimum wage levels are high enough to have any effect, they must increase unemployment, because the labor of some would-be workers will have a market value less than the minimum wage, so employers will not hire them. The higher the minimum wage level, the more would-be workers will be excluded in this way. If there were no minimum-wage law, these would-be workers could find jobs at wages proportionate to the market value of what they can do. Such workers probably would not earn enough to support families of four, but most of them do not have families, as many are adolescents. Those who work but earn too little to avoid poverty could be offered government welfare payments to supplement their low wages. This arrangement would be more efficient than having a minimum wage, since support would go only to those who need it, and the total cost to society of helping the least-well-off would decrease.

Opponents of the minimum wage generally agree with Adam Smith and later classical economists who argued that free market capitalism, functioning without government control over such economic variables as wages and prices, can unleash individual enterprise and make society much richer. Government intervention to set wages will introduce distortions in the allocation of resources, thereby reducing the national income. Instead of emphasizing equality, this way of thinking recommends that members of society tolerate inequality in the distribution of income, in order that total national income will be maximized. Here the idea is that a society is just in which owners who have acquired their property in noncriminal ways are protected in their possession of it, and wages that have been set through free market bargaining will not be altered by government edict. Robert Nozick was an American philosopher who defended this conception of justice.

—*Stephen F. Barker*

Further Reading

Murray, Patrick. *Reflections on Commercial Life: An Anthology of Classic Texts*. New York: Routledge, 1997.

Nicholson, Walter. *Microeconomic Theory*. Cincinnati: South-Western/Thomson Learning, 2002.

Nozick, Robert. *Anarchy, State, and Utopia*. New York: Basic Books, 1974.

Rawls, John. *A Theory of Justice*. Rev. ed. Cambridge, Mass.: Belknap Press of Harvard University Press, 1999.

Smeeding, Timothy M., Michael O'Higgins, and Lee Rainwater, eds. *Poverty, Inequality, and Income Distribution in Comparative Perspective*. Washington, D.C.: Urban Institute Press, 1990.

Smith, Adam. *An Inquiry into the Nature and Causes of the Wealth of Nations: A Selected Edition*. Edited by Kathryn Sutherland. New York: Oxford University Press, 1998.

See also: Child labor legislation; Corporate compensation; Cost-benefit analysis; Equal pay for equal work; Fair Labor Standards Act; Income distribution; Professional athlete incomes; *Theory of Justice, A*; Tipping; Wage discrimination.

Money laundering

Definition: Methods of concealing the source of illegally obtained money

Significance: Money laundering provides the means to fund criminal enterprises, including drug trafficking and terrorism.

Money laundering enterprises are inventive and widespread. The participants vary from small-time gangsters to drug traffickers and international terrorists. In 2002, for example, three clerks were convicted of laundering more than $300,000 at the race track in Saratoga Springs, New York. The same year, executives of a large offshore trust program in Costa Rica were indicted for conspiring to launder $370,000 though a complex network of foreign and domestic accounts. The website for the Internal Revenue Service lists numerous examples of money laundering investigations from Fargo, North Dakota, to Miami, Florida.

Money laundering schemes process criminal finances in order to make the funds appear to have originated from a legitimate source. Money laundering allows the true source of funds to remain hidden while converting the money into assets that appear to have a legal basis. In simple terms, money laundering is cleaning dirty money.

Criminal activity often requires considerable capital and generates substantial profits. Money laundering operations need to control and change the form of the funds while concealing the principal activities and people involved. This usually consists of three stages: placement, layering, and integration.

In the placement stage, the illegal funds enter the financial system. Criminals might attempt to break up large amounts of money into smaller, less conspicuous amounts by employing the services of casinos, banks, and other financial institutions. Money may be moved or placed through a variety of measures: smuggling cash; wire or electronic transfers; purchasing cashier's checks, money orders, traveler's checks, or securities; or cashing third-party checks. During this stage, the funds are most vulnerable to detection and seizure by law enforcement.

Once the money has been placed in the financial system, a series of secondary transactions take place that obscure the trail by moving the funds from location to location. This is called the layering stage. The funds are channeled through the purchase and sale of assets in order to distance them from the original source.

In the final stage, or integration stage, the funds are reintroduced into the economy as legitimate money. This money is used to pay employees, fund business ventures, or purchase luxury items and properties.

Because money laundering is a necessary process in any profit-generating crime, it can occur anywhere in the world. Generally, illegal organizations will use countries that have weak or ineffective anti-money-laundering laws. After the terrorist attacks of September 11, 2001, Congress passed the Patriot Act. The act was passed in order to prevent and detect money laundering and funding of terrorist activities. Under it, financial institutions report suspicious activity, such as large monetary transfers and withdrawals.

According to the U.S. Securities and Exchange Commission, banks develop "watch lists" of clients who have exhibited suspicious behavior and monitor these clients' accounts, screen wire transfers and client backgrounds, and review new account documentation. As of July, 2004, Swiss banks and securities dealers were required to have electronic monitoring systems to identify high-risk transactions and accounts.

—Alison S. Burke

Further Reading

Block, Alan A. All Is Clouded by Desire: Global Banking, Money Laundering, and International Organized Crime. Westport, Conn.: Praeger, 2004.

Lyman, M. D., and G. W. Potter. Organized Crime. 3d ed. Englewood Cliffs, N.J.: Prentice-Hall, 2001.

"Money Laundering." Interpol. Interpol, 2016. Web. 31 May 2016.

"Money Laundering." U.S. Department of the Treasury. U.S. Dept. of Treasury, n.d. Web. 31 May 2016.

Saviano, Roberto. "Where the Mob Keeps Its Money." New York Times. New York Times, 25 Aug. 2012. Web. 31 May 2016.

Monopoly

Definition: Exclusive ownership or control of a good or service in a particular market

Type of ethics: Business and labor ethics

Significance: Monopolies are illegal in the major modern industrialized capitalist nations because they are perceived as unfairly interfering with competition. They are thus said to infringe on the rights of companies to compete equitably in the marketplace, and on the rights of consumers to benefit from that competition

In 1340, an English listing of the "evils of trade" included such things as forestalling (the physical obstruction of goods coming to market, or cornering the supply of goods, which deprived the owner of the market stall his rental),

"I Like a Little Competition"—J. P. Morgan

"I Like a Little Competition"—*J. P. Morgan by Art Young. Cartoon relating to the answer J. P. Morgan gave when asked whether he disliked competition at the Pujo Committee.*

regrating (buying most or all the available goods at a fair for resale at a higher price), and engrossing (contracting for control of goods while they are still being grown or produced). These are all attempts at monopolization of a market, and such actions have been thought wrong since they began. The United States has had laws against monopoly since its founding, based on these terms taken from English common law and justified by reference to an abiding public interest in the maintenance of competition. Competition by ethical individuals results in the completion of mutually beneficial transactions, protects consumers from unreasonable price increases, and, according to Adam Smith (*An Inquiry Into the Nature and Causes of the Wealth of Nations*, 1776), leads to the greatest wealth for the nation.

—*Sandra L. Christensen*

See also: Antitrust legislation; Capitalism; Consumerism; Fairness; Price fixing; Profit economy; Smith, Adam.

Motion picture ratings systems

Definition: Formal systems for classifying films based on content which may be deemed inappropriate for children, detrimental to society, or objectionable on moral or religious grounds

Type of ethics: Arts and censorship

Significance: Ratings systems may be created by third-party organizations independently of film studios, or they may be self-regulatory systems instituted by the studios themselves. In the latter case, they raise issues regarding the boundaries between voluntary self-regulation and institutionally imposed censorship

The motion picture industry of the United States of America has long attempted to forestall government controls by observing self-imposed regulations. Originally, those regulations were proscriptive, intended to make a preponderance of exhibited films palatable to general audiences, but subsequent policy, using ratings to influence public exposure, enabled a wider range of material to appear in major releases. Regulatory systems have been established elsewhere, but the varying U.S. approaches provide excellent studies in the application of standards.

State and local government attempts to censor film date back to a 1907 Chicago ordinance that was upheld by Illinois's supreme court in 1909. The potential impact of such rulings was evident in the proliferation of state and local censor boards as well as a 1915 U.S. Supreme Court determination that cinema was not protected under the First Amendment. With the goal of curtailing widespread government censorship, from 1909 to 1921 the National Board of Censorship assumed some responsibility for the prerelease evaluation of film content. This citizens' group, supported by the film industry, was the nation's first voluntary censorship body.

In 1922, the major Hollywood studios appointed Will Hays the head of their newly formed association, the Motion Picture Producers and Distributors of America (MPPDA). Created to maintain industry sovereignty, the MPPDA in 1934 enacted a code of ethics known as the Production Code, or "Hays Code." Arising out of the Mae West era, the code combined lofty statements of principle ("No picture shall be produced which will lower the moral standards of those who see it") with a battery of specific regulations (for example, "*Methods of Crime* should not be explicitly presented" and "The treatment of bedrooms must be governed by good taste and delicacy").

The Ratings

Two major ratings systems originated during this period. In 1933, the Film Board of National Organizations formulated the MPPDA-supported Green Sheet, which used age and educational criteria to classify films as *A* (Adult), *MY* (Mature Young People), *Y* (Young People), *GA* (General Audience), *C* (Children, unaccompanied), or a combination of those ratings. The following year, a committee of bishops formed the influential Legion of Decency, which rated movies on a scale from *A-I* (morally unobjectionable for general audiences) to *C* (condemned).

Movies without the Production Code Seal were effectively banned from theaters. Code stipulations were, however, periodically amended and perennially subject to administrative give and take (intense lobbying won a place for Rhett Butler's "forbidden" last word in 1939's *Gone with the Wind*). The Code remained in place during the 1940s, as Eric Johnston replaced Hays, the MPPDA became the Motion Picture Association of America (MPAA), and antitrust decisions forced studios to sell their theaters. After the Supreme Court overturned its 1915 ruling in 1952, the newly opened theater market exhibited not only unapproved foreign features but also domestic productions such as *The Moon Is Blue* (1953), which had been denied the Seal for its treatment of virginity. The commercial viability of such films, together with the precedent-setting releases of *Son of Sinbad* (1955) and

Baby Doll (1956)—the first C films to receive the Seal—heralded further shifts in standard application. Additional Court decisions and jolting thrillers such as *Psycho* (1960) and *Cape Fear* (1962) built momentum for extensive Code revision in 1966, when Jack Valenti became the third MPAA president. Early frustrations with language in *Who's Afraid of Virginia Woolf* (1966) and nudity in *Blow-Up* (1966) influenced his replacement of proscription with a voluntary film rating system in 1968.

Officially intended to place responsibility for children's movie-going with parents and guardians, the new system reflected contemporaneous rulings on children and obscenity. Overseen by the MPAA, the National Association of Theatre Owners (NATO), and the International Film Importers and Distributors of America, it classified submitted films according to their appropriateness for one of four possible audience groups. G for General Audiences, M for Mature Audiences (parental guidance suggested), and R for Restricted Audiences were trademarked; *X* (no one under 17 admitted), adopted at the urging of NATO, was not. M, which parents misinterpreted as being sterner than *R*, was initially replaced with *GP* (implying a "General Audience" film for which "Parental Guidance" was suggested) and later with *PG*. In 1984, the young audience categories were expanded to include *PG-13*.

Adult Films

Adult film classification also changed. At first, some *X* features won significant mainstream interest. Soon, however, the rating became identified with pornography, to which it was frequently self-applied. Excluding the young audience market by definition, the rating also precluded advertising in most outlets, leading many major producers to edit movies from *X* to *R*. (Some features, such as *Midnight Cowboy*, 1969, eventually made that transition without cutting.) Ongoing debate over film tailoring and the need for another "adults only" category sparked the creation of the MPAA's federally registered certification mark, *NC-17*, first assigned to *Henry and June* (1990). During the early 1990s, the MPAA also began issuing explanations of specific ratings to theaters and critics. Although criticized for representing an abandonment of moral and ethical responsibility, the shift from proscription to ratings has been praised for enabling major producers to exercise greater freedom of expression. Despite such increased license, the questions of the ratings system constituting a form of self-censorship remained.

Because ratings greatly influence a project's viability, films are not simply rated after completion; throughout the creative process there may be rating-oriented interplay involving filmmakers, the Rating Board, and occasionally (after the code has been assigned) the Appeals Board. This process may receive wide public attention, often dwelling on potentially offensive material and sometimes leading to the creation of alternate versions aimed at different markets. Naturally, content not recognized as potentially offensive may be perceived as implicitly approved. The MPAA uses regular polling to establish that its standards represent the views of a majority of citizens.

Besides advising parents and guardians about film content, the ratings system, which encompasses trailers and film advertising, requires the cooperation of theater owners. At the box office, administrators discriminate according to age and appearance (sometimes requiring potential consumers to identify themselves by birth date), as well as geographic location. This approach reinforces and establishes taboos and hierarchies related to age, appearance, maturity, and media.

The ratings system has been endorsed by the Video Software Dealers Association. Similar systems of self-regulation have been adopted or proposed for recording, video games, and television programming.

—David Marc Fischer

Further Reading

Bernstein, Matthew, ed. *Controlling Hollywood: Censorship and Regulation in the Studio Era.* New Brunswick, N.J.: Rutgers University Press, 1999.
De Grazia, Edward, and Roger K. Newman. *Banned Films.* New York: R. R. Bowker, 1982.
Farber, Stephen. *The Movie Rating Game.* Washington, D.C.: Public Affairs Press, 1972.
Leff, Leonard J., and Jerold L. Simmons. *The Dame in the Kimono.* New York: Grove Weidenfeld, 1990.
Randall, Richard S. *Censorship of the Movies.* Madison: University of Wisconsin Press, 1968.
Schumach, Murray. *The Face on the Cutting Room Floor.* New York: William Morrow, 1964.

See also: Art; Art and public policy; Censorship; Children's television; Consistency; Family values; First Amendment; Freedom of expression; Language; Pornography; Self-regulation.

Multinational corporations

Definition: Large commercial organizations that conduct business in more than a single nation

Type of ethics: Business and labor ethics

Significance: Ethical issues arise due to the very existence of multinational corporations in foreign countries, especially with respect to fundamental human rights and the problem of ethical relativism

The single most important objective of any business enterprise is to create a monetary surplus, which, in turn, allows the business to reinvest in itself in order to continue to pursue the same fundamental objective. Should the business be a corporation with publicly held shares, its financial profits are also used to pay dividends to its shareholders. Should the corporation engage in any business activity with people in any country other than the one in which it is legally incorporated, it achieves the status of a multinational corporation. Such activities include, but are not limited to, the advertising and marketing of the corporation's products or services to people in other countries, the establishment of manufacturing plants in other countries, and the hiring of employees in other countries to work in such plants.

A variety of special ethical issues arises in the context of the normal business practices of any corporation. They concern workplace conditions, including health and safety issues; employee financial compensation issues; employee privacy issues; race, gender, and age discrimination issues; issues of due process when it comes to hiring and firing and the promotion and demotion of employees; product safety issues; issues concerning the environment; and many others. In addition to all these issues is the problem of ethical relativism.

Ethical Relativism

Every culture has, to varying degrees, unique standards of morality that might conflict with those of other cultures; this is an empirical fact and is usually referred to as cultural relativism. Some people assume that, because cultural relativism is a fact, so too is ethical relativism. "Ethical relativism" is the belief that because people in various and different cultures do, in fact, adhere to different and sometimes conflicting standards of morality, there is (and can be) no objective standard of morality that applies equally to all people in every culture and throughout all of human history. In addition to the fact that the belief in the accuracy of ethical relativism does not logically follow from the empirical fact of cultural relativism, there are numerous beliefs that do logically follow from the belief in ethical relativism but that, typically, are found to be un-

acceptable even by proponents of ethical relativism. For example, to take seriously the belief in ethical relativism is to obligate one to accept the belief that there neither exists nor should exist any absolute moral prohibition of any type of human behavior, including murder.

Effects of Ethical Relativism

Through the last four decades of the twentieth century, numerous Western-based multinational corporations attempting to start up business activities in foreign countries such as Indonesia, Nigeria, and Malaysia immediately faced threats of being prohibited from conducting any such business unless they paid what were, in effect, bribes to foreign officials. Despite the fact that most Western multinational corporate executives find such ultimatums to be morally offensive, they tend to attempt to justify compliance with such requirements on grounds of ethical relativism.

One of the most significant cultural distinctions to be found among various nations is the host of different positions of their respective governments on the question of fundamental human rights and the extent to which such rights are, and/or are allowed to be, abused. Historically, relationships between multinational corporations of industrialized Western nations and developing countries in South America, Africa, the Middle East, and the Far East are such that any of a variety of fundamental human rights are routinely neglected, if not abused outright. Again, executives of multinational corporations in such situations typically attempt to justify human rights abuses of foreign citizens on grounds of ethical relativism.

It is not uncommon for Western multinational corporations operating in poor foreign countries to hire children to work in unsafe and unhealthy conditions for long hours each day for the equivalent of only a few dollars per day. Despite the fact that such working conditions might be consistent with what is normally expected in the host countries and the fact that the wages that are paid might actually compare favorably to standard local wages, employing children raises serious ethical questions.

One might reasonably argue that children, in any country, have the right to at least a modicum of a formal education as well as the complementary right to not be coerced to work. Moreover, one could argue that employees (typically, as adults) have the right to reasonably safe and healthy workplace conditions as well as the right to financial compensation that is commensurate with work performance that is both of good quality and of whatever duration. Such rights are consistent with the Universal Declaration of Human Rights that was adopted by the United Nations in 1948. It was designed to be an objective standard by which to measure the extent to which any nation on Earth either respects or abuses the fundamental human rights of its citizens.

Abuse of the Profit Motive

Sometimes, attempts to justify, on grounds of ethical relativism, the business practices in each of the two types of examples as set out above, specifically, the bribery of government officials and the use of child labor (both in poor foreign countries), are really only veiled attempts to justify what is, arguably, the abuse of the profit motive. For multinational corporations, as for any businesses, the more that the executive decision makers are committed to the fundamental objective of creating profits, the more they are tempted to venture into business practices that may be morally suspect.

If bribing government officials is not the normal business practice within a foreign country, then such a practice cannot be justified on grounds of cultural, much less ethical, relativism. In such cases, the most reasonable explanation for bribes is greed on the part of the foreign government officials and abuse of the profit motive on the part of the multinational corporation's executives.

It is arguable that in the vast majority of cases of morally questionable business practices, from workplace conditions to issues concerning the environment, abuse of the profit motive is the most reasonable explanation.

—Stephen C. Taylor

Further Reading

Berberoglu, Berch. *Globalization of Capital and the Nation-State: Imperialism, Class Struggle, and the State in the Age of Global Capitalism.* Lanham, Md.: Rowman & Littlefield, 2003.

Cavanagh, Gerald F. *American Business Values: With International Perspectives.* 4th ed. Upper Saddle River, N.J.: Prentice-Hall, 1998.

DeGeorge, Richard. *Competing with Integrity in International Business.* New York: Oxford University Press, 1993.

_____. "International Business Ethics." In *A Companion to Business Ethics*, edited by Robert Frederick. Oxford, England: Blackwell Publishers, 1999.

Donaldson, Thomas. *The Ethics of International Business.* New York: Oxford University Press, 1989.

_____. "International Business Ethics." In *Encyclopedic Dictionary of Business Ethics*, edited by Patricia Werhane and R. Edward Freeman. Oxford, England: Blackwell Publishers, 1997.

Dunning, John H., ed. *Making Globalization Good: The Moral Challenges of Global Capitalism.* New York: Oxford University Press, 2003.

See also: Agribusiness; Antitrust legislation; Business ethics; Downsizing; Environmental ethics; Ethical codes of organizations; Globalization; Outsourcing; Telemarketing; World Trade Organization.

Napster

Identification: Site on the World Wide Web through which computer users share digital recordings of music

Date: Began operation in early 1991

Type of ethics: Arts and censorship

Significance: Napster's song-sharing software and Web site allowed Internet users to download songs to their own computers for free, prompting lawsuits from artists for copyright infringement, launching a major fight between the newest information technology and established copyright protections. Napster's eventual agreement not to violate copyright law saw the Internet partially brought under the control of the legal system

The Napster Web site, with its song-sharing technology, prompted one of the earliest clashes between the Internet and some of the oldest laws in the United States. Users of Napster downloaded digital files of songs from the site and shared those songs with other users. Most of the songs distributed through Napster were protected under federal copyright law, which required the Web site to pay for their use and distribution. When Napster was sued by the copyright owners, ethical questions were raised about artistic freedom and property rights.

Copyrights are issued by the federal government, providing artists, writers and composers monopoly power over their creations for limited periods of time. Copyrights are given to provide incentives to creative persons, who earn money by selling access to their work. Eventually, all copyrighted works fall into the public domain and can be used by anyone without a fee. The Napster case presented a clash between those competing interests: artists wanting to protect their property and the public seeking to use technology to gain access to popular songs.

Public sharing of copyrighted songs raises ethical concerns about property rights and the right of artists to be rewarded for their efforts by selling their works, rather than having them traded freely. However, another ethical question arose when the artists sued for copyright infringement. Copyrights are intended to advance the creative arts by providing monetary incentives for artists to produce works. However, the protections granted to artists are to advance a general good—the furtherance of knowledge. Using copyright laws to restrict use of the Internet—one of the greatest tool for advancing knowledge ever developed—seems to defeat the purpose intended for issuing copyrights.

Internet users using Napster to download music were violating the copyright laws protecting artists. However, the reaction of the copyright owners, thousands of dollars of fines for people sharing music, was at times seemingly out of proportion to the damage being inflicted. Napster and its song sharing brought another technology under the partial control of government regulation. Napster's agreement to pay copyright owners and charge Internet users downloading songs may have marked a shift in the Internet from a freewheeling new technology to one that could become a center of profit-making activity.

—Douglas Clouatre

Further Reading

Alderman, John. *Sonic Boom: Napster, MP3, and the New Pioneers of Music*. New York: Perseus Publishing, 2001.

Menn, Joseph. *All the Rave: The Rise and Fall of Shawn Fanning's Napster*. New York: Crown Business Publishing, 2003.

Merriden, Trevor. *Irresistible Forces: The Business Legacy of Napster and the Growth of the Underground Internet*. New York: Capstone, 2002.

See also: Computer crime; Computer databases; Computer misuse; Computer technology; Copyright; Intellectual property; Internet piracy; Song lyrics.

National Labor Relations Act

Identification: Labor law outlawing unfair practices by employers and legalizing important labor practices, including collective bargaining and the closed shop

Date: Enacted on July 5, 1935

Type of ethics: Business and labor ethics

Significance: The National Labor Relations Act represented at attempt by the federal government to promote harmony between labor and management and to avoid costly strikes in the midst of an already devastating Depression

Within months of the U.S. Supreme Court's invalidation of the National Industrial Recovery Act of 1933, Congress, led by Senator Robert Wagner of New York, passed legislation to assist employees and at the same time attempt to cure industrial strife by eliminating its chief cause: strikes. The law (known as the Magna Carta of labor) would eradicate the underlying cause of strikes, unfair employer practices, by encouraging collective bargaining, thereby granting employees equal bargaining power with their employers.

Using the National Labor Relations Board to administer its provisions, the act, which applies to all employers engaged in interstate commerce, provides governmental processes for the selection of employee bargaining representatives. The act prohibits employers from interfering with union formation, establishing a "company" union, discriminating against union workers, refusing collective bargaining, or retaliating against workers who file charges under this act. Congress amended the act in 1947 to forbid the closed shop and again in 1959 to monitor union officials' activities.

See also: Arbitration; Congress; Executive Order 10988; Fair Labor Standards Act; Labor-Management Relations Act; National Labor Union; Work.

National Labor Union

Identification: National federation of trade unions organized to secure workers' rights

Date: 1866-1873

Type of ethics: Business and labor ethics

Significance: The National Labor Union (NLU) represented an attempt to create a movement for economic equality which would parallel earlier national movements toward political and religious equality

Fearing the widening economic gap between employer and worker, William H. Sylvis led the Molders' Union and other national labor (craft) unions to join forces to organize the NLU to lobby for the rights of labor. The platform of the highly political NLU provided a plan to maintain its laborers' freedom, equality, and stature in American life. The NLU advocated higher wages, an eight-hour day, cooperative stores, and government action to assist labor. Women and African Americans were encouraged to organize and participate in the NLU. Upon President Sylvis's death in 1869, the NLU split over such ethical issues as women's rights, labor party involvement, and monetary expansion. By 1872, the NLU had become essentially a labor party, and after its lack of success in the election of 1872, both the NLU and the labor party collapsed. The NLU established the first truly national association of labor unions and succeeded in lobbying Congress in 1868 to establish an eight-hour day for federal laborers and artisans.

—*Stephen D. Livesay*

See also: American Federation of Labor; Executive Order 10988; Fair Labor Standards Act; Knights of Labor; Labor-Management Relations Act.

Negligence

Definition: Failure to maintain due standards of care in one's actions, thereby causing or potentially causing harm to another

Type of ethics: Business and labor ethics

Significance: Negligence raises interesting and unique questions about the relationship of intentionality to guilt. Virtually all moral relations have a potential for negligence

Negligence has long been an important concept in both ethics and law. In ethics, the notion of negligence arises out of the conception that one owes a duty of a degree of care toward one's fellow humans in all one's activities and that under given circumstances, one may owe even greater degrees of care arising out of special duties that one takes upon oneself in virtue of the public office or profession one has assumed.

Law and morality both recognize a distinction between advertent negligence, which involves the wrongdoer's proceeding with acts after recognizing the dangerous nature of those actions or omissions, and inadvertent negligence, which involves the wrongdoer's undertaking dangerous acts (or omissions) without having recognized the risk that they impose upon others. The former, which is often called recklessness, is generally regarded as the more culpable form, while the latter raises complex theoretical difficulties for ethicians and legal scholars. The primary problem with inadvertent negligence both in ethics and in law arises from the seeming contradiction between the nature of such negligence and the deliberate intentionality requisite for an act to be culpable. In moral theory, the problem is easily resolved by linking the inadvertent negligence to the idea of culpable ignorance.

The wrongdoer behaved unsafely because he did not know the potential consequences of his actions, but this ignorance does not exculpate him because he should have known. At some time in his past, he failed to acquire the knowledge necessary to recognize the character of his acts. If this failure resulted from deliberate neglect on the part of the wrongdoer—for example, skipping sessions of his job training—then this was culpable ignorance and the wrongs which flowed from it were blameworthy.

In the case of legal negligence, both civil and criminal, more difficult problems seem to present themselves. Criminal guilt usually involves both an *actus reus*, or guilty act, and a *mens rea*, or guilty mind (criminal intention). H. L. A. Hart, the noted British legal philosopher, wrestled with this problem without reaching a conclusive solution: How can inadvertent negligence have a *mens rea*? If one were to recognize the nature and potential consequences of one's act(s), would one not be guilty of advertent negligence, or worse?

The answer to this puzzle may lie in a nonproximate *mens rea* that the law may be seen as assuming to exist in the absence of plausible proof to the contrary. Take, for example, the case of a roofer who has been carefully dropping waste materials from a roof into a dumpster several floors below. Suddenly, after such care, he hurls a bucket off the roof without checking its trajectory and injures a pedestrian below.

The roofer testifies at his trial that he does not know why he threw the bucket as he did and that he gave no thought to the dangers involved in such an act. If he is be-

A decomposed snail in Scotland in case of Donoghue v. Stevenson *[1932] established the modern law of negligence, laying the foundations of the duty of care and the fault principle. By Jürgen Schoner.*

lieved, he will be convicted of an offense connected with inadvertent negligence. If the roofer could provide a plausible explanation of his action that could trace its origins to a cause ultimately outside the roofer's control, however, he might expect acquittal.

Assume that the roofer produces proof that the tar he employed—a newvariety on the market—emitted hallucinogenic fumes and that he was working with that tar just before the allegedly negligent incident. If his proofs were accepted, he would doubtlessly be exonerated, because he had indicated a cause for his actions that lay outside his control.

In the absence of such proof, however, the unstated assumption of the lawmust be that at some earlier time—perhaps even years before—the defendant developed (by omission or commission) habits of mind that were likely ultimately to lead to negligent actions in the future and that in the acquisition of these habits lay the culpability.

The acceptance of those habits of mind constitutes a nonproximate *mens rea* for any negligent acts that might later be done as a result. This interpretation demonstrates that the law of negligence is not a strict liability statute—that is, one enforced without regard to intentionality—as some have maintained.

Other Difficulties

Another difficulty that has perplexed legal theorists involves whether the standard of negligence should be objective or subjective. H. L. A. Hart stated that the objective standard attributes fault to an agent who failed "to take those precautions which any reasonable man with normal capacities would in the circumstances have taken." A subjective standard would give greater weight to the particular circumstances and capacities of the subject.

Finally, there is the question of the relationship of the degree of blameworthiness in negligent acts to the actual results that flowfrom them. A negligent driver (for example, one using excessive speed) might injure somebody or might not. Under one theory, his or her blameworthiness remains the same despite the external circumstances, but others have asserted that effects in the extramental world are a factor in guilt, as a result of so-called "moral luck."

—Patrick M. O'Neil

Further Reading

Cane, Peter, and Jane Stapelton, eds. *The Law of Obligations: Essays in Celebration of John Fleming.* New York: Oxford University Press, 1998.

Feinberg, Joel. *Doing and Deserving.* Princeton, N.J.: Princeton University Press, 1970.

Hart, Herbert L. *Punishment and Responsibility: Essays in the Philosophy of Law.* New York: Oxford University Press, 1968.

Milo, Ronald D. *Immorality.* Princeton, N.J.: Princeton University Press, 1984.

Morris, Herbert. *Freedom and Responsibility.* Stanford, Calif.: Stanford University Press, 1961.

Smith, Holly. "Culpable Ignorance." *Philosophical Review* 92 (October, 1983): 543-572.

See also: Accountability; Business ethics; Duty; Employee safety and treatment; Hart, H. L. A.; Intention; Moral luck; Professional ethics; Prudence; Responsibility.

New York Times Co. v. Sullivan

The Event: U.S. Supreme Court decision that limited states' authority to award libel damages and established "actual malice" as the standard for cases involving public officials, later expanded to include "public figures"

Date: Ruling made on March 9, 1964

Type of ethics: Media ethics

Significance: The Supreme Court's opinion in *Sullivan* significantly expanded the First Amendment protection of the press's right to engage in social criticism and political commentary by specifying that nothing printed about a public official could be deemed libelous unless it was the specific intent of the author to defame the official Thus, even untrue stories are protected in the absence of malicious intent to do harm.

New York Times Co. v. Sullivan was sparked by an advertisement placed in *The New York Times* in 1960 by the Committee to Defend Martin Luther King and the Struggle for Freedom in the South. The advertisement, which was meant to raise support for King's Civil Rights movement, criticized several southern jurisdictions, including Montgomery, Alabama, although it did not name any individuals. In response, Montgomery city commissioner L. B. Sullivan sued the *Times* for libel in circuit court, which found the newspaper guilty under Alabama law. After the Alabama Supreme Court affirmed this judgment, the *Times* appealed to the Supreme Court, claiming violations of its rights of free speech and due process under the First and Fourteenth Amendments to the Constitution.

The Court held unanimously that Alabama law failed to protect adequately freedom of speech and of the press, and that "actual malice" would henceforth be the national standard for determining libel actions involving public officials.

—Lisa Paddock

See also: Due process; First Amendment; Libel; Supreme Court, U.S.

News sources

Definition: Individuals who provide information to reporters for mass media dissemination

Type of ethics: Media ethics

Significance: Journalistic codes of ethics require reporters objectively to evaluate information provided by sources, to verify important information with multiple independent sources, and to protect the privacy of confidential sources by withholding their names and other identifying details from the public

The information conveyed through the mass media is of fundamental importance to American society. On the basis of this information, public opinion is formed, votes are cast, and democracy is enacted. Media professionals, therefore, are obligated to seek out and make use of information sources that are reliable, credible, and well-intentioned. Too often, however, such exemplary sources do not exist, and journalists are left to struggle with questions of conduct and concerns about the ethical treatment of their sources.

Journalistic Ethics

The National Society of Professional Journalists attempts to address the issue by assessing both the journalist's principles and the consequences of his or her actions. Truth-telling is a fundamental governor in a free society and becomes, therefore, an activity that journalists are both morally and socially obligated to pursue. Developing and maintaining reliable news sources is an essential part of this journalistic mission, for without credible sources, reporters may never gain access to the type of information that their "watchdog" role requires.

The U.S. Constitution, through the broad protections offered by the First Amendment, recognizes the unique nature of the press's responsibilities and grants generous latitude in the cultivation and protection of source-re-porter relationships. Strict, absolute rules of conduct are incompatible with this intentionally unrestricted domain, leaving questions of ethics up for examination on a case-by-case basis.

The three main ethical considerations regarding sources of information are anonymity, confidentiality, and the source-reporter relationship. The use of anonymous sources is a fairly common media practice despite industry concerns about both its practical and ethical value. Practically, media professionals agree that the custom detracts from the press's integrity and engenders suspicion about the veracity of the report. Ethically, related considerations range from the erosion of the public trust to the publication of stolen or purchased information and the potential for furthering someone else's purpose by disseminating information that is politically or financially expedient to the source.

Anonymity

Anonymity undermines the journalistic mission of truth-telling because the source is an important part of the story. Failure to disclose the name of the source results in an incomplete or distorted version of truth. Once an anonymous source has been used, the issue of confidentiality arises. Various ethical questions surround this issue. How far is a news organization obligated to go in order to protect the identity of its source? How binding is a reporter's promise of anonymity?

A 1991 Supreme Court decision ruled that the Minneapolis *Star Tribune* violated an implied contract created by the promise of anonymity when the paper publicly revealed a source's identity. The decision reinforced the mutually dependent nature of the source-reporter relationship, one that has long been the subject of controversy. While general opinion agrees that the relationship is frequently characterized by betrayal and manipulation, industry members differ regarding whether it is the reporter or the source who is guilty of malevolence. The debate sparks the question of intention and the ethical implications of using people as a means to further an individual's purpose, journalistic or otherwise.

In general, a liberalized deontological approach is employed to resolve these ethical quandaries. That is, media professionals are expected to adhere to general industry guidelines unless there is a compelling reason not to do so. For example, most news organizations have policies that reflect a cautionary stance regarding the granting of anonymity. Reporters are encouraged to try to get the source to agree to attribution and/or to find alternative ways to verify the information.

Many news organizations require that journalists receive authorization from a superior before quoting from anonymous sources. Typically, editorial approval for anonymity is granted when that anonymity is supported by duty-based principles: when the information is of vital public interest and consistent with the truth-telling ethic; when the justification of minimizing grievous harm is clearly served, such as in the protection of a whistleblower or the victim of abuse; or when a concern for social justice is at stake, as in governmental corruption cases.

In addition, industry guidelines seek to mitigate further the negative effects of anonymous sources by requiring identification as fully as possible, such as by position or title, and by explaining the reason for the use of anonymity.

Because anonymity is zealously guarded, once granted, the promise of confidentiality becomes supreme. The reputation of the press rests on the integrity with which sources are protected, and even the threat of legal action is not justification for exposing a confidential source. Confidentiality may be broken, however, if the news organization discovers that the source has provided false or misleading information.

Malicious intent by a source, as was the case in the Minneapolis *Star Tribune* case, is not an acceptable reason to breach the confidential relationship. Rather, the responsibility lies with journalists not only to examine their own motives for publishing certain information but also to explore the possible motives of their sources. These actions act as safeguards against the likelihood that media professionals will fall prey to sources who are using the press in an effort to damage another's reputation, and reinforce a basic Judeo-Christian principle: Reporters should not treat others or allow themselves to be treated, as a means to someone else's end.

The use of anonymous sources raises a number of ethical considerations in itself, as well as the potential for confidentiality and source-reporter relationship abuses. Therefore, journalists should pursue such a course of action only after thoughtful and deliberate consideration.

—Regina Howard Yaroch

Further Reading

Black, Jay, Bob Steele, and Ralph Barney. *Doing Ethics in Journalism: A Handbook with Case Studies.* Greencastle, Ind.: Sigma Delta Chi Foundation and the Society of Professional Journalists, 1993.

Boeyink, David E. "Anonymous Sources in News Stories: Justifying Exceptions and Limiting Abuses." *Journal of Mass Media Ethics* 5, no. 4 (1990): 233-246.

Christians, Clifford G., et al. *Media Ethics: Cases and Moral Reasoning.* 5th ed. New York: Longman, 1998.

Day, Louis A. *Ethics in Media Communications: Cases and Controversies.* Belmont, Calif.: Wadsworth, 1991.

Meyer, Philip. *Ethical Journalism.* New York: Longman, 1987.

Smith, Rod F. *Groping for Ethics in Journalism.* 5th ed. Ames: Iowa State Press, 2003.

See also: Accuracy in Media; American Society of Newspaper Editors; Confidentiality; Fairness and Accuracy in Reporting; International Covenant on Civil and Political Rights; Journalistic entrapment; Journalistic ethics; Tabloid journalism.

Outsourcing

Definition: Business practice of having important company services performed by other companies or individual persons outside the firm

Type of ethics: Business and labor ethics

Significance: Changing conceptions of corporate efficiency have reconfigured divisions between in-house functions and those that are subcontracted to external agencies, raising new ethical questions about the treatment of employees

Corporations were once largely self-contained and comprehensive collections of functions, some of which might be outsourced, that is, subcontracted to other companies or to individual freelance workers. Keeping functions in-house removed the need to generate profits, and therefore generally saved money; however, costs could easily outweigh savings. Moreover, units of a company that are not expected to generate profits have less reason to use resources effectively. Thus, the same considerations supporting competition in the marketplace would seem to favor competition within the corporation.

In effect, extensive outsourcing brings the competitiveness of the marketplace inside individual corporations, as functions are contracted out to more specialized companies or individual workers. The decade of the 1990s witnessed dramatic developments in this direction, as corporations downsized and otherwise re-engineered their way to being more cost-effective and thus more profitable. Automobile manufacturers do not need to do their own landscaping or package delivery, so one might legitimately ask what other functions such companies could outsource—design, production, sales, accounting, perhaps even management.

One logical result of this line of thought is a distributed, or networked, organization, which has been called the "virtual" corporation. The enterprise becomes a kind of dormant network that can be brought to full life when the need arises, much as a Hollywood film-production company expands its activities when it launches a new film.

Globalization and Its Discontents

Increasingly easy, cheap, and reliable communications and transportation systems make a distributed approach to business possible for corporations. In the government sphere, the same approach is known as privatization. As American manufacturing jobs have moved overseas in search of cheaper labor, other functions, such as software design and financial services, can be imported as needed. An ethically positive consequence of this new globalized flexibility is increased possibilities of productive, synergistic linkages among people, resources, and opportunities. This can mean a constant stream of better and cheaper products and services. Ethically negative consequences include destabilization of companies, greater insecurity for employees whose jobs are being reconfigured or eliminated, and the domination of everyday life by the ceaseless scramble for continuous quality improvement in a world in which everything is new and improved, but nothing is ever good enough.

—*Edward Johnson*

Further Reading

Breslin, David A. "On the Ethics of Outsourcing: A Philosophical Look at A-76." *Program Manager Magazine* (November-December, 1999): 24-26.

Petzinger, Thomas, Jr. *The New Pioneers: The Men and Women Who Are Transforming the Workplace and Marketplace.* New York: Simon & Schuster, 1999.

Wolman, William, and Anne Colamosca. *The Judas Economy: The Triumph of Capital and the Betrayal of Work.* Reading, Mass.: Addison-Wesley, 1997.

See also: Business ethics; Corporate responsibility; Corporate scandal; Cost-benefit analysis; Downsizing; Globalization; Multinational corporations.

Pentagon Papers

Identification: Classified documents at issue in *United States v. New York Times Company*, which the U.S. Su-

preme Court held the federal government could not restrain *The New York Times* from publishing

Date: Court ruling made on June 30, 1971

Type of ethics: Media ethics

Significance: The Pentagon Papers case dealt with the issue of prior restraint, that is, censorship before the fact which prevents the censored material from ever seeing the light of day. Prior restraint is the most extreme form of censorship, and the Supreme Court ruled that the government must meet a heavy burden of justification before it can prevent the press from publishing even top secret information

Popular sentiment against the Vietnam War was on the rise in the spring of 1971, when Daniel Ellsberg, a former U.S. Department of Defense employee, and his friend, Anthony Russo, Jr., stole copies of two massive volumes that have come to be known as the Pentagon Papers. These volumes, "History of U.S. Decision-Making Process on Vietnam Policy" and "Command and Control Study of the Gulf of Tonkin Incident"—which were classified "Top Secret-Sensitive" and "Top Secret," respectively—together constituted a history of American involvement in Vietnam since World War II. Ellsberg and Russo passed the filched documents on to *The New York Times* and *The Washington Post.* In its June 13, 1971, edition, the *Times* began publishing a series of excerpts from the government studies.

Government Attempts Prior Restraint

After the *Times* had published two more excerpts on June 14 and 15, 1971, the federal government filed a motion in the U.S. District Court for the Southern District of New York requesting that the court restrain the *Times* from publishing more passages from the Pentagon Papers. Although the court refused to issue an injunction against the paper, it did grant the government a temporary restraining order, which prevented the *Times* from publishing portions of the Pentagon Papers while the government prepared its case. On June 18, *The Washington Post* also began publishing excerpts from the Pentagon Papers, and the government moved to restrain it, too, in federal court in the District of Columbia. The legal action in the case, however, remained focused on New York City.

On June 18, the district court in New York heard the case, in which the government claimed that the publication of the documents in question would compromise the nation's war effort. Nevertheless, the government's request for an injunction was denied, although the temporary restraining order was extended until the government's appeal to a higher court could be heard. This appeal also was rejected, and on June 24, the government filed a petition with the Supreme Court.

Supreme Court Rejects Government Case

The parties appeared before the Court on June 26, 1971, and the Court delivered its opinion on June 30: The entire litigation had lasted slightly longer than two weeks. Like the lower courts, the Supreme Court rejected the government's attempts to rationalize prior restraint of the press by appealing to national security, dismissing the cases against both the *Times* and the *Post*. The Court was not unanimous in its decision, voting six to three, but writing for the majority, Justice Hugo L. Black delivered a stinging rebuke to the administration of President Richard M. Nixon: "the Solicitor General argues...that the general powers of the Government adopted in the original Constitution should be interpreted to limit and restrict the specific and emphatic guarantees of the Bill of Rights.... I can imagine no greater perversion of history."

Although the dissenters, Chief Justice Warren E. Burger, Justice Harry A. Blackmun, and Justice John M. Harlan II, argued that the Court should defer to the executive branch's concerns, Justice Black's opinion reaffirmed the Court's role as interpreter of the Constitution and guardian of individual rights: "Madison and the other Framers of the First Amendment...wrote in language they earnestly believed could never be misunderstood: 'Congress shall make no law...abridging the freedom...of the press....'"

Continued Prosecution

The government continued, nevertheless, to prosecute Ellsberg and Russo, gaining indictments against them for theft of federal property and violations of the federal Espionage Act. The two defendants were tried in the U.S. District Court for the Central District of California, where the Pentagon Papers were allegedly stolen. Unlike the original Pentagon Papers litigation, the Ellsberg and Russo prosecution dragged on for many months. Although the government had first obtained a preliminary indictment against Ellsberg in June, 1971, the trial of the two defendants did not commence until more than a year later.

The trial was halted almost immediately after it began, however, when it was revealed that the government had been secretly taping the defendants' confidential commu-

According to the Pentagon Papers, the U.S. government played a key role in the 1963 South Vietnamese coup, in which President Ngo Dinh Diem was assassinated.

nications. After the parties had gone through the process of selecting a new jury, the trial recommenced in January, 1973. Shortly thereafter, however, the entire Pentagon Papers case was colored by news of the Watergate imbroglio, which began with the September, 1971, government-sponsored burglary of the offices of Lewis Fielding, Ellsberg's psychoanalyst, committed in an effort to uncover other Ellsberg accomplices. When further revelations of the government's continuing illegal wiretaps of Ellsberg's conversations reached the court, the entire criminal prosecution of Ellsberg and Russo was dismissed. The Nixon administration had not only undermined its reputation and its case against the defendants but had also ensured that future administrative attempts to restrain the press from exercising its First Amendment rights would be more difficult.

—Lisa Paddock

Further Reading

Ellsberg, Daniel. *Secrets: A Memoir of Vietnam and the Pentagon Papers.* New York: Viking, 2002.

French, Peter A. *Conscientious Actions: The Revelation of the Pentagon Papers.* Cambridge, Mass.: Schenkman, 1974.

Meiklejohn Civil Liberties Institute. *Pentagon Papers Case Collection: Annotated Procedural Guide and Index.* Berkeley, Calif.: Author, 1975.

Rudenstine, David. *The Day the Presses Stopped: A History of the Pentagon Papers Case.* Berkeley: University of California Press, 1996.

Salter, Kenneth W. *The Pentagon Papers Trial.* Berkeley, Calif.: Editorial Justa, 1975.

Schrag, Peter. *Test of Loyalty: Daniel Ellsberg and the Rituals of Secret Government.* New York: Simon & Schuster, 1974.

Ungar, Sanford J. *The Papers and the Papers: An Account of the Legal and Political Battle Over the Pentagon Papers.* New York: Columbia University Press, 1989.

See also: Censorship; First Amendment; Invasion of privacy; Journalistic ethics; Public's right to know; Supreme Court, U.S.; Watergate scandal.

Photojournalism

Definition: Profession of news photographers

Type of ethics: Media ethics

Significance: As the tellers of visual stories in the news, photojournalists have special ethical and legal responsibilities to create pictures that are honest reflections of reality

Photojournalism is the journalistic side of photography that visually captures and documents moments in time. Photographers create still-life documentaries that tell stories about politics, sports, disasters, wars, crime, and other situations that involve human emotions, and supplement the written stories of the news. The profession dates back to the mid-1800s, when photographs began being used as the bases for engraved illustrations in news publications. By the end of the century, the halftone process, a technique that enabled printing something closer to true photographs, alongside text, was used worldwide. During the 1930s, candid photography was brought to the masses and photojournalism, as it later became known, was born. During that decade, many picture magazines flourished, most notably *Life*, which then set the world standard for photojournalism. As the profession grew, so did the need for ethical standards.

The Right of Privacy

During the mid-nineteenth century, the journalism profession underwent a major change after two lawyers, Samuel D. Warren and Louis D. Brandeis, argued for the right for privacy in an article published in the *Harvard Law Review*. Their article stemmed from the insensitive coverage by Boston newspapers of a woman's private social life. As a result of the law review article, privacy doctrines were established in journalism that set standards for both writers and photojournalists.

The first principle, called appropriation, forbade the unauthorized commercial use of private individuals' names or identities. This principle protected the property interests people have in their own names and images. Examples of forbidden behavior included photographing formally staged creative performances without permission, photographing images for editorial purposes and then using them for advertising without obtaining written permission, and manipulating and deliberately distorting photographic images without labeling them as "photo illustrations."

The second principle, intrusion and trespass, pertains to the offensive physical, electronic, or mechanical invasion of other people's solitude or seclusion. Historically, this principle has been frequently violated by aggressive photojournalists, who trespass on private property to get their pictures, and photographers of celebrities known as "paparazzi," who are notorious for their intrusiveness and disrespect for the privacy of their subjects.

The second principle is closely related to the third, the prohibition against public disclosure of private information that is offensive or that is of not legitimate concern to the public. Examples include photographing undressed celebrities sunbathing on their private yachts, eavesdropping with telephoto lenses, and shooting pictures with hidden cameras. Another prohibition is falsely portraying, distorting, or fictionalizing a subject's characteristics, conduct, or beliefs, in reckless disregard of the subject's privacy and reputation.

Although all persons are protected under these principles, violations by photojournalists have been common. The subjects of photojournalists who receive the least respect for their privacy are criminals, followed by public officials (both elected and appointed), other public figures, celebrities, short-term heroes in news stories, innocent victims of tragedies, and relatives of prominent people. Photojournalists who adhere to their profession's ethical standards respect the principles of privacy and try to get signed releases from subjects not considered public figures before publishing their pictures.

Professional Code of Ethics

The National Press Photographers Association, a professional society of photojournalists, has created a code of ethics for its members. The foundation of the ethical code is built on truthfulness, honesty, and objectivity. The code also calls for photojournalists to maintain sympathy for humanity and to remember their duty to society. The code advises photojournalists to use common sense and good judgment in situations not covered in the code.

A policy on handling electronic images issued by the Associated Press in 1990 states that photographs should not be manipulated or changed in any way, so that journalistic pictures always tell the truth. The photojournalists' code of ethics does not answer all the questions faced by photojournalists. For example, some of the most frequently occurring issues, including publication of graphic images of nudity, obscene behavior, severe injuries, dead people, and other forms of human suffering, are the focus of many newsroom debates. Even ostensibly innocent photographs of children playing under sprinklers on hot summer days might result in ethical and legal problems.

—*Betty Attaway-Fink*

Further Reading

Clark, Roy P., and Cole C. Campbell, eds. *The Values and Craft of American Journalism.* Gainesville: University Press of Florida, 2002.

Day, Louis A. *Ethics in Media Communications: Cases and Controversies.* 4th ed. Belmont, Calif.: Wadsworth, 2002.

Kovach, Bill, and Tom Rosenstiel. *The Elements of Journalism: What Newspeople Should Know and the Public Should Expect.* New York: Crown Publishers, 2001.

Parrish, Fred S. *Photojournalism: An Introduction.* Belmont, Calif.: Wadsworth, 2002.

Pavlik, John V. *Journalism and New Media.* New York: Columbia University Press, 2001.

Pritchard, David, ed. *Holding the Media Accountable: Citizens, Ethics, and the Law.* Bloomington: Indiana University Press, 2000.

Sloan, David W., and Lisa M. Parcell. *American Journalism: History, Principles, Practices.* Jefferson, N.C.: McFarland, 2002.

See also: Accuracy in Media; American Society of Newspaper Editors; Electronic surveillance; Fairness and Accuracy in Reporting; Invasion of privacy; Journalistic entrapment; Journalistic ethics; Media ownership; News sources; Professional ethics; Tabloid journalism.

Plagiarism

Definition: Unauthorized and unacknowledged appropriation of other persons' work in work that one presents as one's own; usually takes the form of writing but may also occur in such other forms as music, art, computer programming, and even data collection

Type of ethics: Media ethics

Significance: Plagiarism can call into question the unspoken contract between writer and reader, rob original producers of the credit they deserve, and fundamentally disrupt academic integrity and the learning processes. Nonetheless, because definitions of, and reactions to, plagiarism vary across time and cultures and even among academics themselves, its ethical ramifications are often disputed

The word "plagiarism" derives from *plagiarius*, a Latin word for kidnapper. Despite plagiarism's violent etymology and the fact that plagiarism itself is often regarded as theft, plagiarism is a practice that robs its victims of nothing material. It is related to copyright violation and fraud but should not be confused with those practices, which differ from plagiarism in being offenses that are punishable under legal statutes. For professional writers, journalists, and scholars found guilty of plagiarism, however, the practice can be grounds for dismissal and public disgrace. Most universities have policies warning students that if they plagiarize in their coursework, they will fail their courses. Repeat plagiarism violations usually result in expulsion from universities.

Around the turn of the twenty-first century, plagiarism was receiving considerable attention, both in the mainstream media and among educators. Famous—and sometimes controversial—cases included accusations of plagiarism against Martin Luther King, Jr., historian and scholar Doris Kearns Goodwin, and *New York Times* reporter Jayson Blair. Plagiarism was becoming increasingly recognized as a widespread and growing problem, made easier by such new information technologies as the Internet, that allow for both easy research and source retrieval and easy ways to cut and paste without attribution.

Problems with Defining Plagiarism

Statistics about the pervasiveness of plagiarism have revealed certain contradictions. For example, some reports have suggested that anywhere from 45 percent to 80 percent of high school students have admitted to "cheating," while some 15 percent to 54 percent say that have plagiarized from sites on the Internet's World Wide Web. These wide variations in statistics, and the evident discrepancies between cheating and plagiarism rates, may suggest that some students do not consider plagiarism to be "cheating" or that they do not consider what they do to be plagiarism. Indeed, in a 2003 survey conducted by Rutgers University professor Donald L. McCabe, approximately half the students surveyed declared that they did not think it was cheating to copy up to an entire paragraph of text from the Web.

Most of those students' teachers would disagree, although they, too, vary in how they define this problem.

Any sort of blatant fraud—such as downloading or purchasing entire term papers or articles and presenting them as one's own work—is generally reviled as an extreme form of dishonesty. It is also usually considered plagiarism to include in one's paper literal word-for-word copies of substantial portions of others' work when the original sources are not acknowledged.

Plagiaristic practices can also include the failure to credit sources when presenting other writers' ideas, even when they are merely paraphrased or summarized. However, this view is complicated by the fact that what people consider to be "common knowledge"—which usually does not need to be cited—varies from discipline to discipline and among student levels within a discipline. Sometimes, using quotation marks but not citations, or listing sources only at the end of a paper, without providing appropriate footnotes within the text, may be considered plagiarism, though this might more accurately be called improper citation.

Importance of Citation

Because plagiarism involves a failure to provide acknowledgment, it is useful to understand why academics consider citation important. As with the definition of plagiarism, there are multiple rationales. Many people focus on the moral issues, believing that citing is the fair or ethical thing to do because it gives recognition to others whose ideas are important to one's own work. They believe that to deny credit is tantamount to stealing another person's ideas.

Other people focus on the social ethics involved, explaining that citations work to build a community of scholars. They believe that all knowledge is ultimately collaborative and want all persons involved in its creation to be recognized as contributors to the process. Such a rationale, like the first, relies on notions of fairness to earlier producers.

Citations also serve an intellectual purpose, showing the history of ideas and how they have developed over time. At the same time, they also help ensure the accuracy of one's work, as the listed sources can be tracked, traced, and corroborated. Of little ethical significance, though important rhetorically, citations help bolster a writer's authority.

Through citation, writers exhibit knowledge of the field on which they are writing and show the supporting evidence for their ideas, thus giving their work as a whole more credibility and legitimacy in the eyes of their readers.

Finally, there is what may be called the amoral rationale, which considers citations one of many social and genre-specific conventions that writers must emulate in order to demonstrate proficiency in their particular realm of writing. For example, while academic essays demand extensive attribution, a magazine article may rely on paraphrasing or summarizing with few or no references listed. Some workplace writing, especially anonymous or bureaucratic forms, use no citations at all, and even the direct transcription of sources may be acceptable.

Even among educators, however, the understanding of the ethical issues surrounding plagiarism may vary according to one's academic, theoretical, or methodological framework.

Approaches to Plagiarism

The traditional approach calls on universal moral standards in casting all sorts of plagiarism as cheating. It decries plagiarism as fundamentally immoral, equivalent to theft or lying, because it violates tenets of authorial originality. It may place the blame for plagiarism on permissive social values or moral relativism.

There are concerns that this sort of cheating is becoming an acceptable part of the student culture of high schools and colleges. Illustrated in most university policies, this approach fails to distinguish between types of plagiarism or the differing conventions governing writing tasks. It also may not factor in intentionality—whether or not writers purposely set out to deceive their teachers—or deficiencies in understanding the norms of citation use.

In the historical approach, those studying the history of plagiarism view the concept—and its ethical ramifications—as developing in specific and disparate cultural contexts. They assert that plagiarism is not a universally despised example of "theft" or "dishonesty." Instead, they see it as a set of practices that carries diverse moral inflections and receives various ethical treatments. Unacknowledged copying, in other words, may be normative in one era and decried in another. For example, Renaissance writers esteemed imitation, seeing it as a way of exhibiting one's learning and expressing one's debt to earlier writers. Knowledge was believed to be shared, and inspiration was seen as a gift from God.

With the rise of the print marketplace in the eighteenth century, however, the financial stakes were raised. The first copyright law was passed in 1709 at the urging of booksellers; the notion of individual artistic originality developed over the next half century. With a vested interested in seeing their writing as property, a new class of professional writers begin representing plagiarism as a pressing moral and artistic concern.

Literary historians are thus careful, when discussing plagiarism, not to present it as a concept that is "naturally" or "normally" understood as a timeless social ill, but one that bears the imprint of the cultural expectations of specific times and places. Practitioners of this approach have been charged with conveying a dangerous moral relativism, though most do not condone cheating, copying, or fraudulent authorship in an academic environment.

Impact of Technology

As the World Wide Web has increasingly become many students' primary research tool, new technology-based forms of plagiarism have proliferated. Not only can students easily download or cut and paste from a variety of legitimate information sites, but digital "paper mills"—online businesses that sell completed student papers—make the most egregious forms of plagiarism easier than ever. Some observers believe that the only way to combat the increased opportunities for "cyber-plagiarism" provided by these new opportunities is to turn to technology itself. Web-based search engines such as Google can often track down, in seconds, the Web sources copied into student papers.

Furthermore, services have been created that provide online plagiarism-detection software; Turnitin .com is one of the most widely used. Many universities or their individual departments subscribe to such services, knowing that their doing so deters student cheating, even when individual teachers do not use these services themselves. Nonetheless, ethical questions have been raised about possible violations of student privacy—every paper submitted becomes part of the business's database—and the propriety of responding to all student work with suspicion.

Another way of understanding Internet-specific plagiarism, however, suggests that these may be futile—or even reactionary—responses. They see the ease with which students can copy from the Internet not as a temptation, but a new way of thinking about creating texts. Much information on the Web, after all, is collective or anonymous. Web pages often contain chunks of other pages, and graphics freely circulate—mostly without attribution. The Web's ephemeral nature is thought to be fundamentally incompatible with the fixity of text required for "real" plagiarism. Supporters of these ideas draw on historical studies to highlight the different practices of writing supported by modern communication technologies in contrast to those based in market- and property-driven print forms. They believe that new media bring with them a new ethos, and that popular notions of the morality of plagiarism are outdated. Others, however, decry what has been termed the "Napsterization of knowledge" and urge a continuation of print-based ways of understanding and regulating the copying of texts.

Pedagogical Approach

Many of those concerned about student plagiarism—whether they draw on conservative, historical, or technological approaches to understand it—assert that a large part of the ethical responsibility for the problem lies with educators themselves. Many composition instructors, for example, believe that while academic dishonesty should be condemned, proper research methodology, source use, and citation practices should be more rigorously taught to students. Indeed, many believe that "patchwriting," as Rebecca Howard terms the linking together of several paraphrases from unacknowledged sources, is an important stage in the evolution of student knowledge and rhetorical skill.

Such critics may also view plagiarism as a problem in the development of "voice," a reflection of a student's lack of confidence in his or her own opinions and authority, or a misunderstanding of the very purposes of academic writing. Because they see plagiarism as a complex learning issue, these educators question the morality of "prosecuting" students for their ignorance or lack of ability, and they resent the negative effects that the "policing" of plagiarism has on teacher-student relations. Many policy statements written by this camp thus classify plagiarism into two tiers, distinguishing purposeful fraud from accidental source misuse.

The pedagogical approach goes beyond the teaching of writing skills, however. It also focuses on ways instructors can structure classrooms actively to prevent plagiarism. Some insist that academic integrity itself not be taken for granted, but should be routinely explained to, and discussed with, students. Others suggest that teachers should develop more assignments that are difficult to plagiarize because of their specificity, their reliance on course materials, or their relevance to student lives and individual opinions.

Ethical Implications

Clearly, plagiarism is a complex issue with a rich history. There are a variety of ways to define and respond to it. Perhaps the most urgent ethical responsibility of students and educators alike, then, is that they continue to explore together the complicated questions engendered by these multiple approaches.

—Lisa Maruca

Further Reading

Boynton, Robert S. "Is Honor Up for Grabs? Education Isn't About Surveillance." *Washington Post*, May 27, 2001, p. B1. Claims that although the "Napsterization of knowledge" has altered student views of intellectual property, teachers should trust their students instead of policing plagiarism.

Howard, Rebecca Moore. "Plagiarisms, Authorships, and the Academic Death Penalty." *College English* 57, no. 7 (1995): 788-806. This article by an expert in the field of plagiarism and composition uses the history of authorship to argue for a more enlightened view of student patchwriting.

Kewes, Paulina, ed. *Plagiarism in Early Modern England*. New York: Palgrave Macmillan, 2003. Collection of scholarly essays that illustrate the diverse practices and attitudes toward literary borrowing during the sixteenth and seventeenth centuries.

Lathrop, Ann, and Kathleen Foss. *Student Cheating and Plagiarism in the Internet Era: A Wake Up Call*. Westport, Conn.: Greenwood Press, 2000. Guide for educators that discusses the extent of student "high-tech cheating" and provides solutions.

Mallon, Thomas. *Stolen Words*. Rev ed. New York: Harcourt, 2001. Traditionalist approach to plagiarism that covers several case studies. An updated afterword discusses the special problems posed by the Internet.

Vaidhyanathan, Siva. *Copyrights and Copywrongs: The Rise of Intellectual Property and How It Threatens Creativity*. New York: New York University Press, 2003. Broad survey of copyright issues that considers special problems of modern digital resources.

Wherry, Timothy Lee. *The Librarian's Guide to Intellectual Property in the Digital Age: Copyright, Patents, Trademarks*. Chicago: American Library Association, 2002. Handbook designed to give librarians practical advice.

Woodmansee, Martha. "Genius and the Copyright." In *The Author, Art and the Market: Rereading the History of Aesthetics*. New York: Columbia University Press, 1994. This historical study of authorship, copyright, and the concept of originality in the eighteenth century provides important background for understanding historical approaches to plagiarism.

See also: Art; Computer crime; Computer misuse; Copyright; Intellectual property; Internet piracy; Science.

Price fixing

Definition: Agreement by competing sellers of products or services to charge the same prices

Type of ethics: Business and labor ethics

Significance: Price fixing is thought of as creating an "artificially" high price for a commodity by circumventing the "natural" deflationary effects of competition. Consumer advocates assert that it is an unfair practice because it takes advantage of consumers' lack of bargaining power.

Concepts associated with price fixing go back at least to ancient Greece. Philosophers argued about how a "just price," one that was fair to both consumers and producers, could be identified. Debates concerning the ethical issues involved in setting prices concerned the relative power of consumers and producers in the marketplace and behavior that constituted fair play. Opponents of price fixing argued that producers are likely, if allowed, to set prices that give them high levels of profit that are not justified by costs or risks taken in business.

The Sherman Antitrust Act, signed into law on July 2, 1890, forbade contracts, combinations of business, or conspiracies in restraint of trade. Exactly what constituted a restraint of trade remained to be decided by the courts, but price fixing was soon declared illegal under the act. The price fixing laws of the United States are more stringent than are those of other countries. Many countries do not forbid the practice, and some well-known trade organizations, such as the Organization of Petroleum Exporting Countries, exist primarily to fix prices. Even the United States allows some forms of price fixing, such as guaranteed minimum prices for farm products and minimum wages. These exceptions are seen as benefiting sellers of products or services that society has an interest in protecting.

—A. J. Sobczak

See also: Antitrust legislation; Consumerism; Minimum-wage laws; Monopoly; Profit economy; Sales ethics.

Product safety and liability

Definition: Issues relating to questions of who is liable for products that cause harm

Type of ethics: Business and labor ethics

Significance: Two related ethics questions are integrally connected to product safety and liability issues: determination of who is responsible, *prior* to a product's purchase, for ensuring that the product is appropriately safe, and determination of who is responsible, *after* the product is purchased, if someone is injured by it.

Safety is one value among many in transactions between buyers and sellers. Products vary in their degree of riskiness—from cotton balls to butter knives to parachutes—and customers vary in the importance they attach to safety. Automobiles provide an apt example. Howattractive a car is to a customer depends upon its price, style, dependability, fuel efficiency, comfort, capacity, speed, power, maker's service record, and safety features. A young man buying his first car is likely to make speed and style higher priorities, while the parents of a young child who are struggling to make ends meet are more likely to make safety and fuel efficiency their highest priorities.

Two competing ethical models of how to achieve appropriate amounts of safety have been debated. One model emphasizes that both the seller of a product and the product's buyer are self-responsible agents who negotiate appropriate levels of safety in a free market. The other model calls for government regulation of safety on the grounds that sellers do not have enough sufficient incentives to provide appropriate levels of safety, and that buyers often do not have the knowledge or power to negotiate for safety.

The Free Market Model

The free market model sees safety as a value no different in principle than any other value that is produced and consumed. Just as prices, styles, and quality of customer service vary among products and are negotiable between buyers and sellers, optimal amounts of safety are variable and negotiable. Both sellers and buyers are self-responsible agents with their own goals, and both have responsibilities with respect to safety.

The seller's responsibility (*caveat vendor*, let the seller beware) is to manufacture a product within the range of professional standards of competence, to research reasonably foreseeable risks associated with using the product, and, in the case of risks that might not be obvious to consumers, to inform potential buyers of the risks.

The buyer's responsibility (*caveat emptor*) is to become aware of the risks associated with using the product—either by doing firsthand research or by seeking expert advice, such as one might get from physicians or from sources such as *Consumer Reports* magazine. Buy-

ers must then determine their own risk tolerance and learn how to use the products they purchase properly.

Ultimately, sellers and buyers seek each other out and negotiate transactions that are mutually satisfactory, including the question of how safe the products are. On this free market model, appropriate amounts of safety are fixed but vary from product to product and emerge as a result of supply and demand. Different producers emphasize the safety of their products to different degrees and attract to varying degrees customers who are interested in the amount of safety they are providing. The producers' profit motive should lead them to give to consumers the amounts of safety that satisfy them. Some cars, for example, are produced out of heavier materials and have additional safety features, while others are lighter and have extra speed or style features. How many of each kind of car are sold depends on how many customers are interested in their different features. Safety is thus a market value like any other, and the optimal levels of safety are set by supply and demand.

The Government-Regulation Model

The free market model assumes that customers are knowledgeable about both the relative safety of given products and their own risk tolerances, or that they can become knowledgeable by research. It also assumes that producers are responsive to consumer demands for safety. By contrast, the governmentregulation model is skeptical of both assumptions, so it concludes that safety should be provided primarily via government regulation rather than through free market forces.

Producers have a profit motive, which leads some to cut corners on safety. Since safety can be costly, an obvious way to cut costs is to avoid spending money on either research or additional safety features. Correspondingly, consumers are often unaware of risks involved in using many products, particularly new or complex products, and are consequently often unwilling to pay the extra costs associated with safer products.

Therefore, the government-regulation model assumes that many consumers will end up injured or worse because of an unregulated market. Therefore, to protect consumers from both themselves and producers, an informed third party with the power to regulate safety is needed. The government, therefore, should act paternalistically to shield consumers from their own lack of knowledge and poor judgment, and it should act protectively to shield consumers from careless, profit-seeking producers.

According to the government-regulation model, government experts should research products and decide uniform safety standards. The government should craft regulations and communicate them to producers. The producers should be given incentives to produce the specified amounts of safety—the incentives being the avoidance of fines, losing their licenses, or going to prison. Consumers can then purchase products confident in the knowledge that the government has made sure that their production meets adequate safety standards.

The two models of safety differ over two key ethical issues. Both agree that safety is a value but disagree over whether safety is a value that varies from consumer to consumer or is a uniform value that all products in a given category should possess equally.

Both sides also agree that assigning responsibility for safety is crucial—but disagree over whether producers and consumers can be self-responsible for safety or whether government regulators can best handle that responsibility.

Liability

During the 1960's, American liability law began shifting from its long-standing emphasis upon a standard of individual negligence to an emphasis upon strict liability. Common law traditionally analyzed liability in terms of individual responsibility. Plaintiffs were responsible to show that acts of negligence by identifiable defendants caused their injuries. Negligence is ignoring or hiding a reasonably foreseeable harm to a person. The argument for negligence-based liability relies on the concept of rational self-responsibility. Manufacturers sell goods for profit, and customers purchase them for consumption. Since no product can be completely risk-free, traditional liability requires that both sellers and buyers be responsible.

Manufacturers have two basic responsibilities to consumers. They must identify and address foreseeable risks in their products and must inform consumers of the risks. Under traditional liability, consumers have three responsibilities to protect themselves from injury. First, they must educate themselves about the products they buy and the companies that make them. Second, they must accept the foreseeable risks associated with the products. When a company issues directions indicating proper use, the consumers' third responsibility is to use the products properly.

If someone is harmed in using a product, determining liability requires identifying who, if anyone, was negligent in upholding his or her responsibilities. However, even when producers and consumers act responsibly, accidents may still happen. If a manufacturing company provides proper warnings of a product's risks, and the consumer accepts those risks, or if the accident that occurs is not foreseeable, then the costs fall to the consumer. Part of being an ethically responsible consumer is to recognize that accidents may happen and to protect oneself through insurance. Under the negligence standard, however, a producer is liable only if the company has been negligent.

Strict Liability

Although the negligence standard of liability has a long history of solving disputes between parties, proponents of strict liability argue that that standard does not adequately address social concerns, such as large liability claims and complex products. To address these concerns, strict liability eliminates the requirement of having an identifiable negligent party as the cause of the harm. Negligence by the producer or consumer is not necessary for legal liability. Strict liability is a harm-only concept. Additionally, strict liability collectivizes the concepts of harm and liability, in contrast to the negligence standard's individual focus.

Strict liability has created two new concepts in litigation, the class action lawsuit and collective liability. A group of people who have suffered the same harm can bring about a single lawsuit in which the question of plaintiff responsibility is irrelevant. Collective liability occurs when more than one producer contributes to the manufacture of the same harm-causing product. If the product cannot be isolated to one company, then all the producers may be held liable.

Strict liability's use of class action lawsuits and collective liability is intended to solve the perceived gaps left by traditional negligence liability. From the negligence-standard perspective, strict liability may seem unfair to a producer who has not been negligent; however, proponents of strict liability argue that it provides two main social benefits. First, strict liability gives manufacturers a greater incentive to make the safest possible products. If a manufacturer is liable for any of its products that causes harm, then rational economic thought dictates that the manufacturer should market only extremely safe products.

Second, strict liability functions as a social insurance policy. Some people who are harmed have no way to pay their medical costs under traditional liability. If, however, companies are legally required to accept the responsibility for harm done to people, then the medical and other costs will be transferred from the victim to the manufacturers of the product. Manufacturer will then simply add liability as a cost of production.

In wealthy nations such as the United States it may be easier to make everyone share the cost of liability rather than leaving it as an individual responsibility.

Ethical Controversies

Proponents of traditional liability find two problems with strict liability. The first problem is with the safety incentive. Under strict liability, companies should produce safer products; however, their incentive to innovate will decline. Since innovative products involve unknown risks, manufacturers will rationally decide in some cases that the costs of innovation combined with unknowable liability exposure is not compatible with the profit motive.

The second criticism of strict liability is a result of ethical differences. Traditional liability holds self-responsibility as its ethical ideal, while strict liability demands sacrifices of some for the sake of others. Therefore, the negligence view believes strict liability is unjust to manufacturers and will lessen consumers' self-responsibility; advocates of strict liability, by contrast, believe that the negligence model is unfair to individuals who cannot pay for their medical costs.

—Stephen R. C. Hicks and Todd M. Krist

Further Reading

Cane, Peter. *The Anatomy of Tort Law*. Oxford, England: Hart, 1997. Analysis of tort law as an ethical system.

Goldberg, Richard. *Causation and Risk in the Law of Torts: Scientific Evidence and Medicinal Product Liability*. Oxford, England: Hart, 1999. Surveys the legal and scientific issues relating to proof of causation in cases of alleged drug-induced injury.

Huber, Peter W. *Liability: The Legal Revolution and Its Consequences*. New York: Basic, 1990. Survey of the transformation of tort law since the 1960's.

Owen, David G., et al. *Products Liability and Safety*. New York: Foundation Press, 1998. Contains cases and other materials.

Vandall, Frank J. *Strict Liability: Legal and Economic Analysis*. Westport, Conn.: Greenwood Press, 1989. Discusses the legal and economic consequences arising from the expansion of strict liability.

See also: Consumerism; Corporate responsibility; Employee safety and treatment; Genetically modified foods; Industrial research; Marketing; Nader, Ralph; Public interest; Sales ethics; Tobacco industry; Warranties and guarantees.

Professional athlete incomes

Definition: Money that professional athletes make from salaries, product endorsements, appearance fees, and other sources

Type of ethics: Business and labor ethics

Significance: The dramatic rise in the earning power of professional athletes that began during the closing decades of the twentieth century raised numerous ethical questions about income distribution and the role of athletes in society.

Until the late twentieth century, financial compensation for professional athletes typically varied according to each individual athlete's level of competition, experience, and achievement. Athletes at lower levels of professional competition often earned wages that were below subsistence levels. Those at higher competitive levels typically earned comfortable salaries, while a select few were paid handsomely but not out of proportion to the top earners of other professions. In 1930, for example, baseball star Babe Ruth earned an annual salary of $80,000—approximately equivalent to a $800,000 salary in 2003 dollars. At the same time, the average salary of Major League Baseball players was approximately $6,000, or $60,000 in 2003 dollars.

Athletes competing in sports emphasizing individual excellence sometimes earned much more. In 1927, for example, heavyweight boxing champion Gene Tunney earned $990,000—equal to almost $10 million dollars in 2003—for a single boxing match against former champion Jack Dempsey. However, most rank-and-file competitors of the past earned salaries commensurate with national averages for skilled and professional workers.

After World War II, as the advent of mass media made professional athletics increasingly popular and profitable, many professional athletes began to resent team owners and event promoters who were reaping ever higher profits while restricting increases in athlete compensation. In 1966 Major League Baseball players organized the first successful professional athletes' union and, after a series of contentious court cases, won the right to negotiate with other teams when their contracts expired. Andy Messersmith and Dave McNally exercised this option in

1975 and became the first "free agents" in professional sports.

Other professional sports soon followed suit by enacting their own systems of free agency, resulting in dramatic increases in player salaries. By the end of the twentieth century, the *minimum* salary for rookie Major League Baseball players was $200,000, and the highest-paid baseball player, Alex Rodriguez, was earning approximately $25 million per year. In addition to their salaries as players, many top athletes were receiving additional money from product endorsement contracts that often paid them millions of dollars per year.

Impact on Sports

Although most observers agree that higher compensation for athletes has exerted a profound influence upon professional sports, disagreements exist as to whether the aggregate impact has been positive or negative. Supporters maintain that higher earnings have provided athletes with increased motivation to improve their performances, resulting in more intense competition among athletes and higher overall standards of athletic excellence. Moreover, since professional athletes no longer have to work during their off-season months to supplement their incomes as they did in the past, they have more time and energy for training.

Some critics argue, however, that high salaries and lucrative endorsements negatively affect performance by compromising team loyalty, fostering jealousy and friction among team players, and diminishing the desire of individual athletes to achieve their full potentials. In order to enhance their "market value," team-sport athletes are often encouraged to prioritize individual achievement over team success. Thus, critics argue, high salaries and endorsements serve either to distract and spoil athletes or to saddle them with unrealistic expectations.

Defenders of rising compensation rates for professional athlete pay often cite past and present inequalities between athlete pay and the profits of their employers or sponsors. This argument is rooted in the assertion that team owners, event promoters, and corporate sponsors have profited handsomely from the growth of the professional sports industry, and that athletes—without whom the industry would not exist—are ethically justified in their efforts to share in the financial success of their sports.

Societal Implications

The ethical implications of higher athlete pay upon society have also been the subject of contentious debate. Many argue that paying athletes large amounts of money damages both sport and society by fostering gross inequalities in income, and that salaries should thus be limited through regulation. Proponents of free market capitalism insist that owners, promoters, and sponsors are ethically justified in compensating athletes according to freely conducted negotiations and the demands of the market, and that athletes reserve the right as contract employees to sell their services to the highest bidders. Proponents of regulation argue that larger payrolls are unethical because they give sports teams in large markets—such as New York and Los Angeles—unfair advantages over those in small markets, and result in increased costs that are routinely passed along to fans in the form of much higher prices for tickets, concessions, souvenirs, and parking.

Some people view the disproportionately high earnings of top professional athletes as an example of growing disparities between rich and poor people in developed societies. Others argue that it is inequitable, and therefore unethical, to pay top athletes amounts totaling hundreds of times the salaries of persons in such essential occupations as education, health care, public safety, and social work.

Effects on Youth

Many critics also assert that higher athlete pay also damages society by setting a negative and unrealistic example for youth that is inherently unethical. The conspicuous presence of multimillionaire athletes, they argue, encourages youth to value athletic achievement over educational accomplishment, character, and citizenship. Moreover, the lure of immense wealth often encourages young people, especially those from disadvantaged backgrounds, to make sports a higher priority than education or personal growth in the often-unrealistic belief that they will themselves eventually succeed in professional sports. This assertion is supported by numerous examples of athletes who have interrupted their educations to "turn pro."

Proponents of the free market can cite numerous examples of athletes who emerged from modest backgrounds to become rich and famous athletes. By contrast, only a tiny minority of athletes are ever afforded the opportunity to compete professionally, and fewer still ever achieve the level of success required to command large earnings. Therefore, those who are persuaded single-mindedly to pursue careers in professional sports and do not succeed often lack the skills necessary to become healthy, productive members of society.

—*Michael H. Burchett*

Further Reading
Abrams, Roger I. *The Money Pitch: Baseball Free Agency and Salary Arbitration.* Philadelphia: Temple University Press, 2000.

Gorman, Jerry, et al. *The Name of the Game: The Business of Sports.* Indianapolis, Ind.: John Wiley & Sons, 1994.

Meier, Klaus V., et al., eds. *Ethics in Sport.* Champaign, Ill.: Human Kinetics Publishers, 2001.

Simon, Robert L. *Fair Play: The Ethics of Sport.* Boulder, Colo.: Westview Press, 2003.

Staudohar, Paul. *Playing for Dollars: Labor Relations and the Sports Business.* Ithaca, N.Y.: Cornell University Press, 1996.

See also: Betting on sports; Corporate compensation; Drug testing; Greed; Income distribution; Minimum-wage laws; Poverty and wealth; Role models; Taxes; Title IX.

Profit taking

Definition: Selling one's securities or property for more money than one expended to acquire them, especially when the sale occurs immediately after a rise in their market value.

Type of ethics: Business and labor ethics

Significance: Profit taking by many people at once is often the cause of a temporary drop in the price of the security being sold, following the laws of supply and demand. This situation raises ethical issues to the extent that profit takers harm the interests of long-term shareholders to benefit themselves.

In its broadest context, profit taking simply refers to the action of an investor in cashing in an investment and realizing whatever profit has been made. There are at least three circumstances, however, in which profit taking raises ethical questions. Especially during the 1980's, when corporate restructuring became commonplace, insider or management buyouts and firms "going private" often meant that investors with privileged knowledge about a company would offer stockholders more than the market value for their shares but less than the true value of those shares.

Then, sometimes after only a brief period of reorganization, the investors would "go public" again, sell some or all of their shares at a considerably higher price, and thus engage in profit taking.

Such practices raised questions of a conflict of interest on the part of the managers involved, who were operating in their own interest rather than upholding their fiduciary responsibility to the company's shareholders.

A second circumstance that raises ethical questions occurs when an investor realizes excessive profit from a transaction based on some standard of social acceptability, and a third such circumstance occurs when an investor gains profit by using unreasonable economic power.

—*D. Kirk Davidson*

See also: Capitalism; Free enterprise; Greed; Insider trading; Profit economy.

Public's right to know

Definition: Notion that government agencies, and some private companies, have an obligation to disclose their plans and actions to the public

Type of ethics: Media ethics

Significance: A guiding principle behind the public's right to know is the idea that citizens in a representative democracy have the inherent right to be informed about decisions, especially those of government, that may affect them and their communities.

On July 4, 1967, President Lyndon B. Johnson signed the Freedom of Information Act (FOIA). That law effectively required the federal government and, by implication, the various state and local governments, to provide fuller disclosure of their actions and decisions to citizens, especially through the news media.

The law was the logical result of a long series of campaigns to enact "sunshine laws" ensuring that government would be conducted more in the public view.

Those campaigns also grew to include information about significant activities of private corporations that could have impacts on potential health hazards in the air, water, and land, as well as in food and other consumer products. The concept of the public's right to know is not confined to the United States; however, it and the FOIA have special relevance in the United States because of direct connections to the free press clause of Article I of the U.S. Constitution's Bill of Rights.

As the concept is generally accepted, the public's right to know covers several broad categories. The first is that maximum disclosure is favored over partial revelations. Protected areas may include trade secrets and other exceptions, but supporters of the right to know say exceptions should be kept to an absolute minimum. A second broad category is the promotion of open government, the "sunshine" portion of FOIA. Wherever possible, government decisions should be discussed and made in public meetings freely reported by the media.

A fourth area covered by most FOIA and right-to-know legislation is the imperative for government agencies to facilitate use of their information by the news media and citizens. This goal should be achieved through open meetings, limited costs to copy requested documents, and processes that help spread information freely. These are required obligations on the part of government—and, to some extent, the private sector as well. Finally, protection is often afforded to "whistleblowers," those individuals who come forward with previously withheld information covered by the right to know provisions of the law.

There are opponents to the principle of the public's right to know, especially in sensitive areas involving national security or competitiveness. However, courts have generally been favorable to the concept, perhaps shown nowhere more clearly than in the U.S. Supreme Court's ruling that the government could not use prior restraint to prevent *The New York Times* (1971) from publishing excerpts from the Pentagon Papers that revealed how the United States became secretly and heavily involved in the Vietnam War. The ethical obligations of a democracy to inform its citizens as fully as possible, especially about decisions that affect public policy, has clearly been established as a keystone of media operations, although there are those in and out of government who remain unhappy with the concept and its application.

—*Michael Witkoski*

Further Reading

Gorman, Lyn, and David McLean. *Media and Society in the Twentieth Century*. Oxford, England: Blackwell Publishing, 2003.

Kovach, Bill, and Tom Rosentiel. *The Elements of Journalism*. New York: Crown Publishers, 2001.

Levy, Beth, and Denis M. Bonilla, eds. *The Power of the Press*. New York: H. W. Wilson, 1999.

Pavik, John. *Journalism and the New Media*. New York: Columbia University Press, 2001.

See also: Ethics in Government Act; Freedom of Information Act; Information access; Journalistic ethics; Pentagon Papers.

Reality television

Definition: Television programs that involve reallife people engaging in contrived nonfiction situations

Type of ethics: Media ethics

Significance: Much of reality television consists of programs that encourage subjects to compete in actions that might be deemed as violating common social norms.

During the early twenty-first century, reality television programs emerged as a staple of American television network programming because they were comparatively inexpensive to produce and often attracted large audiences. So-called reality programs might be subdivided into four genres: competitive game shows, such as *Survivor*, *Big Brother*, and Donald Trump's *The Apprentice*; romantic or sexually oriented competitions such as *ElimiDATE*, *Who Wants to Marry a Multi-Millionaire?*, and *For Love or Money*; talk shows such as *Jerry Springer* and *Maury*; and crime dramas such as *Cops* and *America's Most Wanted*. Beyond depicting real-life people, what many reality television shows have in common is that their main theme is to portray subjects engaging in behaviors that tend to violate social norms.

Like traditional competitions, reality game shows generally pit contestants against one another, but with a fundamental difference: Their contestants are encouraged to engage in devious, unsportsmanlike conduct that frequently crosses common moral boundaries, in exchange for success—which is typically measured in large cash prizes. Romantic and sexually oriented competitions are often similar in nature, requiring participants to change or violate loyalties or social contracts, or engage in morally compromising behaviors, in order to win.

Reality talk shows take a different approach, depicting subjects who have allegedly already violated some form of social contract or norm—such as those against marital infidelity, abuse, or abandonment—and confronting them with their victims. Just as critics have assailed reality game and romance shows, critics have contended that ubiquitous portrayals of inappropriate behaviors on reality talk shows tend to normalize or glamorize misconduct.

Reality crime dramas depict real-life criminals or suspects by reenacting or documenting actual crimes. Similarly, some shows, such as *Cheaters*, act as on-air private investigators. While supporters claim that such shows may serve as deterrents to inappropriate behaviors, other critics argue that such shows depict society's "tawdry underbelly," and like reality talk shows, tend to normalize or overemphasize morally ambiguous or contradictory behaviors, leading the public to believe that crimes occur more frequently than they actually do.

—Cheryl Pawlowski

See also: Accuracy in Media; Advertising; Children's television; Media ownership; Skepticism; Tabloid journalism; Televangelists.

Redlining

Definition: Systematic exclusion of residents of certain areas, especially low-income, inner-city neighborhoods, from home mortgage lending and property insurance coverage

Type of ethics: Business and labor ethics

Significance: Critics charge that redlining is an unjust practice, because it denies opportunities to those who could qualify for financial services simply because they reside in particular areas; it results in *de facto* discrimination. Practitioners of redlining defend the practice on the grounds that it is based on what they claim to be objective economic science.

In looking for an efficient way to screen out high-risk applications for home mortgages, rehabilitation loans, and home and auto insurance, banks and insurance companies adopted the practice of "redlining," which involves excluding entire low-income neighborhoods from consideration or charging excessively high prices in these areas.

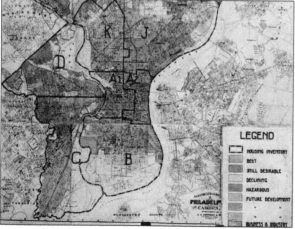

A HOLC 1936 security map of Philadelphia showing redlining of lower income neighborhoods.

Predictably, the burden of these practices fell most heavily on poor African Americans, and civil rights organizations charged that this amounted to systematic discrimination.

The U.S. Congress passed the Community Reinvestment Act in 1977, followed by the Home Mortgage Disclosure Act, to deal with redlining and the more general problem of directing loans and insurance coverage to low-income areas. The former requires banks and thrifts to make a certain proportion of their loans in the areas where their depositors live, and the latter requires them to report their mortgage lending by census tract. The question remains, however, how much responsibility banks should take for providing loans to low-income borrowers as a matter of social policy, especially if such loans conflict with sound business practice.

—D. Kirk Davidson

See also: Civil rights and liberties; Discrimination; Economics; Fairness.

Retirement funds

Definition: Savings that individuals invest in stock markets and other places in the expectation that their investments will steadily grow and provide them with secure income after they retire from working

Type of ethics: Business and labor ethics

Significance: When working people invest funds for their retirement, they understand the risks but also expect to be treated fairly and count on government agencies to regulate the ethical practices of the security firms in which they place their investments.

Until the Great Depression of the 1930's, American security firms regulated themselves, and the result was that influential investors received preferential treatment and had access to information not made available to the general public. However, after the collapse of the New York Stock Exchange in 1929, it became painfully clear to the public that the stock market was effectively rigged to favor certain investors over others. Those who had inside information about the impending collapse of stock values sold their shares before the crash occurred, while average investors lost their investments. Although investors lost much of their faith in the stock market, President Herbert Hoover was philosophically opposed to government regulation of security markets. Things changed, however, after Franklin D. Roosevelt's inauguration in March, 1933.

Roosevelt realized that the federal government needed to regulate the stock market in order to save capitalism by restoring public trust in the market.

During his first two terms, he signed three important bills that imposed ethical values on the security industry and created a Securities and Exchange Commission (SEC) with the power to regulate the security industry and to punish violators with fines and jail terms. These laws were the Securities Act of 1933, the Securities Exchange Act of 1934, and the Investment Company Act of 1940. Among other things the new laws made fraudulent financial reports, insider trading, unequal treatment of investors, and deceptive selling techniques federal crimes. The SEC also created the National Association of Security Dealers (NASD) to regulate securities representatives.

Responsibilities of Securities Representatives

Candidates for certification as securities representatives must pass a qualifying examination that tests their understanding of what a representative can and cannot do. About one-quarter of the examination deals with ethical issues. For example, when securities representatives advise investors, they must propose stocks, bonds, or mutual funds that are appropriate to the specific investors' needs. For investors who are opposed to risks or who are elderly, appropriate investments might be government bonds or conservative bond funds.

By contrast, significantly younger investors who are willing to accept higher risks in the hope of reaping high returns in the future might be directed toward such riskier investments as growth or international mutual funds, junk bonds, or stocks in unproven new companies. In all presentations to their clients, securities representatives must make appropriate recommendations and repeatedly remind investors that investments in stock markets are not guaranteed and that they might even lose their principal.

Managing Retirement Funds

Investment companies and security companies must also behave in an ethical manner in managing retirement funds. Many investors choose to invest in mutual funds and not in individual stocks because they wish to spread out risks over the many different companies in which individual mutual funds invest their members' money. The federal Investment Company Act of 1940 requires that mutual funds establish the values of their shares right ev-

ery day, immediately after the closing of stock markets. This regulation was designed to prevent insider trading and to make sure that all investors receive equal treatment.

Mutual fund managers must also adhere to the philosophies announced in their prospectuses. For example, a mutual fund that states that its intention is to invest 70 percent of its funds in blue-chip American companies and 30 percent in government guaranteed bonds cannot suddenly decide to invest it funds in foreign companies or in junk bonds. If managers of such funds do not respect their announced approaches, the SEC can bring criminal charges against them, and investors can sue such managers for losses caused by investments that contradict the announced goals and philosophies of a specific fund.

These ethical and legal protections are important because they give investors legal rights and remedies.

A scandal that became public in 2003 illustrates the importance of such protection. Managers of several mutual funds, including the Putnam and Strong funds, made illegal trades after the 4:00 p.m. closing time of the New York Stock Exchange that gave them profits that were not shared by other investors. Not only were these managers and their investment companies forced to pay large fines to state and federal regulators, but individual investors in the funds also had the legal right to sue the mutual fund companies and their managers for real losses and punitive damages.

Some investors oppose investments of their retirement finds in industries that may conflict with their ethical beliefs. Many people, for example, do not want their money used to support the production and sale of alcoholic or tobacco products because of their opposition to tobacco and alcohol for personal or religious reasons. Many investment companies offer such mutual funds, which are often called "social choice" funds, that do not invest any funds in tobacco or alcohol companies. In this way, investors can be sure that their retirement funds are not being used to promote activities that are incompatible with their ethical beliefs.

—Edmund J. Campion

Further Reading

Braithwaite, Valerie, and Margaret Levi, eds. *Trust and Governance*. New York: Russell Sage, 1998.

Dardi, Yo Dav. *Misbehavior in Organizations*. Mahwah, N.J.: Lawrence Erlbaum, 2004.

Davis, E. P. *Pension Funds*. New York: Oxford University Press, 1999.

Machan, Tibor R. *Primer on Business Ethics*. Lanham, Md.: Rowman & Littlefield, 2002.

Mitchell, Olivia, ed. *Innovations in Retirement Financing*. Philadelphia: University of Pennsylvania Press, 2002.

Soule, Edward. *Morality and Markets: The Ethics of Government Regulations*. Lanham, Md.: Rowman & Littlefield, 2003.

See also: Ageism; Gray Panthers; Income distribution; Insider trading; Profit taking.

Sales ethics

Definition: Formal and informal codes of conduct defining the morally proper and improper ways to sell things to people.

Type of ethics: Business and labor ethics

Significance: Sales is often perceived, by both buyers and sellers, as the art of convincing people to purchase things they do not really need or to pay more for a commodity than it is really worth. This act raises ethical concerns involving who is ultimately responsible for the decisions of consumers and the extent to which purveyors of commodities can or cannot be said to manipulate buyers or the marketplace itself.

The selling of goods and services has long been the subject of moral and, sometimes, theological concern. Economic theorists at least since the time of Adam Smith have assured people that when a buyer and a seller with equal knowledge of a product reach agreement and a transaction occurs in the marketplace, the situations of both buyer and seller are improved; otherwise, one or the other would not have agreed to the transaction. Nevertheless, since both buyer and seller are seeking to maximize their positions and since their interests are diametrically opposed, one seeking the lowest possible price and the other seeking the highest, it is natural to expect each to try to take advantage of the other, sometimes unfairly. The problem is rooted in whether buyer and seller have equal knowledge; as products and services have become increasingly complex and as manufacturers and sellers have grown into multibillion-dollar corporations, equal knowledge, and therefore equal power, in the marketplace has become the exception rather than the rule.

Marketing Ethics

The ethics of marketing, a broader and more current interpretation of sales, can be viewed in terms of the natural dimensions of the marketing function. The first concerns the safety and appropriateness of the product or service being marketed, normally considered under the subject of product liability. Here the question is: Who has responsibility and liability for any harm done to individuals or to society by the product? This has become an enormously complex and rapidly changing area of the law and of moral concern as well. Traditionally, common law and social thought relied on contract theory, which holds that buyer and seller come as equals to the marketplace, and once the deal has been struck, the buyer is responsible for the product, including any harm it might cause. Especially since the 1950's, however, more and more of the responsibility and liability have been placed on the seller and, particularly, the manufacturer.

It has been argued that the manufacturer has the most knowledge of the product, is in the best position to prevent harm from occurring, and is better able to bear the financial liability for harm than is the buyer, especially when the latter is an individual consumer. No longer is it necessary to show that manufacturers have been negligent in any way; they are now expected to anticipate any potential hazards or possible misuse by customers.

Pricing and Promotion Issues

Ethical questions can arise also in the pricing function of marketing. Here the question is whether a price is considered fair, especially when the product is a necessity such as a basic food item, housing, or medical care. The introduction of revolutionary pharmaceutical products—for example, Burroughs Wellcome's AZT for the treatment of acquired immunodeficiency syndrome (AIDS) patients and Genentech's TPA for heart attack victims—has often triggered complaints that the manufacturer's high price puts an unfair burden on the buyer. Some retailers have been accused of unfairly charging prices in low-income areas that are higher than those that they charge in more affluent neighborhoods for the identical merchandise.

Sophisticated advertising and other promotional tactics are often the subject of ethical questioning. Critics charge that advertisers, usually the manufacturers, manipulate and exploit consumers, and thus use unfair means to encourage them to buy. Manufacturers and some social scientists respond that unless the advertising is actually dishonest, and therefore illegal, consumers cannot be coerced by legal advertising messages into buying anything that they do not really want to buy. This issue takes on added significance when so-called "vulnerable" groups are the target. Cigarette companies have been criticized for targeting African Americans and women; breweries for targeting young, inner-city African Americans for high-alcohol-content beverages; breakfast cereal and toy manufacturers for targeting children; and door-to-door sellers of safety devices for targeting older people. Other ethical questions raised about advertising include the promotion of inappropriate values; for example, materialism and the exploitation of women by emphasizing sex.

In the distribution function of marketing, ethical questions are raised when retailers close stores in inner-city areas (for example, after the Los Angeles riots of May, 1992), when major food retailers collect "slotting fees" from manufacturers just for agreeing to carry new products, and when direct marketers buy and use confidential demographic and consumer behavior information in compiling lists of potential customers.

Corrective Action

Action to correct these ethical problems comes from three sources. First, various industries and business associations agree to exercise self-restraint through company-wide or industry-wide codes of conduct and through the formation of organizations such as the Better Business Bureaus to monitor corporate behavior. Second, dozens of watchdog consumer organizations, such as the Center for Auto Safety, Co-op America, and the Center for Science in the Public Interest, have been formed to guard consumers' interests and call attention to what they perceive as improper behavior on the part of sellers. Third, since the 1970's, many laws have been passed to help protect consumers, such as the Consumers Products Safety Act, the Child Protection and Safety Act, and the Hazardous Substances Act at the federal level.

—D. Kirk Davidson

Further Reading

Davidson, D. Kirk. *The Moral Dimension of Marketing: Essays on Business Ethics*. Chicago: American Marketing Association, 2002.

Galbraith, John Kenneth. *The Affluent Society*. 40th anniversary ed. Boston: Houghton Mifflin, 1998.

Hunt, Shelby D., and Lawrence B. Chonko. "Marketing and Machiavellianism." *Journal of Marketing* 48 (Summer, 1984): 30-42.

Laczniak, Gene R., and Patrick E. Murphy. *Marketing Ethics: Guidelines for Managers*. Lexington, Mass.: Lexington Books, 1985.

Levitt, Theodore. "The Morality (?) of Advertising." *Harvard Business Review*, July-August, 1970: 84-92.

Milne, George R., and Maria-Eugenia Boza. *A Business Perspective on Database Marketing and Consumer Privacy Practices*. Cambridge, Mass.: Marketing Science Institute, 1998.

Schlegelmilch, Bodo B. *Marketing Ethics: An International Perspective*. Boston: International Thomson Business Press, 1998.

Smith, N. Craig, and John A. Quelch. *Ethics in Marketing*. Homewood, Ill.: Richard D. Irwin, 1993.

See also: Advertising; Business ethics; Consumerism; Marketing; Price fixing; Telemarketing; Warranties and guarantees.

Sedition Act of 1798

Identification: One of four "Alien and Sedition Acts" designed to suppress domestic opposition to Federalist policies during a period of European anti-American aggression

Date: Passed in 1798

Type of ethics: Media ethics

Significance: The Sedition Act challenged the First Amendment's guarantees of free speech and a free press, an attempt that ultimately served to broaden the scope of both rights and to limit governmental restraint of political dissent.

The Sedition Act was prompted by Federalist fears that growing Republican opposition to Federalist policy would weaken popular support and lead to the end of Federalist control at a time when the United States was caught between rival international powers. The act sought to apply the English common-law tradition of "seditious libel" by making it unlawful to "write, print, utter, or publish...any false, scandalous, or malicious writing...against the government of the United States...or to bring [it]...into contempt or disrepute." On that basis, ten newspaper editors were convicted, one of them a congressman, by courts made up exclusively of Federalist judges.

Advocates justified the act by interpreting the First Amendment as pertaining only to "prior restraint," meaning that the government could not prevent the publication of dissent but could prosecute the result. Opponents protested that the First Amendment prevented the government from suppressing political speech at any stage, and they pronounced the act unconstitutional. Republican opposition was carried out through the Kentucky and Virginia Resolutions (written by Thomas Jefferson and James Madison, respectively), which asserted the right of states to "nullify" unwanted federal intrusions on individual rights. The act expired with the inauguration of

Thomas Jefferson, and no subsequent attempt to suppress political dissent has ultimately been successful.

See also: Constitution, U.S.; First Amendment; Freedom of expression; Jefferson, Thomas; Politics; Sedition.

Self-regulation

Definition: Imposition of a code of conduct or set of ethical standards by an organization or profession upon its own members

Type of ethics: Business and labor ethics

Significance: The term self-regulation generally implies that measures have been taken to preempt or otherwise render superfluous government intervention or statutory regulation of an industry. Essentially, a group promises to act ethically in order to avoid being forced to act legally. To the extent that members of the group may disagree with the action taken on their behalf, self-regulation raises issues about individual autonomy.

During the late nineteenth century, social critics began to promote increased government regulation of business, industry, and various professions. In an attempt to stave off additional government intrusion into commercial affairs, many Self-Regulatory Organizations (SROs) were formed. SROs function as private rule-making and enforcement bodies that govern the activities of their members. Exemplary among such SROs is the American Institute of Certified Public Accountants (AICPA), which was founded in 1887 to self-regulate the accounting profession.

The AICPA states that its mission is to "provide standards of professional conduct and performance," "monitor professional performance," and "promote public confidence in the integrity, objectivity, competence, and professionalism" of public accountants. SROs such as the AICPA possess the power to censure or disbar their members from practice if they violate professional standards of conduct. Proponents of SROs contend that voluntary professional organizations are inherently more capable of encouraging ethical behavior than is a centralized government agency. Critics of SROs charge that the organizations merely act in the self-interest of their members rather than in the interest of society at large.

—W. Jackson Parham, Jr.

See also: Mozi; Price fixing; Professional ethics.

Song lyrics

Definition: Expressions of a wide range of subjects by means of words set to music

Type of ethics: Arts and censorship

Significance: The lyrics of contemporary popular music challenge the boundaries of taste and public notions of propriety and are central to the debate over limits to free expression.

Bawdy and subversive lyrics are as old as music, and the impulse to suppress them is as old as social hierarchy. There is an ancient underground tradition of songs that defy the prevailing order, satirize the ruling class, and challenge commonly accepted precepts. Anthems such as France's "Marseillaise" and the communist "Internationale" began as oftenbanned incitements to revolution. In nineteenth century Italy, the politics of the reunification movement, the Risorgimento, circumscribed the texts of Giuseppi Verdi operas. Richard Strauss's opera *Salome* was shut down after one performance in New York in 1908, in part because of its allegedly indecent German libretto, which was based on a play by Oscar Wilde.

Modern Popular Culture

With the invention of sound recording and the advent of broadcast media, arguments favoring limits to the content of commercially distributed songs gained currency in the United States. Before the 1950's, most censorship incidents involved the proscription or laundering of Harlem Renaissance blues lyrics or Broadway show tunes such as Cole Porter's "Let's Do It." On occasion, records such as the Andrews Sisters' "Rum and Coca-Cola," whose unexpurgated lyrics refer to a mother-and-daughter team of Trinidadian prostitutes "working for the Yankee dollar," would be banned from the radio. During the Joseph McCarthy era, the socially conscious lyrics of leftist folksingers such as Woody Guthrie were widely suppressed as "communist" propaganda.

With the rise of rock and roll during the 1950's, the verbal content of popular music began to ignite moral panic. Rock, which evolved from African American rhythm and blues in the early 1950's, was considered "jungle music," a destructive combination of primitive rhythms and lewd lyrics. Early antirock music campaigns were sometimes unapologetically racist and always maintained that the music spread violence and promiscuity. The lyrics of some songs, such as the Kingsmen's "Louie Louie," did not even have to be decipherable to be deemed obscene by the Federal Bureau of Investigation and the Federal Communications Commission.

Although the sexual frankness that crept into pop lyrics as the 1960's progressed became increasingly overt, rock songs of that decade were most commonly censored or banned because of real or imagined references to drugs. The Beatles' "Lucy in the Sky with Diamonds" (1967), for example, was reviled in some quarters because it was assumed to describe the effects of LSD. More overt allusions to drug use, such as the Jefferson Airplane's "White Rabbit" (1967), with its exhortations to "feed your head," often caused the song to be denied radio play.

Drug-culture jargon and four-letter words at times provided authorities with convenient excuses to keep antiwar and social protest songs off the air. Within the United States, organized efforts to clean up rock music lyrics have come from across the political spectrum. Leaders of such campaigns have ranged from right-wing ideologue David Noebel to civil rights activist Jesse Jackson. In the late 1970's, the messages of punk bands such as the Sex Pistols, along with the continuing popularity of "heavy metal" music among young teenagers, created concern that "morbid" and "occult" lyrics were causing a rise in teenage suicide. In the late 1980's, artists were threatened with legal action by bereaved parents and in some cases sued. Evangelists and radio personalities such as Bob Larson popularized the idea that satanic messages were encoded in rock lyrics or subliminally injected into certain albums through sound engineering.

Upset by masturbation references in Prince's song "Darling Nikki" in 1985, Tipper Gore, the wife of future vice president Albert Gore, cofounded the Parents Music Resource Center (PMRC), an organization aimed at curbing the excesses of popular music. Congressional hearings held at PMRC's request resulted immediately in censorship activity at the state level. By 1990, the Recording Industry of America (RIAA)was pressured into instituting a voluntary warning-label system whereby some records would carry stickers with the label "Parental Advisory/ Explicit Lyrics." The labeling scheme created a climate of censorship within the music industry and provided a foundation for efforts to restrict sales and criminalize certain lyrics in Louisiana, Washington state, and elsewhere.

The Demonization of Rap
In the late 1980's, Florida attorney Jack Thompson began enlisting allies in a campaign against rap, an African

American art form that he considered an affront to "traditional values." Thompson helped to inspire the arrest and obscenity conviction of a record-store owner who was guilty of selling the Miami rap group 2 Live Crew's album *Nasty as They Wanna Be* (1990); the band itself was arrested in Fort Lauderdale following a live performance of such songs as "Me So Horny." Although 2 Live Crew was acquitted, Thompson continued to hound them and other outspoken rap musicians—especially NWA (Niggas With Attitude)—across the country and as far as the United Kingdom, where 22,000 copies of an NWA album were impounded. Hysteria over "gangsta" rap reached fever pitch in 1992 with the release of Ice-T's *Body Count* album (technically a heavy metal record), an outpouring of rage over forms of racism. Its climactic song, "Cop Killer," was condemned for its venom:

I got my twelve gauge sawed off.
I got my headlights turned off.
I'm 'bout to bust some shots off.
I'm 'bout to dust some cops off.
COP KILLER, it's better you than me.
COP KILLER, f—— police brutality!

Iran-Contra figure Oliver North retained Jack Thompson as counsel in July, 1992, for the express purpose of mobilizing his lobbying operation, Freedom Alliance, against musicians. North's strategy included encouraging police organizations to use various means to eliminate the sale, broadcast, or commercial release of "seditious" music. Ice-T and his distributor, Time Warner, were finally driven to excise "Cop Killer" from future pressings of the *Body Count* album. Other artists who were legally threatened or economically pressured included Ice Cube, Tupac Shakur, Almighty RSO, and Paris, whose "Bush Killa" vented rage at the White House.

Censorship During the 1990's
In 1994, mounting a fresh campaign to force the recording industry to clean up rap and heavy metal lyrics, the PMRC created the unlikely team of liberal Democrat C. Delores Tucker, chairman of the National Political Congress of Black Women, and conservative Republican William J. Bennett, secretary of education under President Ronald Reagan. In joint press releases, op-ed columns, and public appearances, Tucker and Bennett decried "lyrics from the gutter" while paying little attention to actual content.

In 1995, Tucker and Bennett successfully pressured Time Warner to drop its controlling interest in Interscope

Records, which carried such controversial artists as Snoop Doggy Dogg.

U.S. senators Joseph Lieberman of Connecticut and Sam Nunn of Georgia joined Tucker and Bennett in public condemnation of "obscene music," citing such songs as Dove Shack's "Slap a Ho." In 1997, Senator Sam Brownback of Kansas held hearings designed to showcase complaints about objectionable lyrics and other elements of what Senator Lieberman, in testimony, called our "broken culture." In Brownback's media-tailored forum, the voices of artists, serious analysts of American culture, and freespeech advocates were almost absent; witnesses who deplored the moral turpitude of popular music were welcomed warmly. As Congress continued its attack, the Recording Industry Association of America, once fiercely opposed to censorship, began wavering in its support for freedom of expression.

By the mid-1990's, the $12 billion U.S. recording industry began backing away from nonmainstream music. The climate of censorship was aggravated by pressure from retailers and distributors. Wal-Mart, the largest record retailer in the nation, refused to sell albums with "parental-advisory" warning stickers and went so far as to demand censored versions of certain record albums, with problematic songs edited for content or dropped altogether.

After students gunned down fellow classmates at Littleton, Colorado's Columbine High School in 1999, and similar incidents occurred elsewhere, the campaigners against rock and rap were eager to blame the incidents on the troubled teenagers' taste in music. When it was erroneously reported that the Columbine shooters were fans of "goth-rock" singer Marilyn Manson, Senator Brownback and nine of his colleagues demanded that Seagram's, which owned Manson's record label, put an end to the performer's career. They also called for an investigation into popular culture by the U.S. surgeon general.

In an era during which commercial music veered away from political content, the popular art being demonized was often material daring to critique contemporary American life. The so-called gangsta rap genre vented the outrage of an underclass whose real grievances received scant attention in congressional hearings. Critic Lawrence Stanley describes gangsta rap an "unmistakably black art form" that emerged at a time when white institutions were indifferent, if not hostile, to the concerns of African Americans.

For young people of all races who felt numbed by American middle-class life, Marilyn Manson offered an invigorating challenge to traditional gender roles, religious fundamentalism, and pressure to conform.

White rapper Marshall Mathers III, who performs under the name Eminem, was vociferously condemned by everyone from Joan Garry of the Gay and Lesbian Alliance Against Discrimination (GLAAD) to Republican activist Lynne Cheney, wife of future vice president Dick Cheney, when his *Marshall Mathers LP* (2000) gained popularity, praise, and award nominations. Accused of nihilistic, misogynist ranting, Eminem was in fact an articulate chronicler of the ills of working-class Detroit. Describing the blighted industrial city in his song "Amityville," Eminem sings:

we don't call it Detroit, we call it Amityville ('Ville).
You can get capped just having a cavity filled (filled).
Ahahahaha, that's why we're crowned the murder capital still (still).
This ain't Detroit, this is m———n' Hamburger Hill (Hill!).
We don't do drivebys, we park in front of houses and shoot.
and when the police come we f———n'shoot it out with them too!
That's the mentality here (here), that's the reality here (here)....

Through the 1990's, song-lyric censorship in the United States was opposed by the National Campaign for Freedom of Expression, the National Coalition Against Censorship, and grassroots advocacy groups such as Rock Out Censorship and the Massachusetts Music Industry Coalition. The American Civil Liberties Union (ACLU) Arts Censorship Project worked to provide legal aid to embattled musicians, producers, and retailers, helping to overturn an "erotic music" law in Washington state and to defend record stores across the country. Citing federal court rulings on speech, ACLU attorneys maintained that song lyrics, even if they extolled armed rebellion, did not constitute a direct and imminent threat—and that First Amendment protections did indeed apply to such works as "Cop Killer." The irreconcilable disagreements in this controversy illustrated a growing rift between opposing visions of American democracy.

Inspired by a growing worldwide concern about content restrictions on music, activists and musicians held the first World Conference on Music and Censorship in Copenhagen, Denmark, in November, 1998. In the twenty-first century, the debate over song lyrics and other popular expressive media pitted human aspirations toward freedom against a perceived need, real or imagined, for increased authoritarian social control in response to a growing terrorist menace.

—James D'Entremont

Further Reading

Blecha, Peter. *Taboo Tunes: A History of Banned Bands and Censored Songs*. San Francisco: Backbeat Books, 2004.

Cloonan, Martin. *Policing Pop*. Philadelphia: Temple University Press, 2003.

Gore, Tipper. *Raising PG Kids in an X-Rated Society*. Nashville, Tenn.: Abingdon Press, 1987.

Korpe, Marie, ed. *Shoot the Singer: Music Censorship Today*. London: Zed Books, 2004.

Martin, Linda, and Kerry Segrave. *Anti-Rock: The Opposition to Rock 'n' Roll*. Hamden, Conn.: Archon Books, 1988.

Nuzum, Eric D. *Parental Advisory: Music Censorship in America*. New York: Perennia, 2001.

Petley, Julian, et al. "Smashed Hits." *Index on Censorship* 27, no. 6. London: Writers and Scholars International, 1998.

Stanley, Lawrence A, ed. *Rap: The Lyrics*. New York: Penguin Books, 1992.

See also: Art and public policy; Book banning; Children's television; Freedom of expression; Internet piracy; Jackson, Jesse; Napster; Pornography; Violence.

Stewart, Martha

Identification: Entrepreneur and television personality
Born: August 3, 1941, Jersey City, New Jersey
Type of ethics: Business and labor ethics
Significance: Stewart parlayed her homemaking and fashion skills into a multimillion dollar business empire and became a national icon of style and domesticity, but her ethical reputation took a severe blow when she was charged with insider trading and other offenses and was convicted on all counts in 2004.

Beginning with a modest catering service in 1976, Martha Stewart gradually built a homemaking and style empire of books, articles, syndicated television shows, magazines. and a line of products sold through her own mail-order business and at Kmart department stores all over the United States. Her total worth after she consolidated her enterprises as Martha Stewart Living Omnimedia and went public in 1999 put her for two years running on *Forbes Magazine*'s list of the four hundred wealthiest citizens of the United States.

In December, 2001, the day before the stock of the ImClone company fell sharply because the Federal Drug Administration had refused to approve ImClone's anticancer drug, Erbitux, Stewart sold her ImClone shares. Her timely move gave the appearance of having been improperly influenced by inside information. Federal investigators were led to Stewart because of the arrest of Samuel Waksal, the chief executive officer of ImClone and a personal friend of Stewart's, on insider trading charges in the summer of 2002. Now suspected of insider trading herself, Stewart told investigators that she had ordered her broker to sell her ImClone stock if the price per share went down to sixty dollars. The broker corroborated her statement, but his assistant, who had handled the sale, later said that he knew of no "stop-loss" order in this case. Stewart protested her innocence of any wrongdoing.

On June 4, 2003, Stewart was indicted, not for insider trading, but for conspiracy, making false statements, obstruction of justice, and securities fraud. The last charge was based on the allegation that she defrauded investors in Martha Stewart Living Omnimedia by making false statements about her company's worth. Stewart again maintained her innocence of all charges but immediately resigned from the directorship of Omnimedia, though she remained on its board as "creative director."

Stewart's indictment occasioned much speculation about the reason for federal interest in a case involving a stock transaction worth less than forty-six thousand dollars—a tiny fraction of Stewart's total assets—when nothing was being done about more serious cases, such as the multimillion dollar misdeeds of Kenneth Lay, the former chief executive officer of Enron. Many claimed that Stewart was singled out for attention not because she had committed a major transgression, but because she was a self-made and eminently successful business woman and a celebrity or because prosecutors believed that they would win an easy conviction.

Other speculation centered around the reasons why the original basis of the investigation of Stewart for insider trading was abandoned for the lesser, and perhaps far-fetched, charge of misleading her investors. That charge was based on Stewart's public claim in June, 2002, that she had done no wrong. It was also suggested that charges of insider trading are notoriously difficult to prove and more easily left to the jurisdiction of the Securities and Exchange Commission.

Federal Prison Camp, Alderson, where Stewart was confined. By Christopher Ziemnowicz.

Before the scandal over ImClone broke, Stewart had been regarded as a paragon of competence, style and good taste. However, the apparent inconsistencies in the three accounts of the sale of her ImClone stock tarnished her reputation for honesty and forthright dealing, and her financial worth began to decline. CBS-TV cancelled her regular appearances on its weekday *Early Show* and relegated her popular daily homemaking show, *Martha Stewart Living*, to a 2 a.m. time slot.

Although Stewart retained the enthusiastic support of tens of thousands of her admirers and experienced no immediate decline in her line of products sold at Kmart stores, the popularity of her formerly best-selling magazine, *Living*, fell precipitously.

Most damaging, however, was the nearly 50 percent fall between June of 2002 and June of 2003 in the value of Omnimedia stock, of which Stewart herself was the major shareholder. This was especially damaging because Stewart's image and that of her company were virtually identical. Recovery of a lost reputation under such a circumstance is extremely difficult, if not impossible.

On March 5, 2004, Stewart and her stockbroker were convicted on all charges of obstructing justice and lying to the government about her stock sale. In July, she was fined thirty thousand dollars and sentenced to five months in a federal prison. She began serving her term in a West Virginia minimum-security facility on October 8, 2004. In 2005 Stewart began her comeback and the company returned to profitability in 2006. Stewart rejoined the board of directors of Martha Stewart Living Omnimedia in 2011[7] and became chairwoman of her namesake company again in 2012. In the fall of 2016, VH1 premiered a new show featuring Martha and her friend Snoop Dogg called *Martha & Snoop's Potluck Dinner Party*.

—*Margaret Duggan*

Further Reading
Byron, Christopher M. *Martha Inc.: The Incredible Story of Martha Stewart Living Omnimedia*. New York: John Wiley & Sons, 2002.

See also: Corporate scandal; Insider trading.

Tabloid journalism

Identification: Popular form of news reporting in weekly newspapers and television programs
Date: First emerged during the 1920's
Type of ethics: Media ethics
Significance: Tabloid journalism provides readers with news in condensed and highly sensationalized forms that often sacrifice journalistic integrity for marketability.

The term "tabloid" originally referred to the physical size of tabloid newspaper pages, which were smaller than the standard twelve-by-twenty-four-inch pages of broadsheet papers. During the 1920's, when tabloid newspapers first arose to significance, the term "tabloid" expanded to include the content of the newspapers as well as their size, especially referring to the papers' preference for stories involving crime, scandals, and sexual escapades of celebrities. Among the most famous and influential of the early tabloid newspapers were the *New York Daily News*, the *Daily Graphic*, and the *Daily Mirror*—all of which were published in New York City. During a well-publicized "war of the tabs" those three newspapers established the tabloid format and style that have continued into the twenty-first century.

Although the tabloids never entirely disappeared—indeed, the *New York Daily News* enjoyed one of the largest circulations in the nation—they faded in importance during the 1950's and 1960's. Then, toward the end of the 1960's, tabloids began to re-emerge, this time in a weekly format with greater attention given to celebrities, such as television and movie stars, and an emphasis on the private lives of their subjects. The tabloids also generally included highly sensationalized stories about alleged alien abductions, births of monstrous babies, prophecies of coming disasters, and similar items. Buoyed by such content and filled with often lurid photographs, individual tabloids such as the *Star* and the *National Enquirer* achieved enormous circulation figures through their national sales, often at the checkout lines of supermarkets.

A spin-off phenomenon was known as "tabloid television," or shows which featured stories about celebrities, especially their more scandalous activities. Highly visible and publicized crimes, such as the murder of O. J. Simpson's former wife, were also key elements of television tabloid journalism. Like their newspaper tabloid counterparts, these television programs featured stories that were short, sensational, long on illustrations, and short on reliable factual information.

The ethical standards of both print and televised tabloids have been low. Representatives of both forms have been remarkably unconcerned with the actual truth of the stories on which they report, as they freely report rumor and innuendo as fact. Both forms have traditions of paying large amounts for "inside" information, often obtained from relatives and friends of the lead characters in their stories.

Photographs and film of intimate moments, including the aftermath of shocking crimes, are highly prized and have included such dubious achievements as the *National Enquirer*'s printing photographs of the dead body of Elvis Presley in a Memphis morgue.

No matter how low the standards of tabloid journalism, however, there is a pervasive fear among media watchers that, because of their high circulation and ratings, the tabloids' methods and outlook may in time be copied by the more mainstream media.

—*Michael Witkoski*

Further Reading
Fox, Richard, and Robert Van Sickel. *Tabloid Justice*. Boulder, Colo.: Lynne Rienner, 2001.
Gorman, Lyn, and David McLean. *Media and Society in the Twentieth Century*. Oxford, England: Blackwell, 2003.
Levy, Beth, and Denis M. Bonilla, eds. *The Power of the Press*. New York: H. W. Wilson, 1999.
Mott, Frank Luther. *American Journalism*. 3d ed. New York: Macmillan, 1962.
Pavlik, John V. *Journalism and New Media*. New York: Columbia University Press, 2001.

See also: Advice columnists; American Society of Newspaper Editors; Invasion of privacy; Journalistic entrapment; Journalistic ethics; News sources; Photojournalism; Reality television; Truth.

Telemarketing

Definition: Fast-growing international industry that reaches customers through direct telephone calls

Type of ethics: Business and labor ethics

Significance: Although it is recognized that telemarketing provides useful services to consumers, the industry is known for ethically questionable practices that annoy uninterested persons and undermine consumer trust and faith in the marketplace generally.

Telemarketing can be an efficient method of selling products, services, and philanthropic opportunities. It can also disseminate useful information to interested consumers. However, telemarketers are notorious for harming vulnerable consumers and businesses, providing misinformation, annoying people with unsolicited calls, and creating animosities and suspicions that limit the benefits of telemarketing itself.

During the first years of the twenty-first century, it was estimated that the American public was losing an estimated forty billion dollars per year to fraudulent telemarketers. Voluntary telemarketing codes of conduct and state and national criminal codes require that telemarketers make disclosures to consumers, prohibit lies, regulate hours of operation and sales tactics, and allow call recipients to request placement on do-notcall lists. Ethical issues arise when the marketing tactics are unfair, intrusive, or excessively forceful; the sellers, solicitors, buyers, or donors engage in deception or fraud; the marketing targets are vulnerable or exploited; or the products or benefits are exaggerated or misrepresented.

Unethical Practices

Such telemarketing tactics as after-hours or repeated calls, calls to private homes during private hours, calls that clog business telephones and message centers, and sales pitches implying negative consequences for resisting sales calls are considered both unethical and unfair. Some anti-telemarketing tactics are considered unethical. These include fraudulently accepting sales agreements or charitable pledges, injuring telemarketers' ears with loud whistles or horns, insincere and repeated requests for callbacks and written materials, and providing telemarketers with false or misleading information. Both telemarketing callers and the people who take their calls are unknown to each other, making enforcement of applicable laws difficult to enforce.

Some telemarketing companies practice what are known as fly-by-night tactics: After their unfair practices are detected and targeted for investigation, they close their operations, hide their assets, and reopen their businesses under new names with new corporate identities. Companies operating out of foreign countries may be beyond the enforcement reach of U.S. national and state authorities. At the same time, some buyers engage in equally fraudulent behavior by taking delivery of products or services for which they have no intention to pay.

Telemarketing sales pitches that target the elderly, persons with disabilities, geographically and socially isolated persons, or persons with limited financial resources are considered especially unfair. Pitches exploiting the victims' greed, avarice, ego, or emotional sensitivities are also unfair but are often viewed less harshly by the public.

The Federal Trade Commission (FTC) and other enforcement agencies have been lenient in allowing puffery, exaggeration, and hyperbole in marketing. The marketing companies themselves may provide honest and forthright scripts for their callers to read to potential customers; however, they may also encourage their callers to deviate from their scripts to make sales. It is difficult to bring legal charges on oral sales pitches that are delivered by anonymous salespersons. In some cases the product, services, or charities do not even exist. Some telemarketing is a cover for credit card or identity theft, or is used to gather financial and consumer information used by other telemarketers at later dates.

—Gordon Neal Diem

Further Reading

Ditch the Pitch: Hanging Up on Telephone Hucksters. Washington, D.C.: Federal Trade Commission, Office of Consumer and Business Education, 2001.

O'Dea, Valerie. *Better Business by Phones: A Guide to Effective Telebusiness.* West Lafayette, Ind.: Ichor Business Books, 1999.

Sisk, Kathy. *Successful Telemarketing: The Complete Handbook on Managing a Profitable Telemarketing Call Center.* New York: McGraw-Hill, 1995.

See also: Business ethics; Electronic mail; Etiquette; Identity theft; Invasion of privacy; Marketing; Privacy; Sales ethics.

Tipping

Definition: Gratuitously awarding money to persons who provide services, such as waiting on tables

Type of ethics: Business and labor ethics

The first usage of the term "tip" in the sense of giving a gratuity dates back to 1706 (pictured here are European waiters from the early 1900s).

Significance: From the point of view of customers, the central ethical question relating to tipping is whether the action should be regarded as voluntary or involuntary.

In modern Western societies, tipping is regarded as a custom whereby customers receiving services give to the providers additional direct compensation, usually in the form of cash. Service providers such as a taxi drivers, restaurant waiters, hairstylists, and porters are examples of workers who accept tips. Custom generally dictates that tips from satisfied customers should range from 10 to 15 percent of the cost of the services provided, not including sales taxes. Owners of businesses themselves are generally regarded as exempt from tipping. For example, taxicab owners, barbers who own their barbershops, and restaurant owners are exempt.

There are two primary ways one might consider the ethics of tipping. The first is to understand a tip to be a voluntary reward and therefore an evaluation of the service rendered. The second is to consider a tip as an expected form of additional compensation over and above what the workers receive from their employers.

If one chooses to think of tipping as a reward for good service, the giving of tips, as well as the amounts of the tips, are entirely voluntary and left to the discretion of the customer. Seen in this light, generous tips serve as signals to workers that their performance is above average. Conversely, the absence of tips or ungenerous amounts are meant to indicate to workers that their performance needs improvement. From this market perspective, it is ethical to tip only if performance warrants it. In Europe, where tipping is less frequent than in the United States, tipping is considered just such a signal of exemplary service and gratitude on the part of the customer.

In the United States, the public custom of tipping is more complex. Some people consider tipping, as in the European custom, a reward of exemplary service. More often however, American tipping is regarded as customary; tipping is therefore an expected and routine part of the exchange. Customers thus tip 10 to 15 percent of the costs of the services they receive, regardless of the quality of service. Since tips are viewed as part of the overall charges, they are routinely expected by workers. From this perspective, the tip as part of the compensation owed to the server is simply a portion of the total compensation provided by the customer rather than the employer.

The expectation that tipping is customary has arisen, in part, in response to minimum wage laws. Many service workers—particularly those who are most likely to be tipped—are paid below minimum wage levels. Therefore customers, and certainly the workers themselves, view tipping as a just way to close the gap.

—*Steve Neiheisel*

Further Reading

Schein, John E., Edwin F. Jablonski, and Barbara R. Wohlfahrt. *The Art of Tipping*. Wausau, Wis.: Tipping International, 1984.

Segrave, Kerry. *Tipping: An American Social History of Gratuities*. Jefferson, N.C.: McFarland, 1998.

Tuckerman, Nancy, and Nancy Dunnan. *The Complete Book of Etiquette*. New York: Doubleday, 1995.

See also: Cheating; Equal pay for equal work; Etiquette; Generosity; Income distribution; Minimum-wage laws; Service to others; Taxes.

Tobacco industry

Definition: Producers and distributors of tobacco products

Type of ethics: Business and labor ethics

Significance: The American tobacco industry has come under fire for marketing products known to have links to severe health problems—a fact that raises questions as to the industry's ethical responsibility for the illnesses and deaths attributed to tobacco use. The issue also involves questions about the personal responsibility of adults who choose to use products they know are harmful.

During the 1990's, the American tobacco industry came under unprecedented attack from state and federal officials who sought compensation from the companies for the cost of medical treatments of tobacco-related illnesses. Government representatives argued that their publicly funded health care systems were swamped with payments for tobacco-related illnesses for which the tobacco industry was largely responsible.

Industry Liability to Society

Even with the addition of federal warnings of health problems associated with cigarettes, smoking remained a popular if declining activity in American culture. Prior to the 1990's the federal government conducted low-key antismoking campaigns, limited mainly to advertisements and surgeon general reports highlighting the dangers of smoking. By the early 1990's, a burst of antismoking activity broke out, starting with a 1993 Environmental Protection Agency (EPA) report, followed by congressional hearings and continuing into regulations by the Clinton administration. The impetus behind the antismoking campaign was the rising costs in government-funded health care programs.

The ballooning Medicare and Medicaid program budgets were blamed on tobacco-related illnesses including cancer and heart disease. The federal and state governments demanded that tobacco companies reimburse them for these health costs, which were partly caused by their products. This demand became part of a lawsuit filed by state governments seeking damages from the tobacco companies. A settlement was reached in 1998, with the major tobacco companies agreeing to pay more than $200 billion to the states in return for an end to lawsuits over smoking. This money was to be used to reimburse states for health care costs and to pay for antismoking campaigns.

Antismoking advocates argued that the tobacco industry owed society and the government for taking care of those made ill by cigarette smoking. This was a different argument from the one offered by individual smokers who were suing the tobacco industry for smoking-related illnesses they personally suffered.

The governments' lawsuits sought reimbursement not for direct damage caused to government or society by cigarette smoking, but for indirect damage—in the form of higher health care costs brought on by more smoking-related illnesses. This made a single industry responsible for a product voluntarily used and known by the users to be dangerous to human health.

The state governments' arguments were not entirely convincing. Governments have agreed to pay for the poor and elderly's health care costs until their death. Many of those costs would exist with or without smoking because death is inevitable. While smoking may contribute to certain types of terminal illnesses, it does not necessarily produce or increase the costs of caring for terminal patients. Forcing tobacco companies to pay government for terminal illnesses linked to their product makes those companies responsible for the inevitable: terminal illness.

The 1990's also saw another, indirect, government assault on the tobacco industry in the former of rising excise taxes on cigarettes in order to discourage people from taking up smoking and to raise revenues.

For many years most states had imposed taxes of only a few cents per pack on cigarettes. By 2004, however, the average state tax on a pack of cigarettes was sixty cents, and sixteen states had raised their taxes to more than one dollar a pack. Not surprisingly, the states with the lowest tax rates were all tobacco-producing southern states. Meanwhile, smokers in New York City faced a double tax: one dollar and fifty cents went to both the city and the state, adding a total of three dollars in taxes to each pack of cigarettes. In early 2004, New York City added to smokers'difficulties by outlawing all smoking in restaurants.

Industry Liability to Individual Smokers

In addition to lawsuits filed by state and federal governments, tobacco companies faced suits from individual smokers seeking damages for their own terminal illnesses. Other companies have suffered considerable economic damages when their products were found to have contributed to illness or death of consumers. The asbestos industry, the producers of silicon breast implants, and the producers of the Dalkon Shield all paid huge sums to those who suffered medical problems from their products.

However, there was a significant difference between those products and tobacco products. For nearly forty years consumers had been aware of the dangers of cigarette smoking, while those who used the other products were unaware of potential health problems attributed to the products' use. However, prior knowledge of the potential health problems caused by cigarette smoking can shift only part of the responsibility from the industry to the consumer.

Smokers can also attribute specific illnesses and possibly early death and considerable suffering to tobacco products. Individuals suffering because of asbestos exposure or the negligence of makers of breast implants were paid directly by the companies involved. By contrast, no government claimed that it should be reimbursed for the costs of caring for those who suffered lung cancers because of asbestos exposure.

The tobacco industry also had to accept responsibility for other ingredients in cigarettes, including nicotine. Studies have shown that nicotine is an addictive drug, partly explaining the difficulty many smokers have in "kicking the habit" of cigarettes. During the 1990's further evidence was uncovered suggesting that tobacco companies had manipulated nicotine levels in cigarettes in order to create addicted smokers of their products. If to-bacco companies were guilty of adjusting nicotine levels and knew about the addictive qualities of nicotine, then that fact raises new questions about the industry's accountability for the health problems of cigarette smokers.

While an individual might be considered responsible for choosing to smoke, an addictive and dangerous product might condemn that person to serious illness or death. An addictive product, not revealed as such to the consumer, places responsibility for its effects squarely on the tobacco industry. Deliberate manipulation of nicotine levels would suggest the companies were attempting to create an addiction to a product that all knew was potentially unsafe. Health problems including disease and death traced to cigarettes and their addictive qualities would make the tobacco industry responsible for the damage caused by smoking.

Responsibility to Nonsmokers

Another issue of responsibility for the tobacco industry is the cost to nonsmokers and their exposure to smoking. During the 1990's, the federal government and private antismoking organizations used a 1993 EPA report to warn of the dangers of what became known as secondhand smoking—the cigarette smoke inhaled by nonsmokers exposed to cigarette smoking. The EPA report linked secondhand smoking to asthma in children or heart disease and cancer in adults. The report prompted the federal government to seek new methods of limiting exposure to smoking.

Cigarette smoking was tied to the health problems of nonsmokers, breaking the chain of responsibility usually placed on smokers. Nonsmokers did not choose to smoke yet suffered negative effects of the product. They could thus blame any ill effects they suffered on the industry.

With secondhand smoking possibly contributing to negative health effects, local governments began limiting where and when people could smoke within public spaces. Starting in the mid-1990's, laws were passed prohibiting smoking in many public buildings including airports, courtrooms, and government offices.

Supporters of the bans argued that nonsmokers in those buildings had no choice but to inhale cigarette smoke unless smoking was banned. The bans became broader as many cities and some states began prohibiting smoking within private businesses including bars, restaurants, and stores. These bans, initiated throughout the United States, were supported by the public based on the fear that secondhand smoke was dangerous. However, when it came to secondhand smoking, it was the antismoking advocates who faced ethical questions.

Ethics of Tobacco Critics

When the EPA issued its 1993 report claiming that private studies linked secondhand smoking to health concerns, it did not explain the methodological problems associated with its report. The EPA report was actually a combination of nine studies, none of which showed a significant connection between secondhand smoking and health problems for nonsmokers.

The EPA combined those nine studies and produced a report that contradicted the results of the nine. The greatest concern raised by this is the public policy that was based on the distorted results. Laws passed restricting public smoking were based on public belief that secondhand smoke was dangerous to nonsmokers. Lack of definitive scientific proof of this casts doubt on the wisdom of limiting the right to smoke. It also raises concerns about the tactics of antismoking advocates. Those seeking to limit smoking are limiting the rights of other individuals to pursue activities—smoking—that they enjoy. Such a limitation of freedom must be accompanied by some national goal promoting the general welfare. If smoking does not harm nonsmokers, then the rush to limit exposure to secondhand smoking may be an unnecessary limit on individual choice.

Ethics of Advertising

Known health dangers of smoking raise questions about the ethics of tobacco advertising. Companies use advertising to create new markets for their products, drawing in new consumers. These advertisements highlight the popularity of products and suggest that use of the products will enhance a person's social standing and make him or her more popular among others. Like all other advertising, cigarette advertisements promote products, attempting to attract youths into using tobacco. However, even with the warning labels attached to such ads, there is little information about the potential harms associated with smoking. Young people have less experience with those dangers.

Antismoking advocates point to print ads, sponsorship of athletic events by tobacco companies, and placement of products in television shows and movies as examples of the industry's attempt to glamorize smoking to youth. The companies clearly attempt to gloss over the dangers of smoking while highlighting its social acceptability. Those

seeking to regulate cigarettes contend that smoking should never receive any positive public relations because of the serious health problems caused by it. Recruiting people to engage in smoking would expose them to the addictive nature of nicotine and possibly to higher rates of cancer and heart disease. To meet this criticism, the tobacco industry agreed to implement voluntary limitations on its advertising and mounted another ad campaign attempting to limit youth smoking. For the first time in any industry's history, the makers of products were spending money attempting to dissuade consumers from using their products.

—Douglas Clouatre

Further Reading

Hayes, Eileen. *Tobacco U.S.A: The Industry Behind the Smoke Curtain.* New York: Twenty-first Century Books, 1999. This work focuses on the tobacco industry's attempt to hide information linking smoking to health problems while claiming that no such evidence existed.

Hilts, Philip, and Henning Gutmann, eds. *Smokescreen: The Truth Behind the Tobacco Industry Cover-up.* New York: Addison-Wesley, 1996. A series of articles attacking the tobacco industry for hiding the results of studies linking smoking to health problems.

Johnson, Paul. *The Economics of the Tobacco Industry.* Westview, Colo.: Praeger Publishing, 1998. Short work explaining how the tobacco industry remains profitable even as it comes under attack from government and private antismoking organizations.

Milloy, Steven. *Junk Science Judo: Self Defense Against Health Scares and Scams.* Washington, D.C.: Cato Institute, 2001. This work criticizes "scientific" studies used to advance a political goal. In one chapter, Milloy takes special aim at the 1993 EPA report linking secondhand smoking to heart disease and shows how the EPA manipulated data to reach its desired conclusion.

Oakley, Dan. *Slow Burn: The Great American Anti-Smoking Scam.* New York: Eyrie Press, 1999. This book takes aim at antismoking advocates and their attempts to eliminate smoking within the public sphere.

Pampel, Fred. *Tobacco Industry and Smoking.* New York: Facts On File, 2004. Evenhanded work that describes the controversy over smoking and how the tobacco industry has handled it.

Sullivan, Jacob. *"For Your Own Good": The Antismoking Crusade and the Tyranny of Public Health.* New York: Touchstone Books, 1999. Critical work on the efforts by public health officials to use studies in order to restrict smoking in public and private areas.

Zegart, Dan. *Civil Warriors: The Legal Siege on the Tobacco Industry.* New York: Delacorte Press, 1996. Examination of the work of an attorney suing the tobacco industry for damages for smokers made ill by years of smoking and the efforts of tobacco companies to win those suits at any cost.

See also: Advertising; Business ethics; Drug abuse; Health care allocation; Medical insurance; Product safety and liability; Taxes.

Warranties and guarantees

Definition: Assurances made by manufacturers or dealers to consumers that if the products or services they sell fail to meet certain standards, they will repair or replace the goods or otherwise compensate buyers

Type of ethics: Business and labor ethics

Significance: In modern society, warranties and guarantees represent legally binding contracts between manufacturers and consumers. Ethical issues relating to warranties include consumer fraud (a consumer may pretend that a product had a defect when it was really damaged through carelessness), evasion of duty (a company may pretend that damage resulted from consumer carelessness rather than defect), and the proper calculation of a fair and reasonable warranty period.

The terms "guarantee" and "warranty" are virtually synonymous in their marketplace meanings. Laws in the United States generally use the term "warranty," while "guarantee" is perhaps more common in everyday speech. Both terms imply some sort of assurance of quality or standards to the buyer of a product or service. Sellers of products have probably always offered some form of guarantee, if nothing more than their reputation. During the Middle Ages, guilds for various professions set standards for the training and qualifications of their members. This could be considered to be the first formal type of guarantee.

Product warranties can take the form of written or oral statements. Some warranties are implied and are in force even though they are not directly communicated from seller to buyer. Sellers have some protection, in that they can specify that products are warrantied only for "reasonable use" or can attach warnings that products are not suited for particular uses. Many product liability lawsuits hinge on the meaning of "reasonable use" and whether a product is as safe as could reasonably have been expected.

In the United States, written warranties are covered by the Magnuson-Moss Warranty Act of 1975. According to the provisions of that act, a warranty must describe the specific coverage offered and what the purchaser of a product has to do to obtain it, as well as what the warrantor must do to remedy a problem.

Prior to passage of the act, a warranty could be used to limit the seller's responsibility to what was stated on the warranty, thus breaking some reasonable expectations on the part of the buyer. The act states that warranties must be available in writing and must be available for purchasers to read before a purchase is made.

The Magnuson-Moss Warranty Act specifies two types of implied warranties that almost always are in force even though they are not stated in a seller's written warranty. In most cases, sellers are not able to release themselves from these implied warranties.

The implied warranty of merchantability states that the product or service is suited for ordinary use. The implied warranty of fitness for a particular purpose states that sellers are responsible for providing correct information regarding particular uses to which a buyer might put a product. Sellers in this case represent themselves as experts whom consumers can trust for advice. For example, a consumer might tell a vacuum-cleaner salesperson what types of carpets the vacuum cleaner is being purchased to clean. The salesperson then would make a recommendation based on this information. The consumer has a right to expect that the vacuum cleaner will perform, even if the use to which it is put is not ordinary.

Warranties can be either full or limited. The Magnuson-Moss Warranty Act states conditions that must be met for a warranty to be labeled as "full." Limited warranties restrict the promises made by sellers. They can include clauses calling for payment of labor charges by the purchaser, reinstallation charges, or pro-rata refunds based on how long the product had been in use.

Many warranties apply only to new products. Consumers have less protection when they buy used goods, particularly if the goods are specifically sold "as is." Implied warranties most often do not apply to such sales.

Ethical Implications

Warranties and guarantees protect consumers both from unscrupulous behavior and from unanticipated consequences. An honest seller may unintentionally sell a defective product. His or her guarantee to the purchaser may be a simple oral statement that the product can be returned if it is defective. It may also take a formal contractual form. In either case, buyers face little risk when dealing with honest sellers.

Written warranties protect consumers from sellers who misrepresent their products, perhaps lying about the characteristics or expected performance of the product or about what the sellers will do to remedy defects or other consumer dissatisfaction. In the absence of enforceable warranties, sellers would be able to make any claims about their products, and consumers would have no way of making judgments other than basing them on the reputation of the seller. Unscrupulous sellers could then make sales based on exaggerated claims, then refuse to back those claims.

The marketplace might even offer an incentive for such behavior, since consumers would be drawn to products for which exaggerated claims had been made, at least until the sellers' dishonesty had been established.

Warranties thus provide protection against dishonest marketplace behavior. They serve to make marketplaces more efficient, because consumers can be more certain of the information provided to them rather than having to rely on reputation. Warranties also increase the rewards to honest sellers, who are not faced with dishonest competitors who can make sales through false claims about their products. Warranties thus serve to enforce and reward ethical behavior.

—A. J. Sobczak

Further Reading

Eiler, Andrew. *The Consumer Protection Manual.* New York: Facts On File, 1984.

Eisenberger, Kenneth. *The Expert Consumer: A Complete Handbook.* Englewood Cliffs, N.J.: Prentice-Hall, 1977.

Kurer, Martin, et al., eds. *Warranties and Disclaimers: Limitation of Liability in Consumer-Related Transactions.* New York: Kluwer Law International, 2002.

Maynes, E. Scott. *Decision-Making for Consumers: An Introduction to Consumer Economics.* New York: Macmillan, 1976.

Sapolsky, Harvey M., ed. *Consuming Fears: The Politics of Product Risks.* New York: Basic Books, 1986.

Weinstein, Alvin S., et al. *Products Liability and the Reasonably Safe Product: A Guide for Management, Design, and Marketing.* New York: John Wiley & Sons, 1978.

See also: Business ethics; Consumerism; Product safety and liability; Sales ethics.

Whistleblowing

Definition: Publicly revealing, or reporting to appropriate authorities, that one's employer is guilty of corporate or professional wrongdoing

Type of ethics: Business and labor ethics

Significance: Whistleblowing may violate both ethical values, such as loyalty and confidentiality, and specific legal requirements, such as nondisclosure agreements. It is generally defended, however, on the grounds that it serves the public interest and protects third parties from harm. Whistleblowing laws have been passed in many states to protect whistleblowers from corporate reprisals such as lawsuits, dismissal, or demotion.

Blowing the whistle on a person or activity is intended to bring to a halt some activity that will cause harm to the public. Since it is generally recognized that one should prevent harm to others if one can do so without causing great harm to oneself, whistleblowing would seem to be morally required. It is also generally recognized, however, that one should be loyal to one's employers and professional colleagues.

Since whistleblowing by an employee appears to breach this loyalty by reporting the harmful activity to those outside the organization, the employee who discovers misconduct is faced with a moral dilemma.

Some writers argue that such "ratting" on one's employer is always wrong. Others argue that those who are

American whistleblower Edward Snowden. By Laura Poitras.

willing to risk their futures to expose wrongdoing are heroes. Still others assess individual acts of whistleblowing by asking various questions: Have all the internal reporting channels been exhausted without results? Is the harm to the public without a report significantly greater than the harm to the organization with a report? What is the likelihood that the report will actually prevent the harm; that is, is the report believable and substantiatable?

—Ruth B. Heizer

See also: Business ethics; Confidentiality; Corporate responsibility; Corporate scandal; Loyalty; Obedience; Professional ethics.

White-collar crime

Definition: Criminal activity in the corporate, commercial, professional, and political arenas
Type of ethics: Business and labor ethics
Significance: The treatment of white-collar crime both by law enforcement officials and by the media raises fundamental issues of social justice and equal treatment under the law, since such crime is often under-prosecuted in comparison with similar crimes committed by working-class people.

White-collar crimes are distinguished by the fact that they most commonly take place at the workplace and involve activities related to otherwise legitimate occupations. In addition, white-collar criminals rarely use violence or weapons.

The lowest level of white-collar crime, and the one easiest to identify and prosecute, is employee theft, ranging from taking office supplies for nonwork use to the theft of products intended for sale. Higher levels of white-collar crime typically involve manipulations of bookkeeping accounts or legal documents.

These crimes are more difficult to trace, particularly as more records are kept in electronic form, with fewer "paper trails" to identify wrongdoing. A variation of this type of crime involves violating the terms of a business contract or law with the intent of earning a profit in a way not intended by the other contracting parties or by society. An example is insider trading, in which stock, bond, or commodity traders use information they have learned earlier than other traders in order to make a profit in their trading.

This example points out a difficulty in prosecuting some white-collar crime: It is difficult to say what information is illegal to use, since financial markets are designed to reward those who make effective use of information. The lines of ethical and legal behavior are also difficult to draw in cases of political corruption; "constituent service" to one person might be considered to be political favoritism or graft to another.

—A. J. Sobczak

See also: Business ethics; Corporate responsibility; Corporate scandal; Corruption; "Everyone does it"; Fraud; Insider trading.

Science, Technology & the Environment

Self-driving vehicles are increasingly likely to be playing a significant role in public transportation in the very near future. Scientists, engineers and automakers are now confident that their designs and manufacturing facilities are significantly advanced from a technological perspective—particularly in key areas like artificial intelligence and machine perception, or situational awareness—to enable the manufacture and sale of safe, reliable, affordable and energy-efficient alternatives to conventional, human-operated vehicles. Similar advances in intelligent robotic technology likewise promise quite soon to yield self-flying aircraft and self-navigating, sea-going freighters—all incorporating technologies that were thought to be the stuff purely of fantasy and science-fiction only a few years earlier.

According to a principle known as Moore's Law, the rate of technological innovation doubles every two years (or less). That headlong pace of technological development in these and countless other areas sometimes threatens to overwhelm our abilities to comprehend and adjust socially to the new prospects afforded by exponential advances in computer programming, data collection, analysis, and storage, not to mention in robotics, artificial intelligence and machine cognition. These advances impact not only our modes of transportation, but also communication, financial transactions, domestic security, personal safety and privacy, and national defense.

The impact of technology in each of these (and a myriad of other) sectors of civilization are further enhanced by networking—connecting each person and a range of devices with everyone and everything else through social media and the Internet of Things. An intelligent home assistant, for example, wirelessly linked to the global internet as well as to other devices in the home (your refrigerator, heating and air conditioning unit, home security system, as well as to your smartphone) can order food and groceries, make appointments with dentists and physicians, and remind you of important upcoming events the next day, all while selecting your preference of music or television for you to enjoy while relaxing in your living room.

That convenient home assistant, and the devices to which it is connected in your home, however, are all vulnerable to cyberattacks by criminals or even agents of a foreign government, who can hijack the computational power of each device and weave them into a large botnet of networked devices that could be used to attack a city's electrical power grid, overwhelm government and public services, and even rob banks electronically. The helpful home assistant itself could presumably record our every activity and transmit these personal data to massive data storage and analysis systems operated either by commercial organizations (desiring to sell us a variety of goods and services), or by our own police and government agencies (allowing them to track our movements, and perhaps attempt to modify or control our individual behavior).

Scientific and technological advances of these sorts present us with a bewildering array of promises and perils. Human drivers, in our first example, struggle to cope with sudden emergencies caused by a child or a dog suddenly running into their path, or a pedestrian crossing against traffic. How should the automated car be programmed to respond to such unforeseen events? In most instances, the safety of passengers is of paramount importance for the car's designers, of course. But the driverless car's sensors may enable it to have a quicker reaction time to emergencies, and thus avoid hitting the children, pets, or pedestrians by quickly steering off the main road, damaging the car and possibly injuring the driver. How is the car supposed to weigh those alternatives, and assess the risks involved? This is not simply a computational or algorithmic problem. It appears to require something like *a moral judgment* from the intelligent system. And even if the car itself is enabled by its designers to react in this complex fashion, to whom (or what) should police or insurance companies assign liability in the event of injuries or death resulting from its choices?

The prospect of massive surveillance raised in our second example of scientific and technological advance may sound ominous to many. But those ominous perils threaten to blind us to a host of beneficial outcomes that this technology also promises. If I am an elderly person increasingly confined to my home, for example, my need to acquire groceries and prescription refills may still be easily detected and accommodated through use of that networked home assistant. And if I suffer a medical emergency—a heart attack or a serious fall—that sinister-sounding prospect of government surveillance may instead lead to the immediate and welcome notification of police, the fire department, and even summon an ambulance to administer emergency care and transport me to the nearest hospital.

These prospects of promise and peril arising from the pursuit of ever more detailed and accurate scientific knowledge and rapid technological advances seem likewise intertwined and networked. We may ask ourselves (as many before us have likewise wondered when confronted with the endless prospects of scientific inquiry and technological advance): "May I avail myself of the enormous and often unanticipated *benefits* of scientific research and technological innovation, without having to expose myself and society to unanticipated and *perverse consequences* or risk of harm these might also (or instead) inflict?" It seems unavoidable as well as frustrating that the positive benefits afforded by science and technology are virtually inseparable from their potentially negative impact. Researchers in these fields often refer to these unavoidable side effects of their efforts by the acronym, ELSI—denoting the ethical, legal, and social impact of their explorations. Many of the articles in this final section of Volume 3 deal with these profound ELSI questions.

Such ethical questions are posed with a special urgency when contemplating the prospective *military* uses of new and exotic technologies, such as lethally armed autonomous weapons systems, or prospects for the human enhancement of combatants themselves. Elderly persons in Japan at present—even those well into their eighties—are increasingly helping to ease a growing shortage of labor in the workforce by donning robotic exoskeletons which enable the older employees to lift and move heavy loads, or otherwise perform essential tasks that would have previously exceeded their physical capacities. In France, meanwhile, leading technological firms, like CTA Internationale, Nexter Systems and the Thales Group, offer similar robotic exoskeletons for their armed forces, greatly magnifying the capacities of French soldiers both to fight more effectively and avoid injury during combat. Military forces in other nations such as Sweden, the U.K. and Israel are following suit, increasingly relying for enhanced combatant capabilities on genuine analogues to the popular fictional characters, Captain America and Iron Man.

The military is often the chief client for AI and computer-networked technology. Beyond the increasing familiarity of pilotless aircraft like U.S. *Predators* and *Reapers*, countries like China, Israel and the U.K. are experimenting with distributed intelligence, in which information and reasoning capacities may be shared among the individual members of a swarm of small, expendable robots that together (functioning much like ants or locusts) can confuse and overwhelm an adversary's antiaircraft defenses. We have already experienced the manner in which the military's use of drones has spawned a civilian-use counterpart or blowback effect. Small, inexpensive drones can be used for reconnaissance in fighting massive forest fires, or in search and rescue missions following major national disasters like hurricanes, earthquakes, and floods. But those same drones can pose a grave hazard when operated carelessly in the civilian airspace, and even be used to spy and pry into the private lives of neighbors.

The promise and the peril in such instances once again go inseparably hand-in-hand. Additional articles in this section explore the need for scientists and engineers, as well as for the general public, to reflect carefully on the specific ethical challenges accompanying the development and use of such technologies. One of the gravest questions explored in this section is whether or not a lethally-armed, autonomous weapons system should ever be permitted to deliberately target and take a human life—even that of a military adversary or dangerous criminal—absent direct human oversight and control. It is our collective moral responsibility to avoid engaging in what we ourselves might come to regard as thoughtless, reckless, or even criminally negligent behavior when encouraging or participating in the development and use of such technologies.

Finally, scientific research has proven essential in understanding and protecting our natural environment, including the very conditions which make life itself on this planet possible. Ironically, that same research frequently reveals the manner in which our business and industrial activities, along with technological innovations that otherwise lead to marked improvements in everyday human existence, can simultaneously pose grave threats to our surrounding environment, including the plants and animals with whom we share the planet, and on which we depend (often without our full knowledge) for our own survival, safety, and enjoyment.

A profoundly influential naturalist and environmental ethicist writing in the early twentieth century, Aldo Leopold, warned scientists and industrialists in particular to be cautious when exploring—let alone when intervening, consuming, or destroying—any of the individual components of a complex ecosystem. It is foolish, he argued, to dismiss or ignore the possibly vital importance of features (or creatures) whose individual role or function, not to mention interdependence with other elements, in our immediate environment we do not yet fully grasp. "Preserving every cog and wheel," he responded, "is the first rule of intelligent tinkering." An article on his life and influence on the environmental movement, together with others ranging from the ethical challenges of ozone-layer depletion and acid rain to climate change and global warming comprise the remaining articles in this section.

Anthropological ethics

Definition: Study of the moral issues raised in the course of conducting fieldwork in anthropology

Type of ethics: Scientific ethics

Significance: An ethical approach to anthropology that tries to minimize negative effects of the anthropologist's presence and behavior upon the peoples being studied.

Anthropology studies human culture and behavior primarily through the observation of participants living intimately with and observing a community. Anthropologists risk negatively affecting a community or individuals within it by their presence, actions, or reportage of information.

Anthropology originated only during the mid-nineteenth century, and its early practice betrayed its colonialist roots. Field anthropologists often were government agents sent on espionage expeditions to colonies or territories, informants typically were misled regarding the uses to which information would be put, and concern for informants often was sorely lacking. As early as 1916, Franz Boas and other prominent anthropologists had decried these abuses in print.

World War II proved to be a watershed in terms of concern about ethics in anthropology. The second half of the twentieth century saw the development of formal ethical codes for most of the major anthropological organiza-

tions, including the American Anthropological Association, the Society for Applied Anthropology, and the Association of Social Anthropologists of the Commonwealth. These codes contain a core of generally accepted principles, though controversy flourishes regarding other issues.

Core Principles

Formal ethical codes in anthropology emphasize the obligations of the anthropologist to the people under study, the discipline, and the sponsors of the research. The anthropologist's greatest responsibility is to the people under study. These people are critical to the study and can be hurt by it. Furthermore, in some cases, cultural differences make people unlikely to understand fully the possible ramifications of their participation. Consequently, anthropologists must use extreme care to protect their informant-hosts. Knowledge of the political or social structure of a community, even if it is divorced from the specifics of individual officeholders, can be used by governments and others to control, terrorize, or punish a community, and individuals should be aware of what level of risk they are taking by providing that information to anthropologists. Only if the informants find these conditions acceptable should the research continue. The anthropologists must be prepared to withhold information if necessary to protect the people under study. Many ethnographic reports use pseudonyms or nonspecific reporting in attempts to disguise informant and community identities. Recognizing the trust placed in them, anthropologists should be very sensitive to issues of confidentiality and reveal nothing that is likely to harm the study community or its individual members.

Ethical obligations to the discipline revolve around publication. Anthropologists are obligated to publish the results of their studies, lest they become mere self-indulgent "custom collectors." In order to achieve the greater goals of anthropology, the broadest possible corpus of evidence is necessary. Clearly, falsification and distortion are intolerable. Sponsors of ethnographic fieldwork vary greatly. Academic funding agencies sponsor much research, and they typically are sympathetic to anthropological ethics. Other funding, however, may come from private foundations or government agencies that may be unfamiliar with ethical standards or even antagonistic toward them. Project Camelot, for example, was sponsored by the Special Operations Research Office of the U.S. Army between 1964 and 1967. As described in the prospectus, which was mailed to many anthropologists and other social scientists, the goal of this project was "to predict and influence politically significant aspects of social change in the developing nations of the world," particularly Latin America. This kind of a project can place an anthropologist in an untenable position, since it may require providing information that will harm (in the anthropologist's judgment) the people under study.

While many anthropologists argue that anthropologists should never accept funding from agencies with questionable motives, ethical codes typically are less dogmatic. They stress the need for a clear agreement regarding what information is to be made available to the sponsor. Obviously, the anthropologist should reject funding if agreement cannot be reached. If agreement is reached, the anthropologist has an obligation to provide accurate, though not necessarily complete, reporting.

Intervention vs. Scholarly Neutrality

Under the leadership of Franz Boas, early twentieth century anthropology was committed to preserving information about "traditional" societies before they were transformed by the spread of Western civilization. This led to a nonintervention ethic maintaining that anthropology should dispassionately describe and analyze societies but not try to change them.

The twentieth century, however, showed that these societies were changing in response to Western civilization and would continue to do so. An emerging cadre of applied anthropologists argued that anthropology properly should help direct this change in the manner least damaging to these societies. Not all anthropologists, however, have accepted the tenets of applied anthropology, and critics argue that anthropological understanding is too rudimentary to permit control of cultural change. Further concern derives from the fact that most funding for applied anthropological research comes from governments that may not be particularly concerned about the welfare of the people under study; pressure placed on an anthropologist by such a sponsor can be considerable.

Issues of Relativism and Cultural Conflict

In response to ethnocentrism in early anthropology, Boas and others argued for cultural relativism, the recognition that all cultures are equally valid and worthy of respect. Cultural relativism remains entrenched in anthropology, but twentieth century ethnogenocide and human rights violations have led some anthropologists to reconsider, ar-

guing that cultures advocating these and other unacceptable practices are not compatible with world values and must change.

Another related issue occasionally arises. The ethics of anthropology are culture-bound, closely tied to Western precepts, and they may conflict with the ethics of another society. When living in and studying a society whose ethics are very different, should anthropologists cling to their own culture's ethical standards?

"The Delicate Balance of Good"

The ethical perspectives discussed above are full of contradictions. Obligations to the discipline require that studies be published fully; obligations to the people studied require that sensitive information be withheld. These and other conflicts should be resolved by reference to what Erve Chambers calls "the delicate balance of good." The anthropologist must examine the likely results of actions, assess their impact on all parties concerned, and follow the path that is most likely to lead to the best overall outcome.

—*Russell J. Barber*

Further Reading

Beals, Ralph. *Politics of Social Research.* Chicago: Aldine, 1969.

Cassell, Joan. "Ethical Principles for Conducting Fieldwork." *American Anthropologist* 82 (March, 1980): 28-41.

Fluehr-Lobban, Carolyn, ed. *Ethics and the Profession of Anthropology: Dialogue for Ethically Conscious Practice.* 2d ed. Walnut Creek, Calif.: AltaMira Press, 2003.

MacClancy, Jeremy, ed. *Exotic No More: Anthropology on the Front Lines.* Chicago: University of Chicago Press, 2002.

Murphy, Michael Dean, and Agneta Johannsen. "Ethical Obligations and Federal Regulations in Ethnographic Research and Anthropological Education." *Human Organization* 49 (Summer, 1990): 127-138.

Rynkiewich, Michael, and James Spradley. *Ethics and Anthropology.* New York: John Wiley & Sons, 1976.

See also: Colonialism and imperialism; Custom; Durkheim, Émile; Ethnocentrism; Professional ethics; Relativism; Social Darwinism; Sociobiology; Taboos.

Artificial intelligence

Definition: Electronic processes that simulate human thinking

Date: Earliest developments began around 1945

Type of ethics: Scientific ethics

Significance: Artificial intelligence research is creating increasingly complex, computer-generated processes that are increasingly affecting the lives of humans. Because of this development, human beings must address the ethical behavior of such machines and the possible ethical treatment of future thinking machines.

Secret research in British and U.S. military labs during World War II spawned the age of modern digital computers. The house-sized machines of that era performed vast number of computations at speeds no human could match. Soon, however, researchers sought to build machines that did more than compute numbers. Their goal was to create artificial intelligence (AI), electronic processes that simulate human thought patterns.

During the late 1940's, the English mathematician and computer pioneer Alan Turing was the first scientist to suggest that the key to creating artificial intelligence lay in developing advanced software, not more advanced hardware. From that moment, computer labs around the world began investing increasing resources in software development. As a result, AI software is everywhere. Online shopping, voice recognition systems, robotic probes that

Talos, an ancient mythical automaton with artificial intelligence. By Thomas Bullfinch.

search Mars for sign of life, automated climate-controlled "intelligent" buildings, and "smart" credit cards are all made possible by advances in artificial intelligence. Researchers have also developed "expert systems," or software programs that replicate human decision-making processes to aid corporations in marketing, research, costing, management, and billing operations. AI systems work quickly and consistently, and they eliminate much of the tedium and drudgery of modern work. Coupled with the power of the Internet, they also give human beings astounding personal power in the privacy of their own homes.

Behavior of Artificial Intelligence Machines

Artificial intelligence is, however, also provoking concern. Critics argue that too little research is going into addressing the question of how the machines themselves should behave. Some ethicists argue that AI systems that function automatically and independently of human control pose great dangers. Because AI systems lack the ability to emulate human empathy, compassion, and wisdom, they have no ability to use discretion over when to act. Also troubling to ethicists are AI systems programmed with malicious intent that can release confidential information, steal from bank accounts, and disrupt communication and transportation systems. Virulent computer viruses—a malicious form of artificial intelligence—already create havoc on the Internet worldwide. Artificial intelligence offers such tantalizing prospects in weaponry that by the early twenty-first century military organizations were pouring billions of dollars into creating software designed to disrupt the daily operations of modern nations and cause widespread misery, deprivation, and death.

Many ethical questions arise over the use of modern "smart weapons." By 2004, several nations possessed a host of AI-based missiles, bombs, and electronic monitoring systems, programmed to detect enemy targets and automatically attack them, often without human intervention. Enabling machines, and not humans, to decide whether to inflict death upon human beings strikes many thinkers as morally and ethically repugnant. By distancing humans from the killing, artificial intelligence may also entice them to ignore their moral responsibilities. Moreover, argue critics, when human beings are fighting in a war, they often experience profound abhorrence over killing other human beings and may thus be moved to stop further bloodshed. By contrast, AI weaponry may be programmed to continue killing with cold, mechanical efficiency, without compunctions.

In addition, the absence of human beings from the decision-making of waging war might trigger the loss of innocent lives when a smart weapon errs. Such was the case in July, 1988, when an American warship, the USS *Vincennes*, destroyed an Iranian passenger jet flying over the Persian Gulf and killed 290 civilians. The mishap occurred when the ship's electronic detection system on the *Vincennes* incorrectly profiled the Iranian aircraft as a warplane and alerted its crew to launch a missile attack.

When Artificial Intelligence Becomes Self-Aware

Smart weapons and similar forms of rules-following technologies are often called "soft" artificial intelligence, as they are not truly independent, intelligent agents capable of reason or any form of true human thought. Some researchers, however, believe it is simply a matter of time until researchers produce "hard" artificial intelligence—artificial intelligence that is truly alive, or at least appears to be. Computer entities already exist that imitate biologic systems. They move, reproduce, consume other computer-generated entities, and react to external stimuli. Advanced synthetic thinking systems also exit. Deep Blue—an advanced AI system—now plays chess well enough to defeat a human world-class master. Some researchers also predict that before the middle of the twenty-first century advanced AI systems will be more than high-tech problem solvers. They may also become conscious, or semi-conscious, of their own mental states. If and when that develop occurs, will such machines be entitled to ethical treatment from humans? Will artificial beings deserve civil rights or due process of law? Who should decide such questions? Will AI systems themselves be designed to evaluate ethical questions? Some ethicists suggest that if machines ever do become aware of their own existence, they should be included in the growing rights movement, which bestows rights on animals and other living things that are not conscious, such as plants and ecosystems.

Skeptics, such as philosopher John Searle of the University of California, dismiss such concerns. They argue that there is a marked difference between machines that appear to think and machines that really do create intelligence. Machines may be programmed to respond in human ways, but only actual human beings can reflect intelligently on what they are experiencing. Some critics also suggest that emotion is a necessary ingredient of intelligence—something that artificial intelligence lacks. Moreover, they ask, does artificial intelligence have needs? A psyche?

Nonetheless, some ethicists envision a near future when AI systems will interact with human brains. Some speculate that nanotechnology will make possible electronic replicas of human brains. In such an event, it could be theoretically possible to implant a memory chip with an electronic copy of the mind of a deceased person into the consciousness of a living person and create an after-death existence. Some observers believe that AI systems may one day even surpass human beings in intelligence. In fact, philosopher Nick Bostron at Oxford University believes that super-intelligent machines will be the last invention humans ever need to make.

Ethical Precautions

Although ethicists can only speculate about the future of artificial intelligence, they do offer some practical suggestions. Ethical safeguards, for example, might be programmed in soft AI systems to protect privacy and reduce automated decision making. Hard AI systems, however, would require more complex programs that impart a deep, universal understanding of ethics that benefit both human and machines. Otherwise, as some futurists warn, the possibility of a super-intelligent sociopathic machine may someday be realized. Other ethicists wonder if artificial intelligence should be allowed to evolve its own ethics, as humans have done. Perhaps, they suggest, artificial intelligence could develop ethics superior to those of humans.

Finally, some thinkers wonder if humans ought to be creating life at all, and whether Earth really needs another highly developed intelligence. They also point out that if super-intelligent artificial intelligence ever emerges, it may be so profoundly different from what is predicted that all ethical questions now being asked will become irrelevant.

—John M. Dunn

Further Reading

Bentley, Peter J. *Digital Biology: How Nature Is Transforming Our Technology and Our Lives.* New York: Simon & Schuster, 2001.

Gershenfeld, Neil. *When Things Start to Think.* New York: Henry Holt, 1999.

Grand, Steve. *Creation: Life and How to Make It.* Cambridge, Mass.: Harvard University Press, 2000.

Hogan, James P. *Mind Matters: Exploring the World of Artificial Intelligence.* New York: Ballantine, 1997.

Kurzweil, Ray. *The Age of Spiritual Machines: When Computers Exceed Human Intelligence.* New York: Viking, 1999.

Menzel, Peter, and Faith D'Alvisio. *Robosapiens: Evolution of a New Species.* Cambridge, Mass.: MIT Press, 2000.

Mulhall, Douglas. *Our Molecular Future: How Nanotechnology, Robotics, Genetics, and Artificial Intelligence Will Transform Our World.* Amherst, N.Y.: Prometheus Books. 2002.

See also: Computer misuse; Computer technology; Exploitation; Robotics; Sentience; Technology.

Atom bomb

The Event: Creation of an extremely powerful bomb utilizing the process of nuclear fission

Date: 1939-1945

Type of ethics: Scientific ethics

Significance: Scientists ordinarily prefer to regard themselves as members of an international brotherhood devoted to the expansion of knowledge; however, the race to create an atom bomb during World War II highlighted the fact that scientific knowledge also has direct nationalist and military applications.

Among those caught in the ferment of World War I were members of the international scientific community. Early in the war, scientists in the United States were shocked to find that distinguished Germans such as Wilhelm Roentgen had signed a manifesto justifying the destruction of the famed library at Louvain, Belgium, by German armed forces. Soon, however, the imperatives of the war effort placed greater and more direct demands upon scientists, who generally were eager to use their abilities to advance the causes of their respective nations. Although chemists bore the moral burden most directly, thanks to their essential role in the development of increasingly lethal poison gases, physicists also shared in the war efforts of the various belligerents, making significant contributions to the development of acoustic devices for detecting enemy submarines and of flash-ranging and acoustic apparatuses for ascertaining the location of enemy artillery positions.

Demands of World War II

World War II demanded still more of scientists, and physicists in particular, for several of the war's most far-reaching new technologies demanded their expertise: the proximity fuze, radar, and the atom bomb. "Almost overnight," a scientist at a midwestern state university remarked, "physicists have been promoted from semiobscurity to membership in that select group of rarities which include rubber, sugar and coffee." Colleges and universities readily made their facilities available for various wartime endeavors, weapons research among them. In wartime, ethical distinctions between defensive and offensive weaponry can easily be blurred, for physicists who entered radar work labored over devices ranging from microwave apparatuses used to detect enemy submarines and approaching aircraft to equipment designed to enable Allied bombers to drop their bombs with greater accuracy.

At all stages of the conflict, ethical concerns about the war and its weapons were revealed in the thinking of various groups and individuals, including military personnel. Before the war and early in it, air force officers preferred to think of strategic bombing as so precise that only targets of direct military value such as the submarine pens at Wilhelmshaven, Germany, or the ball-bearing plants at Schweinfurt would be attacked. Precision bombing was much more difficult to accomplish than prewar theorists had argued, however, and area bombing, in which not only the plants but also the surrounding communities were designated as target areas, was increasingly used. It was only a matter of time until the communities themselves became targets. Japan's great distance from Allied bases meant that sustained bombing of Japanese targets could not even be undertaken until well into 1944, by which time American forces had had more than a year of experience in the air war against Germany. Area bombing therefore played an especially large role in the air war against Japan. Would the use of an atom bomb represent something altogether different or would it simply expand the still uncertain boundaries of area bombing?

Almost as soon as the discovery of nuclear fission was revealed in 1939, physicists began to discuss an atom bomb. Such a bomb would be a weapon of enormous destructive potential, and using it would claim the lives of many thousands of individuals. First it had to be asked whether an atom bomb could be developed. American physicists and their émigré colleagues rallied to the war effort, nearly five hundred going to the Radiation Lab at the Massachusetts Institute of Technology and many others entering the Manhattan Project (organized in 1942 to coordinate and push forward ongoing fission research) and its various facilities: Among these were the Metallurgical Lab at Chicago, where a controlled chain reaction was first achieved; Oak Ridge, Tennessee, where weapons-grade uranium was processed; and Los Alamos, New Mexico, where work on the bomb itself—it was innocuously called "the gadget" for security reasons—was undertaken. Even when their own efforts seemed disappointing, Manhattan Project scientists could not know whether their German counterparts, such as Nobel laureate Werner Heisenberg, had achieved an insight that had eluded them and had therefore put the atom bomb into Adolf Hitler's hands.

Preoccupied with the work before them, these scientists rarely took time to reflect upon what they were doing. The surrender of Germany in the spring of 1945 was the occasion when scientists should have paused to ask themselves whether work on the atom bomb should continue. A young physicist at Los Alamos did raise the question of resigning from atom bomb work en masse, only to be told by a senior colleague that if work were suspended it would be easy for another Hitler to pick up where they had left off.

At the Met Lab, where work was nearly done by 1945, scientists did join in issuing the Franck Report, which asked that a demonstration of the new weapon be made on an uninhabited area before any use of it was made against Japan. Some half dozen of the most eminent scientists involved in war work, however—those with access to policymakers in Washington—rejected such a recommendation. A direct use of the atom bomb against a Japanese city would be far more likely to bring the war to a prompt conclusion and to increase the likelihood of maintaining peace afterward, they reasoned. Although many scientists involved in the Manhattan Project did at one time or another speculate upon the ethical questions that the development of an atom bomb posed, their concern that Hitler might secure prior access to this weapon sufficed to keep their efforts focused on developing the atom bomb. Moreover, mastering the physics involved in creating an atom bomb was an immensely challenging and absorbing scientific and technological problem. "For most of them," Michael Sherry has observed, "destruction was something they produced, not something they did," an attitude that helps explain the wagers these scientists made on the magnitude of the explosive yield of the bomb used in the July, 1945, Trinity test.

German Scientists

Ironically, some German physicists might have pondered the ethical dimensions of the atom bomb more keenly than had their Allied counterparts. Unlike the Manhattan Project scientists, the Germans knew that their own research could give Hitler the atom bomb. After the war had ended, scientists were more likely to step back and ask what the atom bomb meant and whether international control of it or further development of nuclear weapons should take precedence.

Among those who went on to develop a far more devastating weapon, the hydrogen bomb, the fear of Joseph Stalin and the Soviet Union provided the ethical justification that the thought of a Nazi atom bomb had provided for their Manhattan Project colleagues. By the same token, however, as historian Daniel Kevles put it, "To maintain their scientific, political, and moral integrity, the Los Alamos generation on the whole declared...that scientists could 'no longer disclaim direct responsibility for the uses to which mankind...put their disinterested discoveries.'"

—*Lloyd J. Graybar*

Further Reading
Batchelder, Robert C. *The Irreversible Decision, 1939-1950.* Boston: Houghton Mifflin, 1961.
Boyer, Paul. *By the Bomb's Early Light: American Thought and Culture at the Dawn of the Atomic Age.* Chapel Hill: University of North Carolina Press, 1994.
Powers, Thomas. *Heisenberg's War.* New York: Knopf, 1993.
Rhodes, Richard. *The Making of the Atom Bomb.* New York: Simon & Schuster, 1986.
Rigden, John S. *Rabi: Scientist and Citizen.* New York: Basic Books, 1987.
Schaffer, Ronald. *Wings of Judgment: American Bombing in World War II.* New York: Oxford University Press, 1985.
Schweber, S. S. *In the Shadow of the Bomb: Bethe, Oppenheimer, and the Moral Responsibility of the Scientist.* Princeton, N.J.: Princeton University Press, 2000.
Serber, Robert. *The Los Alamos Primer: The First Lectures on How to Build an Atomic Bomb.* Berkeley: University of California Press, 1992.
Smith, Alice Kimball. *A Peril and a Hope: The Scientists' Movement in America, 1945-47.* Chicago: University of Chicago Press, 1965.
Van De Mark, Brian. *Pandora's Keepers: Nine Men and the Atomic Bomb.* Boston: Little, Brown, 2003.

See also: Biochemical weapons; Hiroshima and Nagasaki bombings; Manhattan Project; Military ethics; Mutually Assured Destruction; Nazi science; Nuclear arms race; Nuclear energy; Union of Concerned Scientists; Weapons research.

Atomic Energy Commission

Identification: Federal government agency established to provide joint military and civilian supervision of nuclear power

Date: Founded in 1946; superseded 1974-1975

Type of ethics: Scientific ethics

Significance: After World War II, it became clear that nuclear energy called for special regulation, and the Atomic Energy Commission (AEC) was created to provide it.

When World War II was ended by the atom bombs that were dropped on Hiroshima and Nagasaki, nearly all that the general public knew about nuclear energy was that it could be devastatingly destructive. The many medical and industrial uses of the atom lay mostly in the future, and only its horrific power was known. Furthermore, advocates of military applications of nuclear energy insisted on continuing development and testing of atomic weapons.

In this atmosphere, the Atomic Energy Act of 1946 was signed into law. It provided for the formation of a presidentially appointed commission, with separate military and civilian committees under it. The AEC devoted much attention to military weaponry in its early years, but the Atomic Energy Act of 1954 provided for civilian industrial participation in the research and manufacture of atomic materials and in the construction of atomic power installations, licensed by the AEC.

In 1974, the AEC was disbanded, and in 1975 two new organizations took up changed functions: the Nuclear Regulatory Commission, charged with the investigation and licensing of all uses of atomic energy—medical, industrial, and power, as well as the health aspects connected with these uses; and the Energy Research and Development Administration, which later became the Department of Energy, with the narrower function implied by its name. The weapons applications have been less prominent since then.

—Robert M. Hawthorne, Jr.

See also: Hiroshima and Nagasaki bombings; Nuclear energy; Nuclear Regulatory Commission; Union of Concerned Scientists; Weapons research.

Biodiversity

Definition: Genetic diversity of all forms of life on Earth, measured in terms of both numbers of species and genetic variability within species

Type of ethics: Environmental ethics

Significance: An ethical mandate for the preservation of biodiversity can be derived either from the potential usefulness of the organisms to human beings or from the viewpoint that humans are stewards of the earth's resources and have no moral right to destroy a unique biological species.

The importance of conserving biodiversity is an idea that attracted increasing international attention during the 1980's; previously, conservationists had concentrated their efforts on preservation of conspicuous and economically important organisms. The 1992 United Nations Conference on Environment and Development ("Earth Summit") arrived at a convention on biodiversity with protocols for protecting endangered species and international cooperation on biotechnology. Species are undoubtedly becoming extinct at a rapid rate because of pollution, habitat destruction, deforestation, overexploitation, and other human activities. The approximately seven hundred extinctions that have been recorded in the last three hundred years are only a small fraction of the total, which is estimated by some scientists to be approaching fifty thousand species per year. Much of the world's genetic biodiversity is concentrated in inconspicuous insects, fungi, aquatic invertebrates, and herbaceous plants that have never been fully described.

Efforts to conserve biodiversity involve balancing known present needs with projected future needs and balancing the conflicting demands of local, national, and international agencies. Frequently, corporate and national policy have favored overexploitation. The well-being of the indigenous population of an area is an important consideration. Resource management by stable traditional societies, which is more sophisticated than is commonly realized, favors biodiversity, but global upheaval and the population explosion have destroyed the delicate balance between society and the biosphere in much of the developed and developing world.

The rise of genetic engineering has served to highlight the economic value of biodiversity and raise the question of ownership. Historically, species have been regarded as common property, but advocates for the rights of indigenous peoples have suggested that something akin to patent rights should belong to the group of people on whose territory an economically important organism is discovered.

—Martha Sherwood-Pike

See also: Conservation; Deforestation; Dominion over nature, human; Earth and humanity; Ecology; Endangered species; Environmental ethics.

Clean Air Act

Identification: Federal law that directs the states to take action to control and prevent air pollution, on the premise that air pollution is essentially a state or local problem

Date: Enacted in 1963

Type of ethics: Environmental ethics

Significance: The Clean Air Act acknowledged that air pollution was a problem of the commons rather than an individual problem, requiring action by the community to protect the health of the public.

The federal Clean Air Act of 1963 superceded the Air Pollution Act of 1955, which had authorized studies of air pollution and recognized air pollution as an emerging national problem. The 1963 Act was passed as a result of a report by the U.S. surgeon general that found that motor vehicle exhaust can be dangerous to human health. The 1963 Act, however, did not permit action by the federal government; instead, grants were made available to state and local governments to undertake initiatives to control pollution in their areas.

The act was amended in 1970 and again in 1977, both times to set or change national standards for air quality in response to state and local government inaction. In 1990, significant changes were made to the 1963 Act to deal with remaining lower atmosphere pollution and, particularly, to act against upper atmosphere problems such as acid rain and the thinning of the ozone layer, which could damage forests, animal life, and the ability of humans to live a healthy life.

—Sandra L. Christensen

See also: Biodiversity; Clean Water Act; Ecology; Environmental ethics; Environmental Protection Agency; Global warming; Greenhouse effect; Pollution; Pollution permits.

Clean Water Act

Identification: Federal law enabling broad federal and state campaigns to prevent, reduce, and eliminate water pollution

Date: Enacted in 1972

Type of ethics: Environmental ethics

Significance: The Clean Water Act recognized the nation's waters as a part of the commons, of benefit to all. With its passage, the federal government accepted the responsibility for ensuring the safety of those waters for human health, and for maintaining the biological diversity of the waters.

The Federal Water Pollution Control Act (FWPCA) of 1972 (known as the Clean Water Act) was an amendment to the FWPCA of 1956. It continued a line of federal legislation of water pollution that began with the Rivers and Harbors Act of 1899, which required a permit to discharge pollutants. In the FWPCA of 1972, responsibility was generally left to the states to control pollution, with the federal government providing grants for local construction of sewage treatment plants.

Other acts, such as the Water Pollution Control Act of 1956 and the Clean Water Restoration Act of 1966, set federal standards for water quality and imposed fines on source point polluters. The goals of the Clean Water Act were to achieve waters clean enough for recreation use by 1983 where such uses had been discontinued because of pollution, and, by 1985, to have no discharge of pollutants into the nation's waters. The act established a National Pollutant Discharge Elimination System that required permits for all source points of pollution, focusing attention on specific polluters rather than on specific bodies of water. The Clean Water Act criminalizes the act of pollution by imposing fines and prison terms for persons found guilty of polluting the waters.

—Sandra L. Christensen

See also: Biodiversity; Clean Air Act; Ecology; Environmental ethics; Environmental Protection Agency; Pollution; Pollution permits.

Computer crime

Definition: Direct or indirect use of computer technology to break the law

Type of ethics: Scientific ethics

Significance: Computer technology has provided both new tools and new targets of opportunity for criminals, spies, and vandals.

Computer crimes typically involve breaches of well-defined ethical issues, but one aspect of the nature of computers raises the possibility of new interpretations of these issues. This is true because computers represent and exchange information in the form of digital electronic signals rather than as tangible objects. This distinction raises the question of whether copying programs or information from computers is really theft if the original programs and data remain in place after the illegal copies are made. Also, are people really trespassing if they remain thousands of miles away from the computer system on which they intrude?

Motives

The psychological motives of persons and groups who engage in computer abuse fall into three categories. The first set of motives include personal gain of money, goods, services, or valuable information. The second is revenge against another person, company, institution, government, or society at large. A variation on the motive of revenge is political motivation. The third type of motivation is to gain stature in one's own mind or those of one's peers by demonstrating mastery over complex technology.

These motivations serve as the bases for several types of activity, which include theft, fraud, espionage, vandalism, malicious mischief, and trespassing.

Theft and Fraud

Theft in computer crime takes many forms. Embezzlement is one of the most publicized. One type of scheme involves the transfer of small amounts of money from bank accounts over a period of time into accounts established by the thieves. One of the most notorious forms of computer crime in the early years of the twenty-first century was the so-called "Nigerian scam," through which con artists in developing countries had bilked citizens of wealthy countries out of millions of dollars. Thieves use e-mail to canvas millions of prospects at minimal cost. Offers of low-priced merchandise that buyers never receive, fraudulent investment opportunities, and false charitable solicitations, abound. Computers make unauthorized use of credit cards particularly easy. Criminals need only the card numbers, expiration dates, and names of the cardholders to order merchandise over the Internet. Such information is often available on discarded credit card receipts or may be procured from the victims through trickery.

Another common and well-known form of theft is software piracy, which is the unauthorized copying of proprietary programs. The scope of piracy is broad. Well-organized groups mass-produce "bootleg copies" of popular personal computer programs. These are then sold to unsuspecting people as legitimate copies. At the other end of the piracy spectrum are isolated individuals who make copies of computer games for friends without even realizing that they are breaking any law.

Sometimes computers themselves are the targets of theft, either for their intrinsic value or for information they may contain. One celebrated case involved the theft of a staff officer's portable computer from his car in the Middle East late in 1990. The computer contained strategic plans for the impending U.S. Operation Desert Storm. The thief was evidently unaware of the computer's sensitive contents, however, and the act did not result in a serious breach of security.

Vandalism and Malicious Mischief

Computer systems are often the targets of vandalism, either by disgruntled individuals or by organized groups. Some of the most serious cases of vandalism against computers were committed in France and Italy by the radical Red Brigades during the late 1970's. One of their attacks resulted in the loss of all computer records of automobiles and drivers' licenses in Italy.

Commercial sites on the World Wide Web have been vandalized and their contents altered. In August, 2000, for example, a British supermarket site was defaced with a hoax message announcing price increases and urging viewers to shop elsewhere. Perpetrators of malicious mischief on computer systems have come to be known as "hackers." Hackers are motivated by a desire to demonstrate mastery over computer technology, especially among their peers. One of their methods is to write programs that, when executed, cause damage to other programs and data files or even cause other computers to crash. These programs vary widely in their nature and are variously known as Trojan horses, worms, and viruses. Worms and viruses are usually programmed to replicate themselves on every computer system with which they come into contact. One of the most notorious was the Internet Worm, the work of a young computer scientist who placed it on the world's largest computer network in 1988. Within a matter of hours it spread to thousands of computer installations, including those of the U.S. Defense Department and many universities, causing tens of millions of dollars in damage.

Later attempts have been even more disruptive. The Melissa virus in 1999 multiplied by e-mailing copies of itself to all names in recipients' Internet address books, thus reaching computers throughout the world at an astonishing speed. In the United States the Melissa virus disabled more than one million computers and caused damaged that cost hundreds of millions of dollars to correct. The Love Bug worm of May, 2000, shut down e-mail servers in a majority of American corporations, reportedly doing several billion dollars worth of damage.

In February 2000, a "Denial of Service" attack launched by a fifteen-year old Canadian high school student identified only as "Mafiaboy," rendered Web sites of major American corporations inoperable. Using automated tools and scripts easily available on the Internet, Mafiaboy planted Trojan horses within many innocent computers, using them to send a flood of simultaneous messages that overwhelmed service at such computer-savvy online companies as Amazon.com, eBay, CNN News, and Yahoo!.

Trespassing

In the context of computer crime, trespassing is unauthorized access to a computer system. The most common form of trespassing is committed by hackers, who often have no intention of causing damage to the systems they break into but are lured by the challenge of overcoming another system's security measures. Once inside a system, they are often content to view its contents and exit without damaging anything. Some hackers, however, have been prosecuted for such acts as breaking into telephone company installations and circulating private access codes.

Spyware programs, which track the buying habits of computer users, are often installed on the computers of user who are downloading free music and game programs. Criminals try to sneak in less benign spyware as e-mail attachments that permit them to control other people's computer from a distance. The intruders can then read files and discover passwords, and Social Security and other account numbers. The acquisition of such information makes theft of the computer owners' identities easy.

Another form of trespassing is committed by persons engaging in espionage. Companies engage in industrial espionage by breaking into rival companies' systems to look for trade secrets and other proprietary information. A rarer variation of espionage occurs when agents of one country break into the computer systems of another government. This occurred during the late 1980's, when West German hackers were discovered using the Internet to access classified information from the U.S. Defense Department.

Online Harassment and Prevention

Internet stalking may appear less threatening than physical harassment, but the emotional impact, and sometimes the tangible results, can be equally damaging. Stalking can include sending continual abusive, obscene, or threatening e-mail messages; placing victims' names on mailing lists so they will receive hundreds of unwanted messages every day; or impersonating the targets and sending fraudulent or abusive mail in their names. In one case a stalker posted a message purporting to come from a woman having unfulfilled fantasies of being raped, including her name, address, and telephone number. Her phone rang endlessly and six men came to her apartment.

Computer crime has become so widespread that most Western industrialized countries have enacted laws against it. In the United States, much of this legislation has been enacted at the state level. Most U.S. states had computer crime laws on their books by the late 1970's or early 1980's. Federal statutes on computer crime are printed in Title 18 of the United States Code, especially sections 1029 and 1030.

The rapidly developing countries of eastern Asia have lagged behind in efforts to police computer crime, and in many of those countries software piracy has become a flourishing business.

Attention to security by programmers, systems managers, corporate management, and government agencies is the single most effective method of computer crime prevention. Many recorded cases of computer crime have been committed by previously honest individuals who spotted opportunities created by lax security methods and succumbed to temptation.

The trend of replacing large mainframe computer systems with networks of personal computers raises further problems, because networks and personal computer operating systems do not have security features as effective as those designed for large systems. Personal computers are also the most vulnerable to attacks by viruses. Virus detection and "disinfection" programs are available from a variety of vendors, sometimes on a free trial basis. Firewalls have also become vital equipment for Internet users having broadband connections, either through cable or via telephone company dedicated subscriber lines (DSL). Because these connections are always open, they present tempting targets for criminals who continually test them to see if they can enter and take control of other computers.

It is generally recognized that if the ethics of computer use were routinely incorporated into computer science and vocational training, people would have a better understanding of responsible behavior. They should know it is wrong to duplicate copyrighted programs and that it is wrong to access other computer systems without proper authorization.

—Charles E. Sutphen; Updated by Milton Berman

Further Reading

Betts, Mitch. "What About Ethics?" *Computerworld* 27 (June 7, 1993): 84.

Furnell, Steven. *Cybercrime: Vandalizing the Information Society.* Boston: Addison-Wesley, 2002.

Harley, David, Robert Slade, and Urs Gattiker. *Viruses Revealed.* Berkeley, Calif.: Osborne/McGraw-Hill, 2001.

Hunter, Richard. *World Without Secrets: Business, Crime, and Privacy in the Age of Ubiquitous Computing.* New York: J. Wiley, 2002.

Jewkes, Yvonne, ed. *Dot.cons: Crime, Deviance, and Identity on the Internet.* Cullompton, Devon, England: Willan, 2002.

Kizza, Joseph Migga. *Computer Network Security and Cyber Ethics.* Jefferson, N.C.: McFarland, 2002.

Parker, Donn B. *Fighting Computer Crime: A New Framework for Protecting Information.* New York: J. Wiley, 1998.

See also: Computer databases; Computer misuse; Computer technology; Fraud; Identity theft; Internet piracy; Napster.

Computer databases

Definition: Collections of information electronically stored on computers and organized in systematic ways designed to facilitate information retrieval

Type of ethics: Legal and judicial ethics

Significance: Rapid advances in computer technology have made it necessary for courts to set forth legal standards governing the use of the information contained in databases. In addition to the legal principles governing database information, general ethical imperatives also govern the use of this data.

In a modern computerized and technologically oriented society, information and the ability to rapidly and accurately retrieve data are of paramount importance. Names, addresses, medical and credit card information are among the kinds of sensitive data being stored for retrieval in computer databases. As technology progresses, the sophistication, size, and relative invisibility of information-gathering activities increases.

Among the general ethical principles that govern computer databases are the needs to respect the privacy rights and confidentiality of individual persons and groups. Ownership rights in data must be respected by the users of information contained in databases, regardless of whether the data are protected by copyright, patent, trade secret or other intellectual property law provisions. Another ethical principle, avoiding harm to others, is also important in this connection.

Privacy and Confidentiality

Many types of data in computer databases are inherently sensitive in nature. In order to obtain many goods and services, such as credit cards, mortgages, insurance, and even medical attention, much personal information must be provided. Compilers of such information are responsible for ensuring that its accuracy and privacy are maintained. When databases are integrated, information from various sources may become available to unintended recipients. When that happens, the unintended recipients of the data should be mindful of their ethical obligation to safeguard the privacy rights of others.

Related to the issue of privacy is the question of maintaining confidentiality of information contained in a database. When information provided to a database is subject to promises to safeguard it from disclosure, it is the ethical obligation of the database maintainers to protect that information. From time to time, individuals or organizations, including the government, may demand access to the information contained in databases. The moral right to access to database information should certainly presuppose a need to know on the part of the requestor. If requests for information are granted, the recipients should be subject to responsibilities similar to those of the database maintainers.

Avoiding Harm

Enormous amounts of information are contained in databases, and those amounts were increasing exponentially at the beginning of the twenty-first century. Since information can become obsolete quickly, constant updating and revising are essential. In the rush to update and revise data, errors are inevitable.

Database maintainers should be required to ensure that the information contained in their databases is as error-free as possible. In the event that erroneous data find their way into databases, and innocent persons suffer harm as a result, the injured parties should have recourse to remedies.

—Gloria A. Whittico

Further Reading

Mackall, Joseph. *Information Management.* Chicago: Ferguson, 1998.

Mason, Richard O. "Four Ethical Issues of the Information Age." *Management Information Systems Quarterly* 10, no. 1 (March, 1986).

Wessells, Michael G. "The Challenge to Privacy." In *Computer, Self, and Society.* Englewood Cliffs, N.J.: Prentice Hall, 1990.

See also: Computer crime; Computer misuse; Computer technology; Electronic mail; Electronic surveillance; Espionage; Identity theft; Information access; Inside information; Privacy.

Computer technology

Definition: Electronic devices for storing, manipulating, and retrieving data.

Type of ethics: Scientific ethics

Significance: The advent of the Information Age and the proliferation of computers creates a wide range of ethical issues, from the personal conduct of individuals using computers to public policy questions involving the equitable distribution of technological resources.

Many computer professionals face ethical dilemmas in their work. These dilemmas relate to protecting people's privacy by guarding against unauthorized access to confidential data and preventing the misuse of personal data. Computer professionals are obligated to design and program systems that ensure the accuracy of data, since critical decisions are made based on the output of their systems. Inaccurate information can have grave economic consequences and in some situations can even place people's lives in danger.

Computer professionals have opportunities to enrich people's lives. Conversely, through the improper application of their knowledge and talents, they can have devastating effects on large segments of society. This reality makes clear the necessity of an ethics for computer technology.

Background

Traditionally, computers and their use were looked upon as value-neutral. By the late 1960's, however, some ethicists and computer professionals were questioning this assumption. By the late 1980's, computer ethics was being recognized as a legitimate academic pursuit and a professional necessity. As a field between science and moral studies, computer ethics has attempted to define the values inherent in computer technology. Pioneers in this field include Walter Maner, Donn Parker, Deborah G. Johnson, James H. Moor, and Terrell Ward Bynum.

Privacy Issues and Surveillance

Computers are used to store massive amounts of information, much of which is personal and the subjects of which are deserving of protection against misuse of these data. Computer networking over various communication facilities, including ordinary telephone lines, allows electronic access to this confidential information. This environment requires a heightened awareness of the potential for political abuses of personal liberties and commercial exploitation through insensitive misuse and inappropriate manipulation of personal information.

Computers can and are used to monitor activities in the workplace. They track work done on computer terminals, monitor phone calls, and browse electronic mail without the individual's knowledge of this activity. While some of these activities may be historically grounded in efficient business management practices (Fred Taylor introduced time and motion studies at the beginning of the twentieth century), the intensity of monitoring activities with computers raises ethical issues. Awareness of monitoring produces stress and contributes to health problems; employees who know that they are monitored feel that they are in an electronic straitjacket.

The invasion of privacy threat posed by computer monitoring is real. Improperly applied, monitoring is nothing short of eavesdropping on individuals' private lives. Employers may argue that every act by an employee while "on the clock" is their concern. This ethical dilemma needs to be evaluated on the basis of principles of fairness and quality of life in the workplace.

Poor System Design and Assigning Responsibility

One of the greatest obstacles to the ethical uses of computers is caused by incompetent system designers, however well intentioned, who develop and program systems that do not accomplish the required tasks, create frustration and aggravation for the users of the systems, and even generate erroneous information. In terms of their cumulative cost to organizations, individuals, and society, poorly designed systems that fail to utilize properly the power of the technology create the greatest and most persistent ethical quandaries. Error-prone, inflexible, unimaginative, and insensitive systems are an ethical issue because of the toll they take on human well-being.

Computers themselves do not have values: They do not make independent decisions, they do not make mistakes, and they can do only what they are programmed to do. The utilization of computer technology, however, is not a value-neutral activity. Faulty programs, invalid data, or lack of proper controls creates computer errors. It is unethical for computer professionals and users to attempt to transfer blame for errors away from themselves. This constitutes denying responsibility and lying. Also key to this issue is that ethical norms must be applied to situations in which the computer is essentially involved, not passively involved; that is, where computer technology is used, or misused, in the actual perpetration of moral wrongdoing. For example, using a computer to gain unauthorized access to company secrets essentially involves the computer; stealing computer equipment, wrong though it may be, only passively involves the computer.

Using computers to do dull, repetitive, noncreative tasks is useful. Using them to replace workers simply for the purpose of reducing payrolls raises serious ethical questions of fairness and obligation. Computer technology ought to be applied in the workplace in ways that allow time for and actually encourage the pursuit of more creative activities.

Intellectual Property

Computer technology focuses attention on the whole issue of intellectual property because computer software is often viewed as such. Some people argue that programmers who write software create in much the same way that an author or an artist creates. Others argue that programming is simply stringing together series of instructions and algorithms that are in the public domain. Therefore, programming is not truly creative, and the end product is not someone's intellectual property.

For those who subscribe to the argument that software is intellectual property, the question of ownership must be answered. Does the programmer, as creator, own the software? Does her employer, who is paying her to create the software, own it? Should those who work to develop software or pay others to develop it expect to be reimbursed by those who use it? Still others argue that all software is in the public domain, since it is nothing more than ideas and thoughts, actualized on a computer, and therefore is not intellectual property at all. Proponents of this latter view oppose exclusive "ownership" of any software. If the ownership of software can be established, however, then unauthorized use of the software raises serious ethical questions.

—Edwin R. Davis

Further Reading

Edgar, Stacey L. *Morality and Machines: Perspectives on Computer Ethics.* 2d ed. Sudbury, Mass.: Jones and Bartlett, 2003.

Forester, Tom, and Perry Morrison. *Computer Ethics.* 2d ed. Cambridge, Mass.: MIT Press, 1994.

Hunter, Richard. *World Without Secrets: Business, Crime, and Privacy in the Age of Ubiquitous Computing.* New York: J. Wiley, 2002.

Johnson, Deborah G. *Computer Ethics.* 3d ed. Upper Saddle River, N.J.: Prentice Hall, 2001.

Kling, Rob, ed. *Computerization and Controversy: Value Conflicts and Social Choices.* San Diego, Calif.: Academic Press, 1996.

Langford, Duncan. *Internet Ethics.* New York: St. Martin's Press, 2000.

Mossberger, Karen, Caroline J. Tolbert, and Mary Stansbury, eds. *Virtual Inequality: Beyond the Digital Divide.* Washington, D.C.: Georgetown University Press, 2003.

Parker, Donn B., Susan Swope, and Bruce N. Baker. *Ethical Conflicts in Information and Computer Science, Technology, and Business.* Wellesley, Mass.: QED Information Sciences, 1990.

Spinello, Richard A. *CyberEthics: Morality and Law in Cyberspace.* 2d ed. Boston: Jones and Bartlett, 2003.

See also: Artificial intelligence; Computer crime; Computer databases; Computer misuse; Internet piracy; Robotics; Technology; Virtual reality.

Conservation

Definition: Prudent use of natural resources

Type of ethics: Environmental ethics

Significance: As increasing amounts of the earth's resources are used up, conservation for many people ceases to be merely a prudent course of action and acquires the status of an ethical imperative. At the same time, the involuntary imposition of strategies of conservation upon individuals, corporations, or governments may be seen as an ethical violation of their rights or freedoms.

The conservation ethic has its American roots in colonial times with the imposition of game limits at Newport, Rhode Island, in 1639, the limitation of timbering in Pennsylvania in 1681, and many other similar regulations that were intended to protect resources for the future. Later, authors such as Henry David Thoreau and Ralph Waldo Emerson emphasized the ethical interrelationship of humankind and nature.

At the beginning of the twentieth century, Theodore Roosevelt and Gifford Pinchot wrote extensively on the conservation ethic; they are widely considered as the founders of modern conservationism. Their programs,

Much attention has been given to preserving the natural characteristics of Hopetoun Falls, Australia, while allowing access for visitors. By David Iliff.

such as the Reclamation Act of 1902, the Inland Waterways Commission of 1907, and the massive expansion of National Forest lands, reflect their emphasis on wise use of resources. They also were concerned with the preservation of natural and cultural assets, as in passage of the Antiquities Act of 1906. Harold Ickes, Henry Wallace, and their associates continued the advocacy of the wise consumption ethic during the 1930's, emphasizing land planning and soil management. Again, wise use was the principal concern. Preservation of unique natural entities, however, continued to be part of the mainstream conservation ethic. Preservationism as a part of conservation, however, has been more heavily promoted since World War II, leading to the vigorous reevaluation of many conservation-for-use programs.

—Ralph L. Langenheim, Jr.

See also: Deforestation; Ecology; Environmental ethics; Leopold, Aldo; Muir, John; National Park System, U.S.; Sierra Club; Sustainability of resources; Thoreau, Henry David.

Deep ecology

Definition: Branch of environmental ethics asserting that all creatures and ecosystems have inherent rights that exist independently of the needs and judgments of humans

Date: Concept formulated in 1949; term coined in 1972

Type of ethics: Environmental ethics

Significance: As the world's human population expands and exerts greater demand on the planet's resources, deep ecology provides an ethical guide to how humans may coexist with other life-forms. Critics see deep ecology as a misguided attempt to thwart the satisfaction of important human needs.

Although the world of nature has long commanded the attention of philosophers, it was not until the late twentieth century that they began exploring whether humans had ethical duties to the natural world. Like so many others, modern ethicists were shocked and dismayed by the persistent destruction of natural habitat, the extinction of wildlife, the pollution of air and water, and the depletion of natural resources. The causes of these destructive forces were an ever-expanding industrialism and a growing human population. In fact, many thinkers predicted an ecological catastrophe was fast approaching. Out of this anguish came several "ecophilosophies" that came to frame an ongoing debate about environmental ethics. Among the most prominent and controversial of them is deep ecology.

Basics of a New Environmental Ethic

More of an intellectual movement than a specific philosophy, deep ecology is nonetheless based on a few core principles. Among them is a rejection of the "human-centered" view of nature that assumes human beings alone have ethical value and are superior to other life-forms. Deep ecology also spurns the Judeo-Christian assertion that the Bible gives human beings a divine right to hold dominion over nature. To deep ecologists these beliefs form the foundation for many of the attitudes in the West that are morally indefensible because they breed arrogance and indifference to the natural world and lead to the destruction and despoliation of living things.

Deep ecologists also argue that any opposition to environmental destruction merely because it is detrimental to human beings is morally shallow. Instead, they advocate a deeper ethic—one that holds that all living creatures and biological systems also have a right to exist. Moreover, this intrinsic value does not depend on how much pleasure or usefulness it provides human beings. Every life-form is unique and exists as an end onto itself. Deep ecology holds that it is morally wrong to assume that nature exists primarily to serve as raw material for human exploitation, consumption, and overproduction. No one, deep ecologists argue, has the moral right to jeopardize the richness and variety of life on Earth, unless to meet basic survival needs.

Origins of Deep Ecology

A Sand County Almanac (1949), a book by American forester and professor Aldo Leopold, heralded the deep ecology movement with his "land ethic." According to Leopold, humans have a moral duty to preserve the biological integrity of living things and ecosystems. Humans, says Leopold, share a biotic community, or ecosystem, with other living creatures.

Drawing upon the thinking of Ezekiel and Isaiah in the Old Testament of the Bible that says despoliation of nature is wrong, Leopold concludes that humans must not act as conquerors of nature. Instead, they should respect fellow living things and biotic communities and work to preserve them.

Other thinkers found common ground with Leopold. One of them was Norwegian philosopher Arne Naess, who coined the expression "deep ecology" in 1972. According to Naess, an appreciation for deep ecology develops when human beings undergo a transformation of consciousness that creates within them new "ecological selves" that provide deeper and clearer perspectives of interconnected relationships among all living things, including human beings. This consciousness, it is suggested, spawns an ethical conscience concerning the natural world.

For many deep ecologists, this realization often accompanies a transcendental experience in nature. Others seek enlightenment in various religious and philosophies found in Asia, such as Buddhism and Daoism, and among the cultures of certain indigenous peoples in North America and in some nonindustrialized countries. However, some deep ecology philosophers also believe it is possible to re-interpret Judeo-Christian scripture and discover a case for revering nature, rather than exploiting it.

Ethics by Which to Live

Deep ecology offers more than a critique of Western culture; it also offers ethical principles by which people may live. Among these principles is a call to oppose immoral acts of destruction against nature.

Deep ecology also admonishes human beings to turn away from materialism and consumerism, and instead use alternative "soft" energy sources, such as those produced by solar and wind power. Such actions are ethical, suggest deep ecologists, because they help reduce human demands on nature. Deep ecology also instructs humans to live by personal codes of conduct that are more spiritual and natural than those generally demonstrated in industrialized society. Finally, it demands that elected leaders discard economic systems that measure the quality of human life solely in terms of production and consumption. In its place should come new economic systems that consider preservation of the natural world as their highest priority.

Critics of Deep Ecology

Despite its growing influence, deep ecology faces an array of critics. For example, some environmentalists point out that concentrating on the preservation of the integrity of ecosystems at all costs is misguided. They argue that ethical concern should focus on dynamics in nature, not ecosystems. For example, these critics point out that the violent destruction of an ecosystem, as by a hurricane or a forest fire, is part of a larger interplay of natural forces that relentlessly restructures ecosystems and is often essential to the survival of some species. Others argue that human intervention is often morally good, because it can, at times, preserve and conserve nature using methods that exceed the restorative power of nature. Some opponents also claim that deep ecology itself is ethically flawed because it is "antihuman." Moreover, they argue that a "human-centered" approach to nature is ethical because it meets the needs of human beings. Ecofeminists, on the other hand, insist that not all humans are responsible for the current environment crisis—that only those with power and money are—elite, white men.

In response, many advocates of deep ecology steadfastly insist that humans have no inalienable right willfully to destroy the natural world for their own selfish interests. Deep ecologists also deny their ideas are antihuman. Rather, they say, they are rooted in an ethical creed that commands humans to treasure all living things—including members of their own species. They suggest that if all humanity lived by deep ecology ethics, the natural world, including human beings, might be spared from annihilation.

—John M. Dunn

Further Reading

Barnhill, David Landis, and Roger S. Gottlieb, eds. *Deep Ecology and World Religions: New Essays on Sacred Ground.* Albany: State University of New York Press, 2001.

Devall, Bill, and George Sessions. *Deep Ecology.* Salt Lake City: Peregrine Smith Books, 1985.

Katz, Eric, Andrew Light, and David Rothenberg, eds. *Beneath the Surface, Critical Essays in the Philosophy of Deep Ecology.* Cambridge, Mass.: MIT Press, 2000.

Leopold, Aldo. *A Sand County Almanac: With Essays on Conservation from Round River.* New York: Ballantine Books, 1970.

Rolston, Homes, III. *Environmental Ethics: Duties to and Values in the Natural World.* Philadelphia: Temple University Press, 1988.

See also: Biodiversity; Conservation; Deforestation; Earth and humanity; Ecofeminism; Ecology; Endangered species; Environmental ethics; Environmental movement; Nature, rights of; Rain forests.

Deforestation

Definition: Destruction of forest cover and forest ecosystems by agriculture, urbanization, and the direct exploitation of timber, ores, and other forest resources in ways that prevent forests from being restored

Type of ethics: Environmental ethics

Significance: Forests are important to human society for food, energy supplies, building materials, natural medicines, and recreation and as spiritual sites. They are also important to global ecology for atmospheric cleansing, climate control, soil and water conservation, and biodiversity. Deforestation thus threatens the future of human society and the sustainability of the global ecology.

Ethical issues posed by deforestation transcend cultures, human generations, geographic locations, and species. Throughout history, advancing human societies both increased forest resource exploitation and increased efforts to sculpture forests to meet human ideals of beauty and utility. Hunter-gatherers, slash-and-burn farmers, timber-frame builders, charcoal manufacturers, pulp and plywood producers, and royal and wealthy estate owners all have used forests in their own ways and limited use by others. Many forests are eventually destroyed by overuse. The modern developed world's demand for timber and pulp is especially devastating. By the early twenty-first century, European forests were virtually extinct, and tropical forests had been reduced by one-half from their pre-exploitation states.

Deforestation creates social inequalities. The modern developed society's demand for timber and pulpwood in manufacturing limits the availability of wood for homes and fuel in the developing world and the availability of forests for subsistence and indigenous societies. Excessive exploitation by a single human generation of forest resources that required many centuries to grow leaves future human generations poorer. While the sale of forest resources is often necessary to raise capital in the developing world, such sales leave developing nations poorer in resources.

Deforestation in one location also creates social problems in adjacent and distant regions by damaging shared soil, surface water, and biodiversity resources; allowing desertification to destroy agricultural and grazing lands; altering rainfall patterns and agricultural production; impacting economically important migratory species; and allowing greenhouse gasses and other pollutants to accumulate. Deforestation by humans thus has global and ecological significance for all species and for the survival of the earth itself.

Well-intentioned efforts at forest management, conservation and husbandry, as alternatives to deforestation, often promote species extinction or species dominance and increase threats of natural disasters such as floods, fires, and insect infestations. The results may negatively affect innumerable unmanaged forest resources and place management demands and resource-use limits on future generations. While outright deforestation is prevented, the forests themselves may be left in degraded states with questionable future viability.

—*Gordon Neal Diem*

Further Reading

Des Jardins, Joseph R. *Environmental Ethics: An Invitation to Environmental Philosophy*. Belmont, Calif.: Wadsworth, 2001.
Eisenberg, Evan. *The Ecology of Eden*. New York: Alfred A. Knopf, 1998.
Orr, David W. *Earth in Mind*. Washington, D.C.: Island Press, 1994.
Sandler, Todd. *Global Challenges: An Approach to Environmental, Political and Economic Problems*. New York: Cambridge University Press, 1997.

See also: Biodiversity; Bioethics; Deep ecology; Ecofeminism; Ecology; Environmental ethics; Land mines; Rain forests; Sustainability of resources.

Dominion over nature, human

Definition: Idea that humanity has the right to use nature to further its own ends
Type of ethics: Environmental ethics
Significance: Some ethical systems hold that nature has been given to humanity to dispose of as it sees fit, while others claim that humans have an obligation to the natural world. Moreover, human dominion over nature has increased to such an extent that humanity may place its own future existence and happiness in jeopardy, which raises practical ethical concerns regardless of one's theoretical value system.

Human beings have always exploited natural resources for their own well-being. Early in human history, people learned how to domesticate plants and animals—to collect or capture them, to breed them selectively, and to harvest them for human use. People also learned how to "capture," "tame," and "harvest" many inanimate resources, such as fire, water, minerals, and fossil fuels.

In most societies, it was either assumed or explicitly taught that human dominion over nature was a natural, or even God-given, right, and as long as human populations were small, this philosophy posed no major problems. As the human population increased and technology made it increasingly easy to harvest natural resources, however, many natural resources began to disappear. Many people are now questioning the idea of the human right of dominion over nature, on both practical and ethical grounds.

—*Linda Mealey*

See also: Animal rights; Biodiversity; Conservation; Deep ecology; Earth and humanity; Ecology; Endangered species; Environmental ethics; Exploitation; Future generations.

Earth and humanity

Definition: Human beings' attitudes and behavior toward Earth and its ecosystems
Type of ethics: Environmental ethics
Significance: The relationship of humankind to the earth has ethical significance within the context of many religious traditions, including Native American religions which require respect of the land and the Judeo-Christian belief that nature is the dominion of humanity. In more recent times, the need to preserve dwindling resources and the plight of endangered species have created new ethical dilemmas.

Human beings have a combination of qualities that are unique among other forms of life on Earth: the capacity for symbolic thought and communication, hands with opposable thumbs, and a predilection to accumulate goods. Their impact on Earth's ecosystems has been significant and distinctive.

History

Earth's origin is dated at 4.5 billion years ago. Humankind's earliest humanoid ancestors appeared approximately five million years ago. The span of human existence, then, has been limited to a mere one-tenth of one percent of the earth's existence. Human evolution has not been strictly linear. There were both extinctions and overlappings among the variety of human species that existed between *Australopithecus*, the earliest-known human ancestor, and the modern species, *Homo sapiens*. The most anatomically modern human appeared 100,000 years ago.

Despite the seeming antiquity of the human presence on Earth, for most of that time, the species survived by gathering vegetation and scavenging meat until successful hunting methods were established; throughout all this time, the species had very little impact on Earth and its ecosystems. It was not until humankind began to domesticate animals and plants and had learned how to generate fire that the human species could begin making notable changes in the course of its future and in the future of the earth's ecosystems. This power was acquired between nine thousand and twelve thousand years ago.

Humankind's psychosocial awareness—the basis for the development of an ethical system—emerged very gradually. In the earliest years, there was no recognition of being distinct as a species or as individuals. Life was a series of instinctive responses to the environment and to physical needs. Jean Gebser describes it as "a time of complete nondifferentiation of man and the universe."

With humankind's growing awareness of its separateness from the rest of the ecosystem came a sense of insecurity about its relationship to the external world. As human societies began to experiment with their potential autonomy, they developed rituals to support their systems of magical beliefs in order to maintain an amicable relationship with the all-powerful outer world and to avoid any punishment for their "defection." Killing animals for food, for example, was no longer an instinctive behavior. It involved asking permission from some life-sustaining force. When disaster struck—or perhaps to forestall it—sacrificial rituals were offered to appease the force. Using rituals based on magical beliefs is evidence of perceiving an adversarial position between the human and outer worlds.

When human beings began to understand Earth's rhythms, some fears were resolved. The Earth-human relationship changed. Myth systems were developed to record and pass on the body of knowledge that humankind had been accumulating. It became possible to predict future occurrences based on past experiences and observations. This development, then, made it possible to begin taking advantage of predictable beneficial conditions and to try avoiding harmful ones. Agriculture made permanent settlements possible. The resultant increase in the size and density of human populations began overtaxing the environment. Cheryl Simon Silver reports that as early as eight thousand years ago, areas around the Mediterranean showed that wild animal populations were being replaced by domesticated ones. Plant communities there have been disrupted so badly and for so long that it is now difficult to determine what constituted the indigenous vegetation.

When humans turned their vision of the life-giving force from being Earth centered to being heaven centered, humankind assumed dominion over the rest of Earth's life-forms and its nonliving "resources." Based on this concept, the most aggressive human societies have exercised their presumed rights through activities such as strip mining, clear-cut logging, growing monocultures, using nuclear power, damming or channelizing rivers, forbidding human contraception, and causing the deliberate extinction of other species.

Modern Environmental Concerns

Because humanity's ethical systems have evolved along with humanity's awareness of its uniqueness on Earth, it might seem that these models exist along a continuum. In fact, they exist as diffuse elements within a mosaic design. They all still survive throughout the world and guide human behavior.

It does not seem likely or practical that individually any of these paradigms will or can solve the problems of environmental damage. The range of proposed solutions, however, is a reflection of each of them. Totally opposite conclusions, both of them based on faith, exist within the dominion-of-humankind paradigm. In humanistic ethical systems there is the belief that progress in technology will find solutions to overturn ecological damage. In religion-based systems, there is the belief that humanity should continue to take advantage of the provided resources and not be concerned about Earth's future, because a transcendent god will rescue at least a portion of humankind in times of mortal danger. Elements of the magical and mythical systems are expressed by groups such as the Nature Conservancy and Releaf, which advocate the preservation or rehabilitation of the environment. The first model, in which there was no differentiation between humankind and its environment, is expressed in groups such as Earth First! or those that represent the deep ecology movement. They define their views as "ecoethics," because they hold that all other approaches to the environment are arrogantly egocentric, based entirely on human self-interest, and have little to do with the reality of humankind's minuscule time span in the total scheme of Earth's existence.

Because there has been evolution in ethical systems, however, there is reason to assume that humankind may evolve some other ethical system that might solve the problems that now threaten both Earth and human beings. Indeed, Daniel Kealey and Gebser believe that the new paradigm is emerging and that it is based on an integration of all the previous ethical systems.

—Marcella T. Joy

Further Reading

Allsopp, Bruce. *Ecological Morality*. London: Frederick Muller, 1972.

Attfield, Robin. *Environmental Ethics: An Overview for the Twenty-First Century*. Malden, Mass.: Blackwell, 2003.

Gebser, Jean. *The Ever-Present Origin*. Translated by Noel Barstad and Algis Mickunas. Athens: Ohio University Press, 1985.

Kealey, Daniel. *Revisioning Environmental Ethics*. Albany: State University of New York Press, 1990.

Light, Andrew, and Holmes Rolston III, eds. *Environmental Ethics: An Anthology*. Malden, Mass.: Blackwell, 2003.

Maguire, Daniel. *The Moral Choice*. Garden City, N.Y.: Doubleday, 1978.

Miller, Alan. *Gaia Connections: An Introduction to Ecology, Ecoethics, and Economics*. Savage, Md.: Rowman & Littlefield, 1991.

Regan, Tom, ed. *Earthbound: New Introductory Essays in Environmental Ethics*. New York: Random House, 1984.

Silver, Cheryl Simon, with Ruth DeFries. *One Earth, One Future: Our Changing Global Environment*. Washington, D.C.: National Academy Press, 1990.

See also: Biodiversity; Conservation; Deep ecology; Dominion over nature, human; Earth Day; Ecology; Environmental ethics; Environmental movement; Global warming; Nature, rights of; *Silent Spring*.

Earth Day

The Event: Day set aside to celebrate the earth and focus attention on the relationship of people to Earth

Date: Begun on April 22, 1970

Type of ethics: Environmental ethics

Significance: Earth Day was the first nationwide event to focus on the environment; it emphasized individual and consumer responsibility for environmental quality.

Earth Day was first organized by Senator Gaylord Nelson of Wisconsin as an opportunity for "teach-ins" on the environment and on the effects of human actions on the environment. Many teach-ins focused on air and water

President Richard Nixon and First Lady Pat Nixon plant a tree on the White House South Lawn to recognize the first Earth Day. By White House Photo Office.

pollution, the relationship between environmental quality and human health, and the individual consumer's responsibility for environmental quality. Grassroots activities included picking up litter along roads and streams. Colleges, universities, and public schools were the locales of many of the first Earth Day activities and continued to be the centers for organized Earth Days in subsequent years.

In 1970, a reported twenty-five million Americans participated in Earth Day activities. Through intensive media coverage of Earth Day, information about the environment reached millions more. Following Earth Day, public opinion polls reflected increased awareness of environmental problems and increased support for maintaining environmental quality. Earth Day both reflected and increased public, media, and official interest in environmental quality and in individual responsibility for the environment. The media continue to present stories on environmental trends and issues on Earth Day each year.

—Marguerite McKnight

See also: Conservation; Earth and humanity; Ecology; Environmental ethics; Environmental movement; Environmental Protection Agency; Nature, rights of; Pollution.

Ecology

Definition: Study of relationships among organisms and between organisms and the environment

Type of ethics: Environmental ethics

Significance: The discipline of ecology forms the scientific basis for an ethic of environmental conservation and preservation.

Ecology is broadly divided into "autecology," pertaining to individual organisms or species, and "synecology," or the ecology of communities of organisms. Synecology places humankind in organic "communities," or ecosystems, thus positing a human ethical responsibility to the environment as broadly defined. Since World War II, an "ecological movement" has advocated programs designed to ensure that humankind will live within the limitations of the earth's resources. By means of these programs, communities modify their environments, thus causing successional replacement and moving toward stable, organic "climax communities" that are adapted to current environmental conditions. Short-term changes in community character, especially retreat from "climax," is a practical measure of humankind's effect on the ecosystem.

Biogeography refers to community distribution, while paleo-biogeography considers succession over geologic time. Ecology arose from Alexander von Humboldt's approach to natural history and from Carolus Linnaeus's studies of plant life histories. Plant ecology in America became well established during the early twentieth century in Nebraska, where Frederic Clements established the community concept and coined an overabundance of technical terms.

Victor Shelford of the University of Chicago contemporaneously developed the fundamentals of animal ecology. Among subdivisions of ecology are limnology, oceanography, plant ecology, animal ecology, phenology, biogeography, and paleo-biogeography.

—*Ralph L. Langenheim, Jr.*

See also: Biodiversity; Conservation; Deforestation; Earth and humanity; Endangered species; Environmental ethics; Environmental Protection Agency; Greenpeace; Sierra Club; Sustainability of resources; Wilderness Act of 1964.

Endangered species

Definition: Living creatures that are threatened with extinction in all or part of their geographical range
Type of ethics: Environmental ethics
Significance: Advocates of environmental ethics believe that it is morally wrong for humans to cause the extinc-

tion of a species, while more anthropocentric arguments are made on the basis of the potential utility of existing species for humanity and the inadvertent self-destruction which may result from the destruction of other members of an ecosystem. As a result, endangered species are recognized and protected by law.

An endangered species is one that has so few individual survivors that it could soon become extinct in all or part of its range. Examples include animals such as the California condor and plants such as orchids and cacti. Those species classified as threatened are presently abundant in their range but likely to become endangered within the near future because of a decline in numbers. Examples include the grizzly bear and the bald eagle.

Wildlife Protection

There are three general methods to prevent wildlife from becoming endangered. These methods are to establish treaties and laws to protect a particular species from being killed and to preserve its habitat; to use gene banks, zoos, botanical gardens, and research centers to preserve species and possibly breed individuals of a critically endangered species to reintroduce them to the wild; and to preserve a variety of unique and representative ecosystems, which tends to save a variety of species rather than an individual species.

The U.S. Congress has passed a variety of laws for the protection of endangered species. Legislation to prohibit the illegal collection of species began in 1900 with the Lacey Act. In 1966, the Endangered Species Preservation Act made an official list of endangered species and authorized the expenditure of funds to acquire their habitats. The Endangered Species Conservation Act of 1969 banned the importation and sale of wildlife threatened with worldwide extinction. These legislative acts applied only to vertebrate animals; they did not protect species that were threatened, and they provided no absolute protection against major federal projects that could exterminate a species.

The 1973 Endangered Species Act protected endangered and threatened species and provided a program for the recovery of those species. The 1973 act included all plants and animals except a few that had been determined to be pests. The act recognized the relationship between a species and its environment by requiring the Department of the Interior to determine the critical habitat of endangered and threatened species. The act authorizes the Na-

The Siberian tiger is an Endangered (EN) tiger subspecies. Three tiger subspecies are already extinct. By Dave Pape.

tional Marine Fisheries Service of the Department of Commerce to identify and list marine species, and the Department of the Interior's Fish and Wildlife Service to identify all other plant and animal species threatened in the United States or abroad. Any decision by either agency to add or remove a species from the list must be based solely on biological grounds without economic consideration.

The 1973 Endangered Species Act also prohibits interstate and international commercial trade involving endangered plant or animal species. Section 7 directs federal agencies not to carry out, fund, or authorize projects that would jeopardize endangered species or destroy habitats critical to their survival. This section was challenged in 1975 when conservationists filed suit against the Tennessee Valley Authority to stop construction on the $137 million Tellico Dam on the Little Tennessee River because the river would flood the only known breeding ground of the tiny snail darter, an endangered species. Courts stopped construction on the dam, though the dam was 90 percent complete. In 1979, Congress passed special legislation exempting the project from the Endangered Species Act. The case of the Tellico Dam raises the ethical problem that if one interprets the 1973 act as favoring species over development in all cases, then the value of the species would be so high that it could not be exceeded by the benefits of development.

The ethical principle of saving endangered species is a high one, but it is not absolute. In some cases, there are higher values that must take precedence over endangered species preservation. Although environmentalists understand this principle, they have argued that the Endangered Species Act is not being carried out as directed by Congress because of budget cuts and administrative rules.

Ethical Principles

The ethical principle of preserving all plant and animal species often entails practical costs that are extremely high. There will continue to be situations in which a development project that is truly necessary for human well-being will come into conflict with the existence of one or more species. With only limited resources, a priority system must be devised so that the maximum number of species is saved. The ecological value of a species is the value of the species in question to its native habitat or what the impact of its extinction will be on the ecosystem. The uniqueness of a species places greater value on a species if it is the only existing member of a family rather than one of many members of a given family. Those species with a current or promising biological, medical, or chemical utility have a high preservation effort. Those species with a commercial value should not be allowed to be harvested to extinction.

In some cases, extinctions may be ethically justifiable. The following reasons may apply in such cases: benefits accrue to large numbers of people and not merely a chosen few; the beneficial action is related to genuine human needs, not luxuries; the preservation costs are too great to be borne by society; the species is not unique and has no known medical value; or alternate habitats are not available. Justifiable extinctions include those of the smallpox virus and of some nonharmful animals in East Africa.

By saving endangered species and preserving Earth's genetic pool, options are kept open for nature and science to maintain a healthy environment in the future. There is a growing understanding that all life forms are part of one interdependent ecosystem and that the declining health of one species signals danger for all species, including humans.

—*David R. Teske*

Further Reading

Allen, Thomas B. *Vanishing Wildlife of North America*. Washington, D.C.: National Geographic Society, 1974.

Attfield, Robin. *Environmental Ethics: An Overview for the Twenty-first Century*. Malden, Mass.: Blackwell, 2003.

Fritsch, Albert J., et al. *Environmental Ethics: Choices for Concerned Citizens*. Garden City, N.Y.: Anchor Press, 1980.

Kohm, Kathryn, ed. *Balancing on the Brink of Extinction: The Endangered Species Act and Lessons for the Future*. Washington, D.C.: Island Press, 1991.

Korn, Peter. "The Case for Preservation." *The Nation* 254 (March 30, 1992): 414-417.

Miller, G. Tyler, Jr. *Environmental Science: Working with the Earth*. 9th ed. Pacific Grove, Calif.: Brooks/Cole, 2003.

Wilson, Edward O. *The Future of Life*. New York: Alfred A. Knopf, 2002.

See also: Animal rights; Biodiversity; Darwin, Charles; Deep ecology; Deforestation; Earth and humanity; Ecology; Environmental ethics; Evolutionary theory; Nature, rights of; Rain forests.

Environmental ethics

Definition: Standard of conduct which treats the preservation of the integrity of the environment as a moral good and the needless destruction of any part of nature as a moral evil

Type of ethics: Environmental ethics

Significance: In contrast to many other branches of moral thought, environmental ethics is based primarily upon the concept of obligation—recognizing obligations to the natural world, future generations, and one another—rather than upon virtues, rights, or freedoms.

Humans have long exploited nature in the belief that their planet was so vast and enduring that people could never inflict devastating harm on it. Events since the 1980's have called this perception into question. Half the biospheric change caused by humans has taken place since World War II. Humans have transformed or manipulated half the ice-free ecosystems on the planet and have made a significant impact on most of the rest. People have steadily reduced the number of other species in the world through pollution, hunting, and the destruction of natural habitat.

Projections vary. Some argue that if human activity continues at the present rate, within a few decades humans will "overshoot" the carrying capacity of the biosphere and precipitate a collapse. Other scientists say that the earth itself is in no danger at the hands of humans. Still others acknowledge harm to the biosphere but justify it because of the benefits received from growth, development, and technology. They assert that some degree of harm to the biosphere is a cost of the Western lifestyle. Increasingly, complex problems are reduced to a "jobs or owls" choice. Is it possible to prevent broad damage to the biosphere while accommodating the economic needs of a growing population? The answer is no, unless the world adopts a new model for environmental ethics—one based on common values. Once people agree at a values level, they can begin to communicate and develop solutions to perhaps the greatest challenge faced by humanity.

Do No Harm—Unless...

Much of the debate about business and the environment has involved harm versus benefits. Industrial accidents happen, factories shut down, the stock market takes a plunge, pollutants are released into the atmosphere; in all cases, some people suffer harm.

The benefits of economic activity are weighed against the harm they cause. In this model of environmental ethics, decisions are based on whether the harm is offset to a significant extent by a corresponding benefit. For example, clear-cutting tropical rain forests causes long-term ecological harm. That harm may outweigh any immediate economic concerns, but the argument is that stopping the activity would deprive many people of their only means of livelihood and further impoverish developing countries. If one can prove that its benefits outweigh its harmful effects, then a destructive activity is permitted. Few people disagree with this trade-off, provided it protects existing human beings. The controversy occurs when people consider the harm done to future generations of humans, animals, plants, or the planet itself.

Costs and profits guide corporate behavior in this ethical model. If an incident's long-term damage is small, it pays to adopt a strategy of reaction or defense. If the long-term damage is perceived to be high, the strategy should be one of proaction or accommodation. Introduced during the 1960's, this management model, called the mechanistic school, entails an anthropocentric view in which humanity perceives itself to be the center and ultimate goal of the universe, viewing the environment as existing for its convenience.

Nature is viewed as a mere storehouse of raw materials for human use. The environment is seen as relatively stable, unlimited, and well understood. Although many businesses now embrace newer models of environmental decision making, many large, hierarchical, rigid corporations are stuck at this level.

During the 1970's came the organic school. In this more adaptive model of decision making, the goal is the exploitation of rapid changes through innovations and the exploration of new opportunities. It views the environment as highly unpredictable, turbulent, dangerous, and presenting unlimited new market opportunities.

Organizations embracing this model look for opportunities in the environmental movement. Consumers and investors are voting with their dollars, and businesses see the opportunities. Sacha Millstone and Ferris Baker Watts, in *The Greening of American Business* (1992), cite surveys indicating that 77 percent of Americans say that a company's environmental reputation affects what they buy. Too often, however, businesses operating in this management model exploit the trend rather than integrate and fully embrace environmental responsibility.

One example of this type of thinking is explored in David Chittick's writings in *The Greening of American Business*. Chittick makes a strong financial case for proactive environmental programs. By being environmentally responsible, a corporation can save millions of dollars by avoiding costs of waste disposal, costs of penalties and fines for noncompliance, costs of handling hazardous materials (insurance, protective equipment), costs of negative publicity, and costs of decreased employee morale and community confidence. The emphasis, however, is on taking advantage of the opportunity presented by environmental programs.

Shift to Biocentrism

By the late 1980's, more and more individuals and businesses began shifting to a model of environmental ethics that embraces biocentrism, viewing the planet Earth as a living system of interdependent species. This approach's "do no harm" principle provides an adaptive model of decision making. It takes a holistic view in which ethical and environmental considerations enter into all decisions. A balance is sought between organizational goals and environmentally based values. The environment is viewed as fragile, limited in resources, and vulnerable to organizational actions. The approach sees the planet as a community of life-forms in which each contributes to and depends upon all the others.

Every act of pollution and resource depletion is viewed not as an isolated event, but as a contributing factor to a collective impact of increasingly accelerating global proportions. As Brian Edwards Brown, an attorney and professor at Iona College, explains:

"Nature is not merely an object of anthropocentric concern, an environment that, if contaminated or otherwise damaged, interferes with human use and enjoyment.

...Nature is a subject in its own right, a totality of diverse, unique, interdependent life-forms, of which the human is but one and without which the human would not be possible."

A Difference of Values

The difference in values prohibits the development of workable solutions. The anthropocentric view is the older one. The biocentric view reflects strides that the science of ecology has made in discovering and understanding the intricate interdependence of species, as well as the interconnectedness of their habitats. It reflects an increased understanding of the environment and its problems. It is an ethically based view. These value differences contribute to difficulties in communication between holders of the two views. They lead to mistrust and misinterpretation of the other's arguments and proposals.

Both groups have an obligation to seek to understand the other's views and arguments. Candid, honest, and respectful communication can lead to the creation of shared values. Communication should include education. The anthropocentrics should undertake to know and understand the workings and interdependencies of the biosphere. The biocentrics should seek to understand the concerns of business.

A holistic view considers all the parts of the problem. It is not realistic to attempt to eliminate all business, to retreat to a lifestyle of a prior century, or to prevent growth in developing countries. People must, however, evaluate the ways in which they live and make appropriate changes. People must consider ethics and the environment in all of their decision making.

We Are All Responsible

If, for example, one asks who is responsible for the pollution caused by automobiles, the answer is the auto manufacturers, the gasoline manufacturers, the auto users, and perhaps even the members of the community that do not provide mass transportation. Everyone shares the responsibility, and everyone must work together for solutions.

Environmental problems are ethical dilemmas. People begin to solve any ethical dilemma with an acknowledgment of facts and perceptions. Next, with a new model, people change their perception of the biosphere and their relationship to it. Then, as in solving all ethical dilemmas, it is necessary to begin with an analysis of the alternatives and their various effects on each stakeholder. A new model of environmental ethics broadens the stakeholder concept. The old model did not include all components of the biosphere, or future generations, as stakeholders. It is not surprising that the solutions put forth have been less than adequate. With the stakeholder analysis complete, it is possible to proceed to synthesis, choice, action, and communication.

This new model creates a permanent shift in the way business operates. With an environmental ethics view, the mission of a corporation is to "manage in an ethical and effective manner in order to maximize shareholder value,"

replacing the less restrictive, "maximize shareholder value."

In 1989, the Coalition for Environmentally Responsible Economies (CERES) adopted the Valdez Principles, which define guidelines for responsible corporate behavior regarding the environment. Although the Valdez Principles are a good start, they are noticeably general. They do not identify specific standards of conduct. There are also loopholes, in that these principles are expressed in terms of "take every effort" or "minimize." Still, they set the stage for a new look at environmental ethics.

Collaboration is a keyword in successful environmental programs. For example, a joint effort of the Environmental Defense Fund and McDonald's Corporation sought solutions to McDonald's environmental problems. The organizations jointly commissioned four scientists to examine ways in which McDonald's could reduce and recycle waste. The result was a set of sound proposals, including the phasing out of bleached paper; the testing of reusable cups, coffee filters, and shipping containers; the use of recycled materials; and continuing experimentation.

More and more companies are looking at what consultant Joel S. Hirschhorn calls taking a total approach to environmental ethics. In this approach, the company culture is permanently changed to include environmental values. Since culture can be broadly defined as the collection of the individual values of the people in the organization, a total approach must begin with individuals. It recognizes the importance of having every person in the organization passionately interested in environmental responsibility.

In this new model, a company does not look at regulatory compliance, which concentrates on better management of wastes and control of pollutants. It looks instead at the beginning of the process—at what the company produces, how it produces it, and how it markets its products and services.

An example of this new type of company is The Body Shop, which not only uses posters, pamphlets, and window displays in the shop to promote environmental messages but also starts with the product. The Body Shop manufactures and markets naturally based skin and hair products. It actively seeks out suppliers in remote parts of the world, including many developing countries. It has an ambitious recycling program and does not test cosmetics on animals. Its marketing programs do not promote idealized notions of beauty or claim that the company's products will perform cosmetic miracles. Practicing what it preaches, The Body

Shop encourages its employees to devote time and energy to volunteer projects in their communities.

First Steps

Hirschhorn calls for setting three priorities in redefining the corporate culture: First, focus on people and the corporate culture to develop and deepen the commitment to corporate environmental responsibility.

Second, focus on technology, manufacturing facilities, and products to improve environmental performance.

Third, focus on products and customers to incorporate effective "green marketing" into the strategic planning of the firm.

A significant first step was taken in June, 1992, when most of the world's top political, spiritual, and business leaders gathered with leading environmentalists in Rio de Janeiro for the historic United Nations Conference on Environment and Development—the Earth Summit. The purpose of the Summit was to reconcile the conflicting demands of the environment and development into global strategies that will ensure a viable future. Among the Summit's accomplishments were the following:

- Establishing the environment as an international issue—a point of transition on how to deal with global issues;

- An agreement on the concept that human development and protection of the earth's environment are inextricably intertwined;

- A legally binding treaty that recommends curbing emissions of carbon dioxide, methane, and other "greenhouse" gases thought to warm the climate by trapping the sun's heat close to Earth;

- A legally binding treaty that requires making inventories of plants and wildlife and planning to protect endangered species;

- A realization of the difficulties of negotiating worldwide solutions to worldwide problems;

- Gathering together the greatest number of world leaders ever assembled with a single aim;

- The creation of a Sustainable Development Commission to monitor compliance with the promises made at Rio. The commission will rely on evidence gathered by private environmental groups and will use peer pressure and public opinion to shame countries into following the policies agreed to at the Summit;

- The realization that there is no common model for environmental ethics. There is a gap between those who say that humans are at the center of concerns and those who say that by putting humans at the center of things, with the implied right to dominate and exploit the rest of nature, humans perpetuate existing problems and create new ones.

The Earth Summit, by its very purpose, was a major step toward adopting a new model for environmental ethics. The human species now ranks with grand natural forces such as volcanoes as a transformer of the earth's life-support system. The model that people will embrace to solve environment and development conflicts will determine not only the very survival of the human race but also the quality of life for future generations.

—*Kathleen D. Purdy*

Further Reading

Attfield, Robin. *Environmental Ethics: An Overview for the Twenty-First Century.* Malden, Mass.: Blackwell, 2003. Surveys the field through both theoretical discussion and practical case studies; argues in favor of consequentialist and objectivist ethics.

Gore, Albert. *Earth in the Balance: Ecology and the Human Spirit.* Boston: Houghton Mifflin, 1992. Embracing the new model in environmental ethics, Gore argues that only a radical rethinking of the human/Earth relationship can save Earth's ecology for future generations. The book presents a comprehensive plan for action.

Hargrove, Eugene. *Foundations of Environmental Ethics.* Englewood Cliffs, N.J.: Prentice-Hall, 1989. Presents a justification for protecting nature using an argument called "ecocentric holism."

Light, Andrew, and Holmes Rolston III, eds. *Environmental Ethics: An Anthology.* Malden, Mass.: Blackwell, 2003. A comprehensive collection of essays, representing both traditional work and more innovative points of view. Both mainstream and alternative approaches to the field are included.

National Conference on Business Ethics. *Business, Ethics, and the Environment: The Public Policy Debate.* Edited by W. Michael Hoffman, Robert Frederick, and Edward S. Petry, Jr. New York: Quorum Books, 1990. A collection of essays addressing the public policy questions of how and whether to regulate corporations to deal with important environmental issues.

_____. *The Corporation, Ethics, and the Environment.* Edited by W. Michael Hoffman, Robert Frederick, and Edward S. Petry, Jr. New York: Quorum Books, 1990. A companion book to *Business, Ethics, and the Environment.* This collection addresses the role of business in protecting the environment. Presents a series of cases and analyses, corporate strategies, and suggestions.

Scherer, Donald, and Thomas Attig, eds. *Ethics and the Environment.* Englewood Cliffs, N.J.: Prentice-Hall, 1983. A basic book that puts forth a range of ecocentric approaches to environmental issues.

Sullivan, Thomas F. P., ed. *The Greening of American Business.* Rockville, Md.: Government Institute, 1992. Readings on the impact of the green movement on business. Topics include labeling, liability, market opportunities, and investing.

See also: Clean Air Act; Clean Water Act; Deep ecology; Dominion over nature, human; Ecology; Environmental movement; Environmental Protection Agency; Gaia hypothesis; Muir, John; Nature, rights of.

Environmental movement

Identification: Cooperative effort of individuals, organizations, and governments to make others aware of environmental issues and attempt to solve environmental problems

Date: Began during the 1960's

Type of ethics: Environmental ethics

Significance: The environmental movement has successfully changed the ways in which many people in industrial societies understand their relationship to the environment. It has also created controversy in the business world, where it is sometimes perceived as an obstacle to maximizing profits.

The environmental movement—if it can properly be called a "movement"—is a loose, shifting, often sharply divided coalition of individuals and organizations concerned about environmental degradation.

The modern movement began during the early 1960's, prompted by Rachel Carson's book *Silent Spring* (1962) and by concern over nuclear war and weapons testing, overpopulation, and the damage caused by postwar growth and technology.

Silent Spring was a widely read account of how pesticides damaged the environment. In 1963, in the face of industry attacks on Carson and her book, President Kennedy's Science Advisory Committee reviewed pesticide use, confirmed Carson's conclusions, and issued a call for legislative measures to safeguard the land and its people against pesticides and industrial toxins. In 1970, the Environmental Protection Agency (EPA) was established, and in 1972 it banned production and use of DDT in the United States. Within fifteen years of *Silent Spring*'s publication, Congress enacted the Endangered Species Act (1972), the Pesticide Control Act (1972), the Clean Air Act (1977), and other landmark environmental legislation. Carson's poetics were thus transformed into public policy.

Government Involvement

Since its founding, the EPA has grown to more than thirty times its original size. Moreover, dozens of other federal agencies and hundreds of state agencies, bureaus, and services deal with the environment.

Around the turn of the twenty-first century, however, successful efforts were made in Congress and the executive branch to repeal or loosen laws and regulations in the name of economic efficiency. Internationally, the United Nations Environment Programme has been called upon to coordinate the environmental efforts of numerous U.N. bodies with diverse international and regional organizations, both governmental and private sector. The Regional Seas Programme, for example, fosters cooperation among 140 nations to improve environmental quality in thirteen regional seas, including the Mediterranean, Caribbean, Red, and Black Seas.

Diverse Approaches

The environmental movement in the United States is diverse and fragmented. Constituents differ not only in their approaches to environmental action but also in their philosophies. Most of the movement—mirroring American society—is from the Western anthropocentric tradition holding that, to one degree or another, the environment is here for the benefit of humankind and that the purpose of the environmental movement, whether through preservation or conservation or development of new resources or efficiencies, is to benefit people. This is exemplified historically by Theodore Roosevelt and Gifford Pinchot's efforts to create a National Park System and by twenty-first century environmentalists who would open the national forests to logging and recreation.

At the other end of the spectrum are the ecophilosophers who view human beings and their culture as part of the seamless web of nature. They trace their roots to sources as varied as St. Francis of Assisi, Zen Buddhism, Baruch Spinoza, and Daoism. Represented by deep ecologists and the Gaia movement, their emphasis is on the necessity of adapting human behavior to nature's terms, rather than controlling nature for the benefit of human beings. This broad range is reflected in the variety of organizations in the United States. Conservationist organizations constitute the largest category; these broad-based membership groups, such as the Sierra Club, are typically moderate in their positions.

Legalist organizations, such as the Environmental Defense Fund and the Natural Resources Defense Council, were founded to litigate environmental issues and are fighting to build a body of case law establishing a right to a clean environment. Other groups have a strong grass-roots presence, professing citizen empowerment—getting ordinary people involved in local environmental problems. They may not have significant technical expertise, but they are experts on local conditions.

Outside the mainstream, organizations such as Earth First!, the Earth Liberation Front, and People for the Ethical Treatment of Animals (PETA) have opted for direct, often illegal, action aimed at halting or delaying projects they deem environmentally unsound. The nature of their activities—heavily inspired by Edward Abbey's novel *The Monkey-Wrench Gang* (1975)—makes reliable data difficult to obtain, but destruction of sport utility vehicles (SUVs), sabotage of earth-moving equipment, release of laboratory animals, and arson at construction sites in environmentally sensitive areas make occasional headlines.

The Sea Shepherds carry out similar, sometimes illegal, operations against whaling and other controversial maritime activities, but do so openly.

Influence

Environmental groups that were on the political fringes as 1960's activists were integral parts of the political process by the twenty-first century. The Green Party, though never gaining more than a few percent of votes nationally, has won local offices and may have altered the course of the 2000 presidential election, in which its candidate, Ralph Nader, may have taken away votes that would have given Democrat Al Gore the election. Some organizations have acquired economic clout similar to that of large industrial concerns. Greenpeace's worldwide revenues, for example, amounted to $175 million in 2000. If the annual revenues of all the conservation groups in the United States were collected together, the sum would exceed $1 billion. This political and economic success has spawned countermovements and even sham environmental organizations, set up by industries to advance their positions under the guise of environmentalism. One influential countermovement is the Wise Use Movement, which borrowed its name from Gifford Pinchot but fights environmental preservation and regulation.

Religious Concerns

Environmental movements began to take root in the religious community simultaneously with the birth of the popular movement. Early evangelical thinking suggested that the chief value of creation was to fuel human industry, but in 1961, at the World Council of Churches Assembly in New Delhi, Lutheran theologian Joseph Sittler pointed out the declining health of the world's environment, sparking widespread Christian concern over environmental issues.

In 1967, *Science* published an address by Lynn White, "Historic Roots of Our Ecologic Crisis." It asserted that through such ideas as human dominion, the desacralizing of nature, and the belief that ultimate human destiny is with God and not with Earth, Christendom has encouraged a destructive use of creation. Christian missions and relief organizations have come to recognize that environmental and developmental needs are not only compatible but also inseparable. During the 1990's, a significant environmental movement began developing within evangelical and Pentecostal Christianity.

The Islamic concept of *khalifa* rejects the Judeo-Christian doctrine of human dominion over creation, holding stewardship of the earth to be humankind's sacred duty, a concept also long held in several strains of Judaic theology. Care for the natural environment and the rights of animals and natural resources play a fundamental role in *sharia*, Muslim religious law. In stark contrast to James Watt, a fundamentalist Christian and former U.S. secretary of the interior who denied the importance of environmental stewardship in light of the impending destruction of the earth on doomsday, the Prophet Muhammad said: "When doomsday comes, if someone has a palm shoot in his hand, he should plant it."

The aboriginal religions of the Americas and Australasia have inspired considerable activism with their emphases on the interrelatedness of land, knowledge, and human identity. A common theme is reverence for the land and the incomprehensibility of treating it as a commodity, to be bought and sold.

Critical Issues

Many view overpopulation as the most serious environmental problem in the twenty-first century and the root of most other problems. Modern Malthusians, such as Paul Ehrlich and Garrett Hardin, predict that population will eventually outstrip resources and cause widespread poverty, starvation, and general disaster. Some governments have tried to encourage or mandate small families, with some success, but most leave this to individual families.

In U.S. constitutional law, family-planning decisions constitute a fundamental right, subject only to narrow governmental interference under the most compelling circumstances. The population issue is vexing for religious groups concerned about the environment, as many oppose certain birth-control methods such as contraception and especially abortion.

Another concern of the environmental movement, spanning national boundaries, is that of nuclear weapons and energy. The threat of nuclear weapons proliferation appears not to have ended with the Cold War, as many had hoped. "Rogue states" and terrorists have replaced the Soviet Union as the West's primary concern. Even peaceful uses of nuclear energy pose serious threats. The 1979 accident at the Three Mile Island nuclear power plant, which called the American public's attention to the dangers of nuclear energy, paled in comparison to Soviet-era incidents at Chernobyl and the lesser-known but far more serious accidents at Chelyabinsk during the 1950's and 1960's. Since then, people of the Chelyabinsk region have become the core of the young but growing environmental movement in Russia.

A dilemma facing modern environmentalists is that nuclear technology promises cheap energy without depleting nonrenewable fossil fuels or polluting the atmosphere with burned hydrocarbons—on its face an environmentalist's dream. Opponents reply that "cheap" does not include the price of health and environmental threats or the yet-unknown costs of long-term disposal of nuclear waste, which has a half-life of up to fifty thousand years. On the whole, the environmental movement favors replacing nuclear energy with solar energy and renewable organic sources such as ethanol made from grain.

The U.S. government's announcement in 2004 that it intends to put astronauts on Mars by the year 2030 was certain to ignite another environmental debate, over the ethics of militarization, colonization, and exploitation of the resources of outer space.

—David R. Teske; Updated by William V. Dunlap

Further Reading

Desjardins, Joseph R. *Environmental Ethics: An Introduction to Environmental Philosophy*. Belmont, Calif.: Wadsworth, 1993.

Dobson, Andrew, ed. *Green Political Thought*. 3d ed. New York: Routledge, 2000.

Jamieson, Dale. *A Companion to Environmental Philosophy*. Oxford: Blackwell, 2003.

Marietta, Don E., and Lester Enbree, eds. *Environmental Philosophy and Environmental Activism*. Lanham, Md.: Rowman & Littlefield, 1995.

Miller, G. Tyler, Jr. *Environmental Science: Working with the Earth*. Belmont, Calif.: Wadsworth, 1997.

Sessions, George, ed. *Deep Ecology for the Twenty-first Century*. Boston: Shambhala, 1995.

Stone, Christopher D. *Should Trees Have Standing? And Other Essays on Law, Morals, and the Environment*. Dobbs Ferry, N.Y.: Oceana, 1996.

Walker, Melissa. *Reading the Environment*. New York: W. W. Norton, 1994.

See also: Conservation; Earth and humanity; Earth Day; Ecology; Endangered species; Environmental ethics; Environmental Protection Agency; Green parties; Greenpeace; Sierra Club; *Silent Spring*.

Environmental Protection Agency

Identification: Independent federal government agency responsible for the development, implementation, and direction of all federal environmental management programs in the United States

Date: Established on December 2, 1970

Type of ethics: Environmental ethics

Significance: The Environmental Protection Agency (EPA) monitors and regulates industrial activity in order to protect the well-being of the nation's environment and the health of its citizens.

President Richard M. Nixon created the EPA by Executive Order, as Reorganization Plan 3 of 1970 (dated July 9, 1970) to be effective December 2, 1970. The Reorganization Plan brought fifteen separate components of five executive departments and agencies with programs related to the environment under one independent executive agency that reported directly to the president.

The EPA took responsibility for the control of pollution in seven environmental areas: air, water, solid and hazardous waste, pesticides, toxic substances, radiation, and noise. The EPA was created in response to rising public concerns about the increasing degradation of the environment in those areas.

The job given to the EPA was to set and enforce standards that would adequately protect the environment, which constituted an acknowledgment of the seriousness of the problems of pollution and a recognition of the interrelated nature of environmental problems.

The role of the EPA grew over time as the U.S. Congress passed more environmental protection legislation, although the issues upon which the EPA focuses shift from public health to the ecological depending on political and social concerns of the times.

—*Sandra L. Christensen*

See also: Clean Air Act; Clean Water Act; Congress; Environmental ethics; Environmental movement; Pollution permits; Toxic waste; Wilderness Act of 1964.

Experimentation

Definition: Conduct of practical scientific or medical research

Type of ethics: Scientific ethics

Significance: Experiments conducted on humans and animals are governed by formal and informal codes of ethics designed to protect the rights and welfare of the subjects, to ensure that the experiments serve a legitimate public interest, and to regulate the use of the information obtained as a result of the experiments.

What are the moral principles to be considered in evaluating the rightness or wrongness of using humans as research subjects? In *The Patient as Partner* (1987), Robert M. Veatch summarized the ethical principles and issues involved in research: The principle of beneficence, which has its roots in the ethics of medical treatment, states that research with humans is justified only when some good can come from it; this is the minimum justification for human research.

Research may do good (therefore meeting the criterion of beneficence) but may also cause harm. Research that causes harm is morally wrong; that is, it does not meet the principle of nonmaleficence. When research causes both good and harm, which principle, beneficence or nonmaleficence, takes priority? If avoiding harm takes priority, then a vast amount of research with human subjects with the potential for doing much good would be considered unethical. Therefore, the ratio of benefit to harm is a more reasonable criterion for justifying human experimentation.

If benefit/harm is adopted as the moral principle, a new problem emerges, because this principle would justify inhumane experimental procedures such as those employed by the Nazis as long as it could be shown that severe harm or death to a few human subjects was of benefit to large numbers of people.

Benefit/harm, a form of beneficence, is therefore a necessary but insufficient justification for research with hu-

man subjects. Additional principles are required. The principle of autonomy recognizes that among the inalienable rights of persons is the right to liberty. The principle of autonomy implies a right to self-determination, including the right, when informed of the benefits and harms, to consent to participate in research that may entail certain risks to the subject. Therefore, autonomy is the basis for the use of informed consent in research with human subjects; informed consent helps to mitigate some of the problems posed by sole reliance on beneficence as a moral criterion.

Still another principle involves considerations of justice (fairness) in the conduct of human research. According to one theory of justice, distributive justice, fairness involves attempting to equalize the benefits and harms among the members of society. This principle has implications for the selection of subjects for research in the sense that disadvantaged subjects—for example, members of minority groups—should not be chosen as subjects, since this would add another burden to an already unduly burdened group. This principle would not apply when minority status was a variable under study in the research.

The principles of beneficence, autonomy, and justice form the basis for some of the criteria set by the U.S. Department of Health and Human Services (DHHS) and used by institutional review boards (IRBs) for judging whether proposed research involving human subjects is ethically sound. These criteria are (1) risks to subjects are minimized, (2) risks are reasonable relative to anticipated benefits, (3) prior informed consent will be obtained from subjects or their legal representatives, (4) informed consent will be documented, and (5) selection of subjects will be equitable. Two additional criteria are that (6) subjects' privacy and confidentiality will be maintained and that (7) the research plan involves monitoring the data, when applicable, so as to ensure subject safety.

The application of ethical principles to particular instances of research with human subjects highlights the complexities involved in the use of these principles. One question that arises concerns the obligations of a scientist when the nature of the research precludes informed consent, as in psychological research that involves the use of deception. While many people believe that deception is permissible under certain limited conditions—for example, when there is little or no risk to subjects and there are no alternative ways of gathering the data—others feel that deception is intrinsically harmful to subjects and is never justified.

Another question has to do with the issue of informed consent with subjects who may not be competent to give informed consent; for example, in cases involving children or individuals who were formerly competent but are no longer so (such as individuals who have some form of dementia). When risks are minimal, informed consent by parents of children and informed consent by guardians of the formerly competent have been employed as criteria. In circumstances in which the subject is competent but informed consent may be obtained under potentially coercive conditions, as in the case of prisoners or clinic patients, complex ethical questions are raised.

The ethics of experimentation also extend into such other areas as issues of animal care and rights, and the ethical obligations of scientists with regard to the integrity of the research process.

—Sanford Golin

Further Reading

Caplan, A. L. *When Medicine Went Mad: Bioethics and the Holocaust.* Totowa, N.J.: Humana Press, 1992.

Cothran, Helen, ed. *Animal Experimentation: Opposing Viewpoints.* San Diego, Calif.: Greenhaven Press, 2002.

Foster, Claire. *The Ethics of Medical Research on Humans.* New York: Cambridge University Press, 2001.

Garattini, Silvio, and D. W. van Bekkum, eds. *The Importance of Animal Experimentation for Safety and Biomedical Research.* Boston: Kluwer Academic, 1990.

Group for the Advancement of Psychiatry. *A Casebook in Psychiatric Ethics.* New York: Brunner/ Mazel, 1990.

Institute of Medicine Committee on Assessing the System for Protecting Human Research Participants. *Responsible Research: A Systems Approach to Protecting Research Participants.* Edited by Daniel D. Federman, Kathi E. Hanna, and Laura Lyman Rodriguez. Washington, D.C.: National Academies Press, 2003.

Sieber, J. E., ed. *Fieldwork, Regulation, and Publication.* Vol. 2 in *The Ethics of Social Research.* New York: Springer-Verlag, 1982.

Veatch, R. M. *The Patient as Partner: A Theory of Human-Experimentation Ethics.* Bloomington: Indiana University Press, 1987.

See also: Animal research; Animal rights; Bioethics; Consent; Medical research; Milgram experiment; National Commission for the Protection of Human Subjects of Biomedical and Behavioral Research; Nazi science; Science.

Facebook

Definition: Online social network.
Type of ethics: Scientific ethics

Significance: Facebook is the symbol for the contradictory nature of an online social network.

Facebook was created in 2004 by Harvard University student Mark Zuckerberg. It was based on the concept of the university's "facebook" — a directory of student names with a picture, typically organized by graduating class year. In its first iteration, Facebook was a program called Facemash, which Zuckerberg developed, that allowed Harvard students to rank photographs of their classmates according to attractiveness. Zuckerberg obtained the photographs by hacking into Harvard's database of student identification images. Harvard University administration shut down the site a few days after Zuckerberg began disseminating it. However, a few months later Zuckerberg began development of the thefacebook.com. Thefacebook.com was launched in February 2004 and only allowed Harvard University students to join. In March of 2004, thefacebook.com expanded to Columbia University, Stanford University, and Yale University. At this time Eduardo Saverin, Dustin Moskovitz, Andrew McCollum, and Chris Hughes joined Zuckerberg in the development and management of the website. Very quickly, thefacebook.com expanded to include Ivy League universities and Boston-area colleges. It continued to expand and by 2006 Facebook was available to anyone over the age of 13. By 2012, Facebook announced it had reached its one-billionth user. Facebook is now a publicly-traded company that has a net worth in the billions of dollars. Its primary source of revenue is through advertising, with a small amount of additional revenue coming from fees and payments for virtual services, such as games.

In many ways, Facebook has become the symbol for the contradictory nature of an online social network. One facet of Facebook is its ability to assist people in maintaining social connections that extend beyond the sphere of everyday life. Conversely, Facebook is a publicly-traded company with responsibilities to its shareholders to maintain a certain level of profitability. Also, its primary source of revenue is advertising. Advertising, by its nature, must respond to its audience. Facebook, must, therefore, be able to define the characteristics of its users. This tension between the use of Facebook as a personal mode of expression, as well as a generator of revenue, informs the question of privacy and Facebook.

The impact on the privacy of individuals using Facebook has been an issue from its initial iteration as

Facemash. When the Harvard University administration shut it down one of the reasons they gave was the privacy concern of disseminating students' pictures without their consent. This concern has persisted, despite Facebook's continued effort to assure its users that the information they generate by using Facebook is adequately protected.

Facebook's data policy does not explicate the specific types of data and information it gathers from its users, but it does collect a large amount of data on its users. Facebook states that it collects "content and other information" provided by the users, including information from posts and information from users' messages and communications with other users. The information collected by Facebook extends beyond a user's actions on Facebook to include information on the device or devices being used to access Facebook. This information details the device's operating system, hardware settings, device locations, and connection information, including network provider, browser type, language, time zone, IP address, and mobile phone number. Facebook also collects information from third-party partners and companies owned or operated by Facebook, such as Instagram.

Users of Facebook are impacted by two facets of online privacy—what the user shares with other users and how Facebook uses the information it gathers on the user. First, users are able to manipulate various privacy controls to limit what information other users can access; however, each user must proactively set the limits. The default privacy settings on Facebook allow for other users, even if not a "friend" of the user, to view a large amount of personal information, such as photographs and where the person lives. In 2015, Facebook changed the default privacy setting for a user's wall posts from the public to "friends" only. However, Facebook recently indexed users' previous post content. This allows users' posts, many going back years, to be searched and accessed.

Secondly, Facebook users have little control over how this information is used by Facebook or disseminated by Facebook to other entities. One facet of this is Facebook's policy on users quitting Facebook. It is impossible for users to delete their Facebook profile and all of its content. Facebook only allows for account deactivation. Deactivation takes the profile out of search results and other users cannot access the profile. However, the profile remains on Facebook servers and information and data from that account can continue to be gleaned by Facebook.

It has been reported that Facebook has participated in lobbying for the passing of the Cybersecurity Information Sharing Act (CISA) of 2015. This act allows companies to share cybersecurity threat information with federal agencies such as the Federal Bureau of Investigations and the National Security Agency. Privacy advocates argue that the definition of a cybersecurity threat under CISA is too broadly defined and will allow companies to actively monitor users without a warrant. This information could then be provided to various federal agencies. While Facebook denies the claims it supports CISA, Facebook does not actively assist users in protecting their profiles and personal information from third party harvesting, as each Facebook user must actively manage the privacy controls for their account, as well as for each third party entity that accesses the user's profile. Many argue that requiring users to proactively manage the privacy settings of their profile is an inadequate way to protect user's privacy. It has also been argued that the current privacy settings in Facebook do not adequately address Facebook's own gathering and use of individual user information.

—*Rachel Jorgensen*

Further Reading
Cohen, Julie E. "Inverse Relationship Between Secrecy and Privacy." *Social Research* 77.3 (Fall 2010): 883-898.
Newton, Lee. *Facebook Nation: Total Information Awesomeness.* New York: Springer, 2014.
Rubenstein, Ira S. and Nathaniel Good. "Privacy By Design: A Counterfactual Analysis of Google and Facebook Privacy Incidents." *Berkeley Technology Law Journal* 28.2 (Fall 2013): 1333-1413.
Trottier, Daniel. *Identity Problems in the Facebook Era.* New York, Routledge, 2014.

Gaia hypothesis

Definition: Theory holding that the earth is a living entity whose biosphere is self-regulating and is able to maintain planetary health by controlling its chemical and physical environment

Date: Developed between 1969 and 1979

Type of ethics: Environmental ethics

Significance: The Gaia hypothesis creates a model of earthly existence that is fundamentally biocentric rather than anthropocentric. Such a model might be seen ethically to require the maintenance of balanced relationships between humans and other forms of life. It might also be seen, however, as an indication that humans are no more responsible for their environmental effects than are any other organisms, since the system as a whole actively maintains itself independently of its individual living components.

While working on a project that would send a space probe to determine whether life exists on Mars, British geochemist and inventor James Lovelock theorized that one could answer the question by observing the activity in the planet's lower atmosphere. Lovelock developed his idea and came to recognize its implications through discussions with U.S. biologist Lynn Margulis. His thinking culminated in the book *Gaia: A New Look at Life on Earth* (1979), which presented his hypothesis that life and its natural environment have coevolved and that the lower at-

Gaea, by Anselm Feuerbach (1875).

mosphere provides the raw materials for life to exist on the planet. The original title of the theory was the Biocybernetic Universal System Tendency (BUST), but novelist William Golding suggested that the theory be named for Gaia, the Greek Earth goddess who is also called Ge (from which root the words "geography" and "geology" are derived).

Although the Gaia hypothesis did not generate much scientific activity until the late 1980's, it was supported by both industrialists (who believed that it supplied a justification for pollution, since the earth could theoretically counteract any harmful effects) and some environmentalists. Other environmentalists, however, believe that the theory argues against any attempt by humans to try to correct environmental degradation.

—Sandra L. Christensen

See also: Biodiversity; Deep ecology; Dominion over nature, human; Environmental ethics; Exploitation.

Gene Editing and CRISPR (Clustered regularly interspaced short palindromic repeats)

Definition: An RNA-mediated bacterial defense system which in combination with Cas9 endonuclease allows for a revolutionary method of genome editing.

Type of ethics: Bioethics

Discovery and Mechanism of the CRISPR System
Clustered regularly interspaced short palindromic repeats (CRISPR) are encoded by prokaryotic genomes. After these sequences are transcribed and processed, the RNAs encoded by the CRISPR sequences associate with an endonuclease such as CRISPR-associated system (Cas), which provides a natural immune system that defends the prokaryotic organism from invading exogenous DNAs and RNAs, such as bacteriophages and plasmids. The CRISPR system is found in about 40% of bacterial and archaea species. The RNA segment associated with CRISPR/Cas guides the CRISPR/Cas to the invading target, binds to complementary sequences in the invading exogenous DNA or RNA, cleaves and degrades the sequence thereby preventing its transmission and/or function. When the CRISPR system cleaves invading DNA, some of the short (about 20 base pairs) fragments of that DNA are incorporated into the CRISPR locus to provide for an "immunological memory." When these short frag-

ments are transcribed into CRISPR RNA (crRNA), the crRNA seeks out complementary sequences in invading DNA and degrades that DNA.

The discovery of the CRISPR system, its function and mechanism was made over several years by several scientists around the world. In 1993, Francisco Mojica at the University of Alicante in Spain started to characterize the CRISPR system. In 2005, Francisco Mojica suggested that the CRISPR system functioned in bacterial immunity.

Perspective and Prospects

The CRISPR/Cas system has numerous applications especially in genetics, medicine and agriculture. The CRISPR/Cas9 system is effective in editing genomes in a variety of organisms. The system can be used to develop knockout and knockdown mice and other organisms including human cells to be used as research models for human disease. Disease models increase the possibility of developing drugs and other methods of treatment.

The CRISPR/Cas9 system has potential to edit the genomes and/or germline of human embryos. In early 2017, scientists in China successfully altered the genome of human embryonic cells. In July 2017, it was reported that a team led by Shoukhrat Mitalipov of Oregon Health & Science University's Center for Embryonic Cell and Gene Therapy, reported that they had targeted and repaired in several embryo cells a specific gene related to a disease. The altered embryos were allowed to develop only for a few days and there was no intention of implanting them, and this paper claimed that CRISPR technique has the potential to correct disease in human embryos. However, the results of this paper and its original interpretations been strongly challenged by Dieter Egli and his colleagues at Columbia University, and more work will need to be done to confirm it.

Many of the applications of CRISPR have raised ethical, moral and environmental issues and concerns. In December 2015, an International Summit on Human Gene Editing was held in Washington, D. C. where scientists expressed concern over human germline, heritable modification since these modifications could be transmitted to future generations. Although the United States Congress has blocked the United States Food and Drug Administration from approving clinical trials that would create a baby from an edited embryo, most countries have not prohibited the procedure.

—*Charles L. Vigue, PhD*

Further Reading

Doudna, Jennifer A. and Emmanuelle Charpentier. "The new frontier of genome engineering with CRISPR-Cas9." Science 2014; 346(6213): 1258096.

Doudna, Jennifer A. and Samuel H. Sternberg. A Crack in Creation: Gene Editing and the Unthinkable Power to Control Evolution. New York: Houghton Mifflin Harcourt, 2017.

Kozubec, Jim. Modern Prometheus: Editing the Human Genome with Crispr-Cas9. New York: Cambridge University Press, 2016.

Lander, Eric. The Heroes of CRISPR. Cell 2016; 164: 17-28.

Roidos, Paris. Genomeeditingwith the CRISPR Cas9system. Saarbrücken, Germany: Lambert Academic Publishing, 2016.

Reis, Alex, Breton Hornblower, Brett Robb and George Tzertzinis. CRISPR/Cas9and Targeted GenomeEditing: A New Era in Molecular Biology. New England BioLabs, Inc. (NEB) *Expressions*, 2014. https://www.neb.com/tools-and-resources/feature-articles/crispr-cas9-and-targeted-genome-editing-a-new-era-in-molecular-biology

Global warming

Definition: Gradual increase of the earth's surface temperatures

Type of ethics: Environmental ethics

Significance: Global warming is a source of longterm but increasing danger to human beings and to all ecosystems on Earth that raises questions about the point at which future problems become present ethical concerns.

During the twentieth century, the earth's average surface temperature increased about 0.5 degree Celsius, arguably as a result of concurrent human generation of "greenhouse" gases. Furthermore, some environmental modeling indicates another 0.7 to 2 degrees Celsius of warming after the oceans reach equilibrium, plus a further 2 to 5 degrees by the year 2020 if no action is taken.

Even greater changes, however, occurred many times in the more remote past when no human activities could have caused them. Repeated glaciation and deglaciation in the last million years repeatedly exceeded the hypothesized changes without human influence, and the causes of glaciation are not thoroughly understood. The major environmental effects of global warming include the poleward shift of climatic belts, the sea level's rising as much as 6 meters by 2020, and drastically changed atmospheric and oceanic circulation. All these occurrences will disrupt present human activity. Thus, regulation or abolition of activities that may be responsible for warming, such as the burning of fossil fuels, is an ethical issue that has provoked proposals for action at both national and international levels. The prohibition of combustible fuels, for example, entails massive social and economic changes, which should not be undertaken lightly in view of substantial lack of consensus regarding the causes and future course of currently observed global warming.

—Ralph L. Langenheim, Jr.

See also: Bioethics; Earth and humanity; Ecology; Environmental ethics; Future generations; Greenhouse effect; Nature, rights of; Rain forests.

Green parties

Definition: Diverse political parties that are most widely known for promoting environmental issues.
Date: First organized during the 1980s
Type of ethics: Environmental ethics
Significance: Greens were the first political parties promoting environmental issues to win seats in national legislatures.

Green parties, or Greens, make environmental issues the focus of their political goals. They criticize the social, political, and economic structures and policies of industrialized countries as the causes of the environmental crisis. Greens consider environmental, economic, social, and political problems to be interrelated and global. Because of this relationship, Greens variously espouse grassroots democracy, social justice and equality, peace, and small-scale economics. They often oppose capitalism, the construction of nuclear power plants, and the testing and production of nuclear weapons.

Most Green parties were established during the 1980s in industrialized countries and became active in every Western European country, as well as in Australia and New Zealand. West Germany's Green Party (*die Grünen*), one of the most powerful Green parties, in 1983 became the first to win seats in a national legislature.

Support for the Greens was strongly linked with active involvement in social movements. The majority of voters supporting the German Green party in 1983 were active in the ecology, antinuclear, or peace movements. Green parties have also won seats in Austria, Belgium, Finland, Luxembourg, the Netherlands, Romania, Sweden, Switzerland, and the European Parliament.

In the United States, the Association of State Green Parties (ASGP), later the Green Party, was formed after the presidential elections of 1996. The first Green state-wide officeholder was Audie Bock, who was elected to the California Assembly in 1999, and the Green Party's choice to run Ralph Nader as its presidential candidate in 2000 arguably changed the outcome of that election.

—Marguerite McKnight; Updated by the editors

See also: Environmental ethics; Environmental movement; Nader, Ralph; Social justice and responsibility.

Greenhouse effect

Definition: Increase in the earth's surface temperature caused by the absorption of reflected infrared radiation by atmospheric "greenhouse gases."
Type of ethics: Environmental ethics
Significance: The greenhouse effect poses a potential danger to all human life and societies, as well as other species. It raises the issue of the extent of each individual person's and corporation's ethical responsibility to alleviate a threat to the species and to the planet.

The "greenhouse gases"—water vapor and small amounts of carbon dioxide, methane, nitrous oxide, ozone, and chlorofluorocarbons—absorb reflected infrared radiation, thus raising the atmospheric temperature. Without this increase, the earth's mean surface temperature would be about 15 degrees Celsius rather than the observed 17.3 degrees Celsius (approximate); therefore, the "greenhouse effect" makes the earth habitable. The warming primarily results from absorption and restricted diffusion rather than reflection and is more properly referred to as the "atmospheric effect."

Human production of carbon dioxide, chlorofluorocarbons, nitrous oxide, and ozone may have caused the global warming that has been noted since industrialization. Atmospheric carbon dioxide is increasing about 0.3 percent annually, an increase closely paralleling rates of fuel consumption. Some scientists predict doubled atmospheric carbon dioxide by the year 2080. Chlorofluorocarbons, which are entirely of industrial origin, are increasing by 5 percent per year.

Actions to control greenhouse gas emissions include attempts to restrict fossil fuel combustion, which generates carbon dioxide, and reforestation and forest preservation, which remove carbon dioxide from the atmosphere. An international agreement made in 1987 required the halving of chlorofluorocarbon emissions in thirty-one countries by the next century.

—*Ralph L. Langenheim, Jr.*

See also: Clean Air Act; Earth and humanity; Global warming; Nuclear energy; Pollution; Rain forests.

Greenpeace

Identification: International organization dedicated to the protection of the environment.
Date: Founded in 1971
Type of ethics: Environmental ethics
Significance: Greenpeace helped introduce the practice of organized interference with environmentally destructive activities, including governmental activities. The group helped extend the principles of civil disobedience to the environmental movement.

In 1971 Jim Bohlen, Paul Cote, and Irving Stowe formed the Don't Make a Wave Committee, in Vancouver, Canada, and it sent a protest vessel, the *Rainbow Warrior*, to Amchitka in the Aleutian Islands to provoke publicity regarding nuclear testing at that site. An attempt to disrupt the test failed, but the resultant publicity established Greenpeace, the new name of the group, as a major factor in environmental activism. Also, no further tests were held at that site.

Among the notable continuing campaigns of Greenpeace is the attempted disruption of French nuclear tests at Mururoa in the South Seas. This effort led to violence on the high seas when French agents sank the *Rainbow Warrior* in Auckland Harbor, New Zealand, killing one activist.

In 1973, Greenpeace began expanding from antinuclear activity to general environmental protest. Interference with sealing and whaling in the St. Lawrence estuary and on the high seas, also involving physical conflict at sea, became prominent. The organization also spread to Europe, the United States, Argentina, and elsewhere, initiating numerous acts of protest and physical interference with such activities as waste disposal.

See also: Civil disobedience; Earth and humanity; Ecology; Environmental movement; Green parties; Nature, rights of.

Industrial research

Definition: Technical inquiry and experimentation to develop newproducts, newmanufacturing technologies, or more profitable and efficient techniques for creating and distributing commodities
Type of ethics: Scientific ethics
Significance: Industrial research raises a host of ethical issues involving fair employment practices, intellectual property rights, environmental responsibility, industrial espionage, workplace safety, and government oversight

During the mid-twentieth century, the sociologist Robert Merton stated the norms of the scientific research community: communality, organized skepticism, originality, universality, and disinterestedness. To these should be added self-motivation, an openness in sharing results, and a readiness to change when objective evidence calls for it. To some degree, all these ethical norms are challenged by the practice of industrial research. The discussion that follows identifies some of these challenges, both to the individual and to the corporation.

The Individual Scientist

People with research degrees (usually doctorates) in the sciences are accustomed from their university experience to being their own bosses in choosing and executing research projects. In industry, by contrast, they are assigned a research problem and must report regular progress to a boss who reports to a higher boss, on up to the research director, with results appearing not in professional journals, but only in internal reports. The problem is less acute in very large, research-oriented companies, where the projects are correspondingly larger and more interesting. In companies with very small research operations, the problems can be depressingly trivial (for example, it is difficult to care how to lengthen the time it takes cornflakes to become soggy in milk). It is also less uncomfortable for graduates without university research training to be trained in a particular company's laboratory and absorb the company's goals with the training. Nevertheless, nearly all industrial researchers occasionally feel that they are compromising true science and must find their own way to be comfortable with this.

Research Practices Within Corporations

Companies must make money to survive. The problem for their research divisions, then, is to do as wide-ranging and complete research as possible within budgetary restraints. The urge to cut off research projects that do not pay off quickly must be resisted, as must the urge to stop a successful project the instant a product becomes possible. A more pernicious ethical problem is that of actually doing the research. Chemical procedures have sometimes been made up out of whole cloth, because "we knowthat's how they'd come out anyhow," and products have been represented as research breakthroughs that were nothing of the kind. Patent policy is worth mentioning: American firms customarily claim patent protection not only for a specific invention, the patent's subject, but also for any similar device or process that can be related to it, thus closing out research efforts by other firms. A topic that is too large to deal with here is the ethical handling of animals in industrial laboratories.

Relations with Other Corporations

All companies examine competitors' products with the idea of improving their own or claiming a share of the market. So long as this practice does not infringe patents, it is legitimate. What is not legitimate is deliberate industrial espionage—hiring a firm to place a person on the competitor's payroll to ferret out secrets of process or formulation that can be obtained in no other way. Equally unethical is the hiring away of key employees to exploit their privileged knowledge. Some firms have explicit policies that forbid this practice; many require professional employees to sign contracts that forbid their working for a competitor for a specified time after leaving the company. A separate issue of marketing that touches on the research side is that of firms that compete, not by improving manufacturing and distribution processes to reduce costs, but by blitzing competitors with a steady flow of new products. A weak firm can be driven out of business by such practices.

Responsibility to Customers

Customers need to know a great many things that only the industrial research laboratories can tell them—for example, about product safety. The Food and Drug Act was passed in 1906 to ensure the purity of foods and the safety and efficacy of drugs; even so, many errors have been made that have stemmed from careless, if not unethical, practices: the pediatric syrup of sulfa drugs marketed during the late 1930s that used toxic ethylene glycol as solvent; the grossly teratogenic drug thalidomide, which was withdrawn from the market during the 1960s; diethylstil-

bestrol (DES), which is carcinogenic in women even to the second generation; and a host of other drugs and food additives, some quietly taken off the market when studies that should have been done in the original research showed unacceptable side effects. Environmental effects should be investigated (although these cannot always be anticipated): for example, pesticide residue toxicity, chlorofluorocarbon depletion of the ozone layer, and so forth. Finally, customers need to knowthat newresearch products are genuine innovations: Could the ingredients of a new two-drug pill have been prescribed separately more cheaply?Will this new research-hyped cosmetic really make one sixteen years old again? Do automotive gimmicks such as rectangular headlights or hideaway headlights make a car safer or mechanically superior? Although some of these examples border on marketing and salesmanship, many relate to the research laboratory.

Conclusion

As the foregoing discussion indicates, industrial research deviates in many respects from pure research. Nearly all these points of deviation call for ethical decisions. No attempt has been made here to say what decisions should be made; the purpose of this article is descriptive rather than prescriptive.

—Robert M. Hawthorne, Jr.

Further Reading

Amato, Ivan. "The Slow Birth of Green Chemistry." "Can the Chemical Industry Change Its Spots?" and "Making Molecules Without the Mess." *Science* 259 (March 12, 1993): 1538-1541.

Blevins, David E. "University Research and Development Activities: Intrusion into Areas Unattended? A Review of Recent Developments and Ethical Issues Raised." *Journal of Business Ethics* 7 (September, 1988): 645-656.

Carboni, Rudolph A. *Planning and Managing Industry-University Research Collaborations.* Westport, Conn.: Quorum Books, 1992.

Kornhauser, William. *Scientists in Industry: Conflict and Accommodation.* Berkeley: University of California Press, 1962.

Krimsky, Sheldon. *Science in the Private Interest: Has the Lure of Profits Corrupted Biomedical Research?* Lanham, Md.: Rowman & Littlefield, 2003.

Vagtborg, Harold. *Research and American Industrial Development.* New York: Pergamon Press, 1976.

Wilks, Stephen. "Science, Technology, and the Large Corporation." *Government and Opposition* 27, no. 2 (Spring, 1992): 190-212.

See also: Business ethics; Environmental ethics; Marketing; Product safety and liability; Science; Weapons research.

Leopold, Aldo

Identification: American scientist and writer
Born: January 11, 1887, Burlington, Iowa
Died: April 21, 1948, near Baraboo, Sauk County, Wisconsin
Type of ethics: Environmental ethics
Significance: Leopold was responsible for the establishment of the first U.S. Wilderness Area. His *A Sand County Almanac* (1949) put forward the "Land Ethic," which placed humanity within, rather than in charge of, the ecosystem.

Aldo Leopold's boyhood was dominated by sports and natural history. After completing one year of postgraduate work in forestry at Yale, Leopold spent fifteen years with the U.S. Forest Service in Arizona and New Mexico.

Leopold's entry in the Yale Sheffield Scientific School year book, 1908.

There, he developed the idea of preserving large, ecologically undisturbed areas for ecological preservation; in 1924, he precipitated the establishment of the first U.S. forest Wilderness Area in the Gila National Forest of New Mexico. In 1933, he became professor of wildlife management at the University of Wisconsin. In 1934 he became a member of the federal Special Committee on Wildlife Restoration. He was a founder of the Wilderness Society in 1935.

Leopold made a family project of restoring the ecosystem to its original condition on an abandoned farm he had purchased near Baraboo, Wisconsin. His posthumous publication relating to this experience, *A Sand County Almanac,* has become an environmentalist classic, and the farm has become a research center, the Leopold Reserve. Four of Leopold's five children became prominent, environmentally oriented scientists. Three of them, Starker, Luna, and Estella, became members of the National Academy of Sciences. His son Carl became an established research scientist, and his daughter Nina became director of the Leopold Reserve.

—*Ralph L. Langenheim, Jr.*

See also: Conservation; Deep ecology; Ecology; Environmental movement; Exploitation; Muir, John; National Park System, U.S.; Nature, rights of; Wilderness Act of 1964.

Lifeboat ethics

Definition: Concept that likens the ethical principles of living on Earth with those of sharing an overcrowded lifeboat
Date: Concept developed during the 1970s
Type of ethics: Environmental ethics
Significance: Lifeboat ethics is a neo-Malthusian response to human population growth, overpopulation, and hunger that advocates the denial of food aid to starving peoples

Garrett Hardin, who first articulated the concept of lifeboat ethics during the 1970s, employed three metaphors to explain the idea. First, he described he relatively few truly affluent nations as living in wellstocked lifeboats, while the much more numerous poor nations' populations continuously fall out of their own overcrowded lifeboats, while hoping to board affluent lifeboats. As in real overcrowded lifeboats, Hardin argues that it is suicidal to help the poor, even if a lifeboat has extra room, as the affluent have a primary obligation to provide for their own future generations.

Hardin's second metaphor is the tragedy of the commons, a term used historically for shared pasturelands using for grazing livestock. Open to all livestock raisers, commons lands invited overuse and consequent destruction. Hardin sees modern immigration—which moves poor people to food—and the World Food Bank—which moves food to the poor—as forms of commons lands. The former accelerates environmental destruction in affluent countries, while the latter leads to exhaustion of the environment.

Hardin's third metaphor is what he calls the ratchet effect. When population increases in poor countries lead to crises, the humanitarian food aid that pours into the countries spurs further population increases, setting up vicious cycles. Food aid thus ultimately contributes to enormous population crashes and untold suffering. Hardin's conclusion challenges altruistic practices and employs a utilitarian approach: Withholding food aid will prevent massive global starvation and suffering in the future.

Assessment

Lifeboat ethics requires a careful assessment of the premises and facts. Hardin assumes that Earth's human population is close to the planet's biological carrying capacity. However, no one actually knows what that capacity really is. World population has historically risen geometrically without the massive starvation that Hardin's theory should expect. Moreover, starvation may have political or economic causes, as it is often occurs in countries involved in wars or beset by irresponsible governments.

The degradation of arable land, overfishing, and global climate change present real threats to the future of the ability of the earth to feed its increasing human population. Moreover, some argue that food aid reinforces governmental irresponsibility in poor nations. Among the countertheories is the cornucopian argument of Julian Simon, which suggests that technological innovations will keep up with population increases, forestalling a crash. Sharing modern technology, and not merely giving food, could become a moral obligation of the affluent.

Ethical responses to lifeboat ethics include the problem of distributive justice, a much discussed difficulty with utilitarianism. While Hardin believes that survival overrides justice, Peter Singer argues that affluent nations have an obligation to ameliorate world suffering. Singer and others also argue that eating meat—which is generally done mostly by the affluent—is unethical, as well as inefficient, as the food given to livestock could be better used to feed the hungry poor. Others treat food aid as supererogatory, an optional as opposed to an obligatory action.

—*Kristen L. Zacharias*

Further Reading

Boucher, Douglas M. *The Paradox of Plenty: Hunger in a Bountiful World*. Oakland, Calif.: Institute for Food and Development Policy, 1999.

Lappe, Frances Moore, Joseph Collins, and Peter Rosset. *World Hunger: Twelve Myths*. Emeryville, Calif.: Grove Press, 1998.

Lucas, George R., Jr., and Thomas W. Ogletree, eds. *Lifeboat Ethics: The Moral Dilemmas of World Hunger*. New York: HarperCollins, 1976.

See also: Agribusiness; Distributive justice; Famine; Future-oriented ethics; Hunger; Malthus, Thomas; Mercy; Population control; Triage; Utilitarianism; Zero-base ethics.

Manhattan Project

Identification: Research and development program established by the U.S. War Department to create a superexplosive utilizing the process of nuclear fission

Date: Established in June, 1942

Type of ethics: Scientific ethics

Significance: The Manhattan Project created the first atom bombs and the only such bombs ever to be used against human targets. The morality both of creating and of employing those weapons has been a matter of debate ever since

In 1939, physicists in the United States learned of Nazi Germany's attempts to develop a fission bomb of unprecedented power and alerted President Franklin D. Roosevelt to the situation in a letter written by Albert Einstein. Given the brutality of the Nazis, the ramifications of such a weapon were frightening. On December 6, 1941, the president directed the Office of Scientific Research and Development to investigate the possibility of producing a nuclear weapon. The head of the office, Vannevar Bush, reported back in early 1942 that it probably would be possible to produce sufficient fissionable uranium or plutonium to power such a weapon. Accomplishing that task was by far the greatest obstacle to building an atom bomb.

In strict secrecy, in June of 1942, the Army Corps of Engineers established the Manhattan Engineer District, a unit devoted to building the bomb. On September 17, then-colonel Leslie R. Groves was appointed to head the

Oppenheimer and Groves at the remains of the Trinity test in September 1945, two months after the test blast and just after the end of World War II. The white overshoes prevented fallout from sticking to the soles of their shoes. By U.S. Army Corps of Engineers.

entire effort (plan and organization), which by this time was called simply the Manhattan Project. Groves was promoted to general shortly thereafter. Physicist J. Robert Oppenheimer directed the scientific group that was responsible for actually designing the weapon.

By 1944, the Project was spending one billion dollars per year—a situation that some people believed was out of control. Project scientists detonated a prototype bomb in New Mexico on July 16, 1945, producing an energy yield that was beyond their expectations. Two more bombs were readied and dropped in early August, and Japan surrendered soon after. At the time, only some contributing scientists protested the use of the atomb bomb against a live target. Qualms were dispelled by the thought that Germany and Japan would have used it if they had developed it. As the effects of the new weapon became more fully appreciated, however, many began to feel remorse.

—Andrew C. Skinner; Updated by the editors

See also: Atom bomb; Cold War; Hiroshima and Nagasaki bombings; Union of Concerned Scientists; Weapons research.

Milgram experiment

The Event: Series of studies designed to determine the degree to which subjects would be willing to obey an authority's instructions to harm another person

Date: Conducted in 1961-1962

Type of ethics: Scientific ethics

Significance: The Milgram investigations produced unexpected data regarding the willingness of people to violate their own moral values when instructed to do so by an authority figure. They also created extreme stress for their participants, leading to a reconsideration of the ethical guidelines governing such research

Psychologist Stanley Milgram, horrified by the atrocities that had been committed by the Nazis during the Holocaust, conducted a program of research designed to explore the process of obedience to authority. The disturbing nature of his results and the ethical issues raised by his methods make this some of the most controversial and widely discussed research in the history of social science.

Recruited through a newspaper advertisement, a diverse group of adult subjects reported (individually) to Milgram's laboratory at Yale University expecting to participate in a study of memory and learning. Each participant was greeted by an experimenter dressed in a lab coat. Also present was a middle-aged gentleman, an accomplice who was ostensibly another participant in the session. The experimenter then described the research, which would investigate the effect of punishment on learning. Then, through a rigged drawing, the accomplice was assigned the role of "learner," while the actual subject became the "teacher."

The Experiment

Next, the three went to an adjacent room, where the learner was strapped into an "electric chair" as the experimenter explained that shock would be used as punishment. The teacher was then escorted back to the first room and seated in front of a shock generator, the front panel of which consisted of a series of thirty switches that could be used to administer shock. Each was labeled with a voltage level, starting with 15 volts and increasing by 15-volt increments to 450 volts; several verbal labels below the switches also indicated the severity of the shock. After receiving instructions and a demonstration from the experimenter, the teacher presented a sequence of simple memory tests to the learner through an intercom. The learner made "errors" according to a script, and the teacher was instructed to respond to each error by pushing a switch, thus delivering a shock to the learner. The teacher started with 15 volts and was directed to use the next higher switch with each successive error.

The goal of this procedure was simply to determine how long the subject/teacher would continue to obey the order to administer shock. (The accomplice/learner never actually received any shock.) As the shocks grew stronger, the learner began protesting—eventually pleading to be let out, then screaming, and finally ceasing to respond at all. When the teacher balked, the experimenter provided one of several firm verbal "prods" to continue (for example, "you *must* go on"). The procedure was discontinued if the teacher refused to obey after four such prods for a given shock level.

Milgram and other experts felt that few if any participants would demonstrate obedience under these circumstances, particularly after the learner began protesting. Nearly two-thirds of them, however, obeyed the experimenter's orders all the way to the highest level of shock (450 volts). This result occurred with both men and women, even in a version of the study in which the learner was portrayed as having a heart condition.

The typical subject in these studies showed clear signs of distress over the plight of the learner. Subjects often perspired or trembled, and some exhibited nervous laughter or other indications of tension. Indeed, it is this aspect of the research that has been cited most frequently by those who consider the studies unethical. Critics argue that Milgram compromised the welfare of the participants in this research by subjecting them to inappropriately high levels of stress. Many of these same critics have also suggested that Milgram failed to provide his subjects with enough advance information to enable them to make a fully informed decision about whether to participate.

In his defense, Milgram points out that his procedure was not intended to cause stress for the participants. Furthermore, he and other experts did not anticipate the stress that did occur because they expected that subjects would be reluctant to obey these orders. It is also important to note that Milgram did take care to protect these subjects and their dignity, as indicated by the activities that followed the experimental sessions. These measures included a discussion of the experiment and its rationale, a

meeting with the learner involving an explanation that he had not really been shocked, and reassurances that the subject's behavior (obedient or not) was entirely normal given the circumstances. Some three-fourths of all the participants indicated that they had learned something personally important as a result of being in the study, and additional follow-up by a psychiatrist a year later found no evidence of lasting psychological harm in any of those examined.

The Ethical Dilemma

More generally, this research illustrates a basic ethical dilemma faced frequently by experimental social psychologists. These researchers often need to create and manipulate powerful situations if they are to generate enough impact to observe something meaningful about social behavior, but doing so sometimes risks causing undue stress to subjects. This ethical issue is sometimes complicated still further by the need to deceive participants in order to preserve the authenticity of their behavior.

Few will deny that Milgram's research yielded significant insights into how obedience to an authority can prevent a subordinate from taking responsibility for inflicting harm on another person, but does the end justify the means employed to gain this knowledge? Ultimately, decisions of this sort must be made by carefully weighing the costs and benefits involved. Regardless of one's position on the ethics of the obedience studies, Milgram's work has done much to heighten sensitivity to ethical considerations in social research. Since Milgram's investigations were conducted, psychologists have adopted a more conservative set of principles governing research with people—guidelines that today would probably not allow the procedures he used.

—*Steve A. Nida*

Further Reading

American Psychological Association. "Ethical Principles of Psychologists." *American Psychologist* 45 (March, 1990): 390-395.

Baumrind, Diana. "Some Thoughts on Ethics of Research: After Reading Milgram's 'Behavioral Study of Obedience.'" *American Psychologist* 19, no. 6 (1964): 421-423.

Blass, Thomas, ed. *Obedience to Authority: Current Perspectives on the Milgram Paradigm.* Mahwah, N.J.: Lawrence Erlbaum Associates, 2000.

Milgram, Stanley. *Obedience to Authority.* New York: Harper & Row, 1974.

Miller, Arthur G., ed. *The Social Psychology of Psychological Research.* New York: Free Press, 1972.

Myers, David G. *Social Psychology.* 7th ed. Boston: McGraw-Hill, 2002.

See also: Collective guilt; Conscientious objection; Ethical Principles of Psychologists; Experimentation; Harm; Holocaust; Obedience; Psychology; Science.

Muir, John

Identification: Scottish American naturalist
Born: April 21, 1838, Dunbar, Scotland
Died: December 24, 1914, Los Angeles, California
Type of ethics: Environmental ethics
Significance: Muir lobbied for the establishment of Yosemite, Sequoia, and General Grant National Parks; was a founder of the Sierra Club; and increased general public interest in preservationism

John Muir moved to a Wisconsin homestead when he was eleven and attended the University of Wisconsin from 1858 to 1863. After a year of farming while waiting for a draft call, he decamped to stay in Canada from 1863 to 1864. In 1867, he began a fulltime career in nature study, starting with a projected thousand-mile walk to the Gulf of Mexico on his way to South America. Frustrated by serious illness, he went to California and lived in the Yosemite Valley for five years. In 1873, he began a full-time career as a nature writer and preservationist, spending summers hiking and observing natural phenomena in the mountains.

In 1889, Muir began writing and lobbying to preserve Yosemite Valley as a National Park. In 1896, as one of its founders, he became the first president of the Sierra Club; he remained in that position until 1914. He was preeminent in publicity and lobbying (1905-1913) against San Francisco's Hetch Hetchy water project. Although unsuccessful, this effort broadcast the preservationist ethic nationwide.

Muir's contributions to glaciology and geomorphology give him minor scientific status. He published more than 500 articles and essays, many of which were based on his mountaineering journals. His books include *Mountains of California* (1894), *My First Summer in the Sierra* (1911), and *The Yosemite* (1912).

—*Ralph L. Langenheim, Jr.*

See also: Bioethics; Conservation; Endangered species; Environmental movement; Leopold, Aldo; National Park System, U.S.; Sierra Club.

National Park System, U.S.

Identification: Group of over 360 parcels of land owned, administered, and protected by the federal government
Date: First park established in 1872
Type of ethics: Environmental ethics
Significance: The National Park System seeks to preserve environmental resources from industrial development, unregulated tourism, hunting, and other encroachments, on the theory that the nation's populace has an interest in, or benefits from, the conservation of wilderness. The creation of new parks may raise ethical issues regarding federal seizure of private or state land

In 1870, members of the Washburn survey decided, around a campfire, to recommend public ownership and preservation of scenic features in the Yellowstone region rather than claim them for themselves. This led Ferdinand Vandiveer Hayden, director of the U.S. Geographical and Geological Survey of the Territories, to lobby Congress,

1938 poster promoting Yellowstone National Park, the first national park in the world. By the National Park Service.

which established Yellowstone National Park in 1872. In 1886, the park was organized under the Army. In 1916, the National Park Service was established in the Department of the Interior, with Stephen Mather as its first director. Mather organized the system, emphasizing preservation and display. During the mid-1960s, Congress responded to the land ethic by directing the establishment of wilderness areas within existing parks. The park system also has broadened its scope from preserving spectacular scenic areas such as the Grand Canyon to include significant historical sites, outstanding recreational areas, and areas designed to preserve practical examples of important ecosystems, such as the Florida Everglades. National Parks are established by acts of Congress that define their areas and control their operation. Some national monuments, such as Death Valley National Monument, are of the same character as national parks but are established and controlled by Executive Order, a power granted to the president under the Antiquities Act of 1906.

—*Ralph L. Langenheim, Jr.*

See also: Conservation; Leopold, Aldo; Muir, John; Sierra Club; Wilderness Act of 1964.

Nature Conservancy Council

Identification: British agency established to promote the conservation of natural environments
Date: Chartered as Nature Conservancy in 1949; Council established 1973 by an act of Parliament; dissolved December 21, 1991
Type of ethics: Environmental ethics
Significance: The Nature Conservancy Council (NCC) established national nature reserves and conducted research within them, simultaneously preserving wildlife and increasing the scientific community's understanding of the importance of such preservation

The Nature Conservancy Council was established "to provide scientific advice on the conservation and control of the natural flora and fauna of Great Britain; to establish, maintain and manage nature reserves in Great Britain; and to organize and develop the research and scientific services related thereto." While the NCC was not the only conservation organization in the United Kingdom, its mission of scientific research combined with conservation was unique.

Some national nature reserves were owned by the conservancy; others were privately or publicly owned lands that were subject to reserve agreements. The conservancy was given the power to acquire land compulsorily when necessary. Through its land acquisition activities, it provided an alternative to development and played an important role in habitat preservation. The NCC worked with voluntary organizations, universities, and other government organizations in its conservation and scientific efforts. It increased public awareness of ecological processes and support for conservation. The British Nature Conservancy provided a model for the United States organization of the same name, established in 1951. The latter is a private nonprofit organization that conserves critical habitats by acquiring land through purchases or gifts, manages the sanctuaries, and supports research. In 1991, the NCC was divided into three smaller entities: English Nature, Scottish Natural Heritage, and the Countryside Council for Wales.

—*Marguerite McKnight; Updated by the editors*

See also: Biodiversity; Conservation; Endangered species.

Nature, rights of

Definition: Rights which may be said to inhere in the natural world, including both organic life and inorganic aspects of the landscape
Type of ethics: Environmental ethics
Significance: Theories which ascribe rights to nature are generally attempts to construct a moral framework within which to reconcile the human ability to damage and manipulate the environment with the needs of other species and with the sense that lands and waters may themselves have qualitative worth. Such theories are anthropocentric, however, in the sense that they tend to ascribe moral worth to the environment by investing it with human moral characteristics

Western thought, being greatly influenced by Christianity, has historically assumed the dominance of humans over all plant and animal species. The ability to destroy, domesticate, and alter other species has been seen as an inherent argument for human dominance of the natural world. Until the latter part of the twentieth century, little regard was given to the rights of nature to exist within a framework beneficial to species other than humans. The development of environmental crises such as global warming, extinctions, and the depletion of natural resources has led philosophers to consider the rights of nature. When Thomas Jefferson wrote the Declaration of Independence, he declared that all men were created with unalienable rights that allowed them to be treated with equality. Jefferson's ideal, while extended to all humans, was not at the time the reality for all humans.

Darwinism

Approximately one hundred years after Jefferson wrote the Declaration of Independence, Charles Darwin presented the idea of the evolution of species. Darwin's idea suggested that those species that currently exist do so because they were best able to adapt to the changing environment in which they live. It is important to note that Darwin did not put forth the idea that the strongest species survived, but rather that the most adaptable species survived. Darwin's theory was slightly distorted and generally believed to be survival of the fittest or strongest. This distortion of Darwin's theory, coupled with Jefferson's emphasis on the unalienable rights of humankind, led to a popular belief that humans had the right to regard nature as simply a resource to use and dominate without regard for any rights that nature might possess.

As a result of the idea of dispensable natural resources, be they inanimate or animate, human technological development and industrialization led to several ecological problems during the latter half of the twentieth century. Global warming, depletion of the earth's protective ozone layer, increases in harmful gases in the atmosphere, and the extinctions of plant and animal species are a few of these problems. The burgeoning ecological crisis began to illustrate the intricate and dependent relationship of humans with the natural world. As a result, philosophers and other thinkers began to reevaluate the rights of nature and the role of humans. It became clear that all species on the planet were interconnected and that the environment had forced all species into a subtle compact for survival.

Initially, nature was not viewed as possessing inalienable rights. Instead, the argument was made to protect nature for the benefit of human existence. Nature was important only insofar as it provided what was needful for human existence; if a human activity infringed upon nature in a way that was not viewed as destructive to human existence, then the activity was morally acceptable. Indeed, this view is still held; however, a deeper view of nature began to develop from this perspective. This deeper view argued that humans are only a percentage of an eco-logical whole, and that each part of this whole is dependent upon the other parts. The interdependence of the parts means that the rights of any one part are not greater than the rights of other parts of the ecological whole. Each species acts upon the society of other species and is acted upon by this society. This fact is commonly illustrated by such concepts as the food chain. In fact, all species, as a result of their existence in the environment, are involved in a social contract with one another. Those who argue from this perspective point out that humans as well as other animals perceive and react to the environment; therefore, humans and other animals have equal value in an environmental context.

Interdependence of Species

The interdependence of species is the cornerstone for the rights-of-nature argument. The theory of evolution supports the idea that all species are created equal because all species have evolved from common ancestors. The species currently residing on the planet are not historically the strongest or most fit but the descendants of the most adaptable species. It is an error to use one species' ability to manipulate the environment as a sanction to disregard the rights of other species. Furthermore, the fact that humans are able to know many of the details about how nature works as a result of biological science does not mean that humans have the right to disregard the rights of nature. Jefferson's unalienable rights for men do not discriminate upon the basis of intelligence; thus, the argument is applied to nature and humans. Humans are capable of knowing the workings of other species, but this should not justify disregard for these species' rights.

If it is held that nature has rights and that human rights are rights that should be accorded to the entire community of species, then how should actions be judged to be right or wrong? Perhaps the best definition is that of Aldo Leopold, who defines an action as being right when it preserves the integrity, stability, and beauty of the biotic community. If nature is accorded an ethical status that is equal to human ethical status, a benchmark such as Leopold's will be needed to make judgments about the actions that humans take.

—*Tod Murphy*

Further Reading

Attfield, Robin. *Environmental Ethics: An Overview for the Twenty-First Century.* Malden, Mass.: Blackwell, 2003.
_____. *The Ethics of Environmental Concern.* New York: Columbia University Press, 1983.

Brennan, Andrew. *Thinking About Nature: An Investigation of Nature, Value, and Ecology.* Athens: University of Georgia Press, 1988.

Day, David. *The Eco Wars: A Layman's Guide to the Ecology Movement.* London: Harrap, 1989.

Light, Andrew, and Holmes Rolston III, eds. *Environmental Ethics: An Anthology.* Malden, Mass.: Blackwell, 2003.

Miller, G. Tyler, Jr. *Living in the Environment: Principles, Connections, and Solutions.* 12th ed. Belmont, Calif.: Brooks/Cole, 2002.

Pimm, Stuart. *The Balance of Nature? Ecological Issues in the Conservation of Species and Communities.* Chicago: University of Chicago Press, 1991.

Spellerberg, Ian. *Evaluation and Assessment for Conservation: Ecological Guidelines for Determining Priorities for Nature Conservation.* London: Chapman & Hall, 1992.

See also: Animal rights; Dominion over nature, human; Environmental ethics; Global warming; Leopold, Aldo; Moral status of animals; *Silent Spring.*

Nazi science

Definition: Experiments conducted by the German scientific establishment during the period when Adolf Hitler and the Nazi Party dominated Germany

Date: 1933-1945

Type of ethics: Scientific ethics

Significance: The experiments conducted on Jews and other unwilling subjects by Nazi scientists have been used to symbolize the convergence of logic and moral atrocity in the Holocaust and the rationalist, dispassionate evil of the "final solution."

For more than twelve years (January 31, 1933-May 2, 1945), Germany was dominated by a political movement called the *Nationalsozialistische Deutsche Arbeiterpartei* (NSDAP or Nazis, for short). Upon becoming the chancellor of Germany, Nazi leader Adolf Hitler launched the twin programs of *Machtergreifung* and *Gleichschaltung* (the former term meaning "seizure of power" and the latter meaning "coordination"). The Nazis first installed members of their own party or party sympathizers into positions of authority in every government organization in Germany—schools and universities, scientific research institutes, medical facilities, youth groups, women's organizations, museums, philharmonic orchestras, art galleries, and virtually everything else in Germany. Nazis or Nazi sympathizers in those organizations then "coordinated" the activities of the people they controlled with Hitler's view of what all Germans should do and think.

German scientists also had to coordinate their experiments with Hitler's own peculiar view of the universe and humanity's place in it. The ultimate result was the destruction of human lives on a scale so massive as to defy understanding.

Eugenics Theories

Hitler's understanding of human society represented a vulgarized form of ideas that evolved from scientific experiments and theories in Western Europe and the United States during the nineteenth century. Evolutionists, geneticists, and eugenicists from the so-called "hard" sciences, along with psychologists and Social Darwinists from the "soft" sciences, contributed to the construction in the minds of Hitler and many other people of an essentially racial interpretation of human history.

Evolutionists taught that all members of a species of living organisms are involved in a constant struggle for survival. Those organisms that have inherited characteristics from their ancestors that are best suited for survival will outcompete their less genetically blessed rivals and thus pass along those beneficial traits to their offspring. When scientists rediscovered Mendelian genetics immediately after 1900, many of them began to realize that breeding a superior stock of human beings poses no more of a scientific problem than does the selective breeding of plants and animals. A program of selective human breeding would assure that only desirable characteristics would pass from one generation to the next.

Social Darwinists argued that human races (or nations) are engaged in a struggle for survival, as are the members of individual species. If a nation or race does not possess or adopt the physical and intellectual qualities necessary to allow it to outcompete its rivals, it will be swept into the dustbin of history and become extinct or its members will become subservient to superior nations or races. Social Darwinists combined with advocates of selective human breeding to form the international eugenics movement.

Eugenicists included scientists from every discipline, but especially anthropology, medicine, and psychology. They argued that governments should adopt regulations to assure that future generations would enjoy the best physical and intellectual constitutions that their gene pools could supply. Eugenicists advocated that individuals with congenital diseases of the mind or body should undergo mandatory sterilization to prevent their disabilities from being passed along to future generations. During the 1920s and 1930s, governments in many Western European countries and several state legislatures in the United States adopted laws mandating sterilization for persons with inheritable infirmities.

Some of the eugenicists advocated that enlightened governments should adopt euthanasia programs to eliminate persons with mental or physical disabilities that were of a terminal nature or that rendered them incapable of enjoying an ill-defined "quality of life" acceptable to the euthanasists. The euthanasists tried to convince governments that the inmates of medical clinics, hospitals, and insane asylums should be screened by qualified physicians who would determine whether their lives were of any further value to themselves or to society. Those inmates deemed by screening physicians to be incurably ill (mentally or physically) or as "useless eaters" should, according to the euthanasists, be granted "mercy deaths." Only in Nazi Germany did the government adopt euthanasia. The German euthanasia program led directly to mass murders in Nazi concentration camps.

Weapons

The Nazi government also coopted all the other sciences in Germany to advance its own view of how Germany and the world should be organized. The sciences of aeronautical engineering, chemistry, and physics in particular became integral parts of a huge military-industrial complex designed to make advanced weapons of war. In Hitler's Social Darwinistic worldview, war was a natural and necessary condition of human evolution. In his semiautobiographical *Mein Kampf* (1926), Hitler clearly expressed his intent to conquer territory in the Soviet Union into which the German race could expand. As one of his earliest actions after attaining dictatorial power in Germany, Hitler began a massive expansion of the German armed forces. German scientists from every discipline began to devote their research to areas that would further Hitler's military intentions.

Some German scientists began programs that led to the development of the world's first operational jet fighter aircraft. Others began developing experiments in rocketry that culminated in the V-2, a ballistic missile that wreaked great havoc among civilians in Britain. German chemists developed toxic gases (never used) that were more deadly than any that had been used in World War I. Chemists also discovered how to make synthetic rubber as well as synthetic gasoline derived from coal, in an effort to assure that the German war machine could continue to function even if it were cut off from supplies of petroleum and rub-

ber by an enemy blockade. German physicists began research designed to produce revolutionary new weapons of war, including a program that almost produced a nuclear bomb. Other exotic weaponssystems research included plans for a giant mirror that, when placed in low Earth orbit, could focus the sun's rays on any spot on Earth with devastating results.

Medical Research

Perhaps the most flagrant violations of accepted scientific ethical principles in Germany during the Nazi era occurred in medical science. Medical researchers in some concentration camps routinely used unwilling human subjects in macabre experiments that often resulted in the death or disfigurement of the subjects. Physicians in concentration camps, medical clinics, and insane asylums willingly participated in "selections" (determining whether individuals were fit for work or should be summarily executed). In the case of some of the concentration camps, physicians made these selections without conducting even cursory medical examinations. The physicians also extracted organs from the cadavers of those who had been killed and sent them to medical research institutes throughout Germany for experimentation. Physicians perpetrated this dismemberment without the knowledge or approval of the victims or the victims' families.

Many scientists presently condemn the atrocities that were committed in the name of science in Germany during the Nazi era. They believe that German scientists of the period abandoned all accepted ethical principles while they were caught up in a national madness brought on by extraordinary circumstances. A number of the German scientists involved, however, maintained that their actions were entirely ethical, because they were all intended to serve the highest good—the improvement of the human condition.

In the long view of history, they maintained, the human race will benefit enormously from their actions—materially, physically, and intellectually. The Nazi scientists adopted the position that, in science, the end justifies the means. Many scientists in all countries today accept that position, at least to some degree. Perhaps more than any other event in history, the Nazi era underscores the absolute necessity of a universally accepted code of scientific ethics if any semblance of humanity is to be maintained in the wake of an increasingly technological and scientific society.

—*Paul Madden*

Further Reading

Beyerchen, Alan D. *Scientists Under Hitler: Politics and the Physics Community in the Third Reich.* New Haven, Conn.:Yale University Press, 1977.

Bracher, Karl Dietrich. *The German Dictatorship: The Origins, Structure, and Effects of National Socialism.* Translated by Jean Steinberg. New York: Praeger, 1970.

Cecil, Robert. *The Myth of the Master Race: Alfred Rosenberg and Nazi Ideology.* New York: Dodd, Mead, 1972.

Lifton, Robert Jay. *The Nazi Doctors: Medical Killing and the Psychology of Genocide.* New York: Basic Books, 1986.

Muller-Hill, Benno. *Murderous Science: Elimination by Scientific Selection of Jews, Gypsies, and Others, Germany 1933-1945.* New York: Oxford University Press, 1988.

Szöllösi-Janze, Margit, ed. *Science in the Third Reich.* New York: Berg, 2001.

Weale, Adrian. *Science and the Swastika.* London: Channel 4 Books, 2001.

See also: Atom bomb; Concentration camps; Eugenics; Experimentation; Hitler, Adolf; Holocaust; Medical research; Nazism; Nuremberg Trials; "Playing god" in medical decision making.

"Not in my backyard"

Definition: Popular objection to the establishment of socially necessary but unattractive or troublesome facilities, such as landfills, prisons, and group homes

Date: Term first used during the 1980s

Type of ethics: Environmental ethics

Significance: Both proponents and opponents of unpopular projects utilize moral arguments to support their positions

"Not-in-my-backyard" (often represented by the acronym NIMBY) objections are often raised to the introduction of an unwanted facility to an area, particularly one in or near a residential area. Almost all members of the society may recognize the need for the facility and support it in principle, while at the same time not wanting it in their own neighborhoods or communities. Citizen groups may form and noisily oppose projects such as prisons, nuclear waste sites, and low-income housing projects. In acrimonious NIMBY debates among project developers and members of the public, all sides may raise ethical arguments. As in other aspects of life, multiple ethical principles often apply and create conflict of moral rules.

Ethical Arguments in Favor of Projects

The first argument in favor of an unpopular project is that it will serve the common good of society. The project's utilitarian consequences, it may be argued, will bring health, happiness, and general wellbeing to the greatest number. Indeed, a community would have a difficult time surviving without facilities to dispose of its wastes, create its energy, and provide its human services. The question is: Where are the facilities necessary to perform these functions to be located?

Abhorrent consequences may follow if NIMBY advocates succeed. The blocked project will simply be relocated elsewhere, to the detriment of another community. Furthermore, there is a possibility that the alternative site may not be as safe or effective as the site initially selected by scientific planners.

Human beings are ethically required not to cause real harm to others. However, they also are not obligated to abstain from conduct that is erroneously perceived as harmful. Protesters are often ill-informed about plans they oppose. For example, many people do not distinguish between hazardous and nonhazardous types of waste, or they may believe false stereotypes about the dangers of people with mental disabilities. The fact that members of a community are psychologically uncomfortable with a plan does not constitute a morally relevant reason for disallowing it.

Ethical Rules in Opposition

In an ideal society, the costs imposed by essential services should be shared equally by all. Unpopular projects, such as waste dumps and prisons, unfairly burden their closest neighbors. While the community as a whole may be served by having such facilities, the facilities' nearest neighbors receive no compensation for the extra noise, unpleasant odors, extra dangers, inconvenient traffic, and fall in the value of their properties. Furthermore, a basic rule of fairness requires that all members of a community should clean up their own messes. NIMBY neighbors are blameless; they are not any more responsible for community problems such as nuclear wastes, energy shortages, highway congestion, or prison populations that the unpopular facilities are designed to fix.

In a fair contest, the better competitor should win without cheating. Some NIMBY opposition arguments focus on unethical project planning and marketing. Public land uses should be determined in consultation with the public, as community members should have a say in events affecting their own neighborhoods. However, in NIMBY situations, proposals are typically imposed and implemented by outside bodies. Such bodies may promote projects unethically, break their promises, conceal the truth, and intimidate opponents.

Two Types of NIMBY Projects

One class of NIMBY projects poses some type of environmental threat, while at the same time providing a needed service. A large subclass is disposal site proposals, including facilities for nuclear wastes and regular landfills. There are also environment-altering NIMBY proposals that do not deal with waste, such as airports, oil refineries, windmill farms, cellular phone towers, and ballparks.

A second major class of projects provides needed human services such as new prisons, group homes for people with drug or alcohol problems or mental disabilities, and nursing homes that admit AIDS patients. Babies and children are not exempt from NIMBY opposition. Even small day-care facilities have been opposed in some residential neighborhoods. The ethical issues raised about these two project types include the points already discussed, as well as variants for each type of project.

Environmental Projects

When waste disposal sites and polluting farms or factories are planned, the neighbors who are affected are typically poor and nonwhite. The concept of "environmental racism" critiques burdening society's least powerful groups, unable to defend themselves, with exposure to unsafe and unpleasant substances. To add insult to injury, the employment opportunities promised to the poor in return for acceptance of the new facilities often do not materialize.

Some ardent environmental activists contend that all the world's neighborhoods deserve protection from exposure. They argue that it is immoral to export toxins to developing countries. Rich nations should not dump their trash on the world's poor. This viewpoint has been nicknamed NOPE, an acronym for "Not on Planet Earth." Activists urge fundamental changes in materialistic societies such as the United States. They argue that Americans need fewer landfills, not more, and suggest that recycling and less wasteful lifestyles are the answers. According to this view, landfills are the evil products of pollution and materialism.

Proponents of new waste sites contend that they will improve public health and safety, especially in communities whose existing dumps are overburdened and leaky.

Without larger, leakproof facilities, a town's dumps may remain, and dangerous practices such as late-night dumping of wastes by unscrupulous haulers will continue. Furthermore, it is argued, it is morally unfair to put off permanent solutions to waste problems, leaving them for future generations to solve.

Human Service Projects

A moral community is responsive to the needs of all its members. It is compassionate toward its weakest and most needy. All people should be treated humanely, and in ways that allow them to thrive and develop their abilities. Additionally, both law and morality require that people be treated equally unless there are valid reasons for doing otherwise.

There is no morally relevant reason to exclude people with mental disabilities from middle-class neighborhoods. Similar arguments are made by advocates for placing small, moderate-income housing within such neighborhoods. Research has shown that both subgroups are harmed by being segregated off by themselves. Moreover, society as a whole can benefit in that intergroup contact often leads to decreases in intergroup prejudices.

—Nancy Conn Terjesen

Further Reading

Bullard, Robert D. *Dumping in Dixie: Race, Class and Environmental Quality.* Boulder, Colo.: Westview Press, 1990.

Gerrard, Michael B. *Whose Backyard, Whose Risk.* Cambridge, Mass.: MIT Press, 1994.

Hornblower, Margot. "Not in My Backyard, You Don't." *Time* 131 (June 27, 1988): 44, 45.

Inhaber, Herbert. *Slaying the NIMBY Dragon.* New Brunswick, N.J.: Transaction Publishers, 1998.

Morris, Jane Anne. *Not in My Backyard: The Handbook.* San Diego, Calif.: Silvercat Publications, 1994.

See also: Ecology; Environmental ethics; Environmental Protection Agency; Nuclear Regulatory Commission; Toxic waste.

Nuclear energy

Definition: Production of energy via processes that affect the nucleus of the atom

Date: Developed during the mid-twentieth century

Type of ethics: Environmental ethics

Significance: The use of nuclear science to generate power raises ethical issues, because it is unclear whether the significant benefits of atomic power outweigh the actual and potential damage to humans and the environment caused by radioactive materials and nuclear accidents

The invention and utilization of devices to convert energy from natural forms into readily accessible forms has accompanied the technological progress of humans. Humans are continuously searching for methods that efficiently meet their rapidly increasing energy demands.

The "nuclear age" began in 1938 with the discovery by Otto Hahn and Fritz Strassmann that substantial amounts of energy are released when heavy atoms such as uranium are broken into smaller atomic fragments. This process of nuclear fission is one of three types of nuclear reaction that release substantial amounts of energy. The fission of one gram of uranium 235 can keep a 100-watt light bulb continuously lit for twenty-three years, whereas only eight minutes of light can be generated by burning one gram of gasoline. When controlled, the fission process can be used to generate electric power; uncontrolled, it becomes the destructive power of atom bombs.

Peaceful vs. Military Uses

Although the peaceful uses of nuclear power cannot be morally equated with the military uses, events such as the

The Calder Hall nuclear power station in the United Kingdom was the world's first commercial nuclear power station. It was connected to the national power grid on 27 August 1956 and officially revealed in a ceremony by Queen Elizabeth II on 17 October 1956. In common with a number of other Generation I nuclear reactors, the plant had the dual purpose of producing electrical power and plutonium-239, the latter for the nascent nuclear weapons program in Britain. By Energy.gov.

accidents at Three Mile Island and Chernobyl demonstrate the conflict between basic ecological priorities and technological accomplishments. Ethical considerations in the past have focused mainly on human beings. People tend to regard themselves as the only beings of inherent value, with the remainder of the natural world being a resource valued only for its usefulness to humans. While the limitations of past technologies have allowed the survival of the natural biosphere, modern technology, with its potential for impact on future generations, requires an ethics of long-range responsibility.

When Hiroshima was bombed, little was known about radioactive fallout. During the 1950s, it was discovered that the above-ground testing of nuclear weapons introduced radioactive materials into the upper atmosphere to be transported by the winds for deposition in distant places. The strontium 90 produced in these explosions became a concern in 1954. Chemically, it behaves like calcium and is incorporated into the food chain via plants, cows, and milk, ultimately ending up in children's bones. Another radioactive by-product, iodine 131, incorporates itself into the thyroid gland. The radioactive emissions from these incorporated elements can lead to the development of cancer.

Humans can thrive only in the particular environmental niche to which they are adapted. The fact that human bodies cannot discriminate between species such as radioactive iodine and safe iodine shows that damaging the environment jeopardizes the survival of the human race. Radioactive pollutants are particularly insidious because they remain in the environment for long periods of time—it takes almost four hundred years for the radioactivity of a sample of strontium 90 to degrade to a negligible level. These problems led the United States and the Soviet Union to prohibit the atmospheric testing of nuclear weapons in 1963.

On December 2, 1942, a team of scientists at the University of Chicago produced the first controlled nuclear chain reaction, the experiment that led to the harnessing of the atom for peaceful purposes. Nuclear reactors have since been used to generate electricity, to power ships and rockets, and to power water desalination plants.

Safety Issues

Although a modern nuclear reactor is not a bomb, because its concentration of radioactive fuel is too low, environmental safety is still an issue. Major accidents, such as the 1957 Windscale, England, disaster in which the reactor core overheated and a significant amount of radiation was released into the atmosphere and the 1986 Chernobyl catastrophe in which ninety thousand people had to be evacuated from a nineteen-mile danger zone and a large amount of radioactive material was ejected into the atmosphere, are examples of the destructive potential of nuclear energy production. Although absolute safety at nuclear reactors cannot be guaranteed, modern safeguards have decreased the likelihood of such disasters.

Little attention was paid to the disposal of nuclear wastes during the early days of nuclear power generation. Nuclear waste includes all by-products generated in either routine operations or accidents at any point along the nuclear fuel trail (uranium mining, enrichment, fuel fabrication, spent fuel, and so forth). Since these wastes cannot be detoxified, they must be completely isolated from human contact until they have decayed to negligible levels. For plutonium, the most dangerous species in nuclear waste, this time period is at least 240,000 years.

Is it possible to store such materials in isolation for thousands of centuries? Historically, nuclear waste has not been adequately contained. While scientists predicted that the plutonium stored at Maxey Flats, Kentucky, the world's largest plutonium waste facility, would migrate only one-half inch on-site over a 24,000-year period, it actually migrated two miles off-site within ten years. More than 500,000 gallons of waste stored at Hanford, Washington, leaked into the soil, introducing radioactive pollutants into the Columbia River and the Pacific Ocean. The worst example of breached storage occurred in the Ural Mountains of the Soviet Union during the late 1950s, when an unexpected and uncontrolled nuclear reaction occurred in stored waste, rendering more than twenty square miles uninhabitable to humans and other species. Thus, the ethics of using nuclear energy until the technology exists for safe storage repositories must be questioned.

Even if safe storage technology can be developed, storing waste for thousands of centuries remains a gamble. Disposal sites must remain undisturbed by acts of war, terrorism, and natural processes such as ice sheets and geological folding, while storage conditions must not allow the waste to become reactive. History discounts the ability of humans to protect their "treasures" for extended periods of time; for example, the tombs of Egypt were left undisturbed for less than four thousand years.

How humanity generates the energy needed by its technology is a complex issue. The elimination of nuclear energy generation without a concomitant reduction in humanity's energy requirements would only result in the burning of more fossil fuel. Although this occurrence would avoid future nuclear disasters and end the accumulation of radioactive waste, it would also exacerbate the "greenhouse effect" and the resultant global warming, which also puts the biosphere at risk for future generations. Ultimately, the chance of disaster in the present and the legacy of toxic waste that humans neither have the knowledge to make safe nor the ability to contain must be compared to the risks posed by alternative methods of energy production to present and future generations.

—Arlene R. Courtney

Further Reading

Barlett, Donald L., and James B. Steele. *Forevermore: Nuclear Waste in America.* New York: W. W. Norton, 1985.

Cohen, Bernard L. *Nuclear Science and Society.* Garden City, N.Y.: Anchor Press, 1974.

Irwin, Michael. *Nuclear Energy: Good or Bad?* New York: Public Affairs Committee, 1984.

Medvedev, Zhores A. *Nuclear Disaster in the Urals.* New York: W. W. Norton, 1979.

Nye, Joseph S. *Nuclear Ethics.* New York: Free Press, 1986.

Welsh, Ian. *Mobilising Modernity: The Nuclear Moment.* New York: Routledge, 2000.

Williams, David R. *What Is Safe? The Risks of Living in a Nuclear Age.* Cambridge, England: Royal Society of Chemistry, Information Services, 1998.

See also: Atomic Energy Commission; Global warming; Greenhouse effect; "Not in my backyard"; Nuclear arms race; Nuclear Regulatory Commission; Science; Toxic waste; Union of Concerned Scientists.

Nuclear Regulatory Commission

Identification: Independent agency of the U.S. government that licenses and regulates the civilian uses of nuclear energy and materials

Date: Established on October 11, 1974

Type of ethics: Environmental ethics

Significance: The Nuclear Regulatory Commission (NRC) is responsible for protecting the environment from damage caused by nuclear materials

The Energy Reorganization Act of 1974 established the Energy Research and Development Administration (ERDA) and the Nuclear Regulatory Commission (NRC) and abolished the Atomic Energy Commission (AEC). One purpose of the act was "to enhance the goals of restor-

ing, protecting, and enhancing environmental quality." The act separated the licensing and regulation of civilian nuclear energy and materials from their development and promotion. These functions had been joined under the AEC. The act directed the NRC to identify possible nuclear-energy sites and to evaluate potential environmental impacts from their construction and operation. In 1977, the ERDA was abolished and its responsibilities were transferred to the Department of Energy.

The NRC regulates the processing, transport, handling, and disposal of nuclear materials and is responsible for protecting public health and safety and the environment. It licenses and oversees the construction and operation of nuclear reactors that generate electricity. Before licensing reactors, the NRC holds hearings to enable public participation in the process. It also inspects facilities for violations of safety standards and investigates nuclear accidents.

—Marguerite McKnight

See also: Atomic Energy Commission; Nuclear energy; Toxic waste; Union of Concerned Scientists.

Pollution

Definition: Environmental contamination with human-made waste

Type of ethics: Environmental ethics

Significance: Pollution has effects on many different levels, from causing people minor inconvenience and aesthetic displeasure up to and including mass human illness and death, and the extinctions of other species

Pollution must be viewed in the light of natural versus human-based events. A natural event is part of the fundamental cycle of Earth processes that maintain a balance of building up and wearing down, of destruction and recovery. A volcano may spew tons of ash into the atmosphere and darken the sky so much that weather patterns are changed. Mudflows precipitated by loose debris and rapidly melting glaciers clog waterways on which nearby ecosystems rely. Lava kills everything in its path. Despite these drastic, destructive changes, natural processes will clear the air to reestablish customary weather patterns, will create more glaciers whose runoff will establish new river ecosystems, and will produce fertile soils to support life in areas where it was destroyed.

Pollution is the introduction of agents by humans into the environment in quantities that disrupt the balance of natural processes. Its possible detrimental effect on human life is not part of pollution's definition. Neither are human ignorance or lack of foresight, which may greatly influence the course and severity of pollution.

Ethics is a dimension specific to pollution that is not characteristic of natural processes. Humankind has the intellectual capacity to affect its course, and is itself affected morally by pollution's existence.

Pollution started when humans began manipulating the environment. Although pollution is usually characterized as chemicals or by-products of synthetic processes, this characterization is not entirely accurate. Waste from herds of domestic animals, for example, is a natural product, but it causes many environmental problems. Introducing aggressive nonnative species into an established ecosystem is also pollution, since such species frequently overwhelm the natural system's balance and displace native species. It has even been asserted that the human species itself is a pollutant, since it is both an aggressive species and nonnative to many habitats that it occupies and exploits.

In considering pollution created by manufacturing and daily human activities, there is no uncontaminated ecosystem. Even beyond Earth's known biosphere, humankind sends objects into outer space, and those that become defunct or were never intended to return are dubbed "space junk." Invisible pollutants cannot be overlooked. Various types of synthesized and concentrated radiation—from ultralow-frequency sound waves to sonic booms; from artificial lighting in classrooms, offices, and along highways to nuclear radioactivity—bombard and vibrate the molecules of the land, the air, and the inhabitants. As a result of all these different contaminants, plant and animal species suffer from aborted embryos, deformed offspring, poor health, shortened lives, and death. Among those suffering is the human species.

History

Since pollution has an ethical dimension, why has humanity not exercised its moral strength in preventing or halting it? Part of the answer is ignorance. It is not until environmental damage is recognized—usually by detecting injury to some species of plant or animal—that humankind realizes that pollution has occurred.

When gasoline-powered cars were introduced, it never occurred to proponents of modern transportation that the admittedly malodorous exhaust could possibly place large numbers of people in dire respiratory straits, let alone cause Earth to face global warming. Even when auto exhaust was recognized as a major contributor to the unsightly haze of smog, scientists had not yet developed sensing and testing equipment that would give them knowledge of the scope of the air pollution problem.

Another reason that humankind's moral capacity has not been a force in preventing pollution is lack of foresight. This issue illustrates two kinds of humanity's arrogance. Many people assume that humankind has the power and intelligence to solve every problem it recognizes. Many people also have the unrealistic, erroneous belief that there are segments of society that cannot be affected by the dangers that everyone else faces.

When nuclear power plants were developed, the designers were aware that lethal by-products would be generated, and planners incorporated holding ponds and other storage areas in the building complexes. They had not yet developed any means for the safe disposal of nuclear waste, assuming that they would be able to do so as necessary at some future date. Since these designers recognized most of the possible problems of such facilities, did they assume that they were invulnerable to those problems?

Another factor in the pollution situation is the human population's exponential growth. The relationship between technological development and increased human survival has so far been linked in an endless circle. If the human population was only one percent of what it is now, with a corresponding ratio of contaminants in the environment, pollution would be no less real, though it might not seem as serious.

Discussion

The ethics of the survival of life on Earth are shaped by the immediate danger presented by environmental pollution. Most people presume that the survival of the human species is the most important issue. Some reject this conclusion as blatant homocentric speciesism and argue that the survival of human life is inherently no more urgent or legitimate than the survival of any other species. Many people realize, without making claims for the necessity of human survival, that it is dependent on uncountable plant and animal species surviving and upon an environment unsullied enough to support them. All these considerations are based on human acceptance of responsibility for the future. Is humankind responsible for the future? Should humankind assume any responsibility for it?

Perhaps human arrogance causes humankind to presume that such a responsibility exists. Could it be that human history is merely a natural part of evolution on Earth? Are humankind's effects on the environment part of the natural scheme of things to which the environment will eventually adapt? Will that adaptation include mass extinctions and the subsequent development of other life-forms capable of tolerating the changes that humankind has wrought?

Is humankind responsible for all future generations of life? Is humankind morally liable for the future of Earth itself? If humankind does accept any of these responsibilities, what are the exigent considerations? Given the history of discovering pollution by hindsight, it would seem logical that humankind should not introduce any further agents, unknown or known, into the environment. If additional contamination by known pollutants is to be stopped, it cannot be done without accepting the moral consequences of the human misery and death that will follow as a result of the loss of jobs and the decreased availability and less efficient distribution of food and other human necessities.

As with most moral issues, the pollution dilemma has no easy answers. Yet if humankind is to persist, there can be no avoiding the ethical considerations involved in a possible solution to the problems of pollution.

—Marcella T. Joy

Further Reading

Allsopp, Bruce. *Ecological Morality.* London: Frederick Muller, 1972.

Attfield, Robin. *Environmental Ethics: An Overview for the Twenty-First Century.* Malden, Mass.: Blackwell, 2003.

Light, Andrew, and Holmes Rolston III, eds. *Environmental Ethics: An Anthology.* Malden, Mass.: Blackwell, 2003.

Partride, Ernest, ed. *Responsibilities to Future Generations: Environmental Ethics.* Buffalo, N.Y.: Prometheus Books, 1981.

Rolston, Holmes, III. *Environmental Ethics: Duties to and Values in the Natural World.* Philadelphia: Temple University Press, 1988.

Scherer, Donald, ed. *Upstream/Downstream: Issues in Environmental Ethics.* Philadelphia: Temple University Press, 1990.

Silver, Cheryl Simon, with Ruth DeFries. *One Earth, One Future: Our Changing Global Environment.* Washington, D.C.: National Academy Press, 1990.

See also: Clean Air Act; Clean Water Act; Earth and humanity; Environmental ethics; Environmental Protection Agency; Gaia hypothesis; Pollution permits; *Silent Spring*; Sociobiology; Technology; Toxic waste.

Pollution permits

Definition: Governmental exemptions that grant industries the right to release defined amounts of pollution into the environment

Type of ethics: Environmental ethics

Significance: Although pollution permits have proven to be an effective means of controlling and reducing pollution, thus benefiting society, their critics argue that it is ethically wrong to give any industry the right to cause pollution

Pollution is a problem of the common resources that are used by all members of society. Such "commons" include air, water, and the oceans. The problem in protecting these resources is how to deal with the external costs, including environmental degradation and injury to human health. The external costs of pollution are borne by those using the common resources and not by the polluters.

Early proposals to control pollution included taxation, which was favored by economists, and command and control, which was favored by politicians. In the latter method, regulatory agencies determine acceptable levels of pollution and impose the implementation of new technologies to reduce it. Both solutions have difficulties, however. Another mechanism for reducing pollution has been the issuance of marketable or tradable pollution permits, a system that relies on free market forces and economic efficiency. The use of pollution permits has resulted in the elimination of lead additives in petroleum refining, in major reductions of sulfur dioxide (which are responsible for acid rain) and particulate emissions, and in lesser reductions of chlorofluorocarbons and nitrogen oxides. The U.S. Congress incorporated pollution permits in the provisions of its 1990 Clean Air Act.

How Pollution Permits Work

Employing cost-benefit analysis, a regulatory agency determines a permissible level of pollution and allocates permits to the industries producing the pollution. Those able to reduce emissions inexpensively may then sell their unused permits to those less able to afford reductions of their emissions. Unlike the command-and-control approach, the pollution permits system allows polluters to determine how best to reduce pollution.

Many economists prefer the pollution permit system because it allows free market forces to act, while environmentalists like it because it does reduce pollution. However, the system presents ethical difficulties. First, the common resources, such as air and water, belong to all members of society but appear to be treated as private property under the pollution permit system. Defenders respond that the permits only authorize use of the commons, not ownership of some part of it.

Critics also argue that polluting is morally wrong and that the pollution permit systems allows favorites—the permit holders—to do something that no one should be permitted to do. Sellers transfer the right to pollute and thus cause harm, something no one should have the right to sell. Others assert that holders of permits should have no right to sell them, as permits should be given away. Defenders of the system responding to these criticisms argue that the goal of the permits is the benefit of humanity, and that studies of health and the environment determine permissible levels of pollution. In addition, the permissible levels should gradually be lowered until pollutants such as leaded gasoline are eliminated or further reductions in pollution cost more than the benefits accrued from the total elimination of the pollution. Finally, critics argue that pollution permit practices that produce "hot spots"—areas where higher concentrations of pollution develop—often in economically poorer neighborhoods, must be banned.

—*Kristen L. Zacharias*

Further Reading

Girdner, Eddie J., and Jack Smith. *Killing Me Softly: Toxic Waste, Corporate Profit, and the Struggle for Environmental Justice.* New York: Monthly Review Press, 2002.

Steidlmeier, Paul. "The Morality of Pollution Permits." *Environmental Ethics* 15 (1993): 133-150.

Tietenberg, T. H. "Ethical Influences on the Evolution of the U.S. Tradable Permit Approach to Pollution Control." *Ecological Economics* 24 (1998): 241-257.

See also: Bioethics; Clean Air Act; Clean Water Act; Cost-benefit analysis; Environmental Protection Agency; Pollution; *Silent Spring*; Sustainability of resources; Toxic waste.

Population Connection

Identification: Organization established to fight for social and economic stability by advocating that population growth be limited to accord with available resources

Date: Founded in 1968; renamed on May 1, 2002

Type of ethics: Environmental ethics

Significance: Population Connection not only focuses on encouraging individuals to do their part to improve living conditions for all peoples of the world but also mounts political campaigns intended to change national policy in order to limit population growth and destruction of the environment

With a membership during the 1990s of more than forty thousand and an annual budget of more than two million dollars, Population Connection (originally known as Zero Population Growth) promotes protection of the environment through reduction of population growth. Because 1990 figures reflect an increase of 95 million people per year worldwide, scientists fear that the ability of the earth's resources to support the population will be seriously undermined.

Population Connection works in several ways, both within the United States and internationally, to educate legislators, organizations, teachers, and individuals regarding the massive negative impact of the burgeoning population and its consequent demands upon the earth's resources because of increasing food and energy demands, as well as lifestyle choices that result in the wasting of resources and pollution. Among the organization's activities are political action to ensure reproductive rights, including making available safe, reliable family planning information and services and legal abortion when contraception fails; enhancing the economic and social status of women worldwide through both governmental and private efforts; and, most important, educating people regarding the crucial link between continued population growth and environmental degradation, pollution, poverty, and political and social unrest.

—*Mary Johnson*

See also: Abortion; Birth control; Conservation; Ecology; Population control.

Population control

Definition: Attempt to limit human population by various means

Type of ethics: Environmental ethics

Significance: Population control is generally driven by ethical concerns about the effects of human overpopulation upon both the environment and the quality of life of individual members of the human race. Some methods of population control raise ethical concerns of their own, however, about paternalism, the right to privacy, and basic human rights

The human population, like that of other creatures, is limited in growth by its biotic potential, the maximum rate at which a species can produce offspring given unlimited resources and ideal environmental conditions. At this rate of growth, the population would at first grow slowly only to increase rapidly to produce an exponential curve. Neither humans nor any other species in a given ecosystem can indefinitely grow at their biotic potential, since one or more factors always act as limiting agents. The maximum population size an ecosystem can support indefinitely under a given set of environmental conditions is called that ecosystem's carrying capacity.

Growth Potential

Human population has continued to grow as Earth's carrying capacity for humans has been extended as a result of human cleverness, technological and social adaptations, and other forms of cultural evolution. People have altered their ecological niche by increasing food production, controlling disease, and using large amounts of energy and material resources to make habitable those parts of the world that are normally not so.

Observers believe a wide range of populations is possible. Some observers believe that people have already gone beyond the carrying capacity point at which all the earth's inhabitants can be fed, sheltered, and supported. Estimates on the low end of population are that only 1.2 billion people can be supported to U.S. dietary standards and only 600 million at the U.S. rate of energy consumption. These numbers are likely low, since the U.S. rate of food and energy use is high. The higher estimate for human carrying capacity is 45 billion people on a diet similar to U.S. dietary standards, made possible by cultivating all available land, using nuclear power for energy, and mining much of the earth's crust to a depth of 1.6 kilometers for resources. An even higher estimate for human carrying capacity is 157 billion if diets are based solely on grains.

The human population continues to grow, regardless of what the carrying capacity may be. The world population doubles every thirty-five years at growth rates of the 1970s and 1980s. If the population were controlled to zero population growth, the world population would continue to grow for several generations because of decreasing death rates.

Ethical Concerns

Ethically, most nations favor stabilized or low population growth, because problems of peace, poverty, racism, disease, pollution, urbanization, ecosystem simplification, and resource depletion become harder to solve as the population increases. At the same time, many less-developed nations feel that population control, coupled with the continued status quo of international economic order, poses a dire threat to already oppressed people. These nations insist that for population control to become accepted, there must be a reorganization of economic and political power. These nations argue that people are the most vital of the world's resources and that problems of resource depletion and pollution can be solved by human ingenuity and technology. It is argued that the more people there are, the more likely it is that these problems will be solved. Economic growth would be stimulated because with more people there would be more production.

In contrast, others argue that, ethically, the world population should be limited because most people would be added to the least-developed countries, where education, health, and nutrition levels are so low that continued rapid population growth would condemn millions to an early death. Although technological advances do not come only from people who are well educated or well paid, nations that favor limited population growth feel that encouraging rapid birth rates in the hope that someone may be born to solve the world's pollution and resource problems is an inhumane way to preserve the lives of people who already exist. Nations that encourage better education, nutrition, health care, and work opportunities for a smaller population feel that, ethically, that approach has a greater chance of making needed technological breakthroughs without adding to human suffering.

Methods of Population Control

Most nations favor limiting population growth by controlling birth rates. Two approaches to controlling birth rates are economic development and family planning. It is argued that economic development may not be able to help the least-developed countries lower their birth rates, since economic development for these nations is more difficult than it is for those nations that developed in the nineteenth century. In these least-developed countries, expanded family planning programs may bring a more rapid decrease in the birth rate than can economic development alone.

Family planning is a purely voluntary approach whereby information and contraceptives are provided to help couples have the number of children they want when they want to have them. Between 1965 and 1985, family planning was claimed to be a major factor in reducing the birth rates of China, Mexico, and Indonesia. In the same period, moderate to poor results of family planning occurred in the least-developed countries, such as India, Brazil, Bangladesh, and many countries in Africa and Latin America. India started the world's first national family planning program in 1952. Its population then was 400 million; by 1985, it had grown to 765 million, and it topped 1 billion during 2000.

Many people believe that effective population control must include a combination of economic development and the use of methods that go beyond voluntary family planning. Among these methods are voluntary abortion and increased rights, education, and work opportunities for women.

—David R. Teske

Further Reading

Attfield, Robin. *Environmental Ethics: An Overview for the Twenty-First Century*. Malden, Mass.: Blackwell, 2003.

Ehrlich, Anne H., and Paul R. Ehrlich. "Needed: An Endangered Humanity Act?" In *Balancing on the Brink of Extinction*, edited by Kathryn A. Kohm. Washington, D.C.: Island Press, 1991.

Fritsch, Albert J., et al. *Environmental Ethics: Choices for Concerned Citizens*. Garden City, N.Y.: Anchor Press, 1980.

Hardin, Garrett. *Naked Emperors: Essays of a Taboo-Stalker*. Los Altos, Calif.: William Kaufmann, 1982.

Miller, G. Tyler, Jr. *Environmental Science: Working with the Earth*. 9th ed. Pacific Grove, Calif.: Brooks/Cole, 2003.

Newland, Kathleen. *Women and Population Growth: Choice Beyond Childbearing*. Washington, D.C.: Worldwatch Institute, 1977.

See also: Birth control; Environmental ethics; Future-oriented ethics; Immigration; Lifeboat ethics; Malthus, Thomas; Population Connection; Zerobase ethics.

Rain forests

Definition: Large wooded areas characterized by more than one hundred inches of rainfall annually and tall evergreen trees that provide a high canopy

Type of ethics: Environmental ethics

Significance: The potential destruction of the rain forests by humans became both a symbolic issue and a grave practical concern for the environmental movement of the late twentieth and early twenty-first centuries.

The rain forests provide indigenous peoples and the world with a rich source of actual and potential benefits. In their natural state, the rain forests act as filters for the global atmosphere, provide habitats for animal and plant species, and provide food for humans. The rain forests are also harvested as a source of fuel, with the resulting cleared land providing a rich soil for farming. Finding a balance between altering the rain forests for temporary benefit and using them in their natural and sustainable state is the heart of the rain forest debate. In their naturally occurring state, the rain forests of the world act as watersheds for the surrounding land. The rich soil and dense foliage of the forests act as a natural sponge, capturing rainfall and runoff.

These trapped waters are slowly released, recharging aquifers, streams, and natural reservoirs. It is this trapping and slow releasing of water that controls both flooding and erosion in the forests and surrounding areas. When the rain forest is clear-cut and removed, streams, lakes, rivers, and other natural waterways are quickly filled with runoff sediment and lost.

Along with playing an important role in the water cycle, the rain forest is critical in the conversion of carbon dioxide into oxygen. The loss of one of the earth's natural air filters cannot be replaced in any manner. This loss threatens not only to affect local areas but also to have global air-quality effects. With the removal of rain forests, the local area immediately is affected by an alteration in the moisture content of the air and a disturbance in the water cycle. The long-term effects of this disturbance could be the development of arid savanna or desert.

Although the rain forests cover only slightly more than 7 percent of the land masses of the world, they provide habitats for more than 50 percent of the animal and plant species found on the planet. The destruction of plant life in the rain forest not only threatens the water cycle and the planet's carbon dioxide/ oxygen cycle but also removes plant species that may provide important medical benefits. This loss of potential medicines is another example of local action's having worldwide effects. Rain forest plants have already contributed aspirin and many other pharmaceuticals, some of which are used in the treatment of leukemia and Hodgkin's disease. The loss of this rich pharmaceutical research possibility is not recoverable in any way.

Depletion

The reasons for rain forest destruction are myriad; primarily, however, it is a matter of economics and survival. Nearly half of all the trees cut in the forests are used for fuel to cook and heat homes. The vast majority of rain for-

The canopy at the Forest Research Institute Malaysia showing crown shyness. By Mikenorton.

ests are found in less-developed countries where alternative fuels such as fossil fuels, solar power, or hydroelectric power are not available in remote and isolated areas. Yet while the forests provide a rich supply of fuel, local people nevertheless are not able to cut and secure adequate fuel supplies to meet their basic survival needs. Although globally there exist several other fuel sources, local people lack the economic strength to secure these sources of fuel. As a result, the forests are cut and sold for timber products, providing poor communities with a bit of economic freedom.

The newly cleared land, with its rich and fertile soil, is used for farming until it is depleted of all nutrition—usually, within five years. Although the agricultural use of the land is limited to such a short duration, it again provides the community with muchneeded economic benefits. Af-

ter the soil has been used to exhaustion, the farmer cuts more of the forest, sells the timber, and farms the newland until it also is depleted. When the trees have been cut and the soil has been depleted, the forest on that land is gone and the soil can no longer support the life that existed upon it six or seven years earlier.

Clearly, the economic benefits derived from using the forests in such a destructive short-term manner are enough to drive the process on. It is important to present to local people a means of using the forest in its natural and sustainable state that will provide them comparable economic benefit for the long term. There are several possibilities, such as harvesting and selling fruits and nuts from the forests, tourism, and a tax for the use of the rain forests for medical research.

It is the resolution of this dichotomy—the forest in its natural state providing water, oxygen, medicine, and habitat versus the economic and existence needs of local peoples—that must be effected. It is estimated that one tree, over a period of fifty years, provides $196,250 worth of benefits by producing oxygen, reducing erosion, recyclingwater, and creating habitats. The same tree, when sold for lumber, is worth approximately $600. The $600 is actual and usable currency, however, while the nearly $200,000 value exists in the form of benefits. It is the need for hard currency that must be addressed if preservation of the rain forest is to occur and continue. This economic need must be addressed not only by world leaders but also by indigenous peoples. Ultimately, the entire world will suffer the consequences of rain forest destruction; however, it is the local people who will be the first to suffer, and the local people have little economic capability to adjust.

—*Tod Murphy*

Further Reading

Aiken, S. Robert. *Vanishing Rain Forests: The Ecological Transition in Malaysia.* New York: Oxford University Press, 1992.

Attfield, Robin. *Environmental Ethics: An Overview for the Twenty-first Century.* Malden, Mass.: Blackwell, 2003.

Gunn, Alastair S. "Environmental Ethics and Tropical Rain Forests: Should Greens Have Standing?" In *Environmental Ethics and Forestry: A Reader*, edited by Peter C. List. Philadelphia: Temple University Press, 2000.

Kilaparti, Ramakrishna, and George M. Woodwell, eds. *World Forests for the Future: Their Use and Conservation.* New Haven, Conn.: Yale University Press, 1993.

Miller, Kenton, and Laura Tangley. *Trees of Life: Saving Tropical Rain Forests and Their Biological Wealth.* Boston: Beacon Press, 1991.

Park, Chris. *Tropical Rainforests.* New York: Routledge, 1992.

Pimm, Stuart. *The Balance of Nature? Ecological Issues in the Conservation of Species and Communities.* Chicago: University of Chicago Press, 1991.

See also: Deep ecology; Deforestation; Ecology; Endangered species; Environmental ethics; Global warming; Greenhouse effect.

Robotics

Definition: Science and technology of creating machines that mimic the ways in which humans perform tasks

Date: Originated during the 1940's

Type of ethics: Scientific ethics

Significance: The existence of machines that are capable of replacing humans in various activities has a far-reaching impact on society and may eventually redefine humankind's role in the world The word "robot"was first used in 1921 in *R.U.R., or Rossum's Universal Robots*, a play by the Czech writer Karel Capek. In that dramatic work, the term was used to describe machines that performed the work of humans. The word itself is derived from the Czech word *robota*, which means slave labor. Capek's play is a story of mechanical laborers who revolt against their human masters.

The science of robotics draws on two technologies: automatic machine control and artificial intelligence. Devices for automatic machine control, which are called servomechanisms, work by feeding information about a machine's location, speed, and direction back to a computer-based control unit that automatically makes adjustments.

By the 1950's, mathematicians began to explore the possibilities of emulating human logic and behavior in computer programs. In 1956, John McCarthy, then at Dartmouth College, gave this discipline its name—artificial intelligence. The first artificial intelligence researchers began to program computers to play games, prove mathematical theorems, and even play the role of ersatz psychologists. Later efforts focused on the building of robots. The first patent for an industrial robot was awarded to Joseph Engelberger in 1961. His machine, which was called the Unimate, used a feedback control system that was attached to a computer. The Unimate robots were first used to control die-casting machines.

Robotics Development and Applications

Robotics has continued its development through two approaches to design. The first of these is the topdown approach, which focuses on a specific task to be done by the machine. Industrial robots that pick parts from a bin, paint auto body parts, or do welding, drilling, grinding, routing, or riveting from a fixed position on a factory floor are examples of top-down design. Computer programs called expert systems also employ the top-down approach to perform tasks focused in a narrow field—such as identifying mineral deposits or advising doctors about blood diseases—by consulting a body of knowledge in the form of rules.

A more difficult approach to robot design is the bottom-up approach, in which the goal is to build general-purpose machines. Robots of this type tend to be mobile, use camera systems to see the world around them, and employ electronic sensors for touch. They may be programmed to accomplish a variety of tasks. Computer programs for these machines simulate learning by adding observations and experience to their models of the world.

Reliable, quick industrial robots have become regular components of industrial processes. Some applications combine two conventional robotic arms to work together to perform complex assembly tasks, including maintenance operations for nuclear reactors, removal of toxic waste, and loading and unloading machine tools—tasks that are dangerous for humans to perform.

In the medical field, heart surgery is being performed without opening the patients' chests by using robotic arms that are inserted into the chest region through three or four holes, each less than a centimeter in diameter. One robot has a camera for transmitting images to a computer console, while the others are fitted with operating instruments. The robotic movements are guided by a surgeon sitting at a computer, on whose monitor a magnified image of the operating area appears. Bypass surgery and repairs of heart murmurs and valve defects have been successfully performed with this alternative approach to conventional surgery. Similar applications are being used with brain and lung surgeries.

Much of the focus of robotics researchers is on the development of autonomous robots. In the first years of the twenty-first century, robotics researchers at Cardiff University in Wales were developing agile, versatile robots fitted with the latest Pentium-based control systems, vision sensors, video links, and a Global Positioning System for navigation. One application allows farmers to use these robots to check on distant herds of animals, unload feed in selected fields, and inspect gates and fencing. Other applications include robotic wheelchairs and cleaning and security devices.

Another robot, a hexapod, is a two-foot long, sixlegged, self-propelled machine that can avoid obstacles and negotiate rough terrain. This robot has sensors to monitor its position and a charge-coupled device camera and laser to generate a three-dimensional map of the surrounding terrain.

Numerous military applications for robotics are also being explored. An intelligent, mobile robot known as Rhino was developed at the University of Bonn and has been used to conduct guided tours at a museum in Bonn, Germany. Mobile robots have also been used to explore the earth's seafloor and the surface of Mars.

Ethical Issues

The ethical issues of robotics arise from several areas. One fundamental concern is what kind of ethical principles should be built into robots. Sciencefiction author Isaac Asimov began to explore this issue in the 1940's with a series of stories about intelligent robots, which were collected in *I, Robot* (1950) and other books. Asimov's robots had "positronic brains," circuits based on what he called the Three Laws of Robotics, whose principles were protecting the well-being of humans, obeying human orders, and self-preservation—in that order.

Asimov's principles are tested when considering the social consequences of replacing human labor with machine labor. Large-scale factory automation has resulted in the permanent loss of millions of unskilled jobs throughout the industrialized world. As robots continue to be refined and used in more applications, they will replace humans in jobs requiring ever greater degrees of skill. The economic benefits of robot automation reach a point of diminishing returns when the social costs of the unemployed workers—government subsidies, poverty, crime, and political unrest—become too high.

Some experts think that general-purpose humanoid robots will remain too expensive ever to reach widespread use. They contend that society is working itself through an inevitable turbulent period in the wake of the robot automation of industry and will evolve into a period in which skilled workers are used instead of robots. Others believe that advances in computer and robotics technology will inevitably lead to a convergence of the specialized, expert approach and the general-purpose, mobile, artificial intelligence approach. Such a convergence would lead to the development of self-aware machines with sophisticated models of their worlds and the ability to increase their knowledge.

Other ethical issues arise from the prospect of robots becoming more and more like humans in appearance and behavior. Such issues raise questions that have no answers, because there is no way to know what will happen until sentient machines actually make their appearance. Until then, the cost effectiveness of such development is likely to remain a major obstacle.

By 1993, chess computers were playing at tournament level, and in 1997, Deep Blue became the first computer to defeat the reigning world chess champion, Garry Kasparov, in a classical chess match. Given the possibility of intelligent, humanlike robots, what should be their place in human society? Should they be allowed to coexist with people, with their own fundamental rights protected by law, or should they be regarded as a disposable race of slaves?

Legal Issues

Many questions have been raised about the legal status of intelligent robots. If they are accorded rights under the law, should they also have responsibilities? For example, might robots ever manage human workers, serve on juries, or run for elected office? Will they ever vote? Who would be blamed if a robot's "negligence" were to cause the accidental death of a human being? (Many of these issues are raised in Asimov's fictional robot stories.) On May 17, 1992, an industrial robot called Robbie CX30 killed its operator, Bart Matthews, at the Cybernetics corporation in Silicon Heights, California.

Authorities concluded that a software module written by a computer programmer from Silicon Techtronics was responsible for the robot oscillating out of control and killing Matthews. The programmer was charged with negligence. Further investigation revealed that the interface design combined with flawed software was probably the real culprit.

That tragic incident emphasized the need to supply robot designers and programmers with guidelines and handbooks that deal with the ethical issues and principles that should be incorporated into future robot development.

Some robotics experts predict that intelligent machines will eventually be capable of building other, even more intelligent machines. Although robotics research and development currently models robots based upon human senses, actions, and abilities, as the future continues to unfold, people may confront some very disturbing prospects if the machines they have created become more intelligent and powerful than they are themselves. Because machine technology develops millions of times faster than biological evolution, the capabilities of robots could someday so far surpass human ones that the human race could become extinct—not because of war, pestilence, or famine, but because of a lack of purpose. Consequently, future robotics research and development should be carefully governed by the ethical principles advocated by Asimov.

—Charles E. Sutphen, Updated by Alvin K. Benson

Further Reading

Brooks, Rodney A. *Flesh and Machines: How Robots Will Change Us.* New York: Pantheon Books, 2002.

Katic, Dusko. *Intelligent Control of Robotic Systems.* Boston, Mass.: Kluwer Academic Publishers, 2003.

Mulhall, Douglas. *Our Molecular Future: How Nanotechnology, Robotics, Genetics, and Artificial Intelligence Will Transform Our World.* Amherst, N.Y.: Prometheus Books, 2002.

Nehmzow, Ulrich. *Mobile Robotics: A Practical Introduction.* New York: Springer, 2003.

Warwick, Kevin. *March of the Machines: Why the New Race of Robots Will Rule the World.* London: Century, 1997.

Winston, Patrick Henry. *Artificial Intelligence.* 3d ed. Reading, Mass.: Addison-Wesley, 1992.

Zylinska, Joanna, ed. *The Cyborg Experiments: The Extensions of the Body in the Media Age.* New York: Continuum, 2002.

See also: Animal rights; Artificial intelligence;Computer technology; Dominion over nature, human; Exploitation; Sentience; Technology; Virtual reality.

Science

Definition: Formal theorization and experimentation designed to produce objective knowledge, especially knowledge of the general laws governing the natural world.

Type of ethics: Scientific ethics

Significance: Modern standards of scientific inquiry require science to be conducted as far as possible in an impartial, disinterested fashion, but most forms of science cannot be conducted at all without major sources of funding which may influence inquiry either directly or indirectly. Ethical issues raised by science also include appropriate treatment of living research subjects and the practical effects upon the real world of scientific discovery.

Science, ethics, and philosophy interact in a range of arenas. The development of ethical standards—that is, codes of behavior that govern moral decisions—has been a major issue for the great philosophers and thinkers throughout time. Traditionally, metaphysical hypotheses and religious beliefs have governed the attempts of humankind to fathom the unfathomable, to come to grips with mortality, and to hold themselves to a set of standards of conduct. The science of the twentieth century influenced this search, in some cases incorporating, in some cases rejecting, religion as a part of that effort.

The writings of Albert Einstein epitomize the attempt to reconcile science with religion. Einstein holds a central place in modern history because of his groundbreaking ideas on theoretical physics. He writes, "To know what is impenetrable to us really exists, manifesting itself as the highest wisdom and the most radiant beauty which our dull faculties can comprehend only in their most primitive forms—this knowledge, this feeling, is at the center of true religiousness." At the same time, the achievements of science and technology have posed their own moral dilemmas.

For example, the theory of relativity, developed by Einstein during the early twentieth century, set the stage for the development of the atom bomb. In the face of a creation with such awesome destructive potential, however, the question is posed: To what extent should scientists involve themselves in the ultimate consequences of their research? For this generation and for generations to come, the advances in the fields of genetics and biomedicine are likely to give rise to similar dilemmas.

The much-seen film *Jurassic Park* (1993) focused the popular consciousness on the risks inherent in bioengineering technology. With all their inherent potential for good, genetic technologies may carry as yet unknown risks and consequences.

The limited amount of funding available for scientific research has forced both scientists and those responsible for science policy to make choices regarding which projects to fund. Should "big" projects such as the Human Genome Project or the Superconducting Supercollider (SSC) be funded or should many smaller but important projects receive government or private monies? Where should these "big" projects be located? Should basic research be targeted in the hope of eventual payoff or should applications research be the major focus? Are political and economic concerns playing a too-important role in the funding process? To what extent should science and mathematics education be considered a priority?

During the late 1980's and early 1990's, the spotlight turned on ethical conduct and misconduct in scientific research. A major challenge to both the scientific community and the community at large is this: What is the appropriate response to scientific fraud and misconduct? What should be the response to the "gray areas" of even more problematical situations of conflict of interest or "honest mistakes"?

Philosophical Issues

As a guide in an attempt to deal with the range of ethical issues involved in scientific research, the scientific community and the community at large might look to philosophical thinkers who have dealt with issues in this field. In fact, from antiquity through the beginning of the twenty-first century, the great thinkers concerned themselves with issues not only of philosophy, ethics, and morality but also with those of science. Aristotle, René Descartes, and Immanuel Kant made major contributions not only to philosophy but also to the sciences. Wolfgang von Goethe, although best known for his literary works, also wrote extensively on the natural sciences.

At the same time, science has had a major, sometimes even a revolutionary, impact on the values and the worldview of society. The theories of Galileo and Isaac Newton on planetary motion and the views of Charles Darwin on the evolution of species had that kind of revolutionary impact. Similarly, the development of the atom bomb strongly influenced the political and social climate of the latter half of the twentieth century. It is likely that major advances in computer science and bioengineering now taking place will have their impact well into the twenty-first century. It is equally likely that scientists and society will have to deal with the ethical dilemmas posed by the positive and negative capabilities of these technologies.

The analysis of moral and ethical decisions in science might make use of following principles of ethics and philosophy.

The value neutrality of science is epitomized by the vision of the scientist as the ceaseless seeker motivated only by the search for truth. This theory has its basis in features first introduced in the seventeenth and eighteenth century. The theory of the scientific method, which is known as inductivism, has relied on this concept and postulates that science begins with the collection of data, goes on to generalize about laws and theories, and makes predictions that can be proved. The theory of inductivism had its roots in the writings of Francis Bacon in the sixteenth and seventeenth century and in the empiricist theories developed by David Hume in the eighteenth century. The inductivist view was supported by the Cambridge school of Bertrand Russell during the early twentieth century and the Vienna circle of the 1920's and 1930's.

Critics of the Vienna circle and of inductivism have included Karl Popper. Popper maintains that the concepts and postulates (which are ultimately proved or disproved by experimentation) are the products not necessarily of observations but of potentially "unjustified (and unjustifiable) anticipations, by guesses, by tentative solutions to our problems, by conjectures.

The conjectures are controlled by criticism; that is, by attempted refutations, which include severely critical tests." The source of the hypothesis is irrelevant; the originator of the hypothesis or postulate joins in the criticism and testing of the hypothesis that he or she has proposed. Popper is considered to have inaugurated the current era in the philosophy of science.

Misconduct in Science

The embarrassment of the "honest mistake" is far surpassed by the violation of the ethos of science of the outright fraud. Fraud in science impugns the integrity of the research process and destroys the trust on which scientific achievement is built. At the same time, intentionally fraudulent actions undermine the confidence of society and the body politic in science and scientific inquiry. Potentially, the effects of fraud may be horrific; if, for example, a medical treatment should be based on fraudulent results.

Many scientists base their codes of conduct on the example of role models and on what some have termed the "school of hard knocks." A more systematic approach has been contributed by professional organizations who have contributed their expertise. A recent contribution is a 1989 publication of the National Academy of Science, *On Being a Scientist*. Other resources include a 1992 report, likewise from the National Academy of Sciences, called *Responsible Science: Ensuring the Integrity of the Research Process*. These publications and others often cite as examples of fraud and misconduct the actions of William Summerlin at Sloan-Kettering during the 1970's, those of John Darsee at Harvard and those of Stephen E. Breuning in Pittsburgh during the early 1980's, and those of Thereza Imanishi-Kari and Nobel laureate David Baltimore during the late 1980's.

A well-known and rather tragic example of fraud was that of William Summerlin. During the early 1970's, Summerlin came to the Sloan-Kettering Institute as the chief of a laboratory working on transplantation immunology. A laboratory assistant noticed that the supposedly black grafts on white mice could be washed off with ethanol. It turned out that Summerlin had used a black felt-tipped marker to mimic the appearance of black grafts. Additional discrepancies regarding Summerlin's results on corneal transplantations led an internal committee to recommend that Summerlin take a medical leave of absence and to condemn Summerlin's behavior as irresponsible.

During the early 1980's, John Darsee had worked under the supervision of Eugene Braunwauld, a wellknown cardiologist at Harvard University. At Harvard, three coworkers apparently observed Darsee fake data for an experiment. An internal investigation for the next few months found no discrepancies. A subsequent National Institutes of Health (NIH) investigation, however, demonstrated that virtually every paper that Darsee had produced was fabricated.

Another episode involved a professor at the University of Pittsburgh, Stephen E. Breuning, who had become prominent for his expertise in the medical treatment of mental retardation. In 1983, Breuning's former mentor, Robert Sprague, questioned the veracity of his student's research. Eventually, it turned out that much of Breuning's data came from experiments that had not been performed on subjects that had not even been tested.

An exceptionally disturbing case was that of Thereza Imanishi-Kari and Nobel laureate David Baltimore of the Massachusettes Intitute of Technology (MIT). A postdoctoral fellow at Imanishi-Kari's laboratory, Margot O'Toole, uncovered evidence that Imanishi-Kari may have fabricated certain results appearing in a paper in *Cell* on gene transplantation, a paper that was also coauthored by Baltimore. University inquiries at MIT dismissed O'Toole's concerns, but a few years later, the concerns resurfaced, resulting in ultimate retraction of the *Cell* paper and investigations by the NIH, Congressman John Dingell, and the Secret Service. While the U.S. attorney in the case declined to prosecute Imanishi-Kari, as of this writing, clouds continued to obscure her career and that of Baltimore.

During the late 1980's and the early 1990's, more than two hundred allegations of misconduct in science were received by the U.S. government. One study has indicated that approximately 40 percent of the deans of graduate schools knew of cases of misconduct at their institutions. A survey sponsored by the American Association for the Advancement of Science likewise indicated that during the first ten years, 27 percent of scientists indicated that they had personally encountered incidences of falsified, fabricated, or plagiarized research.

In fact, by the late 1980's and into the early 1990's, articles on misconduct in science continued to constitute the vast majority of references on science ethics produced by computerized literature searches. During the late 1980's, incidents of apparent fraud, plagiarism, and misconduct drew the attention of the Subcommittee on Oversight and Investigations of the U.S. House of Representatives, chaired by Congressman John D. Dingell. The threat not only to the research process but also to the autonomy of the scientific community posed by examples of abuse has challenged scientists to developways of dealing with misconduct within their ranks. Congressman Dingell himself acknowledged the drawbacks of resolving issues of misconduct in the congressional hearing. "Encouraging science to police itself is far preferable to the alternatives...But with every case [which is] is covered up or mishandled, pressure builds for such extreme measures."

Gray Areas

Certain instances of apparent fraud violate any accepted standards of moral or ethical conduct. Many other situations, however, fall into what might be termed a "gray area." For example, a vexing question concerns the allocation of credit for scientific achievements. The bitter dispute between Newton and Gottfried Wilhelm Leibniz over who first discovered the calculus is paralleled by the twentieth century quarrel between Robert Gallo, the renowned acquired immunodeficiency syndrome (AIDS) researcher at the NIH, and his counterpart at the Pasteur Institute, Luc Montagnier, over the discovery of the AIDS virus. Also in what might be termed a "gray area" are issues of "conflict of interest." (Outright bribery to promote fabrication of results would violate most standards of conduct.) By the late 1980's and early 1990's, doubts over the degree to which scientists' findings might be influenced by funding sources led journals such as *Science, JAMA,* and the *New England Journal of Medicine (NEJM)* to adopt standards of disclosure for potential conflicts of interest.

The *JAMA* and *NEJM* standards stressed financial conflicts; the *Science* standards also include a range of other relationships that might possibly have influenced the scientist's work. The possibility of abuse inherent in these kinds of standards has led to a "backlash" as scientists and physicians engaged in medical research talked of a "New McCarthyism in Science" and evoked the possibility that not only financial conflicts but also such factors as religion and sexual orientation might be included in the disclosure standards. Kenneth J. Rothman, writing in the *Journal of the American Medical Association,* cites Popper (*The Open Society and Its Enemies,* 1966) in noting the impossibility of achieving full objectivity in any scientific endeavor.

Equally problematical for the scientist—and also in a "gray area"—are the new ethical problems created by scientific discoveries. Are scientists responsible for the ethical and moral uses of their discoveries? For example, should decisions about the use of the atom bomb have been in the hands of the scientists or, as actually occurred, in the hands of the politicians? Should scientists attempt to exert any kind of control over the uses of their discoveries?

A tradition of political neutrality governed science from the seventeenth century through World War I. Bacon, for example, conceived of science as a "new instrument." The chemist Robert Hooke warned the founders of the Royal Society of London that their business was to "improve the natural knowledge of things, not meddling with Divinity, Metaphysics, Moralls, Politicks, Grammar, Rhetorick or Logic." World War I, however, disrupted the tradition of neutrality as technological solutions not only made up for the losses of raw materials caused by the war but also played a major role in enhancing the lethal effect of explosive and chemical weapons.

Political authorities continued to come into the scientific arena with the advocacy by Joseph Stalin's regime of the 1930's and 1940's of the genetic theories of T. D. Lysenko. Nazi Germany purged its Jewish and left-wing scientists. Some disapproving scientists left the country, but others remained, adhering to a tradition that held no place for social responsibility and hoping to exert influence on the Nazi regime.

World War II gave impetus to research in a range of areas, as synthetics replaced raw materials and new drugs such as penicillin became available. Refugee scientists from Nazi Germany encouraged preliminary research on an atom bomb. The ensuing success of the Manhattan Project resulted in the explosion of the atom bombs over Hiroshima and Nagasaki, which was followed by the development of atomic capability by the Soviet Union in 1949.

The dilemma for scientists is this: To what extent should they concern themselves with the ultimate consequences of their discoveries? Is scientific knowledge and discovery an inherent good? Are the risks of scientific and technological advances as important as the potential benefits?

The challenges posed by the development of the atom bomb are paralleled by issues raised by the scientific advances of the 1980's and 1990's. The development of computer and electronic technology raises some important issues of privacy and the possibility of social control.

Equally problematical are issues raised by advances in the biological and medical sciences.

An additional ethical issue concerns the eradication of racism and sexism in science. For example, a particularly shocking example of racism involved the Tuskegee syphilis experiment. During a forty-year study that received federal funds, African American victims of syphilis were denied treatment even after penicillin became available. The apparent justification was that the denial of treatment was essential to the study of the progress of the disease.

A challenge for researchers is to design studies of common illnesses (for example, myocardial infarction, diabetes) that not only provide sufficient data on the white middle-class male population but also include information on which to base the treatment of minority and female patients.

Allocation of Resources

Scientific research in the United States is funded to a large extent by the U.S. government. Major corporations, such as large pharmaceutical companies, support much of the rest. What are the implications of these facts? The marriage of science and government dates back to World War II and Vannevar Bush, who then headed the Office of Scientific Research and Development. In the system that evolved, research proposals are initiated by the researcher, who usually works in a university or institute setting. At the same time, funding was a federal responsibility, and although some research was taking place in government laboratories, most basic research was undertaken in universities. There arose not a single funding agency, as envisioned by Bush, but a multiplicity of agencies—responsible for funding basic research.

By the late 1980's, the numbers of individuals involved in basic research had increased, while the pool of dollars available stayed the same. The result was that a far smaller proportion of grant proposals were being funded. For example, in 1980, the NIH approved up to one in three "meritorious" grants for funding, while by the 1990's, fewer than one in five grants received approval. The system in place through the latter half of the twentieth century achieved scientific productivity, as measured by the numbers of citations; prestige, measured by the numbers of Nobel Prizes; and some degree of economic productivity.

During the late 1980's and early 1990's, the lessened availability of funding and the potential for political abuse and "pork-barrel" science led some experts to question the current criteria for funding scientific research. At the same time, the costs of new technologies and issues relating to the use of those technologies have led some people to question the direction of public policy on science issues. This position has yet to be adopted by public policy makers.

The direction of governmental policy at the beginning of the 1990's is reiterated by Donna Shalala, Secretary of the federal department of Health and Human Services. Shalala states: The last thing we should try to do is try to curb technology in our attempt to deal with costs or to slowdown our investment in research.... The issue is how you use technology, far more than whether we should keep producing technology. Rather than beating up on technology, we need to get scientists and administrators to think about the more appropriate use of it.

—Adele Lubell

Further Reading

Bell, Robert. *Impure Science: Fraud, Compromise and Political Influence in Scientific Research.* New York: John Wiley & Sons, 1992. The author claims to document how some members of the scientific community have fostered influence, misconduct, and fraud in scientific research. The volume is most valuable for its account of some less-well-known examples of alleged fraud or misconduct.

Claude, Richard Pierre. *Science in the Service of Human Rights.* Philadelphia: University of Pennsylvania Press, 2002. Seeks to address the political and ethical dimensions of science and the scientific dimensions of socio-political ethics. Examines such issues as cloning and the rights of African people with AIDS to have access to pharmaceutical treatment.

Dingell, J. D. "Shattuck Lecture: Misconduct in Medical Research." *New England Journal of Medicine* 328 (June 3, 1993): 1610-1615. Congressman Dingell is best known for his role as chairman of the Subcommittee on Oversight and Investigations of the U.S. House of Representatives. Dingell played a major role in governmental investigation into scientific misconduct during the late 1980's and early 1990's. The article is the address he gave to the Massachussetts Medical Society in Boston in May, 1992.

Gillies, Donald. *Philosophy of Science in the Twentieth Century.* Cambridge, Mass.: Blackwell Scientific, 1993. The author discusses some important trends in the philosophy of science in the twentieth century. He particularly focuses on the ideas of Karl Popper, with whom Gillies studied during the late 1960's.

Martino, J. P. *Science Funding.* New Brunswick, N.J.: Transaction, 1992. This volume documents the history and current status of trends in the funding of scientific research, from Vannevar Bush to the present.

Mosedale, F. E., ed. *Philosophy and Science.* Englewood Cliffs, N.J.: Prentice-Hall, 1979. Includes the writings of philosophers, scientists, and others on important issues in science. Many selections discuss ethical and moral concerns.

National Academy of Sciences. Committee on the Conduct of Science. *On Being a Scientist*. Washington, D.C.: National Academy Press, 1989. A booklet that offers the beginning and active scientist an introduction to the ethos of science.

Seebauer, Edmund G., and Robert L. Barry. *Fundamentals of Ethics for Scientists and Engineers*. New York: Oxford University Press, 2001. Practical textbook designed for the student of ethics or of engineering that takes a hands-on approach to scientific ethics. Contains many specific examples of ethical dilemmas in science, some actual and some fictionalized, in order to illustrate the virtue-based principles of ethical practice endorsed by the authors.

United States Committee on Science, Engineering, and Public Policy's Panel on Scientific Responsibility and the Conduct of Research. *Responsible Science: Ensuring the Integrity of the Research Process*. 2 vols. Washington, D.C.: National Academy Press, 1992-1993. Comprehensive volumes that attempt to delineate issues around integrity in science research and devise appropriate procedures for dealing with misconduct.

See also: Bacon, Francis; Bioethics; Darwin, Charles; Experimentation; Hume, David; Industrial research; Manhattan Project; Nazi science; Psychology; Technology.

Sierra Club

Identification: Oldest and largest environmental organization in the United States

Date: Founded in 1892

Type of ethics: Environmental ethics

Significance: Since the organization's foundation, the mission of the Sierra Club has been to protect the natural environment.

The Sierra Club was founded on May 28, 1892, with an initial membership of 182 persons. Naturalist John Muir was selected as the club's first president. Many of the organization's early activities were concerned with the preservation of natural resources and the establishment of national parks in the United States. Its initial campaign in 1892 focused on defeating a proposed reduction of the boundaries of Yosemite National Park in California.

From this beginning, the Sierra Club grew to an international organization claiming a membership of approximately 700,000 people at the beginning of the twenty-first century. It retained as its primary mission today the protection and enhancement of Earth's natural environment by sustaining natural life-support systems, facilitating the survival of species, establishing and protecting natural reserves, controlling population growth and pollution, developing responsible technology managing resources and educating the public about environmental protection.

Theodore Roosevelt and John Muir in Yosemite National Park, c. 1906. by Underwood & Underwood.

Critics of the Sierra Club have charged that the organization's policies to preserve and protect the environment may sometimes infringe on individual rights and restrict public access to property. Some critics also assert that the Sierra Club is composed of an economic, social, and political elite interested in preserving the wilderness for a select few who are not sincerely concerned with environmental justice at the grass-roots level. For example, in 1972 the club opposed the attempt by Walt Disney Enterprises to build a highway through Sequoia National Park in California to a proposed ski resort that was expected to attract fourteen thousand visitors a day. The club argued that the valley should be kept in its natural state for its own sake. The club has also advocated breaching the Glen Canyon Dam on the Colorado River and draining Lake Powell in order to return the region to its natural state. The dam provides flood control and electricity for four million people, and Lake Powell is one of the most popular camping sites in the United States. Controversies such as these illustrate an ethical dilemma repeatedly faced by the Sierra Club: how to balance individual rights and the protection of the environment for all people.

—William V. Moore

See also: Animal rights; Bioethics; Conservation; Deep ecology; Ecology; Environmental movement; Leopold, Aldo; Muir, John; National Park System, U.S.; Pollution.

Silent Spring

Identification: Book by Rachel Carson (1907-1964)

Date: Published in 1962

Type of ethics: Environmental ethics

Significance: *Silent Spring* increased popular awareness of chemical pollution by illustrating the demise and death of organisms that had once been a part of a rural spring.

During the late 1950's, a proliferation of the manufacturing and use of chemical agents as insecticides and herbicides seemed to stimulate the agricultural industry. Initially, these chemicals provided relief to farmers who could now control and obliterate insect pests and weeds from cropland. Insufficient testing and monitoring of the use of these chemicals, however, led to widespread contamination of water and land, resulting in the destruction of a great variety of animals and plants.

The popular book *Silent Spring* aroused public awareness of a sinister development in which streams and springs became silent as birds, frogs, fish, and other organisms died from the toxic chemicals used in adjacent fields. Ethically, the realization that humans can quickly and easily pollute and blight large regions through the careless use of chemicals illustrated the necessity for good stewardship of natural resources. As an alternative to control insect pests, Rachel Carson suggested the use of nonchemical methods that were more environmentally wholesome. Carson's landmark book led to the formation of numerous environmental groups that have committed themselves to protecting natural resources.

—Roman J. Miller

See also: Clean Air Act; Clean Water Act; Conservation; Earth and humanity; Environmental ethics; Environmental movement; Environmental Protection Agency; Nature, rights of; Pollution; Toxic waste.

Social media

Definition: Online social networks.

Type of ethics: Scientific ethics

Significance: Facebook is the symbol for the contradictory nature of an online social network.

Evolving technology platforms allowing ordinary people to disseminate ideas and information simply by establishing a social media account. Social media empowers every person to become a live-streaming news and entertainment source, sharing images and stories that range from the intimately personal to the mundane. Items shared on social media are often referred to as "posts" or "postings." Users share information about themselves, others, current events, recipes, parties, sporting events, beverage and food choices, political issues, and seemingly limitless other topics. Some social media platforms only permit users to share (or "post") photos. Social media can, but does not necessarily, compete with traditional media.

Individuals using social media are not required to provide their real identity or present their actual opinions. Further, individuals can have numerous social media accounts, often cutting across technological platforms. Many individuals will have different social media accounts for their professional and personal lives. Social media is not limited to actual persons. Businesses, restaurants, athletic teams, entertainers, and universities have all begun capitalizing on the low- to cost-free usage of social media.

Many famous individuals have social media accounts. In fact, both the President of the United States (@POTUS) and the Pope (Pope Francis @PONTIFEX) have Twitter accounts. The U.S. Internal Revenue Service also uses social media platforms, including YouTube, Twitter, Tumblr, and Facebook. Overall, the Pew Research Center found that, as of 2014, 74 percent of adults report using social media. This same study indicates that more than 70 percent of adults utilize Facebook, while approximately 25 percent use Twitter, Instagram, Pinterest, and LinkedIn. There is no question that social media usage is expanding across all demographics.

Social media users can "share" information with "friends" and "followers," individuals or entities the user confirms are permitted to access their information. These "friends" and "followers," however, who may not be known acquaintances, can then share that information with other individuals, who can do the same with their "friends" and "followers" until such time that a story goes "viral." Many social media platforms also permit individuals to have their account be entirely public so that any individual or entity can view the information.

Social media primarily differs from traditional media in that the information disseminated is not generally vetted for accuracy or authenticity. In fact, there are many social media accounts that are intended to be fictional or to parody an actual person. One of the more popular social mediaplatforms, Twitter, allows parody but not impersonation. Its website has rules regarding proper usage and how individuals can create "fan" and "parody" accounts that will not be suspended.

Social media posts are generally not censored, except by the individual posting the information. Instead, the only limits placed on social media tend to be after the fact, with a social media platform deleting a post or suspending an account if the post is found to violate usage terms. The most obvious examples have included the deletion of accounts owned by criminals and terrorist groups, such as ISIS, that post graphic depictions of actual crimes.

Social media platforms are numerous and constantly expanding. Some permit posts that include words, images, audios, and videos. Others may be limited solely to words or images (such as photographs). Each platform tends to have a descriptive focus. For example, Facebook is likely the most popular "social" social media platform where users generally share a wide-range of information about themselves, their interests, and their daily lives. Common posts include pictures of what one ate at a particular meal; descriptions of one's exercise regime; requests for advice on particular matters; rants about businesses, entertainers or sports; Biblical quotations and other religious or inspirational passages; political messages; funny photos or cartoons; and calls for help funding a particular person or cause.

Twitter, another highly popular social media network, currently limits its posts to 140 characters or fewer. Individuals can post images and words but in very short, often cryptic fashion. Other Twitter users will simply send numerous "tweets" that allow them to expand their message beyond the 140 characters, as a series of "tweets" can accomplish what a single 140-character message cannot. Still other social media platforms, such as YouTube, Pinterest, and Instagram, focus on visual mediums to allow users to share photos and video recordings.

Other conventional social media platforms include Google+, LinkedIn, About.me, Foursquare, MySpace, Meerkat, Periscope, Tumblr, Blogger, Vox, Reddit, Scribd, SlideShare, Classmates, Friendster, CaringBridge, MyLife, Flickr, and Snapchat. At the moment this list was typed, it was likely obsolete. Social media is literally growing and changing at that furious a pace.

The law relating to technology, in general, and social media, in particular, however, has not grown at the same rate. Few legal restraints are placed on social media users. Instead, most social media platforms provide usage "guidelines" that seek to impose legal norms on users. For example, Twitter (and most other social media platforms, including Meerkat and Periscope) prohibits copyright and trademark infringement, threats and harassment, targeted abuse, "graphic content," and release of "private information." Twitter reserves the right to remove any content violating its "guidelines" and/or to entirely shut down an account, which is consistent with other social media platform rules. While Twitter's rules may impose more restraints than the law itself would, these guidelines—and similar guidelines on other social media platforms—steer users away from potential legal violations. Further, these guidelines ensure that the companies hosting the social media platforms do not, themselves, become subject to legal action for many of the violations they prohibit.

Social media platforms run by independent companies can regulate speech and expression in a much more restrictive manner than the United States government can. The First Amendment, like all constitutional provisions, applies only to governmental action. Thus most social media platforms cannot be found to violate a user's First Amendment rights because the First Amendment does not apply to private restrictions on speech and expression.

To the extent that individuals and companies are subjected to governmental punishment or prosecution for social media usage, that governmental action will be tempered by the First Amendment. Cases involving cyberbullying, for example, may be subject to a First Amendment defense unless the behavior involved a true threat. Under traditional First Amendment jurisprudence, a true threat is considered low-value speech that is not protected by the First Amendment. Similarly, individuals sharing or posting information that is itself criminal in nature—for example, actual child pornography—will not benefit from the First Amendment because it is the very act of sharing or posting such information that constitutes the crime.

Social media platforms also implicate individual privacy concerns. Many individuals constantly provide "status updates" and live-stream stories such that individuals can discern their location and precise activities. It is not uncommon for someone to "check in" on Facebook, which immediately indicates his or her location to "friends"—and, potentially, criminals. Further, a recent experiment posted on YouTube entitled "The Dangers of Social Media" illustrates the serious risk that social media poses to children. Actor Coby Persin, proceeding with the permission and complicity of several teens' parents, easily lured both male and female teens to meet with him (he was posing as someone else) despite the warnings of their parents about the dangers of social media. The experiment demonstrates some of the risks posed by social media—how do parents monitor their children's usage and protect against predators?

Just as criminals can use social media, so can the police and government. Because social media permits individuals to create accounts using a fictitious name and persona, the police have been able to set up stings to arrest (without entrapment) individuals seeking to commit statutory rape, terroristic crimes, or drug-related offenses. Sometimes police officers, posing as someone else, enter chat rooms and observe other individuals' postings and comments. Alternatively, the police may simply benefit from information posted by a criminal about a crime he or she committed, or such information shared with the police by a "friend" or "follower" of the individual. Moreover, with the live-streaming capacity of Meerkat and Periscope, officers also happen upon criminals who foolishly post their crimes online. Posts on Periscope, which appears to be Twitter's video-sharing social media platform, have resulted in the arrest of drunk drivers and burglars who live-streamed their respective crimes.

Social media has also been credited with creating an alternate "community" where activists can help spur political change and revolution. In countries where traditional media sources are controlled by the government and Internet access is limited—particularly during periods of political instability—social media can aid ordinary citizens by helping galvanize this alternative community to bring about change at the grassroots level. The Arab Spring is largely believed to have benefitted from the presence, and leveraging, of social media.

Those desiring negative change, instability, and chaos also resort to social media. ISIS took to social media to depict, in graphic video and still photography footage, the beheading of its captives. Each time, it was not until after the videos surfaced and were shared that these accounts were suspended and the images taken down. By then, many viewers had access to the videos and messages conveyed. And, once these accounts were shut down, ISIS members simply opened new accounts. Brookings Institution scholars J. M. Berger and Jonathon Morgan have suggested that ISIS supporters have between 46,000 and 70,000 Twitter accounts and may post as many as 200,000 tweets per day.

The lesson is that social media can be used for good and it can be used for evil. It can bring people together and tear societies apart. Without clear laws in place—particularly obligations that can be enforced transnationally—there is little hope that those seeking to use social media to harm society or others can be effectively deterred. Social media provides every individual with the opportunity to tell his or her story, be it truth, fiction, or opinion. Thus, as the technology expands, serious consideration should be given to the benefits and risks that social media poses to society.

Social media remains a new and ever-evolving form of communication. Its achievements, potential, and shortcomings are still being assessed. From an international perspective, social media has opened up the world in a myriad of positive ways. Now, without waiting for a traditional media source to filter a story—particularly in a country that depends on state-sponsored media outlets—information can be transmitted literally across the world in seconds. Information is no longer just the property of the traditional media or government. Even in the United States, messages and newsworthy events can be instantaneously shared without waiting for traditional media platforms to vet, package, and present the story.

As social media becomes more entrenched in our daily lives, the law will ultimately need to catch up. There will be increased need to protect the intellectual property rights of business and individuals, through copyright and trademark infringement protections. There will be greater need to protect the vulnerable from predators, whether the vulnerable are our children, the elderly, or persons leaving on vacation who carelessly post a status-update. There will be an increased need to consider the true privacy implications of what we post and share with others. Libel laws, defamation laws, obscenity laws, and intellectual property laws will all need to be refashioned to consider their application in a social media-driven world. Even those who "like" social media must appreciate both the benefits and risk posed by such expansive communicative opportunities operating almost entirely outside the bounds of the law.

—*Mary M. Penrose*

Further Reading

Albarran, Alan B., ed. The Social Media Industries. New York: Routledge, 2013.

Berger, J. M., and Jonathon Morgan. The ISIS Twitter Census: Defining and Describing the Population of ISIS Supporters on Twitter. Brookings Project on U.S. Relations with the Islamic World Analysis Paper no. 20 (March 2015). Available at: http://www.brookings.edu/~/media/research/files/papers/2015/03/isis-twitter-census-berger-morgan/isis_twitter_census_berger_morgan.pdf.

Robert Hannigan, "*The Web Is a Terrorist's Command-and-Control Network of Choice*," Financial Times, November 3, 2014.

Hartley, John, Jean Burgess, and Axel Bruns, eds. A Companion to New Media Dynamics. Malden, MA: Wiley, 2013.

Mandiberg, Michael. The Social Media Reader. New York: New York University Press, 2012.

Parkinson, Hannah Jane. "*James Foley: How Social Media Is Fighting Back against ISIS Propaganda*," Guardian, August 20, 2014.

John Pollack, "Streetbook: How Egyptian and Tunisian Youth Hacked the Arab Spring," MIT Technology Review, August 23, 2011.

Qualman, Erik. Socialnomics: How Social Media Transforms the Way We Live and Do Business. 2d ed. Hoboken, NJ: Wiley, 2013.

Warburton, Steven, and Stylianos Hatzipanagos, eds. Digital Identity and Social Media. Hershey, PA: Information Science Reference, 2013.

Youngs, Gillian, ed. Digital World: Connectivity, Creativity, and Rights. 2013; reprint, New York: Routledge, 2013.

Sociobiology

Definition: Study of the evolutionary basis of human social behavior

Date: Originated around 1975

Type of ethics: Scientific ethics

Significance: Sociobiological studies of humans are based on the premise that human behavior is the result of evolution. Thus, sociobiologists argue that morality has evolutionary value, and indeed that it results from processes of natural selection. This argument has been attacked, however, as a form of biological determinism.

In 1975, E. O. Wilson, a Harvard professor and world-renowned expert on ants, published a massive book in which he tied together decades of empirical research by animal behaviorists with decades of theoretical work by geneticists and evolutionary biologists. In so doing, he defined a new academic discipline, "sociobiology," the name of which is taken from the title of his book, *Sociobiology: The New Synthesis*.

The thesis of Wilson's book was that behavior, like any other attribute of an animal, has some of its basis in genetics, and therefore scientists should study behavior in the same way they do anatomy, physiology, or any other observable feature of an animal; that is, they should not only describe it but also try to figure out its function and the reasons why it evolved. Most biologists found no fault with this logic, and the discipline grew very rapidly, spawning hundreds of books and thousands of articles. Many predictions generated from this new perspective were corroborated, and many previously unexplained behaviors started to make sense.

The majority of biologists were rapidly convinced that this new approach was both useful and valid. Other scientists, however, as well as many sociopolitical organizations and representatives, immediately took a stand against it. In his book, Wilson had included a closing chapter on the sociobiology of human behavior, and his critics believed that the principles and methods used to study nonhuman animals simply could not be applied to humans. Academic critics tended to be psychologists, sociologists, anthropologists, and political scientists who believed that learning and culture, not evolution and genetics, determine most human behavior. Nonacademic critics tended to be either philosophers and theologians who believed that the human spirit makes people qualitatively different from other animals or leftleaning political organizations who believed that violent, discriminatory, and oppressive human behaviors might somehow be justified by calling attention to the existence of similar behaviors in other animals.

The Altruism Debate

The first, and perhaps most significant, debate over sociobiology as it applied to humans involved explanations for altruism. Altruism, by definition, is behavior that helps another individual or group at some cost to the altruist. Since altruistic behavior would appear to help nonaltruistic recipients of altruism to survive and pass on their genes but not help altruists themselves, any genetic tendency toward altruism should rapidly die out; which would imply that altruistic behavior must be nonevolved; that is, either culturally learned or spiritually motivated, as the critics claimed.

Biologists, however, had documented altruistic behavior in a wide variety of nonhuman animals, suggesting either that other animals must also have cultural or spiritual motives (suggestions not accepted by most of the critics) or that altruism really must, somehow, increase the altruist's ability to survive and pass on genes, not merely help the nonaltruistic recipient. Two theoreticians provided explanations for how this might have occurred.

W. D. Hamilton proposed an evolutionary model based on the concept of "kin selection"; according to this model, altruistic behavior does not have to increase the altruist's chances of survival and reproduction, as long as it increases the survival and reproduction of the altruist's relatives. Since relatives share genes, even though an altruist may decrease his or her own chances of survival and reproduction, the genetic tendency for altruism can be passed on to subsequent generations because the altruist has increased the total number of his or her genes in the next generation by increasing the number of collateral, or nondirect, descendants.

Later, Robert Trivers proposed a model based on the concept of "reciprocal altruism"; according to this model, altruists do increase their own chances of survival and reproduction, because the recipients of their altruism remember them and help them out when the tables are turned. (This is often referred to colloquially as the "You scratch my back and I'll scratch yours" model.) Largely on the basis of these two models of altruism, sociobiologists argued that even the most complex and seemingly spiritually motivated behaviors of humans could be explained solely by evolutionary biology. This notion was widely publicized in Richard Dawkins's book *The Selfish Gene* (1976), E. O. Wilson's subsequent book *On Human Nature* (1978), and Richard Alexander's *The Biology of Moral Systems* (1987).

Although many anthropologists and psychologists have converted to the evolutionary perspective and found it fruitful, many remain antagonistic to it, and sociologists, philosophers, and theologians, in particular, remain highly critical. Their argument continues to be that human behavior is qualitatively different from that of other animals because of the complexity of human culture and spirituality. They argue that a reductionist approach to human behavior will inevitably miss the most important features of human nature and social interactions.

In addition, many individuals and political groups remain hostile to sociobiology because of the widespread belief that if something is genetic, it is inevitable and justifiable. Although these conclusions are not logically valid, there is legitimate concern that some people might use sociobiological arguments to try to undermine moral teaching or to promote or rationalize nepotism, aggression, racism, or sexism. To the extent that sociobiology is perceived as an ideological tool rather than a scientific enterprise, it has been argued that sociobiological research should not be funded or otherwise promoted by public institutions (such as universities). The debate has thus become one of politics and social goals as well as one of scientific philosophy and method.

—Linda Mealey

Further Reading

Alexander, Richard D. *The Biology of Moral Systems.* Hawthorne, N.Y.: Aldine De Gruyter, 1987.

Cameron, Donald. *The Purpose of Life: Human Purpose and Morality from an Evolutionary Perspective.* Bristol, England: Woodhill, 2001.

Caplan, Arthur L., ed. *The Sociobiology Debate: Readings on Ethical and Scientific Issues.* New York: Harper & Row, 1978.

Casebeer, William D. *Natural Ethical Facts: Evolution, Connectionism, and Moral Cognition.* Cambridge, Mass.: MIT Press, 2003.

Dawkins, Richard. *The Selfish Gene.* New ed. New York: Oxford University Press, 1999.

Kitcher, Phillip. *Vaulting Ambition: Sociobiology and the Quest for Human Nature.* Cambridge, Mass.: MIT Press, 1985.

Montagu, Ashley, ed. *Sociobiology Examined.* New York: Oxford University Press, 1980.

Ruse, Michael. *Sociobiology: Sense or Nonsense?* Boston: D. Reidel, 1979.

Thompson, Paul, ed. *Issues in Evolutionary Ethics.* Albany: State University of New York Press, 1995.

Wilson, E. O. *Sociobiology: The New Synthesis.* Cambridge, Mass.: Belknap/Harvard University Press, 1975.

See also: Academic freedom; Altruism; Anthropological ethics; Darwin, Charles; Determinism and freedom; Evolutionary theory; Ideology; Political correctness; Social Darwinism; Taboos.

Sustainability of resources

Definition: Ability of natural environments to maintain constant levels of resources in the face of human exploitation

Type of ethics: Environmental ethics

Significance: There is no scientific consensus on how many human beings Earth's natural resources can support because the intensity of resource use varies across societies and regions. Developing ethical principles to guide human interactions with the environment is important to ensure the sustainability of resources and environmental quality across national and cultural boundaries.

Modern societies create enduring tensions between development and conservation. Development is often considered as the means to improve economic growth with the ultimate goal of improving human welfare and quality of life. As populations grow and demands for higher quality of life increase, society's demands for natural resources increase, leading inevitably to further exploration and exploitation of environments that may otherwise be preserved. Moreover, there is substantial evidence that current practices to obtain and redistribute natural resources are adversely affecting the environment, potentially resulting in the depletion of certain essential resources, extinctions of biological species, and the pollution of air, water, and soil to extents that are detrimental to the welfare of human societies. The application of environmental ethics to sustainability science aims to discover globally acceptable standards and practices for balancing development with the conservation of natural resources.

Ethical Issues in Resource Conservation

How many natural resources should the average human being consume? Should societies provide for each individual at the risk of depleting natural resources? The answers to such questions may play a role in determining the fate of human societies on Earth. Innovative scientific approaches to these questions are being developed, but convincing answers will most likely transcend disciplinary science, as ethical issues play greater roles in providing robust guidance.

Nutritional foods, clean water, and clean air are all essential for the growth and development of both individual human beings and human societies. Keeping these most basic resources available requires the expenditure of energy, which was still dominated by combustion of such fossil fuels as coal, petroleum, and natural gas at the beginning of the twenty-first century. Supplies of these resources are finite, and their distribution is uneven across national boundaries. Toxic waste products from industrial development that relies on these sources of energy also threaten communities worldwide, but their impacts are also unevenly distributed, with poor communities and nations suffering more than affluent ones. These problems have raised the profile of equity as a dominant topic of debate among environmental ethicists. Equity issues in resource conservation transcend geographical, generational, and phylogenetic boundaries.

Geographical and Generational Divides

Concerns over global climate change, including its causes, impacts, and mitigation strategies are fundamentally different between industrialized countries of the Northern Hemisphere and the less developed countries of the Southern Hemisphere. Therefore, questions of ethics, fairness, equity, and environmental justice have often stalled agreements at international summits aiming to design long-term solutions to problems associated with global environmental change.

The likelihood that certain natural resources may be depleted in one or two generations and the storage of radioactive waste materials with long half-lives have raised the questions about trans-generational ethics and equity. How should humans living today protect and reserve natural resources and conserve good environmental quality for those who will live tomorrow? Whereas most people will agree that societies should reserve the benefits of abundant natural resources and clean environments for future generations, there is wide disagreement on how much sacrifice individuals and societies must make in the present to ensure satisfactory levels of resources in the future.

Most contributions made by ethicists on these questions have been theoretical, but the time has arrived for practical applications of solutions that have emerged from ethical debates. Indeed, at the beginning of the twenty-first century, some of those applications were being proposed in international conventions on the environment.

The Phylogenetic Divide

Perhaps the most difficult of the numerous ethical questions in resource conservation and global sustainability arises from the phylogenetic divide that forces humans to set monetary values on other organisms. What values should humans place on biological diversity and the extinction of species? Nonhuman organisms rely on humans to make their case for conservation. Therefore, there is an inherent bias in protection and conservation practices that favor organisms that humans find useful or appealing for aesthetic reasons. Given that most of the biological diversity on Earth remains to be classified, while rates of urbanization, desertification, and deforestation are increasing, there is clearly an urgent need for a coherent system of resource conservation that is based on sound ethical principles.

There is a global challenge to resolve the difficult issues surrounding the concept of sustainable development. Is economic development possible without compromising the sustainability of natural resources and a clean environment? The relatively new disciplines of industrial ecology and sustainability science have highlighted the path to possible solutions, but it is imperative for these discussions to include innovations in the study of ethics and human character—if the recommended scientific solutions are expected to be widely accepted and sustainable.

—O. A. Ogunseitan

Further Reading

Armstrong, Susan J., and Richard G. Botzler. *Environmental Ethics: Divergence and Convergence.* New York: McGraw-Hill, 1993.

Boochkin, Murray. *The Philosophy of Social Ecology.* Montreal: Black Rose Books, 1990.

Des Jardins, Joseph R. *Environmental Ethics: An Introduction to Environmental Philosophy.* Belmont, Calif.: Wadsworth/Thomson Learning, 2001.

Dobson, Andrew, ed. *Fairness and Futurity: Essays on Sustainability and Social Justice.* New York: Oxford University Press, 1999.

Kates, Robert W., et al. "Sustainability Science." *Science* 292 (2001): 641-642.

Myers, N., and J. Kent. *New Consumers: The Influence of Affluence on the Environment.* Proceedings of the National Academy of Science (U.S.A.) 100: 4963-4968, 2003.

Ruttan, V. W. *Technology, Growth, and Development.* New York: Oxford University Press, 2001.

See also: Bioethics; Conservation; Deep ecology; Deforestation; Earth and humanity; Ecofeminism; Ecology; Environmental movement; Genetic engineering.

Technology

Definition: Practical application of scientific knowledge
Type of ethics: Scientific ethics
Significance: The ethics of modern technology involved reconsiderations of personal and social values to ensure the wise use of technology and to prevent dehumanization and environmental destruction.

Through technology, humans have developed the means to transcend certain physical and mental limitations of their bodies. In the process, they have modified materials and their environment to better satisfy their needs and wants. Technological change has, however, resulted in an expanded range of choices and newethical dilemmas that necessitate a reconsideration of personal and social values. Ethical analysis of technology involves reviewing whether the social and personal impact, economic costs, environmental damage, and potential risks associated with technology are worth its benefits. Such analysis is used in combination with scientific knowledge to formulate goals and policies to help ensure the responsible development and utilization of technology.

Historical Context

Despite its profound influences on humanity and the environment, technology became a subject of ethical inquiry only relatively recently. A review of how the cultural context of science and technology has changed with time is useful in understanding why technology did not come under the scrutiny of ethical analysis earlier.

Technology is generally considered to be the application of scientific knowledge; however, technology actually preceded science. The first human use of tools and the development of agriculture were early forms of technology. The word "technology" originates from the Greek *technè*, which means "art," "craft," or "skill." In ancient times, science was equated with the search for truth and understanding of the world and of human life. The Greek philosophers were the first to formulate ideas about matter, although they never experimentally tested their ideas. Their discourse focused on determining what was real and unique about humans relative to other forms of matter.

A relationship between science and technology began in the Middle Ages with the practice of alchemy—a sort of mystical chemistry practiced by people with an interest in human health and the quality of life. Alchemists prepared elixirs in efforts to remedy ailments as well as to confer immortality. It was Francis Bacon, however, who first perpetuated the belief that knowledge obtained through science could be utilized to enrich human life through newinventions.

Bacon lived in an age when people first used instruments to collect information about nature and the universe but also considered the influence of the stars upon their destinies and believed in witchcraft. As an alternative, Bacon outlined what was to become the modern scientific

Luddites smashing a power loom in 1812. By Chris Sunde.

method—a process characterized by induction, experiment, and the empirical study of data.

Over the next hundred years, René Descartes, Thomas Hobbes, Robert Boyle, and Sir Isaac Newton further contributed to the philosophical basis of the scientific revolution. Science was viewed as one of humanity's noblest enterprises and one of the best means for gaining an understanding of nature. Of relevance to ethics was the fact that this new image of science differed from previous philosophical thought on at least two major points. First, classical ethics assumed that there were limits on humanity's power over natural phenomena; nature and the future were controlled by fate, chance, or some divine power. According to Bacon, however, the power obtained through knowledge would enable humans to control nature and their own destiny.

Scientific knowledge was also considered objective and tangible. Scientific judgments could be tested by observation of facts and logical analysis; one could provide clear evidence of truth. In contrast, moral judgments were seen as subjective, abstract, and incapable of being empirically tested. Ethical analyses reflected attitudes of the persons involved and were based on values held by an individual or society—all of which have a tendency to be relative to a particular culture and time. Such relativism was not thought to apply to scientific data.

Bacon could not have fully imagined the extent to which his predictions about the enhancement of human life would come true as a result of technological innovations beginning with the Industrial Revolution.

By the mid-twentieth century, numerous dreaded diseases had been virtually eliminated with the discovery of antibiotics and vaccines. Fertilizers, pesticides, and animal breeding had increased and enriched the world's food supply. New materials such as plastics and fibers had brought new products into homes, industrial automation had increased leisure time, advances in transportation and communications had linked remote regions of the world, and humanity had begun to look toward outer space as a new frontier.

The public was content to leave details of scientific concepts to a perceived elite group of experts. What seemed important was that technology, the practical result of this work, was the means to improve the quality of life for the average person both by providing conveniences to simplify tasks and ease the burden of work and by offering new luxuries and expanded time for leisure. Advancements in new weaponry and synthetic pesticides that dra-

matically impacted the course of World War II served to further the public's positive view of technology.

Changing Attitudes

Despite the perceived benefits of technology, several events during the twentieth century contributed to changing attitudes about science and technology. The development of the assembly line in 1913, initially hailed as a means of providing affordable products for everyone, was blamed for the loss of jobs during the Great Depression. Around this same time, philosophical concerns about technological impact on humans were voiced by individuals like William F. Ogburn, Leslie White, Lewis Mumford, and C. P. Snow. They all questioned whether the machine was an amplifier of human power that challenged human productive abilities or something that placed humans into a new serfdom. Despite this, mechanization propagated as the industrial robot and other forms of automation were introduced.

The United States' use of the atom bomb during World War II raised the level of consciousness of responsibility among scientists. Afterward, they protested against nuclear weapons testing, development of antiballistic missiles, and military research being done within university settings. Additionally, scientists (most notably Rachel Carson) pointed out that science and technology had the potential to destroy the world by the irreversible damage to the environment caused by industrial pollution and the rampant use of pesticides. Such testimony by scientists and other experts led to an increased social awareness of environmental hazards resulting from technology, and for the first time, the general public began to question the value of technology.

Philosophers of the technological age, such as Herbert Marcuse, Jacques Ellul, Victor Ferkiss, and Jacob Bronowski, began to formulate the foundations of a new ethic. New methods of analysis emerged. One example was Norbert Wiener's notion of communication and feedback control processes in animals and machines that he introduced in his book *Cybernetics* (1948); it became a discipline of study in the 1960's. Several other books emerged during the middle of the twentieth century in which the authors openly questioned the value of technology. Rachel Carson's *Silent Spring* (1962) was pivotal in this respect. The evils of technology were often emphasized, and it was pointed out that technology had altered the image of humankind. Science-fiction writers portrayed the horrors of technology gone awry; for example,

Kurt Vonnegut's *Player Piano* (1952) detailed the impact of technological change on the human psyche.

Public concerns about science and technology rose dramatically toward the end of the twentieth century. Nuclear energy, resource availability, biomedical and reproductive technologies, genetic engineering, animal welfare, the value of "big science"—such as space exploration, strategic defense initiatives, superconductors, and the Human Genome Project—and the economic and environmental impact of technology were all among the topics of concern.

A growing reliance on computers, the Internet, and new electronic modes of communication were changing models of conducting business, accessibility to information, and perceptions of time and distances around the globe. New ethical concerns were being raised about the artificial extension of the human mind and the changing forms of human interactions.

Life science research and biotechnology methodologies led to gene therapy, genetically modified foods, cloning of mammals, and the use of stem cells for research—all of which have raised to unprecedented levels public awareness of the new ethical dilemmas.

Technology and Public Policy

Despite a move in the United States to isolate scientific research from political control, the opposite situation occurred. Scientists and engineers were consulted by the government for advice on technology—especially, originally, on issues related to atomic energy. Federal government involvement in science expanded during the 1950's and early 1960's, with the formation of funding agencies such as the National Science Foundation and the National Institutes of Health.

Changing economic and political situations in the 1960's, however, led to decreased federal appropriations for research, and there was a new emphasis on accountability. Scientists were expected to be productive, and research was expected to lead to practical applications. Phrases such as "applied science" and "publish or perish" became popular, blurring the distinction between science and technology. The increased involvement of government in research and technology and the increased dependence of science on public funding severely challenged the previously held ideal that these were ethically neutral areas.

Value judgments, social attitudes, and political and economic pressures were clearly influencing the national science agenda, research priorities, and public opinions of technology. After the 1960's, the level of federal funding for science in the United States increased significantly; a large percentage of scientists rely on federal research support. Entrepreneurial partnerships between universities and business have become common, serving to further emphasize applied research and profitmaking—sometimes at the expense of the traditional academic missions of education and basic research.

Social priorities define where research funds are directed; this is evident in the large amounts of funding available for research related to cancer, acquired immunodeficiency syndrome (AIDS), and, in the early twenty-first century, national security—especially in the wake of the events of September 11, 2001.

During the 1970's, private institutes such as the Hastings Center in New York and government advisory groups such as the Office of Technology Assessment and the National Academy of Sciences were established to initiate discussions and studies of ethical issues in technology. Emphasis was on the personal and social impact of technology, regulatory issues, and finding ways to better inform the public about technology. International gatherings of scientists (most notably the meeting on recombinant DNA technology held at Asilomar, California, in 1975) focused on ethical dilemmas related to the safe application of new and controversial technology in scientific research, industry, and agriculture.

The national dialogue about technology and ethics expanded as professional scientific societies began to routinely include sessions on ethics at their annual national meetings. Ethics has become a required component of the curriculum of many science graduate school programs, and researchers often must address ethical issues when submitting grant proposals for federal research funds. Centers of ethics related to technology have been developed at a number of universities; the Center for Bioethics at the University of Pennsylvania and the Markkula Center for Applied Ethics at Santa Clara University in California are prominent examples.

Calls to place limits on, or even ban, certain types of research were beginning to be voiced. Initially these came largely from environmentalists and animal rights activists, but they later expanded to groups concerned about genetically modified foods and reproductive technologies, including cloning. A National Bioethics Advisory Commission was established by executive order during President Bill Clinton's initial term in office. This advisory committee examined issues related to human subjects' protection in research. Growing public concerns about human cloning and embryonic stem cell research led President George W. Bush to establish a new President's Council on Bioethics that met for the first time in January, 2002.

Ethical dilemmas related to the distribution of wealth and knowledge and environmental damage resulting from technology have become a major focus of foreign policy. This is evident in provisions of international agreements such as the Montreal and Kyoto Protocols (which focus on environmental concerns), unilateral agreements on weapons and nuclear power, and discussions about the distribution of AIDS drugs to developing nations where the disease is most prevalent. In October, 2003, the president of France, Jacques Chirac, called for an international convention to address ethics raised by advances in genetic engineering and biotechnology.

Ethical Principles

Traditional ethics were anthropocentric; the fundamental nature of the human entity was presumed to be constant. Classical theories such as Immanuel Kant's theory on moral law focused on similarities between kinds of situations and people. Questions of good or evil actions toward fellow humans were confined to the foreseeable future and to individuals to whom a person was either related or was close in the sense of time or physical location. Actions toward nonhuman objects were considered to be outside the realm of ethical consideration.

Modern technology has altered these premises of classical ethics by changing the nature and the realm of human actions. Individualism and uniqueness, rather than similarities, are valued; society is pluralistic. Innovations in communication and transportation have altered perceptions of time and space, as well as changing the very nature of how humans interact with each other. Humans must think globally in terms of their actions, since they can affect not only living relatives and neighbors but also unknown people living thousands of miles away or someone who might be born several generations in the future.

Modern technology is informed by a much deeper understanding of natural phenomena, yet nature is critically vulnerable to technological intervention. Because of this, the realm of moral consideration has been expanded to include nonhuman living organisms, or even all components of the planet. This has led to the animal rights movement and the development of the field of environmental ethics. Despite this new awareness, humans continue to use technology to construct new environments and alter existing elements of nature—described by some as humans' attempt to re-create Eden.

Contemporary ethics, which emerged in the twentieth century, is usually divided into three components. Through descriptive ethics, one seeks an accurate, objective account of moral behavior or beliefs. Metaethics involves examining the meanings and uses of moral terms such as "good" or "right" and studying moral reasoning and foundations for moral judgments. In normative ethics, moral arguments about what types of conduct are right or wrong, or good or bad, are analyzed. Normative ethics is also concerned with how human beings might best lead their lives and which states of affairs ought to be furthered in society. It is this latter branch of contemporary ethics on which discussions about technology focus. Most ethical considerations of technology are issue or case-oriented (applied ethics) and often focus on specific areas such as bioethics or computer ethics.

Ethical assessments draw on traditional ethical theory and principles when possible, but also rely on scientific evidence and psychological, political, economic, and historical factors. Traditional ethical reasoning involves consideration of utility, right, justice, common good, and virtue, and use of such standards would lead to questions such as the following when assessing technology: What are the benefits and harms of a particular technology? Who will be impacted and do individuals have free choice in determining whether they will use or be impacted, by technology? Are individuals protected from technology being used in ways they do not want? Will there be a fair distribution of the direct benefits and wealth technology brings? However, given the pace at which new information is obtained and put into application, and the inability to foresee all the consequences of technology, it is difficult to conduct such a thorough assessment.

The fundamental ethical question of whether science and its applications through technology are good or evil is frequently debated. Since goodness is a function of both personal and societal sets of values, there is no absolute set of standards from either classical or contemporary ethics that can be used in this area. Such analysis is further complicated by divided views as to whether technology is mechanical or autonomous. In the mechanical view, or instrumental theory, technology is seen as a tool with which to accomplish a humanly defined goal. As such, it has instrumental value depending on its usefulness to humans, and ethical judgments can be made only regarding the goals for which the tools are used. In the autonomous view, or substantive theory, technology has a life of its own and may no longer be under human control. Ethical concerns center both on whether to control or restrict technology and on the moral impact of technology on individuals and society.

New Ethical Issues

Fears that technology might someday begin controlling humans have long been a major ethical concern. Some people believe this to be reality. During the 1980's and 1990's, Neil Postman and Langdon Winner both described how technology had redefined social relationships, culture, ideas of space and time, individual habits, moral boundaries, and political and economic structures. Ironically, technology, which originally led to increased leisure time, has now created a mind-set in business (at least in the United States) that prioritizes efficiency and productivity and promotes a "24-7" mentality. Without free time to pursue friendships, people ironically now turn to their computers for human interaction. Some have noted that the ever-accelerating pace of new knowledge acquisition and implementation of new technologies correlates with fast-paced modern society that is characterized by temporary relationships (consider the high divorce rate, the increasing trend of frequent career changes, and the routine buyouts and mergers in business).

Many have described the seductive power of technology and society's increasing reliance on it. Ruth Conway refers to the "flick of a switch" syndrome where individuals use technology but are unaware of the workings of the machine or the environmental impact of the product and are completely disconnected from the science and creativity that went into the design. She sees this as a debilitating power of technology that can lead to a sense of powerlessness and incompetence. (Consider some people's dependence on remote controls or the common perception that younger generations can no longer do mathematical calculations without the aid of a calculator.) As technology advances, the scientific literacy of the general public lags farther behind. Given the expanding information gap between the experts and the public, who should make decisions about acceptable risks of technology, determine public policy on scientific research, or set limits on technology that threatens to cross some unacceptable moral boundary?

Humans have never before dealt with the types of ethical implications to which modern technology has given birth. Genetic engineering is a good example of a modern technology that leads to a range of new ethical dilemmas including decisions about whether humans should genetically modify themselves or other animals and uncertainties associated with scientists tinkering with evolution and natural selection. However, besides these, there are questions of whom, if anybody should profit from this technology.

In *Diamond v. Chakrabarty* (1980), the U.S. Supreme Court ruled that oil-eating bacteria produced by genetic engineering were living inventions and thus were patentable. This decision further sparked debate over whether life-forms should be engineered, much less patented, and has intensified as a result of the various genome sequencing projects and the patenting of specific DNA sequences isolated from living organisms. A scientist can patent not only a gene responsible for some desirable trait in a crop plant but also a potentially interesting abnormal gene isolated from tissue of a patient with some disease (without the patient's knowledge). Previously unimaginable businesses such as gene prospecting (from humans and other species) and trade in indigenous DNA have emerged.

Computer and communication technologies have also led to new ethical dilemmas—typically in the areas of privacy and intellectual property rights. While some parents may appreciate the ability to check in on their children electronically at a day care center, they might strongly object to the same technology being used in their workplace to monitor their own work. Global positioning systems enable products such as OnStar, which can be used to help a stranded motorist, but also allows companies to track the driving patterns and location of automobile owners without their explicit consent. The Internet and electronic mail communication have many benefits, but they also expand the availability of potential victims, as evidenced by the increase of new breeds of criminals including hackers and online sexual predators.

International Issues

Most countries realize that their welfare is dependent in part on their national scientific and technological capacity. In the past, the poor (including those in technological countries) have benefited least from technology. How is it possible to distribute justly the benefits of technology? Should everyone enjoy some equitable level of quality of life before further technological advances are permitted? Does the inequality in wealth and technology that exists between industrial and developing nations lead to undesirable practices such as black markets for weapons or substances such as chlorofluorocarbons (CFCs)—which were later banned by the provisions of the Montreal Protocols? Should technologically advanced countries continue to use resources obtained from lessdeveloped countries? If so, what constitutes a fair compensation?

The British philosopher David Hume stated that a system of justice was necessary because of human passions, selfishness, and limits of resources. Ethical discussions of technology often refer to the tragedy of the commons. The commons are those provisions of the earth that humans must share; the tragedy is that human nature compels people continually to increase their well-being—often at the expense of fellow humans. Can a spirit of cooperation prevail if competition is instinctual?

Countries may be obligated to share not only the benefits of technology but also certain kinds of knowledge, such as that related to the eradication of disease. For poor countries, the information may be useless unless financial assistance for implementation is also provided. Who becomes responsible for such financial support? Other technical information, such as that linked to national security, may require protection.

Who decides which information is to be shared? New technology raises questions of priorities, especially when resources are limited. Should ending world hunger be of higher priority than having humans explore outer space? Proponents argue that technology stimulates human intellect, national prestige, and pride. Of what value are these? When a nation has a large national debt, how much technology is needed for security (whether to serve as a deterrent or for defense)? What would be the social price of not using technology?

Technology is often blamed for the depletion of many natural resources. Can limited resources be shared or conserved? If technology cannot provide alternatives to scarce resources, what valued material goods and comforts would humans be willing to sacrifice?

What alternative energy sources are acceptable substitutes when traditional ones are depleted? Innovations in agriculture enhanced the world's food supply, but overpopulation threatens the planet. Should birth control (via technological products) be mandated to bring the population back into balance with what the earth can support?

Other new ethical questions relate to responsibilities toward future generations. What impact will continued technological development have on the future of humanity and Earth's ecosystem? Are these even within the realm of human responsibility? The technology accepted in the twenty-first century or any decisions made to set limits on research and evolving technologies will likely have far-reaching consequences for many generations to come.

Has Technology Altered Humans?

Early ethical considerations of technology asked whether it was a threat to the dignity of humans and whether humans were becoming slaves to machines. In contrast, others argue that the machine has freed humans from demoralizing and tedious physical labor, allowing them to more fully develop their intellectual capacities. Modern technological advances have the potential to further blur the boundary between human and machine, including artificial intelligence, neurotechnology—which involves implantable microcomputer chips connected to prosthetic devices—and nanotechnology.

Advances in computing and communication technology allow individuals to access information and regions of the world previously unattainable for the majority of people. To achieve this global connectivity, what has been lost in terms of fundamental human values of family and community? Despite the capability to access almost infinite amounts of information, computers and artificial intelligence are blamed for diminished communication skills and a loss of imagination. Are impersonal interactions and loss of privacy worth the ability to augment intellectual power?

Through technology, scientists have revealed the "secret of life" (DNA structure), and it is theoretically possible to modify humans through genetic engineering. Scientists are identifying the chemical reactions that are responsible for learning, memory, behavior, and the perceptions of pleasure and pain. It has become possible to predict some future health problems, the ability to learn, or an individual's potential for criminal conduct or displaying an addictive behavior—in some cases, before a person is even born. How will such information be used, and by whom? Chemical or genetic modification of behavior, in combination with computers and artificial intelligence, will further enable the expansion of the mental capacities of humans. Researchers have the technology and most of the genetic details to redesign humans should they so choose. What impact does such knowledge have on humanity and spirituality?

Individual value systems are influenced by a person's experiences and environment. Both one's sense of self and decision-making abilities are determined by these values. What happens to human values when the factors that influence them are in constant flux? Values are known to change more slowly than the reality of human experience; what sort of crisis does this present? Humans are confronted with more choices than ever. With shifting values and no set of common societal values, how can decisions be made?

Technological Risk and Responsibility

Although technology provides numerous benefits to society, it also entails risks. Oftentimes, not all potential dangers resulting from technology can be foreseen, since predictive knowledge falls behind the technical knowledge and humankind's power to act. Because of this, risk-benefit analysis (a utilitarian approach) is not relevant in all cases, nor is it always possible to logically determine acceptable levels of risk. Choices must be made regarding things that humans have not yet experienced.

How should people address risk in a way that accommodates the perceptions and values of those who bear it when perceptions of the nature, magnitude, and acceptability of the risk differ tremendously among people? Is it possible to identify common values and consider objectives for technology that different cultures within a society or across international boundaries can accept?

Highly trained science experts have difficulty keeping up with developments in their own specialized areas. Couple this with the view that the general public is relatively scientifically illiterate, and how, in a democratic society, can citizens participate in wise decision making relative to technology? What responsibility do people have to educate themselves about science and technology? How does the public gain access to the relevant information? What are the obligations of scientists and technologists in disseminating complex information to the public? How do scientists and technologists balance loyalties to their employers, their profession, and the public in calling attention to potential risks arising from their work? Is it the role of journalists to provide an adequate set of facts to the public?

Even when intelligent decisions are made, errors can occur. Who becomes responsible for unexpected applications or undesirable consequences of technology? Who could have predicted that terrorists would use jets as weapons of mass destruction or samples from biomedical research for bioterrorism? The unpredictable nature of humans and the complexity of political and economic factors make it impossible to foresee all consequences. How can people know the truth about the future conditions of humankind and the earth? How can people know what might possibly be at stake? How important does trust become when regulating the power that humankind obtains through technology?

If technological change is inevitable, consideration must be given to how it should be controlled and assessed and how progress should be defined. Is continued evidence of technological progress a sufficient measure of the healthful state of modern culture? Ironically, modern decision making is dependent on the collection and analysis of data and the use of technological devices for this process; technology is used to assess and make decisions about technology.

Where does ethical analysis fit into the process? Are there some areas of research and technology that simply should not be pursued? Who should determine the legitimate goals of science and technology, and who will be responsible for setting limits on scientific freedom and bans on certain technologies?

Although difficult, attempts are continually being made to evaluate technological outcomes. Modern pluralistic societies cannot agree on what ends should be served or how conflicting values should be prioritized.

There is a general consensus that technology should be regulated, but the development of public policy has been hampered by the unanswered question of who should decide what the moral boundaries should be. Values of freedom (respect for autonomy) and of individual choice conflict with ideas on what is right for society as a whole (the utilitarian perspective). Such conflict between self-interest and profit on one side and the sense of obligation for the common good on the other is typical of Western philosophy.

A series of profound questions remain unanswered. What are the foundations of an ethic that is applicable to this new technological age? How should the new image of humans be defined in a technological age? How can the survival of humanity, which many people claim is permanently threatened by automation, computers, and genetic engineering, be ensured?

—*Diane White Husic*

Further Reading

Burke, John G., and Marshall C. Eakin, eds. *Technology and Change*. San Francisco: Boyd & Fraser, 1979. Collection of essays dealing with ethics, attitudes toward technology, and policy issues. Includes classic excerpts from philosophers of the technological age.

Conway, Ruth. *Choices at the Heart of Technology: A Christian Perspective*. Harrisburg, Pa.: Trinity Press International, 1999. Explores how technology has changed individuals, society, and human values and summarizes several modern ethical analyses of technology.

D'Souza, Dinesh. *The Virtue of Prosperity: Finding Values in an Age of Techno-Affluence*. New York: Free Press, 2000. Analysis of the spiritual and social consequences of a new technology that has led to a mass affluent class.

Ellul, Jacques. *The Technological Society*. London: Random House, 1967. Classic treatise on how technology controls humans.

Mumford, Lewis. *Technics and Civilization*. San Diego, Calif.: Harvest Books, 1963. Classic book that provides a multidisciplinary analysis of technology.

Ophuls, William, and A. Stephen Boyan, Jr. *Ecology and the Politics of Scarcity Revisited: The Unraveling of the American Dream*. New York: W. H. Freeman, 1992. Broad look at the interweaving of ethics, science, and politics through case studies. The authors make frequent references to classical philosophers and illustrate how their ideas are relevant to modern technological issues.

Postman, Neil. *Technopoly: The Surrender of Culture to Technology*. New York: Vintage Books, 1993. Traces the evolution of technology from its origins as a support system of culture to a phenomenon that controls society.

Shrader-Frechette, Kristin, and Laura Westra, eds. *Technology and Values*. Lanham, Md.: Rowman & Littlefield, 1997. Collection of essays that examine contemporary science- and technologyrelated ethical issues.

Watkins, Bruce O., and Roy Meador. *Technology and Human Values: Collision and Solution*. Ann Arbor, Mich.: Ann Arbor Science, 1977. Cowritten by an engineer and a science writer, this concise book presents several ethical arguments for and against technology. Each side of the debate is critically analyzed, providing a balanced perspective.

Winner, Langdon. *The Whale and the Reactor: A Search for Limits in an Age of High Technology*. Chicago: University of Chicago Press, 1986. A series of essays that investigate technological consequences on society, politics, and philosophy.

See also: Bacon, Francis; Biotechnology; Cloning; Computer technology; Dominion over nature, human; Electronic mail; Future-oriented ethics; Nuclear energy; Robotics; Science; Stem cell research.

Toxic waste

Definition: Poisonous or other dangerous substances needing specialized forms of disposal

Type of ethics: Environmental ethics

Significance: Ethical practices of toxic waste disposal are those that protect the environment and human life.

By the early twenty-first century, toxic waste was spreading throughout the world at an alarming rate. To protect the environment and human life, ethical practices must be employed to dispose of toxic waste materials generated by industry, agriculture, consumers, and individual persons. The numerous toxic waste disposal abuses of the past were sometimes due to ignorance or carelessness; however, many abuses were due to the unethical practices used to save companies or individuals time and money in waste disposal. Disposed toxic substances can be highly detrimental to people, whether the people are aware that they are being exposed to the materials or not. Among other things, careless, unethical dumping of toxic waste has produced dirty streams, greasy drinkingwater, noxious fumes, and human suffering, disease, and death.

Toxic Sites

During the nineteenth and twentieth centuries, many toxic waste substances were spread into the air, soil, andwater. For example, Love Canal, an artificial waterway that was built near Niagara Falls, New York, during the 1890's became a site of industrial toxic waste disposal, with more than forty toxic organic compounds found in the canal and in nearby soil, water, and air samples collected during the late 1970's. In May, 1980, the federal Environmental Protection Agency released a study showing a rate of chromosome damage among babies born to people living near the Love Canal site. Among myriad other sites where dumped toxic wastes have produced documented cancer, mysterious health problems, and other devastating effects are Waukegan Harbor, Illinois; Times Beach, Missouri; Woburn, Massachusetts; Mapleton, Utah; and Bhopal, India.

Many of the more than fifty thousand toxic-wasteproducing firms in the United States contract with waste-disposal companies to provide ethical, scientifically sound, legal ways to dispose of their waste materials. Some companies dump or bury their toxic wastes on-site. In many instances when problems develop, waste disposers claim that the problems are not serious and decline to spend any money to clean up disposal sites. This difficulty led the U.S. Congress to pass the Comprehensive Environmental Response, Compensation, and Liability Act in 1980, which included the establishment of the Superfund to pay for immediate cleanup of abandoned toxic-waste sites and inoperative sites where the owners refuse to clean them up.

As the numbers of toxic waste sites, the amounts and varieties of chemical contamination, and cleanup costs continue to escalate, the only feasible solutions for protecting the environment and human life and rights appear to be regulatory controls that focus on waste minimization and ethical practices of waste disposal. Grassroots organizations across America demand that the government legislate and enforce such action.

—Alvin K. Benson

Further Reading

Crawford, Mark. *Toxic Waste Sites: An Encyclopedia of Endangered America*. Santa Barbara, Calif.: ABC-CLIO, 1997.

Girdner, Eddie J., and Jack Smith. *Killing Me Softly: Toxic Waste, Corporate Profit, and the Struggle for Environmental Justice*. New York: Monthly Review Press, 2002.

Setterberg, Fred, and Lonny Shavelson. *Toxic Nation: The Fight to Save Our Communities from Chemical Contamination*. New York: John Wiley & Sons, 1993.

See also: Bioethics; Birth defects; Business ethics; Environmental ethics; Environmental movement; Environmental Protection Agency; "Not in my backyard"; Nuclear energy; Pollution permits; *Silent Spring*; Sustainability of resources.

Union of Concerned Scientists

Identification: Organization established to examine the uses and hazards of nuclear energy

Date: Founded in 1969

Type of ethics: Scientific ethics

Significance: The Union of Concerned Scientists pursues a vigorous program of public advocacy and education concerning the effects of advanced technology on society and public policy.

At the end of the 1960's, the testing of nuclear weapons had been suspended by the United States, the Soviet Union, and other nations with nuclear arms, but the Strategic Arms Limitation Treaty (SALT) talks that would halt the construction of weapons had not yet begun. In addition, the first nuclear power plants were either on the drawing boards or actually under construction. The Union of Concerned Scientists (USC) was founded at this time to gather information on the nuclear arms race, arms control, nuclear reactor safety, energy policy, and other related matters. (Although the membership of the USC is not made up exclusively of scientists, a core of technically competent

professionals makes its studies definitive and disinterested.) The USC's findings are made available in its own periodicals, in conferences, in public presentations, in the media, in speaking engagements, and in educational packets provided for school use. The USC also provides court testimony and appearances at hearings such as those conducted by the U.S. Nuclear Regulatory Commission (NRC) regarding the relicensing of atomic power plants. More recently, the USC has broadened its scope to deal with the impact of advanced technology in general on society and has organized scientists on a worldwide basis out of concern for the earth's ecology.

—Robert M. Hawthorne, Jr.

See also: Atom bomb; Atomic Energy Commission; Earth and humanity; Mutually Assured Destruction; Nuclear energy; Nuclear Regulatory Commission; SALT treaties; Science.

Virtual reality

Definition: Computer-generated experiences meant to resemble in form or content the perceptual experience of reality

Type of ethics: Scientific ethics

Significance: Virtual reality is designed to be the most visceral possible form of representation. It therefore raises all the issues raised by representation generally, involving responsible and irresponsible portrayals of people, social groups, and issues; the function of ideology within representation; and the ability or desirability of art to instruct people morally. In addition, virtual reality intensifies debates over whether "mere" representation is ultimately innocuous, or whether its effects on the world are significant enough to merit moral concern or even legal regulation.

Virtual reality (VR) is a computerized system of data presentation that allows the user to project himself or herself into a simulated three-dimensional space and move about in that space, introduce other objects into it, change the positions and shapes of objects already there, and interact with animate objects in the space. VR was made possible by the enormous increase in computer memory and data-processing capacity, even in personal computers (PCs), and by the development of miniaturized video and audio devices and motion sensors that give the illusion of motion and of touching and manipulating material objects. Other descriptive names for this technology are artificial reality, virtual environment, telepresence, and immersive simulation, but VR is the preferred term.

Software and Presentation Devices

The memory software of VR consists of many, many points of a three-dimensional grid, built from either an actual scene or a computer-generated space. The array of coordinates must be complete enough to allow the space to be rotated on three axes and the viewpoint to be moved similarly. In addition, other objects, animate and inanimate, must be held in memory with complete manipulability (including the tactile sensing of shape, inertia, texture, and so forth); and provision must be made for the creation of new objects with equal flexibility. Clearly, this technology calls for enormous memory capacity and complex programs to accomplish the apparent motion.

VR presentations can be very simple, such as viewing a scene on a PC monitor, or very complex, such as donning a helmet containing a miniature television screen for each eye, to give stereoscopic vision; headphones for directional sound; motion sensors to slew the scene left or right, up or down as the viewer's head moves; and a so-called Dataglove both to accept motion commands from the hand and to give back pressure information to define objects, motion, and so forth. Presentations between the simple and the complex seem to be missing; at the upper end, a whole-body sensing suit is expected to be available in the future. This very brief description of equipment may suggest why VR had to wait until microchip technology made the necessary memory available within reasonably sized computers.

Positive Applications of Virtual Reality

Many uses of VR raise few if any ethical questions. It is used, for example, to train surgical students on a "virtual" patient before they actually perform an operation. Experienced surgeons can practice a complex new procedure before using it in the operating room. Operators of heavy construction equipment can train on VR devices, and in some cases controls have been redesigned for greater simplicity and efficiency on the basis of such experience. Physiological chemists can manipulate molecules in VR to see—or feel—how they fit together in three dimensions. Attractions and repulsions of functional groups in the molecules are programmed into memory, and the user can actually feel, through the Dataglove, when a drug molecule fits or fails to fit in a cellular structure, or when a vi-

rus clicks into place on a cell receptor. Pilots can be trained in VR simulations so lifelike that an hour of training is considered as effective as an hour of actual flying time. In fact, the Air Force was an early major developer of VR presentations.

Architects and their clients can stroll through a building that has yet to be built, to get the feel of it and to identify where the design needs to be changed for greater comfort. These are all fairly unexceptionable applications.

Possible Ethically Negative Aspects

One of the most frequently voiced criticisms of VR is that it makes possible what might be called participatory pornography—not simply reading, video viewing, or telephone talk, but all these combined but together with the tactile feedback of a whole body suit that will allow virtual sexual experience of all varieties. Some designers and marketers of VR equipment speak enthusiastically of such pornography as an exciting prospect for the future. Critics view it as a real moral menace in a society that is already awash in casual sexuality. Others believe that it is merely an extension of the pornography that has always existed.

One commentator spoke sourly of "the myth that sex and pornography are the keys to understanding the growth of all new technologies." Perhaps the real menace here is that VR can be a powerful new device for furthering the alienation of individuals by making artificial experience easier and more exciting than actual human contact. This is true not only of VR sex but also potentially of all VR experience except training applications. Another aspect of this ethical concern lies in the enormous amount of time and attention that could be wasted because of VR. In a society that already spends a tenth of its time in front of television, imagine what the effect would be if every household had its own VR.

Other questions raised by VR that are perhaps medical rather than ethical but are worth mentioning: Can the tactile feedback become vigorous enough to cause physical damage? VR causes physical reactions for some users (such as nausea and actual vomiting in flight simulations); can it cause mental damage as well? Is this a technology that should be kept away from the undeveloped psyches of children and restricted to adults? All these ethical questions have yet to be addressed.

In sum, VR appears to be simply another new technology that can be used well or badly. Its capacities for good and evil seem not much greater than those of electric power, the automobile, or the telephone. The decisions lie, as always, in human hands.

—*Robert M. Hawthorne, Jr.*

Further Reading

Churbuck, David C. "Applied Reality." *Forbes* 150 (September 14, 1992): 486-489.

Dvorak, John C. "America, AreYou Ready for Simulated Sex and Virtual Reality?" *PC Computing* 5 (May, 1992): 78.

Earnshaw, Rae, Huw Jones, and Mike Gigante. *Virtual Reality Systems.* San Diego, Calif.: Academic Press, 1993.

Hayles, N. Katherine. *How We Became Posthuman: Virtual Bodies in Cybernetics, Literature, and Informatics.* Chicago: University of Chicago Press, 1999.

Hsu, Jeffrey, "Virtual Reality." *Compute* 15 (February, 1993): 101-104.

Rheingold, Howard. *Virtual Reality.* New York: Summit Books, 1991.

Spinello, Richard A. *CyberEthics: Morality and Law in Cyberspace.* 2d ed. Boston: Jones and Bartlett, 2003.

Woolley, Benjamin. "Being and Believing: Ethics of Virtual Reality." *The Lancet* 338 (August 3, 1991): 283-284.

_____. *Virtual Worlds: A Journey in Hype and Hyperreality.* Cambridge, Mass.: Blackwell Scientific, 1992.

Zizek, Slavoj. "Cyberspace: Or, The Unbearable Closure of Being." In *The Plague of Fantasies.* New York: Verso, 1997.

_____. "From Virtual Reality to the Virtualization of Reality." In *Electronic Culture: Technology and Visual Representation,* edited by Tim Druckrey. New York: Aperture, 1996.

See also: Art; Artificial intelligence; Computer technology; Narrative ethics; Pornography; Robotics; Science; Technology.

Walden

Identification: Book by Henry David Thoreau (1817-1862)

Date: Published in 1854

Type of ethics: Environmental ethics

Significance: *Walden* provides a model of the proper ethical treatment of nature and serves almost as a handbook for an environmental ethics.

Henry David Thoreau's two-year experiment of living at Massachusetts's Walden Pond was on one level an effort to determine whether a person really needed the material possessions that were considered essential in mid-nineteenth century America. His book demonstrated that one could attain the good life by living in harmony with nature supplied only with the bare necessities. The first chapter, entitled "Economy," demonstrates that human needs are few; thus, there is no need to exploit nature to attain them.

Henry David Thoreau. By George F. Parlow.

Much of the rest of the book attacks the acquisitive spirit. At bottom, Thoreau argues, materialistic values indicate not enterprise but a basic lack of spiritual self-reliance. In Thoreau's ethic, ownership of the land is invalid. Humans should act as stewards rather than squires.

Thoreau's own love of nature is illustrated in the intricate detail with which he describes the seasons, flora and fauna, natural processes, and Walden Pond itself. If he measures and documents, plumbs the depths of the lake, scrupulously counts every penny spent in the building of his house, and ponders his profit after selling produce from his garden, it is to show that empirical science does have a use, but that it should be subordinate to a guiding spirit that respects and loves the natural environment rather than exploits it. *Walden* continually demonstrates "correspondences"; that is, clear relationships between the ethical life of humankind and nature, an interconnectedness that Thoreau believed deserved more acknowledgment and respect.

—*William L. Howard*

See also: Earth and humanity; Nature, rights of; Thoreau, Henry David; Transcendentalism.

Wilderness Act of 1964

Identification: Federal law setting aside specific tracts of land to be preserved and managed so that the natural conditions of the wilderness ecosystem remain unaltered

Date: Enacted on September 3, 1964

Type of ethics: Environmental ethics

Significance: Designed to ensure that wilderness would be available as a resource for future generations, the Wilderness Act brought into federal law for the first time the principle that nature is valuable for its own sake, not only for the uses to which humans can put it.

A wilderness bill was first introduced in the U.S. Senate in 1956, but because of conflicts between economic interests and conservationists regarding the appropriate uses of land in areas set aside for wilderness, it was not until 1964 that the Wilderness Act was finally made law. The Wilderness Act of 1964 defines wilderness as "an area where the earth and community of life are untrammeled by man, where man himself is a visitor who does not remain."

The act does allow prospecting for minerals and protects mining interests that existed as of January 1, 1964, but it does not allow any new mineral patents after that date. This was a compromise that was difficult to effect. No motorized equipment, motor vehicles, motorboats, or commercial enterprises are allowed in wilderness areas. Supporters of the act stated that these exclusions did not violate the multiple-use principle, which calls for public lands to be used for their highest and best use, but indeed applied the principle by reserving some lands for the whole of the community to enjoy. The act embodies the principle that nature should not be managed, in these wilderness areas, merely to suit people, but so as to preserve and protect the land in its natural condition in accordance with wilderness values.

—*Sandra L. Christensen*

See also: Conservation; Ecology; Environmental movement; Future generations; Leopold, Aldo; Muir, John; National Park System, U.S.; Sierra Club.